THE NEW PRIVATE INTERNATIONAL LAW OF CONTRACT OF THE EUROPEAN COMMUNITY

To my mother

The New Private International Law of Contract of the European Community

Implementation of the EEC's Contractual Obligations Convention in England and Wales Under the Contracts (Applicable Law) Act 1990

PETER KAYE
Reader in Law and Director of the Centre of European Law and Practice at the University of East Anglia

Dartmouth
Aldershot • Brookfield USA • Hong Kong • Singapore • Sydney

© Peter Kaye 1993

All rights reserved. No part of this publication may be reproduced, stored in a retrieval system, or transmitted in any form or by any means, electronic, mechanical, photocopying, recording, or otherwise without the prior permission of Dartmouth Publishing Company Limited.

Published by
Dartmouth Publishing Company Limited
Gower House
Croft Road
Aldershot
Hants GU11 3HR
England

Dartmouth Publishing Company
Old Post Road
Brookfield
Vermont 05036
USA

A CIP catalogue record for this book is available from the British Library.

ISBN 1 85521 276 5

Printed and Bound in Great Britain by
Hartnolls Limited, Bodmin, Cornwall.

Contents

Preface	ix
Table of Cases	xi
Table of Statutes	xxiii
International Conventions and Treaties	xxix
Table of Orders and Regulations	xxxvii
Glossary	xxxix
Abbreviations	xli
1 Introduction	1

PART I 7

2 Pre-existing National English Private International Rules of Contract 9

PART II 27

3 General Impact of EEC's Contractual Obligations Convention 31

PART III Commentary on Individual Provisions of the 1990 Act and Convention 89

4	Contracts (Applicable Law) Act 1990	91
5	Preamble to the Rome Convention	95
6	Article 1: Scope of the Convention	97
7	Article 2: Universal Application of the Convention	143
8	Article 3: Agreement on Choice of Law	147
9	Article 4: Applicable Law in the Absence of Choice	171
10	Article 5: Consumer Contracts	203

11	Article 6: Individual Employment Contracts	221
12	Article 7: Mandatory Rules of Contract Law	239
13	Article 8: Material Validity of Contracts	269
14	Article 9: Formal Validity of Contracts	281
15	Article 10: Scope of Applicable Law	297
16	Article 11: Contractual Incapacity	311
17	Article 12: Voluntary Assignment of Rights	321
18	Article 13: Subrogation to Contractual Rights	327
19	Article 14: Presumptions, Burden and Modes of Proof	331
20	Article 15: Inapplicability of *Renvoi*	343
21	Article 16: *Ordre Public* Exception to Applicable Law	345
22	Article 17: No Retrospective Effect of the Convention	351
23	Article 18: Uniform Interpretation of the Convention	355
24	Article 19: Application of Convention to and in Composite States	359
25	Article 20: Precedence of Community Law over the Convention	365
26	Article 21: Precedence of Other International Conventions over the Convention	367
27	Article 22: Reservations to Full Application of the Convention	371
28	Article 23: Precedence and Procedure for New National Choice of Law Rules	373
29	Article 24: Procedure for New Multilateral Conflicts Conventions	379
30	Article 25: Procedure in Respect of Certain International Agreements	385
31	Article 26: Revision of the Convention	389
32	Article 27: Extensions of the Convention to European Territories of Contracting States	391
33	Article 28: Ratification of the Convention	395
34	Article 29: Entry into Force of the Convention	397
35	Article 30: Duration of the Convention	399
36	Article 31: Notifications in Respect of the Convention	403
37	Article 32: Integration of Annexed Protocol	405
38	Article 33: Authentic Texts of the Convention	407
39	Annexed Protocol	409
40	Schedule 2 1990 Act: The Luxembourg Convention on Greek Accession	411
41	Schedule 3 1990 Act: The First Brussels Interpretation Protocol	415
42	Schedule 4 1990 Act: Revisions to Other Enactments	431

Contents vii

PART IV 437

43 Comparison of Convention and Pre-existing English Private
   International Rules of Contract 439

PART V 447

44 Conclusions 449

Appendix A   *The Contracts (Applicable Law) Act 1990*   459
Appendix B   *Some Authentic Foreign Texts of the Rome Contracts*
            Convention   477
Select Bibliography   507
Index   511

Preface

The EEC's Rome Convention on the Law Applicable to Contractual Obligations of 19 June 1980 entered into force in the United Kingdom on 1 April 1991 under the Contracts (Applicable Law) Act 1990, and it applies to contracts concluded thereafter. The Convention concerns ascertainment of national laws to govern international contracts, and at the time of writing it also operates in the courts of several of the other member states of the European Community. There are in addition two Protocols, yet to be brought into force, (Greece too has now joined ratifying states, on 8 May 1992), providing for references on interpretation of the Rome Convention to be sent to the European Court of Justice by appellate national courts in proceedings before them: in no case is this obligatory, being left to the discretion of the national courts to decide in each individual action. In this work, the Rome Convention is variously described as such, or more frequently as 'the Obligations Convention', 'the Contracts Convention', or simply 'the Convention'. The Contracts (Applicable Law) Act 1990 may simply be referred to as 'the 1990 Act' or 'the Act'. The rapporteurs' report on the Rome Convention (O.J. 1980 No. C 282/1) is stated as 'the Report' or the 'Giuliano/Lagarde Report'; there is also the 'Tizzano Report' on the Brussels Interpretation Protocols (O.J. 1990 No.C 219/1). Since the Rome Convention only superseded the prior English law in relation to contracts concluded after 1 April 1991, and only subject to certain excluded areas of contract such as agency and EEC insurance risks, the traditional rules continue to apply to these matters falling outside the Convention's scope, and are accordingly referred to as the *pre-existing* – rather than previous – private international law of contract.

The Obligations Convention is intended to unify rules on applicable law within the Community in the absence of substantive harmonization of differing contract laws, and joins with the earlier Brussels Convention of 1968 on Jurisdiction and the Enforcement of Judgments in Civil and Commercial Matters ('the European Judgments Convention') as central components of a developing corpus of homogeneous European international procedural and conflicts law designed to further equalisation of rights and legal protection within the EC.

Its introduction into the United Kingdom's legal systems proved controversial and engendered passions previously unsuspected. There were letters to *The Times* newspaper from Convention opponents (14 December 1989) and from its supporters (19 December 1989), and unflattering remarks were made in the House of Lords (*Hansard*, HL Vol.515, Col. 1482, Lord Goff), in particular in respect of arrangements made for references of interpretative questions to be directed to the European Court of Justice (Hansard, HL Vol.515, Col. 1478 and Col.1541, Lord Wilberforce) and in relation to use of reports prepared by Italian and French professors as interpretative aids (Hansard, HL Vol.513, Col. 1261). In spite of the brouhaha however, the Convention eventually became law in the United Kingdom and we are thus left to grapple with its complexities.

This book is meant to assist legal counsel and students of commerce and private international law to understand the new European rules and to become aware of any differences brought about in relation to the traditional treatment of international contracts under the law of England and Wales. This is felt to be essential to the proper conduct of contractual relations and to the overall administration of justice within the European Community.

The support and advice I have received from my publishers, and in particular from the editorial manager, Sonia Hubbard, has been unparalleled, and I am deeply appreciative of this.

I wish too to thank Sallyann Blake of the Law School and Mavis Wesley of the Centre of East Anglian Studies who jointly typed the manuscript, and I am further grateful to Professor Robert Merkin of the University of Exeter for some valuable insights into arbitration practice, and to Mr Nicholas Hodgson of the Lord Chancellor's department for keeping me informed of dates of ratification and the like. Any mistakes of substance in the text are attributable to myself alone.

1 April 1992
Earlham Hall
Norwich
NR4 7TJ

P.K.

Table of Cases

Adams v. *Lindsell* (1818) 1 B & Ald. 681   **352**
Adams v. *National Bank of Greece and Athens* SA [1961] AC 255   **18, 307, 312**
Addison v. *Brown* [1954] 1 All ER 213   **25, 245, 348**
Adoui and Cornuaille v. *Belgian State, Cases* 115 and 116/81 [1982] ECR 1665, [1982] 3 CMLR 631   **349, 423**
The Adriatic [1931] P.241   **11**
A-G of New Zealand v. *Ortiz* [1984] AC1   **245**
Albeko Schuhmaschinen v. *The Kamborian Shoe Machine Co. Ltd* [1961] 111 LJ 519   **15, 84, 269, 272**
Alcock v. *Smith* [1892] 1 Ch 238   **118**
Alves v. *Hodgson* (1797) 7 TR 241   **18, 63, 290, 339**
Amin Rasheed Shipping Corpn v. *Kuwait Insurance Co.* [1984] AC 50   **10, 11, 12, 13, 50, 56, 84, 147, 149, 150, 172, 173, 344**
Anderson v. *Equitable Assurance Society of the United States* [1926] 134 LT 557   **23**
Re Anglo-Austrian Bank [1920] 1 Ch 69   **237**
Re Anziani [1930] 1 Ch 407   **323**
Arab Monetary Fund v. *Hashim* [1991] 2 AC 114   **124, 127, 130**
Sprl Arcado v. *Haviland SA*, Case 9/87 [1988] ECR 1539   **32, 92, 98**
Armar Shipping Co. Ltd v. *Caisse Algérienne* [1981] 1 WLR 207   **51, 150**
Arnott v. *Redfern* (1825) 2 C & P 88   **127**
Ascherberg v. *Casa Musicale Sonzogno* [1971] 1 WLR 173   **98, 104**
The Assunzione [1954] P.150   **12, 56, 84, 172, 442, 453**
A.V. Pound & Co. Ltd v. *M.W. Hardy & Co.* [1956] 1 All ER 639   **301**

Bain v. *Whitehaven Rail Co.* (1850) 3 HL Cas. 1   **133, 334**
Baindail v. *Baindail* [1946] P.122   **19**
Balfour v. *Balfour* [1919] 2 KB 571   **106**
Bank of Africa v. *Cohen* [1902] 2 Ch 129, CA   **16, 65, 113, 311, 443**

Bank voor Handel en Scheepvaart NV v. *Slatford* [1953] 1 QB 248 **240**
Barbaros Denizcilik Isletmesi AS v. *Deval Shipping & Trading Co., Deval Denizcilik V.E. Ticaret SA* (1990) ELD 232 **197**
Baroness Wenlock v. *River Dee Co.* (1883) 36 Ch D 675 n **443**
Baschet v. *London Illustrated Standard Co.* [1900] 1 Ch 73 **306**
Bata v. *Beugro* (1984) N.J. No. 745, 2663 **181**
Bavaria Fluggesellschaft Schwabe v. *Eurocontrol*, Cases 9 and 10/77 [1977] ECR 1517, [1980] 1 CMLR 566 **368**
Berghoefer v. *ASA SA*, Case 221/84 [1985] ECR 2699, [1986] 1 CMLR 13 **275, 278**
Bertrand v. *Ott*, Case 150/77 [1978] ECR 1431, [1978] 3 CMLR 499 **205, 206**
Bettray v. *Staatssecretaris van Justitie*, Case 344/87 [1991] 1 CMLR 459 **222**
Blanckaert and Willems v. *Trost*, Case 139/80 [1981] ECR 819, [1982] 2 CMLR 1 **128**
Bodley Head Ltd v. *Flegon* [1972] 1 WLR 680 **19, 113, 312**
Boissevain v. *Weil* [1950] AC 327, **24, 68, 84, 244, 261, 440, 444**
Re Bonacina [1912] 2 Ch 394 **15, 99, 270**
Bondholders Securities Corporation v. *Manville* (1933) 4 DLR 699 **117**
Bonython v. *Commonwealth of Australia* [1951] AC 201 **11, 12, 172, 298**
Borker, Case 138/80 [1980] ECR 1975, [1980] 3 CMLR 273 **422**
R v. *Bouchereau*, Case 30/77 [1977] ECR 1999, [1977] 2 CMLR 800 **357**
Bowling v. *Cox* [1926] AC 751 **101**
BP Exploration Co. (Libya) Ltd v. *Hunt* (No.2) [1979] 1 WLR 783 **301**
Brack v. *Insurance Officer*, Case 17/16 [1976] ECR 1429, [1976] 2 CMLR 592 **357**
Brinkibon Ltd v. *Stahag Stahl GmbH* [1982] 2 AC 34 **15**
Bristow v. *Sequeville* (1850) 5 Exch 275 **135**
British Controlled Oilfields v. *Stagg* (1921) LT 209 **18, 270**
British Linen Co. v. *Drummond* (1830) 10 B & C 903 **44, 133, 307**
British South Africa Co. v. *de Beers Consolidated Mines Ltd* [1910] 2 Ch 502, CA **12, 13**
Brodin v. *A/R Seljan* (1973) SC 213 **48, 102, 105, 106, 227, 242**
Broekmeulen v. *Huisarts Registratie Commissie*, Case 246/80 [1981] ECR 2311, [1982] 1 CMLR 91 **422**
Brogden v. *Metropolitan Ry* (1977) 2 App Cas 666 **278**
Brown v. *Thornton* (1837) 6 Ad & El 185 **336**
Bulk Oil (Zug) AG v. *Sun International Ltd* [1984] 1 All ER 386 **422**

Bulmer v. *Bollinger* [1974] Ch 401   **421, 423, 426, 457**
Bumper Development Corporation v. *Commissioner of Police of the Metropolis* [1991] 1 WLR 1362   **138**

Cammell v. *Sewell* (1860) 5 H & N 728, Ex Ch   **43**
Campbell, Connelly & Co. v. *Noble* [1963] 1 WLR 252   **323, 324**
Cesena Sulphur Co. v. *Nicholson* (1876) 1 Ex D 428   **185**
Charron v. *Montreal Trust Co.* [1958] 15 DLR (2d) 240   **19, 65, 113, 312, 443**
Chatenay v. *Brazilian Submarine Telegraph Co.* [1981] 1 QB 79   **12, 51, 127, 129, 300**
Chemial Farmaceutici SpA v. *DAF SpA Case* 140/79 [1981] ECR 1, [1981] 3 CMLR 350   **424**
Re *Chesterman's Trusts* [1923] Ch 466   **23, 300, 444**
C.H.W. v. *G.J.H.*, Case 25/81 [1982] ECR 1189, [1983] 2 CMLR 125   **115**
CILFIT Srl v. *Ministry of Health*, Case 283/81 [1982] ECR 3415, [1983] 1 CMLR 472   **78, 357, 419, 426**
Citadel Insurance v. *Atlantic Union Insurance* [1982] 2 Lloyd's Rep 543   **12**
Clegg v. *Levy* (1812) 3 Comp 166   **135**
Cleveland Museum of Art v. *Capricorn Art International* SA [1990] 2 Lloyd's Rep 166   **185, 236**
CMI Corporation v. *ICA (Isis Computer Associates) Europe BV* (1989) ELD 412   **181**
Coast Lines v. *Hudig & Veder Chartering NV* [1972] 2 QB 34   **12, 18**
Re *Cohn* [1945] Ch 5   **48, 136, 333**
The Colorado [1923] P.102   **138**
Compagnie Tunisienne de Navigation SA v. *Compagnie d'Armement Maritime SA* [1971] AC 572   **11, 17, 51, 121, 150, 152, 173, 442**
Compania Colombia de Seguros v. *Pacific Steam Navigation Co.* [1965] 1 QB 101   **324**
Conegate Ltd v. *Customs and Excise Commissioners*, Case 121/85 [1986] ECR 1007, [1986] 1 CMLR 739   **349**
Corocraft Ltd v. *Pan American Airways Inc* [1969] 1 QB 616   **244**
Costa v. *ENEL*, Case 6/64 [1964] ECR 585, [1964] CMLR 425   **420**
Coupland v. *Arabian Gulf Oil Co.* [1983] 1 WLR 1136   **237**
Cox v. *E.L.G. Metals Ltd* [1985] ICR 310   **226**
Cruse v. *Chittum* [1974] 2 All ER 940   **184**

Da Costa en Schaake NV v. *Nederlandse Belastingadministratie*, Cases 28–30/62 [1963] ECR 31, [1963] CMLR 224   **426**

D'Almeida Araujo Lda v. *Sir Frederick Becker & Co. Ltd* [1953] 2 QB 329
24, 44, 135, 305, 444
D'Almeida Araujo: 'The Despina R' [1979] AC 685 **135**
De Cavel v. *De Cavel* (No.1), Case 143/78 [1979] ECR 1055, [1979] 2 CMLR 547 **40, 115**
De Cavel v. *De Cavel* (No.2), Case 120/79 [1980] ECR 731, [1980] 3 CMLR 1 **115**
De Geus v. *Bosch*, Case 13/61 [1962] ECR 45, [1962] CMLR 1 **425**
De Nicols v. *Curlier* [1900] AC 21 **114**
De Thoren v. *AG* (1876) 1 App C 686 **48**
de Wolf v. *Harry Cox BV*, Case 42/79 [1976] ECR 1759, [1977] 2 CMLR 43 **96**
de Wutz v. *Hendricks* (1824) 2 Bing 314 **20, 240**
The Despina R [1979] AC 685 **24, 136**
Dimskal Shipping Co. SA v. *International Transport Workers Federation, The 'Evia Luck' (No.2)* [1990] 1 Lloyd's Rep 319 **10, 50, 100, 104, 105, 344**
Dresser UK Limited v. *Falcongate Freight Management Limited* [1992] 2 WLR 319 **424**
Dubai Electricity Co. v. *Islamic Republic of Iran Shipping Lines* ("*The Iran Vojdan*") [1984] 2 Lloyd's Rep 380 **12**
Duncan v. *Motherwell Bridge and Engineering Co.* (1952) SC 131 **226**
Dunlop Pneumatic Tyre Co. Ltd v. *AG Cudell & Co.* [1902] 1 KB 342 **236**
Dynamit AG v. *Rio Tinto Co. Ltd* [1918] AC 292 **107, 244**

Effer v. *Kantner*, Case 38/81 [1982] ECR 825, [1984] 2 CMLR 667 **103, 273**
E.F. Hutton & Co. (London) Ltd v. *Abdul Ghani Mofarrij* [1989] 2 Lloyd's Rep 348 **116**
Egyptian Delta Land and Investment Co. v. *Todd* [1929] AC 1 **184**
E.I. du Pont de Nemours v. *Agnew* [1987] 2 Lloyd's Rep 585 **139**
Elefanten Schuh v. *Jacqmain*, Case 150/80 [1981] ECR 1671, [1982] 3 CMLR 1 **79, 102**
Embiricos v. *Anglo-Austrian Bank* [1904] 2 KB 870 **118**
Re English and Colonial Produce Co. Ltd [1906] 2 Ch 435 **123**
English v. *Donnelly* 1958 SC 494 **243, 244, 292**
Entores v. *Miles Far East Corporation* [1955] 2 QB 327, CA **15**
Etler v. *Kertesz* (1960) 26 ELR (2d) 209 **310**

Felthouse v. *Bindley* (1862) 11 CB (N.S.) 869 **275**

Fibrosa Spolka Akcyjna v. *Fairbairn Lawson Combe Barbour Ltd* [1943] AC 32   **310**
Fogiia v. *Novello (Nos 1 and 2)*, Cases 104/79 and 244/80[1980] ECR 745, [1981] 1 CMLR 45 and [1981] ECR 3045, [1982] 1 CMLR 585   **424**
Forsakringsiktieselskapet Vesta v. *Butcher* [1986] 2 All ER 488, affd [1988] 2 All ER 43, [1989] 1 All ER 402   **9, 51, 142, 154, 175**
Foss v. *Harbottle* (1843) 2 Ha 461   **126**
The Folias [1979] AC 685   **306**
Foster v. *Driscoll* [1929] 1 KB 470   **19, 25, 68, 70, 84, 240, 346, 441, 445**
Fothergill v. *Monarch Airlines* [1981] AC 251   **80**
The Frank Pais [1986] 1 Lloyd's Rep 529   **119**
The Freccia del Nord [1989] 1 Lloyd's Rep 388   **424**
Re Fry [1946] Ch 312   **324**
Re Fuld's Estate (No.3) [1968] P.675   **49, 333**

Garcin v. *Amerindo Investment Advisors Ltd* [1991] 4 All ER 655   **336**
Garden Cottage Foods Ltd v. *Milk Marketing Board* [1984] AC 130   **421**
G & H Montage GmbH v. *Irvani* [1990] 1 WLR 667   **18, 290**
General Steam Navigation Co. v. *Guillou* (1843) 11 M & W 877   **138, 303**
George Mitchell (Chesterhall) Ltd v. *Finney Lock Seeds Ltd* [1983] 1 All ER 108   **278**
Gerli & Co. Inc v. *Cunard SS Co. Ltd* 48 F 2d 115 (2nd Cir.) (1931)   **169**
Gibbs v. *Société Industrielle et Commerciale des Métaux* (1890) 25 QBD 399   **309**
Golden Acres Ltd v. *Quensland Estates Pty Ltd* [1969] Qd R 378   **13, 148, 243**
Goodwin v. *Gray* (1874) 22 WR 312   **329**
Goodwin v. *Robarts* (1876) 1 App Cas 476   **118**
Gray v. *Formosa* [1963] P.259   **347–348**
Grell v. *Levy* (1864) 9 LT 721   **244**
Guépratte v. *Young* (1851) 4 De G & Sm 217   **18, 60, 443**

Hacker v. *Euro Relais GmbH*, Case C-280/90 (1992) *The Times*, 9 April   **193, 194, 195, 196, 207**
Hamlyn & Co. v. *Talisker Distillery* [1894] AC 202   **9, 175, 442**
Re Helbert Wagg & Co. Ltd's Claim [1956] Ch 323   **9, 18, 175**
R v. *Henn and Darby*, Case 34/79 [1979] ECR 3795, [1980] 1 CMLR 246   **349**

Henry Kendall and Sons v. *William Lillico and Sons* [1969] AC 31 **278**
Hill v. *Hibbit* (1871) 25 LT 183 **333**
Hoekstra (Née Unger) v. *BBDA*, Case 75/63 [1964] ECR 177, [1964] CMLR 319 **222**
Hoffman v. *Kreig*, Case 145/86 [1988] ECR 645 **348**
Hoffman-La Roche AG v. *Centrafarm*, Case 107/76 [1977] ECR 957, [1977] 2 CMLR 334 **421**
The Hollandia [1983] AC 565 **14, 17, 24, 69, 161, 169, 198, 244, 261, 356, 370, 440, 442, 444**

Innes v. *Dunlop* (1800) 8 TR 595 **325**
The Iran Vojdan [1984] 2 Lloyd's Rep 380 **119, 150, 172**
Irish Creamery Milk Suppliers Association v. *Ireland* [1981] ECR 735, [1981] 2 CMLR 455 **423**
Ivenel v. *Schwab*, Case 133/81 [1982] ECR 1891, [1983] 1 CMLR 538 **57, 59, 79, 128, 178, 188, 233**

Jacobs v. *Crédit Lyonnais* (1884) 12 QBD 589 **12, 13, 23, 299, 301, 307, 444**
Jakob Handte GmbH v. *TMCS*, Case 26/91 (1992) *The Times*, 19 August **98, 99**
James Buchanan & Co. Ltd v. *Babco Forwarding and Shipping (UK) Ltd* [1978] AC 141 **77, 356**
James Miller and Partners Ltd v. *Whitworth Street Estates (Manchester) Ltd* [1970] AC 583 **51, 56, 84, 172, 173**
J.H. Rayner (Mincing Lane) Ltd v. *Department of Trade and Industry* [1990] 2 AC 418 **124, 126, 130**
Jones v. *Trollope Colls Cementation Overseas Ltd* (1990) *The Times*, 26 January **350**
Joseph Constantine Steamship Line v. *Imperial Smelting Corporation* [1942] AC 154 **332**

Kahler v. *Midland Bank* [1950] AC 24 **9, 19, 51, 68, 84, 175, 245, 270, 443**
Kalfelis v. *Schröder, Münchmeyer, Hengst*, Case 189/87 [1988] ECR 5565 **38, 99**
Kaufman v. *Gerson* [1904] 1 KB 591 **245, 270, 346, 348**
Kay's Leasing Corporation v. *Fletcher* (1964) 116 CLR 124 **243**
Kelly v. *Selwyn* [1905] 2 Ch 117 **324, 325**
Kempf v. *Statssecretaris van Justitie*, Case 139/85 [1987] 1 CMLR 764 **222**

King's Norton Metal Co. v. *Edridge, Merrett & Co. Ltd* (1897) 14 TLR 98
   157
Kleinwort Benson Ltd and Barclays Bank plc v. *Glasgow City Council* (1992) *The Times*, 17 March   **47, 80, 93, 100, 101, 309, 357**
Kleinwort Sons & Co. v. *Ungarische Baumwolle AG* [1939] 2 KB 678
   23, 241
Kloeckner & Co. AG v. *Gatoil Overseas Inc* [1990] 1 Lloyd's Rep 177
   11, 153, 424
Koechlin et Cie v. *Kestenbaum* [1927] 1 KB 889   **118**
Kohnke v. *Karger* [1951] 2 KB 670   **24**
The Komninoss (1991) *Financial Times*, 16 January   **150, 152**
Korner v. *Witkowitzer* [1950] 2 KB 128   **298, 337**
Re *Korvine's Trusts* [1921] 1 Ch 343   **114**
Kraut AG v. *Albany Fabrics Ltd* [1977] QB 182   **306**
Kremezi v. *Ridgway* [1949] 1 All ER 662   **156**

Re *Langley's Settlement Trusts* [1962] Ch 541   **317–318, 350**
The Lankya Abbaya (1988) I Prax 26   **272**
Re *Lamplugh Iron Ore Co. Ltd* [1927] 1 Ch 308   **328**
Lawrence v. *Lawrence* [1985] Fam 106   **106**
Lawrie-Blum v. *Land Baden-Württemberg*, Case 66/85 [1987] 3 CMLR 389
Lee v. *Abdy* (1886) 17 QBD 309   **323**
Le Feuvre v. *Sullivan* (1855) 10 Moo PC 1   **325**
Lehndorf Property Management Ltd v. *McGrath and Eagle* [1984] 3 WWR 187   **135**
Lemanda Trading Co. v. *African Middle East Petroleum Co. Ltd* [1988] 1 All ER 513   **20, 68, 241**
The Leonidas D [1985] 1 WLR 925   **275**
Leroux v. *Brown* (1852) 12 CB 801   **18, 44, 63, 134, 135, 137, 290, 338, 339**
Les Afféteurs Réunis SA v. *Leopold Walford (London) Ltd* [1919] AC 801
   132
Levin v. *Staatssecretaris van Justitie*, Case 53/81 [1982] ECR 1035, [1982] 2 CMLR 454   **222**
Libyan Arab Foreign Bank v. *Bankers Trust Co.* [1989] QB 728, [1989] 3 All ER 252   **9, 19, 21, 51, 68, 175, 252, 300, 443, 445**
Linden Gardens Trust Ltd v. *Lenesta Sludge Disposals Ltd, and St Martins Corporation Ltd* v. *Sir Robert McAlpine & Sons Ltd* (1992) *The Times*, 27 February   **324**
Lipkin Gorman v. *Karpnale Ltd* [1991] 3 WLR 10   **101**
Lister v. *Forth Dry Dock and Engineering Co. Ltd* [1989] 2 WLR 634
   256

Littauer Glove Corpn v. F.W. Millington (1920) Ltd (1928) 44 TLR 746
     236
Lord Bethell v. Sabena [1983] 3 CMLR 1   **423**
Loucks v. Standard Oil Co. of New York (1918) 224 NY 99   **266**
Lorentzen v. Lydden & Co. [1942] 2 KB 202   **240**
L.T.U. v. Eurocontrol, Case 29/76 [1976] ECR 1541, [1977] 1 CMLR 88
     356

Mackender v. Feldia AG [1967] 2 QB 590   **17, 119, 169, 270, 272**
Mahadervan v. Mahadervan [1964] P.23   **333**
Male v. Roberts (1800) 3 Esp 163   **19, 65, 113, 311, 443**
Marc Rich and Co. AG v. Società Italiana Impianti PA ("The Atlantic Emperor"), Case C-190/89 (1991) *The Times,* 20 September   **41, 102, 120, 271, 423, 457**
The Mariannina [1983] 1 Lloyd's Rep 12   **150**
Maspons v. Mildred (1882) 9 QBD 530   **127**
Matthews v. Kuwait Bechtel Corpn [1959] 2 QB 57   **237**
Maurox v. Sociedade Comercial Abel Pereira da Fonseca SARL [1972] 2 All ER 1085   **127**
Maxim's Ltd v. Dye [1978] 2 All ER 55   **423**
Medway Packaging Ltd v. Meurer Maschinen GmbH & Co. KG [1990] 1 Lloyd's Rep. 383   **102**
Meilicke v. ADV/OGA F.A. Meyer AG, Case C-83/91 (1992) *The Times,* 20 October   **424**
Mercury Publicity Ltd v. Wolfgang Loerke GmbH (1991) *The Times,* 21 October   **57, 79**
Re Metcalfe's Trusts (1864) 2 De G.J. & S. 122   **350**
Meyer v. Dresser (1864) 16 CB (N.S.) 646   **305**
Midland International Trade Services Ltd v. Sudairy (1990) *Financial Times,* 2 May   **300, 305**
Milchkontor v. Hauptzollamt Saarbrücken, Case 19/68 [1969] ECR 165, [1969] CMLR 390   **81, 426**
Miliangos v. George Frank (Textiles) Ltd [1976] AC 443   **23, 306, 444**
Miliangos v. George Frank (Textiles) Ltd (No.2)[1977] QB 480   **24, 135, 300, 305, 444**
Re Missouri Steamship Company (1889) 42 Ch D 321   **23, 241**
Moggré v. Big Dutchman International AG (1989) ELD 454   **234**
Molkerei-Zentrale v. Hauptzollamt Paderborn, Case 28/67 [1968] ECR 143, [1968] CMLR 187   **26**
Monterosso Shipping Co. Ltd v. International Transport Workers Federation, The Rosso [1982] 2 Lloyd's Rep 120, [1982] 3 All ER 841   **18, 135, 137, 222, 290, 338, 339**

Moulis v. *Owen* [1907] 1 KB 746 **40, 116**
Mount Albert Borough Council v. *Australasian Temperance and General Mutual Life Assurance Society* [1938] AC 224 **18, 300, 443**

National Bank of Greece and Athens SA v. *Metliss* [1958] AC 509 **18, 307, 443**
New England Reinsurance v. *Messoghios Insurance Co. S.A.* [1992] 1 Lloyd's Rep 201 **103**
Newtherapeutics Ltd v. *Katz* [1990] 3 WLR 1183 **101, 126, 356**
Nordsee v. *Reederei Mond,* Case 102/81 [1982] ECR 1095 **422**

O'Callaghan v. *Thomond* (1810) 3 Taunt 82 **138, 325**
Oppenheimer v. *Catermole* [1976] AC 249 **350**
Re Oriel Ltd [1986] 1 WLR 180 **236**

P & O Steam Navigation Co. v. *Shand* (1865) 3 Moo P.B. (N.S.) 272 **12, 13, 270**
The Parouth [1982] 2 Lloyd's Rep 351 **10, 15, 271, 272, 442**
Pearce v. *Brooks* (1866) LR 1 Exch 213 **348**
Pender v. *Lushington* (1877) 6 Ch D 70 **125**
Peter Buchanan Ltd and Macharg v. *McVey* [1954] IR 89 **245**
Peters v. *ZNAV,* Case 34/82 [1983] ECR 987 **38, 79, 98, 125**
R v. *Pharmaceutical Society of Great Britain, ex parte Association of Pharmaceutical Importers* [1987] 3 CMLR 951 **421**
Phillips v. *Eyre* (1870) LR 6 QB 1 **105**
Phoenix Assurance Co. v. *Spooner* [1905] 2 KB 753 **328**
Phrantzes v. *Argenti* [1960] 2 QB 19 **136, 306, 336**
Picker v. *London Bank* (1887) 18 QBD 519 **118**
Pickstone v. *Freemans plc* [1989] AC 66 **356**
Pickup v. *Thames & Mersey Marine Insurance Co.* (1878) 3 QBD 594 **332**
Powell Duffryn plc v. *Petereit,* Case C-214/89 (1992) *The Times,* 15 April **98, 126**
Prodexport Co. v. *E.D. & F.M. Man Ltd* [1973] 1 QB 389 **17**

R v. *International Trustee for the Protection of Bondholders AC* [1937] AC 500 **12**
Ralli Brothers v. *Compania Naviera Sota y Aznar* [1920] 2 KB 287 **20, 21, 22, 47, 68, 69, 84, 240, 260, 300, 347, 441, 443**
Ready Mixed Concrete (South East) Ltd v. *Minister of Pensions and National Insurance* [1968] 2 QB 497 **222**

Regazzoni v. *K.C. Sethia (1944) Ltd* [1958] AC 301   **20, 69, 76, 84, 240, 245, 252, 456**
Reichert v. *Dresdner Bank*, Case 115/88 [1990] ECR 27   **195**
Republica de Guatemala v. *Nunez* [1927] 1 KB 669   **323**
Rewe v. *Hauptzollamt Kiel*, Case 150/80 [1981] ECR 805   **218**
Rijksdienst voor Werknemerspensioenen v. *Vlaeminck*, Case 132/81 [1982] ECR 2953   **426**
R v. *International Trustee* [1937] AC 500   **147**
Risdon Iron and Locomotive Works v. *Furness* [1906] 1 KB 49   **124**
The Roberta (1937) 58 L1 L Rep 159   **49, 137, 333**
Robinson v. *Bland* (1760) 2 Burr 1077   **25, 76, 245**
Rösler v. *Rottwinkel*, Case 241/83 [1985] ECR 99, [1985] 1 CMLR 806   **192, 193, 196**
Rossano v. *Manufacturers Life Insurance Co.* [1962] 2 All ER 214, 218   **1, 172**
Rossano v. *Manufacturers Life Insurance Co.* [1963] 2 QB 352   **12**
Rousillon v. *Rousillon* (1880) 14 Ch D 351   **25, 244, 261, 440, 444**
Rowlett Leaky & Co. v. *Scottish Provident Institution* [1927] 1 Ch 55   **298**
Rutili v. *Ministre de l'Intérieur*, Case 36/75 [1975] ECR 1219, [1976] 1 CMLR 140   **349**

S v. *K* (1983) Recueil Dalloz Sirey, Nos 1–27, J 146   **181**
Salotti v. *RÜWA*, Case 24/76 [1976] ECR 1831, [1977] 1 CMLR 345   **119, 278**
Sanders v. *Van der Putte*, Case 73/77 [1977] ECR 2382, [1978] 1 CMLR 331   **102, 192**
Sanicentral v. *Collin*, Case 25/79 [1979] ECR 3423, [1980] 2 CMLR 164   **79, 223**
SAR Schotte GmbH v. *Parfum Rothschild S.a.r.l.*, Case 218/86 [1987] ECR 4905   **128**
Saxby v. *Fulton* [1909] 2 KB 208   **348**
Sayers v. *International Drilling Co.* [1971] 1 WLR 1176, CA   **12, 105, 106, 227, 235, 237, 242, 243, 247**
Scammel v. *Ousten* [1941] AC 251   **451**
Scherrens v. *Maenhout*, Case 158/87 [1988] ECR 3791   **193, 194**
Schwebel v. *Ungar* (1963) 42 DLR (2d) 622   **104, 106**
Segoura v. *Bonakdarian*, Case 25/77 [1976] ECR 1851, [1977] 1 CMLR 361   **119, 278**
Re Selot's Trusts [1920] 1 Ch 488   **317, 350**
Shenavai v. *Kreischer*, Case 266/85 [1987] ECR 239, [1987] 3 CMLR 782   **57, 178, 223, 233**

Six Constructions Ltd v. *Humbert*, Case 32/88 [1989] ECR 341   **57, 79, 80, 93, 178, 233**
Re Soltykoff, ex p Margrett [1891] 1 QB 413   **117**
Somafer SA v. *Saar-Ferngas AG*, Case 33/78 [1978] ECR 2183, [1979] 1 CMLR 490   **96, 128**
Sottomayor v. *De Barros (No.1)* (1877) LR 3 PD 1   **19, 64–5, 113, 311, 443**
South African Breweries Limited v.*King* [1900] 1 Ch 273   **234**
South India Shipping Corpn Ltd v. *Export-Import Bank of Korea* [1985] 1 WLR 585   **236**
Steymann v. *Staatssecretaris van Justitie*, Case 196/87 [1989] 1 CMLR 449   **222**
St Pierre v. *South American Stores Ltd* [1937] 1 All ER 206   **135, 298, 337**

Tescam Distribution Ltd v. *Schuh Mode Team GmbH* (1989) *The Times*, 24 October   **102**
R v. *Thompson*, Case 7/78 [1978] ECR 2247   **357**
Trendtex Trading Corpn v. *Crédit Suisse* [1982] AC 679   **245, 323, 324**

Udny v. *Udny* (1869) LR 1 Sc & Div 44   **112**
Union Transport plc v. *Continental Lines S.A.* [1992] 1 W.L.R. 15, 20–1 (H.L.(E.))   **178**
Union Trust Co. v. *Grosman* 245 US 412 (1918)   **113, 311**
Re United Railways of the Havana and Regla Warehouses Ltd [1960] Ch 52   **10, 12, 50, 156, 172, 173, 175, 321, 344, 442**

Van Duyn v. *Home Office*, Case 41/74 [1974] ECR 1337, [1975] 1 CMLR 1   **349, 357**
Van Gend en Loos v. *Nederlandse Administratie der Belastingen*, Case 26/62 [1963] ECR 1, [1963] CMLR 105   **425**
Van Grutten v. *Digby* (1862) 31 Beav 561   **18, 60, 63, 443**
Verwaeke v. *Smith* [1983] 1 AC 145   **348**
Viral SpA v. *Orbat SpA*, Case 46/80 [1981] ECR 77, [1981] 3 CMLR 524   **424**
Vineh Construction Company Limited v. *Houthandel G. Wijma en Zonen BV* (1989) ELD 252   **181, 269**
Vita Food Products Inc v. *Unus Shipping Co.* [1939] AC 277   **11, 13, 50, 52, 69, 84, 108, 148, 241, 273, 442, 456**

White Cliffs Opal Mines v. *Miller* [1904] 4 SR (NSW) 150   **64, 399**

Whitworth Street Estates (Manchester) Ltd v. *James Miller & Partners Ltd*
  [1970] AC 583   **11, 12**
Williams and Humbert Ltd v. *W. and H. Trade Marks (Jersey) Ltd* [1986] 1
  AC 368   **245**
Wilson v. *Maynard Shipbuilding Consultants A.B.* [1978] QB 665   **234**
Winkworth v. *Christie, Manson and Woods Ltd* [1980] Ch 496   **43**
Worms v. *De Valdor* (1880) 49 LJ Ch 261   **317, 350**

X A/G v. *A Bank* [1983] 2 All ER 464   **12**

The Zinnia [1984] 2 Lloyd's Rep 211   **278**
Zivnostenska Banka v. *Frankman* [1950] AC 57   **175**

Table of Statutes

Arbitration Act 1975
   s.5(2)(b)   **121**
Arbitration Act 1979
   s.1   **422**
   s.2   **422**
Aviation Security Act 1982
   s.19(5)   **432, 434**

Bills of Exchange Act 1882
   General   **116**
   s.22(1)   **117**
   s.72(1)   **40, 117**
   s.72(2)   **40, 117**
   s.72(3)   **117**
   s.97   **117**
Business Names Act 1985
   s.5   **127**

Carriage by Air Act 1961   **198, 244**
Carriage by Air (Supplementary Provisions) Act 1962   **198**
Carriage of Goods by Road Act 1965   **198, 244**
Carriage of Goods by Sea Act 1971
   s.1(2)   **14, 244, 370**
   s 1(3)   **14**
   General   **24, 161**
   Schedule, Article III para 8   **242**
   Schedule, Article X   **14, 198, 244, 370**
Carriage of Passengers by Road Act 1974   **198–9, 244**
Civil Jurisdiction and Judgments Act 1982
   s.16(1)(a)   **192**
   s.16(3)(a)   **101**

Schedule 4, Article 5(1)   80, 101, 102, 309
Schedule 4, Article 5(3)   102
Companies Act 1985
  s.14(1)   125
  s.24   126
  s.35(1)   42, 124
  s.35 A(1)   124, 126, 129
  s.35(3)   126
  s.36(1)(a)   282
  s.36 C(1)   123
  s.117(8)   126
  s.349   126
Companies Act 1989
  s.108(1)   42, 124
Consumer Credit Act 1974
  s.43(2)(c)   431, 433
  s.60–65   292, 338, 340
  s.61   290
  s.67   210, 242
  s.127   292, 338, 340
  s.145(3)(c)   431, 433
  s.145(4)(b)   431, 433
  s.173   84, 210, 242, 293
Contracts (Applicable Law) Act 1990   1, 91
  s.1   362
  s.1(a)   78
  s.1(b)   78
  s.1(c)   1, 78, 81, 415
  s.2   91, 92, 395
  s.2(1)   1, 34, 78, 93, 398, 429
  s.2(2)   3, 47, 52, 69, 71, 73, 74, 93, 104, 214, 231, 238, 249, 282, 305, 309, 371, 372, 441, 451
  s.2(3)   31, 32, 110, 309, 362, 363, 419
  s.2(4)(a)   1, 31, 78
  s.2(4)(b)   1, 31, 78
  s.2(4)(c)   1, 31, 78, 81
  s.3   92
  s.3(1)   1, 2, 40, 79, 92, 108, 358, 408, 427
  s.3(2)   1, 2, 40, 79, 92, 358, 427
  s.3(3)   78, 358, 408
  s.3(3)(a)   94

s.3(3)(b)	**1, 78, 94, 416**
s.4	**36, 93**
s.4(1)	**259**
s.4(1)(b)	**309, 372**
s.4(3)	**93, 392**
s.5	**2, 31, 93, 225, 241, 432, 435**
s.6	**34, 93**
s.7	**1, 31, 34, 78, 79, 93, 395, 429**
s.8	**94**
s.8(2)	**392**
s.9	**94**
Schedule 1	**1, 31, 78, 91, 95**
Schedule 2	**1, 31, 78, 91, 411**
Schedule 3	**1, 31, 78, 81, 91, 415, 417**
Schedule 4	**2, 31, 93, 225, 241, 431–435**

Emergency Powers (Defence) Act 1939
 s.3(1) **244**
Employment Protection Act 1975
 Schedule 6 **433**
Employment Protection (Consolidation) Act 1978
 s.140(1) **55**
 s.141(1), (2), (3), (4) **226, 230, 244**
 s.153 (5) **14, 24, 226, 243**
Equal Pay Act 1970
 s.1(1) **75, 225, 230, 244**
 s.1(11) **14, 24, 225, 244, 431, 432**
Equal Pay Act (Northern Ireland) 1970 **431, 432**

Factories Act 1961 **227**
Family Law Act 1986
 s.46(1) **112**
Foreign Limitation Periods Act 1984
 General **308**
 s.1(1) **44, 46, 307**
 s.1(1)(a) **307**

Health and Safety at Work etc Act 1974
 s.47(1) and (2) **227**
Hire Purchase Act 1954 **243, 244**
Hire Purchase and Small Debt (Scotland) Act 1932 **243, 244**

Income and Corporation Taxes Act 1988
  s.347 B(1)(a)   **432, 435**
Insolvency Act 1986
  s.239   **127**
Insurance Companies Act 1982
  s.94A   **139**
  s.96A   **45, 141**
  Schedule 3A   **139**
International Transport Conventions Act 1983   **198**

Law of Property Act 1925
  s.40(1)   **63, 66, 290, 293, 294, 339, 340, 341**
  s.136   **289, 325**
  s.184   **332**
Law of Property (Miscellaneous Provisions) Act 1989
  s.2   **63, 290**
  s.2(1)   **63, 294, 338, 341**
  s.2(4)   **63, 294, 339**
  s.2(8)   **63, 66, 290, 294, 339, 340**
Law Reform (Personal Injuries) Act 1948
  s.1(3)   **227, 242, 243**

Merchant Shipping Act 1894
  s.24   **290**
Merchant Shipping Act 1979
  General   **199**
  s.14(1)   **244**
Misrepresentation Act 1967
  s.2(2)   **334**
  s.6(4)   **361**

Offices, Shops and Railway Premises Act 1963   **227**

Patents Act 1977
  ss.39–43   **226, 244**
  s.43(2)   **226, 230, 244**
  s.82(5),(6)   **431, 433, 434**
Prescription and Limitation (Scotland) Act 1984   **46, 307**

Recognition of Trusts Act 1987   **132, 133**
  Schedule, Article 2(1), 3(2)   **132, 133**
  Schedule, Article 15   **249**

Table of Statutes xxvii

  Schedule, Article 16   **262**
Rent Act 1977
  s.126(1)   **242**

Sale of Goods Act 1979
  s.6(1)(a)   **210, 215**
  s.6(2)(a)   **210**
  s.12   **14, 52, 53, 72, 73, 160, 161, 211, 242, 243, 440**
  s.12(1)   **210, 215**
  s.12(1)(a)   **206**
  s.12(1)(b)   **206**
  s.13   **14, 52, 53, 72, 73, 160, 161, 211, 242, 243, 440**
  s.14   **14, 52, 53, 72, 160, 161, 211, 242, 243, 440**
  s.14(2)   **206, 210**
  s.14(3)   **206**
  s.15   **14, 52, 53, 72, 73, 160, 161, 211, 242, 243, 440**
  s.56   **24, 70, 73, 161, 211**
  s.56(3)   **14, 161, 211, 243, 244, 263**
  s.61(1)   **204**
Sex Discrimination Act 1975
  s.8   **225**
  s.10(1)   **230**
  Schedule I, Part I, para 1(4)   **225**
Statute of Frauds 1677
  s.4   **290, 338, 339**

Trade Union and Labour Relations Act 1974
  s.18   **222, 226**
  s.29   **221**
  s.30(b)   **14, 24, 226**
  s.30(1)   **221**

Unfair Contract Terms Act 1977
  s.6   **52, 53, 84, 160, 161, 167, 206, 211, 212, 242, 261, 277, 434, 440**
  s.7   **277**
  s.11(2)   **277**
  s.12   **53**
  s.26   **14, 52, 53, 54, 70, 160, 161, 167, 210, 211, 215, 241, 242, 244, 263, 440**
  s.27   **73, 74, 84, 442**
  s.27(1)   **13, 241, 432, 434, 441, 445**

s.27(2)	**13, 24, 160, 167, 212, 226, 242, 261, 263, 440, 444**
Sch.2	**277**

Wages Act 1986
   s.30   **226**

International Conventions and Treaties

1924 Brussels International Convention for the Unification of Certain Rules of Law Relating to Bills of Lading, 25th August 1924 (1931) U.K.T.S. 17 **198, 370, 410**

1930 Geneva Convention Providing for the Settlement of Certain Conflicts of Laws in Connection with Bills of Exchange and Promissory Notes, 7th June 1930 (1934) U.K.T.S. 14 **116, 117**

1931 Geneva Convention Providing for the Settlement of Certain Conflicts of Laws in Connection with Cheques, 19th March 1931, 143 U.N.T.S. 407 **116**

1955 Hague Convention on the Law Applicable to International Sales of Goods, 15th June 1955, 510 U.N.T.S. 147 **367, 369, 382**

1956 Convention on the Contract for the International Carriage of Goods by Road (CMR), 19th May 1956, Cmnd 3455 **198**

1957 EEC Treaty Establishing the European Economic Community (Treaty of Rome), 25th March 1957, 298 U.N.T.S. 11
Article 36 **349**
Article 48 **222**
Article 48(3) **349**
Article 52 **222**
Article 54(3)(g) **122**
Article 56 **349**
Article 177 **83, 420, 421, 422, 423, 457**
Article 188 **418**
Article 220 **95, 400, 416, 417**

Article 227(4) **392**

1958 New York Convention on the Recognition and Enforcement of Foreign Arbitral Awards, 10th June 1958 330 U.N.T.S. 3 **120**

1961 Hague Convention on Conflict of Laws Regarding Testamentary Dispositions, 15th October 1961, 510 U..T.S. 175 **281**

1968 Brussels Convention on Jurisdiction and the Enforcement of Judgments in Civil and Commercial Matters, 27th September 1968, O.J. 1978, L 304/77
Article 1 para 2(4) **40, 120**
Article 5(1) **38, 79, 80, 98, 99, 101, 102, 125, 178, 184, 223, 233, 309, 310**
Article 5(2) **39**
Article 5(3) **38, 98**
Article 5(5) **127**
Article 13 **205, 206**
Article 13(1) **204, 206**
Article 13(2) **204**
Article 13(3) **215**
Article 14 **264**
Article 15 **165**
Article 16(1) **192, 193, 194, 195, 455**
Article 17 **17, 41, 103, 164, 165, 223**
Article 21 **424**
Article 27(1) **349**
Article 60 **392**
Article 63 **396**

1971 Protocol on Interpretation of the Judgments Convention, 3rd June 1971, O.J. 1975 L 204/28
Article 4 **427**

1973 Convention on the Contract for the International Carriage of Passengers and Luggage by Road (CVR) **198**

1974 Athens Convention relating to the Carriage of Passengers and their Luggage by Sea, Cmnd 6326, UKTS 40 (1987) **199**

1978 Hague Convention on the Law Applicable to Agency, 14th March 1978, Cmnd 7020 **249, 368**

1980 Rome Convention on the Law Applicable to Contractual Obligations, 19th June 1980, O.J. 1980, L 266/1   **1**
Preamble   2, 32, 78, 95, 100, 106
Article 1   25, 97, 439
Article 1(1)   2, 32, 33, 38, 53, 98, 105, 106, 107, 108, 110, 125, 146, 159, 161, 170, 172, 195, 203, 210, 244, 297, 350, 363
Article 1(2)   2, 31, 350
Article 1(2)(a)   39, 42, 64, 111, 112, 113, 117, 124, 224, 250, 266, 269, 311, 312, 316, 317, 318, 319, 322, 350, 443
Article 1(2)(b)   39, 40, 113, 115, 133
Article 1(2)(c)   40, 116, 117, 198
Article 1(2)(d)   40, 106, 118, 121
Article 1(2)(e)   41, 42, 64, 111, 121, 122, 123, 124, 125, 126, 127, 269, 311, 322, 443
Article 1(2)(f)   42, 121, 123, 126, 127, 129, 130, 200, 288, 300, 368
Article 1(2)(g)   38, 43, 99, 114, 131, 132
Article 1(2)(h)   24, 43, 44, 46, 48, 49, 66, 67, 85, 133, 134, 135, 138, 152, 232, 294, 295, 298, 299, 307, 308, 309, 325, 332, 334, 338, 339, 340, 444
Article 1(3)   45, 108, 138, 140, 141, 146, 204, 329
Article 1(4)   45, 138, 140, 142
Article 2   31, 34, 143, 145, 153, 392, 412, 416
Article 3   50, 103, 127, 130, 143, 147, 170, 191, 207, 212, 221, 228, 255, 275, 282, 319, 323, 340
Article 3(1)   23, 50, 51, 53, 56, 84, 120, 121, 139, 142, 148, 149, 151, 152, 153, 154, 155, 165, 174, 208, 222, 261, 291, 298, 299, 367, 442, 444, 449, 452
Article 3(2)   51, 84, 98, 148, 149, 151, 154, 155, 156, 157, 158, 159, 261, 283, 442, 456
Article 3(3)   3, 21, 33, 52, 53, 55, 68, 70, 71, 72, 74, 75, 84, 108, 110, 139, 148, 158, 160, 161, 162, 163, 165, 166, 167, 168, 173, 210, 211, 214, 224, 226, 228, 230, 242, 247, 251, 256, 257, 258, 262, 264, 318, 341, 350, 440, 441, 442, 444, 445, 454, 455, 456
Article 3(4)   17, 46, 51, 52, 84, 108, 148, 152, 155, 169, 174, 270, 272, 284, 353, 442, 452
Article 4   50, 52, 55, 107, 109, 153, 155, 170, 219, 255, 275, 282, 291, 319, 323, 340, 359, 452
Article 4(1)   56, 57, 84, 85, 108, 120, 121, 148, 151, 153, 171, 172, 173, 174, 175, 176, 179, 182, 183, 186, 187, 188, 189, 191, 192, 194, 197, 198, 201, 299, 359, 442, 449
Article 4(2)   34, 56, 57, 58, 59, 81, 123, 127, 130, 140, 173, 176,

177, 178, 179, 181, 182, 183, 184, 185, 186, 187, 188, 191, 192, 193, 194, 196, 197, 198, 199, 201, 204, 221, 232, 253, 284, 308, 356, 389, 425, 439, 442, 453, 454

Article 4(3)   58, 62, 183, 191, 193, 194, 195, 196, 208, 219, 293, 439, 442, 455

Article 4(4)   58, 173, 196, 197, 198, 199, 200, 201, 207, 208, 439, 442

Article 4(5)   56, 57, 62, 127, 131, 142, 177, 179, 182, 183, 184, 186, 187, 188, 189, 192, 193, 194, 195, 196, 201, 298, 439, 442

Article 5   21, 45, 53, 62, 203, 217, 221, 297, 319, 359, 439, 444, 445

Article 5(1)   102, 140, 141, 204, 205, 206, 207, 215

Article 5(2)   3, 54, 68, 69, 71, 72, 73, 74, 85, 142, 148, 160, 162, 164, 204, 209, 210, 211, 212, 213, 214, 215, 216, 219, 228, 230, 231, 242, 243, 247, 257, 258, 259, 260, 263, 264, 270, 277, 318, 340, 344, 350, 365, 440, 441, 442, 443, 451, 455, 456

Article 5(3)   59, 188, 204, 213, 214, 215, 219, 220, 238, 270, 292, 442, 454

Article 5(4)   54, 58, 220

Article 5(4)(a)   58, 197, 207, 208, 209, 218

Article 5(4)(b)   208

Article 5(5)   54, 58, 197, 208, 209, 218

Article 6   21, 31, 55, 127, 181, 195, 221, 223, 297, 353, 359, 439, 444, 445

Article 6(1)   3, 55, 68, 70, 71, 72, 73, 74, 85, 148, 160, 164, 210, 214, 222, 224, 225, 226, 227, 228, 229, 230, 231, 232, 242, 243, 247, 257, 258, 259, 260, 263, 264, 270, 277, 282, 318, 341, 344, 350, 440, 441, 442, 443, 451, 455, 456

Article 6(2)   55, 57, 59, 127, 188, 214, 221, 223, 228, 229, 231, 264, 270, 292, 298, 442

Article 6(2)(a)   59, 60, 162, 232, 233, 234, 237, 238, 253

Article 6(2)(b)   59, 60, 71, 79, 230, 233, 234, 236, 237

Article 7   21, 62, 70, 73, 74, 139, 140, 155, 160, 161, 210, 211, 214, 215, 224, 228, 239, 282, 292, 370, 375, 381

Article 7(1)   3, 52, 69, 71, 72, 73, 74, 75, 84, 85, 91, 162, 163, 164, 165, 166, 187, 196, 198, 214, 220, 231, 247, 249, 252, 253, 254, 255, 256, 257, 258, 259, 260, 261, 262, 263, 264, 265, 266, 292, 303, 344, 347, 350, 371, 403, 440, 441, 445, 455

Article 7(2)   3, 21, 66, 68, 69, 71, 72, 73, 74, 75, 77, 85, 127, 162, 163, 164, 196, 214, 219, 220, 232, 247, 250, 251, 256, 260, 261, 262, 263, 264, 265, 266, 282, 292, 309, 318, 339, 341, 344, 347, 350, 374, 440, 441, 442, 443, 444, 445, 455

Article 8	17, 21, 51, 103, 107, 148, 155, 169, 284, 297, 298, 323, 440, 452
Article 8(1)	46, 60, 68, 103, 155, 168, 269, 270, 271, 272, 273, 274, 276, 277, 278, 292, 299, 314, 352, 401, 442
Article 8(2)	60, 84, 123, 168, 269, 270, 273, 274, 275, 276, 277, 278, 279, 323, 356, 425, 443
Article 9	44, 51, 61, 62, 63, 65, 67, 140, 154, 155, 168, 221, 253, 281, 282, 294, 298, 314, 336, 337, 338, 339, 340, 439, 445
Article 9(1)	48, 61, 66, 85, 130, 184, 283, 284, 285, 286, 287, 288, 313, 335, 340, 341, 440, 443
Article 9(2)	48, 61, 66, 85, 130, 283, 285, 286, 287, 288, 313, 335, 340, 341, 440, 443
Article 9(3)	61, 130, 286, 288, 289, 313, 443
Article 9(4)	61, 130, 289, 290, 291, 300, 443
Article 9(5)	62, 140, 220, 221, 283, 292, 335, 443
Article 9(6)	3, 21, 62, 66, 68, 70, 71, 72, 73, 74, 84, 148, 160, 161, 162, 196, 211, 247, 258, 259, 260, 262, 263, 290, 292, 293, 335, 339, 340, 341, 344, 350, 441, 442, 443, 444, 445
Article 10	98, 129, 133, 321, 323, 331, 340, 443, 452
Article 10(1)(a)	23, 46, 152, 169, 174, 298, 451
Article 10(1)(b)	21, 46, 47, 68, 299, 443
Article 10(1)(c)	24, 44, 46, 85, 108, 134, 135, 136, 232, 300, 303, 305, 306, 307, 440, 444
Article 10(1)(d)	21, 44, 46, 68, 85, 134, 156, 284, 299, 300, 307, 308, 350, 443
Article 10(1)(e)	91, 101, 102, 104, 304, 309, 310, 371, 403
Article 10(2)	21, 23, 47, 63, 64, 85, 253, 299, 301, 303, 304, 435, 439, 444
Article 11	2, 33, 51, 64, 65, 111, 113, 117, 123, 130, 155, 224, 250, 266, 269, 286, 298, 311, 312, 313, 314, 315, 316, 317, 318, 319, 322, 350, 356, 359, 360, 439, 440, 443
Article 12	47, 321, 328, 329, 331
Article 12(1)	322, 324
Article 12(2)	322, 324, 325
Article 13	47, 48, 298, 321, 331
Article 13(1)	327, 328, 329, 330
Article 13(2)	330
Article 14	24, 44, 85, 133, 134, 137, 152, 297, 299, 331
Article 14(1)	48, 49, 108, 137, 332, 333, 334, 335, 440, 444
Article 14(2)	44, 62, 64, 66, 67, 68, 107, 134, 282, 290, 292, 293, 294, 295, 298, 334, 335, 336, 337, 338, 339, 341, 440, 444
Article 15	21, 50, 141, 343, 344

Article 16	3, 21, 47, 76, 148, 239–240, 260, 265, 266, 301, 317, 336, 345, 346, 347, 348, 349, 350, 441, 442, 443, 444, 445, 456
Article 17	2, 25, 31, 35, 93, 351, 353, 372, 401, 435
Article 18	76, 77, 85, 98, 174, 190, 277, 298, 355, 356, 357, 407, 408, 419, 457
Article 19	419
Article 19(1)	32, 33, 53, 167, 309, 359, 360, 361, 362, 363
Article 19(2)	31, 32, 33, 92, 110, 359, 362, 363
Article 20	37, 97, 365, 366
Article 21	2, 31, 37, 97, 100, 132, 198, 244, 360, 362, 367, 368, 369, 370, 379, 410
Article 22	92, 97, 371, 403
Article 22(1)(a)	3, 69, 71, 249, 262, 371, 372, 441, 451, 455
Article 22(1)(b)	47, 101, 104, 304, 309, 371, 372
Article 22(2)	371, 372
Article 22(3)	259, 309, 371, 372
Article 23	36, 37, 97, 370, 373, 374, 376, 381, 409, 410
Article 23(1)	375
Article 23(2)	375, 377, 387, 404
Article 23(3)	375, 377, 380, 386
Article 24	37, 97, 360, 362, 369, 379
Article 24(1)	37, 369, 380, 381, 382, 383, 385
Article 24(2)	37, 381, 385, 386, 410
Article 25	37, 97, 369, 380, 383, 385, 386, 387
Article 26	36, 100, 157, 187, 360, 389
Article 27	391
Article 27(1)	392
Article 27(2)	372, 402
Article 27(2)(a)	392
Article 27(2)(b)	392, 421
Article 27(2)(c)	392
Article 27(4)	392, 421
Article 28	395
Article 28 Para 1	395
Article 29	397
Article 29 Para 1	34, 397, 400, 401
Article 29 Para 2	34, 351, 397, 400
Article 30	4, 35, 353, 368, 399, 401, 429, 458
Article 30(1)	400
Article 30(2)	400, 401, 402
Article 30(3)	402
Article 30(4)	400, 401

Article 31	**403**
Article 31(a)	**398**
Article 31(b)	**398**
Article 31(c)	**398**
Article 31(d)	**376, 402, 404**
Article 31(e)	**403**
Article 32	**198, 405**
Article 33	**35, 37, 77, 91, 357, 407, 411**
Annexed Protocol	**405, 409**

1980 United Nations (UNCITRAL) Convention on Contracts for the International Sale of Goods, 11th April 1980, Cmnd 8074

General	**368**
Article 1(1)(a)	**370**
Article 7	**255**
Article 10(a) and (b)	**212**

1980 Berne Convention concerning International Carriage by Rail, CIV and CIM Uniform Rules in Appendix A and B, Cmnd 8535 (1982) **198**

1984 Luxembourg Convention on the Accession of the Hellenic Republic to the Rome Convention, 10th April 1984, O.J. 1984 L 146/1

General	**1, 31**
Article 1	**411**
Article 2	**357, 411**
Article 3	**412**
Article 4	**412**
Article 4 Para 1	**400, 412**
Article 4 Para 2	**397, 400, 412**
Article 5	**398, 413**
Article 6	**77, 357, 407, 413**

1985 Hague Convention on the Law Applicable to Trusts and on their Recognition, 1st July 1985, Cmnd 9494, (1985) U.K.T.S. 43 **131–2**

1986 Hague Convention on the Law Applicable to Contracts for the International Sale of Goods, 22nd December 1986, (1985) 24 I.L.M. 1575 **368**

1988 Lugano Convention on Jurisdiction and the Enforcement of Judgments in Civil and Commercial Matters, 16th September 1988, O.J. 1988, L 319/9
Article 5(1)   **80, 233**

1988 First Brussels Protocol on Interpretation by the Court of Justice of the Contractual Obligations Convention 19th June 1980 O.J. 1989, L 48/1
General	**1, 31**
Article 1	**81, 417, 419**
Article 1(a)	**353, 363, 419**
Article 1(b)	**419**
Article 1(c)	**419**
Article 2	**81, 82, 83, 416, 418, 420, 424, 425, 427, 457**
Article 2(a)	**82, 83, 420, 421, 422, 423, 428, 429**
Article 2(b)	**82, 83, 420, 421, 422, 423, 428**
Article 3	**81, 83, 418, 827**
Article 3(1)	**427**
Article 4	**83, 418, 428**
Article 5	**428**
Article 6	**1, 82, 428, 430**
Article 6(1)	**417**
Article 7	**398, 429**
Article 8	**429**
Article 9	**83, 401, 429**
Article 10	**36, 393, 430**
Article 11	**77, 357**

1988 Second Brussels Protocol on the Interpretation by the Court of Justice of the Contractual Obligations Convention, 19th June 1980, O.J. 1989, L 48/17   **31, 82**
Article 2	**417**
Article 3	**417**

1989 San Sebastian Convention on the Accession of Spain and Portugal to the Brussels Convention, 26th May 1989, O.J. 1989, L 285/1
General	**195**
Article 4	**79, 223, 233**
Article 5	**196**
Article 6	**455**
Article 7	**223**
Article 21	**392**

Table of Orders and Regulations

Contracts (Applicable Law) Act 1990 (Commencement No.1) Order 1991,
S.I. 1991, No.707   **1, 31, 34, 351, 395, 398, 435**

Insurance Companies (Amendment) Regulations 1990, S.I. 1990 No.1333
45

Rules of the Supreme Court

RSC Order 11
General   **15, 272**
rule 1(1)(d)   **101, 435**

RSC Order 38 rule 3   **336**

RSC Order 114   **428**

Glossary

Cheshire and North: Cheshire and North, Private International Law, 11th ed (1987)

Dicey and Morris: Dicey and Morris, Conflict of Laws, 11th ed (1987)

Fletcher: Conflict of Laws and European Community Law (1982)

Graveson: Conflict of Laws. Private International Law, 7th ed (1974)

Kaye, Civil Jurisdiction: Kaye, Civil Jurisdiction and Enforcement of Foreign Judgments (1987)

Lando (ed.): Lando, von Hoffmann and Siehr, European Private International Law of Obligations (1975)

Lipstein(ed.): Lipstein, Harmonisation of Private International Law by the EEC (1978)

North (ed.): North, Contract Conflicts (1982)

Abbreviations

AC	Appeal Cases (Law Reports)
ALL E.R.	All England Law Reports
Am.J.Comp.L.	American Journal of Comparative Law
Am.J.Int.L.	American Journal of International Law
B.Y.B.I.L.	British Yearbook of International Law
Ch	Chancery Law Reports
C.J.Q.	Civil Justice Quarterly
C.L.J.	Cambridge Law Journal
C.M.L.R.	Common Market Law Reports
C.M.L.Rev.	Common Market Law Review
E.C.R.	European Court Reports
E.L.D.	European Law Digest
E.L.Rev.	European Law Review
Fam	Family Division (Law Reports)
I.C.L.Q.	International and Comparative Law Quarterly
I.L.Pr.	International Litigation and Procedure
I. Prax.	Praxis des Internationalen Privat- und Verfahrensrechts
J.B.L.	Journal of Business Law
Lloyd's Rep.	Lloyd's Law Reports
L.M.C.L.Q.	Lloyd's Maritime and Commercial Law Quarterly
L.Q.R.	Law Quarterly Review
M.L.R.	Modern Law Review
Neths.Int.L.Rev.	Netherlands International Law Review
P.	Probate Divorce and Admiralty Law Reports
O.J.	Official Journal of the European Communities
Rabel's Zeitschrift	Rabel's Zeitschrift für ausländisches und internationales Privatrecht
R.S.C.	Rules of the Supreme Court
Virginia J.Int.L.	Virginia Journal of International Law
W.L.R.	Weekly Law Reports
Ybk.E.L.	Yearbook of European Law

1 Introduction

The Contracts (Applicable Law) Act 1990 implements in the United Kingdom the Rome Convention on the Law Applicable to Contractual Obligations of 19 June 1980 (O.J. 1980, No. L266/1) and the Luxembourg Convention on Greek Accession thereto of 10 April 1984 (O.J. 1984, No. L146/1), set out for ease of reference in Schedules 1 and 2 respectively thereto (s.2(4)(a) and (b)). The Act refers to 'the Rome Convention' and 'the Luxembourg Convention' (s.1(a) and (b)): in this book, the Rome Convention is referred to variously as 'the Obligations Convention', or 'Rome Convention', or simply 'the Convention'.

Section 2(1) of the 1990 Act gives the force of law to the Conventions in the United Kingdom, and s.2 itself, together with all other provisions of the Act, with the exception of s.3(1), (2) and (3)(b) relating to interpretative references to the European Court and rapporteur's report thereon, was brought into force by Order in Council, in accordance with s.7, as from 1 April 1991 (see The Contracts (Applicable Law) Act 1990 (Commencement No. 1) Order 1991, SI 1991, No. 707: the first Brussels Protocol on Interpretation of the Rome Convention by the European Court, of 19 December 1988, O.J. 1989, No. L48/1, set out for ease of reference in Schedule 3 to the 1990 Act under s.2(4)(c), and referred to in the Act as 'the Brussels Protocol' in accordance with 1990 Act s.1(c), has been ratified by the United Kingdom, Greece and the Netherlands, but is not yet in force according to the conditions laid down therefor under its Article 6 requiring *inter alia* seven Rome Convention – 'Contracting' – states to have ratified it, and consequently, the Brussels Protocol is excepted from the effects of s.2(1) for the time being under SI 1991, No. 707 para. 2, and the Tizzano Report on the Brussels Protocol, O.J. 1990 No. C219/1, need not be referred to under s.3(3)(b) for interpretation of the Protocol).

Other original Contracting States were Belgium, Denmark, France, Germany, Greece, Italy and Luxembourg; the Conventions entered into force for the Netherlands on 1 September 1991, and for Ireland on 1 January 1992.

In interpreting the Conventions, Contracting States' courts may take into account the report of Convention rapporteurs Professors Giuliano of Milan and Lagarde of Paris (O.J. 1980, No. C282/1: see 1990 Act s.3(3)(a)), referred to in this work as 'the Giuliano/Lagarde Report', or more frequently simply as 'the Report'. Eventually, when the Brussels Interpretation Protocol has entered into force, it will become possible for highest and appellate courts of Contracting States to suspend national court proceedings in order to request the European Court to rule on interpretation of the Convention's provisions, and any such European Court case law will have to be followed thereafter (1990 Act s.3(1) and (2)).

The Obligations Convention, unlike the Brussels Convention of 1968 on Jurisdiction and the Enforcement of Judgments in Civil and Commercial Matters ('the Judgments Convention') before it, is not derived from any provision of the EEC Treaty, but was drawn up by member states' representatives *au sein de la Communauté*, as representing member states' desire to continue the unifying work of the Judgments Convention in the field of Community private international law and thereby to equalize the legal protection of persons established within the Community (see Obligations Convention, Preamble para. 2).

The effect of the United Kingdom's implementation of the Obligations Convention is to replace its prior system of private international law of contract by the Convention's uniform rules as from 1 April 1991. Even the old terminology – *proper law of the contract* as the governing law – is gone, replaced by the Convention expression 'applicable law', including in relation to existing statutes (see 1990 Act, s.5 and Schedule 4).

However, the Convention only applies within its international (Article 1(1)), subject-matter (Articles 1(2)–(4) and 11) and temporal (Article 17) scope, and cedes priority to any other international contract conflicts conventions to which a Contracting State may be party (Article 21), so that certain types of contract will remain subject to the previous law, as will all contracts not concluded after 1 April 1991 when the Convention entered into force in the United Kingdom. Thus, the traditional English private international law of contract developed by the English courts over the past two centuries has not wholly disappeared: it remains in force for contracts excluded from the Convention's effects (together with any novel EC or other regulation of specific areas, such as EC insurance – and doubtless, its underlying principles will continue to constitute a major source of experience to be drawn upon in applying the Convention), and accordingly it is referred to in this book as *pre-existing*, rather than previous or past, national English contract conflicts.

Rome Convention law has four main pillars:

1 autonomy of contracting parties to select a law to govern their contracts;
2 applicable law based upon closest connection of contracts with countries in the absence of parties' choice;
3 safeguards for operation of mandatory rules of law of countries other than those of applicable law;
4 the principle and mechanism of uniform interpretation (and, in the first case, application) of the Convention as between different Contracting States.

Of the preceding primary elements of the new law, the first two are likewise central features of the pre-existing system of English contracts conflicts, whilst the fourth has not of course been of fundamental concern, notwithstanding the underlying willingness to consult authorities in different parts of the United Kingdom and elsewhere in the Commonwealth and United States. The third of the preceding areas, that of mandatory protection and extraterritoriality of otherwise inapplicable legal systems has had an – at least covertly – more inhibited development in England than, say, in France, where *droit international public* traditionally has a higher dynamic within the overall conflicts system than in the case of public policy in English private international law of contract. Certainly too, the attention previously paid in England to protection of application of imperative *foreign* laws not otherwise to be referred to under mainstream conflicts rules has been sporadic and unsystematic, its principles remaining largely to be worked out, hitherto being founded on relatively vague notions of comity and public policy, rather than specified connectional or party-protective considerations. The Convention's treatment, aside from certain constructional and technical problems, could not be more different from the pre-existing English approach described, in attempting to provide a comprehensive network of provisions on mandatory safeguards as to types of contract (Articles 5(2), 6(1), 9(6)), degrees of connection (Articles 3(3), 7(1)), and overriding interests of the forum (Articles 7(2), 16), as a counter-balance to the first Convention principle of party autonomy in applicable law – no surprise, then, that the United Kingdom (along with Germany, Ireland and Luxembourg, as it happens) found the general Convention safeguard for mandatory laws of contract of closely connected foreign countries unpalatable (see North, in North (ed.), *Contract Conflicts* (1982), pp. 19–20) and accordingly exercised the reservation against application of Article 7(1) in the United Kingdom's courts (Article 22(1)(a); Contracts (Applicable Law) Act 1990 s.2(2)), although, presumably, if contracting parties were to stipulate in their contract that Article 7(1) should apply in the event of any dispute arising between them, courts might then be obliged to give effect to their wishes in this respect by virtue of the same fundamental Convention principle of party autonomy as governs in respect of general applicable law (see below, p.251).

Whatever the respective merits of Convention and pre-existing English contract conflicts, however, the die has now been cast: the Convention exists and is in force. Whether it was right or not to base its applicable law upon parties' agreements and necessarily then to provide for safeguards of mandatory contract rules of other countries' laws, has become less important in practice (at least for the Convention's initial duration of ten years, and thereafter in the absence of denunciation under Article 30) than the need to explain and to assess its effects and mode of operation, and changes from previous English private international rules of contract.

Those latter objectives are the subject matter of the remainder of this book.

Introduction 5

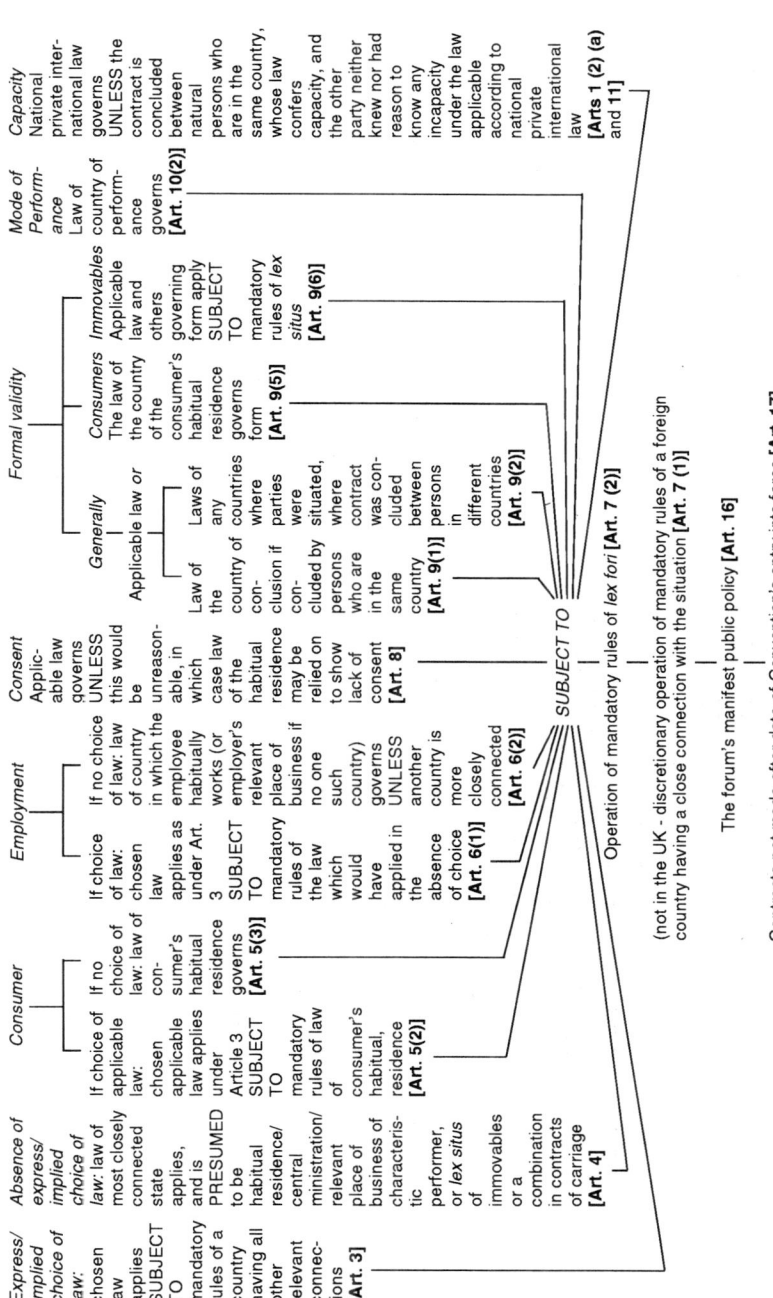

Figure 1.1 Applicable law under the Obligations Convention

PART I

2 Pre-existing National English Private International Rules of Contract

Pre-existing English private international law of contract rules were, in large part, built up by the courts from the middle of the nineteenth century, founded upon the liberal principles of *freedom of contract* characteristic of that period and latterly subjected to certain controls and to the desire not to pursue the idea of party autonomy to unreasonable lengths.

The quest under the pre-existing law is to identify the 'proper law' of the contract, as that law which is to govern relations subsisting under the contract as a whole, subject to the possibility of its optional displacement by a different law or laws in respect of certain aspects of the contract (such as capacity and form), and to its non-application in favour of other connecting factors in the case of a minority of contractual issues (mode of performance, money of account).

The following brief points may be made with regard to the pre-existing proper law doctrine, which are of interest in the context of the overall consideration of the Convention:

1   In principle, albeit exceptionally, there may be two or more proper laws chosen by the parties to govern different elements of the contract (*Hamlyn & Co.* v. *Talisker Distillery* [1894] AC 202, 207; *Kahler* v. *Midland Bank* [1950] AC 24, 42; *Re Helbert Wagg & Co. Ltd.* [1956] Ch 323, 340; *Forsakringsiktieselskapet Vesta* v. *Butcher* [1986] 2 All ER 488, 504–5, affd on other grounds [1988] 2 All ER 43, [1989] 1 All ER 402; *Libyan Arab Foreign Bank* v. *Bankers Trust Co.* [1989] 3 All ER 252, 267). Cheshire and North state that as a matter of legal logic and commercial sense there cannot be a 'floating' proper law, that is, non-existent when the contract is concluded, but subsequently crystallized by the unilateral act of one of the parties (p. 451). This seems inconsistent

with their support (*ibid.*) for ability of parties to vary the proper law following contract.

2   *Renvoi* is inapplicable in contract law (*Re United Railways of the Havana and Regla Warehouses Ltd* [1960] Ch. 52, 96–7; *Amin Rasheed Shipping Corpn* v. *Kuwait Insurance Co.* [1984] AC 50; *Dimskal Shipping Co. SA* v. *International Transport Workers Federation, The 'Evia Luck' (No. 2)* [1990] 1 Lloyd's Rep. 319, 327).

3   It is not settled whether contractual *existence* is subject to the subjective – not solely objective – proper law (*The Parouth* [1982] 2 Lloyd's Rep. 351).

4   It is unclear whether English *lex fori*, or the law allegedly chosen by the parties, or the law which would have applied to the contract as proper law in the absence of choice by the parties, governs validity and existence of the choice of law agreement itself and consent of the parties thereto, the former (*lex fori*) seeming to have much to commend it, given the procedural and policy nature of the very process of applying an English choice-of-law connecting-factor rule to the question of applicable law of contract, although, objective applicable law may be the *practical* solution (see Cheshire and North, p.454).

5   It is uncertain whether parties may subsequently change the proper law (*Armar Shipping Co. Ltd.* v. *Caisse Algérienne* [1981] 1 WLR 207, 216); Cheshire and North (p.451) indicate that the parties should be allowed to do so, which would seem sensible; arguably, however, this should only be the case if permitted by the original proper law, or at least if the new 'agreement' on choice of law is contractually valid thereunder.

It is now proposed to deal with, firstly, the method of determining the legal system which governs as proper law under the pre-existing system, and, secondly, the latter's scope in relation to the contract as a whole, and whether other laws are able to be applied to particular aspects of the contract as an alternative to, or in place of, the proper law.

ASCERTAINMENT OF THE PROPER LAW

The *Subjective* Proper Law

(a) Express choice

Where parties expressly choose the law to govern their contract, their choice will be given effect to. In *Vita Food Products Inc.* v. *Unus Shipping Co.* [1939] AC 277, a contract made in Newfoundland, for the carriage of goods by sea from Newfoundland to New York, which presumably might well have been governed by Newfoundland law in the absence of choice, was expressly subjected to English law by the parties. Newfoundland law applied the Hague Rules to outward shipments, as also did English law to outward shipments from England alone at that time. The cargo was damaged owing to the master's negligence, and the Judicial Committee of the Privy Council, on appeal from the courts of Nova Scotia, held that the carriers were exempt from liability, not by virtue of the Hague Rules, as part of Newfoundland law, but under the expressly chosen English proper law which also upheld the contractual exclusion clause, notwithstanding the contract's obvious lack of connection with England.

(b) Implied choice

Where the parties have not expressly chosen a law to govern their contract, courts will attempt to infer an implied intention on their part from the terms of the contract and surrounding circumstances, greater importance being attached to the former (*Amin Rasheed Shipping Corpn* v. *Kuwait Insurance Co.* [1984] AC 50, pp.64–7, *per* LORD DIPLOCK). Factors taken into account, therefore, will include: existence of jurisdiction or arbitration clauses, giving rise to a strong inference (though, no longer conclusive presumption) of choice of the same law (*Compagnie Tunisienne de Navigation SA* v. *Compagnie d'Armement Maritime SA* [1971] AC 572); form, language and terminology of the contract (*The Adriatic* [1931] P. 241 CA; *Whitworth Street Estates (Manchester) Ltd* v. *James Miller & Partners Ltd* [1970] AC 583, HL) – although, given the wide use of English language and forms in international commerce, too much significance is not to be accorded to this factor in choice of law (*Amin Rasheed Shipping Corpn* v. *Kuwait Insurance Co.* pp. 65 and 70–1); a party's status as a government or state (*Bonython* v. *Commonwealth of Australia* [1951] AC 201); previous and related transactions (*The Adriatic; Kloeckner & Co AG* v. *Gatoil Overseas Inc* [1990] 1 Lloyd's Rep 177, 206); the fact that a particular law upholds contractual relations (*P.&O. Steam Navigation Co.* v. *Shand* (1865) 3 Moo. P.B. (N.S.) 272); parties' residence and nationality (*Jacobs* v. *Crédit Lyonnais* (1884) 12 QBD 589); country of the flag in the case of charter parties or contracts of affreightment (*Compagnie Tunisienne*), law of the insurer's place of business in insurance contracts (*Rossano* v. *Manufacturers Life Insurance Co.* [1963] 2 QB 352); law of country in which the insurance market is situated in the case of reinsurance contracts (*Citadel Insurance* v. *Atlantic Union Insurance* [1982] 2 Lloyd's Rep. 543); law of the bank branch where an account is kept (*X A/G* v. *A Bank* [1983] 2 All ER 464); law of the state of a common employer's place of business (*Sayers* v. *International Drilling Co.* [1971] 1 WLR 1176, CA); law of the place in which an agent acted in regard to obligations between principal and third party (*Chatenay* v. *Brazilian Submarine Telegraph Co.* [1981] 1 QB 79).

The *Objective* Proper Law

In the absence of an express or implied choice of law between the parties, courts will abandon the attempt to deduce any fictitious intention, and will proceed to determine the law with which the transaction embodied in the contract has its closest and most real connection, the localization of the contract (*The Assunzione* [1954] P.150; *Coast Lines* v. *Hudig & Veder Chartering NV* [1972] 2 QB 34).

There is some uncertainty over whether the connection has to be with a particular legal system, or with a country (see *James Miller & Partners Ltd* v. *Whitworth Street Estates (Manchester) Ltd* [1970] AC 583). *Amin Rasheed* [1984] AC 50, 61, *Bonython* v. *Commonwealth of Australia* [1951] AC 201, 219, *Rossano* v. *Manufacturers Life Insurance Company* [1962] 2 All ER 214, 218, and *Dubai Electricity Co* v. *Islamic Republic of Iran Shipping Lines* ('*The Iran Vojdan*') [1984] 2 Lloyd's Rep 380, 383 col. 1, suggest the former; *Re United Railways of Havana* [1961] AC 1007, 1068 seems to indicate the latter. The Convention is concerned with closest connections with *countries*, and it is suggested that, whilst this may be logically correct, and itself inclusive of connections with systems of law as such, the latter itself would have had much to commend it as a matter of practical expediency and flexibility.

Courts will take *all* material facts and circumstances into account in determining objective proper law, without applying presumptions (*The Assunzione*). These will include those mentioned in connection with implied subjective choice of proper law, as well as others not specifically related to the expression of the contract, for example, currency and place of payment (*R.* v. *International Trustee for the Protection of Bondholders AG* [1937] AC 500), nature and location of subject matter (*British South Africa*

Co. v. de Beers Consolidated Mines Ltd [1910] 2 Ch. 502 CA), place of making the contract (*P.& O. Steam Navigation Co. v. Shand* (1865) 3 Moo. P.C. (N.S.) 272), place of performance or delivery (*Jacobs v. Crédit Lyonnais* (1884) 12 QBD 589). Cheshire and North (p.461) suggest that in the absence of an express subjective choice of law in the contract, courts should proceed at once to determine the objective proper law, without attempting to infer an implied choice lacking any real foundation, and LORD WILBERFORCE's judgment in *Amin Rasheed Shipping Corpn v. Kuwait Insurance Co.* (pp.69–71) is cited in support.

Limitations on Subjective Choice of Law

(a) Choice must be bona fide and legal, and not against public policy.

LORD WRIGHT set these limitations in the *Vita Foods* case ([1939] AC 277, p.290). Much uncertainty has surrounded their meaning. The '*bona fide*' qualification may have been intended to confirm the courts' ultimate power to find that choice of a completely unconnected law could not have been seriously meant and that it was a sham (in Australia, HOARE J in *Golden Acres Ltd v. Queensland Estates Pty Ltd* [1969] Qd R 378, held absence of *bona fides* to denote evasionary intent); 'legal' might have referred to the contract as a whole, of which the choice of law was part, or purely to the agreement itself on choice of law, of which the effectiveness was also to be judged in accordance with *objective* proper law's domestic or private international law, if that law was not the same as the subjective proper law; and 'public policy' would simply have covered the usual savings for non-application of any foreign legal rule, of contract or otherwise, which was considered to be unsuitable for application in English courts on the ground that its effects would be contrary to English public policy.

(b) Unfair Contract Terms Act 1977 s.27(1)

Where English law is proper law only because it has been chosen to be so and would not otherwise have governed but for the choice, the restrictions on contractual exclusion of liability laid down in the Act will not apply.

(c) Unfair Contract Terms Act 1977 s.27(2)

Where a non-United Kingdom law is chosen, the Act's restrictions on contractual exclusion of liability continue to operate notwithstanding the choice of foreign law (other than in international contracts for the sale or supply of goods, as defined under s.26), if the choice appears to have been wholly or mainly to enable the party imposing it to evade the Act; or

one party dealt as a consumer, was habitually resident in the United Kingdom, and the essential steps to conclude the contract were taken in the United Kingdom by him or others on his behalf.

(d) Carriage of Goods by Sea Act 1971

The Act implements in the United Kingdom the Hague–Visby Rules in its Schedule, imposing, and fixing financial limits on, a sea carrier's liability. Article X makes the Rules applicable where the carriage is between ports in two different states and the Rules are chosen *or* the bill of lading is issued in a contracting state *or* the carriage is from a port in a contracting state. In *The Hollandia* [1983] AC 565, the carriers argued that the controls in the Rules were inapplicable, because Dutch – not English – law (applying the unamended Hague Rules) had been expressly chosen to govern the contract. The House of Lords held that the revised Hague Rules were meant to prevent avoidance in this way (s.1(2) of the 1971 Act gave the Rules the 'force of law' in the United Kingdom, and s.1(3) specified that they would apply where the port of shipment was a port in the United Kingdom, whether or not the carriage was between ports in two different states within the meaning of Article X of the Rules); consequently, they would be applied by an English court in accordance with Article X, regardless of the proper law (which would possibly also include *objective* proper law, not just expressly chosen law, as a matter of policy, even if not also construction of the Rules). Furthermore, choice of foreign *courts* which would not apply the Hague Rules, would not be given effect to, as an attempt at indirect avoidance of the Rules (contrary to the prohibition on their exclusion under Article III para. 8 in the English Act's Schedule: [1983] AC 565, 575–7).

(e) Sale of Goods Act 1979 s.56

Choice of foreign proper law will not have the effect of excluding implied terms under ss.12–15 of the 1979 Act, where English law would be objective proper law but for the agreement on applicable law (other than in international contracts, as defined under s.56(3)).

(See too, for further examples of controls on otherwise applicable law, Equal Pay Act 1970 s.1(11) as amended by 1990 Act, Schedule 4, para. 1, Trade Union and Labour Relations Act 1974 s.30(6), and Employment Protection (Consolidation) Act 1978 s.153(5).)

SCOPE OF THE PROPER LAW

Aspects Subject *Exclusively* to the Proper Law

(a) Creation of the contract

Where courts have to decide where a contract has been concluded for purposes of jurisdiction, or, arguably, as a factor in determining objective choice of law, there is evidence that they will apply English law as *lex fori* (*Entores* v. *Miles Far East Corporation* [1955] 2 QB 327, CA; *Brinkibon Ltd* v. *Stahag Stahl GmbH* [1982] 2 AC 34, HL). However, in order to settle merits questions such as offer and acceptance, binding nature of offers, silence as acceptance, the need for consideration, and effects of mistake and duress, it would seem that the proper law will have to govern (*Re Bonacina* [1912] 2 Ch. 394; *Albeko Schuhmaschinen* v. *The Kamborian Shoe Machine Co. Ltd* [1961] 111 LJ 519; *The Parouth* [1982] 2 Lloyd's Rep. 351).

Three points should be made regarding application of the proper law to such matters of creation of the contractual bond.

'Putative' proper law governs contractual existence The logical difficulty of applying the proper law of a contract to the issue of contractual existence is of course that, until it is known whether there *is* a contract, there can be no governing law in relation thereto; yet the former question is itself precisely the object of the quest to discover the governing law.

In *The Parouth*, therefore, the Court of Appeal indicated (at p.353) (in a RSC Order 11 jurisdiction context of determining whether the plaintiff had a good arguable case on the merits that a contract existed under applicable law) that the 'putative' proper law should decide the matter, that is to say, the law which *would* be the proper law if the contract *were* validly concluded. Cheshire and North (p.475) agree with this approach.

'Objective' putative proper law governs contractual existence Whilst Cheshire and North support the principle of the putative proper law as governing contractual existence (pp. 473–6), they nevertheless wish to limit its application to the *objective* proper law, and disagree with the position that putative proper law should also be able to be referred to where *chosen* by the parties. *The Parouth* is regarded as unsatisfactory for not having expressly made this distinction (pp.474 and 476). Dicey and Morris appear to agree, where there is no absolute certainty as to parties' consensus on choice of law (pp. 1200–1). Collier, on the other hand, considers that

there are few public policy elements in the rules of offer and acceptance such as would prevent subjective putative proper law from being given effect to (*Conflict of Laws*, 1987, p.164).

It is submitted that, on the one hand, there is no *logical* objection against applying subjective putative proper law to contractual existence, since ultimately, applicable law is a *legal, procedural* decision for the courts and is not founded *directly* upon the parties' agreement: the latter is merely a factor – overwhelmingly influential in most cases it is true – to be taken into account by courts in reaching the decision as to applicable law, even if, in the end, the contract is held not to exist thereunder. (Indeed, if objective proper law were applied instead, and the contract were found not to exist thereunder, it might then be argued that the putative approach itself was incorrect, given non-existence of the contract to which such contract choice of law rule was applicable, and in respect of which *non-existent* contract, objective factors were taken into account in ascertaining objective proper law!) Nevertheless, on the other hand it has to be said that there are various *policy* objections against the subjective approach: if a party denies existence of the contract at law, so too, therefore, is the choice of law clause contained in the alleged agreement also presumably disclaimed, so that it would be wrong for courts to ascribe any significance thereto in their decision on applicable law, when it is not known whether parties were in fact agreed on choice of law itself. Limitation of the putative method to the objective proper law in the matter of contractual existence is the less likely to encounter this objection (although, as seen, not immune, where a party can be taken also to deny the *contracts*-existence of objective factors); as will be seen, however, such is not the approach adopted under the Convention.

'Objective' putative proper law governs existence and validity of choice of law agreement itself   If there is any doubt over whether objective putative proper law alone governs existence and creation of the contract as a whole, arguably there should be none in relation to its operation in respect of the choice of law agreement itself, whether part of or separate from the main contract in regard to which it allegedly lays down applicable law (although, even in the case of the objective applicable law, it has to be admitted, the party denying contractual existence might just as well deny any consent to or participation in the factors and circumstances claimed to surround the alleged choice of law, as he would in relation to his very agreement to enter the contract itself). Indeed, it is difficult to see how *any* aspect of the law agreement – whether relating to contractual creation and existence and consent or not – could possibly be assigned to any proper law other than objective, given the former's purported nature and effect. The only other possible course might be to apply English law itself as *lex fori*, on the basis

that English choice of law rules are procedural and policy matters which should be applied and understood according to English concepts and meanings. There is some evidence to the effect that courts will apply *lex fori* to determine validity and existence of *jurisdiction* clauses, rather than the law applicable to the contract (*Mackender* v. *Feldia AG* [1967] 2 QB 590; Brussels Convention, Article 17 – although, see *Prodexport Co* v. *E.D. & F. Man Ltd.* [1973] 1 QB 389, 397). However, it is clear that the question of ascertaining consent to jurisdiction has a far greater procedural complexion than that of deciding upon agreement on choice of law once jurisdiction is confirmed, and, from this perspective, there seems less to object to in respect of application of objective proper law to a law agreement than would be the case where jurisdiction clauses were involved (although, conversely, it has to be said, there is less *circularity* in applying *lex causae* to jurisdiction agreements than to choice of law); the Obligations Convention itself, it will be seen, governs existence and validity of consent of the parties to choice of applicable law, by subjective or objective applicable law, as the case may be (Articles 3(4) and 8), and resort to *lex fori* does also encounter the usual charge of encouraging forum shopping.

Dicey and Morris take the following line (pp.1177–8): where the issue relates to *existence* of the choice of law agreement, it is suggested that English law should apply, as *lex fori* (thus, in *Mackender* v. *Feldia, supra*, the Court of Appeal might have been willing to disregard a foreign jurisdiction and law clause, had the plea been that the contract as a whole was void *ab initio* rather than merely voidable, which the court seemed to treat as a matter to be decided according to *lex fori* for such purposes; and in *Compagnie Tunisienne*, LORD DIPLOCK indicated that English law would govern construction of the contract as to choice of law – although, whether this would include matters of offer and acceptance would seem questionable); in the case of *validity* of a choice of law agreement, held to have come into existence, by whatever law, the tentative suggestion of Dicey and Morris is that invalidity by objective foreign proper law should be disregarded where *English* law is chosen, but invalidity under an overriding rule of English law should operate where a foreign law is chosen (*The Hollandia*); however, *invalidity under objective foreign* proper law should be applied where a different, unconnected *foreign* law is chosen, and of course invalidity under the chosen foreign law itself will render the choice ineffective. It is considered that the initial exception in favour of validity under chosen English law is questionable, but that, in general, such cumulative application of objective and subjective proper law has its attractions.

(b) Essential validity

Effects of exemption or indemnity clauses (*Coast Lines Ltd* v. *Hudig and Veder Chartering NV* [1972] 2 QB 34), misrepresentation (*British Controlled Oilfields* v. *Stagg* (1921) 127 LT 209), excuses for non-performance (*Jacobs* v. *Crédit Lyonnais*), effects of moratoria (*Re Helbert Wagg & Co. Ltd.'s Claim* [1956] Ch. 323), and the substance of performance (*Mount Albert Borough Council* v. *Australasian Temperance and General Mutual Life Assurance Society* [1938] AC 224) are subject to the proper law.

(c) Interpretation

The proper law's rules of contractual interpretation and construction – but not necessarily its own meanings as such – govern the contract (*Bonython* v. *Commonwealth of Australia* [1951] AC 201 PB): for example, whether 'dollars' means Canadian, Australian or American dollars (although, the *value* of the contractual currency of account is for *lex pecuniae*, as will be seen below).

(d) Discharge of the contract

The proper law governs contractual discharge, whether, for example, by frustration, war, legislation, death, bankruptcy, amalgamation or novation (*National Bank of Greece and Athens SA* v. *Metliss* [1958] AC 509; *Adams* v. *National Bank of Greece and Athens SA* [1961] AC 255).

Aspects Governed *Non-Exclusively* by the Proper Law

(a) Formal validity

It is sufficient for a contract to comply with the formal requirements of *either* (i) *lex loci contractus* (*Guépratte* v. *Young* (1851) 4 De G. & Sm 217), *or* (ii) the proper law (*Van Grutten* v. *Digby* (1862) 31 Beav 561). Requirements held to be procedural (negativing contractual enforcement), rather than substantive formal (negativing existence or validity), are subject to *lex fori* (*Leroux* v. *Brown* [1852] 12 CB 801; *Alves* v. *Hodgson* (1797) 7 TR 241; *Monterosso Shipping Co. Ltd* v. *ITF* [1982] 3 All ER 841; *G. & H. Montage GmbH* v. *Irvani* [1990] 1 WLR 667).

(b) Capacity

The authorities are in a state of uncertainty at common law. There is support for a number of laws:

1 *lex loci contractus* (*Male* v. *Roberts* (1800) 3 Esp. 163; *Baindail* v. *Baindail* [1946] P.122);
2 *lex domicilii* (*Sottomayor* v. *De Barros (No. 1)* (1877) LR 3 PD 1);
3 *lex situs* in the case of contracts relating to land (*Bank of Africa* v. *Cohen* [1902] 2 Ch. 129 CA);
4 the proper law (*Charron* v. *Montreal Trust Co*.(1958) 15 DLR (2d) 240; *Bodley Head Ltd* v. *Flegon* [1972] 1 WLR 680).

Cheshire and North support the latter in modern conditions of trade, where law of a party's domicile in respect of capacity may not be expected to be known by the other (pp. 480–2); and Dicey and Morris are in accord (p. 1203).

'Objective' proper law   Cheshire and North further assert that the *Charron* and *Bodley Head* decisions lend support to their view that the proper law to govern capacity is that which is objectively ascertained; people are not to be allowed to confer capacity upon themselves through the device of choice of law (p.482).

(c) Illegality

A number of laws are influential in this sphere:

1 Proper law. Contracts illegal by their proper law will not be enforced (*Kahler* v. *Midland Bank Ltd* [1950] AC 24; *Libyan Arab Foreign Bank* v. *Bankers Trust Co* [1989] 3 All ER 252).
2 Public policy. Contracts that are illegal under *any* law may not be enforced, on the rather nebulous ground that it would be contrary to comity and public policy if the English courts were to assist in the breach of the laws of foreign friendly countries. Presumably, breach of any public or criminal rule would not be sufficient for public policy to be invoked: the breach of rule would surely need to have involved a particularly serious offence against the public order of the foreign state and such as might have imperilled the relations of the Crown therewith were English courts to have agreed to lend their aid in enforcement of the contract. Examples are: (a) *Foster* v. *Driscoll* [1929] 1 KB 470, where the contract, governed by English law, was for the supply of whisky,

the *purpose* being to smuggle it into the United States, to be sold there in contravention of the latter's prohibition laws; (b) *Regazzoni* v. *K.C. Sethia (1944) Ltd* [1958] AC 301, where the English contract for the sale of jute in India to a Swiss buyer, for delivery in Italy, was made in the full knowledge of the buyer's intention to resell the jute for export to South Africa, which was prohibited under Indian criminal law; (c) *de Wutz* v. *Hendricks* (1824) 2 Bing 314, involving an English contract to finance a rebellion abroad. On the other hand, it may be that merely being contrary to the *public policy* of the foreign, friendly country might not be sufficient to invoke the English comity ground of refusal to enforce a contract, and that what is required is the violation of *provisions of law* of the foreign legal system – although, the fact that the transaction was thus contrary to the public policy of the foreign state would nonetheless be relevant in assessing whether enforcement of the contract would offend against the English proper law's public policy on general principles of morality (see *Lemenda Trading Co Ltd* v. *African Middle East Petroleum Co Ltd* [1988] 1 All ER 513, 519, PHILLIPS J).

3   Law of place of performance. There can be few doubts that where English law is that of the place of performance and the latter is illegal thereby, enforcement of the contract will be refused by the English courts on public policy grounds (see *Kahler*). However, what of the case of illegality in general, under non-English *lex loci solutionis* where the latter is a law other than the proper law? Will enforcement be affected? The facts of *Ralli Brothers* v. *Compania Naviera Sota y Aznar* [1920] 2 KB 287 can be taken to support the proposition that contracts illegal under *lex loci solutionis* will not be enforced in the English courts (see too [1991] E.L.D. 261, for a corresponding principle in German and Dutch cases 209 and 210). Jute was sold under an English contract, to be carried by sea from Calcutta to Barcelona, the freight to be paid for at £50 a ton. Before the ship arrived, a Spanish decree made it illegal to pay freight of more than £10 a ton on jute. The action in the English courts for the balance of £40 a ton was unsuccessful: performance was illegal under Spanish law. It has however been suggested that the *Ralli* case does not constitute any such authority for the general proposition that *lex loci solutionis* governs illegality – at least of performance aspects of the contract – alongside the proper law: the argument runs that *Ralli* concerned supervening illegality, following conclusion of the contract, which under the *internal* – not private international – rules of the *governing English proper law*, would constitute a frustrating event, and that had the proper law not been English but some other law, supervening Spanish illegality would only then have been able to have been referred to, if capable of affecting contractual enforcement under

the internal rules of contract of that other, foreign proper law; whereas, *initial* illegality of the contract according to *lex loci solutionis* – or any other foreign law – would already be covered by the principles against enforcement on the grounds of comity and public policy previously referred to (see Cheshire and North, pp. 488–9, and *Libyan Arab Foreign Bank v. Bankers Trust Co* [1989] 3 All ER 252, 265–6). In view of the ambiguity of the various statements in the cases and of the differences of opinion amongst commentators as to the role of *lex loci solutionis* in illegality of contracts, it is desirable to consider what ought to have been the appropriate rule under pre-existing English conflicts. This remains of importance in the Convention context. The latter contains no express ground referring illegality, supervening or otherwise, to the *lex loci solutionis*. However, if *Ralli* really were to be regarded as justifying *indirect* resort to *lex loci solutionis*, via internal rules of a proper law, relating to frustration, this would clearly be to admit the operation of *lex loci* in respect of supervening illegality into the Convention regime, where it was taken into account under domestic applicable law. Apart from that, illegality thereunder will be exclusively for applicable law (see Articles 8 and 10(1)(b) and (d) – and as a matter of construction, it would be somewhat far-fetched to argue that *manner* of performance, referred to *lex loci solutionis* under Article 10(2), must necessarily be regarded as in issue, where performance as a whole, including, therefore, *manner* thereof, is illegal thereunder!): it is questionable whether Article 16 on public policy is wide enough to cover refusal of contractual enforcement on comity and illegality grounds under *lex loci*; Articles 3 (3), 5, 6, 7 and 9(6) safeguarding mandatory rules are also of questionable applicability to general illegality (although, if the *domestic-English-rule* interpretation of *Ralli* were to be accepted, it might then be possible to rely upon Article 7(2), safeguarding the forum's mandatory rules, if the former alleged rule were held to be mandatory for purposes thereof, notwithstanding a foreign applicable law: obviously, if English law itself governed the contract, the alleged principle would then simply apply in any event); and *renvoi* (to *lex loci*, from a non-Contracting State applicable law) is excluded under Article 15. In all such cases, therefore, applicable law alone should govern illegality under the Convention, even where *England* is the place of performance, by whose law the contract is illegal (subject to Article 7 (2) on mandatory rules of the forum, and possibly also Article 16 whereby illegality of performance in *England* as place of performance would conceivably invariably be held to be manifestly in breach of English public policy).

In the present submission, the view consigning at least initial *lex loci solutionis*-illegality to the forum's comity and public policy ground of enforcement-refusal under national conflicts has the advantage of flexibility; and the accompanying proper law approach towards supervening illegality also has a certain sophistication. However, on analysis, each is rather seriously flawed: the comity consideration is unacceptably vague in a proper system of commercial conflicts, whilst the internal proper law argument is illogical. If internal English (or any other country's) law, as the proper law, regards a contract suffering supervening illegality as unenforceable through frustration, this still fails to provide an answer to the question of which law or laws decide upon such illegality, apart from the proper law itself? If the court in *Ralli* did in fact refer to Spanish law, merely for the purpose of applying internal English proper law, nonetheless, is it not also consequently to be concluded therefrom that the reference to Spanish *lex loci solutionis* on supervening illegality of performance, as an *incidental question*, must have been made in accordance with inferred English 'private international law' (either as that of the forum, or of English *lex causae* on the main issue of contractual subsistence and enforceability), thereby implicitly confirming the existence of *lex loci* as a rule of English conflicts on illegality?

If the latter argument is correct, it will not be possible under the Convention to pay regard to supervening illegality under *lex loci* by virtue of private international law of the legal system applicable thereunder, where it is that of a Convention state, because clearly such private international law of contract will be that laid down in the Convention itself, making no provision for application of *lex loci* to illegality. On the other hand, there is one situation in which recourse to *lex loci* would be possible: this is where, *as a matter of contractual construction*, the parties can be taken to have intended that the contract should be unenforceable if illegal according to *lex loci solutionis*, or any other law for that matter. This would be distinct from their having chosen *lex loci* to govern illegality as applicable law (solely or alongside the law generally applicable to the contract, if different), in that – as in the case of any other contractual term – technically, the effectiveness of their term would be governed by the law applicable to the contract. (*Lex loci* would thus be referred to by virtue of a contractual term, rather than as a matter of private international law of *lex fori*, or of *lex causae* on the main issue of contractual effectiveness, not possible, as seen, under the Convention, where the main law involved is that of a Convention state.) Indeed, it could be argued that on a proper reading of SCRUTTON LJ's judgment in *Ralli* itself, construed contractual intention of the parties (as to substantive terms, not choice of law) is precisely the reason why Spanish law – the *lex loci* – was referred to in the matter of illegality in that case. It was not that internal contract rules of the English proper law *required* supervening illegality under Spanish *lex loci* to be taken into account as a frustrating event, but simply that the parties were to be taken to have *intended* that it should be, and the English proper law, as was to be expected, placed no obstacles in the way of giving effect to their intentions in this respect ([1920] 2KB 287, at pp.301 and 303–4).

Finally, illegality under neither *lex loci contractus* (*Re Missouri Steamship Company* [1889] 42 Ch. D 321) nor law of the defendant's domicile, residence or nationality (*Kleinwort Sons & Co* v. *Ungarische Baumwolle A/G* [1939] 2 KB 678) is to be taken into account under pre-existing English conflicts, other than, of course, on the ground of comity and public policy.

Aspects *Not* Governed by the Proper Law

(a) Mode of performance

The 'method and manner' of performing contractual obligations held to exist and to be valid under the proper law are controlled by *lex loci solutionis*, unless some other law is chosen (*Jacobs* v. *Crédit Lyonnais* (1884) 12 QBD 589; Dicey and Morris, Rule 186(2)): matters included will be hours for payment and delivery, currency of payment, need for an export licence.

(b) Units of monetary account

Value and identification of the contractual money of account are matters for the law of the money of account – *lex pecuniae* – specified in the contract (*Re Chesterman's Trusts* [1923] 2 Ch. 466); but revalorization, affecting value of the debt rather than currency, is for the proper law (*Anderson* v. *Equitable Assurance Society of the United States* (1926) 134 LT 557). Money of payment, as an aspect of mode of performance, is for *lex loci solutionis* (*Miliangos* v. *George Frank (Textiles) Ltd* [1976] AC 443). Under the Convention, there is no express provision safeguarding application of *lex pecuniae*. Nevertheless, it is submitted that this would have been unnecessary: Article 3(1) permits parties to select, expressly or impliedly, the law applicable to the whole *or a part only* of their contract. Their designation of the money of account would seem to constitute at least an implied selection of *lex pecuniae* to govern value and legal unit of the chosen currency – although, interpretation would be a matter for the law generally applicable to the contract under Article 10(1)(a), and currency of payment would remain to be decided in accordance with *lex loci solutionis* under Article 10(2).

(c) Procedural remedies

Quantification and assessment of contractual damages, as well as currency of award, are procedural matters for English *lex fori* (*D'Almeida Araujo Lda v. Sir Frederick Becker & Co. Ltd* [1953] 2 QB 329; *Kohnke* v. *Karger* [1951] 2 KB 670; *The Despina R* [1979] AC 685); whereas, remoteness of damage (*D'Almeida*), and liability to pay interest on damages for breach of contract (*Miliangos* v. *George Frank (Textiles) Ltd (No. 2)* [1977] QB 480 – although possibly not the rate thereof, *ibid.*) are substantive and for the proper law. The procedural treatment of these rules may not survive the Convention, because although Article 1(2)(h) excludes evidence and procedure generally from the Convention's scope, Articles 10(1)(c) and 14 make major inroads into that exclusion, in the matter of damages and proof.

(d) Mandatory rules of the forum

Section 27(2) of the Unfair Contract Terms Act 1977, preserving application of the Act's restrictions on liability exclusion, in favour of United Kingdom habitually resident consumers, where a foreign proper law is chosen, and Sale of Goods Act 1979 s.56, preventing liability avoidance through selection of foreign law, have previously been referred to.

In addition, other English statutes may expressly have provided for their operation whatever the proper law (for example, Bills of Exchange Act 1882 s.72(1)(a); Trade Union and Labour Relations Act 1974 s.30(6); Employment Protection (Consolidation) Act 1978 s.153(5); Equal Pay Act 1970 s.1(11) as amended).

Furthermore, even if a statute does not contain a provision expressly overriding the normal rules of conflict of laws, its objectives may have been adjudged to be so important that the courts would hold it to have *extraterritorial* effect, notwithstanding foreign applicable law (*Boissevain* v. *Weil* [1950] AC 327, HL). Thus, it was seen, in *The Hollandia* [1983] AC 565, 573–4, the House of Lords held the Carriage of Goods by Sea Act 1971, implementing the Hague–Visby Rules in its schedule, to apply as *lex fori* whatever the law (or jurisdiction: pp. 575–7) chosen to govern (or, possibly, otherwise applicable to) the contract, by reason of the prohibition on contracting-out under Schedule, Article III para. 8.

(e) Public policy, and mandatory foreign rules

Finally, English law might also apply on the ground that enforcement of the contract in contravention of, for example, English *lex fori*'s rules on restraint of trade would be contrary to public policy, at least where *English* trade is affected (see *Rousillon* v. *Rousillon* (1880) 14 Ch. D 351; and *Addison* v. *Brown* [1954] 1 All ER 213).

Naturally too, a foreign rule of applicable law will not be given effect to if held to be repugnant and unconscionable, as against public policy: for example, a foreign rule upholding a contract promoting sexual immorality (*Robinson* v. *Bland* (1760) 2 Burr 1077 at p.1084, *per* WILMOT J).

Further, it was previously noted that mandatory rules of a *foreign* law, not otherwise applicable to the contract, may nonetheless be applied by English courts so as to deny effectiveness to the contract, on the ground that it would be in breach of comity and public policy for English courts to uphold a contract which, though valid under the relevant contract rules of the proper law, would nevertheless contravene the mandatory laws of the former, being those of a foreign friendly country (*Foster* v. *Driscoll*).

Such, then, in briefest outline, are the *pre-existing* English rules of conflicts of law relating to contract, which continue to govern contracts concluded prior to 2 April 1991, under Convention Article 17, and (subject to any *special* national provisions, for example, in relation to insurance: see below, Chapter 6) those otherwise not included within the Convention's scope in accordance with Article 1 thereof.

PART II

Contents

CHAPTER 3   GENERAL IMPACT OF EEC'S CONTRACTUAL OBLIGATIONS CONVENTION

Introduction	31
Scope of Convention	32
International Contracts	32
Universal Application	34
Date of Operation of Convention	34
No Retrospective Operation	35
Termination of Convention	35
Revision of the Convention	36
Relations with other Laws and Conventions	36
National laws of Contracting States	36
Other Conventions and community laws	37
Contractual Obligations	38
Listed Exclusions	39
Status and capacity	39
Wills and succession	40
Negotiable instruments	40
Arbitration and choice of court	40
Companies	41
Agency	43
Trusts	43
Evidence and procedure	44
Insurance	45
Law Applicable to General Aspects of Contracts	46
Scope of the Applicable Law	46
Substance of the contract	46
Voluntary assignments	47
Subrogation	47
Presumptions and burden of proof	48
Renvoi excluded	50
Agreements on Applicable Law	50
General: Article 3	50
Consumers: Article 5	53

Individual employment contracts: Article 6	55	Modes of Proof: Article 14	65
		Illegality	68
Applicable Law in the Absence of Choice	55	Mandatory Laws and Public Policy	69
General: Article 4	55	Scope of Convention provisions on mandatory rules	70
Consumers: Article 5	59		
Individual employees: Article 6	59		
		Contracts-Mandatory and conflicts-mandatory	72
Laws Applicable to Particular Aspects of Contracts	60	Public Policy	76
Consent: Article 8	60	Interpretation of the Convention	77
Form: Article 9	60		
		Sources	78
General	61		
Consumers	62	Procedure to Obtain Rulings from the European Court	81
Immovables	62		
Mode of Performance: Article 10(2)	63	Figure 3.1	86–7
		Figure 3.2	88
Capacity: Article 11	64		

3 General Impact of EEC's Contractual Obligations Convention

INTRODUCTION

The Contracts (Applicable Law) Act 1990 implements the 1980 Rome Convention on the Law Applicable to Contractual Obligations (O.J. 1980, No.L 266/1) and the 1984 Luxembourg Convention on Greek Accession thereto (O.J. 1984, No. L146/1), which are set out for ease of reference in Schedules 1 and 2, respectively, to the Act (see s.2(4)(a) and (b)), in the United Kingdom, as from 1 April 1991 (see 1990 Act s.7, and SI 1991, No. 707).

The United Kingdom has ratified the two Brussels Protocols of 1988 (O.J. 1989, No. L48/1 and 17) providing for references to be made by national courts to the European Court of Justice for interpretation of the Conventions, the first of which is set out for ease of reference in Schedule 3 to the 1990 Act (s.2(4)(c)), but these are not yet in force, needing first the required number of ratifications by the other Contracting States (see first Brussels Protocol, Article 6, and second Brussels Protocol, Articles 2 and 3).

The Convention replaces pre-existing English private international rules of applicable law in international contracts (and substitutes the new expression 'applicable law' for the previous term 'proper law': see 1990 Act s.5 and Schedule 4) except in regard to types of contract expressly excluded from its scope under Article 1(2)–(4), those the subject of other international conventions under Article 21, and all contracts not concluded after 1 April 1991, the date of its entry into force in the United Kingdom (see Article 17).

Where it does apply, however, the Convention is not limited to the determination of applicable law of parts of the United Kingdom (see Article 19(1); 1990 Act s.2(3) and Article 19(2)) or of that of other Contracting

States; to this extent, its scope is universal, irrespective of whether the law specified by its provisions is the law of a Contracting or non-Contracting State (Article 2).

At the present time, the Convention has entered into force for Belgium, Denmark, France, Germany, Greece, Italy, Luxembourg, the United Kingdom (all on 1 April 1991), the Netherlands (on 1 September 1991), and Ireland (1 January 1992). Portugal and Spain hope to accede in due course.

SCOPE OF CONVENTION

International Contract Disputes

The Convention is meant to apply to international contractual relations, not to domestic disputes (see Report, p.10): that is to say, it is applicable to contractual obligations 'in any situation involving a choice between the laws of different countries', under Article 1(1). Paragraph 2 of the Preamble to the Convention further refers to unification 'in the field of private international law', and the long title to the 1990 Act states the latter's object to be to make provision as to the law applicable to contractual obligations 'in the case of conflict of laws'.

In relation to the United Kingdom, the question of contracts' internationality has an additional dimension, in that three separate legal systems – the English and Welsh, Scottish and Northern Irish – host their own laws of contract within the single political entity, raising the issue of whether situations involving a conflict between two or more of those laws, but concerning no country other than the United Kingdom, would amount to a choice between the laws *of different countries* for purposes of Article 1(1). Article 19(1) resolves the problem, by specifying that in such circumstances in which a state comprises more than one separate law district with their own rules of contract, each of these latter is to be deemed to be a 'country' for purposes of identifying applicable law under the Convention, the effect of which provision is not merely to confine prescribed Convention contact points to connections with territorial law units rather than with states as such where these do not coincide, but also to bring disputes within the Convention's scope, as being international under Article 1(1), should dispersal of connections involve a choice between separate such legal systems of a single political state but of no other country. Under Article 19(2), the opportunity is provided for courts of the *composite* Contracting State itself not to apply the Convention to contracts conflicts involving solely its separate law districts; but the United Kingdom declined to take this course, and s.2(3) of the 1990 Act specifically states that the Convention is to be applied in the United Kingdom's courts even in the case of conflicts entirely between the laws of different parts of the United Kingdom. (Still, difficulties may arise with Article 19. For example, if a French court, seised of Convention proceedings, were to discover that, whilst French law had been expressly chosen by the parties to govern their contract under Article 3, all other connections relevant to the situation were established with the United Kingdom, would *mandatory* contract rules of the latter's legal systems nonetheless remain inapplicable for purposes of Article 3(3), unless *all* such contacts were located in *one* of the three internal legal systems within the United Kingdom? Presumably, this would be so, according to the wording and policy of Articles 19(1) and 3(3); and the same solution would apply if it were English courts seised of the dispute over a contract expressly subjected by the parties to English law, and all other connections were with either of Scotland or Northern Ireland, or vice versa in the case of choice of the latters' laws: by virtue of Article 19, separate countries' laws would be involved for the purposes of the Convention's application under Article 1(1) and for those of operation of mandatory rules under Article 3(3).)

A further question which might occur under Article 1(1) is that of whether foreign connections capable of giving rise to a choice between different applicable laws should be assessed as at the date of contractual conclusion or as at that of the subsequent dispute, where, for example, parties reside in the same country at the former, but not at the latter, point in time – the word 'situation' in Article 1(1) seemingly being able to cover either circumstance. In the present writer's opinion, as a general Convention principle, relevant connections to be taken into account in determination of applicable law are restricted to those existing at the date of contractual conclusion, to the exclusion of events occurring subsequently thereto, and consistent with this, so should Convention applicability, according to the criterion of choice between different countries' laws under Article 1(1), be assessed.

Additional complications are whether connections taken into account for this purpose of international scope of Convention application, and others under the Convention (for example, in the case of Article 3(3), previously referred to), should encompass every conceivable link which the situation may have with a particular country or only those which are in some way 'relevant' to the case, and, if the latter is correct, whether 'relevance' of points of contact should be assessed in accordance with Convention provisions on applicable law themselves, or alternatively under national private international law rules outside the Convention, or both (see below, Part III, Chapter 6): in the case of contractual capacity of natural persons for example, *lex domicilii* is a connectional factor under national English private international law, but not (at least not directly) under the Convention (see Article 11). Presumably in such a capacity case where the sole foreign connection was the party's domicile, the contract should be held to be international by reason thereof, and the Convention consequently to apply, since to disregard the *national* domicile factor as irrelevant *under the Convention*, subsequently to be held applicable, would be to ignore the fact that choice of law for Article 1(1) is not only *under* the Convention or *under* national conflicts, but also *as between* those two systems of applicable law in contract.

Universal Application of Convention

There is a natural temptation to assume that the Convention only applies where the law applicable thereunder would be that of another Contracting State (just as, for example, the Judgments Convention's jurisdiction grounds are founded upon connections with *Contracting* States). This would be incorrect. Article 2 of the Obligations Convention makes it perfectly plain that applicable law thereunder may be that of a Contracting or *non*-Contracting State (see Report, p.13) – a dimension of the Convention's scope which proved highly controversial during the passage of the legislation in the United Kingdom's parliament (where LORDS WILBERFORCE and GOFF supported an amendment, ultimately defeated, which would have limited the Convention's operation to those contracting parties having their habitual residence, or in the case of businesses, their central administration, in a *Contracting* State: see Hansard, HL Vol.515, cols 1474, 1481–2).

It ought also to be stated that the 1990 Act expressly binds the Crown (s.6).

Date of Operation of Convention

In accordance with Article 29(1), the Convention came into force on 1 April 1991 as between the United Kingdom and Belgium, Denmark, France, Germany, Italy and Luxembourg – the first day of the third month following that of the seventh ratification (by the United Kingdom, on 29 January 1991) – and as between the same states and Greece on that date, in accordance with Article 4 para. 1 of the Luxembourg Convention on Greek Accession to the Obligations Convention; and under Article 29(2), the Obligations Convention subsequently entered into force for the Netherlands on 1 September 1991 and for Ireland on 1 January 1992, as did the Luxembourg Convention therefor on those dates under Article 4 para. 2.

In the United Kingdom, internal effect is given to the Obligations Convention and to the Luxembourg Convention on Greek Accession, by s.2(1) of the Contracts (Applicable Law) Act 1990, brought into force (other than

General Impact of EEC's Contractual Obligations Convention 35

in respect of the Brussels Interpretation Protocol) by Order in Council, as specified under s. 7 of the Act (see The Contracts (Applicable Law) Act 1990 (Commencement No. 1) Order 1991, SI 1991 No. 707), on 1 April 1991.

No Retrospective Operation

Although the Convention entered into force for the original Contracting States on 1 April 1991 and for the Netherlands and Ireland on 1 September 1991 and 1 January 1992 respectively, Article 17 expressly provides that in individual Contracting States the Convention only applies to contracts *made after the date* of its entry into force in those states: that is to say, in the United Kingdom and other Contracting States, apart from the Netherlands and Ireland, contracts concluded on 2 April 1991 and thereafter, and in the Netherlands and Ireland, those made respectively on 2 September 1991 and 2 January 1992, or subsequently, are subject to the Convention's rules on applicable law.

Pre-existing English contract conflicts consequently continue to operate in relation to contracts falling within the Convention's subject-matter scope, where these were concluded on or before 1 April 1991. According to which system of private international law, however – Convention or pre-existing national – should the question of *date of conclusion* of a contract for such purposes be determined (see below, Part III, Chapters 22 and 35)?

Termination of the Convention

The Report explains that since the Obligations Convention is not imposed by any provision of the EEC Treaty, but freely entered into by Contracting States, under Article 30 it has a defined period of duration of ten years from 1 April 1991, the date of its original entry into force, automatically renewable for five-year terms thereafter, except in Contracting States in which it has been denounced not less than six months before the expiration of the period of ten or five years, in which latter states it then ceases to have any further effect at the end of the relevant period (Report, p.41).

It has to be said that it is a little difficult to comprehend why the Obligations Convention, viewed as part of the overall effort to harmonize private international legal relations within the Community (see Preamble, paras 2 and 3), should thus have had its projected period of duration limited in this way simply because this was *permitted*.

Furthermore, there are other difficulties with Article 30. First, there happens to be no equivalent provision in the Luxembourg Convention for denunciation of Greek accession. Technically, therefore, it could be argued that, if a Luxembourg Convention state were to denounce the Obligations Convention, Greece would nonetheless remain bound thereto to apply the Obligations Convention (in the absence of its own denunciation) at the public international level!

Secondly, were a Contracting State to denounce the Convention under Article 30, would the text of the Convention in that state's language remain equally authentic for interpretative purposes under Article 33? Presumably it would (just as it does thereunder *prior* to a state's Convention ratification) and a revision conference would have to be called under Article 26 in order to amend Article 33 if thought desirable or necessary.

Revision of the Convention

On the request of any Contracting State, a conference *must* be convened in order to discuss revision of the Convention (Article 26; see too Brussels Protocol, Article 10, and 1990 Act s.4).

Relations with Other Laws and Conventions

National laws of Contracting States

Within its scope of operation, the Convention supersedes all pre-existing national rules of private international law of contract of the Contracting States.

However, *after* the Convention has entered into force for a Contracting State, the latter may, in accordance with Article 23, adopt a new national choice of law rule in place of the corresponding Convention provision

- provided that the new national rule in question is restricted to a particular category of contract, rather than being generalized; and
- the Contracting State communicates its intentions to the other signatory States in the prescribed manner; and
- consultations must then take place over the proposed derogation from the Convention's provisions, if so requested by another signatory State.

The Report explains that this safety-net rule, possibly leading to a weakening of the mandatory force of the Convention, was included because of the very wide scope of the Convention and the general character of most of its rules. Thus:

The case was envisaged where a State found it necessary for political, economic or social reasons to amend a choice of law rule and it was thought desirable to find a solution sufficiently flexible to enable States to ratify the Convention without having to denounce it as soon as they were forced to disregard its rules on a particular point (p.40).

Accordingly, the provision may simply be regarded as an extension of excluded areas in Article 1(2), which covers certain categories of contract known *at the present time* to be unsuitable for regulation by the Convention's rules.

One further provision should be mentioned in the current connection. This is the Protocol annexed to the Convention (forming an integral part thereof, by virtue of Article 32). According to the Protocol, Denmark is to be permitted to retain its *existing* choice of law rules laid down in paragraph 169 of its Statute on Maritime Law, concerning contracts for the carriage of goods by sea, and if it wishes to revise these or substitute new laws therefor, it need not follow the communication and consultation procedure prescribed under Article 23. The reason for the exception is that the Danish law in question is in the nature of an approximation of rules amongst Scandinavian countries, more akin to an existing international convention – enjoying precedence and excluded from the consultation procedure under Articles 21 and 24(2), respectively, of the Convention – than to a mere pre-existing national conflicts provision (Report, p.42).

Other conventions and community laws

Under Article 21, other international conventions, existing or future, within the Convention's scope, *take precedence* over the Convention to the extent that they are inconsistent therewith.

However, in the case of Contracting States wishing to become parties to a multilateral contract conflicts convention *after* the Convention has entered into force in respect thereof, they are required to undergo the communication and consultation *procedure* laid down in Article 24(1), unless one of the exceptional sets of circumstances specified in Article 24(2) (another Contracting State or one of the European Communities is already a party to the other convention, or the object of the other convention is to revise a convention to which the Contracting State concerned is already a party, or the other convention is concluded within the framework of the EC Treaties) is found to exist – although, even in the latter case, under Article 25 a Contracting State may request consultations if it thinks that Convention unification would be prejudiced by the conclusion of such conventions (and in para. II of the first Joint Declaration annexed to the Convention, signatory states declared their intention to consult with each other even prior to the Convention's entry into force, if any of them wished to become a party to an Article 24(1)-type convention: see O.J. 1980, No. L266/14).

In addition, it should be noted that in accordance with Article 20, the Convention's provisions must defer to any contract choice of law rules laid down in existing or future acts of EC institutions, or in national laws harmonized in implementation thereof, *in relation to particular matters*: such EC *leges speciales* must therefore be given priority − although, para. I of the first Joint Declaration annexed to the Convention does express the wish that EC institutions will try to ensure that any such choice of law rules are consistent with those of the Convention, where the need for them arises.

Contractual Obligations

Tucked away in the wording of Article 1(1) of the Convention is the key term 'contractual' in relation to obligations, the subject matter of the Convention's rules. Convention negotiators, who began their task by pinpointing a somewhat broader range of legal relationships to be covered by the new uniform rules than purely the contractual, eventually restricted their efforts to the latter alone (Report, pp.5–7), and the Convention is the outcome of that decision.

The problem, of course, is that, as is well known, the concept of *contractual* relations may differ from one national law to another, as may the classification of causes of action as such. Accordingly, 'contractual' in Article 1(1) is effectively a *code word* enabling courts of Contracting States, and eventually the European Court itself, to reach policy decisions as to the types of legal relations and causes of action which are to be drawn into the Convention's scope through being classified as contractual, and there can be few doubts that, as in the case of Article 5(1) of the Judgments Convention (jurisdiction in matters relating to a *contract*, to be distinguished from Article 5(3) on torts), the European Court and national courts will seek to apply an independent Community concept of contractual obligations for purposes of Article 1(1) of the Obligations Convention (see, for example, Judgments Convention cases *Peters* v. *ZNAV*, Case 34/82 [1983] ECR 987; *Sprl Arcado* v. *Haviland S.A.*, Case 9/87 [1988] ECR 1539; *Kalfelis* v. *Schröder, Münchmeyer, Hengst*, Case 189/87 [1988] ECR 5565), in particular, in view of the express requirement laid down in Article 18 of the Obligations Convention that the latter's provisions should be interpreted and applied having regard to their international character and to the need for uniformity to be achieved.

Thus, the Report indicates that matters of property, physical or intangible, are outside the concept of contractual (p.10) – although, clearly, contracts themselves, relating to the transfer of property, fall within the Convention's scope notwithstanding such exclusion of their proprietary effects. *Gifts*, furthermore, to the extent that they are promissory and contractual (and not, for example, proprietary or constitutive of a trust: see Article 1(2)(g)), and generally unilateral promises (see *Re Bonacina* [1912] 2 Ch. 394), are believed to be within the Convention's scope, provided of course that they do not fall within either of the family law or succession exceptions in Article 1(2)(b) (Report, pp.10–11; and see below Part III, Chapter 6). It is further submitted that claims in quasi-contract and restitution, even arising from contracts, should be held to fall outside the Convention's scope as non-contractual (see below, Chapter 6).

Listed Exclusions from the Convention's Subject-Matter Scope

Article 1(2) contains a list of miscellaneous matters which are expressly excluded from the Convention's scope of operation for a number of reasons.

Status and legal capacity of natural persons: Article 1(2)(a)

To the extent that 'transactions' affecting status, such as marriage or engagement, are held to pertain to a contract between the parties thereto, in accordance with the relevant national legal system, they nonetheless remain excluded from the Convention's scope, as being too closely associated with the main status relationship for general Convention contract rules to be allowed to replace the special, social policy choice-of-law rules on status under national private international law systems.

Legal capacity of natural persons to enter contracts, as an aspect of international contractual regulation, is excluded from the Convention, because it would seem to be the case that civil lawyers prefer to view the matter as one involving status, rather than contract (see North, in North (ed.) *Contract Conflicts* (1982), p.10). This being so, it is difficult to understand why an exception to the exclusion was permitted to be included in Article 11, to which Article 1(2)(a) is expressly made subject. It would seem that drafters were overcome by a desire to protect parties, who in good faith believed themselves to be contracting with a party of full capacity, against the latter's incapacity and consequent invalidity of the contract under national rules of private international law (Report, p.34).

Wills and succession, matrimonial property and family relations: Article 1(2)(b)

Maintenance agreements fall within the scope of the Judgments Convention (see Article 5(2) thereof), but are excluded (including those in respect of illegitimate children) from that of the Obligations Convention *to the extent that* they give effect to an existing legal obligation to maintain (Report, p.10). All other such agreements, therefore, even if they provide maintenance for a member of the *family* towards whom there are no legal maintenance obligations, are within the Obligations Convention's scope (*ibid.*).

European Court jurisprudence concerning the meaning of 'rights in property arising out of a matrimonial relationship' under Article 1 para. 2(1) of the Judgments Convention will need to be taken into account in construing the equivalent expression in Article 1(2)(b) of the Obligations Convention (1990 Act s. 3(1) and (2), and Obligations Convention Article 18: see *de Cavel v. de Cavel (No.1)*, Case 143/78 [1979] ECR 1055, and below, Chapter 6).

Bills of exchange, cheques and promissory notes and other negotiable instruments, to the extent that the obligations under such other negotiable instruments arise out of their negotiable character: Article 1(2)(c)

It is not the contractual transaction in respect of which the cheque or other negotiable instrument is given in payment which is excluded from the Convention's scope, but the contractual elements of the instrument itself (see *Moulis v. Owen* [1907] 1 KB 746); nor are ordinary dealings with the latter, not arising from its negotiability, excluded (Report, p.11). Documents of transfer which lack the quality of *negotiability* – the latter to be characterized, according to the Report (p.11), by reference to national private international law of the forum – such as bills of lading, are not within the exclusion (*ibid.*).

Thus, the original contract comprised in the negotiable instrument, and those supervening on indorsement, are excluded from the Convention and consequently subject to national English choice of law rules in the Bills of Exchange Act 1882 s.72(1) and (2).

Arbitration agreements and choice of court: Article 1(2)(d)

The European Court recently ruled in connection with the arbitration exclusion under Article 1 para. 2(4) of the Judgments Convention that proceedings for appointment of an arbitrator, even involving existence or validity of the arbitration agreement as a preliminary issue, were covered by the latter exclusion, on the ground that arbitration was already the subject of international conventions (admittedly, to which not all member states were parties), and that although procedure for appointment of arbitrators was not covered by those conventions, nevertheless, arbitration was intended to be excluded in its entirety from the Convention, and arbitral appointment remained part of the process for setting the excluded arbitration proceedings in motion; further, whatever the independent status of existence and validity proceedings might be, excluded or otherwise, they could not affect the excluded nature of main appointment proceedings simply through being raised as a preliminary issue in the course thereof (see *Marc Rich and Co AG v. Società Italiana Impianti PA*, Case C-190-89 (1991) *The Times*, 20 September).

Under the Obligations Convention too, therefore, it would seem that the arbitration exclusion is to be construed expansively, as including formation, validity and effects, as well as any contractual aspects relating to procedural elements, and whether the arbitration agreement is entered into independently or forms part of a larger, non-excluded contract (as to which, it may still be taken into account as an implied indication of applicable law) (Report, p.12). The United Kingdom's Convention negotiators thought that arbitration should not be excluded, because not all member states were parties to the international agreements, and these latter did not cover all areas of choice of law in any event; but other voices prevailed on the grounds of complexity and unsuitability of certain Convention provisions in relation to arbitration (Report, *ibid.*).

The Report (p.11) considers that, in the case of choice of court agreements, the question of the law applicable to consent will not arise in practice, because Article 17 of the Judgments Convention generally requires jurisdiction agreements (which will normally accompany the choice of law clause) to be either in, or evidenced in, writing – a viewpoint which rather assumes that the consensus required thereunder is in substitution for, rather than in addition to, national rules of contractual agreement required for effectiveness of agreements on choice of court.

Questions governed by the law of companies and other bodies corporate or unincorporate, such as the creation, by registration or otherwise, legal capacity, internal organization or winding up of companies and other bodies corporate or unincorporate and the personal liability of officers and members as such for the obligations of the company or body: Article 1(2)(e)

To the extent that formation and winding up of companies and associations may be regarded as contractual, rather than purely administrative, as between promoters or other parties involved, such creation or termination is excluded from the Convention – although, according to the Report, preliminary contracts creating obligations solely between promoters are not excluded, whereas agreements for mergers and groupings are so (p.12).

Matters of internal organization – for example, concerning the calling of meetings and rights to vote – which may be deemed to be founded upon a contract as between the company and its members, and as between members *inter se* (see Companies Act 1985 s. 14(1)), together with provisions imposing personal responsibility upon officers and members of the company or body for the latter's contracts (see Companies Act 1985 s. 349), are also expressly mentioned as being excluded.

As in the case of natural persons under Article 1(2)(a), legal capacity of companies and bodies is excluded too – although, in this instance, not subject to the special rule in Article 11. (Arguably, in the case of partnerships, which the Report (p.12) says are included within Article 1(2)(e), in spite of their lack of separate legal personality under English law, legal capacity is therefore covered by the unqualified exclusion in Article 1(2)(e), rather than by the qualified equivalent in Article 1(2)(a): however, capacity to *enter into* a partnership agreement should surely be held to fall within the latter, notwithstanding its direct bearing upon *creation* of the firm within Article 1(2)(e); and doubts may even be felt over whether such legal capacity of a partner in an English firm personally to be bound in contract towards a third party is itself within Article 1(2)(e) rather than (a) – where not turning upon agency in Article 1(2)(f) – and even the reference in Article 1(2)(e) to personal liability of officers and members for the body's obligations would seem to presuppose that the body as such is capable, in the first place, of assuming such obligations, possible under certain legal systems, in spite of a lack of independent legal personality: see Kaye, *Civil Jurisdiction* (1987), p.404.)

The Report further specifies that the exclusion of legal capacity under Article 1(2)(e) covers 'limitations, which may be imposed by law on companies and firms, for example in respect of acquisition of immovable property' and not also the effects of *ultra vires* upon the body, which is instead a question for the agency exclusion under Article 1(2)(f) (pp.12–13). Neither Article 1(2)(e) nor (f) specifically refers to cases in which *the third party* seeks to escape contractual liability towards the company by relying upon a defence that the transaction was beyond the company's capacity (see now, however, Companies Act 1985 s. 35(1), by virtue of Companies Act 1989 s.108); nevertheless, the better view would seem to be that the latter too would be a question *governed by the law of companies and other bodies corporate or unincorporate* within the meaning of Article 1(2)(e), and its exclusion from the Convention's scope would be consistent with the treatment of the converse case in which the company seeks to use *ultra vires* as a defence in contract.

Binding nature of agency: Article 1(2)(f)

Questions of whether an agent is able to bind a principal, or an organ to bind a company or body corporate or unincorporate, towards third parties, are also excluded from the Convention's scope.

Thus, existence and effects of acts *ultra vires* the company or its representative officers are excluded from the Convention's scope hereunder, according to the line taken in the Report (pp.12–13) – although, whether the former falls within Article 1(2)(f) rather than (e) is, in the present submission, open to question (see below, Part III, Chapter 6).

The Report draws attention to the fact that the provision is only expressed to apply to creation of binding principal–third party relations, in respect of which it was considered too difficult to accept the Convention principle of freedom of contract, and that the rule does not therefore extend to principal–agent and agent–third party relationships, which were seen as in no way differing from other obligations and consequently were to be included in the Convention, in so far as they were of a contractual nature (p.13).

Constitution of trusts and relationship between settlors, trustees and beneficiaries: Article 1(2)(g)

As in the case of company matters under Article 1(2)(e), it is the *internal*, not external, relations of the trust which were considered to be unsuitable – to the extent of their being contractual in nature – for regulation according to the Convention's rules. It is not entirely clear why this particular exclusion should have been felt to be necessary, since the Report makes it plain that the English word 'trusts' – also used in foreign authentic texts of Article 1(2)(g) – is intended to be understood in the common law sense (and analogous Continental institutions will only be equated therewith to the extent that they exhibit the same characteristics) (p.13), in view of which, it ought to have been possible, in any event, to treat contractual and excluded proprietary elements of the trust separately for purposes of applicable law, so that the Convention's application to the former would not automatically have led to difficulties: thus, a contract for the transfer of assets on trust, or in the execution thereof, could have been subjected to the law of a country of which the legal system contained no trust concept, without also having had an effect upon proprietary trust aspects according to the law applicable to the latter, provided that the *contract* were held to be valid and effective under Convention applicable law (see *Cammell* v. *Sewell* (1860) 5 H. & N. 728, Ex. Ch.; *Winkworth* v. *Christie, Manson and Woods Ltd* [1980] Ch. 496).

Evidence and procedure, without prejudice to Article 14: Article 1(2)(h)

Matters classified as evidential or procedural – for example, requirements for proof of contractual existence and enforceability (*Leroux* v. *Brown* (1852) 12 CB 801), and quantification of damages for breach of contract (*D'Almeida Araujo Lda* v. *Becker & Co. Ltd* [1953] 2 QB 329) – are traditionally for regulation according to *lex fori* rather than the proper law of contracts, and Article 1(2)(h) maintains this practice by excluding evidential and procedural elements relating to the contract from the scope of the Convention's rules on applicable law. The general principle is that solely matters classified as substantive will be governed by the Convention; and in accordance with Article 18, classification as such ought to take place in an internationalist spirit so as not to foster divergencies between the courts of different Contracting States.

Article 1(2)(h) is specifically stated to be without prejudice to Article 14. The latter secures operation of applicable law *et alia* under the Convention – and, by necessary implication, therefore, the Convention's application itself – in relation to certain matters which *might* otherwise have been regarded as being excluded, as procedural or evidential issues for national laws under Article 1(2)(h): namely, presumptions of law, burden and modes of proof of contract. (Difficult questions may arise as to whether particular formalities of contracting are to be classified as substantive rules of formal *validity* within Article 9, or *modes of proof* for purposes of Article 14(2), or *neither*, in which latter event they may be subject to *lex fori* under national private international law of procedure by virtue of Article 1(2)(h), excluding the Convention from applying.)

In addition, it is possible, as a matter of Convention construction, that quantification of damages, as an aspect of *assessment* thereof within the meaning of Article 10(1)(c), which includes the latter within the scope of applicable law under the Convention, and consequently (if also by necessary implication) of the Convention itself, is also an exception to the Article 1(2)(h) procedural exclusion, notwithstanding the absence of any express reference therein to Article 10 (although, the latter omission is significant, since it would seem that both of Articles 10 and 14 *pre-dated* Article 1(2)(h): see Report, p.36). This would be to bring about a change from the previous law, classifying the question as procedural (*D'Almeida Araujo Lda*), whereas limitation of actions, on the other hand, referred to as falling within the scope of applicable law (and consequently of the Convention) under Article 10(1)(d), is now also for *lex causae* under pre-existing national English conflicts (see Foreign Limitation Periods Act 1984 s.1(1)), having previously been treated as procedural for *lex fori* thereunder (*British Linen Co. v. Drummond* (1830) 10 B. & C. 903).

Contracts of insurance (but not reinsurance) covering risks situated in the territories of member states of the EEC (such situation to be determined in accordance with courts' internal laws): Article 1(3) and (4)

EEC insurance risks were excluded because of work being carried out in the Community in the field of insurance, including choice of law (Report, p.13). Thus, in the case of non-life insurance, Regulation 6 of the Insurance Companies (Amendment) Regulations 1990 (SI 1990 No. 1333) implemented in the United Kingdom as from 1 July 1990 the Second Council Directive on Non-Life Insurance of 22 June 1988 (88/357/EEC, O.J. 1988 L172/1) through insertion of s.94A and Schedule 3A into the Insurance Companies Act 1982 containing choice of law rules based upon the insured's home member state; and life assurance will be governed by Article 4 of the Second Council Directive on Life Assurance of 8 November 1990 (90/619/EEC, O.J. 1990 L330/50) when implemented in the United Kingdom in the course of 1992, subjecting the contract *inter alia* to law of the country of the policyholder's habitual residence or establishment, until which time pre-existing national English conflicts, founded upon proper law of the insurance contract – often the insurer's law (Dicey and Morris, pp. 1289–90) – should apply.

In respect of reinsurance, where the same need for protection of insured parties will not exist (Report, p.13), and of non-EEC risks, the Convention will be applicable, and it is possible that insurance contracts may be held to constitute 'consumer contracts' within the meaning of Article 5 and to be subject therefore to its special rules of protection as to applicable law (Report, p.13).

Article 1(3) requires courts to apply their own internal law (which means domestic rules, to the exclusion of private international law: see Article 15; Report, p.13) in order to determine situation of risk for such purposes. This is not a matter which appears to have received a great deal of attention according to previous English conflicts. However, s.96A of the Insurance Companies Act 1982, referred to earlier, contains some rules for ascertaining situation of risks under that Act, including *inter alia* place of registration of the vehicle in the case of motor insurance, and of habitual residence in other types of policy.

LAW APPLICABLE TO GENERAL ASPECTS OF CONTRACTS

Scope of the Applicable Law

Substance of the contract: Articles 8 and 10

The following matters of substance are specifically referred to as falling within the scope of applicable law:
- existence and validity of the contract and of its terms (Article 8(1)): this will include matters of formation such as offer and acceptance and requirement of consideration (existence), as well as initial illegality, and effectiveness of liability exclusion clauses (validity), and even existence and validity of consent to a choice of law agreement itself (see Article 3(4));
- interpretation of the contract (Article 10(1)(a));
- substance of performance (but not manner thereof: Article 10(2)) (Article 10(1)(b)): this probably also includes valuation and legality of the money of account, as the law applicable thereto (severably, if necessary, under Article 3(1)), as well as, arguably, initial and supervening illegality of performance;
- within the court's procedural powers, consequences of breach of contract, including the assessment of damages in so far as it is governed by rules of law (Article 10(1)(c)): as previously seen in connection with Article 1(2)(h), it is possible – yet uncertain – that the formula in Article 10(1)(c) includes quantification (procedural for *lex fori*, under pre-existing English conflicts), and not merely remoteness, of damage, except to the extent that the former is purely factual, and the reference to *rules of law* in Article 10(1)(c) does not greatly clarify the question (see Report, p.33); *consequences of breach* will include any requirement of service of notice on a party to assume his liability (Report, *ibid.*), as a pre-condition of the latter's existence, although, availability of remedies for breach, such as specific performance and injunctions, will expressly be subject to the limits of the forum's procedural powers thereunder;
- extinction of obligations, and prescription and limitation of actions (Article 10(1)(d)): discharge through frustration and supervening illegality *et alia* will be for applicable law, as will, as has previously been seen, time bars on actions, as under pre-existing national laws as laid down in the Foreign Limitation Periods Act 1984 and the Prescription and Limitation (Scotland) Act 1984: it would seem, therefore, that there is no separate choice of law rule under the

Convention, consigning legality of performance to law of the country of performance (see *Ralli Bros* v. *Compania Naviera Sota y Aznar* [1920] 2 KB 287) (except, of course, to the extent that illegality is merely as to *manner* of performance under Article 10(2), and other than possibly where such rules on legality are regarded as *mandatory* for purposes of Convention provisions safeguarding application thereof, or as activating public policy comity refusal of the courts to apply a conflicting rule of applicable law under Article 16: see below, Chapters 12 and 21);

- **[not in the United Kingdom: 1990 Act s. 2(2); Article 22(1)(b)]** the consequences of nullity of the contract (Article 10(1)(e)): the United Kingdom reserved the right not to apply this provision under Article 22(1)(b); the latter was included on the ground of non-contractual nature of laws of restitution under various Contracting States' legal systems, including those of the United Kingdom (see *Kleinwort Benson Ltd. and Barclays Bank plc* v. *Glasgow City Council* (1992) *The Times*, 17 March).

Contracts of voluntary assignment of rights: Article 12

Article 12 distinguishes between two related, yet different, types of legal relations involved in a contract for the voluntary assignment of a right – contractual or otherwise – against another person (referred to as 'the debtor'): (1) the contractual relationship between assignor and assignee, the law governing their mutual obligations being that which is applicable to their contract under the Convention; and (2) the relationship between assignee and debtor, the law governing the right to which the assignment relates applying to this, together with the right's assignability in the first place, conditions under which the assignment may be invoked against the debtor and the question of whether the debtor's obligations have been discharged. Clearly, where the right assigned is itself derived from a contract falling within the Convention's scope, law applicable thereto and relations between assignee and debtor will themselves be subject to the Convention even in respect of assignability thereof, where, according to national private international principles on assignability of intangible property rights, 'the law governing' the latter is that applicable to the source transaction (see Report, p.35; below, Chapter 17).

Subrogation to rights: Article 13

According to the legislation of various Contracting States, where a third person has a duty to satisfy a debtor's creditor, or has in fact discharged that duty, the third person becomes entitled – subrogated – to the creditor's rights against the debtor, for example, in the case of a guarantor of another's debt to a creditor. Thus, the question arises of which law to apply in order to determine whether the third person possesses such rights of subrogation, where the third person's duty to satisfy the creditor arises from a contract between them. Is it the law governing the latter, or alternatively, that conferring the creditor's rights against the debtor? Under Article 13(1), where the claim satisfied by the third person is contractual, it is the law governing the third person's duty to do so which applies in order to determine whether the third person is entitled to exercise the creditor's rights against the debtor arising under the law governing the creditor–debtor relationship, in full or in part, subject, of course, to the terms of any contract existing between the third person and the debtor, itself governed by the law applicable thereto under the Convention and unaffected by Article 13 (Report, p.35). (Surely too, the same rule should be applied in any event, aside from Article 13, to contractual succession of a third person to a creditor's rights against a debtor of a *non-contractual* nature, subject also to the law governing the non-contractual creditor–debtor relations in this instance: see *Brodin* v. *A/R Seljan* (1973) SC 213, in an analogous context); and similarly, under Article 13(2), this is the case where one of several persons subject to the same contractual claim has satisfied the creditor.

Presumptions of law and burden of proof: Article 14(1)

It has already been seen that Article 1(2)(h), generally excluding evidential and procedural matters from the Convention's scope, is expressly made subject to Article 14, the implication being that but for this saving such issues as are dealt with under the latter might have had to have been held to fall outside the Convention's scope as procedural. Article 14, however, has the further effect that these questions are not only within the Convention's overall scope, but also within that of the contract's *applicable law* under the Convention (and also via Article 9(1) and (2), in the case of *modes of proof* of contract under Article 14(2): see below, Chapter 19). The Report explains that, whatever the view may be at national law, presumptions of law, relieving a party in whose favour they operate from the need to produce evidence, and rules on burden of proof, are really rules of substance 'which in the law of contract contribute to making clear the obligations of the parties and therefore cannot be separated from the law which governs the contract' (p.36). Thus, under national English conflicts, irrebuttable presumptions of law seem to be treated as substantive (*Re Cohn* [1945] Ch. 5), as well as possibly also in the case of rebuttable (*De Thoren* v. *AG* (1876) 1 App. Cas. 686); however, the position as to burden of proof appears to be more doubtful in this respect (see *The Roberta* (1937) 58 Ll. L. Rep 159; *Re Fuld's Estate (No.3)* [1968] P. 675).

There is nevertheless one limitation expressed in Article 14(1), upon the operation of applicable law: the latter only applies to presumptions and burden of proof *to the extent that it contains in the law of contract* rules on such matters. The meaning of this restriction is far from clear (see below, Part III, Chapter 19). The difficulty is whether, in the construction of the expression *law of contract*, greater emphasis should be placed upon the word 'law', to be read as *substantive* law rather than procedural, or upon the words 'of contract', so that solely those presumptions and rules of burden of proof specifically applicable to contracts, rather than those of more general operation, should be regarded as being required to be regulated according to applicable law. The first approach would seem to undo most of the effects of the safeguard for Article 14 in Article 1(2)(h) in so far as it relates to Article 14(1), in that to the extent that presumptions and burden of proof were to be classified as procedural by national courts, they would fall outside Article 14(1) on scope of applicable law and consequently also outside the Convention's scope under Article 1(2)(h)! On the other hand, however, the second possible interpretation of the limitation in Article 14(1) might also be felt to be unduly restrictive. The Report in fact offers a means of resolving the problem: the words in question in Article 14(1) should be read as referring to presumptions and rules on burden of proof which are non-procedural ('in effect rules of substance'), that is, the first meaning above, but *procedure* is then apparently to be given a very narrow meaning in this context, basically as relating to the conduct itself of forensic proceedings and pleadings, which are clearly part of procedural law and should properly be subject to the forum's rules rather than to those of contract applicable law:

> This is the case, for example, with the rule whereby the claim of a party who appears is deemed to be substantiated if the other party fails to appear, or the rule making silence on the part of a party to an action with regard to facts alleged by the other party equivalent to an admission of those facts ... Such rules do not form part of 'the law of contract' and accordingly do not fall within the choice of law rule established by Article 14(1) (p.36).

Accordingly, only *substantive* rules on presumptions and burden of proof fall within the scope of applicable law under Article 14(1), and these are not confined to those specifically operating in relation to contracts; however, excluded *procedural* such rules are narrowly confined in meaning to rules of actual pleading and process.

Renvoi is excluded: Article 15

Applicable law under the Convention means domestic rules of contract of the law referred to, minus its rules of private international law, as under pre-existing English conflicts (*Re United Railways of Havana and Regla Warehouses Ltd* [1960] Ch. 52; *Dimskal Shipping Co. SA* v. *ITWF, The 'Evia Luck' (No. 2)* [1990] 1 Lloyd's Rep 319, CA). The Report justifies this approach on the ground that chosen law under Article 3 is clearly intended to indicate substantive provisions of the chosen law, whilst it would further be unreasonable for courts to subject a contract to a law other than that of the most connected country under Article 4 by introducing *renvoi* solely because the latter's conflicts rules contained different connecting factors from those of the forum (p.37) – an approach founded solidly upon commercial pragmatism rather than on any compelling arguments of principle. At least, however, there is a limit to the exclusionary scope of the rule in Article 15, in that it is expressly restricted to provisions of *private international law*, which, presumably, will not include those national spatial limitations imposed in respect of particular substantive legal norms, for example, under s.1(1) of the Equal Pay Act 1970, as amended, restricting the equality clause in contracts to those of employees at establishments in Great Britain. It would be rather strange if the latter type of territorial limitation were excluded from applying, as constituting rules of private international law under Article 15, so that by virtue of the Convention such specific national policy restrictions were ignored and the projected territorial reach of the laws in question consequently extended.

Agreements on Applicable Law

General: Article 3

Express and implied choice of law agreements will be given effect to under Article 3(1): the choice must be expressed or 'demonstrated with reasonable certainty by the terms of the contract or the circumstances of the case'. This basically accords with pre-existing national English contract conflicts (see *Vita Food Products Inc.* v. *Unus Shipping Co. Ltd* [1939] AC 277, 290; *Amin Rasheed Shipping Corpn* v. *Kuwait Insurance Co.* [1984] AC 50, 61), as well as with that of other Contracting States (see Report, p.15). Factors from which a choice of a country's law may be implied will be, for example, use of a standard form widely known to be characteristic of a particular country's legal system, a previous course of dealing between the parties subjected to a certain law, and choice of court or arbitration – as under the previous law (see *Chatenay* v. *Brazilian Submarine Telegraph Co. Ltd* [1891] 1 QB 79; *The Adriatic* [1931] P. 241; *Compagnie d'Armement Maritime SA* v. *Compagnie Tunisienne de Navigation SA* [1971] AC 572) (Report, p.17). Severable choice is expressly permitted: under Article 3(1) parties may choose X law to govern one part of their contract, and Y law to apply to another or the remainder (presumably, law of the money of account specified in the contract – *lex pecuniae* – will be regarded as severable applicable law in relation thereto); or they may simply select X law to govern part, leaving the rest to be regulated according to Convention rules on applicable law in the absence of choice. (National English law appears to correspond: see *Forsakringsiktieselskapet* v. *Butcher* [1986] 2 All ER 488, pp. 504–5; although, there is caution over splitting a contract unnecessarily: see *Kahler* v. *Midland Bank* [1950] AC 24, 42; *Libyan Arab Foreign Bank* v. *Bankers Trust Co* [1989] 3All ER 252, 267). The only control over such severance seems to be that laws severably applicable should be logically reconcilable (Report, p.17).

Article 3(2) goes on to provide that parties are permitted to *vary* the law otherwise applicable to their contract (whether through Article 3 agreement or in the absence thereof under the Convention) subsequent to conclusion of the contract. This clarifies the previous position under English conflicts where there seemed to be a division of opinion over whether parties' ability so to vary the original proper law should be governed by the latter or by *lex fori* (see Dicey and Morris, p.1168; in *James Miller and Partners Ltd* v. *Whitworth Street Estates (Manchester) Ltd* [1970] AC 583, 603, LORD REID contemplated that parties could vary the proper law, but failed to indicate which system of law would govern the variation; in *Armar Shipping Co. Ltd* v. *Caisse Algérienne d'Assurance et de Réassurance* [1981] 1 WLR 207, CA, MEGAW LJ, at 215–16, delivered *dicta* against subsequent change of applicable law, but these were in fact made in the context of an attack upon a floating proper law, to be concretized according to occurrence of events specified in the contract, which is not quite the same thing; note too, Report, pp.17–18, for a comparative survey of national treatments). Article 3(2) indicates, however, that the attempted variation will be ineffective in either of two situations: first, to the extent that its effect would somehow be to prejudice the contract's formal validity under Article 9; and secondly, where it would adversely affect the rights of third parties, for example, those entitled to benefit from stipulations in the contract made in their favour under Continental civil law systems.

It should further be noted that under Article 3(4), existence and validity of consent to a choice of law agreement itself is not a matter for *lex fori*, but also for *applicable law* – that is to say, including that which is supposedly chosen under Article 3! – in accordance with Articles 8 and 9 (and 11, as subjectively chosen or objective proper law under national English private international law: see below, Chapter 16), just as, under Article 8, existence and validity of the contract as a whole and of any term thereof are also subject to the law which would govern the contract *as if the contract or term were valid*, that is to say, to subjectively chosen applicable law under Article 3, as well as to that applicable in the absence of choice under Article 4.

According to pre-existing national English conflicts, there were certain rather vague restrictions upon parties' power to agree on any law whatsoever to govern their contract, based on LORD WRIGHT's dicta in *Vita Food Products Inc.* v. *Unus Shipping Co. Ltd* [1939] AC 277, 290 (PC) to the effect that a choice should be *bona fide* and legal and not avoidable on public policy grounds if it was to be given effect to. Presumably, the *bona fide* qualification was intended to indicate that the expressed (or implied) choice should be seriously meant (Dicey and Morris, p.1172), which may not be held to be so where the ostensibly chosen law has absolutely no connection whatsoever with the parties or transaction, whilst legality and public policy would bear their normal conflicts meanings. The Convention is far more specific (although, possibly less flexible), in providing under Article 3(3) that where a particular country's law is chosen, and yet the contractual situation at the time of choice is otherwise wholly connected with *one* other country, the choice is not to prejudice the application of the mandatory rules of law of the latter country – even if the former's courts as well as law were agreed upon. Thus, whilst Article 3(3)'s constraints on parties' choice of applicable law are more clearly defined than those of national English conflicts, the former simply safeguard the operation of *mandatory rules* of the otherwise wholly connected law rather than that of the latter as a whole – *mandatory* being defined thereunder as rules of law 'which cannot be derogated from by contract': for example, contractual exclusion of ss. 12–15 of the Sale of Goods Act 1979, implying certain terms into sale of goods contracts, is restricted under s.6 of the Unfair Contract Terms Act 1977 (in *non*-international cases under s.26 of the 1977 Act). It is possible that courts might still find a law chosen under Article 3(1) to be so unconnected as to be considered a sham, not seriously meant; yet, in view of the express inclusion of Article 3(3), this possibility appears unlikely to have been intended, and Article 7(1) – albeit inapplicable in the United Kingdom (1990 Act s.2(2)) – further provides a safeguard for operation of mandatory rules of law of a country other than that of applicable law, with which the situation has a close, even if not the closest, connection. (Moreover, according to the Report, p.18, the United Kingdom in particular amongst negotiating states was concerned not to limit parties' freedom of contract to choose applicable law even where there was apparently no connection with the contract, so that autonomy should only be departed from in exceptional circumstances such as application of mandatory rules.) One final point concerning Article 3(3) is that in accordance with Article 19(1), where countries possess several different contracts legal systems, as in the case of the English and Welsh, Scottish, and Northern Irish within the United Kingdom, each of such separate law districts is to be regarded as a 'country' for purposes of applicable law under the Convention (even by courts within the United Kingdom itself, if it so elects, as has occurred: see 1990 Act s.2(3); Article 19(2)). Choice of English law under Article 3(1) may therefore be subject to mandatory rules of Scottish or Northern Irish contract law under Article 3(3) where either of the latter is otherwise wholly connected, and vice versa (provided that, generally, Article 3(3) still applies where it is the forum's law which is so chosen: see below, Part III, Chapter 8).

Consumer contracts: Article 5

There is a major constraint upon choice of applicable law in the case of consumer contracts within Article 5: under Article 5(2), a choice of law agreed to in accordance with Article 3 is not to have the result of depriving a consumer party of the protection afforded to him by mandatory rules of law of the country in which he has his *habitual residence*.

'Mandatory rules' are as defined under Article 3(3), in so far as they are applicable to consumers within the meaning of Article 5, that is to say, in accordance with Article 5(1), persons supplied with goods or services or credit therefor, for a purpose which can be regarded as being outside their trade or profession. The example of ss. 12–15 of the Sale of Goods Act 1979, by virtue of Unfair Contract Terms Act 1977 s.6, in so far as these apply to Article 5 consumers, has previously been seen (the meaning of 'deals as consumer' in s.12 of the 1977 Act is narrower than, and therefore covered by, Article 5's definition of consumer, the former requiring that the person neither makes the contract in the course of a business nor holds himself out as so doing, and that the other party does make the contract in the course of a business, and that in sale of goods and hire-purchase *et alia*, the goods are of a type ordinarily supplied for private use or consumption). Section 6 of the 1977 Act, controlling exclusion of 1979 Act ss.12–15, is limited in its application, to contracts other than those which are international under 1977 Act s.26, and consequently, since the Convention, as explained, only applies to international transactions raising conflicts of laws under Article 1(1), it might be thought that there is little scope for the operation of such national mandatory rules described. This would be incorrect, however, because the Convention's concept of internationality, triggering its applicability, is far wider than equivalent national conceptions, in only requiring very tenuous contacts to exist with another country for the test to be satisfied, whereas, under 1977 Act s.26, parties must have their respective places of business or habitual residences in different states and the goods must be transported from one state to another, or offer and acceptance carried out in different states, or the goods delivered to a state other than that of offer and acceptance.

It should in addition be stated that Article 5's operation is subject to two further sets of conditions.

First, under Article 5(4), Article 5 is inapplicable to

- contracts of carriage, and
- contracts under which services are to be supplied to a consumer exclusively in a country other than that of his habitual residence

    EXCEPT where, in either case, the contract provides for a combination of travel and accommodation, at an inclusive price (the 'package tour': Report, p.25), which specifically falls within Article 5, by virtue of Article 5(5).

Secondly, Article 5 only applies in any of three alternative situations involving consumer contracts, namely, under Article 5(2)

- where the consumer took all steps necessary to conclude the contract in the country of his habitual residence, and contractual conclusion was preceded by a specific invitation addressed to him or by advertising, in that country: the Report states that the purpose of this condition is to protect the consumer against international mail order or doorstep selling aimed at consumers, and the reference to *steps necessary* to conclude contracts seeks to avoid the classic problem of law applicable to determine time and place of contractual conclusion for these and other purposes (Report, p.24; and see below, Part III, Chapter 10);
- where the consumer's order was received by the other party or his agent in the country of the consumer's habitual residence: here, the other party solicits the consumer's order, for example, through a permanent branch or agency, or at a fair or exhibition, in the consumer's country, without having advertised there or specifically invited the consumer to attend (Report, p.24);
- where the seller arranged for the consumer in a sale of goods contract to travel from the latter's country of habitual residence to another country where he was induced to place his order: 'border-crossing excursion-selling' is how the Report (p.24) describes this form of transacting, where a store-owner in country A arranges one-day bus

trips for consumers in a neighbouring country B, with the main purpose of inducing the consumers to buy in his store, an increasingly common practice; and provided that the seller has undertaken overall contractual, or agent's, or even mere *organizational* responsibility ('arranged'/'*organisé*'/'*herbeigeführt*') for the ferry-, coach- or other type of journey to be undergone by the consumer, the former need not personally convey the latter to the agreed destination for the condition to be satisfied.

Individual employment contracts: Article 6

As in the case of consumer contracts, there is special protection under Article 6 for the weaker party to employment contracts – the employee – against complete party freedom to select applicable law under Article 3. Under Article 6(1), therefore, such choice of law must not have the result of depriving the employee of the protection afforded to him by the mandatory rules of the law which *would be applicable under Article 6(2) in the absence of choice* (see below). 'Mandatory' again has the meaning in Article 3(3) (*hereinafter*) – that is, rules of law which cannot be derogated from by contract: for example, rules of protection of employees in the Employment Protection (Consolidation) Act 1978 are unable to be excluded by a contractual term, under s.140(1) thereof; and according to the Report (p.25), such mandatory rules consist not only of those to be included in the contract of employment itself, but also of laws 'concerning industrial safety and hygiene which are regarded in certain Member States as being provisions of public law' – a view relating to the scope of Article 6(1) which is not without its difficulties (see below, Part III, Chapter 11). Collective employment agreements between trade unions and employers' associations, where these are enforceable contracts under Contracting States' laws, are not included within the protective provisions of Article 6 (Report, p.25), except, of course, to the extent that their terms are incorporated into individual employees' employment contracts.

Applicable Law in the Absence of Choice

Generally: Article 4

Under national English contract conflicts, the modern rule for ascertainment of the law applicable to contracts, in the absence of express or implied choice of law by the parties, is perfectly clear: the court will seek to determine the law with which the transaction has the closest and most real connection (see *Amin Rasheed Corpn* v. *Kuwait Insurance Co.* [1984] AC 50, 61), on a consideration of all material facts and circumstances, without the previous reliance upon presumptions (*The Assunzione* [1954] P. 150).

The general Convention system differs from the pre-existing English in certain important respects, as will be apparent from the following description thereof.

General rule of closest connection   Article 4(1) prescribes the general rule that, in the absence of choice by the parties, law applicable to the contract shall be that of the country with which the contract is most closely connected, which basically corresponds with pre-existing English law (except that, according to the latter, it may, first, be the *transaction*, rather than the perhaps narrower concept of *contract*, which must be most closely connected, and, second, it is probably *laws* rather than *countries* with which connections should be established under the existing law: see *James Miller & Partners Ltd* v. *Whitworth Street Estates (Manchester) Ltd* [1970] AC 583). Exceptionally (Report, p. 20) courts may find a contract to be *severably* governed by different laws, where a severable part has a closer connection with another country under Article 4(1), or in any event where a law has been chosen under Article 3(1) to apply to part only of the contract.

Rebuttable presumptions as to most connected law   The main difference from national English conflicts is that Article 4 contains a number of rebuttable presumptions – general and special – as to most closely connected country for purposes of Article 4(1).

(a) General presumption in Article 4(2)   It is to be rebuttably (Article 4(5)) presumed that the contract is most closely connected with the country *where the party who is to effect the performance which is characteristic of the contract* has at the time of conclusion of the contract

- his habitual residence, *or*, in the case of a body corporate or unincorporate, its central administration

    EXCEPT THAT if the contract is entered into in the course of such party's trade or profession, the country of closest connection is presumed to be that of the party's
- principal place of business, *or*
- where, under the contract, performance is to be effected through a place of business other than the principal place of business, the former place of business.

Article 4(2) has proved to be controversial amongst commentators for two main reasons. In the first place, it is intended – together with other, special presumptions in Article 4 – to introduce a degree of certainty into operation of the broad *closest connection* rule in Article 4(1), and yet the very fact that the presumption may be rebutted under Article 4(5) might be thought to reinstate the very element of uncertainty sought to be removed through Article 4(2), with an even higher level of complexity than would otherwise have existed on a simple application of Article 4(1)! Secondly, the concept of *characteristic performance* of a contract is new to English jurisprudence (see the Judgments Convention cases of *Ivenel* v. *Schwab*, Case 133/81 [1982] ECR 1891, *Shenavai* v. *Kreischer*, Case 266/85 [1987] ECR 239, *Six Constructions Ltd* v. *Humbert*, Case 32/88 [1989] ECR 341, and the Court of Appeal's decision in *Mercury Publicity Ltd* v. *Wolfgang Loerke GmbH* (1991) *The Times*, 21 October), and may not be particularly easy to apply other than in the clearest cases. Obviously, in a contract of employment (not in fact subject to Article 4 – see below on Article 6(2)), the obligation to work would plainly be regarded as that characterizing the contract, rather than the payment of wages (see *Ivenel* v. *Schwab*, *supra*); in addition, delivery in sale of goods, agency in agents' contracts, and perhaps too provision of the guarantee in guarantors' contracts are also likely to qualify without much dissent (Report, p.21). Beyond these individual cases, however, it is difficult to establish a general principle for deciding on characteristic obligation. The Report talks of the latter as defining the connecting factor from the inside, not from the outside by 'elements unrelated to the essence of the obligation such as the nationality of the contracting parties or the place where the contract was concluded', and relates the concept to the 'function which the legal relationship involved fulfils in the economic and social life of any country' and to the 'social and economic environment of which it will form a part' (p.20), concluding that characteristic performance will not consist of the obligation to pay a sum of money in return for the other party's performance, but of the latter itself 'the delivery of goods, the granting of the right to make use of an item of property, the provision of a service, transport, insurance,' banking operations, security, etc.' (*ibid.*). At least, nevertheless, where it proves impossible to say which performance obligation is characteristic of the contract in a particular case – for example in a contract of exchange or part-exchange, when delivery obligations of respective parties, based in different countries, are equivalent – Article 4(5) specifically provides ('if the characteristic performance cannot be determined') that Article 4(2) will not apply, and accordingly courts must fall back upon the country of closest connection test in Article 4(1) in such event. Furthermore, as precedents develop, the uncertainty arising from Article 4(2) should be greatly reduced, although, continuing national divergencies in meaning and application thereof will remain virtually inevitable (notwithstanding Article 18).

(b) Special presumption in the case of immovables in Article 4(3) Understandably, Article 4(3) displaces the characteristic performance presumption in Article 4(2), to the extent that the subject matter of the contract is a right in or to use immovable property, with a presumption that the contract is most closely connected with the country where the property is situated – although, the Report makes the point that the presumption does not extend to contracts for the construction or repair of immovable property, because the main subject matter thereof is the constructing or repairing activity rather than the immovable property itself (p.21).

(c) Special presumption in the case of contracts for the carriage of goods in Article 4(4) Again, Article 4(2) is inapplicable. Instead the contract is presumed to be most closely connected with the country in which at the time of its conclusion

a   the carrier has his principal place of business, *and*
b   the place of loading, or discharge, or principal place of business of the consignor is situated.

The exclusion of Article 4(2) in favour of a combination of connecting factors is due to the 'peculiarities' of this type of transport, frequently the subject of international conventions (Report, pp.21–2). 'Carrier' means the party to the contract who undertakes to carry the goods, whether or not he performs the carriage himself, and 'consignor' refers to any person who consigns goods to the carrier (*ibid.*). Contracts for the carriage of passengers remain subject to the general presumption in Article 4(2), by virtue of Article 5(4)(a), to the extent that they are not those for combined travel and accommodation, within the consumer protection provisions of Article 5 by virtue of Article 5(5). Article 4(4) remains applicable to contracts for the carriage of goods, even in relation to contracting parties who are consumers, under Article 5(4)(a). Article 4(4) provides expressly that single voyage charter-parties, and other contracts the main purpose of which ('in so far as that is their substance': Report, p.22) is the carriage of goods, are to be treated as contracts for the carriage of goods within Article 4(4).

Rebuttal As intimated, both the general presumption in Article 4(2) and special presumptions in Article 4(3) and 4(4) are expressly rebuttable under Article 4(5) *if it appears from the circumstances as a whole that the contract is more closely connected with another country.* Given that the general presumption in Article 4(2) is founded upon country of characteristic performer's habitual residence or central administration, it may be expected that in many instances rebuttal, if it occurs, will be in favour of the country in which characteristic performance is actually to take place, where that and other factors are sufficient to amount to the closest (or at least closer) connections with the contract.

Consumer contracts: Article 5(3)

Under Article 5(3), where a consumer contract (as defined in Article 5(1), (4) and (5): see above, p.53, on applicable law agreements) is entered into in any of the circumstances set down in Article 5(2) (see p.54), Article 4 is inapplicable in the absence of choice of law under Article 3, and the contract is instead governed by the *law of the country in which the consumer has his habitual residence* (presumably, under Article 4(2), law of the country of the seller's/creditor's central administration or relevant place of business would otherwise have applied, presumptively, as that of the characteristic performer).

Individual employment contracts: Article 6(2)

Here too, Article 6(2) displaces Article 4 in the absence of agreement upon applicable law under Article 3, with the following laws

- law of the country in which the employee *habitually carries out his work* in performance of the contract, even if he is temporarily employed in another country (Article 6(2)(a)), *or*
- law of the country in which the place of business through which the employee was engaged is situated, where the employee does not habitually carry out his work in any one country (Article 6(2)(b))

    EXCEPT THAT in either case where it appears from the circumstances as a whole that the contract is more closely connected with another country, the contract will be governed by the law of the latter country.

Under Article 4(2), doubtless, law of the country of the employee's habitual residence would have been presumptively applicable, as that of the employee as characteristic performer (see *Ivenel* v. *Schwab*); although, in many cases of course, that law will correspond with that of the country of habitual place of work under Article 6(2)(a) in any event, and where this is not so, it may be that the latter law could nevertheless be displaced by the former as that of the more closely connected country, under the proviso to Article 6(2)(a) and (b).

LAWS APPLICABLE TO PARTICULAR ASPECTS OF CONTRACTS

In respect of certain aspects of contracts, laws denoted under Articles 3 to 6 may not be exclusively applicable, nor possibly even applicable at all.

Consent

It has previously been seen that existence and validity of contracts and terms are governed by applicable law, in accordance with Article 8(1).

However, this provision was felt to leave an offeree potentially vulnerable at the hands of an offeror, who might subject the 'contract' to a law which would regard the offeree's silence in response to the offer as an acceptance thereof (Report, p.28). Accordingly, Article 8(2) was included – though not solely – as the means to avoid such an unfortunate result from the offeree's point of view: a party is permitted to rely on the *law of the country in which he has his habitual residence* in order to establish that he did not consent, if it appears from the circumstances that it would not be reasonable to determine the effect of his conduct in accordance with the law otherwise applicable to the contract under Article 8(1).

As to circumstances in which resort to applicable law on consent would not be reasonable, this is a matter of speculation. Use of standard forms by one of the parties, and their relative bargaining power, are likely to be relevant, as, according to the Report (p.28), are parties' previous business relationships and practices *inter se* (presumably, meaning that it would be unreasonable to subject consent to a law not usually applicable to their dealings).

Either party, offeror or offeree, may rely upon Article 8(2) as to his lack of consent, but resort to the rule may only result in the release of such party from otherwise binding obligations under applicable law according to Article 8(1), not the reverse (*ibid.*).

Form of Contracts

At national law, contractual form may comply alternatively with the proper law (*Van Grutten* v. *Digby* (1862) 31 Bear 561) or *lex loci contractus* (*Guépratte* v. *Young* (1851) 4 De G. & Sm 217) (or possibly *lex situs* in the case of formal validity of contracts relating to immovables: Graveson, p.440 – although, see Dicey and Morris, pp.1210–11 and 1257 on this).

The Convention's regime on formal validity is more elaborate, and consists of a number of general rules which seek to remove additional technicalities from the process of determination of applicable law, together with specially appropriate rules for particular types of contracts.

General: Article 9(1)–(4)

Laws applicable to form of contracts in general under Article 9 are as follows:

1. where the contract is concluded between persons who are in the same country

   — applicable law under the Convention, *or*
   — law of the country of conclusion (Article 9(1));

2. where the contract is concluded between persons who are in different countries
   — applicable law under the Convention, *or*
   — law of either of the countries in which the parties concluded the contract (Article 9(2)).

Thus, reference to either of the parties' countries' laws under Article 9(2) is intended to avoid the difficulty of deciding upon time and place of technical conclusion of the contract – itself involving choice of law – for such purposes (Report, p.31). Furthermore, where it is the agent of one or more of the contracting parties, as opposed to the latter themselves, who actually concludes the contract on behalf of his principal, it is expressly provided by Article 9(3) that the country in which the agent acts is that which is relevant for the purposes of Article 9(1) and (2).

A special choice of law rule on form is included in Article 9(4) in respect of *acts* intended to have legal effect relating to an existing or contemplated contract: the act is formally valid if it satisfies the formal requirements of either

a. the law which governs or would govern the *contract* under the Convention; *or*
b. the law of the country where the *act was done.*

The Report explains that this provision was included for the sake of clarity, and that 'acts' may include notice of termination of a contract, declaration of rescission and repudiation (p.29) (as well as, arguably, offers themselves, which may be binding and irrevocable for a period under certain laws, for example German) – that is to say, not mere factual acts relating to contracts, but those which may have definite legal consequences according to applicable law of the relevant legal system. (It is submitted below, p. 303, that *methods* of carrying out any such formal steps and acts in the event of defective performance – for example, appropriate times and days – are for *lex loci solutionis* under article 10(2).)

Finally, it will be recalled that by virtue of Article 3(4), form of choice of law agreements themselves is governed by Article 9.

Consumer contracts: Article 9(5)

Article 9(1)–(4) is inapplicable to consumer contracts within Article 5. Instead, Article 9(5) governs their formal validity by the law of the country *in which the consumer has his habitual residence*, in order to ensure maximum protection for the consumer (Report, p.31). (The rule on applicable law in the absence of choice, in the case of employment contracts under Article 6(2) however, was felt to be too uncertain to govern their form – and consequently, the main protection in respect of form thereof will have to be found in the general safeguard for mandatory laws under Article 7: Report, p.32.)

Immovables: Article 9(6)

The special rule on form in relation to contracts of which the subject matter is a right in, or to use, immovable property, is that Article 9(1)–(4) applies, but SUBJECT TO

- the *mandatory* requirements of form of *lex situs* if by that law such requirements are imposed irrespective of country of contractual conclusion and of applicable law governing the contract.

Applicable law in the absence of choice under Article 4(3), of course, would be *lex situs* in any event – but only *presumptively* so, subject to rebuttal under Article 4(5), so that at least if the latter were to take place, mandatory requirements of form of the *situs* would still be protected under Article 9(6).

Formal validity Article 9 only affects requirements of 'formal validity' of contracts. This expression is undefined in the Convention, and must be distinguished from *modes of proof* of contract, subject to *lex fori* in the alternative to Article 9 laws under Article 14(2) (see below, p.66). The Report considers 'form' for the purposes of Article 9 to include 'every external manifestation required on the part of a person expressing the will to be legally bound, and in the absence of which such expression of will would not be regarded as fully effective' (p.29) – not a particularly illuminating explanation, it has to be said.

Presumably, as under pre-existing English conflicts, the distinction will somehow have to turn upon the effects of non-compliance with particular requirements and the latters' purpose: if the consequence is invalidity of the contract, the rule will obviously relate to formal validity (*Van Grutten* v. *Digby* (1862) 31 Beav 561); if the effect is not invalidity, but contractual unenforceability, and the purpose of the law is to provide appropriate evidence of existence of contractual intent, the matter would be one of mode of proof rather than of formal validity of contract (*Leroux* v. *Brown* (1852) 12 CB 801: *English* procedural requirement; *Alves* v. *Hodgson* (1797) 7 TR 241; *foreign* stamping requirement). Thus, for example, in the case of contracts for the sale or other disposition of land or of an interest therein concluded prior to 27 September 1989, s.40(1) of the Law of Property Act 1925 (superseded as from that date by the Law of Property (Miscellaneous Provisions) Act 1989 s.2 – see s.2(8)) requires written evidence of the contract for the latter to be enforceable; whereas, s.2(1) of the Law of Property (Miscellaneous Provisions) Act 1989, replacing the former in relation to contracts made on or after 27 September 1989, requires such contracts to be made in writing if they are to be held to exist and to be valid at all (see s.2(4)). There can be few doubts but that s.2(1) will be regarded as a mandatory rule of form of English *lex situs* for purposes of Article 9(6), whatever uncertainties may otherwise surround the status of s.40(1) as form, mode of proof, or otherwise possibly excluded from the Convention's scope for such purposes (see below, Chapters 15 and 19).

Mode of Contractual Performance

Article 10(2) provides that in respect of manner of performance of the contract, and steps to be taken in the event of defective performance, 'regard shall be had to the law of the country in which performance takes place'.

At national English conflicts, mode of performance is also for *lex loci solutionis*, seemingly to the exclusion of the proper or any other law, in the absence of evidence that parties intended these latter to apply (Dicey and Morris, Rule 186(2), p.1236). Article 10(2), however, seems rather less insistent upon the operation of that law ('regard shall be had'), and the Report actually states that the court may consider whether *lex loci* has any relevance to the manner in which the contract should be performed and that the court has a discretion whether to apply it in whole or in part, so as to do justice between the parties (p.33). This would mean that not only would *lex loci* not be exclusively applicable to mode of performance under the Convention, but also not even alternatively so, but merely so as a matter of discretion! (The Report, *ibid.*, replaces the word 'shall' in English and foreign texts of Article 10(2) with 'may'.) Such a vague prescription for the governance of manner of performing contracts would seem highly undesirable in commercial relations, and it is submitted that stress should be laid on the word 'shall' rather than on the relatively weak word 'regard' thereunder, so that the effect of Article 10(2) is precisely that: regard *must* be had to compliance with *lex loci* on mode – *lex loci solutionis must* be complied with.

The usual problems of imprecision exist with regard to the meaning of *manner* of performance, as opposed to substance thereof. Dicey and Morris provide illustrations based on the authorities (pp.1237–8): usual business hours (but effects of frustration and liability for defects are substance; arguably too, time and date for performance according to a particular time zone are also issues of substance rather than mode, at least as a matter of contractual interpretation: see *White Cliffs Opal Mines* v. *Miller* [1904] 4 SR (NSW) 150 – although the question is debatable); requirement of an export licence and customs clearance (but whether the seller or buyer is under a contractual duty to obtain the licence, and liability for failing to fulfil such duty, are substance); ship's readiness to discharge its cargo; whether payment should be made in cash or by cheque and in which currency (but rate – except possibly in the case of damages for breach of contract, which may be procedural for *lex fori* – and right to interest, and value and validity of currency of account are matters of substance). The essence of mode, therefore, would seem to be that it revolves around those legal regulations which concern the actual process of change in the previous mutual commercial or other status of parties to be brought about under and as a consequence of their contract as a result of acts or omissions of human agents, rather than the legal standard or effects thereof.

Yet, even viewed as such, it is admitted that there will be blurs at the edges.

Contractual Capacity

Article 1(2)(a) and (e) excludes contractual capacity of natural and legal persons, respectively, from the scope of the Convention – in the former case, subject to Article 11.

Accordingly, pre-existing national English conflicts rules govern contractual capacity in principle: *lex domicilii* (*Sottomayor* v. *De Barros (No.1)*

(1877) 3 PD 1), *lex situs* in the case of immovables (*Bank of Africa* v. *Cohen* [1902] 2 Ch. 129 CA), and (probably objective) proper law (*Charron* v. *Montreal Trust Co.* (1958) 15 DLR (2d) 240), may each confer capacity upon individuals as contracting parties thereunder (as well as possibly also *lex loci contractus*: *Male* v. *Roberts* (1800) 3 Esp. 163), whilst corporate capacity is a matter for company statutes, as subjected to the law of incorporation and objective contractual proper law (Dicey and Morris, Rule 174).

However, as said, in the case of natural persons' capacity to contract, operation of national conflicts is subject to Article 11, intended to protect a party who in good faith believed himself to be contracting with a person of full capacity – especially serious where a person's capacity is governed by some remote and unexpected *lex nationalis* according to national private international law (Report, p.34).

Article 11 provides for the mandatory displacement of national conflicts incapacity of natural persons where

- the contract is concluded between persons who are in the same country;
- the otherwise incapacitated party has capacity under the law of the preceding country;
- the other party was not aware of the incapacity, nor negligently unaware thereof, at the time of conclusion of the contract.

Thus, the incapacitated party cannot invoke his incapacity under national conflicts where this would be unjust to the other party and capacity exists according to *lex loci contractus*. The wording suggests that the burden of proof is on the incapacitated party to show knowledge or negligence of the other party: good faith is therefore presumed.

Modes of Proof of Contract

Under Article 14(2), modes of proof of contracts are for regulation according to, *alternatively*

- *lex fori*; and
- any of the laws referred to under Article 9, under which the contract is formally valid, provided that any such mode of proof is able to be administered by the forum.

Article 14(2), consequently, has two main effects: (1) it brings within the Convention's overall subject-matter scope, matters which might otherwise have been excluded therefrom as being evidential and procedural under Article 1(2)(h) (the latter being expressly stated to be *without prejudice to*

Article 14) (see *Bain* v. *Whitehaven Rly Co.* (1850) 3 HL Cas. 1, 19); (2) it removes modes of proof from the exclusive sphere of *lex fori's* rules of evidence and procedure, and subjects such matters in the alternative to Article 9 laws on formal validity. This 'liberal' solution is apparently favoured in France and the Benelux countries and serves to protect the legitimate expectations of parties at the time of making the contract, when they will not know with certitude the identity of the forum for the settlement of any future dispute (Report, p.36).

As was seen in discussion of Article 9 on formal validity of contracts, it may sometimes be difficult to discern immediately whether a particular requirement is a contractual formality or a rule of evidence and procedure. In the case of Article 14(2), for the purpose of designating a rule as one of mode of proof within the latter, or as a contractual formality outside it, not merely must it be shown that non-compliance leads to mere unenforceability rather than to non-existence or invalidity, under the relevant rule, but it will also be a matter of determining the underlying objective of the written, stamping, registration or other such formal requirement, in order to determine whether this is intended to provide evidence of contractual conclusion and terms – consequently, a mode of proof within Article 14(2) – or to fulfil some other objective, for example to protect the weaker party against overhasty conclusion of a contract or to bring important terms to his attention, in which case the matter lies outside Article 14(2) and is governed by general Convention rules on applicable law. Even where the purpose is evidential, it is not certain that contracting formalities (as opposed to, say, rules on competence and compellability of witnesses) are intended to be included within the concept of *modes of proof* under Article 14(2), and this will be a matter for the European Court to interpret. If they do fall within Article 14(2) and a contract is enforceable according to a foreign law referred to thereunder, it will nonetheless be the case that mandatory formalities of the forum will continue to apply by virtue of Article 7(2) (although, note that arguably, the situation could not come about in any event in which an informal contract relating to English land was enforceable under a foreign law to which it had been expressly subjected by the parties, by virtue of Article 9(1) or (2) and in accordance with Article 14(2), because Article 9(6) itself subjects such applicable law to mandatory rules of the *situs* and there can be few doubts that English courts would regard s.40(1) of the Law of Property Act 1925 (applicable to pre–27 September 1989 contracts, under s.2(8) of the Law of Property (Miscellaneous Provisions) Act 1989), requiring written evidence for such contracts to be enforceable, as *mandatory* for purposes of Article 9(6) and Article 14(2) referring thereto – provided that, of course, in the particular context of Article 14(2), the courts were prepared to disregard the fact that, strictly speaking, the reference in Article 9(6) would still actually be to mandatory rules of 'form', presumably, meaning formal validity thereunder.) If however such contractual formalities were held *not* to be included within the scope of Article 14(2), their evidential and procedural character would mean that they would have to be regarded as excluded from the Convention's scope under Article 1(2)(h), and consequently they would be governed by *lex fori* as procedural under national English private international law.

The Report makes the point that where an Article 9 law on mode of proof is resorted to under Article 14(2), this should be one of the laws referred to in Article 9 according to which the contract is in fact formally *valid* (or any thereof, if valid under more than one such law) (p.37). There is, however, a safeguard included in Article 14(2) against application of a foreign mode of proof under an Article 9 law, which appears to be too different from those permitted by *lex fori*: the words 'provided that such mode of proof can be administered by the forum'. The purpose of this proviso is that the liberalism of Article 14(2) 'should not lead to imposing on the trial court modes of proof which its procedural law does not enable it to administer' (*administration* of modes of proof not being dealt with by Article 14(2)) (Report, p.37). Thus, the court may (without needing to resort to public policy) disregard modes of proof which its procedural law cannot generally allow, such as affidavit evidence, a party's testimony or common knowledge (*ibid.*).

(Evidential value of acts and documents, not expressly referred to in Article 14, is apparently outside the Convention's scope (Report, *ibid.*). This could prove problematic, and, on the contrary, must surely be subject to Article 14(2), where a mode of proof is not otherwise admitted according to *lex fori*, since the evidential value, according to *lex fori*, of such mode of proof, admissible under a foreign Article 9 law, would otherwise inevitably be nil! On the other hand, of course, where a particular type of evidence is generally admitted by the forum, as well as by the Article 9 law, and yet has different evidential value under each – say, conclusive under the former, but *prima facie* according to the latter, or vice versa – there would seem to be no strong objection against application of *lex fori*'s evidential standard to the common mode of proof. Difficulties remain, however:

(i) is, for example, the parol evidence rule of English law, according to which oral evidence of terms alleged to form part of an otherwise written contract is not permitted to add to or vary the latter, a mode of proof, in which case it may have no effect upon such oral evidence of contract admissible under a foreign Article 9 law by virtue of Article 14(2), or is it merely a rule of (*nil*) evidential value of *lex fori*, whereby such admissible foreign mode of proof of contract would automatically be reduced to ineffectiveness, unless operation of *lex fori* on evidential value were subordinated to that of Article 14(2) in such circumstances, as advocated above; and

(ii) does Article 14(2) simply apply to modes of proof of contractual conclusion and existence, or also to proof of terms – as under the parol evidence rule – of an admitted contract, the latter construction seeming to have much to commend it, both in logic and practicality?)

Illegality

There is no specific Convention rule dealing with the law applicable to illegality of contracts. General principles apply therefore: initial contractual illegality, preventing its existence or validity from the earliest possible point in time, is covered by Article 8(1), referring such matters to applicable law; whilst, initial illegality of performance, and supervening illegality leading to discharge of the contract, are also questions for applicable law according to Article 10(1)(b) and (d) respectively.

Under pre-existing national English conflicts, illegality is for

- the proper law (*Kahler* v. *Midland Bank Ltd* [1950] AC 24; *Libyan Arab Foreign Bank* v. *Bankers Trust Co* [1989] 3 All ER 252);
- possibly *lex loci solutionis* in the case of supervening (if not also initial) illegality of performance (*Ralli Bros* v. *Compania Naviera Sota y Aznar* [1920] 2 KB 287);
- English *lex fori* of extraterritorial application, and public policy (*Boissevain* v. *Weil* [1949] 1 KB 482);
- any imperative foreign law (although, possibly not merely public policy: *Lemanda Trading Co.* v. *African Middle East Petroleum Co. Ltd* [1988] 1 All ER 513) of a friendly foreign country, contravention of which would be a breach of comity and public policy in the United Kingdom (*Foster* v. *Driscoll* [1929] 1 KB 470; *Libyan Arab Foreign Bank* v. *Bankers Trust Co.* [1989] 3 All ER 252).

Of the preceding laws applicable under national English conflicts, only the proper law and English laws of extraterritorial operation are the subject of definite Convention provision – the former, as seen, under Articles 8(1) and 10(1)(b) and (d), and the latter under Article 7(2), preserving application of *lex fori*'s rules of law in a situation where they are mandatory irrespective of the law otherwise applicable to the contract (see below, p.69 *et seq*).

In the case of foreign laws on legality, these will be preserved against chosen applicable law, under special Convention safeguards for otherwise wholly connected laws (Article 3(3)), consumers (Article 5(2)), employees (Article 6(1)), and formal validity of contracts for rights in or to use immovable property (Article 9(6)), *provided that* they are able to be treated as *mandatory* at national law for Convention purposes; and furthermore, mandatory laws on legality, generally, of foreign countries with which the situation has a close connection, will be protected under Article 7(1) – although not in the United Kingdom (nor in Germany, Ireland or Luxembourg), in which Article 7(1) is inapplicable (see Article 22(1)(a); 1990 Act s.2(2)). However, it is questionable whether the general public policy comity ground of refusal to enforce a contract, illegal under a friendly foreign country's law (see *Regazzoni* v. *K.C.Sethia (1944) Ltd* [1956] 2 QB 490), remains: Article 16 enables the court to refuse to apply a foreign law which is manifestly incompatible with the forum's public policy; but this appears to be limited to individual rules of foreign law which offend. Can it be said that a *notional* such rule, *not* striking down a transaction as illegal, may be so classified? This seems doubtful.

Lex loci solutionis – unless it happens also to be the same law as those mandatory rules protected by Convention provisions previously referred to – seems to be the loser under the Convention. There is one possible means of avoiding this outcome, however. Cheshire and North (pp. 486–9) appear to believe the true construction of the *Ralli* case to be not that *lex loci solutionis* is to be referred to as a conflicts rule in the matter of legality of performance, but simply that in that case there was held to exist a rule of *domestic English* proper law governing the contract, to the effect that contracts suffering from supervening illegality according to foreign *lex loci solutionis* would not be enforced under the former (*ibid.*). If such an argument were to be accepted – and this must be the subject of considerable doubt (see below, Part III, Chapter 12, and earlier Part I, Chapter 2) – it would mean that at least where English law was applicable law under the Convention (as well as any other law reputed to have a similar domestic rule), illegality under foreign *lex loci solutionis* could then be given effect to; and even where applicable law was that of a foreign country under the Convention, the same result could ensue by virtue of Article 7(2), provided that the alleged rule of domestic English contract law, protecting illegality under foreign *lex loci solutionis*, were held to be mandatory for the purposes of that provision.

Mandatory Laws and Public Policy

Under national English contract conflicts, the courts have been gradually moving towards a doctrine of extraterritoriality of mandatory English laws, so as to prevent avoidance of the latter through the conflicts process in international transactions where important connections nonetheless exist with the forum's territory (see, for example, *Vita Food Products Inc.* v. *Unus Shipping Co. Ltd* [1939] AC 277, 290 (JC); and *The Hollandia* [1983] AC

565): and statute has also expressly sought to control the exclusion of liability arising under English law in non-international cases through evasionary intent or otherwise choice of a foreign law (see, for example, Sale of Goods Act 1979 s.56), limited, if necessary, so as to favour consumers (see, for example, Unfair Contract Terms Act 1977 ss. 26 and 27).

The Convention has an elaborate – and not always easily comprehensible – system of protection of mandatory rules of laws other than those generally applicable to the contract, in recognition of the fact that certain rules may be so important to a state that their observance is required even in preference to laws of another country which may have been chosen by the parties to govern their contract (Report, p.26). Pre-existing English law has no fixed principle for giving effect to *foreign* mandatory rules of extraterritorial operation, other than that which is based upon the discretionary public policy ground of comity, to the effect that English courts will not lend their assistance to the enforcement of contracts in contravention of the imperative laws of foreign, friendly states (see *Foster* v. *Driscoll* [1929] 1 KB 470; and *Regazzoni* v. *K.C. Sethia (1944) Ltd* [1956] 2 QB 490). The Convention makes no such distinction generally between mandatory rules of law of the forum and those of foreign countries, the same basic protection being given to each thereunder according to provisions safeguarding their application (see Articles 3(3), 5(2), 6(1), 7 and 9(6)).

Scope of Convention provisions on mandatory rules

It is possible to detect three different policies underlying the various Convention provisions which seek to safeguard mandatory rules of national laws other than those applicable to the contract:

- consumer and employee protection: Articles 5(2) and 6(1) specifically try to ensure the application of mandatory rules of law of a country favourable, respectively, to consumers and employees, notwithstanding choice of another law to govern the contract, on the basis of connections with such country which might not otherwise necessarily have been considered to be closer and more real than other competing contacts;
- particular degree or type of connection with a country, deemed most appropriate, at least in respect of its mandatory rules, for these latter to apply notwithstanding choice, or otherwise the application of, another country's law in respect of the contract (anti-evasionary): Articles 3(3) (mandatory laws of country with which contract is wholly connected apart from choice of law and possibly also choice of jurisdiction), 7(1) (inapplicable in the United Kingdom – as well

as in Germany, Ireland and Luxembourg, and possibly also Portugal and Spain when they accede – under Article 22(1)(a), and 1990 Act s.2(2): mandatory laws of country with which the situation has a close connection), and 9(6) (mandatory laws of form of the country in which immovable property is situated in the case of contracts for rights in or to use such);
- the special claim of the forum to apply its own mandatory laws of extraterritorial operation: Article 7(2) preserves this possibility, even if the forum has no, or merely any nationally prescribed spatial (and, in Convention terms, otherwise not closest), connection with the contract.

Further categorizations are of course also possible: for example, Articles 5(2), 6(1) and 9(6) on, respectively, consumers, employees and form of contracts for immovables, could all be classified together as being restricted to contracts having a particular type of subject matter, whereas Articles 3(3) and 7 apply to contracts of any sort within the Convention's scope; alternatively, Articles 5(2) and 6(1) are limited in their application to certain only of the designated law's mandatory rules, being solely those protecting the parties concerned, consumers and employees respectively, whereas, Articles 3(3), 7 and 9(6) bring into operation mandatory rules generally of the specified legal system; again, the fact that application of mandatory rules under Article 7(1) is merely discretionary (effect 'may' be given ... regard shall be had to their nature and purpose and to the consequences of their application or non-application) might serve to separate the latter from the other, obligatory safeguards of mandatory laws.

Clearly, some overlap between these various provisions' scope of operation will be inevitable. Presumably, however, where this occurs, obligatory mandatory safeguards will be resorted to before those which are discretionary: for example, place of engagement of an employee under Article 6(1) and (2)(b) may also have a close connection with the situation under Article 7(1) (not in the United Kingdom of course), but it will be according to the former that its mandatory rules apply in the case of choice of another law; and special subject-matter provisions will be applied rather than the more general: for example, consumer's habitual residence under Article 5(2) may also be country of the overwhelmingly closest connection under Article 3(3) or that of the forum under Article 7(2), but it should be the former which is referred to for safeguards; only where the safeguard sought is beyond the scope of special subject-matter provisions will the more general rules have to be referred to: for example, where the consumer's or employee's law contains mandatory safeguards not in fact for consumers' or employees' protection, but, say, for that of the state or economy, such as price or credit controls, those rules lie outside the scope of Articles 5(2) and 6(1) (see below, Part III, Chapters 10 and 11), and Articles 3(3), 7 and 9(6) would have to be called in aid if also satisfied, as where consumer and employment contracts were not involved. As for the position where more than one of the *general* Convention provisions safeguarding mandatory rules are satisfied, it is submitted that Article 7(2) has primacy by virtue of its wording ('Nothing in this Convention shall restrict ...'), and this is plainly correct, since Article 7(2) is far easier to apply and to interpret than, say, Article 3(3) or 7(1), and accordingly, only where it is not *the forum* which is the otherwise wholly connected country, should Article 3(3) have to be referred to – and if the forum is such most connected country, Article 7(2) is the easiest means for protection of the forum's mandatory laws.

One potentially major – and unfortunately, at the present time, rather uncertain – qualification, however, to the preceding relationship between the various Convention provisions safeguarding national mandatory rules of contract is that there *may* be inferred from the Convention system, and from its mandatory provisions as a whole, a distinction between two main different types of national mandatory law, with one of which, certain of those Convention rules are concerned, and to the second of which the others would appear to apply. In this book, the two sorts of mandatory rule which the Convention seems to contemplate as existing at national law are referred to as *contracts*-mandatory and *conflicts*-mandatory.

Contracts-mandatory and conflicts-mandatory laws

Article 3(3) defines 'mandatory rules' *hereinafter* as rules of law *which cannot be derogated from by contract*. The phrase 'mandatory rules' (*dispositions impératives/zwingende Bestimmungen*) is then used again in Articles 5(2), 6(1), 7(1), and , arguably, also on a construction of Article 9(6). Article 7(2), on the other hand, refers to rules of law which are *mandatory irrespective of the law otherwise applicable to the contract* (Article 7 is headed *Lois de Police/Zwingende Vorschriften*). The latter formula, with slight variations in the wording, is also used in Articles 7(1) and 9(6).

It will immediately be appreciated that there are possible differences as to the types of national 'mandatory rules' which may be covered by each definition:

a   in the first case, what appears to be contemplated is a national rule of contract law, which parties are prohibited by national law from excluding in their contract: an example would be ss.12–15 of the Sale of Goods Act 1979, implying various terms into sale of goods contracts,

and unable to be excluded by the parties under their contract in prescribed circumstances under s.6 of the Unfair Contract Terms Act 1977;
b   whereas, an example of the second type of national contract rule, unable to be avoided through application of a foreign law of contract, would be s.6 itself of the 1977 Act, together with other provisions thereof restricting contractual exclusion of liability (as well as ss.12–15 themselves of the 1979 Act, by virtue of s.56 of the latter), unable to be avoided through choice of a foreign law to govern the contract, when the conditions set out in s.27 are satisfied.

As a result of the distinct effects of the two different types of national mandatory rule contemplated by the Convention, therefore, the expressions *contracts-mandatory* and *conflicts-mandatory* are here used to describe each *alleged* type of national rule, respectively.

The importance of the distinction referred to, if it truly exists at national law, for the scope and interrelationship of the Convention's individual provisions on mandatory safeguards, is that

1   Articles 3(3), 5(2) and 6(1) appear to be concerned solely with national *contracts*-mandatory rules.
2   Articles 7(1) and 9(6) seem to be limited to national rules which are *both* contracts-mandatory and conflicts-mandatory.
3   Article 7(2) applies solely to national *conflicts*-mandatory rules.

Accordingly, if the preceding conclusions as to construction of the relevant Convention provisions are correct, these latter must consequently be applied subject to such further ensuing restrictions upon their respective mutual and individual scope of operation. Article 5(2) on consumer protection, for example, concerned solely with national *contracts*-mandatory rules, would be unable to safeguard application of a rule of the law of the consumer's habitual residence to the extent that it was also conflicts-mandatory under that national law, whereas Article 7(1), applicable to national laws both contracts- *and* conflicts-mandatory, would be able to do so, if, as seems likely, the country of the consumer's habitual residence were held to have a close connection with the contract for purposes of Article 7(1) (inapplicable in the United Kingdom, of course: 1990 Act s.2(2)).

It has to be said, however, that, whilst it is necessary to bear in mind the possible existence of these two different types of national mandatory contract rule to be inferred from the Convention system, and the effects thereof upon scope of operation of the various Convention safeguards referred to, in practice the distinction is unlikely to create too much difficulty of differentiation and consequent selection of the appropriate Convention provisions, for a number of reasons.

First, the construction of the relevant Convention rules here put forward may be wrong – or, at least, not accepted! Articles 3(3), 5(2) and 6(1) may be held also to apply to national contract rules which are solely conflicts-mandatory, as well as to those solely contracts-mandatory; whilst, Article 7(2) may be thought to be capable of safeguarding contract rules of the forum which are solely contract-mandatory, as well as those solely conflicts-mandatory – constructions which, one is bound to comment, would seem to fly in the face of the strict text, certainly of the latter, if not also of the former provisions and their definitions.

Secondly, even if the construction previously contemplated above *were* correct, nevertheless this would not necessarily be wholly to exclude the possibility that Article 3(3)-type national contract rules would not be restricted solely to those which were contracts-mandatory at national law. This is because the definition of mandatory rules thereunder, as those which 'cannot be derogated from by contract', is, as may be seen, capable of covering not only those cases where parties are prohibited at national law from derogating from mandatory contract rules *directly* through a term of their contract, but also national restrictions upon their attempt to do so *indirectly* through incorporation of a term into the contract selecting a foreign law to govern the latter (for example, those covered by s.27 of the Unfair Contract Terms Act 1977, referred to earlier – such national contract rules, protected against choice of foreign law, but not also against operation of foreign applicable law in the absence of choice, being sub-categorized in this book as '*half*-conflicts-mandatory' national contract laws, as opposed to the latter type above, called '*full*-conflicts-mandatory' rules herein: see below, Part III, Chapters 8, 10, 11, 12 and 14). Thus, each such instance is essentially one of *derogation by contract* from national mandatory rules of law (and if this construction is correct, the only type of national mandatory contract rule which the definition in Article 3(3) would not cover would be a national rule applicable extraterritorially whatever the law otherwise governing the contract in the absence of choice). Accordingly, to the extent that applicable law were that selected by the parties in accordance with Article 3, Articles 3(3), 5(2) and 6(1) could then be resorted to to safeguard the operation of the half-conflicts-mandatory national rules against application of the chosen law. (If the construction were not accepted, Article 7(2) would consequently have to be turned to where the mandatory rules in question were those of the forum and any national territorial limitation for application of the national mandatory rule – such as employment at an establishment in Great Britain: see, for instance, Equal Pay Act 1970 s.1(1) – was satisfied. Where, of course, the national conflicts-mandatory contract rule in question was not that of the forum but of a foreign country, Article 7(2) would be inapplicable – and even in those countries in which Article 7(1) applied, the latter would be unable to be referred to in order to safeguard such conflicts-mandatory contract rules of a foreign law, as being those of a country having a close connection with the situation, because Article 7(1) safeguards national rules which are *both* contracts- and conflicts-mandatory, not those solely the latter as may be the position in the case under discussion.)

Thirdly, however, preceding potential negative conflicts of laws and limitations on scope of Convention safeguards may not in practice occur with great frequency. It is felt that this is so, because where a national contract rule is stated by statute to be (half- or full-) conflicts-mandatory (or, conversely, as the case may be, contracts-mandatory) – and *a fortiori* where this is not expressly decreed, but held to be so by judicial construction – it seems most unlikely that the particular mandatory contract rule in question would not also be held to be contracts- (or, as the case may be, conflicts-) mandatory, so that the situation in which Article 3(3)-type safeguards would be unable to be applied to national conflicts-mandatory laws would be unlikely to arise, since such laws would probably also be contracts-mandatory at national law, a category to which Article 3(3) does apply (and furthermore, the latter is not expressed to safeguard such national rules only when there has actually been an attempt by parties to derogate therefrom *directly* by contract – it simply says that chosen law shall be without prejudice to application of such rules, *which cannot be* so derogated from). Similarly, national conflicts-mandatory rules protected by Article 7(2) should also be found to be contracts-mandatory at national law as a matter of construction (although, in this instance, the wording of Article 7(2) seems to indicate that the latter is concerned solely with the conflicts-mandatory operation of the national rules: 'in a situation where'). How, after all, could it be regarded as satisfactory for parties to be restricted from excluding rules of law directly by contractual terms and yet not also from choosing a foreign law, or arranging their transaction so that a foreign law applied in the absence of choice, where the chosen or otherwise applicable legal system contained no equivalent contract rules – or vice versa?

It is to be hoped, therefore, that the potential difficulties over which Convention provision to refer to for mandatory safeguards, and over how to avoid missing out on any of them through absence of prescribed Convention connections for the particular type of national mandatory rule, may in practice be avoided.

Nevertheless, it will pay to be aware of the possibilities open to be argued for by the opposing side as a result of the inferences capable of being drawn from the Convention system as to the different types of mandatory national contract rules, the alleged existence of which is apparently contemplated thereunder.

Public policy

The ultimate power to refuse to apply a foreign law of contract on the ground of public policy, for example, because the effect of enforcement of the contract would be repugnant and offensive to fundamental moral attitudes prevailing in the forum (see, for example, *Robinson* v. *Bland* (1760) 2 Burr 1077, 1084), is preserved by Article 16 of the Convention, according to which application of a foreign rule *may* be refused if such *application* would be *manifestly* incompatible with the forum's public policy.

Thus it is the effect of application of the foreign rule which has to be seen to offend, rather than the rule as such (Report, p.38); and the power to refuse to apply the latter is discretionary, not mandatory. The word 'manifestly' demonstrates that the provision, endangering Convention unity, must be restrictively applied, and the French term *ordre public*, used both in the heading to Article 16 and in parentheses in the text, also shows that Article 16 should be interpreted and applied in a unificationist manner, in accordance with the general prescription for such uniform treatment of Convention rules under Article 18 thereof.

Finally, as previously mentioned, it may be possible to construe Article 16 as also covering the case in which a contract, valid and legal according to applicable law, would nonetheless be illegal according to the law of another foreign country, whether of performance or otherwise, on the ground that it would be contrary to public policy comity grounds of the forum for the latter to lend its assistance to enforcement of a contract in breach of the imperative laws of a foreign, friendly country even though not that of applicable law, as under pre-existing national English conflicts (see, for example, *Regazzoni* v. *K.C.Sethia (1944) Ltd*, above). However, such a construction would seem unlikely, since Article 16 does appear to contemplate that it has to be a particular legal norm of a foreign applicable law – which may not, therefore, include a notional positive such norm to be deduced from the absence of any specific norm negating legality of the contractual performance in question! – which gives rise to the public policy objection; and the very existence of Article 7(1) (albeit inapplicable in the United Kingdom), providing an express, discretionary safeguard for mandatory rules in general of foreign countries having a close connection, would further seem to detract from the overall acceptability of the possible construction of Article 16 referred to.

INTERPRETATION OF THE CONVENTION

The Convention is uniform European law, as is essentially its national implementing legislation. In accordance with modern principles of judicial interpretation of international conventions and statutes giving effect thereto (see, for example, *James Buchanan & Co. Ltd* v. *Babco Forwarding and Shipping (UK) Ltd* [1978] AC 141), both Convention and 1990 Act must be construed in an internationalist spirit, without undue emphasis being placed upon a particular national text or meaning thereof, so as to preserve the uniformity achieved and to prevent serious national divergencies in interpretation and application from arising in the courts of different Contracting States. There are in fact two provisions in the Convention which give expression to this uniform approach:

- Article 18, stating that, in the interpretation and application of the Convention's uniform rules, regard shall be had to their international character and to the desirability of achieving uniformity in their interpretation and application; and
- Article 33, stating that all Community language texts there referred to (seemingly, even if not yet of *Contracting* States) are equally authentic (see too Luxembourg Convention on Greek Accession Articles 2 and 6, and Brussels Interpretation Protocol Article 11).

Thus, for example, in deciding upon mandatory nature of national English contract rules of the forum under Article 7(2) (*application*), and upon the meaning itself of mandatory therein for Convention purposes (*interpretation*), English courts should exercise appropriate restraint so as to reduce the risk that uniform Convention aims and primacy of applicable law thereunder will be undermined by excessive qualification thereto.

The European Court itself in dealing with European Community or uniform European law will adopt what is referred to as a *teleological* or *purposive* interpretation thereof, that is to say, based upon the spirit and object of the text, even if not wholly consistent with its literal meaning where such departure from the latter is justified by the fundamental underlying purpose of the particular law in question (see Kaye, *Civil Jurisdiction*, pp. 1694 *et seq* and authorities there referred to, concerning the Judgments Convention and EC laws in general).

Sources of Interpretation

There are a number of sources as interpretative aids to construction of the Convention's provisions which may be turned to in the name of uniformity:

a   as seen, the Convention's text, in *all* authentic languages under Article 33 (see *CILFIT Srl* v. *Ministry of Health*, Case 283/81 [1982] ECR 3415, 3430): in accordance with s.2(4)(a)–(c) of the 1990 Act, English texts of the Convention, Luxembourg Convention on Greek Accession and Brussels Interpretation Protocol (referred to in the Act, in accordance with s.1(a)–(c), as the Rome Convention, the Luxembourg Convention, and the Brussels Protocol) are set out in Schedules 1, 2 and 3 to the Act for 'ease of reference' only, and accordingly, it is the Conventions, as international instruments as such, and as reproduced in the EC Official Journal (see O.J. 1980 L266/1; O.J. 1984 L146/1; O.J. 1989 L48/1), which have the force of law internationally and internally within the United Kingdom under s.2(1) of the 1990 Act (although, not yet, in the case of the Brussels Protocol: see SI 1991 No. 707);

b   the Preamble to the Convention (see, too, long title to 1990 Act) mentions certain goals and objects to be achieved by the Convention, and may therefore be referred to for an indication of the parameters of the Convention: paragraph 2 demonstrates that the Convention is to be looked upon as a continuation of the work already carried out towards unification of private international law within the EEC, most notably in the field of jurisdiction and the enforcement of foreign judgments under the European Judgments Convention (see (d), below), and paragraph 3 emphasizes the contractual scope of the Obligations Convention and its uniform purpose;

c   the Giuliano/Lagarde report of rapporteurs on the Convention (O.J. 1980 No. C282/1), which s.3(3)(a) of the 1990 Act states 'may be considered in ascertaining the meaning or effect of any provision of the Convention' (and, at some future date, when s.3(3)(b) of the Act shall have been brought into force by statutory instrument under s.7, the Tizzano Report on the Brussels Interpretation Protocols, O.J. 1990 No. C219/1, which, under s.3(3)(b), may also be so considered) – these reports constituting the agreed content as between rapporteurs, in their personal capacity, and Convention negotiators, rather than official *travaux préparatoires* representing drafters' actual intentions, albeit highly authoritative in view of their inclusion in the Official Journal of the Community; in addition, s.3(3) specifically states that those reports are *without prejudice to any practice of the courts as to the matters which may be considered apart therefrom* – to be taken as a reference to

leading English and foreign academic commentaries on the Convention (see Hansard, HL Vol. 515, cols 1488–90; Vol. 517, cols 1541–43);
d principles laid down by the European Court as part of its interpretative jurisdiction: s.3(1) of the 1990 Act – yet to be brought into force by statutory instrument under s.7 (see SI 1991 No. 707) – provides that any question as to the meaning or effect of any Convention provision *shall*, if not referred to the European Court in the case at hand under the Brussels Interpretation Protocol (not yet in force), be determined in accordance with the principles laid down by, and any relevant decision of, the European Court, and, as a matter of evidence, s.3(2), also not yet in force, states that judicial notice shall be taken of any decision of, or expression of opinion by, the European Court on any such question; it is believed that such *relevant* decisions *et alia* of the European Court will not be confined to those solely in relation to the Convention, but will also be likely to include those on EEC law in general, as well as those on the EEC Judgments Convention where relevant (see below, Part III, Chapters 11 and 21); (in the Judgments Convention case of *Ivenel* v. *Schwab*, Case 133/81 [1982] ECR 1891, 1900, conversely, the European Court expressly referred to the Obligations Convention and to the report thereon, in interpreting the Judgments Convention: see too *Sanicentral* v. *Collin*, Case 25/79 [1979] ECR 3423, 3434; *Elefanten Schuh* v. *Jacqmain*, Case 150/80 [1981] ECR 1671, 1698; *Peters* v. *ZNAV*, Case 34/82 [1983] ECR 987, 1007; and *Mercury Publicity Limited* v. *Wolfgang Loerke GmbH* [1991] *The Times*, 21 October – although, in *Six Constructions Ltd* v. *Humbert*, Case 32/88 [1989] ECR 341, 362–363, the European Court declined to follow Article 6(2)(b) of the Obligations Convention, in the matter of *jurisdiction* in respect of litigation involving employees who did not normally perform their work in a single country, on the ground that such competence of courts of the place of business through which the employee was engaged would depart significantly from the actual terms of Article 5(1) of the Judgments Convention and fail to pay sufficient regard to the protection of the socially weaker party, namely, the employee; and, subsequently, therefore, the version of Article 5(1) of the Judgments Convention, as amended by Article 4 of the San Sebastian Convention on Spanish–Portuguese Accession thereto, O.J. 1989 L285/1, largely incorporated the provision made by Article 6(2)(b) of the Obligations Convention in relation to employees, *but* limited jurisdiction of courts of the place of business through which the employee was engaged, to actions brought by employees against employers, and not the reverse, in order to take account of the European Court's ruling in *Six Constructions Ltd* v. *Humbert* – see Almeida Cruz/Desantes Real/Jenard Report on Spanish–Portuguese

Accession, O.J. 1990 C 189/35 pp.44–5; Article 5(1) of the Lugano Convention, O.J. 1988 L319/9, extending the Judgments Convention as between EC and EFTA countries, simply reproduced the connection in Article 6(2)(b) of the Obligations Convention, without the limitation referred to in Article 5(1) as amended by the San Sebastian Convention, the former having been drafted before the European Court's ruling in *Six Constructions Ltd* v. *Humbert* – see Jenard/Möller Report on the Lugano Convention, O.J. 1990 C189/57 para 38); indeed, it will be noted that express reference is made to the Judgments Convention under paragraph 2 of the Preamble to the Obligations Convention, referred to above; quite rightly, however, in the Judgments Convention case of *Kleinwort Benson Ltd and Barclays Bank plc* v. *Glasgow City Council* (1992) *The Times*, 17 March, HIRST J held that, whilst it was legitimate to take account of the provisions of the Obligations Convention in construing Article 5(1) of the Judgments Convention (or more accurately, in that case, Article 5(1) of Schedule 4 to the Civil Jurisdiction and Judgments Act 1982, based on Article 5(1) of the Convention and governing internal jurisdiction in the United Kingdom), concerning jurisdiction of courts of the place for performance of a contractual obligation (the question being whether a restitution claim consequent upon payment of sums in pursuance of agreements which were *ultra vires* and void *ab initio*, was nonetheless to be classified as relating to contract), nevertheless, the Obligations Convention could not properly be treated as determinative of the Judgments Convention's construction, and doubtless the converse would also be the case;

e it is axiomatic that in applying the Convention in accordance with the unificationist design given expression to by Article 18, English courts should be prepared to take account of foreign Contracting States' courts' case law on the Convention, and to accord it such persuasive influence, if any, as the merits of the decision and the position and prestige of the foreign court in its national hierarchy appear to demand (see *Fothergill* v. *Monarch Airlines* [1980] 2 All ER 696, 708, LORD DIPLOCK); and, in this connection, it will be noted that the first Joint Declaration annexed to the first Brussels Interpretation Protocol (O.J. 1989 No. L48/8), in order to ensure that the Convention is applied as effectively and as uniformly as possible, declares the readiness of Contracting States to organize an exchange of information on certain national Convention judgments through the offices of the European Court.

It may also be the case that courts should be willing to consider authorities of *non*-Contracting States where Convention principles have been influenced thereby: for example, the characteristic performance doctrine under Article 4(2) was apparently influenced by certain Swiss developments (see below, Chapter 9). However, it is considered that any such non-Contracting State source, lying outside the dynamics of unifying Community law, would simply be illustrational and contextual, rather than in any sense authoritative or persuasive, and of even less relevance when occurring subsequent to the Convention's entry into force rather than prior to the date of its drafting.

Procedure to Obtain Interpretative Rulings from the European Court

In the Second Joint Declaration annexed to the Obligations Convention (O.J. 1980 No. L266/17), future Contracting States declared themselves ready to examine the possibility of conferring jurisdiction to interpret the Convention upon the European Court of Justice, in order to ensure that the Convention would be applied as effectively as possible and differences of interpretation prevented from impairing its unifying effect. *Eight* years later, on 19 December 1988, two Protocols on interpretation by the European Court were signed at Brussels after much negotiation.

The first Brussels Protocol on the Interpretation of the Contractual Obligations Convention, of 19 December 1988 (O.J. 1989 No. L48/1) (referred to in the 1990 Act as 'the Brussels Protocol': s.1(c)) is set out for ease of reference (s.2(4)(c)) in Schedule 3 to the 1990 Act, and provides for specified courts of Contracting States (Article 2) or designated authorities thereof (Article 3) to request the European Court to give rulings on interpretation of the Convention, Luxembourg Convention on Greek Accession and any future accession convention in relation to Portugal and Spain (para. III of the First Joint Declaration annexed to the Rome Convention, O.J. 1980 No. L266/14, expresses the view, having regard to the Convention's contribution towards uniformity of contract conflicts within the European Communities, that any state becoming a member of the Communities should accede to the Convention, and the Second Joint Declaration annexed to the first Brussels Interpretation Protocol, O.J. 1989 No. L 48/13, does the same in respect of accession thereto), and the Brussels Protocol itself (Article 1). Such rulings will be binding upon the requesting court, as in the case of European Court decisions on the Judgments Convention under the 1971 Protocol on Interpretation thereof, and on the EEC Treaty itself under Article 177 of the latter (*Milchkontor* v. *Hauptzollamt Saarbrücken,* Case 19/68 [1969] ECR 165, 180).

The Brussels Protocol is not yet in force. The United Kingdom, Greece and the Netherlands have so far ratified it, but Article 6 requires seven Convention Contracting States to ratify it for it to enter into force in accordance therewith: but even then, under Article 6, it is not to enter into operation, unless the *Second* Brussels Protocol Conferring on the European Court of Justice Certain Powers to Interpret the Contractual Obligations Convention (O.J. 1989 No. L48/17), of the same date as the first, is also in force.

How so? What is this *second* interpretation Protocol referred to in Article 6 of the first?

The Report by Professor Tizzano of Naples (O.J. 1990 No. C219/1, 3–12) explains the background to the *two* Brussels Protocols on Interpretation: the Obligations Convention is not founded upon any provision of the EEC Treaty (unlike the Judgments Convention: see EEC Treaty, Article 220), and accordingly, unanimous assent of EEC member states is required for power to be conferred upon the European Court, as a Community institution, to give interpretative rulings on the Obligations Convention. However, certain member states, notably Ireland, might encounter constitutional difficulties in so granting jurisdiction to a supranational judicial body when not derived from the EEC Treaty. In order therefore to avoid the delay caused by Irish measures to overcome their national obstacles, it was decided to formulate *two* Protocols, rather than one, concerning European Court interpretation: the second alone requires unanimous EEC member state ratification for it to enter into force under its Articles 2 and 3, and Article 1 thereof confers the power upon the European Court to grant rulings on interpretation under the first Protocol; thus, the latter, as seen, need only then be ratified by seven Convention States for it to enter into force *for those States* under its Article 6. In this way, delays in implementation can be reduced, and countries like Ireland can join in conferring power upon the European Court (under the second Brussels Protocol) – but not necessarily also in relation to its own courts (under the first Brussels Protocol) until it is constitutionally ready to do so. The United Kingdom, Greece and the Netherlands have ratified the two Protocols, and Ireland the Second Protocol.

Article 2 of the first Brussels Protocol lists the national courts which are empowered to request interpretative rulings, generally the highest in the land (see too Article 8 as to future amendments). In the case of the United Kingdom, the courts referred to are

- the House of Lords and other courts from which no further appeal is possible (Article 2(a));
- courts of the United Kingdom acting as appeal courts (Article 2(b)).

Thus, Article 2(b) applies to Contracting States' courts generally, including the United Kingdom's, and accordingly, the express reference in Article

2(a) to United Kingdom courts from which *no further appeal* is possible (presumably, included at a stage when it was contemplated that references under Article 2(a) would be obligatory, as in the case of the Judgments Convention) is largely superfluous – especially since in practice, Article 2(b) will be easier to construe and to rely on than Article 2(a) and therefore preferred to the latter in the United Kingdom (see below, Part III, Chapter 41).

One difference from the Judgments Convention's Interpretation Protocol and Article 177 of the EEC Treaty is that there is no *obligation* upon the highest courts of Contracting States to request interpretation by the European Court under Article 2 of the Brussels Protocol: there is merely a *discretion,* accorded to all courts listed, to do so ('may request'). As in the case of the Judgments Convention, however, courts of first instance are excluded from those capable of making a reference.

Conditions for making a preliminary reference to the European Court in Article 2 follow those of the Judgments Convention and Article 177

- The question of interpretation must arise from a case *pending* before the national court, and may not be hypothetical: by way of qualification to this, Article 3 permits competent authorities of Contracting States to request rulings outside actual forensic proceedings, where judgments of courts of those states are in conflict either with a European Court decision or with the judgment of one of the Article 2-courts of another Contracting State.
- There must be a question *raised* in the pending national court proceedings, and the question must concern *interpretation*, not application, of the Convention: questions will not be regarded as raised – or at least, not to be those concerning *interpretation* – where there has been a previous European Court ruling thereon in another case, not desired to be departed from, or the meaning is obvious and free from ambiguity, or there is no genuine dispute between the parties in respect thereof (see below, Part III, Chapter 41).
- The national court must believe that a decision on the question is *necessary* to enable it to give judgment.

EEC Treaty procedural provisions generally apply to Brussels Protocol interpretative references to the European Court (Article 4), and the Brussels Protocol is to remain in force for as long as the Obligations Convention itself does so (Article 9).

CONCLUSION

The notable feature of the Convention is its attempt to be *candid*.

There are many elements of the pre-existing English private international rules of applicable law in contract which are rather vague and uncertain or not entirely satisfactory: limits, if any, upon ability of parties to select an unconnected law to govern their contract (*Vita Foods*); procedure on finding the parties to have included no express provision on applicable law in their contract – whether to look for an implied choice, or to proceed immediately to determine the law most closely and really connected with the transaction, as objective proper law (*Amin Rasheed*); extent of scission of applicable law possible (*Kahler*); ability to vary applicable law subsequent to contracting (Dicey and Morris, p.1168); law to govern existence and validity of contracts and of choice of law clauses (*Albeko*; *Brinkibon*; *The Parouth*); whether the transaction should be most closely connected with a law, or a country, in the absence of choice (*James Miller & Partners Ltd*); applicable law on a balance of all facts and circumstances in the absence of agreement between the parties (*Assunzione*); absence of general consumer protection provision on applicable law in the absence of choice by parties, and limitation generally of consumer protection to application of *English* law notwithstanding choice of a *foreign* proper law, or contractual exclusion of *English* legal liability (Unfair Contract Terms Act 1977 ss. 6 and 27 – see though, s.27(1); Consumer Credit Act 1974 s.173); wholly undeveloped system for protection of mandatory *foreign* laws having an interest in their extraterritorial operation, the matter being left to the vagaries of public policy comity objections (*Foster*; *Regazzoni*); a rather patchy development of mandatory English extraterritoriality (*Boissevain*; *Hollandia*); normal preliminary problems of location of *lex loci contractus* for purposes of applicable law of form; uncertainty over applicability of *lex loci solutionis* as a conflicts rule to govern (supervening) illegality of contractual performance (*Ralli*); lack of precision as to the law to govern individuals' contractual capacity (Cheshire and North, p.480).

In all such cases, the Convention's rules are comparatively easy to discern and are openly presented. The Convention displays its goods on the stall rather than under the counter: Article 3(1) specifies plainly the principle that parties may freely select applicable law, and the exceptions on the basis of relative lack of sufficient connections are expressly stated and limited to safeguard of mandatory rules of other laws (Articles 3(3), 7(1) and 9(6)); where there is no expressly chosen law, courts are first required to determine whether there is a reasonably certain implied choice before proceeding to find the law of the most connected country (Article 3(1)); *dépeçage* is openly sanctioned (Article 3(1)), although, only exceptionally in the absence of choice (Article 4(1)); subsequent variation of applicable law is explicitly permitted and controlled (Article 3(2)); chosen or otherwise applicable law specifically governs existence and validity of contracts and terms (Article 8(1)), including consent to choice of law itself (Article 3(4)), subject to a protective rule in the case of absence of consent (Article 8(2)); the Convention makes it quite clear that it is law of most closely connected country, rather than most closely connected law, which must be sought to be determined as applicable law in the absence of choice (Article 4(1)); rebuttable presumptions of closest connection, based upon express points of contact, operate to determine applicable law in the absence of choice (Article 4(2)–(5)); consumer protection on applicable law in the absence of choice is included (Article 5(3)), and safeguards are provided for mandatory rules of a consumer's law against choice of another, irrespective of whether the former is English or foreign (Article 5(2): see too Article 6(1) on employee protection); Convention mandatory protection extends to foreign, not just English, laws (Articles 3(3), 5(2), 6(1), 7(1) and 9(6)); a clear statement is included to the effect that nothing in the Convention is to restrict the application of mandatory extraterritorial laws of the forum (Article 7(2)); difficulties over defining *lex loci contractus* as applicable law in the case of contractual form are avoided (Article 9(1) and (2)); the Convention contains no rule of applicable law based on *lex loci solutionis* to govern illegality, which is a matter for normal applicable law (Articles 8 and 10(1)(b) and (d)); a uniform rule on applicable law of individuals' contracting capacity is provided as an alternative to resort to national conflicts on the matter in certain circumstances (Article 11).

True it may be that the Convention has its own uncertainties and inadequacies: for example, the rather esoteric *characteristic performance* obligation at the heart of the presumption of most closely connected applicable law in the absence of choice under Article 4(2), and possibilities of rebuttal thereof, are highly controversial; the concept of *reasonableness* of applicable law in relation to consent under Article 8(2) is a difficult one to be definite about; scope of applicable law in respect of *quantification* of damages under Articles 1(2)(h) and 10(1)(c) is made unnecessarily complicated to determine ('within the limits of the powers conferred on the court by its procedural law ... in so far as it is governed by rules of law'), as is that of *lex loci solutionis* in relation to manner of contractual performance under Article 10(2) ('regard shall be had') and of applicable laws in the case of presumptions of law and burden and modes of proof under Article 14 ('in the law of contract'; 'can be administered by the forum'); the interpretation and operation of the Convention mandatory protection system is undesirably complex; and misgivings may be felt over whether the mechanism for achieving fairness in the case of law governing contractual incapacity under Article 11 is the best that could have been devised.

However, at least it may be said of the preceding Convention inadequacies and problems over meaning and application that they are *secondary* difficulties, deriving from a comprehensively presented, detailed set of uniform rules of applicable law for the entire Community, to be subjected to a uniform system of interpretation and application (Article 18) under the guidance and unifying influence of the European Court itself (Brussels Protocol), rather than existing in and as to the very content and fabric of partly-developed, and sometimes merely suppositional, divergent national rules of contract conflicts.

Figure 3.1   Applicable law under the Obligations Convention

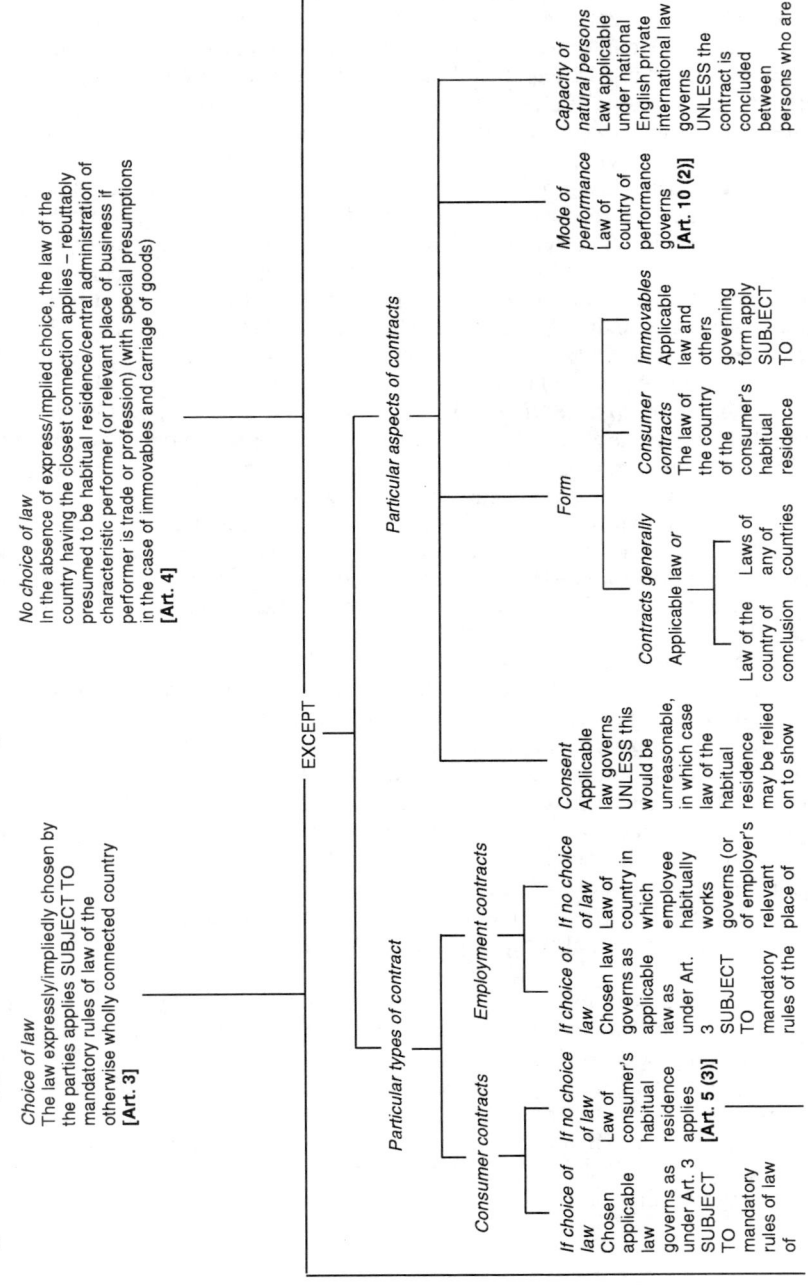

General Impact of EEC's Contractual Obligations Convention 87

Figure 3.1 continued

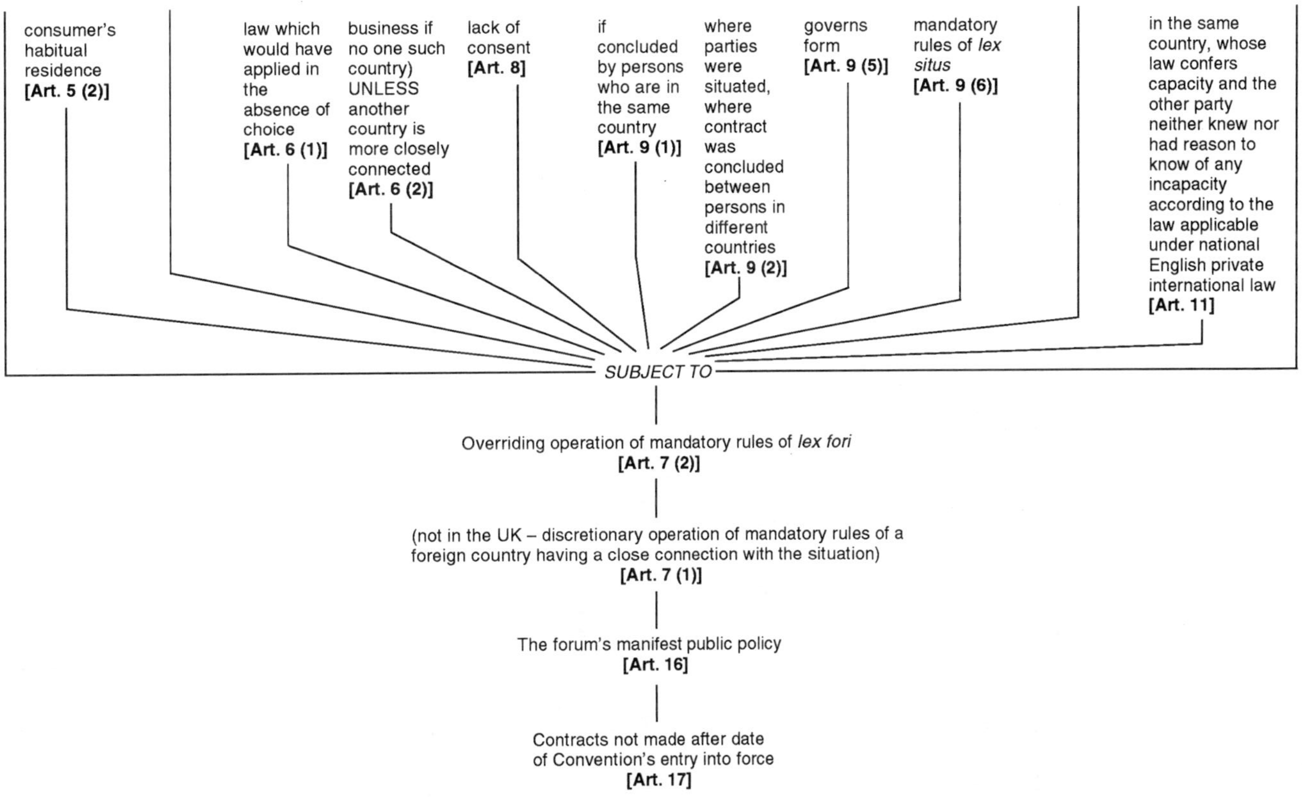

- consumer's habitual residence **[Art. 5 (2)]**
- law which would have applied in the absence of choice **[Art. 6 (1)]**
- business if no one such country) UNLESS another country is more closely connected **[Art. 6 (2)]**
- lack of consent **[Art. 8]**
- if concluded by persons who are in the same country **[Art. 9 (1)]**
- where parties were situated, where contract was concluded between persons in different countries **[Art. 9 (2)]**
- governs form **[Art. 9 (5)]**
- mandatory rules of *lex situs* **[Art. 9 (6)]**
- in the same country, whose law confers capacity and the other party neither knew nor had reason to know of any incapacity according to the law applicable under national English private international law **[Art. 11]**

SUBJECT TO

- Overriding operation of mandatory rules of *lex fori* **[Art. 7 (2)]**
- (not in the UK – discretionary operation of mandatory rules of a foreign country having a close connection with the situation) **[Art. 7 (1)]**
- The forum's manifest public policy **[Art. 16]**
- Contracts not made after date of Convention's entry into force **[Art. 17]**

**Mandatory rules of law of a country with which *all other relevant connections are established* apply notwithstanding choice of a different country's law to govern the contract
[Art. 3 (3)]**

**Mandatory rules of law of a foreign country with which the situation has a close connection *may* apply in place of applicable law, having regard to their nature and purpose and to the consequences of their application or non-application
[Art. 7 (1)]**
(Inapplicable in the UK: 1990 Act s. 2 (2))

**Mandatory rules of form of *lex situs* govern contracts concerning rights in or to use immovables, where those requirements are irrespective of country of conclusion and of the law governing the contract
[Art. 9 (6)]**

**Mandatory rules of *lex fori* must be applied (according to national law) irrespective of applicable law
[Art. 7 (2)]**

**In *consumer contracts* mandatory rules of the law of the country in which the consumer has his habitual residence apply to protect the consumer notwithstanding choice of a different country's law under Article 3
[Art. 5 (2)]**

**In *employment contracts* mandatory rules of the law of the country in which the employee habitually works (or in which the place of business through which he was engaged is situated if he does not habitually work in any one country) apply to protect the employee notwithstanding choice of a different country's law to govern the contract under Article 3, unless the contract is more closely connected with another country, in which case the mandatory rules of the latter's law shall apply
[Art. 6 (1)]**

**Application of any rule of a law specified under the Convention may be refused on the ground that such application is *manifestly incompatible with the public policy of the forum*
[Art. 16]**

Figure 3.2 Circumstances in which mandatory rules displace other laws under the Convention

PART III

Commentary on Individual Provisions of the 1990 Act and Convention

4 Contracts (Applicable Law) Act 1990

1990 CHAPTER 36

An Act to make provision as to the law applicable to contractual obligations in the case of conflict of laws [26 July 1990].

The long title mirrors the Convention Preamble, which emphasizes the need for a unificationist solution to the problem of applicable law in international cases within the European Economic Community.

Section 1

[*Shortened form references in the Act to the Obligations Convention, Luxembourg Convention on Greek Accession, and the first Brussels Interpretation Protocol, referred to, respectively, in the Act, as 'the Rome Convention', 'the Luxembourg Convention', and the 'Brussels Protocol', and, collectively, as 'the Conventions'.*]

Section 2

[*Provision is made for Rome and Luxembourg Conventions, and the Brussels Protocol, English texts of which are set out for ease of reference in Schedules 1, 2 and 3, respectively, to the Act, to be given the force of law in the United Kingdom* (so that technically it is the *Conventions* – all language versions, not just English, under Article 33 and equivalents – *not the Schedules*, which are authoritative) *with the exception of Convention Articles 7(1) (application of foreign mandatory laws generally) and 10(1)(e) (applicability of applicable law under the Convention, to the consequences of nullity of contract), which the United Kingdom reserved the right not to apply, in accordance with Article 22(1), on ratifying the Obligations Convention. The Convention's rules cover conflicts of laws within the United Kingdom, as well as those involving a legal system other than another within the United Kingdom, notwithstanding Article 19(2), which latter would otherwise relieve the United Kingdom's courts from having to apply the Convention to intra-United Kingdom conflicts. Pre-existing national rules of contract conflicts are thus replaced by the Convention's provisions within the latter's scope.]*

Section 3

[Regard 'must' be had to European Court jurisprudence ('principles laid down by, and any relevant decision of') in interpreting the meaning or effect of any provision of the Conventions, if the question at issue is not referred to the European Court under the Brussels Protocol (to be brought into force), in the case at hand; and, without prejudice to this or other methods and practices of interpretation, the Giuliano/Lagarde Report on the Obligations Convention (O.J. 1980, No. C282/1) – hereinafter 'the Report' – 'may' also be considered in ascertaining the meaning or effect of any Convention provision, as 'may' any report on the Brussels Interpretation Protocol (to be brought into force), which appears in the Official Journal of the Communities – see The Tizzano Report (O.J. 1990, No. C219/1). The words 'Without prejudice to any practice of the courts as to the matters which may be considered apart from this subsection' are meant to indicate that express mention of the reports is not to give rise to the inference that other academic commentaries may not be considered, for what they are worth, by the courts: see Hansard, HL Vol.515, cols 1488–90; Vol.517, cols 1541–3.

Seemingly, from s.3(1), even relevant European Court decisions on the European Judgments Convention may be followed in interpreting the Obligations Convention (a fortiori, where the Court's pronouncements in a Judgments Convention case actually relate to the Obligations Convention! See for example SPRL Arcado v. Haviland SA, Case 9/87 [1988] ECR 1539, p. 1555 – although, the policies under both Conventions will not necessarily always coincide, see Six Constructions Ltd v. Humbert, Case 32/88 [1989] ECR 341, 362–363, and Kleinwort Benson Ltd and Barclays Bank plc v. Glasgow City Council (1992) The Times, 17 March: above, pp. 79–80); and from s.3(2) on judicial notice (European Court decisions need not be proven as fact, by expert evidence, as though they were foreign law), mere expressions of opinion by the European Court may also be taken into consideration.]

Section 4

[Provision for appropriate amendment of the Act, or of any other statute, by Order in Council, at any time, as a consequence of revision of any of the Conventions, and in particular, in connection with accession of states to the Rome Convention, or where the United Kingdom decides that either or both of Articles 7(1) and 10(1)(e) are to have the force of law in the United Kingdom.]

There are wide definitions of 'modifications' and 'revision' (as well as 'statutory provision') for the purposes of the section, in s.4(3): in particular, it may be noted that 'revision' includes *inter alia* replacement of any of the Conventions 'to any extent' by another convention *et alia*, which may thus be carried out in this manner by Order in Council.

A draft of the Order in Council must be laid before parliament and approved by a resolution of each House.

Section 5

The enactments specified in Schedule 4 to this Act shall have effect subject to the amendments specified in that Schedule.

The words 'proper law of', redolent of pre-existing English contract conflicts and used in various statutory provisions listed in Schedule 4, are substituted by the Convention expression 'law applicable to' in those enactments.

In respect of contracts concluded prior to 2 April 1991, to which the previous conflicts law continues to apply (Article 17), the alterations in Schedule 4 should produce little or no effect.

Section 6

[The Act binds the Crown: see Hansard, HL Vol.513, cols 1265–6, 1267.]

Section 7

[Dates of entry into force of the Act in accordance with statutory instrument – see The Contracts (Applicable Law) Act 1990 (Commencement No.1) Order 1991, SI 1991 No. 707. Provisions brought into force under the latter on 1 April 1991 were s.1; s.2(1) in so far as it relates to the Rome and Luxembourg Conventions (but not the Brussels Protocol); s.2(2) to (4);

s.3(3)(a) (report on Rome Convention – but not yet s.3(1) and (2), on authority of European Court decisions, or 3(3)(b), as to the *Tizzano* Report on the Brussels Protocol); ss. 4 to 9; and Schedules 1 to 4.]

Section 8

[*The Act extends to Northern Ireland; and it may be extended by Order in Council to all or any of the Isle of Man, any of the Channel Islands, Gibraltar, and the Sovereign Base Areas of Akrotiri and Dhekelia, subject to any modifications and supplementary provisions considered appropriate.*]

Section 9

[*Short title*]

5 Preamble to the Rome Convention

[SCHEDULES]

[SCHEDULE 1]

[THE ROME CONVENTION]

[The High Contracting Parties to the Treaty establishing the European Economic Community] [Have agreed as follows:]

Anxious to continue in the field of private international law the work of unification of law which has already been done within the Community, in particular in the field of jurisdiction and enforcement of judgments,

Wishing to establish uniform rules concerning the law applicable to contractual obligations,

The Convention's objective is to unify the private international law of contract amongst Contracting States (see Report, p. 4, paras 1 and 2): this aim is set forth in the Preamble (inserted in Schedule 1 to the Act at the Report stage of the legislation: see Hansard, HL Vol. 515, cols 1490–1; Vol. 517, col.1544), which should be read together with Article 18, requiring regard to be had to the international character of the rules and to their unificationist goals, in interpretation and application of the Convention, and with the Second Joint Declaration annexed to the Convention (O.J. 1980, No.L266/17), concerning the importance of uniform development and European Court interpretative jurisdiction.

The scarcely veiled reference in the Preamble to the European Judgments Convention is not merely an indiscreet form of diplomatic name-dropping! The two Conventions are parallel developments in the same movement towards harmonization and equalization of commercial legal regulation and protection throughout the separate states of the European Community (although, the Obligations Convention itself, unlike the Judgments Convention, is not derived from Article 220 of the EEC Treaty) and are thus closely linked, which means that in practice judicial trends and European Court interpretative decisions and approaches in either sphere, as well as those in the wider EC law context, are of mutual interest and influence (see *de Wolf* v. *Harry Cox BV*, Case 42/76 [1976] ECR 1759, 1768, and *Somafer SA* v. *Saar-Ferngas AG*, Case 33/78 [1978] ECR 2183, 2190, for European Court references to the Judgments Convention's Preamble). Furthermore, the very fact that plaintiffs could have a choice of more than one possibly applicable jurisdiction under the Judgments Convention made the need to unify Contracting States' laws of contractual conflicts even more essential, for the purpose of preventing divergencies and forum shopping within the Community (see [1985] 2 CMLR/49).

The Report (p. 5) sets out the guiding motives of those who promoted negotiation of the Obligations Convention:

- the avoidance of delays from the attempt to unify *everything*;
- the urgent need for greater legal *certainty* in some sectors of major economic importance;
- the wish to forestall any aggravation of *differences* in the rules of private international law amongst the various member states.

6 Article 1: Scope of the Convention

TITLE I
SCOPE OF THE CONVENTION

Article 1 determines the positive and negative subject-matter scope of the Convention.

The Convention applies to *contractual* obligations.

Excluded contracts, generally, are those either closely related to non-commercial, status matters, or in respect of which other international or EEC agreements are in existence or anticipated.

Article 1

Scope of the Convention

1   **The rules of this Convention shall apply to contractual obligations in any situation involving a choice between the laws of different countries.**

(A) CONVENTION RULES *SHALL* APPLY ...

The Convention's application is obligatory, not optional or discretionary. Within its scope of operation, national private international rules of contract are excluded, except to the extent that these, or rules laid down in other international instruments or conventions on choice of law in contract, are expressly preserved by the Convention (see Articles 20, 21 and 23–5). (Public, or private, bodies for settlement of contract disputes, which make their own provision on applicable law, are naturally not bound by the Convention, which is primarily intended for application by *courts*, as procedural *law* of the forum: see Morse, 'The EEC Convention on the Law Applicable to Contractual Obligations' (1982), 2 *Yearbook of European Law* 107, p.111.)

The standard rule of English law is that foreign law has to be pleaded and proved in the courts as a matter of fact: in the absence of pleading, English law is applied, and in the absence of proof, foreign law is presumed to be the same as English (*Ascherberg* v. *Casa Musicale Sonzogno* [1971] 1 WLR 173, p.1128). (Morris, in *The Conflict of Laws*, 3rd edn (1984), p.41, prefers to say that *English law* applies also in the latter circumstances.)

Strictly, if English courts were to fall back on these traditional procedures in Convention cases, the United Kingdom could find itself in breach of its public international treaty obligation to apply the Convention. It seems highly desirable, therefore, that judges should be willing to apply the Convention of their own motion where necessary and to request the parties to provide evidence and to plead applicable law under the Convention in the appropriate manner. The parties may, in any event, expressly or impliedly agree to vary the law otherwise applicable – including any previously chosen by them – in accordance with Article 3(2), which permits them to do so at any time, including the pleading stage of proceedings and thereafter: own motion application of the Convention is, accordingly, not necessarily inconsistent with party autonomy (although, such variation *is* subject to previous formal validity and to third party rights).

(B) CONTRACTUAL OBLIGATIONS

Contractual

In view of Article 18, providing for a uniform, internationalist interpretation of Convention rules, there seems little doubt that the fundamental concept of 'contractual' obligations in Article 1(1) must be given an independent, Community meaning, as opposed to that of the national law of the forum as such. This is certainly the approach which has been adopted by the European Court in relation to the interpretation of 'matters relating to a contract' in Article 5(1) of the Judgments Convention (see *Peters* v. *ZNAV*, Case 34/82 [1983] ECR 987; [1984] 2 CMLR 605; *Jakob Handte GmbH* v. *TMCS*, Case 26/91 (1992) *The Times*, 19 August; and note *Powell Duffryn plc* v. *Petereit*, Case C-214/89 (1992) *The Times*, 15 April, in that case, specifically as to *jurisdiction* agreements within Article 17 – below p.126). In *S.p.r.l. Arcado* v. *Haviland S.A.*, Case 9/87 [1988] ECR 1539, a claim for compensation for wrongful repudiation of an independent commercial agency agreement was held to conform to the independent Judgments Convention concept of matters relating to a contract within Article 5(1), rather than to amount to a quasi-delict within Article 5(3), and interestingly, the European Court, at p.1555, pointed to Article 10 of the Obligations Convention as confirming the contractual nature of such proceedings 'as it provides that the law applicable to a contract governs the consequences of a total or partial failure to comply with obligations arising under it and consequently the contractual liability of the party responsible for such breach' (see Article 10(1)(c)). (In the subsequent case of *Kalfelis* v. *Schröder, Münchmeyer, Hengst,* Case 189/87 [1988] ECR 5565, the European Court went on to define *tort* for Judgments Convention purposes as an independent concept, covering all actions which seek to establish a defendant's liability and which are not related to a contract within Article 5(1).) Under pre-existing national English private international law too, the courts have in the past adopted a liberal approach, in classifying contracts as not being required to possess all attributes – such as consideration – which would be necessary for a valid contract to exist under English *lex fori,* where the agreement was entered into under a foreign legal system containing no such requirement (see *Re Bonacina* [1912] 2 Ch. 394: such matters would instead be regarded as concerning validity, rather than classification).

The European Court should, therefore, be requested to formulate a definition of 'contractual', based upon the common elements of Contracting States' national laws of contract and the appropriate policy to be pursued in applying the Convention.

A suggestion is made elsewhere for a meaning based upon 'an agreement between parties capable of giving rise to legal rights and duties on satisfaction of prescribed legal norms' (see Kaye, *Civil Jurisdiction and Enforcement of Foreign Judgments* (1987), p.490 – there, specifically for purposes of the EEC Judgments Convention). (Lipstein, in *Harmonisation of Private International Law by the EEC* (1978), pp. 1, 2–3, suggests that courts should look behind any formal classification of a legal rule as contractual or not by its host national legal system, in order to determine its true nature: take, for example, the French action in *tort* for breach of promise to marry, essentially contractual, but derived from a reluctance to acknowledge the engagement to marry itself as being legally enforceable.)

Such a definition will obviously exclude liability which is held to be criminal or tortious (notwithstanding that the same facts may also give rise to a claim for breach of contract – see too *Jakob Handte GmbH* v. *TMCS,* Case 26/91 (1992) *The Times,* 19 August: Article 5(1) Judgments Convention inapplicable to claim by sub-purchaser against manufacturer who was not the vendor), as well as *internal* relationships arising under the law of trusts (the latter themselves being expressly excluded in any event from the Convention's scope, by Article 1(2)(g) – see below, p.132) and proprietary disputes, including those regarding rights of persons claiming under a contract concluded with a non-owner.

The Report itself expressly specifies that property rights and intellectual property are not covered by the Convention (see p.10 – there was an express provision to this effect in the original preliminary draft, subsequently regarded as superfluous). It seems clear that, in either case, the exclusion encompasses proprietary or tortious claims, although not those of a purely contractual nature, having the tangible or intellectual property right as their subject matter. (LORD LLOYD OF KILGERRAN's proposed amendments to the Preamble para. 3 during the passage of the legislation, so as to exclude contractual obligations involving intellectual property rights from the Convention's scope were subsequently withdrawn: see Hansard, HL Vol. 513, cols 1264–5; Vol. 515, cols 1473–4; Vol. 517, cols 1544–6. LORD LLOYD had considered the area of contractual obligations and situations relating to intellectual property to be too complex and technical for regulation by the Convention, and the latter's provisions on choice of law for employment contracts wholly unsuitable for consultants employed on research and development in different countries, *ibid.*; the Lord Chancellor, however, pointed out that the Convention was not for alteration by a national legislature and that the proper course would be to conclude a separate convention, having precedence over the Obligations Convention under Article 21 thereof, or to convene a revision conference under Article 26: HL Vol. 517, col. 1547.)

Thus, for example contractual aspects of a transaction for a loan secured by way of a mortgage on property are governed by the Convention, as, similarly, are those in respect of intellectual property rights, where not otherwise the province of the law of tort (see *Tyburn Productions Ltd* v. *Conan Doyle* [1990] 3 WLR 167, commented upon in Kaye, *Private International Law of Tort and Product Liability* (1991), pp. 60–1), and promises to make gifts and donations – treated as binding and contractual in nature under many legal systems – as opposed to the proprietary gift transaction itself (see French Civil Code Article 931: Tous actes portant donation entre vifs seront passés devant notaires, dans la forme ordinaire des *contrats* ....; German Civil Code Article 518(1): Zur Gültigkeit eines *Vertrags*, durch den eine Leistung schenkweise versprochen wird ....).

Nonetheless, problems may arise. In the first place, relationships *at the edges of* the contractual bond may or may not be felt to fall within the suggested concept of contractual: for example, quasi-contract and restitution (recompense in Scotland) (see *Dimskal Shipping Co. SA* v. *International Transport Workers' Federation, The 'Evia Luck'* [1991] 4 All ER 871, 875, HL; *Kleinwort Benson Ltd and Barclays Bank plc* v. *Glasgow City Council* (1992) *The Times*, 17 March), and pre-contractual liability (tortious under English law, but regarded as pertaining to contracts in some other legal systems, such as the German – see Kaye, *Civil Jurisdiction*, p. 562). Opinions will differ, but in the present writer's submission none of the preceding matters ought to be held to be included within the Convention's meaning of contractual, since even where the liability is consequent upon the outcome of a contractual relationship, and certainly when it is not, such relations, it is felt, lack the essential *consensual* characteristic (albeit, that they may be based upon some deemed implied obligation) required for the contractual element to be held to be present (see Bennett, 'Choice of Law Rules in Claims of Unjust Enrichment' (1990) 39 *ICLQ* 136, for the fallacy in treating 'quasi-contract' claims arising from a situation involving contract, or otherwise of course, as *contractual*; also Collier, 'The Draft Convention and Restitution or Quasi-Contract', in Lipstein (ed.), *Harmonisation of Private International Law by the EEC* (1978), pp. 81, 83). Recent case law is thought to confirm a *sui generis* classification of restitution and unjust enrichment claims under general legal doctrine, freed from the historical terminological analogies of contract *et alia* (see *Lipkin Gorman* v. *Karpnale Ltd* [1991] 3 WLR 10 (H.L.); Law Commission Consultation Paper No.120, Restitution of Payments Made under a Mistake of Law, pp.50–1; and (1991) LMCLQ 473). On the other hand, it is conceded that Article 10(1)(e) expressly subjects 'the consequences of nullity of the contract' to applicable law under the Convention, to which an express reservation must be made (as in the case of the United Kingdom) under Article 22 (1)(b) if it is not to apply in a Contracting State, from which provision majority support in favour of a contractual classification may be inferred (see Report, p.33); and furthermore, it may be noted that in *Newtherapeutics Ltd* v. *Katz* [1990] 3 WLR 1183, KNOX J, at p. 1206, referred to *Bowling* v. *Cox* [1926] AC 751, as a case in which the Privy Council had held a rule on a par with RSC Order 11, concerning assumed jurisdiction over contracts, to include quasi-contract within the reference to contract therein (see Order 11 r 1(1)(d)). However, an alternative construction would be to treat such 'consequences' in Article 10(1)(e) as referring to the effects of nullity upon performance of their obligations by parties *under the contract*, as opposed to any such consequent rights of restitution, or otherwise as meaning the *contractual* consequences of nullity, when so classified. In addition, even if 'consequences' in Article 10(1)(e) were to be construed in the quasi-contractual sense, HIRST J discounted the very argument put above on that basis as possibly favouring a contractual classification thereof, in the Judgments Convention case of *Kleinwort Benson Ltd and Barclays Bank plc* v. *Glasgow City Council* (1992) *The Times*, 17 March. The proceedings in question involved an attempt – unsuccessful as it turned out – by the plaintiffs to establish the jurisdiction of the English courts over a claim for the restitution of sums paid by the plaintiffs to the defendant under transactions which were *ultra vires* the latter and consequently void *ab initio*. The defendant had its seat as domicile in Scotland, and accordingly, the only basis upon which the English courts might have been entitled to adjudicate was Article 5(1) of Schedule 4 to the Civil Jurisdiction and Judgments Act 1982 (regulating internal jurisdiction amongst legal systems within the United Kingdom and following Article 5(1) of the Judgments Convention itself, interpretation of which would be relevant to Schedule 4 – see 1982 Act s. 16(3)(a)). This provided for jurisdiction of courts for the place of performance of the obligation in question in matters *relating to a contract*. HIRST J held that English courts lacked jurisdiction over the Scottish domiciled defendant: to regard as a matter relating to 'contract' for such purposes transactions which were treated as being void *ab initio* was said to place a severe strain on the language of Article 5(1), in the light of case law thereon; HIRST J, as indicated, considering Article 10(1)(e) of the Obligations Convention as an aid to interpretation of Article 5(1), noted that it provided for law applicable to consequences of nullity of contract and that the United Kingdom had had to declare it inapplicable in order to prevent such matters from being governed by the Convention in the United Kingdom; he nevertheless concluded that, whilst it had no doubt been proper and necessary for the Obligations Convention to stipulate a law applicable to consequences of nullity of contract, if it was to fulfil its function as a comprehensive code of conflicts, it by no means followed therefrom that these were matters relating to a contract, since *ex hypothesi* no contract existed (a strong point, given that Article 5(3) of Schedule 4 was equally considered to be inapplicable to confer jurisdiction in tort upon the English courts).

Rights of third parties under a contract, where these are conferred according to a possibly applicable law, are plainly to be regarded as contractual for Convention purposes, where not constituted under a proprietary trust: this, it is believed, will include the rights of third-party victims of tort to sue the tortfeasor's insurers directly under relevant legislation, although the matter has been the subject of some debate (see English and Scottish Law Commissions' *Private International Law. Choice of Law in Tort and Delict* (1984) Working Paper No. 87 and Consultative Memorandum No. 62, para. 6.67, in support of the contractual classification – although, in their subsequent Report, 1990 LAW COM. No. 193 and SCOT. LAW COM. No. 129, para. 3.51, the Commissions seemed to prefer a tortious construction in the light of views received from consultants). Furthermore, contractual exclusion of tortious liability continues to be regarded as contractual, in so far as *contractual* effectiveness of the exclusion is involved (*Brodin* v. *A/R Seljan* 1973 SC 213), even though effects upon tort liability of a contractually effective exclusion clause are properly a question for the law of tort (see Kaye, *Private International Law of Tort and Product Liability*, 1991, p.62).

Secondly, questions have arisen in the case of Article 5(1) of the Judgments Convention, conferring jurisdiction in contract upon courts for the place in which the obligation in question has to be performed, over whether the provision continues to apply where the subject matter of the dispute concerns the very existence and validity of the contract (see *Effer* v. *Kantner*, Case 38/81 [1982] ECR 825; [1984] 2 CMLR 667; *Medway Packaging Ltd* v. *Meurer Maschinen GmbH & Co. KG* [1990] 1 Lloyd's Rep. 383; *Tesam Distribution Ltd* v. *Schuh Mode Team GmbH* (1989) *The Times*, 24 October; *New England Reinsurance* v. *Messoghios Insurance Co. S.A.* [1992] 1 Lloyd's Rep 201: a good arguable case for conclusion must be shown, p. 202; see too *Sanders* v. *Van der Putte*, Case 73/77 [1977] ECR 2382, as to existence of tenancy agreements under Article 16(1); *Elefanten Schuh* v. *Jacqmain*, Case 150/80 [1981] ECR 1671, as to jurisdiction agreements under Article 17; and *'The Atlantic Emperor'*, Case C-190/89 (1991) *The Times*, 20 September, as to existence of arbitration agreements). Clearly, in the case of choice of law, the problem of a contrived contractual claim or denial is not so acute as in that of jurisdiction where the very competence of the court applied to may depend upon the existence of the alleged contract (although, even in contract choice of law, a party might plead existence of a contract in the knowledge that the particular law applicable under the Convention would uphold the contractual relationship; yet, in such a case, the deficiencies, if any, must surely lie in the domestic rules of the applicable law rather than in the operation itself of the latter to matters of contracts-existence under the Convention). Fortunately, furthermore, in the case of the Obligations Convention it is made perfectly clear that the Convention applies even where the existence or validity of the contract is in issue, by reason of the inclusion of a provision dealing expressly with applicable law in such cases, namely Article 8, determining existence and validity of a contract or of any term thereof, principally, according to applicable law, *as if the contract or term were valid.* (Article 8 para.1, therefore, is not only a so-called 'bootstraps' rule, in the sense of governing existence of contracts by *inter alia* laws agreed to by parties to contracts (under Article 3) as a term thereof *before* it has in fact been established that the agreement, including that term, is a valid, subsisting contract, but also as treating the Convention as being applicable at all in the first place, notwithstanding that a contract may yet be found not to have entered into existence thereunder – and as *not* then permitting Contracting States' courts to go on to apply their national private international laws of contract, should it be held that no valid contract exists according to applicable law under the Convention, in which event, technically, where the voidness was *ab initio*, the relationship in issue falls outside the Convention's contractual scope.)

Thirdly, how is the defendant's alleged liability to be characterized as contractual or otherwise, say tortious, in accordance with independent Convention criteria, to be developed by the European Court, for the purpose of ascertaining whether the Convention applies to determine applicable law, *before* the very nature of such liability has been able to be established according to applicable law? How should this problem of circularity be dealt with? It is submitted that the correct course for the court to pursue is to decide whether the facts of the claim would amount to a cause of action according to laws applicable to both contract (under the Convention) and tort (under national private international law), and thereafter to classify such species of liability as are found to exist. If the liability under applicable laws is contractual and tortious respectively, the plaintiff has a claim in both contract and tort; if solely contractual, only the first-mentioned law applies; if solely tortious and non-contractual, only the second law(s) referred to would govern (arguably, however, subject to any contractual liability existing under the proper law according to *national*, non-Convention private international law of contract); if liability under applicable laws is tortious and contractual respectively, there is a false conflict and the defendant escapes liability (again, possibly subject to any contractual liability found to exist under national private international law of contract), the latter being a consequence of the fact that Convention and national choice of law rules in contract and tort respectively, as well as the contemplated future Convention definition of contractual, are but policy norms for selection of the appropriate law to govern a particular type of relation on the basis of prescribed connections.

Finally, there are three further points which should be borne in mind.

The first is that under the legal system of England and Wales, courts will largely be reliant upon the parties' pleadings and submissions for information as to nature and content of foreign legal liability in the classificatory process, in the absence of which, foreign law will be assumed to be the same as English (*Ascherberg* v. *Casa Musicale Sonzogno* [1971] 1 WLR 173, p.1128) (or, according to Morris, *Conflict of Laws,* p.41, the court simply applies English law to liability: see above, p.98).

Secondly, in the case of consequences of nullity of a contract, referred to applicable contract law under Article 10(1)(e), yet regarded as restitutionary in nature in the United Kingdom, the latter has specifically entered a reservation against application thereof, under Article 22(1)(b) and 1990 Act s.2(2).

Thirdly, in *The 'Evia Luck'* [1991] 4 All ER 871, HL, a contract (pre-Convention) governed by English law as its proper law was alleged to be void as a result of economic duress exerted in Sweden, where the action complained of was said to be quite lawful. The House of Lords held by a majority (Lords Ackner, Keith, Goff and Lowry, with Lord Templeman dissenting) that the issue of effects of economic duress upon the existence of the contract was a matter for the English proper law of contract to decide, regardless of whether the conduct in question was lawful or not, or would affect contractual validity or not, according to the law of the Swedish place of commission (pp.880-881, 881-882). This was apparently because under domestic English law governing effects of duress upon contractual existence, it was not a requirement that the duress exerted should actually amount to a tort (pp. 881, 882, 883). Presumably, had the latter been the case, then, as an *incidental question* of tort conflicts, to be decided according to English private international law of the English *lex causae* on the main contracts cause (see *Schwebel* v. *Ungar* (1963) 42 DLR (2d) 622), the matter would have had to have been referred by the English courts to Swedish law, as *lex loci delicti*, as well as to English *lex fori*, as laws governing tort, in accordance with the rule laid down for torts in *Phillips* v. *Eyre* (1870) LR 6 QBI, in order to determine whether the conduct amounted to a tort, as a pre-requisite to their decision as to the contractual effects of such tort under the proper law of the contract. Thus, the position as to classification and applicable law may be said to be the converse of that which may be thought to be appropriate in respect of effects of contractual exclusion clauses upon liability in tort: the latter main issue is for applicable laws of *tort*, whereas *contractual* validity and effectiveness of the exclusion clause should be for the applicable law of contract (see earlier, *Brodin* v. *A/R Seljan* 1973 SC 213, and Kaye, *Private International Law of Tort and Product Liability*, 1991, pp. 62-3 – and note *Sayers* v. *International Drilling Co.* [1971] 1WLR 1176 for the contrary approach by the majority of the Court of Appeal, treating the issue as purely contractual). LORD TEMPLEMAN, dissenting in *The 'Evia Luck'* (pp. 874 and 875), held that Swedish law should properly apply to determine whether the claimants were entitled to a remedy, and since the actions to which objection was taken by them were perfectly lawful in Sweden where they were carried out, the proceedings would fail. However, the reasons for LORD TEMPLEMAN'S dissent did not seem to be based upon any disagreement in principle with the majority as to classification and laws to govern contractual and tort issues arising out of contractual effects of alleged duress, or on whether the latter was required or not to amount to a tort under English proper law governing the contract. LORD TEMPLEMAN simply construed the respondents' claim as being one for the tort of economic duress and intimidation and inducement of breach of contract, remedies for which would include restitution of sums paid under contracts coerced and declaration of avoidance of the latter, rather than as a claim for contractual avoidance and restitutionary remedies therefor. It is a little difficult to discern from the law report of the proceedings whether the latter construction was correct, but it must be subject to some doubt from the facts of the case and the majority's approach. Even if LORD TEMPLEMAN's reading of the claim were to be accepted, however, it would still surely be the case that effects upon existence of the contract of alleged economic tortious liability would remain a matter for the law governing the coerced contract, instead of such contractual avoidance having to be held to constitute a remedial measure of the forum.

Obligations

Although Article 1(1) refers to contractual 'obligations' as falling within the Convention's scope, it is clear that this expression has to be construed in the broadest sense, as including not only actions for a remedy for breach of contractual obligations by a defendant, but also those for avoidance of contracts, even *ab initio* (where no obligations would have arisen under the contract), and for a declaration of rights thereunder.

Furthermore, even if the main question in the proceedings is not one of contract, the Convention must nevertheless be applied to any question of the law applicable to an incidental issue involving a contractual obligation, whether as *lex fori*'s private international law (see *Lawrence* v. *Lawrence* [1985] Fam. 106) or that of the Contracting State of *lex causae* on the main cause (see *Schwebel* v. *Ungar* (1963) 42 DLR (2d) 622, affd (1964) 48 DLR (2d) 644). For example, in possession or theft proceedings, themselves outside the Convention's contractual scope, there may be a defence based on a valid contract conferring rights; or in a tort case, the defendant may seek to establish a valid contractual exemption clause (see *Brodin* v. *A/R. Seljan*, 1973 SC 213; *Sayers* v. *International Drilling Co.* [1971] 1 WLR 1176).

Similarly, in the converse case of an *excluded* incidental matter, the Convention continues to govern the main contract issue, as where a husband seeks to rely on the presumption of absence of intention to create legal relations in a contract with a woman whom he alleges to be his wife (*Balfour* v. *Balfour* [1919] 2 KB 571, CA), and the latter denies that they ever went through a valid ceremony of marriage. Unlike the Judgments Convention, therefore, where the jurisdictional implications thereunder require that only the principal, not merely the incidental, nature of proceedings is to be taken into account in determining matters of scope, the Obligations Convention would appear to lay down no corresponding principle: and obligations under a contract, which fall within the Convention's scope, continue to do so, notwithstanding that other terms of the contract – for example, on choice of court (Article 1(2)(d)) – or main elements of liability – such as criminal – are not themselves included.

(C) SITUATIONS INVOLVING A CHOICE BETWEEN THE LAWS OF DIFFERENT COUNTRIES

The Convention is not intended to apply to purely domestic disputes, but only where the situation involves a choice between the laws of different (not necessarily Contracting) countries. This is specifically confirmed by Article 1(1), and the 1990 Act's long title states that it is an Act to make provision as to the law applicable to contractual obligations 'in the case of conflict of laws' (see too Convention Preamble para.2).

Choice Between

The Report states the purpose of the provision to be 'to define the true aims of the uniform rules', and goes on to explain that the true aim is to govern contracts uniformly by a foreign country's law where *lex fori* is not the most appropriate to do so (p.10).

The implications of the approach described in the Report are as follows:

1   a choice between laws of different countries should be held to exist where the situation involves one or more material connections with a country or countries (the German text of Article 1(1) expressly refers to the requirement for a connection with the law of different countries) *other than that of the forum*; and
2   even if *all* relevant connections are established with a *foreign* country as opposed to the forum, the condition in Article 1(1) is apparently still to be regarded as being satisfied, presumably on the basis that – apart from the Convention – courts would always retain the option of deciding to apply *lex fori* rather than foreign law (note LORD PARKER, in *Dynamit AG v. Rio Tinto Co. Ltd* [1918] AC 292, 302), so that a choice (albeit notional) exists notwithstanding exclusivity of connections with the single foreign territory. (The original preliminary draft Convention referred to 'situations of an international character', subsequently dropped for uncertainty and inflexibility: see North, *Contract Conflicts* (1982), p.9; Lando, 'International Situations and Situations Involving a Choice Between the Laws of Different Legal Systems', in Lipstein (ed.), *Harmonisation of Private International Law by the EEC* (1978), pp. 15, 16–17 and 19–20.)

In practice, it is thought, it may not make a great deal of difference whether national private international law or Convention rules govern in such circumstances in which all relevant connections are established with a single foreign country. However, this is not automatically the case: English rules of subjective and objective proper law, and Convention Articles 3 and 4 on applicable law, respectively, are similar, but not entirely on all fours, nor is the scope of proper and applicable law under national and Convention systems respectively, necessarily co-extensive. Thus, for example, under the Convention system, if the latter applies, consent to choice of law may be subjected to applicable law itself (Articles 3(4) and 8); and assessment of damages (Article 10(1)(c)), burden of proof (Article 14(1)) and modes of proof of contract (Article 14(2)) are also for regulation according to that law; whereas, under national private international law rules, *lex fori* may be expected to be referred to in respect of some or all of such matters.

The Report provides examples of foreign connections giving rise to choice of law: foreign nationality or habitual residence of one or all parties to the contract, the fact that the contract was made abroad, foreign place of performance of one or more obligations of parties *et seq.* – thereby giving the legal systems of several countries potentially competing claims to govern the contract. 'These are precisely the situations in which the uniform rules are intended to apply' (p.10).

In addition, it is clear that *choice* of a foreign country's law, where all other connections are with the forum, will also be a factor bringing the Convention into operation, because – as seen – of the existence of a choice as between *lex fori* and the chosen foreign law (similarly in the case of choice of the law of a *foreign* state X, in a situation where all other connections are with *foreign* state Y, by reason of the existence of choice as between (*lex fori* and) the laws of states X and Y – and this is further reinforced in such instances by the express provision made for application of mandatory rules of state Y under Article 3(3) in the circumstances).

A difficult question is whether the foreign connection to be shown under Article 1(1) (as under Article 3(3) – below, Chapter 8) is limited to those which may in some way be said to be *material*, in the sense of being capable of leading to an applicable law. The problem is that few connections are really capable *on their own* of founding applicable law in contract under Convention or other choice of law systems, and will only be *decisive* depending upon the exact circumstances of an individual case and balance of connecting factors therein. Furthermore, if relevant connections were limited to those employed by Convention provisions themselves, this would exclude potentially important factors, including those referred to in the Report, such as nationality, domicile, and previous lengthy habitation. On the other hand, is it right that, under Article 1(1), the Convention should govern a contract entirely connected with England simply because one of the parties' great-grandparents was an Irish immigrant? Obviously not.

It is submitted that the practical compromise solution to the question is for courts only to take *material* connections into account under Article 1(1), but that

1 Convention connections should automatically and irrebuttably be deemed to be material (these will include *inter alia* choice, place of habitual residence, central administration, or place of business of characteristic performer, consumer's habitual residence, employee's place of work, *situs* of immovables, place of conclusion and performance, and situation of insurable risk abroad in a non-EEC state; Article 4(1) on applicable law in the absence of choice in fact permits *any* connection to be considered in assessing country of closest connection – but this need not open the doors to all connections for present purposes, because, unlike the others, such a connection does not necessarily *per se* lead to applicable law, even though it could be decisive in the circumstances of the individual case); and

2 any other connections should be rebuttably presumed *not* to be material, until shown to the court's satisfaction to be capable of being decisive as to applicable law in the case at hand (the onus of proof being heavy, in order to reduce uncertainty for contracting parties), for example, where the parties can be shown to have concluded all of their previous transactions in a particular country of which they are both nationals. (Lipstein, in *Harmonisation,* pp.1,2, considers that a foreign insurer of one of the parties would constitute the otherwise domestic contract *international* and the Convention applicable. This is doubted – not least where the insurance contract is itself outside the Convention's scope under Article 1(3). Similarly, it seems questionable whether the fact that an otherwise domestic contract of guarantee relates to a main contract governed by a foreign law, or to be performed abroad, is necessarily sufficient to constitute the former *international* for Convention purposes.)

Thus, where all material connections are with the forum and no other country, the Convention is inapplicable and national English private international law rules govern. Obviously, in the circumstances, English law will apply thereunder, as would have been the position under the Convention. For all intents and purposes, therefore, the situation is the same as if the Convention had applied, unless, in the case of an express choice of English law, the latter were for some unlikely reason held to be *mala fide* according to national English conflicts rules (*Vita Food Products Inc.* v. *Unus Shipping Co.* [1939] AC 277, p.290 PC, LORD WRIGHT), in which case English law would instead govern as objective proper law (although arguably a sham choice would also have been ineffective under the Convention as well), or in the case of objective proper law in the absence of choice, some foreign connection – not found independently in the Convention, such as law of a ship's flag – were to be accorded overriding influence in the circumstances under national conflicts (but then, such would also surely have been proved to be *material* as a connection under Article 4 for Convention purposes, so as to bring the latter into operation under Article 1(1)). An obvious difference would be that Convention application is subject to any European Court rulings on interpretation (1990 Act s.3(1)), whereas national conflicts is of course free of that particular source of influence – at least on an obligatory basis.

Finally, with regard to the question of whether connections should be assessed for their effects upon internationality as at the time of contracting or as at the later date of institution of proceedings, it is considered that – as is expressly the position in respect of the safeguard for application of mandatory rules of the most connected law but for parties' choice, under Article 3(3) – the former should be regarded as the date of primary importance for such purposes, except to the extent, if any, that matters occurring subsequently thereto are able to be taken into account as being relevant to applicable law according to the rules applied to the question (see below, Chapter 9). If time of institution of proceedings were instead to be adopted as the relevant date, there would be a risk that one of the parties, contemplating commencement of litigation relating to the contract, would then attempt to manipulate the situation – for example, by establishing or discontinuing his residence in the same country as that of the other party – in order to avoid or to secure the Convention's application to the contract as the case may be.

Between the Laws of Different Countries

Article 1(1) is subject to Article 19(1), according to which separate territorial law units, having their own rules of contract, are each to be considered as 'countries' for purposes of identifying applicable law under the Convention – and, consequently, it is implicit, for purposes of assessing applicability of the Convention at all under Article 1(1) – notwithstanding that they form part of a single political country, such as the United Kingdom or the United States (Report, p.10).

Effectively, for present purposes, this is only of relevance for courts within the composite state itself, since for other countries' courts, the foreign connection with *any* part of the former would be sufficient to trigger the Convention's operation as involving a choice of law between the forum and a foreign country or countries under Article 1(1). For English courts, therefore, a material connection with Scotland or Northern Ireland involves a choice between the laws of 'different countries', namely England and Wales and Scotland or Northern Ireland. Article 19(2) specifically permits courts of the different territorial units within such a composite state not to apply the Convention 'to conflicts solely between the laws of such units' (that is to say, where the material foreign connection is solely with another territorial unit). In the United Kingdom, however, it is expressly stated by s.2(3) of the 1990 Act that notwithstanding Article 19(2) of the Convention, the Convention applies 'in the case of conflicts between the laws of different parts of the United Kingdom'.

(D) PRIVATE LAW NATURE OF CONVENTION SCOPE

It is doubted whether 'public' law contracts are included with the scope of the Convention – essentially, an instrument for the selection of, and avoidance of conflicts between, national rules governing private contractual relations. Should, for example, a question involving a French administrative law contract arise incidentally in the course of English main proceedings which are governed by the Convention, it is submitted that Convention rules on applicable law should not apply. It is a pity that the Convention did not so specify by express provision, not only for the sake of certainty, but also because, in the absence thereof, and of the consequent opportunity for the European Court to develop a uniform, independent concept of 'public law contract', it would seem that courts must instead apply the Convention in the first instance, in order to ascertain the private or public law character of the contract, according to applicable law thereunder, a rather circular and potentially unsuitable process where French law, in the example, is found to be inapplicable (see generally, Lipstein, *Harmonisation* (1978), pp.3–4).

2   THEY SHALL NOT APPLY TO:

(a) questions involving the status or legal capacity of natural persons, without prejudice to Article 11;

Status of natural persons, together with its incidents, such as lack of contractual capacity, is excluded from the Convention, with the express exception of provision made under Article 11, according to Article 1(2)(a).

This is so whether the contractual incapacity involved exists in relation to the entire world, as, for example, in the case of a minor, mentally disordered person or prodigal, or solely in relation to a particular person, for example where a wife enters a contract with her husband.

(Legal capacity of companies and associations is separately excluded under Article 1(2)(e) – see below, p.122.)

The Report explains that the intention was to exclude all matters of *family law*, which would include, for example, agreements relating to custody of children (pp.10 and 11). (Exclusion of custody was not mentioned expressly in Article 1(2), in order to avoid an *a contrario* interpretation of the Judgments Convention, which also does not refer expressly to custody in its Article 1 provision on exclusion.) However, it has to be said that, whilst conferral of status is clearly not a matter for applicable law in contract, whether under the Convention or otherwise, and although it may be appreciated that, once a particular status had been conferred according to the national law applicable thereto, it would then have been difficult for equivalent incidents to be attached to such a status according to the applicable law in contract, especially where the latter itself conferred no similar status, nevertheless, it is still by no means clear that the issue of contractual capacity ought necessarily to have been excluded from the Convention (see Hoyer, in *European Private International Law of Obligations* (1975), p. 115, critical of the exclusion of capacity; on the other hand, North, *Contract Conflicts*, p.10, provides as the reason for the exclusion the fact that, while common lawyers classify capacity to contract as being contractual, civil lawyers regard it as a matter of status – see too Dicey and Morris, pp.1205–6). It has been pointed out that whereas, under Article 1 para.2(1) of the Judgments Convention, status and legal capacity are only excluded where they are the principal subject matter of proceedings, the exclusion in the Obligations Convention applies even as an incidental matter, for example where incapacity is raised as a defence (see Lasok and Stone, *Conflict of Laws in the European Community* (1987) p. 351): hence the phrase 'involving…' in Article 1(2)(a) (not in fact to be found in foreign texts).

The effect of the exclusion is that national English rules of private international law govern the conferral of status and contractual capacity upon natural persons – subject to the gloss placed thereon under Article 11.

STATUS

The traditional general rule of English private international law is that *lex domicilii* governs status (*Udny* v. *Udny* (1869) LR 1 Sc. & Div. 44; Graveson, *Conflict of Laws, Private International Law,* 7th edn (1974), p.230) – although, other laws, for example, that of the habitual residence or nationality, may be referred to in particular cases, such as that of recognition of a foreign divorce (see e.g. Family Law Act 1986 s.46(1)).

CONTRACTUAL CAPACITY

There is some uncertainty as to the precise law to govern contractual capacity under national English private international law outside the Convention. Authority exists for each of

- *lex domicilii* (*Sottomayor* v. *De Barros (No.1)* (1877) 3 PD I; *Union Trust Co.* v. *Grosman* 245 US 412 (1918));
- *lex situs* in the case of immovables (*Bank of Africa* v. *Cohen* [1902] 2 Ch. 129 CA);
- *lex loci contractus* (*Male* v. *Roberts* (1800) 3 Esp. 163);
- proper law (probably objective) (*Charron* v. *Montreal Trust Co.* (1958) 15 DLR (2d) 240; *Bodley Head* v. *Flegon* [1972] 1 WLR 680).

Dicey and Morris suggest that capacity according to either the objective proper law or *lex domicilii* should be sufficient for the contract to be upheld (p.1202, Rule 182): and Morris writes

> the law which an English court would apply to the question is obviously anybody's guess. The best solution, it is suggested, is to say that if a person has capacity either by the proper law of the contract or by the law of his domicile and residence, then the contract is valid, so far as capacity is concerned (Morris, *Conflict of Laws*, p.288).

ARTICLE 11 GLOSS

As will be seen, notwithstanding general exclusion of individuals' contractual capacity from the Convention and the consequent operation of national private international law in relation thereto, Article 11 nevertheless provides that a natural person who possesses contractual capacity under the law of the country in which both parties concluded the contract, if such was the case, may only invoke his incapacity under the law otherwise applicable thereto (according to national private international law), if the other party was aware of the incapacity at the time of conclusion of the contract or was not aware thereof as a result of negligence. This means that parties concluding a contract in a particular country are not to be taken by surprise by the other's incapacity under a foreign law: for the latter to apply, the first party must have been, or ought reasonably to have been, aware of the incapacity.

Finally, arguably capacity to make a will or to marry should be held to fall within the broader exclusions of wills and succession, and possibly also marriage, in Article 1(2)(b), rather than the specific capacity category in Article 1(2)(a) – the significance of the distinction being that the latter, but not the former, is subject to Article 11.

(b) contractual obligations relating to:

— wills and succession;
— rights in property arising out of a matrimonial relationship;
— rights and duties arising out of a family relationship, parentage,

marriage or affinity, including maintenance obligations in respect of children who are not legitimate.

WILLS AND SUCCESSION

An agreement to confer a benefit upon somebody under a will, or not to execute a will, would, it is submitted, fall within the Convention's scope in respect of its purely *contractual* effectiveness; whereas, effectiveness of a contractually valid agreement of this nature under the law of *wills and succession* would be excluded. (Lipstein, in Lipstein (ed.)(1978), p.3, considers that contracts to institute heirs – *Erbverträge* – and claims for a statutory portion according to German law, are also thus excluded.) The Hague Convention of 1 August 1989 on the Law Applicable to Succession to the Estates of Deceased Persons would permit a limited choice of law to govern succession matters falling within its scope.

Donatio mortis causa, may be felt to lack the necessary contractual, as opposed to proprietary, element in any event for it to be included within the Convention, whether or not it is to be regarded as a disposition *inter vivos* or as relating to succession (see *Re Korvine's Trusts* [1921] 1 Ch.343, classified as an *inter vivos* transfer; Kaye, *Civil Jurisdiction*, pp.126–7).

On the other hand, promises to make *inter vivos* gifts, where capable of giving rise to a binding contractual obligation, according to an independent Convention classification on the basis of a comparative study of Contracting States' laws of contract, clearly do fall within the Convention's scope, provided that they are not covered by excluded family law (Report, pp.10–11). (Since trusts are excluded under Article 1(2)(g), problems of deciding whether testamentary trusts are excluded matters of succession or not are avoided; contrast the position in the case of the Judgments Convention, which does not exclude trusts from its scope.)

RIGHTS IN PROPERTY ARISING OUT OF A MATRIMONIAL RELATIONSHIP

Similar questions are posed as those under the Judgments Convention, which contains an identical exclusion in Article 1 para.2(1).

Clearly, agreements entered into between spouses, which have no direct bearing upon, nor specific association with, the marital state, fall outside the exclusion.

As for contracts to transfer property, which are made in fulfilment of a financial order or settlement on divorce, annulment or separation, and community property regimes, where these are regarded as being founded upon some sort of implied contract (see *De Nicols* v. *Curlier* [1900] AC 21), it seems clear that such contracts are to be regarded as excluded from the Convention's scope, as being closely associated with and following upon the matrimonial relationship.

Thus, in the Judgments Convention case of *de Cavel* v. *de Cavel (No. 1)*, Case 143/78 [1979] ECR 1055, the European Court distinguished between, on the one hand, disputes concerning or closely connected with proprietary legal relationships between spouses *resulting directly from the matrimonial relationship or the dissolution thereof*, and, on the other hand, proprietary legal relations existing between them *which have no connection with the marriage*, the former, but not the latter, being excluded from the Judgments Convention (*ibid.*, p.1066). As to whether a particular transaction falls within one or other category, it should not be too difficult a task for courts to determine whether the contract stems from the matrimonial bond or is, on a common-sense view, independent thereof (see Kaye, *Civil Jurisdiction*, pp.101–2, and *C.H.W.* v. *G.J.H.*, Case 25/81 [1982] ECR 1189).

One difference which exists, however, between respective scope of Judgments and Obligations Conventions is that, whereas the former applies to maintenance claims between husband and wife (see *de Cavel* v. *de Cavel (No.2)*, Case 120/79 [1980] ECR 731), the Report states that maintenance agreements 'which parties under a legal maintenance obligation make in performance of that obligation' are excluded from the Obligations Convention's scope under Article 1(2)(b) – presumably, as a right or duty 'arising out of a family relationship' (p.10). All other contractual obligations nonetheless – even if providing for *maintenance* of a member of the family, towards whom there are no legal maintenance obligations other than those existing under the contract (for example, where an uncle promises an allowance to his favourite niece: or vice versa!) – are within the Convention's scope. Difficult questions, therefore, which arise under the Judgments Convention, concerning whether provision for financial support amounts to excluded matrimonial property matters between spouses or to non-excluded maintenance (see Kaye, *Civil Jurisdiction,* p.103 *et seq.*), do not occur in connection with the Obligations Convention.

RIGHTS AND DUTIES ARISING OUT OF A FAMILY RELATIONSHIP, PARENTAGE, MARRIAGE OR AFFINITY, INCLUDING MAINTENANCE OBLIGATIONS IN RESPECT OF CHILDREN WHO ARE NOT LEGITIMATE

As with the matrimonial property exclusion, agreements intended to be excluded are those which are materially affected in some legal way specifically by the familial bond, and which either alter, confirm or create parties' legal rights and duties by reason of their family membership. Agreements relating to an existing legal obligation, under the relevant legal system, to maintain an illegitimate child, are expressly referred to as being excluded from the Convention's scope. (This is for the avoidance of doubt, and as seen, therefore, it should not be concluded therefrom that such maintenance *generally* is within the Convention's scope. It is not. Presumably too, however, in accordance with the general principle referred to, agreements to maintain an illegitimate child, where there is not otherwise a legal obligation to do so, are included within the Convention's scope.)

(c) obligations arising under bills of exchange, cheques and promissory notes and other negotiable instruments to the extent that the obligations under such other negotiable instruments arise out of their negotiable character;

EFFECT OF EXCLUSION

The effect of this exclusion is that the contract comprised in the *original* transaction on the drawing up of the instrument between the drawer and payee, and the *supervening* contracts taking place on indorsement, and on acceptance of the instrument, are excluded from the Convention's scope and are governed by national choice of law rules: *except that* neither the contract – for example, for the sale of goods – in respect of which the negotiable instrument is used as a method of payment, nor a contract for the purchase and sale of the instrument itself (that is to say, its transfer other than by way of negotiation) is covered by the exclusion (Report, p.11; note *Moulis* v. *Owen* [1907] 1 KB 745, where a loan and the cheque given in payment were governed respectively by different applicable laws; see too *E. F. Hutton & Co. (London) Ltd* v. *Abdul Ghani Mofarrij* [1989] 2 Lloyd's Rep. 348 CA).

The Report provides reasons for the exclusion: Convention provisions were not suited to regulation of such obligations (arguably, greater certainty is required in this area of commerce than would be possible under the Convention's choice of law rule in Article 4, in the absence of express selection by the parties); some EEC states regard such obligations as non-contractual; international regulation is already available under *inter alia* the Geneva Convention of 7 June 1930 for the Settlement of Certain Conflicts of Laws in Connection with Bills of Exchange and Promissory Notes, and the Geneva Convention of 19 March 1931 for the Settlement of Certain Conflicts of Laws in Connection with Cheques (to each of which the United Kingdom itself is not a party) (*ibid.*).

Thus, national English conflicts rules relating to bills of exchange are contained in the Bills of Exchange Act 1882: formal validity of the instrument is governed by the law of the place of issue, as place of first delivery, and interpretation and formal and essential validity of contracts comprised in bills of exchange are referred to the law of the place in which any such contract is made (Bills of Exchange Act 1882 s.72(1), (2); *G. & H. Montage GmbH* v. *Irvani* [1988] 1 WLR 1285, affd [1990] 1 WLR 667 (CA) – although, *lex fori* will classify the transaction as involving a negotiable instrument, or indorsement, or not, albeit in taking into account a foreign *lex loci contractus's* concepts, *ibid.*; see too *Banco Atlantico S.A.* v. *British Bank of the Middle East* [1990] 2 Lloyd's Rep.504 (CA)). The place where each such supervening contract is *made* is the place where that contract is completed by delivery (*Chapman* v. *Cottrell* (1865) 3 H. & C. 865) (presumably, this is according to English *lex fori*: Graveson, however, in *The Conflict of Laws*, p.452, recognizes that choice of law ought to be involved in determining place of conclusion itself). Need for protest or notice of dishonour is for the law of the place where the bill of exchange is dishonoured (Bills of Exchange Act 1882 s.72(3) – *G. & H. Montage GmbH*).

Choice of law on capacity to draw a bill of exchange or to become liable under any of its supervening contracts is not specifically regulated by the 1882 Act and is accordingly subject to normal English private international rules of contract (see Bills of Exchange Act 1882 ss.22(1) and 97(2) – capacity co-extensive with normal contractual capacity; the 1930 Geneva Convention refers capacity to *lex nationalis*,to which the United Kingdom could not agree). This means, as seen, principally the proper law, and possibly also *lex domicilii* and *lex loci contractus* in the alternative (see *Bondholders Securities Corporation* v. *Manville* (1933) 4 DLR 699; *Re Soltykoff, ex p.Margrett* [1891] 1 QB 413). These national applicable laws are not subject to the special rule in Article 11 of the Obligations Convention, because although the latter is an express exception to the exclusion of individuals' contractual capacity from the Convention's scope under Article 1(2)(a), the specific exclusion of negotiable instruments in Article 1(2)(c) overrides the more general exclusion in Article 1(2)(a) and is consequently not subject to Article 11.

NEGOTIABLE INSTRUMENTS

The Report provides two hints as to the characterization of negotiable instruments for Convention purposes.

In the first place, by way of a partial definition of negotiable instrument, it indicates that a document may be transferable, yet not also negotiable, in which case it is not covered by the exclusion. This means, according to the Report, that (i) 'such documents as bills of lading, similar documents issued in connection with transport contracts, and bonds, debentures, guarantees, letters of indemnity, certificates of deposit, warrants and warehouse receipts' are only excluded by Article 1(2)(c) if they can be regarded as negotiable instruments; and (ii) 'even then the exclusion only applies with regard to obligations arising out of their negotiable character' (p.11 – see too von Hoffmann, in Lando (ed.) (1975), *European Private International Law of Obligations*, p.30).

In the second place, as a choice of law indication, the Report states that whether a document is to be characterized as a negotiable instrument or not, is *not* governed by the Convention, but is a matter for the forum's law, including its rules of private international law (*ibid.*). According to English private international law therefore, such 'negotiability' is to be conferred by the law of the country in which the instrument is transferred (see Dicey and Morris, p.1322; *Alcock* v. *Smith* [1892] 1 Ch.238 (CA); *Embiricos* v. *Anglo-Austrian Bank* [1904] 2 KB 870; *Koechlin et Cie* v. *Kestenbaum* [1927] 1 KB 889).

It is submitted that there is no real inconsistency between the two preceding lines of approach in the Report: their effect is simply that, whereas legal characteristics of a documentary transaction, alleged to be a negotiable instrument, are to be attached in accordance with the law applicable thereto under national private international law rules of the forum, the question of whether a transaction of such nature by virtue of applicable national law *amounts to a negotiable instrument for purposes of the Convention* is to be decided according to whether its characteristics are in conformity with an independent Community definition of negotiable instruments or not. Thus, under pre-existing English private international law, documents are classified as negotiable instruments where according to statute or the custom of merchants they are recognized as possessing such qualities as conform to a general concept of negotiability for the purposes, evidently including the ability to confer upon the transferee by delivery (and indorsement) in good faith and for value a better claim than that possessed by the transferor with defective title (Graveson, *The Conflict of Laws*, p.445; *Picker* v. *London Bank* (1887) 18 QBD 519; *Goodwin* v. *Robarts* (1876) 1 App. Cas. 476).

For Convention purposes, therefore, the preceding national concept is simply replaced by a Convention meaning of negotiable instrument, with which the attributes conferred are to conform. Presumably, the Community definition to be developed will not differ greatly from the national English meaning referred to.

(d) arbitration agreements and agreements on the choice of court;

The Report reveals that exclusion of these areas proved contentious (pp.11–12).

CHOICE OF COURT AGREEMENTS

These are excluded as forming part of procedure and the administration of justice, as well as possibly also being affected by public policy considerations limiting freedom of contract, and as displaying such disunity as might have threatened the ratification of the Convention.

Furthermore, their validity was said to be subject to *lex fori* rather than applicable law of contract: and within the EEC, most important matters of form and validity were governed by Article 17 of the Judgments Convention (p.11).

It is submitted that some of these arguments are spurious.

First, Article 17 does indeed govern form, and the underlying purpose of the provision is certainly to establish existence of consensus between the parties as to choice of court (see S*alotti* v. *RÜWA*, Case 24/76 [1976] ECR 1831; [1977] 1 CMLR 345; *Segoura* v. *Bonakdarian*, Case 25/76 [1976] ECR 1851; [1977] 1 CMLR 361). However, it is argued forcefully elsewhere that there is no reason to believe that such rule operates *in place of* national applicable law requirements as to contractual consent and essential validity of the jurisdiction agreement, rather than merely *in addition thereto* in Convention cases (see Kaye, *Civil Jurisdiction*, pp.1070–81).

Secondly, whereas the question of *effect* to be given to a valid jurisdiction clause is a matter of procedure and administration of justice for courts applied to, to be decided according to their own rules, whether of the Judgments Convention or otherwise, nevertheless this does not also entail that the initial question of the jurisdiction agreement's *contractual validity* should also be subject to *lex fori*'s rules on contract, or alternatively, discarded altogether as a precondition of the agreement's effectiveness (see Dicey and Morris, p.405; Lipstein, in Lipstein (ed.) (1978), p.3; *Kahn-Freund* (1977), 26 ICLQ 825; *Mackender* v. *Feldia AG* [1967] 2 QB 590; '*The Iran Vojdan*' [1984] 2 Lloyd's Rep. 380; *The Frank Pais* [1986] 1 Lloyd's Rep. 529).

ARBITRATION AGREEMENTS

The United Kingdom wished these to be included in the Convention's scope, as presenting standard contract questions and as not sufficiently harmonized by international conventions, which were ratified by only some of the EEC states and not by others. However, the views of the French and German Convention negotiators, in favour of exclusion, were to prevail, on the grounds that procedural and contractual aspects – the former necessarily being excluded – were hard to separate; that the matter was complex and the Convention's closest connection principle in the absence of choice of law (Article 4(1)) difficult to apply in the case of arbitration agreements; that separate treatment of arbitration clauses from other aspects of the main contract was quite in accordance with the Convention principle of severability (Article 3(1)); and that there were a sufficient number of international conventions in the area and the International Chamber of Commerce felt there to be no need for further regulation (Articles II and V of the New York Convention of 1958 on the Recognition and Enforcement of Foreign Arbitral Awards concerned the validity of arbitration agreements; other international arbitration conventions were the Geneva Convention of 1927 (and 1923 Protocol), the Hague Convention of 1965, and the European (Geneva) Convention of 1961) (Report, p.12). The decision was consequently taken to exclude arbitration in its entirety from the Convention and then to return to study the question of arbitration and choice of court agreements separately, with a view to placing their regulation in a separate protocol. (In the recent Judgments Convention case of *Marc Rich and Co. AG* v. *Società Italiana Impianti PA*, *'The Atlantic Emperor'*, Case C-190/89 (1991) *The Times*, 20 September, the European Court ruled, on a reference from the English Court of Appeal for interpretation of the scope of the arbitration exclusion in Article 1(4) of the Judgments Convention, that proceedings for appointment of an arbitrator and concerning the existence or validity of an arbitration agreement as a preliminary issue, were covered by the exclusion.)

As in the case of court jurisdiction agreements, it is submitted that a distinction *could* have been drawn between procedural effects of valid arbitration clauses, to be subjected to *lex arbitrii*, and contractual validity of the arbitration agreement, which might have been subjected to applicable law of contract and, consequently, to the Convention's rules. (Giardina, in North (ed.) (1982), *Contract Conflicts*, p.248, thinks that application of the Convention could offer arbitrators and national judges a unifying and practical means of applying common criteria to validity of arbitration clauses, in place of the developing trend according to which arbitrators decide on existence and validity of arbitration agreements autonomously of national procedural laws.)

SCOPE OF EXCLUSION

The Convention is inapplicable not merely to effects of arbitration and jurisdiction agreements, but also to matters such as their form, validity and consent thereto. In addition, it is submitted, in accordance with the approach of the European Court in *'The Atlantic Emperor'* (*supra*), in relation to the arbitration exclusion under Article 1 para. 2(4) of the Judgments Convention, the corresponding exclusion of arbitration and jurisdiction agreements in Article 1(2)(d) of the Obligations Convention should receive a broad interpretation. Thus, not merely the agreement itself to arbitrate, or on courts to adjudicate, should be held to be excluded: other terms relating thereto, for example, as to costs, curial law and arbitral appointment, should also be considered to fall outside the Convention's scope.

However, as the Report points out:

a   where an arbitration clause is an integral part of a larger contract and not an independent agreement, the exclusion only relates to the arbitration clause and not to the remainder of the contract – although, law governing the main contract under the Convention may still be influential as to law applicable to the arbitration term under national private international law (which may otherwise often be that of state of arbitration – see Arbitration Act 1975 s.5(2)(b) in the enforcement context: enforcement of a Convention award may be refused if the person against whom it is invoked proves ... that the arbitration agreement was not valid under the law to which the parties subjected it or, failing any indication thereon, *under the law of the country where the award was made*); and (conversely)

b   an excluded arbitration or jurisdiction agreement may still be taken into account for purposes of deciding upon implied choice of law to govern the main contract under Article 3(1) or country of closest connection under Article 4(1) (p.12; and *Compagnie d'Armement Maritime SA v. Compagnie Tunisienne de Navigation SA* [1971] AC 572) (and note the express exclusion of choice of court as preventing application of mandatory rules in the particular situation dealt with under Article 3(3)).

(e) questions governed by the law of companies and other bodies corporate or unincorporate such as the creation, by registration or otherwise, legal capacity, internal organisation or winding up of companies and other bodies corporate or unincorporate and the personal liability of officers and members as such for the obligations of the company or body;

Internal contractual relationships within companies and other legal or commercial entities, such as partnerships and associations, are excluded from the Convention under Article 1(2)(e).

Their *external* contractual relations on the other hand – other than in the matter of their legal capacity to contract, excluded under Article 1(2)(e), and the effects of agency upon liability, excluded generally, and specifically in relation to such entities, under Article 1(2)(f) – fall within the Convention's scope of operation. To this extent, companies' contracts are no less subject to Convention rules on applicable law than are those concluded by natural persons.

The reason for the particular exclusion is not of course lack of economic importance of companies in the EEC; far from it! It was simply that drafters were desirous not to interfere with harmonization work on company law to be conducted separately through Directives within the Community (Report, p.12; see too EEC Treaty, Article 54(3)(g)).

ENTITIES COVERED BY THE EXCLUSION

The Report explains that the list of bodies mentioned as covered by the exclusion in Article 1(2)(e) was made as broad and flexible as it is because of the diversity of national laws as to the types of body which may exist and the consequent need to prevent certain relationships from being held to be governed by the Convention in some countries, and excluded therefrom in others (*ibid.*).

Thus, Article 1(2)(e) refers to questions governed by *the law of*

- companies; or
- other bodies corporate; or
- other bodies unincorporate.

In addition, the Report states that the body may be with or *without legal personality*, and profit-making or *non-profit-making* – and specifically indicates *inter alia* that a *partnership* is included within the exclusion, as an unincorporated 'body' (*ibid.*), as, it would seem, would be an unincorporated association (see Kaye, *Civil Jurisdiction,* p.404).

AREAS COVERED BY THE EXCLUSION

The exclusion expressly includes contractual aspects relating to

- *creation* of the body;
- *legal capacity*;
- *internal organization*, for example, calling of meetings, right to vote, quorum, appointment of officers;
- *winding up*, voluntarily or by operation of law, or for reorganization or merger and the like (mergers and groupings generally are excluded, even though not referred to expressly: Report, p.12; they may be covered by the reference to creation by registration *or otherwise*: see Hansard, HL Vol.513, col.1264);

- *personal liability* of officers and members as such for the obligations of the body.

Accordingly, actions concerning the effect, effectiveness or interpretation of the very constitution of a company or partnership or other such body, or contractual elements arising from such, are excluded. However, the Report points out that pre-incorporation contracts between promoters and third parties, or as between promoters *inter se*, are not excluded (*ibid.*). The latter point is somewhat debatable. The capacity of a company to be bound by transactions made in its name or on its behalf prior to formation, or its incapacity to be or to become so (see *Re English and Colonial Produce Co. Ltd* [1906] 2 Ch. 435 CA), would seem to be a matter of company law, no less than post-formation capacity, notwithstanding that it may also correspond with general, non-corporate legal doctrine according to applicable law; and furthermore, even if viewed as a matter of 'agent's'/'organ's' ability or otherwise to bind a 'principal'/'company' towards a third party (see Companies Act 1985 s.36 C(1)), the issue is excluded in any event under Article 1 (2)(f). (The contrary argument would be that the latter provision is inapplicable according to its terms, there being no 'agent' and no 'principal' by definition; and since 'agent's' personal liability towards the third party is a matter for applicable law under the Convention (see below, p.130), the latter would possibly be inconsistent with that regulating *excluded* corporate liability under national conflicts in the case at hand, and the two matters should be governed by the Convention. The trouble with this argument of course is that ascertainment of common applicable law in the absence of choice under the Convention would be problematical, where 'agent's' and 'principal's' respective habitual residences or central administration were different for purposes of determining applicable law under Article 4(2) or consent to contract under Article 8 para.2.)

The Report explains that as regards exclusion of legal capacity of corporations and associations (note, Article 11 only applies to *natural* persons), the reference is to 'limitations, which may be imposed by law on companies and firms, for example in respect of acquisition of immovable property, not to *ultra vires* acts by organs of the company or firm, which fall under subparagraph (f)' (pp.12–13). The problem with the preceding statement, which could be taken to exclude from Article 1(2)(e) general legal incapacity to transact outside a company's constitution, is that it may well be the case that such legal capacity of a company does nonetheless seem to amount to a question 'governed by the law of companies', as prescribed by Article 1(2)(e): the *law* may state, for example, that a company (other than charitable) is bound contractually to third parties notwithstanding that its acts are beyond its powers and objects (Companies Act 1985 s.35(1), as substituted by Companies Act 1989 s.108(1)). Such matters of acts *ultra vires* the company and their effect upon contractual liability are surely to be considered as being excluded under Article 1(2)(e). The statement above from the Report should therefore not be taken to refer to acts beyond the capacity *of the company itself*, but should be limited to the matter of companies' contractual liability (incurred by virtue of Companies Act 1985 s.35 A(1)) as a result of acts *ultra vires* their *organs and officers*, which latter fall instead within Article 1(2)(f). In either case, whether the defence raised is that a contract sued on is *ultra vires* the company itself, or its officers, so as not to bind the company or third parties, the issue of capacity is governed by national private international law rules (namely, law of the place of incorporation, as corporate seat and domicile: *Risdon Iron and Locomotive Works* v. *Furness* [1906] 1 KB 49 (CA); *J.H.Rayner (Mincing Lane) Ltd* v. *Department of Trade and Industry* [1990] 2 AC 418; *Arab Monetary Fund* v. *Hashim* [1991] 2 AC 114 (H.L.(E.)); Dicey and Morris, *The Conflict of Laws*, 11th edn [1987], p.1134, Rule 174 – subject to any further restrictions according to corporate statute or objective *lex causae* governing the transaction, Dicey and Morris, *ibid.*, p.1135), even though the remainder of the contract may be subject to a different law under the Convention (as may also be the position in the case of natural persons, by virtue of Article 1(2)(a)).

In respect of matters of internal organization, where members have a contractual right against the company or association that prescribed rules and procedures affecting their rights should be observed, and vice versa (or, in theory, *inter se*), such disputes are excluded under Article 1(2)(e). It is possible to argue that such internal *contractual* matters do not fall within the sphere of Article 1(2)(e) as 'questions governed by the law of companies and other bodies corporate or unincorporate', given precisely their nature as contractual rather than company law questions, if *governed by the law of companies* is so to be construed as meaning regulation according to principles and norms applying specifically to or for the purposes of such company issues, as opposed to operation of general legal and contractual doctrine thereto. In the present submission, the latter would be incorrect: in the first place, so restrictive an interpretation of the text of Article 1(2)(e), effectively reducing the latter to mere declaratory status, would produce complexities and divergencies inimical to the unificationist objectives of Article 1(2)(e) and the remainder of the Convention's provisions on scope, in requiring courts to define so restrictively the amorphous term 'company law', which may even have different connotations from one Contracting State's law to another's (see *Peters* v. *ZNAV*, Case 34/82 [1983] ECR 987, 993, as to Dutch law on the relationship between associations and members in the Judgments Convention context of jurisdiction over *contracts*; and

Kaye, *Civil Jurisdiction,* p.492); and secondly, if questions governed by the law of companies under Article 1(2)(e) were to be construed as being limited to those which were not of such contractual nature, it would then be difficult to comprehend why it should thus have been felt necessary to exclude such *non-contractual* matters from the Convention's scope, limited as the latter is to *contractual* obligations under Article 1(1) in any event. Accordingly, it is considered that internal corporate contractual issues should be regarded as 'questions governed by the law of companies' for purposes of Article 1(2)(e) for the sake of simplicity, uniformity, principle, and compliance with the text: simply because the matter is essentially one of contractual legal principle, this does not then mean that it cannot also be held to constitute a question of company law – on the contrary, it is exactly the *internal* corporate functioning of such principle that renders the latter part of the overall corpus of company law, irrespective of its wider source in the general law of contract.

Thus, the memorandum and articles of an English registered company constitute a contract, binding the company and members to each other, under Companies Act 1985 s.14 (1) (see too *Pender* v. *Lushington* (1877) 6 Ch. D 70); and in the Judgments Convention case of *Peters* v. *ZNAV*, Case 34/82 [1983] ECR 987, the European Court held that proceedings brought by a Dutch association against a German member, to enforce the latter's obligations towards the rest under the rules of the association, were matters relating to a *contract* for purposes of Article 5(1) of the Judgments Convention, and that this was so whether the obligation in question arose simply from the fact of becoming a member or from that act in conjunction with a decision of an organ of the association; (interestingly, in that case, the exclusion provision under Article 1(2)(e) of the Obligations Convention was variously referred to by participants in the European Court proceedings as either being in support of the view that, given the Article 1(2)(e) exclusion, internal association relations were consequently *non*-contractual for Judgments Convention purposes (p.993), or of the view that existence of the exclusion under Article 1(2)(e) demonstrated that internal association matters would not otherwise have been held to fall outside the Obligations Convention's scope and that these were consequently contractual (pp.995 and 1011–Advocate General Mancini), together with contractual aspects of other matters dealt with under Article 1(2)(e), such as creation or winding up of corporate and unincorporate bodies – the former of the preceding two lines of argument having been criticized above, as being based upon the fallacious assumption that excluded *company law* questions under Article 1(2)(e) would necessarily entail their exclusive corporate, *non-contractual* status, an approach justified neither on principle, textual analysis, nor practical and uniform expedience); while, again, in the Judgments Convention case of *Powell Duffryn plc* v. *Petereit*, Case C-214/89 (1992) *The Times*, 15 April, the European Court held that a German company's articles of association constituted a *contract* between both company and shareholders, and shareholders *inter se*, and that consequently a choice of jurisdiction clause contained in the articles amounted to an agreement conferring jurisdiction as between those parties, so as to satisfy the requirements for effectiveness laid down in Article 17 of the European Judgments Convention. Proceedings to enforce such internal corporate contracts therefore are excluded under Article 1(2)(e).

Furthermore, actions excluded under Article 1(2)(e) are not limited to those brought by members in respect of their personal rights under the constitution: derivative actions for an injunction to prevent the directors from acting for, or binding (see Companies Act 1985 s.35 (3)) the company in contract beyond its powers are also covered by the exclusion. However, actions to injunct directors from acting beyond *their own* powers, so as to bind the company under s.35 A(1) of the Companies Act 1985, are excluded under Article 1(2)(f), rather than (e); and derivative actions against directors for breach of their fiduciary duties, under one of the exceptions to the rule in *Foss* v. *Harbottle* (1843) 2 Ha. 461, would not even seem to be *contractual* in nature in any event (see *Newtherapeutics Ltd* v. *Katz* [1990] 3 WLR 1183,1206, where KNOX J declined to treat the mere office of director, without the existence of a separate service contract, as being contractual, in the strictly defined context of RSC Order 11 r.1(1) discretionary jurisdiction grounds).

In addition, contractual obligations undertaken in the course of a winding up or merger – for example, agreement by the company or other shareholders to purchase a dissenting minority's shares, or a share exchange agreement, or purchase of undertaking – fall within the exclusion in Article 1 (2)(e).

Excluded personal liability of officers and members as such for the obligations of the company or body, as well as including matters such as partner's liability for acts of the others in the course of a partnership business, will also cover, for example, personal liability of an officer of a company towards a contracting party under Companies Act 1985 s.349, where the company's name has been used incorrectly, or of directors of a public company under s.117(8) when the contract is made before the company is entitled to commence business, in prescribed circumstances, or of a member for the company's debts under s.24, when the number of members falls below the minimum. (On the other hand, any *personal* – non-quasi- – contractual liability of an officer acting beyond his agent's-authority, towards a third party, under general legal principle, would not seem to be a matter of company law under Article 1(2)(e), nor within the terms of

Article 1(2)(f), and accordingly is to be regarded as falling within the Convention's scope – a potential source of confusion and disruption where the latter law is inconsistent with that exculpating the company itself from such liability under national conflicts.)

In *J.H. Rayner (Mincing Lane) Ltd* v. *Department of Trade and Industry* [1990] 2 AC 418, it was confirmed that members' personal liability for a corporation's debts was a matter for the law of the place of its incorporation under English private international law – although, any such liability under *public* international treaty law would be non-justiciable in national domestic courts of the United Kingdom (see too *Arab Monetary Fund* v.*Hashim* [1991] 2 AC 114, 164, 169 (H.L.(E.))).

Article 1(2)(e) merely provides *examples* of excluded matters governed by company law, not an exclusive list ('questions ...such as ...'). Other issues may therefore be within the exclusion, provided that they are subject to company law, such as the setting aside of transactions as preferences under s.239 of the Insolvency Act 1986, and inability of companies, which fail properly to publicize their business name, to enforce their contracts, under s.5 of the Business Names Act 1985.

(f) the question whether an agent is able to bind a principal, or an organ to bind a company or body corporate or unincorporate, to a third party;

PRINCIPAL–AGENT RELATIONS NOT EXCLUDED

Questions involving the contractual relations between principal and agent themselves (for example, agent's commission, extent of actual authority, principal's duty to provide information and supply goods to the agent, and agent's remuneration and liability to removal) – governed according to pre-existing national English conflicts rules by the proper law of the contract creating the agency (*Maspons* v. *Mildred* (1882) 9 QBD 530; affd (1883) 8 App. Cas. 874) – are not covered by the exclusion and thus fall within the scope of the Convention. Under pre-existing English private international law, proper law of the principal–agent contract will frequently be that of the country *in which the agent is to perform the contract* (*Chatenay* v. *Brazilian Submarine Telegraph Co.* [1891] 1 QB 79), but not necessarily so, especially if the agency extends to a number of countries (*Mauroux* v. *Sociedade Comercial Abel Pereira da Fonseca SARL* [1972] 2 All ER 1085): thus, the law of the place where the principal carries on business is given considerable weight, especially where the agent sought out the principal there (*Arnott* v. *Redfern* (1825) 2 C. & P. 88); and Dicey and Morris (p. 1339, Rule 200) state that an agent's authority as between himself and the principal is governed by the law with reference to which the agency is constituted, which in general is the law of the country where the relation of principal and agent is created. According to Article 4(2) of the Convention, however, in the absence of express or implied choice of law under Article 3, the law of the country in which the party performing the characteristic obligation under the agency contract – clearly, the agent rather than the principal – *has his habitual residence or its central administration, or otherwise its relevant place of business in the course of a trade or profession* governs, as that of the country presumed (rebuttably, under Article 4(5)) to have the closest connection with the contract. Unless, therefore, courts were to follow the previous law's decisions, through permitting the presumption to be rebutted in favour of place of agent's performance in such agency cases, there is a possibility that a different applicable law may prevail SUBJECT TO

- operation of any mandatory rules of the forum under Article 7(2); and
- the possibility that agency contracts will be equated with *employment contracts* under Article 6(2), according to which, in the absence of choice, law of the country in which the employee habitually works, or of his employer's relevant place of business, if he does not habitually carry out his work in any one country, governs the employment contract: a solution which plainly bears a close relation to the position on applicable law on agency under pre-existing English rules referred to.

As to whether an agent's contract may thus be equated with contracts of employment under Article 6:

a the concept of 'contract of employment' should be interpreted in a uniform, autonomous manner, independently of specific national meanings under individual Convention States' laws; and
b assistance may be derived from European Court rulings on the meaning of 'branch, agency or other establishment' under Article 5(5) of the Judgments Convention, as distinguishing agents and employees: the distinction would seem to turn on the relative levels of control and independence of principal and representative respectively, insufficiency of the former suggesting absence of the employment- and, depending upon the extent thereof, even agency (under Article 5(5), as opposed to legal *agent's*)-relationship, and lack of the latter pointing to existence of employment (and even agency – if not mere legal agent's – under Article 5(5), provided that a necessary degree of independence re-

mains) (see *Ivenel* v. *Schwab*, Case 133/81 [1982] ECR 1891; *Somafer* v. *Saar-Ferngas*, Case 33/78 [1978] ECR 2183; *Blanckaert and Willems* v. *Trost*, Case 139/80 [1981] ECR 819; *SAR Schotte GmbH* v. *Parfums Rothschild S.a.r.l.*, Case 218/86[1987] ECR 4905).

EXISTENCE OF PRINCIPAL–THIRD PARTY RELATIONS EXCLUDED

Once it has been decided according to relevant applicable law (see below) that principal and third party are bound contractually towards each other as a result of the agent's representation activities, the contract thus concluded between the former is subject to applicable law *under the Convention* in all its facets to the extent that these fall within the latter's scope, including standard and mode of performance, interpretation and discharge (see Article 10).

However, the question whether an agent has bound a principal, or an organ a company or body corporate or unincorporate, to a third party in the first place is excluded from the Convention under Article 1(2)(f), because it was considered 'difficult to accept the principle of freedom of contract on this point' (Report, p.13). (Surely though, agency could have been made the subject of a special Convention provision, limiting party autonomy?)

National conflicts rules (see too below, p.368, for international convention law) consequently govern the issues of whether the principal is bound towards a third party by apparent and ostensible authority of an agent where the latter exceeded his actual authority or lacked any at all through revocation or otherwise, or whether an undisclosed or unidentified principal can sue or be sued on a contract made by an agent with a third party, or whether a company is bound by transactions exceeding the directors' authority (Companies Act 1985 s.35A(1)), or whether shareholders can obtain an injunction to prevent the company from becoming bound thereby.

The national conflicts rule in such cases is that the 'rights and liabilities of the principal as regards third parties are, in general, governed by the proper law of the contract concluded between the agent and the third party' (Dicey and Morris, *The Conflict of Laws* (1987) p.1341, Rule 201). This may be the law of the country in which the agent acts (*Chatenay* v. *Brazilian Submarine Telegraph Co.* [1891] 1 QB 79), or of another country, if the latter is more closely connected with the contract made by the agent (Dicey and Morris, *The Conflict of Laws* (1987), pp.1341–6; Cheshire and North, *Private International Law* (1987), p.494 – which perhaps may be the case where the breach of actual authority by the agent consists of, or includes, his acting in the former). Arguably, in order to determine the law governing the contract between agent and third party for such purposes of deciding whether the principal is bound under national conflicts, it should be the Convention's rules which operate to identify that law, rather than national private international law itself, since it would seem strange for the former to govern all aspects of contractual performance and validity other than that of whether the principal is actually a party thereto, especially if Convention applicable law took a different line from national proper law on the latter issue. On the other hand, it could be put that such a course should not be followed, because to apply a 'principal's' law *putatively* to the question of applicable law under Article 4(2) in the absence of choice (or *a fortiori*, any law, as a result of the 'agent's' choice under Article 3) before it is established that the principal–agent relationship exists and has been given effect to, simply begs the question of whether such steps are at all justified. (A similar question arises in connection with Article 9(3), which provides, for the purposes of applicable law on formal validity of contracts under Article 9(1) and (2), that where the contract is concluded by an agent, the country *in which the agent acts* is the relevant country; presumably, before Article 9(3) can be applied, it must first be established according to relevant applicable law that the 'principal' is able to be bound by such 'agent's' acts in relation to contractual conclusion or otherwise. National conflicts rules, in accordance with Article 1(2)(f), must provide the answer, and not – as might simply be assumed – *lex fori*'s agency law. Indeed, it could be argued that the same considerations apply to the special rule on capacity of natural persons to contract under Article 11, even though the latter does not expressly refer to the country in which an agent acts.)

Needless to say, where the alleged liability of undisclosed principals is said to derive from public international treaty law, the matter is not justiciable in the domestic English courts (see *J.H.Rayner (Mincing Lane) Ltd* v. *Department of Trade and Industry* [1990] 2 AC 418; and *Arab Monetary Fund* v. *Hashim* [1991] 2 AC 114).

RELATIONS BETWEEN AGENT AND THIRD PARTY NOT EXCLUDED

The Report states that the exclusion in Article 1(2)(f) does not affect relations between principal and agent and, notably, 'agent–third party relationships' (p.13).

Thus, rights and obligations arising as between the agent himself and the third party are not excluded. This means that the Convention governs matters such as whether the agent has created privity of contract between himself and the third party, rights and liabilities of agents acting for undisclosed or unidentified principals, and agent's liability for breach of warranty of authority.

It seems rather remarkable that these latter relations are not also excluded from the Convention by Article 1(2)(f). At national private international law, relations between agent and third party are subject to the law according to which the agent purported to act and governing alleged contractual relations between himself and the third party, as in the case of principal–third party relations (Dicey and Morris, p.1346). Under the Convention, in the absence of express or implied choice of law, as indicated, law of the country of the habitual residence, central administration or relevant place of business of the agent (if performer of characteristic obligation as between himself and third party) is rebuttably presumed to be most closely connected applicable law under Article 4(2). Failing rebuttal, therefore, under Article 4(5), a situation could arise in which the law of the agent's habitual residence under the Convention were to treat the agent as being in breach of his warranty of authority due to lack of actual or apparent authority to bind the principal, whereas the law of the country in which the agent acts, governing relations between principal and third party at national private international law, would hold the principal to be bound to the third party through ostensible authority of the agent, thereby affording the third party *two bites at the litigational cherry* (unless it were considered that the question of agent's possession of authority in such a case should be governed by national private international law, and solely the issue of whether the agent was liable for warranting any authority alleged to be lacking thereunder, by applicable law under the Convention); or the converse might be the case, in which event the third party would have recourse against no one. (The situation would be even more complicated if the matter were regarded as relating to *consent* to contract, in consequence of which different laws could apply to principal and agent under Article 8 para.2.) Principal–third party and agent–third party relations would seem to be so interwoven that both should be governed by a common system of choice of law, likely to lead to the same applicable law. If the former is excluded from the Convention's scope, then the latter should also have been so.

(g) the constitution of trusts and the relationship between settlors, trustees and beneficiaries;

SCOPE OF EXCLUSION

The proprietary and internal relations of the trust are excluded from the Convention, as they should be. The mutual rights and liabilities of settlor, trustees and beneficiaries under a completely constituted trust are governed by the law of trusts, not contract. Similarly, the creation of an express or implied trust by declaration or otherwise is proprietary, not contractual. (The 1986 Hague Convention on the law applicable to trusts and on their recognition, given effect to in the United Kingdom by the Recognition of Trusts Act 1987, to which it is scheduled, would have to be accorded precedence under Article 21 of the Obligations Convention in any event, even if such internal matters were to be classified as contractual.)

External contracts, between trustees or beneficiaries and third parties, in the course of administering the trust, are not covered by the exclusion however, and therefore fall within the Convention's scope.

Furthermore, it is submitted, contracts entered *in the course of constituting* a declared trust – as, for example, where the settlor executes a contract in a deed agreeing to transfer property to declared trustees of a newly created or existing trust prior to effecting the actual transfer (or where the settlor ineffectively attempts to transfer the property under a binding contract to create a trust) – or *in the course of distributing trust assets* to beneficiaries – for example, where the transfer is ineffective and operates as a contract to do so – are also not to be regarded as excluded from the Convention. Generally therefore, it is believed, a distinction should be drawn between rights to property or other benefits and services under the trust – excluded from the Convention – and contractual rights under formal contracts preceding transfer – not excluded from the Convention, according to the view here canvassed.

Trusts

The Report states that 'trust' in Article 1(2)(g) is to be understood in the English common law sense: 'The English word "trust" is properly used to define the scope of the exclusion. On the other hand similar institutions under continental laws fall within the provisions of the Convention because they are normally contractual in origin' (p.13).

'Trust' is therefore to be given the English meaning, as a Convention concept. This will clearly exclude from the notion of trusts the Continental doctrines whereby the contract in favour of a third party – *Vertrag zugunsten Dritter* (Article 328, German Civil Code)/*stipulation au profit d'un tiers ou pour autrui* (Article 1121 French Civil Code), *stipulazione a favore di un terzo* (Article 1411 Italian Civil Code) – is given effect to on a purely contractual basis, as well as those cases in which English law itself is prepared to allow the third party to join the promisee as co-plaintiff, as trustee of the benefit of the contract, in an action against the promisor in favour of the third party (*Les Affréteurs Réunis SA* v. *Leopold Walford (London) Ltd* [1919] AC 801, HL).

On the other hand, the Report goes on to say that it is open to judges to treat Continental institutions in the same way as the common law trust, 'when they exhibit the same characteristics', the latter not also being defined by the authors (p.13). It would seem unlikely however that the *Auftrag* (mandate), *Treuhand* (fiduciary holding) or *Sicherungsübereignung* (security transfer) could be regarded as equivalent to trusts, since the remedies they afford are essentially contractual in nature, while the *Stiftung/fondation* (foundation) is founded upon legal personality and rights and duties attached thereto; and the French wives' matrimonial dowry regime (*biens dotaux*), inalienable, safe from seizure by creditors, and administered by the husband, during the marriage, resemblant in some respects to the trust, is otherwise excluded in any event under Article 1(2)(b), as relating to rights in property arising out of a matrimonial relationship. (The Recognition of Trusts Act 1987, Schedule, Article 2(1) may also be referred to for a definition of trusts for purposes of the 1986 Hague Convention, as 'the legal relationship created – inter vivos or on death – by a person, the settlor, when assets have been placed under the control of a trustee for the benefit of a beneficiary or for a specified purpose'; Article 2(2) proceeds to describe various characteristics of such a trust, namely (a) the assets constitute a separate fund and are not a part of the trustee's own estate; (b) title to the trust assets stands in the name of the trustee or in the name of another person on behalf of the trustee; (c) the trustee has the power and the duty, in respect of which he is accountable, to manage, employ or dispose of the assets in accordance with the terms of the trust and the special duties imposed upon him by law – although, Article 2(3) goes on to specify that reservation by the settlor of certain rights and powers, and the fact that the trustee may himself have rights as a beneficiary, are not necessarily inconsistent with the existence of a trust.)

(h) evidence and procedure, without prejudice to Article 14

EVIDENCE AND PROCEDURE

These are excluded from the Convention under Article 1(2)(h), and, under national English conflicts rules, are governed by English law, as *lex fori* (*British Linen Company* v. *Drummond* (1830) 10 B. & C. 903; *Bain* v. *Whitehaven Rail Co.* (1850) 3 HL Cas.1).

However, Article 1(2)(h) is expressed to be without prejudice to Article 14, which attracts within the Convention's scope and, in particular, that of, *inter alia*, applicable law thereunder, certain matters which might be classified as procedural or evidential and, consequently, as otherwise for national *lex fori*; and, in addition, Article 10(1), concerning scope of applicable law, may be of similar effect, in including within the latter's scope, and therefore also the Convention's itself, such possibly procedural issues.

Thus, Article 14 specifically regulates choice of law in respect of

- presumptions of law;
- burden of proof;
- mode of proof of contracts.

Article 10(1)(c) and (d) additionally subject *inter alia* the following aspects to Convention rules

- consequences of breach, including assessment of damages in so far as it is governed by rules of law;
- limitation of actions.

Accordingly, it is necessary to try to define those procedural and associated areas which emerge as being excluded from the Convention's scope through this patchwork of provisions. As ever, uncertainties are possible as to the degree of excluded subject matter in this vital area of the Convention's scope as a result of difficulties of construction of the extent and effect of some of the relevant provisions.

NON-EXCLUDED AREAS

(a) Matters Which Are Not Procedural

(i) Formal validity

Complexities may exist in deciding whether rules prescribing written form or record of contract are substantive requirements of formal validity and consequently subject to applicable *lex causae* under the Convention Article 9, or procedural and evidential in nature and therefore matters for national conflicts and *lex fori* (subject to the possibility that such procedural formalities may nonetheless be held to fall within the concept of 'modes of proof' of contractual existence within the meaning of Article 14(2), which subjects the same to *lex fori* or Article 9 laws optionally, and incidentally thereby attracts them within the Convention's overall scope in derogation of the general exclusion in Article 1(2)(h)). A judicial tendency to favour the procedural classification has been evident at times in the past (see for example *Leroux* v. *Brown* (1852) 12 CB 801). It may be the case that requirements of writing or stamping are to be regarded as *form* where non-compliance would lead to non-existence or invalidity of the contract under the relevant legal system *(Clegg* v. *Levy* (1812) 3 Comp. 166; *Monterosso Shipping Co. Ltd* v. *International Transport Workers' Federation, The Rosso* [1982] 2 Lloyd's Rep. 120; *Lehndorf Property Management Ltd* v. *McGrath and Eagle* [1984] 3 WWR 187), and *procedure* when the effect of failure to comply is to render the contract merely unenforceable through the courts (*Alves* v. *Hodgson* (1797) 7 Term Tep. 241; *Bristow* v. *Sequeville* (1850) 5 Exch. 275; *Leroux* v. *Brown* (1852) 12 CB 801).

(ii) Contractual interpretation

Certainly, if the rule in question is one of contractual interpretation rather than evidence of terms (for an example of the latter, see *Korner* v. *Witkowitzer* [1950] 2 KB 128, in which the English forum's parol evidence rule was applied to a contract governed by Czech law), the matter is not excluded under Article 1(2)(h) (Article 10 (1)(a); *St Pierre* v. *South American Stores Ltd* [1937] 1 All ER 206: Chilean proper law applied to interpret a lease).

(iii) Remoteness of damage on breach of contract

This isue is regarded as substantive and as consequently subject to *lex causae* under pre-existing English conflicts (*D'Almeida Araujo* v. *Sir Frederick Becker and Co. Ltd* [1953] 2 QB 329); that this position will continue under the Convention is confirmed by Article 10(1)(c) which expressly includes within the scope of applicable law under the Convention – and consequently, of the latter itself overall – the consequences of breach, including assessment of damages, in circumstances there prescribed. The same is true of liability to pay interest on damages for breach of contract (*Miliangos* v. *George Frank (Textiles) Ltd. (No.2)* [1977] QB 480).

(b) Procedure and Evidence, and Associated Matters

(i) Possibly quantification of damages (and rate of interest on damages for breach, probably procedural at national law – see *Miliangos (No.2)*). It is possible, as a matter of construction, that financial measure of damages, including ability or not to award damages in a foreign currency, is covered by the expression 'assessment of damages' in Article 10(1)(c), expressly referring the latter to applicable law under the Convention. This would be in conflict with pre-existing English private international law, holding the question to be one of procedure for *lex fori (D'Almeida Araujo; The Despina R* [1979] AC 685), to the extent that such matters are more than purely factual for the courts. There are, however, limits on scope of applicable law in Article 10(1)(c) itself, in relation to damages assessment *et alia*: in the first place, the latter is included 'in so far as it is governed by rules of law', and it is possible to construe this condition as restricting its operation to *substantive* – as opposed to procedural – rules of damages law, effectively neutralizing the provision in respect of quantification of damages (see below, p.304 *et seq*); and in the second place, consequences of breach and assessment are only covered 'within the limits of the powers conferred on the court by its procedural law', so that even if, contrary to the preceding argument, *procedural* rules of law are held to be included with Article 10(1)(c), foreign procedural rules – for example, providing for damages to be awarded by way of periodical payments rather than in a lump sum, or in a foreign currency – are inapplicable if these are contrary to the practices of administration of justice of the forum (see below, p.304 *et seq*).

(ii) Types of remedy available. According to pre-existing English conflicts, availability and types of remedies in contract are procedural for *lex fori*, irrespective of *lex causae*'s remedies (except that a foreign substantive right will not be enforced if it would be distorted or incapable of enforcement according to English remedies: *Phrantzes* v. *Argenti* [1960] 2 QB 19). As in the case of assessment of damages, it would seem that this principle may not survive under the Convention, since Article 10(1)(c) expressly refers 'the consequences of breach' to applicable law thereunder; however, as with damages assessment, this is subject to procedural competence of the forum to administer such remedies, and accordingly, for example, specific performance will continue to be available only on a discretionary basis (see below, p.304 *et seq*).

(iii) Limitation of actions. This is specifically subjected to applicable law and Convention scope, by Article 10(1)(d), which accords with its treatment at national law under the Foreign Limitation Periods Act 1984 s.1(1)(a).

(iv) Presumptions of law. Article 14(1) expressly states that presumptions of law in contract are subject to applicable law under the Convention – and by necessary inference therefore they fall within the latter's scope. This is consistent with national conflicts, according to which such presumptions are to be classified as substantive in any event (*Re Cohn* [1945] Ch.5).

(v) Burden of proof. In the face of academic opposition, burden of proof appears to have a procedural classification under national English conflicts (*The Roberta* [1937] 58 Ll. L. Rep. 159). Article 14(1), however, specifically subjects burden of proof to applicable law and accordingly to the Convention's scope. There is a limitation in Article 14(1) in relation both to presumptions – as seen, substantive and within the Convention's scope according to English conflicts in any event – and burden of proof: this is that such matters are only affected by Article 14(1) to the extent that they are contained 'in the law of contract'. It may be the case that the effect of this limitation is that burden of proof (though not presumptions, substantive as seen) remains a matter of procedure, excluded from the Convention's scope, where the rule in question is not specifically derived from contract law: although, such a narrow interpretation is criticized elsewhere (see below, p.332 *et seq*).

(vi) Modes of proof of contract. These are brought within the Convention's scope, in spite of their procedural classification under national conflicts, by virtue of Article 14(2), which subjects them to various alternative choice of law rules. They will include forensic rules of proof, such as admission of affidavit or oral evidence, and rules on competence and compellability of witnesses – although, only to the extent that such modes of proof 'can be administered by the forum', which presumably excludes those methods of proof with which English judges are so inexperienced or unfamiliar that it would be a threat to the due administration of justice for them to be applied in the forum, even if not repugnant to public policy (see Chapters 19 and 21 below). Arguably, too, included within modes of proof for purposes of Article 14(2) are those formalities of contract – such as written evidence or registration – non-compliance with which makes the contract unenforceable (*procedural*, according to *Leroux* v. *Brown*), though not invalid (as *substantive* requirements of form, within the scope of the Convention in any event, and specifically of Article 9) (see *Monterosso Shipping Co. Ltd* v. *ITF* [1982] 3 All ER 841, 846 and 848) – provided that the nature and objective of the formality in question is one of proof of contractual existence (for example, s.4 of the Statute of Frauds 1677) as opposed to, say, protection of the weaker party to contract from being pressured to conclude the contract without properly understanding its terms or having an adequate period to reflect (outside Article 14(2) – and the Convention itself, if classified as procedural, which latter is surely of doubtful authenticity; national propensities to treat such rules as procedural – not to mention those on proof of contractual existence themselves – ought to be curtailed at least in the Convention context, in favour of a more realistic substantive classification and consequent subjection to general Convention scope: see below, Chapter 19, and *Monterosso Shipping Co. Ltd* v. *ITF* [1982] 3 All ER 841, 846 and 848, CA). However, if contracting formalities referred to above are held *not* to amount to modes of proof under Article 14(2), in spite of their evidential purpose, they will then, as previously seen, be subject to procedural rules of *lex fori* under national private international law of the forum, given their evidential and procedural status, excluded from the Convention's scope under Article 1(2)(h) thereof.

EXCLUDED AREAS

In the preceding section, matters non-procedural and certain otherwise of a procedural or evidential nature, falling within the Convention's scope, unaffected by the general exclusion of evidence and procedure under Article 1(2)(h), were alluded to.

Remaining areas of national procedural law will therefore fall within the exclusion from the Convention's scope under Article 1(2)(h) and remain subject to *lex fori* according to national conflicts provision: for example, rules on proper parties to sue or be sued, when of a procedural character and not affecting substantive liability (*O'Callaghan* v. *Thomond* (1810) 3 Taunt. 82; *General Steam Navigation Co.* v. *Guillou* (1843) 11 M. & W. 877; *Bumper Development Corporation* v. *Commissioner of Police of the Metropolis* [1991] 1 WLR 1362, 1371 (CA) – although, conferral of legal personality for the purposes of suit according to *lex fori*, is a matter for the appropriate applicable law, subject to public policy of the forum, and not for *lex fori* itself, *ibid.*, pp. 1371–3), and priorities of contractual creditors (*The Colorado* [1923], P. 102).

3   The rules of this Convention do not apply to contracts of insurance which cover risks situated in the territories of the Member States of the European Economic Community. In order to determine whether a risk is situated in these territories the court shall apply its internal law.
4   The preceding paragraph does not apply to contracts of reinsurance.

GENERAL EXCLUSION OF EEC INSURANCE

Insurance was generally excluded from the Convention so as to take account of Community unifying work in the field, although, the Report indicated that Contracting States might wish to apply rules to insurance, based on those in the Convention, on a voluntary basis in their implementing legislation while Community harmonization was awaited (p.13). (English and Scottish Law Commissions in fact criticized parallel existence of the then proposed EEC Directive on insurance, in relation to choice of law, in their Report of 11 April 1979 on the Choice of Law Rules in the Draft Non-Life Insurance Services Directive: see Fletcher, *Conflict of Laws and European Community Law* (1982), pp.155 and 181.) Under the previous national English conflicts law, contracts of insurance are governed by the proper law, subjective or objective, the latter (especially in life assurance) apparently often being taken to be the law of the country in which the insurer carries on its business, or of its head office if business is carried on in two or more countries, except in the case of marine insurance, in which the form of the policy and the market in which it is issued may be more important (see Dicey and Morris, *The Conflict of Laws*, 11th edn, pp.1289–90. Rule 193, and *E.I. du Pont de Nemours* v. *Agnew* [1987] 2 Lloyd's Rep. 585 (CA)).

The new or, as the case may be, prospective, law governing EEC insurance policies falling outside the Convention's scope is as follows.

Non-life Insurance

Regulation 6 of the Insurance Companies (Amendment) Regulations 1990 (SI 1990 No. 1333), implementing in the United Kingdom, as from 1 July 1990, the Second Council Directive on Non-Life Insurance of 22 June 1988 (88/357/EEC, O.J. 1988 L172/1), inserts s. 94A and Schedule 3A into the Insurance Companies Act 1982, governing such insurance contracts, where these constitute 'general business' (s.1(1) and Schedule 2, Part I), by special choice of law rules in relation to EEC risks (see 1982 Act s. 96A(3), for the United Kingdom definition of location of risk – and below, p.141), basically amounting to law of the insured's home member state.

(Under Article 7 of the Directive, relating to law applicable to insurance of risks situated in member states, or parts thereof in the case of composite states (i) where the policyholder is habitually resident or has its central administration in the member state of the risk, the latter's law governs the contract of insurance, subject to parties' choice of law where the former so permits; (ii) but where neither the habitual residence nor central administration is situated in that state, the parties may choose to apply either the law of the member state of the risk or law of the state in which the policyholder is habitually resident or has its central administration. In the case of policyholders conducting commercial, industrial or professional activities to which the policy risk relates and which are carried out in different member states, any of the latters' laws may apply. There are equivalent provisions to those in Article 3(1) and (3) of the Obligations Convention relating to implied choice of law and safeguard for mandatory rules of the law of a wholly connected member state other than that whose law was chosen by the parties. In the absence of choice of law by the parties, law of the most closely connected country from amongst Article 7 laws will govern – that of the situation of risk being rebuttably presumed to be most closely connected. Exceptionally, severability of applicable law is possible. See below, p.141, as to place of situation of risk for such purposes.)

The Obligations Convention, of course, applies in the case of *non-EEC* risks.

Life Assurance

Choice of law in relation to EEC risks (to be defined by implementing legislation as being located in the member state of the commitment) will be governed by Article 4 of the Second Council Directive on Life Assurance of 8 November 1990 (90/619/EEC, O.J. 1990 L330/50) when it is implemented in the United Kingdom in the course of 1992 (law of the member state of the commitment – defined as that of the policyholder's habitual residence or establishment – subject to choice of another law if the former allows, or to choice of *lex nationalis* where the policy holder is a natural person habitually resident in a member state other than that of his nationality, and to mandatory rules of the forum and member state of the commitment in prescribed circumstances, and otherwise to general private international law of contract). Pre-existing conflicts governs EEC risks prior thereto (see above, p. 45).

INSURANCE CONTRACTS TO WHICH THE CONVENTION APPLIES

There are two circumstances in which the exclusion of insurance from the Convention's scope is expressly *inapplicable*.

(1) Cases Where a Risk Covered by the Policy is Not Situated in Any of the Territories of the EEC States (Article 1(3))

In this situation the Convention's rules on choice of law govern the insurance contract: characteristic performer under Article 4(2) must surely be the insurer (Report, p.20 – provision of cover, rather than payment on occurrence of risk) and form of contracts is governed by laws applicable under Article 9, subject to any mandatory rules safeguarded by Article 7. Notwithstanding contrary indication in the Report (p.13), however, it is considered that provision of insurance is not *automatically* to be construed as falling within the concept of the supply of 'services' to a person outside his trade or profession, within the meaning of Article 5 laying down protective choice of law rules in relation to consumer contracts (see too Article 9(5) on form), in particular, since Article 5(1) expressly distinguishes between supply of goods or *services* on the one hand and provision of credit for that object on the other (each being included within its ambit). If provision of credit – arguably analogous to award of insurance cover – were already a 'service', why should it have been specifically referred to? On the other hand, the policies behind exclusion of EEC insurance from the Convention's scope (that is, *inter alia*, to ensure greater protection for the insured under

EEC Directives), and inclusion of reinsurance therewithin (lack of need for protection), provide support for construction of Article 5 as covering insurance (and it may be put that express reference in Article 5(1) to provision of credit *for that object* may simply have been intended to *restrict* the operation of the consumer protection rule therein to contracts for the provision of credit – otherwise one for services in any event – where the credit is to be used for acquisition of goods or services, as opposed to, for example, gambling or making a gift); and Article 61(2) of the EEC Treaty certainly treats insurance as a service. However, even if insurance were thus to be regarded as falling within Article 5(1), as supply of services, it remains questionable as to just how frequently the conditions for operation thereof laid down in Article 5(2) would be satisfied (see, however, Merkin, 'Contracts (Applicable Law) Act 1990' (1991) *Journal of Business Law* 205, 211, as to the likely growth of cross-border insurance, in line with EC free movement of services and rights of establishment principles).

In deciding whether a 'risk is situated' in the EEC territories for these purposes, Article 1(3) requires courts to apply their internal law, that is to say, English rules, exclusive of private international law (excluded generally in any event as part of *renvoi*, under Article 15) (Report, p.13, para 10), and 'territories' of EEC member states include those further territories specified in Article 27, subject, where necessary, to the appropriate declaration being made thereunder.

Where, then, is an insurance risk situated according to English law?

This matter appears to be undecided according to pre-exisiting English conflicts. However, help may be derived from s.96A of the Insurance Companies Act 1982 (inserted by Insurance Companies (Amendment) Regulations 1990, Regulation 2(1)), whereby *situs* of risk for such purposes is (a) place where the property is situated in the case of buildings insurance; (b) place of registration in the case of vehicles insurance; (c) place where the policyholder took out the policy in the case of travel or holiday insurance lasting up to four months; and (d) in other cases (i) place of habitual residence where the policyholder is an individual; and (ii) otherwise, place of establishment of the policyholder to which the policy related (and presumably, category (d)(i) could also be extended to life assurance). Clearly, therefore, a policy covering different categories of insurance – say, home and contents, including garaged vehicles – could be subject to (possibly different) applicable laws, under both national conflicts and the Convention, respectively: for example, a building is situated inside the EEC, but the garaged vehicle is registered outside thereof. It is possible to conclude from the wording of Article 1(3) that this is not in fact the case, and that if *any* part of the policy is concerned with EEC risks, the *entire* contract is to be held to be excluded from the Convention thereunder: thus, Article 1(3) provides that Convention rules are inapplicable to insurance contracts 'which cover' such risks, not merely 'to the extent that' they do so. However, it is felt that the latter is the correct sense of the provision, in accordance with its underlying specialization policy objective.

(2) Reinsurance

Article 1(4) expressly provides that contracts of reinsurance are not excluded from the Convention's scope, because 'these contracts do not raise the same problems as contracts of insurance, where the need to protect the persons insured must necessarily be taken into account' (Report, p.13). Presumably, the previous English rules on choice of law in insurance contracts, described earlier, will be reflected in the law held to be most closely connected, in the absence of expressed or implied choice, under Article 4, if necessary, in rebutting the presumption that country of reinsurer's relevant place of business is the most connected thereunder. (Furthermore, there may well be cause for inferring an implied intention under Article 3(1) – or otherwise for finding rebuttal under Article 4(5) – to the effect that the law governing the reinsurance contract (or, at least, construction and effects of certain related clauses thereof), should be the same as that applying to the original insurance policy: see *Forsikringsaktieselskapet Vesta v. Butcher* [1986] 2 All ER 488, affd [1989] AC 852.)

7 Article 2: Universal Application of the Convention

Article 2

Application of law of non-contracting states

Any law specified by this Convention shall be applied whether or not it is the law of a Contracting State.

When a law is indicated as applicable under the Convention, it governs whether it is the law of a Contracting or non-Contracting State. Convention rules are thus universal, applicable *erga omnes*, without requiring reciprocity from the state of the law chosen under Article 3 or most closely connected in accordance with Article 4. The aim was to reduce confusion from existence of parallel sets of choice of law rules in relation to Contracting and non-Contracting States' laws (Report, p.13). (Giardina, in North (ed.) (1982), *Contract Conflicts*, pp.248–9, is concerned that reciprocity and mutual trust, preconditions for operation of foreign mandatory rules under Article 7(1), may be lacking in respect of non-Contracting States' mandatory laws. However, such matters can be taken into account in exercising the discretion thereunder.)

There is no limitation upon the scope of operation of the Convention according to whether the parties are nationals, domiciliaries, or residents of Contracting States.

On the second reading of the implementing legislation in the House of Lords, LORD WILBERFORCE questioned whether the Convention – *all well and good and very useful* as a law governing as between members of the EEC and people resident in the Community and carrying on business there – should also apply to contracts between, say, English and American companies, or Belgian and Norwegian companies (Hansard, HL Vol.513, col. 1269), and at the Committee stage in the Lords, he moved that the Act should be expressed to apply as between any parties to a contract who, at the time of its conclusion, had their *habitual residence*, or, in the case of bodies corporate or unincorporate, their *central administration*, in a *Contracting* State (HL Vol 515, col. 1474); it was clear from the Convention's Preamble that the Convention, like other EEC conventions, was a 'closed family contract between the 12 member states which aims at harmonisation of the law relating to contracts as between those member states' (col. 1475); the common formula for giving effect to the Convention, namely that it should 'have the force of law' in the United Kingdom, under s.2(1) of the 1990 Act, was not intended to be construed in such manner as would lead to the Convention's application to contracts having no EC connection at all, where no party had anything to do with the EC, and none of the contracts had any reference to the EC or to any member state (cols 1475–6); it was not unusual for legal relations to be governed in one area by an international convention and in another by the common law or another convention, whereas the 'universal' approach would mean also governing contracts between US and Swedish companies, or between Japanese and Norwegian companies, by the Convention, which would be extremely serious (col. 1476). There were thus, according to LORD WILBERFORCE, *practical*, *constitutional* and *constructional* objections to the universal approach.

Practical Considerations

The English Commercial Court and London 'Court' of International Arbitration – each of the very highest international repute and accustomed to hear cases, many of which were between parties having nothing to do with the United Kingdom – applied the highly regarded English system of the conflict of laws in choice of law in contract, built up by the judges over the years and set down in *Dicey and Morris on the Conflict of Laws* as a certain and comprehensive code, which could flexibly be changed as new judicial decisions emerged; these worldwide authorities would all be superseded by the new, imprecise, 'strange' language of the Convention, subject to interpretation according to the report of the Italian and French professors and by the European Court of Justice (col.1477); thus, the practical objection to universal application of the Convention was that non-Contracting State parties would no longer wish to litigate in England according to unfamiliar rules, commented on in inaccessible reports and interpreted by the non-representative European Court, whereas previously they would have obtained fast, certain and cheap adjudication within the English jurisdiction (col. 1478).

Constitutional Problems

There was also a not negligible constitutional objection that substitution of an entire mini-code in the conflict of laws should be carried out by parliamentary draftsmen and submitted to parliament for discussion, rather than being introduced 'by the back door, brought in holus-bolus by schedule which is not capable of discussion and not capable of amendment' (*ibid.*).

Construction of the Text

There was nothing express in the general words of Article 1(1) or 2 which required the Convention to be applied to *all* contracts; and having regard to the object and purpose of the enactment, it was perfectly legitimate to construe them as limited to EC parties, in order to facilitate the flow of goods and services in the EEC, so that under Article 2 a contract between French and German companies to build a plant in Nigeria might then be governed by Nigerian law under the Convention; this was what was meant by 'universal' application of the Convention in the report. However, LORD WILBERFORCE went on: 'What Community interest is there in laying down the law which our Commercial Court or arbitrators are to apply to a contract between an Indian company and a New York company?' (cols 1479 and 1480). LORD GOFF supported LORD WILBERFORCE's view that the Act should expressly limit operation of the Convention to EC contracts and that this was not inconsistent with the Convention itself (cols 1481–2); a large proportion of Commercial Court cases and London arbitrations involved overseas parties, many of whom would be startled at the impact of the Convention, not least in the matter of certainty of legal advice and effects on jurisdiction based on choice of law, and would ask 'why England of all countries should apply a European test to contracts between parties, both of whom come from outside Europe?' (*ibid.*). In his response, the Lord Chancellor demonstrated that both the Report and *Dicey and Morris* indicated the Convention also to be applicable to contracts with non-EEC elements and in relation to parties domiciled and resident in, and nationals of, non-EEC states, so that the option to limit its application was not available (cols 1483–4); the main Convention principles were very similar in broad terms to pre-existing English conflicts, and there was a constitutional duty to give the Convention the force of law in the United Kingdom (cols 1484–5). (Furthermore, delays from interpretative references to the European Court were dealt with in the interpretation protocol, permitting solely appellate courts to request rulings: *ibid.*) The Wilberforce amendment was thereafter withdrawn in Committee (in the midst of some confusion over whether or not the Convention had already been ratified by the United Kingdom in any event at the relevant time: it had not). The amendment was moved again at the Report stage (HL Vol.517, col. 1537), where it was defeated (the Lord Chancellor contrasted Article 1(1) with Article 1(3) on insurance, the latter alone expressly referring to EEC connections, col. 1538; the Preamble too, together with leading English academic writers and foreign EEC governments, all seemed to contemplate the Convention's universal application to contracts, cols 1539–40; EC limitation in the United Kingdom would be against the Convention's unificationist objective and not even allowed thereunder, *ibid.*).

Thus, the only realistic construction of Convention Articles 1(1) and 2 must surely be that Convention rules govern, irrespective of whether parties' nationality, domicile or residence is located within or outside the EEC.

8 Article 3: Agreement on Choice of Law

Article 3

Freedom of choice

1 **A contract shall be governed by the law chosen by the parties. The choice must be express or demonstrated with reasonable certainty by the terms of the contract or the circumstances of the case. By their choice the parties can select the law applicable to the whole or a part only of the contract.**

GENERAL PRINCIPLE ALLOWING EXPRESS OR IMPLIED CHOICE OF LAW

Autonomy in contract choice of law is universal throughout national systems of private international law in the EEC (Report, pp.15 and 16; Williams, 'The EEC Convention on the Law Applicable to Contractual Obligations' (1986) 35 ICLQ 1, 11, footnote 24; *R.* v. *International Trustee* [1937] AC 500; *Amin Rasheed Shipping Corpn* v. *Kuwait Insurance Co.* [1984] AC 50), and beyond (see, for example, US Second Restatement of the Conflict of Laws (1971) sections 186 and 187). Professor Juenger informs that a choice of law clause was even contained in the marriage contract between El Cid, the Castilian reconquistador, and the lady from Leon whom he wed in 1074 (see North (ed.), *Contract Conflicts* (1982), p.297)! Reasons of certainty, freedom, commercial convenience and morality of agreements dictate that this should be so.

Article 3 of the Convention enshrines this principle.

National conflicts laws may sometimes limit the freedom of parties' choice, by permitting the chosen law only to govern where it is to a greater or lesser extent connected in some way with the parties or contract (section 187(2)(a) of the US Second Restatement requires a substantial relationship with, or some other reasonable basis for, the choice, in respect of certain aspects: see North (ed.) (1982), pp.150 and 297; note too von Hoffmann, *ibid.*, p.222, as to the position in Germany; in *Vita Food Products Inc.* v. *Unus Shipping Co. Ltd* [1939] AC 277, 290, LORD WRIGHT indicated that the choice should be *bona fide* – see *Golden Acres Ltd* v. *Queensland Estates Pty Ltd* [1969] Qd R 378 – and *legal* and not avoidable on the ground of *public policy*).

Article 3 contains no such anti-evasion limitation upon the general applicability of the chosen law: parties may select a completely unconnected law (or a law according to which the contract is invalid – see below p.272), and provided that, as a matter of contractual construction, the choice is serious and not a sham (a 'real choice of law': Report, p.17), that law will then be generally applicable to their contract (see, for example, von Hoffmann, in *European Private International Law of Obligations* (1975), p.4, as to choice of English law under the standard form of the London Corn Trade Association). Indeed, Article 3(3) specifically concerns the situation in which the chosen law governs generally when *all* other relevant connections are with another country (thereby additionally indicating Article 16 to be inoperative to destroy the choice on public policy grounds); and further, the Convention itself may only be applicable to the proceedings by virtue of that choice, where the dispute would not otherwise involve an international conflict of laws for purposes of Article 1(1).

The only partial restraint on autonomy is that under the Convention, *mandatory* rules of laws other than those selected by parties will override their choice in certain circumstances (Articles 3(3), 5(2), 6(1), 9(6), and 7), and rules of the chosen law whose application is manifestly contrary to public policy of the forum may also be inapplicable (Article 16).

English courts and arbitrators may now, therefore, in principle, even if not significantly in practice, feel themselves, to this extent, to be even less restricted than before, in giving effect to parties' choice of law to govern their contractual relations. This makes sound commercial sense, especially where English law is generally recognized as being more advanced than others in the particular field of commerce involved.

In the present writer's submission, furthermore, there should be no objection in principle to giving effect to a 'floating' choice of law under Article 3(1) – or, perhaps more accurately, Article 3(2) – once the *crystallization* has taken place (prior thereto, Article 4(1) governs, as on absence of chosen applicable law) – subject to insufficient contractual certainty being held to exist under applicable law of contract (under Articles 3(4) and 8). Thus, parties have only themselves to blame if they are uncertain as to the law which will ultimately regulate their rights and duties, through reference to several potentially applicable laws, one of which is to be designated by a party at a later date. Cheshire and North take a contrary view, against giving effect to floating proper law (p.451), but this is hard to reconcile with their subsequent support for allowing parties to change the proper law following conclusion of contract, explicitly permitted − as will be seen below − under Article 3(2) of the Convention.

IMPLIED CHOICE OF LAW

This is permitted by Article 3(1), which states that the choice must be express 'or demonstrated with reasonable certainty by the terms of the contract or the circumstances of the case'. The key word is 'choice', which means that, if the parties have failed to express a choice, the court should not then simply proceed to determine the most closely connected country's law under Article 4 (see LORD WILBERFORCE in *Amin Rasheed Shipping Corpn v. Kuwait Insurance Co.* [1984] AC 50, 69–71, under pre-existing conflicts), but should try to ascertain whether they nonetheless possessed a common intent as to the law to govern their contract (see LORD DIPLOCK in [1984] AC 50, 61). The test, moreover, is a subjective one, not objective (Report, p.17): the court must seek to discover whether *these* parties had a particular, unexpressed choice of applicable law (i) whether such choice can be said to be commercially sensible and reasonable or not from the objective point of view ('reasonable certainty' in Article 3(1) concerns evidence of implied choice, and is not a criterion for making such); (ii) whether or not the law alleged to have been impliedly selected is that of the most connected country; and (iii) on the basis of connections amongst the totality, which may be thought to be especially relevant to implied choice, even if not otherwise the most substantial: indeed, to a certain degree, implied choice of law under Article 3 is really only of significance to the extent that this differs from the law which would otherwise have been applicable in the absence of choice under Article 4, and this consideration may well be taken into account by courts in operating the former (for example, connections with a *law*, as opposed to those with *countries* required for Article 4, may be expected to be accorded the greater significance under Article 3, given the latter's preoccupation with choice of *law*).

(a) Demonstrated with Reasonable Certainty

The line must be drawn somewhere; courts cannot be expected to go on fishing expeditions to find an implied choice (see Diamond, 'Conflict of Laws in the EEC' (1979), 32 *Current Legal Problems*, 155, 160). 'Reasonable certainty' is the standard set, although, this is of course merely a signpost, indicating that courts should act with regard to commercial needs and realities ('reasonable' certainty may, however, be less restrictive than LORD DIPLOCK's 'by necessary implication' in *Amin Rasheed Shipping Corpn v. Kuwait Insurance Co.* [1984] AC 50, p.61). In the Court of Appeal proceedings in *Compagnie D'Armement Maritime SA v. Compagnie Tunisienne de Navigation SA* [1969] 3 All ER 589, even the *express* selection of 'laws of the flag of the vessel carrying the goods' was held to be insufficiently certain to be given effect to, where the contract contemplated performance in a number of different vessels flying different flags (the House of Lords reached the contrary view – [1971] AC 572); similarly, in *'The Iran Vojdan'* [1984] 2 Lloyd's Rep. 380, 385 Col. 1, BINGHAM J held a 'floating proper law' clause, permitting selection between Iranian, German and English law, to be too uncertain for application (see too *Armar Shipping Co. Ltd v. Caisse Algérienne d'Assurance et de Réassurance* [1981] 1 WLR 207, 215–216, CA) – although, this is to be distinguished from a fall-back provision in the contract, stating that the law of Y shall govern if the parties' choice of law of X is for any reason held by the courts to be ineffective, said by the Court of Appeal in *The Mariannina* [1983] 1 Lloyd's Rep. 12 to make sound commercial sense and consequently to be acceptable. On the other hand, in *The Komninos S* (1991) *Financial Times*, 16 January, the Court of Appeal held that an express choice of 'British' courts in a bill of lading was to be construed as meaning English (not Scottish, Northern Irish nor colonial) courts in the particular context of international maritime contracts, given the renown and reputation of the English Commercial and Admiralty Courts, for the purpose of inferring implied choice of English law to govern the contract.

Professor Merkin has raised the issue of effects on choice of law under the Convention of inclusion in the contract of an *amiable compositeur* arbitration clause in which:

a) there is an express choice of law, but the arbitrator is given the power to disregard technical and strict constructions, in favour of equitable principles; or

b) where there is no such choice of law – or there is, but the arbitrators are empowered to disregard rules of law as well as of construction; or

c) the arbitrators are delegated the power to decide upon applicable law.

In the first of the preceding cases, there is ostensibly an express choice within the meaning of Article 3(1): although, it may be that matters of contractual construction removed from its scope, must then be consigned – severably from expressly chosen law – to the law of the most connected country applicable under Article 4(1), even if only in order to determine whether the arbitrator is permitted to construe on equitable, rather than legal, principles, if not solely for the latter purpose itself, in accordance with the Convention system. Where, however, the choice of national law in such circumstances is sought to be *implied* under Article 3(1), as in the second of the cases mentioned above, then it may well be the case that the *amiable compositeur* element will be held to be destructive of what would otherwise have been the 'reasonable certainty' of such implied choice under Article 3(1), so that the national applicable law is then to be determined according to Article 4(1) – whether or not the *amiable compositeur* specification is thereafter to be applied thereto within the English jurisdiction or arbitration. In either of the two preceding instances, if the arbitrator is authorized to disregard rules of law, as well as of construction, it is submitted that the effectiveness of such party provision must again be determined according to national law applicable under Article 3(1) or 4(1). Below it is questioned whether choice of 'de-localized' legal principles to govern the contract as a whole may be given effect to under the Convention system, and it is believed that similar considerations will apply to the situation at present under discussion in which the arbitrator is empowered to disregard rules of law. Finally, cases where power to select applicable law under Article 3 is delegated by parties to the arbitrators are in effect akin to that of the 'floating applicable law' referred to above, in that – perhaps with even less certainty than in the examples given in the previous discussion – a mechanism is provided by the parties for applicable law to be settled subsequent to contract through the act or declaration of one of the parties, or on the occurrence of an event. The position will be recalled that existing authorities, and certain commentators, tend to support the view that such a floating choice of law ought not to be given effect to, as being insufficiently certain of application. If this were so, subject to the unlikely possibility of the clause being held to give rise to implied choice of law by the parties under Article 3(1), applicable law would be that of the most closely connected country under Article 4(1). It may be reminded that in the present writer's opinion there was said to be nothing objectionable in principle in giving effect to a floating choice of law under Article 3(1) (or 3(2), depending upon the manner in which the time factor is perceived, retrospectively or otherwise), once the law-concretizing event has occurred – subject to sufficient certainty of consent by parties to such agreement being held to exist in conformity with the national law so determined in accordance with

Articles 3(4) and 8. The same comment therefore applies to delegated arbitral power to select applicable national law.

(b) By the Terms of the Contract or the Circumstances of the Case

The factors to be taken into account by courts in inferring an implied choice of law under Article 3(1) will correspond with those previously considered to be relevant to implied choice under pre-existing English conflicts (see Cheshire and North, pp.457–61; and von Hoffmann, in North (ed.) (1982), p.224, for similar practices in the German courts).

(i) *Terms of the contract* will include the following: choice of jurisdiction (see *The Komninos S* (1991) *Financial Times*, 16 January) or arbitration (even if this fails to give rise to an implied choice under Article 3(1), chosen jurisdiction will nonetheless remain an objective factor to be taken into account in determining applicable law of the most closely connected country under Article 4(1)); reference to provisions of a certain law or use of technical language redolent thereof (perhaps concerning, say, an English trust); use of a particular language, standard (or other) forms and documentation; selection of currency for payment; a failed attempt to express a choice of law (*Compagnie d'Armement Maritime SA* v. *Compagnie Tunisienne de Navigation SA* [1971] AC 572). (*Quaere*, in this connection, whether selection of 'law of the flag' is express or implied. Presumably, the actual meaning of the expression, as opposed to its effects – governed by Article 3(1) – is a matter of contractual interpretation, though nonetheless subject to *lex fori*'s interpretative rules, since reference to Article 10(1)(a) is absent from Article 3(4), as is reference to Article 14, so that procedural rules of evidence which may be adduced in order to deduce the existence of an implied choice of law from 'the circumstances of the case', as opposed to the terms of the contract, also remain matters for *lex fori* alone, in accordance with Article 1(2)(h)). In the present submission, the formula constitutes an express choice of law; if it were held not to be so, however, it would then have to satisfy the reasonable certainty test.

Supposing the parties select a 'de-localised' law to govern their contract, that is, the decision on the merits is to be reached according to general principles of countries' laws, equity and international commerce. Is this to be regarded as an express or sufficiently certain implied choice of law under Article 3(1)? The traditional response under English private international law is for courts to refuse to give effect to such a stipulation in the contract, on the ground of its non-juridical nature (see *Amin Rasheed Shipping Corpn* v. *Kuwait Insurance Co.* [1984] AC 50, 65 LORD DIPLOCK), in which event, if this approach is retained, law of the most closely connected country will govern instead under Article 4(1). However, there are two possible textual arguments which may be adduced in order to effectuate such a de-localized choice under the Convention regime in England:

a) first, it may be argued that the law of a country, the legal system of which *would* give effect to the de-localized choice of law, ought to be regarded as having been impliedly chosen in accordance with Article 3(1) if other sufficient connections are also established with that country for purposes of implied choice under Article 3(1), and that the de-localized principles might then be regarded as effectively incorporated into the applicable legal system, so as to amount to impliedly chosen applicable 'law' within the meaning of Article 3(1); and

b) secondly, in the alternative, it might in any event be felt that the de-localized principles chosen by the parties for application by the courts *are*, effectively, express choice of 'law' within the meaning of Article 3(1), since Article 2, concerning Convention scope, refers to any 'law' specified by the Convention, rather than to law *of a country* applicable thereunder, as does Article 3(1) itself in respect of parties' choice – although, admittedly, the words *même si* (even if) and *auch ...wenn* (also/even...if), followed by 'it is the law of a non-Contracting State', in French and German texts of Article 2, in place of the English 'whether or not', in relation to the subsequent words 'it is the law of a Contracting State' thereunder, may be taken to indicate that such law should be that of a state, specifically, Contracting or non-Contracting, under the Convention.

Arbitrators themselves, on the other hand, are less likely to raise objections to operation of de-localized law in relation to contracts (as opposed to its application to the arbitration agreement itself, or to its curial law – see Palmer, 'Can International Commercial Arbitration be Delocalised?' (1989), *International Litigation and Arbitration* 10, and cases there cited).

(ii) *Circumstances of the case* will comprise matters such as nature and location of subject matter; parties' residence or nationality (especially if common to both of them); connection with a related or previous transaction subject to a chosen law (Report, p.17 – and see *Kloeckner & Co AG v. Gatoil Overseas Inc* [1990] 1 Lloyd's Rep. 177, 206 col. 2). These latter circumstances are to be assessed according to their evidential weight as indicating a possible shared intent as to applicable law as between parties, rather than as connections possessing an objective weight and influence, cumulatively considered, as constituting the closest connection, which is the province of Article 4.

Von Hoffmann (in North (ed.), *Contract Conflicts* (1982), pp.224–5) considers that mode of pleading in court should be able to be regarded as a material factor (just as Article 18 of the Judgments Convention permits submission to jurisdiction at the date of proceedings). This would seem to be correct on the basis put forward by von Hoffmann himself, namely, that defendant's failure, for example, to challenge the plaintiff's unsubstantiated assertions as to implied choice of law under the contract amounts to an agreement to vary the law otherwise applicable under Article 4, which is allowed to be made at any time under Article 3(2) (although, this will differ in its effects from the defendant's response – or lack thereof – being held to amount to *implied choice of law under the main contract, by virtue of Article 3(1)*, because had the latter been the case, then conceivably, absence, say, of required form of contract according to the law thereby applicable to that main contract under Article 9 could thereupon have affected formal validity of the choice of law itself, not so under Article 3(2) – and indeed, it is submitted that as a matter of general underlying principle, and following the text itself of Article 3(1), factors considered in inferring an implied original choice of law should be restricted to those existing at the date of contract, to the exclusion of any coming into being subsequently thereto).

SEVERABILITY OF APPLICABLE LAW (DÉPEÇAGE)

Parties have a fairly wide formal freedom to select a law (or laws) to apply to only part of their contract, and severability of the contract itself is not a condition of such choice (nor is severable choice limited to express) (Report, p.17).

Furthermore, under Article 3(1) parties are not restricted to choice of law to govern a single part of the contract; they can select different laws in respect of each part (see *Forsakringsiktieselskapet Vesta* v. *Butcher* [1986] 2 All ER 488, affd [1988] 2 All ER 43 and [1989] 1 All ER 402, at national law). In the former case, the part of the contract to which the chosen law is inapplicable is governed by the law applicable in the absence of choice under Article 4. (Express choice of law to govern a part does not give rise to a presumption as to its implied choice to apply to the contract in its entirety:Report, p.17.)

The only control on severability is probably that of general jurisprudential practicability: a partial or multiple choice should be logically consistent and not give rise to contradictions, for example, by subjecting sellers' and buyers' rights and duties to different laws, conflicting with each other; in the latter event, the choice would be ineffective and recourse would have to be made to Article 4 for applicable law (Report, p.17).

Finally, the usual distinction should be drawn between *choice of law* (*kollisionsrechtlich*) and *incorporation* of rules of a particular law as static terms of the contract (*materiellrechtlich*): Article 3 applies to the former, but not to the latter. Ability to incorporate by reference is a matter for applicable law (see, for example, Sale of Goods Act 1979 s.56(1)), whether chosen, expressly or impliedly, under Article 3, or referred to in the absence of choice, by virtue of Article 4; (although, indirectly, even if applicable law gives effect thereto, such terms will still be subject to mandatory controls under Article 7 *et alia*).

2 **The parties may at any time agree to subject the contract to a law other than that which previously governed it, whether as a result of an earlier choice under this Article or of other provisions of this Convention. Any variation by the parties of the law to be applied made after the conclusion of the contract shall not prejudice its formal validity under Article 9 or adversely affect the rights of third parties.**

MAY AT ANY TIME AGREE

Article 3(2) uses the language of *agreement* on applicable law, in contrast to Article 3(1) which refers to *chosen* law. However, nothing would seem to turn on the difference in terminology in English and foreign texts: the very purpose of Article 3(2) would appear to be to provide a *choice of law rule* whereby parties are permitted to avail themselves of the power in Article 3(1) to select a law to govern their concluded contract, *expressly or implicitly* (for example, from an agreement to arbitrate), *and subsequent to conclusion, where the law so chosen differs from the law otherwise applicable thereto*. According to the Report, the agreement on new applicable law may even be reached in the course of legal proceedings, subject to national procedural rules of the forum as to cut-off points *et alia*; and in all cases under Article 3(2), the new choice of law is subject to Articles 8, 9 and 11 as to existence and validity of consent, by virtue of Article 3(4), in the same way as any original choice of law would have been so (p.18).

It is quite clear that Article 3(2) makes the new choice of law effective without the otherwise applicable law having to be referred to in order to determine whether the variation or subsequent choice is valid and permitted. The latter is a matter of choice of law for the forum, and thereby subject to the Convention's rules, no less than any original choice of law would have been. (The variation thus goes ahead under Article 3(2), even where invalidity of the contract – including the new choice of law itself – results from the operation of the newly chosen law, in accordance with Articles 3(4) and 8(1).) The Report calls this a logical and liberal solution, said to be in accordance with French, German and Dutch (and possibly

American – Juenger, in North (ed.), p.298; but not, it would seem, Italian – Pierce, 'Post-Formation Choice of Law in Contract' (1987), 50 *MLR* 176, 198) judicial practice (*ibid.*). In England the issue seems undecided (Cheshire and North, p.451, simply state that, if the parties have chosen a new law to govern the contract, there is a strong case for giving effect to their intentions, without further elaboration).

Dicey and Morris (p.1168) state 'the better view is that it depends on English law as the law of the forum', that is to say, their approach is that in Article 3(2) (see too Kahn-Freund, *General Problems of Private International Law* (1976), p.256; and Pierce (1987) 50 *MLR* 176,195). Fletcher (p.159) attacks Article 3(2) on logical and practical grounds: once a contract has been concluded, and legal relations formed, change of applicable law should be for its existing governing law to assess; Diamond, in 'Conflict of Laws in the EEC' (1979), 32 *Current Legal Problems,* 155, 162–5, is in agreement (see too Wolff, *Private International Law* (2nd edn 1950), p.426, and Mann, 'The Time Element in the Conflict of Laws' (1954), 31 *BYBIL* 217, 222); and where the alteration is to a *non*-EEC applicable law, the latter cannot be presumed to allow it (pp.159–60). Fletcher further considers that both old and new applicable laws should have been required to be referred to for efficacy of the variation (*ibid.*). It is submitted that Fletcher is quite correct to describe the rule as illogical: furthermore, it is considered that since the subsequent variation may well affect substantive contractual relations – *a fortiori*, if executed *after* a breach! – it follows that novation of the entire contract – not merely choice of law – is sought to be brought about from the date of the new choice of law, and that strictly such novation should therefore have been referred to old and new laws in accordance with established practice (see Article 10(1)(d); and *Re United Railways of the Havana and Regla Warehouses* [1960] Ch. 52, 84–5, affd [1961] AC 1007), thereby enabling deletion of the saving in Article 3(2) for formal validity and third-party rights under the original law, which would each have been subject to old and new laws *in any event*. (The same could still actually be achieved under the existing Article 3(2), by the very means of a novation: see Giardina, in North (ed.) (1982), p.245; and *Kremezi* v. *Ridgway* [1949] 1 All ER 662,663, HILBERY J.) (Morse argues, however, that Article 3(2)'s effect could have been brought about in relation to subsequent choice of *English* law in any event, simply through failure of parties to plead and prove the original foreign applicable law in the course of English procedure: see (1982) 2 *Yearbook of European Law,* 107, 120–1. The accuracy of this analysis rather depends upon whether or not courts are bound to apply the Convention of their own motion; if they are not, Morse is correct – but such a finding could pose a serious threat to the Convention's overall effectiveness where actions are brought in default of appearance.)

Thus, it may be seen that a previously invalid contract may be rescued by means of a new choice of law, and vice versa (subject to savings for formalities and third parties), under Article 3(2). Purists will object. Supporters of Article 3(2) will refer to commercial convenience. In the final analysis, Article 3(2) exists, and revision conferences under Article 26 are things for the future.

SUBJECT THE CONTRACT TO A LAW OTHER THAN THAT WHICH PREVIOUSLY GOVERNED IT

It is expressly provided in Article 3(2) that the original applicable law can be the result of an earlier choice (express or implied) under Article 3, or of other provisions of the Convention, such as Article 4 in the absence of choice. Indeed, the earlier choice may itself have been made under Article 3(2).

VARIATION NOT TO PREJUDICE FORMAL VALIDITY OR ADVERSELY AFFECT THIRD PARTY RIGHTS

The variation in applicable law may confer formal validity under Article 9 upon a previously invalid contract, as well as any third party rights, but it must neither *prejudice* the former (as distinct from formal validity of the new choice of law itself, which obviously lies outside the saving provision in Article 3(2)) nor *adversely affect* (which perhaps would have been regarded as not being a *bona fide* choice of law under national English conflicts) the latter (the German text uses the single term 'affect' for both). One would have thought that the latter would naturally have followed in any event from the former, and need not therefore have been mentioned expressly; nevertheless, this may not always be so, for example, where, under the original applicable law, the contract is actually voidable through formal defect, but the seller has failed to avoid before the buyer resold to the third party in good faith, so that the third party obtained good title (see generally, *King's Norton Metal Co.* v. *Edridge, Merrett & Co. Ltd* (1897) 14 TLR 98); if the new applicable law states that the contract is formally void, it could be argued that this *should be given effect to* as not 'prejudicing' formal validity as between buyer and seller themselves under Article 3(2), in which event, but for the express saving for third parties thereunder, they might otherwise have been deprived of their previous rights, as a consequence of application of the new law. In this and other cases (for example, where the contract is formally *valid* under *both* laws), therefore, where according to original applicable law a third party is entitled to benefit under or as a result of a contract to which he is not privy, contractual invalidity or otherwise, or lack of privity, under the new law, is not permitted adversely to affect the third party's rights. It is not wholly clear why essential validity of the contract is not also to be protected from being prejudiced through application of the new law under Article 3(2). The Report simply indicates that the saving for formal validity was intended to avoid uncertainty in the period between contractual conclusion and change of applicable law, where parties specifically complied with formalities of the original law at the former date. However, this does not deal with the point that they might also have been aware of the contract's essential validity under the original law at that time. At least, nonetheless, in the case of third parties, these are not to be prejudiced by invalidity, whether the latter is formal or essential (although, in the latter case, it is unclear whether the newly chosen law would nevertheless govern essential validity as between the contracting parties, *inter se*, notwithstanding that third parties remain unaffected, or whether the variation is struck down *in toto erga omnes* – the latter, presumably). Yet, what is to be done where there are conflicting third party rights: for example, a contract of sale is essentially *invalid* under the original law, but valid under the new; prior to the variation, the seller, knowing the contract with the buyer to be invalid, sells to third party X; but the buyer, erroneously believing himself to have concluded a valid contract, resells to fourth party Y; if the variation is given effect to, Y will benefit, but X's rights are adversely affected; if it is not, X is protected, but Y loses out? It is submitted that 'rights' in Article 3(2) should be taken to refer to those existing under, or as a result of, the *original* applicable law – X's rights, in the example – rather than those which *would be* acquired under or as a result of the new choice – Y's in the example – and that accordingly, the variation in the example would not be permitted adversely to affect X's rights, even though this would be to the detriment of Y's expectations under or as a consequence of the attempted new law.

Finally, it should be reminded that *mandatory* rules of law of the country with which the situation 'at the time of the choice' is otherwise wholly connected are safeguarded under Article 3(3) notwithstanding choice of another law. Clearly, where the choice is varied under Article 3(2), relevant connections may be different from those existing at the date of the original choice, and this may consequently lead to application of different mandatory rules, or avoidance of those previously applicable – undoubtedly, a danger to the unwary. (This also brings to light the fact that, technically, where the law originally chosen was that of the country with which all other relevant connections were established, Article 3(2) is displaced, because the Convention would previously have been inapplicable thereto in such non-international circumstances under Article 1(1), and Article 3(2) does seem to assume that the original law would have been applicable *under the Convention*. It is suggested, however, that Article 3(2) should nonetheless be applied to the variation question in place of divergent national conflicts in such cases, since plainly Article 3(1) itself is inappropriate, as being tailored to original choices made in relation to the main contractual conclusion. In the converse situation, where, at the time of the subsequent choice of law, the connections are such that the contract is no longer international as it originally was (assuming that the original law may thus be eliminated as a factor from the subsequent internationality enquiry – not at all clearly the case), it is suggested that, whereas ability of the original applicable law under the Convention to be varied is subject to provision made therefor under Article 3(2), nevertheless, effectiveness of the new choice is a matter for national (private international) law outside the Convention in view of the subsequent non-international character of the contract.)

3 The fact that the parties have chosen a foreign law, whether or not accompanied by the choice of a foreign tribunal, shall not, where all the other elements relevant to the situation at the time of the choice are connected with one country only, prejudice the application of rules of the law of that country which cannot be derogated from by contract, hereinafter called 'mandatory rules'.

GENERAL CONSIDERATIONS

The Report explains that Article 3(3) is a compromise between those negotiators who believed that a choice of law should not be given effect to at all, where all other connections with the contract were established with another country, and others, in particular those representing the United Kingdom, who felt that such a choice could be justified even in the absence of any other foreign element: thus, the latter view was accepted, but protection is conferred under Article 3(3) in respect of 'mandatory rules' of that otherwise wholly connected law (p.18 – see Chapter 44 below, for criticism of the solution).

Accordingly, Article 3(3) forms part of the rather complex Convention regime (if indeed the latter description is even merited!) of safeguards for mandatory provisions of laws other than those otherwise applicable under the Convention.

(a) Effects of Article 3(3)

In the United Kingdom, Article 3(3) requires the application of ('shall not ... prejudice the application of')

- *English* contract-mandatory rules, when a foreign applicable law has been chosen, but England is otherwise wholly connected with the situation at issue;
- *foreign* contract-mandatory rules, when another law, possibly only foreign and not English (depending upon whether the word 'foreign' in the first line of Article 3(3) means, on the one hand, that the chosen law is *foreign to the English forum* or, on the other hand, that it is *foreign to the country with which the contract is otherwise wholly connected*), has been chosen.

It will further be seen from consideration of Article 7 – the general mandatory-protection provision under the Convention – that the Convention appears to adopt four different types of mandatory classifications in respect of national laws, which may be termed as follows:

1. *contracts-mandatory* (Articles 3(3), 5(2), 6(1), and including 7(1) and 9(6)) – national contract rules from which parties are not permitted to derogate by contractual exclusion under national laws (as so defined in Article 3(3)): for example, ss. 12–15 of the Sale of Goods Act 1979, under s.6 of the Unfair Contract Terms Act 1977 (other than in international cases under 1977 Act s.26);
2. *half-conflicts-mandatory* (Articles 7 and 9(6), and possibly also 3(3), 5(2) and 6(1)) – these are rules of national law which national conflicts law states cannot be avoided by choice of a foreign law, perhaps where the legal system of which they form part would otherwise apply in the absence of such choice (and subject to any national territorial or other qualification on application of the national contract rule, e.g. residence of parties in that state): for example, restrictions on contractual exclusion of liability in s.6 of the Unfair Contract Terms Act 1977, under s.27(2) thereof (other than in s.26 international cases); it seems fairly clear that such half-conflicts rules are covered by Articles 7 and 9(6), and it is even arguable that they are included within Article 3(3) itself (not to mention Articles 5(2) and 6(1)) on the basis that *derogation by contract*, prohibited thereunder, also covers derogation *by contractual choice of law*, although, this is open to debate since the texts thereof are ambiguous;

3   *full-conflicts-mandatory* (Articles 7 and 9(6)) – these are national contracts rules which apply according to national conflicts (subject to any spatial qualifications) whether the otherwise applicable foreign law would have governed on the basis of choice or as most connected or otherwise: for example, the Carriage of Goods by Sea Act 1971 (see *The Hollandia* [1983] AC 565); clearly, Articles 7 and 9(6) cover this type; (the question is, are they limited thereto, to the exclusion of *half-conflicts*-mandatory rules? It is thought not: see *infra*);
4   *full-conflicts-mandatory-plus* (Article 9(6)) – these are as the preceding category, but in addition the national contracts rules must be applicable irrespective of the country of contractual conclusion; only then may mandatory rules of form of *lex situs* apply in contracts for rights in or to use immovables under Article 9(6).

In all such cases, the nature of a particular national contract rule, as falling within one or other of these Convention categories, if any, is a matter of construction of the national law concerned: not simply express statutory designation as such will be taken into account, but also common law classification thereof carried out by the courts – even in the Convention case at hand, if not in the course of previous proceedings.

Furthermore, a national contract rule may actually come within two or more of these categories, where, say, parties are prohibited both from contracting out and from avoiding the latter restriction through choice of a foreign law: for example, ss.12–15 of the Sale of Goods Act 1979, implying terms into contracts for the sale of goods, are both *contracts-mandatory*, by virtue of s.6 of the Unfair Contract Terms Act 1977, which controls their direct exclusion under the contract, and *half-conflicts-mandatory*, by virtue of s.56 of the Sale of Goods Act 1979, which prevents their indirect avoidance through choice of a foreign law to govern the contract (in both cases, other than in international contracts, under 1979 Act s.56(3) and 1977 Act s.26: note that international contracts under these latter are defined as where parties' places of business or, if none, habitual residences, are in different states, and (a) the goods are, at conclusion of the contract, in the course of carriage, or to be carried, from one state to another; or (b) the acts constituting offer and acceptance have been done in different states; or (c) the contract provides for the goods to be delivered to the territory of a state other than that of offer and acceptance; clearly, therefore, the Convention – and with it Article 3(3), together with the other Convention provisions on national mandatory rules – may thus apply under its far less restrictive test of internationality for purposes of Article 1(1), even where the contract is not also international according to the national statutory definitions, so that such national contracts- or conflicts-mandatory rules are operative in relation to the national *non-international* contract). Furthermore, an argument may be put to the effect that it is virtually inevitable as a matter of construction that contracts-mandatory rules should also be held to be conflicts-mandatory at national law, and vice versa – or that, if not, Convention mandatory-protection should not necessarily have been conferred in respect of both types (see below, p.163, 211, 244, 246).

(b) Independent Role of Article 3(3)

Does Article 3(3) have such under the Convention mandatory system? Or are its effects obtainable by alternative means?

The answer is that as an anti-evasion, as opposed to party-protective, provision, it can have a specific role to play.

1   In the case of *English* contract-mandatory rules:
    (a) where wholly connected English law is that of a consumer's habitual residence (Article 5(2)), or place of habitual employment (Article 6(2)(a)), mandatory English rules are applicable in any event (except any which are not specifically for the consumer's/employee's protection) under Articles 5 and 6, and Article 3(3) is not needed (although, it may be easier to apply than Articles 5 and 6);
    (b) but where a consumer or individual employment contract is not involved, then, unless the English rule is also conflicts-mandatory (or conflicts-mandatory-plus, in the case of immovables formalities), Article 7(2) (or, as the case may be, Article 9(6)) is inapplicable: *Article 3(3) would then need to be relied on for application of the English rule*; if, however, the contract-mandatory rule *is* also conflicts-mandatory, Article 7(2) (or Article 9(6)) would seem to be the easier provision to rely on.
2   In the case of *foreign* contract-mandatory rules:
    (a) again, Articles 5 and 6 make Article 3(3) unnecessary in the case of mandatory consumer- and employment-protection rules;
    (b) in non-consumer- and non-employee-protection cases, however, if the foreign rule is not also conflicts-mandatory-plus, Article 9(6) is inapplicable (or, in Contracting States in which, unlike the United Kingdom, Article 7(1) applies, if not also conflicts-mandatory, in which case Article 7(1) would be inapplicable): *Article 3(3) must then be relied on for application of the foreign rule* (although, possibly, not when it is English law which was chosen, in English courts – see below, p.164). (Even if Article 7(1) were to

apply in the United Kingdom, and the foreign rule *was* also conflicts-mandatory, Article 7(1) is merely discretionary, whereas Article 3(3) is obligatory and consequently to be relied on, when its conditions are satisfied, instead of Article 7(1).)

In formal terms, therefore, it can be seen that Article 3(3) does possess some independent scope of operation.

However, whether the existence of separate provision on mandatory rules under Article 3(3) is justified or not, is another matter, which should be briefly alluded to at this stage.

(c) Justification for Article 3(3)

It is by no means clear whether the fundamental distinction implicit in the Convention system between mere contract-mandatory rules of national law and those which are conflicts-mandatory ought to be given credence. For it is difficult to accept, at least as a matter of construction (albeit, at present, in most cases, not yet decided) of contracts-mandatory rules, if not of express statutory provision, that such rules would be permitted to be avoided by choice of another law (if not by foreign applicable law in the absence of choice), or that, conversely, conflicts-mandatory rules would not also be considered to be contracts-mandatory at national law, so that parties are not allowed to contract on other terms. The significance, for the Convention system, of deciding whether the distinction is acceptable or not is as follows:

1 If the distinction between mere contract-mandatory and conflicts-mandatory is sustainable: then it has to be asked how it may be that Article 3(3) could possibly have been justified in *converting* into half-conflicts-mandatory rules those which were not even such, but merely contract-mandatory, at national law?

2 If the distinction is not sustainable: then Article 3(3) ought not to have been necessary for the Convention system, because in principle Article 7(2) and (1) would have operated so as to make such English or foreign contract- and conflicts-mandatory rules apply, except that (a) Article 7(1), as it happens, is inapplicable in the United Kingdom, so that Article 3(3) does have some effect; (b) Article 7(1) is merely discretionary, whereas Article 3(3) – presumably, because of the almost total connection – is obligatory; and (c) it is arguably the case – although, it is submitted, highly unlikely – that Article 7(1) and (2) is inapplicable to *half*-conflicts-mandatory rules, whereas Article 3(3)

could be construed as also applying thereto, and not merely to contracts-mandatory laws.

In the present writer's belief, the distinction may be admitted, but should not have been permitted to infiltrate the Convention system via Article 3(3) (or 5(2) and 6(1)). The latter should have been restricted to half-conflicts-mandatory rules, and could then have been justified, if restricted to safeguarding *foreign* such mandatory rules of an almost totally connected law (making it somewhat clearer that this is so even when English law is that chosen by the parties), since, as seen (a) English such rules are already able to be protected under Article 7(2) (provided that the latter does in fact apply to half-, not merely full-, conflicts-mandatory rules); and (b) although foreign such rules are the subject of Article 7(1), nevertheless the latter is inapplicable in the United Kingdom *et alia*, and is in any event merely discretionary (the connection thereunder simply being required to be 'close', and not almost complete). Mere contract-mandatory national rules, if they exist (see further, below, Article 7), on the other hand, should have been allowed to *go to the wall* if national law itself – as a matter of construction or statutory provision – thought fit to give them no further, conflicts protection, and they ought never to have made an appearance in Article 3(3).

CONDITIONS OF OPERATION OF ARTICLE 3(3)

There are six basic conditions according to which Article 3(3) is required to operate.

(a) Parties Have Chosen a Foreign Law

As stated, it is not clear from English or foreign texts whether 'foreign' is to be understood as meaning, on the one hand, *foreign to the English (or other) forum*, in which case, chosen foreign, but not English, law is displaced by mandatory rules of the otherwise wholly connected law under Article 3(3) in English fora, or, on the other hand, *foreign to the wholly connected law*, whereupon chosen English, as well as any other, law may be overridden thereunder in English proceedings. In the circumstances, it can hardly be objectionable for the latter interpretation to be allowed to prevail: and this is especially so, since, as will be seen, if English courts are also agreed on for any disputes (expressly not a factor preventing operation of Article 3(3)), they may be bound to accept such jurisdiction under Article 17 of the Judgments Convention, notwithstanding absence of any real connection with England; while, conversely, the scope for protection of *foreign* wholly connected laws from other *foreign* chosen laws may be reduced by jurisdictional constraints in the English courts.

(b) Whether or Not Accompanied by the Choice of a Foreign Tribunal

Even choice of the courts of the 'foreign' country whose law is chosen (*a fortiori* where such latter choice is actually implied from the former) will not prevent Article 3(3) from operating (nor, or course, where a third country's courts are selected). If England is the chosen country, the court may (dependent upon parties' Contracting State domicile: Article 17 para.1) be required to adjudicate under Article 17 (as well as possibly 15 in consumer cases) of the Judgments Convention (in the case of defendants not domiciled in a Judgments Convention State, English courts would possess discretionary jurisdiction on the basis of chosen English law of contract, under RSC Order 11 rule 1(1)(d)(iii)) on the other hand, if a foreign Judgments Convention country is chosen, English courts may have to decline jurisdiction in favour thereof; and if a non-Judgments Convention country is agreed on, it is likely that in such circumstances the English court may feel inclined to stay its jurisdiction in favour of the former or of courts of the most connected country. Accordingly, Article 3(3)'s operation, in practice, may be confined to protection of mandatory rules of (i) wholly connected English law, where a foreign law is chosen (provided that the latter is not also that of a Judgments Convention State, whose courts are agreed on); (ii) wholly connected foreign law, where English law and courts are chosen (provided that Article 3(3) operates to displace English law – see above, p.164); and (iii) wholly connected foreign law X, where foreign law Y is chosen, and English courts are agreed on under Article 17 of the Judgments Convention – to the exclusion of cases where the law (if not also courts) of foreign country Y is chosen, but foreign country X has all other connections, in which case English courts are unlikely to possess or to exercise national jurisdiction on a non-choice basis. Those who object, therefore, to the inclusion of Article 3(3) in the Convention, as an unnecessary intrusion into the sphere of Article 7(1), may not be too disturbed by any such jurisdictional restrictions upon its actual scope in practice.

(c) All the Other Elements

Article 3(3)'s *raison d'être* is that not just some, but all (with the exception of any agreement on jurisdiction) other elements are attached to a country other than that whose law is chosen, thereby giving the former's law a legitimate claim to govern in mandatory areas.

(d) Relevant to the Situation

'Relevant' (missing from foreign texts of Article 3(3), yet offering courts a degree of flexibility otherwise lacking in the absence of discretion thereunder) is the great imponderable – conceivably, every single factor could have some effect upon applicable law in the absence of choice. As in the case of deciding upon internationality of a contract as a precondition of the Convention's applicability as a whole therefore, courts will need to adopt a reasoned, commercially-minded approach in deciding which connections with third countries (or fourth, if the forum's sole connection is that of parties' choice of jurisdiction) are so overwhelmingly neutralized by those of the most connected country as not even to retain what would otherwise have been their competing relevance to choice of law. The fact that the contract for the car purchased by one Italian from another in Italy *was made in France* should not prevent Article 3(3) from operating to safeguard mandatory Italian rules from the application of chosen English law in English courts, since the French connection can hardly be thought to be of any real relevance at all. It should also be noted in this connection that choice of courts of country X, where Y law is chosen to govern the contract and all other connections are with country Z, is not to be taken as a relevant factor detracting from Z's otherwise totality of connections for purposes of Article 3(3), because, as indicated, the latter does not in fact appear to assume, neither in English nor in foreign texts, that chosen law and courts are necessarily those of the *same* country, when expressly discarding these accompanying factors as restraints on operation of Article 3(3). As for relevance to the 'situation', this is clearly intended to enable courts to take account of all factors which might otherwise have been found to be material to applicable law in the absence of choice – such as parties' residence and perhaps also law governing previous dealings – rather than being confined to the specific terms of the contract. (Arguably too, as in the case of Article 7(1) – 'with which the situation has a close connection': see below, Chapter 12 – elements relevant to the *situation* may be held to be confined to those which are of special significance in relation to the issue in dispute before the court, rather than having to be established with the contract as a whole; although, in the present submission, it is questionable whether such an approach is practicable in the case of Article 3(3), under which, first, *all* relevant connections have to be shown to exist with a particular country, in contrast to the far more vague and flexible test of 'close connection' to be satisfied under Article 7(1), and where secondly, the elements are required to be relevant 'at the time of the choice' (see below) as opposed to some later date of dispute, which suggests that the situation in question under Article 3(3) *is* the contract and surrounding circumstances as a whole.)

(e) At the Time of the Choice

This time limitation prevents subsequent manipulation of factors by parties in order to secure the operation of mandatory rules of a particular law following conclusion of contract.

(f) Connected With One Country Only

As seen, this is the basis of obligatory Article 3(3). Choice of another law itself is obviously discounted, and – as previously indicated, on the basis of the text and of any desire which may be felt to accord Article 3(3) a wider practical scope than would otherwise be the case – choice of a third (not just chosen law's) country's courts may also be disregarded as detracting from the otherwise totality of most connected country's connections. Once again, it is reminded that in the case of connections totally with the United Kingdom notwithstanding choice of another law, by virtue of Article 19(1), it will be England and Wales, Scotland and Northern Ireland which may (that is, if they have separate laws of contract on the issue) have to be treated as 'countries' for this and other Convention purposes, so that unless the connections are with one of these 'countries' on its own, Article 3(3) will not apply, even if the connections are otherwise exclusive to the United Kingdom as a whole.

OPERATION OF THE MANDATORY RULES

(a) Rules of the Law of That Country Which Cannot be Derogated from by Contract, Hereinafter Called 'Mandatory Rules'

It was earlier questioned whether Article 3(3) ought not to have been restricted to operation of rules which were already *half-conflicts-mandatory* at national law, for example, s.6 of the Unfair Contract Terms Act 1977 (by virtue of s.27(2) of the latter, other than in international cases under s.26), rather than merely contracts-mandatory, if the latter were even truly to exist (see too below – chapters 11 and 12). In addition, as seen, it could actually be argued that the former *are* in fact included, because derogation 'by contract' might be said to include derogation by contractual provision for choice of foreign law, as much as any direct contractual exclusion of substantive legal liability.

(b) Shall Not ... Prejudice the Application of

Article 3(3) uses this somewhat reticent formula, rather than simply prescribing application of mandatory rules. The message, in particular taking into account foreign texts, such as the German and French, seems to be that it is the *content* of the mandatory rules which should be preserved, rather than the application thereof as such: provided that chosen law's substance and effects are broadly the same therefore as those which would result from operation of the mandatory rules of the otherwise wholly connected law, it would seem that the functioning norms will be those of the former rather than the latter. In addition of course, in spite of the imperative nature of the rule in Article 3(3), any national law element of discretion as to applicability of mandatory laws, and naturally also any spatial and territorial limitations thereunder, are incorporated.

4   The existence and validity of the consent of the parties as to the choice of the applicable law shall be determined in accordance with the provisions of Articles 8, 9 and 11.

EXISTENCE AND VALIDITY OF CONSENT

Matters of offer and acceptance, mistake, and duress and undue influence (*existence*), formal validity, misrepresentation and contractual capacity (*validity*) in relation to *the choice of applicable law term*, are governed according to applicable law under the specified Convention provisions, in the same manner as these latter apply to the substantive contract itself (and the choice of law agreement may be separately valid or invalid according to the governing law, irrespective of validity or otherwise of the main contract). Arguably, Article 8(1) ('or of any term of a contract') could have applied to choice of law in any event.

LAW APPLICABLE TO CHOICE OF LAW

- Essential validity and existence of consent are matters for the law chosen itself (Article 8(1)), unless a party would be taken not to have consented according to the law of his habitual residence and it is unreasonable for the law alleged to have been chosen to govern consent (Article 8(2)).
- Formal validity of the choice of law agreement is for Article 9.
- Capacity is excluded from the Convention's scope, subject to Article 11 in the case of natural persons.

Article 3(4), therefore, is the final word in 'bootstrapping' (see *Gerli & Co. Inc* v. *Cunard S.S. Co. Ltd* 48 F 2d 115 (2nd Cir. 1931)): not only is the existence and validity of a main contract to be assessed according to a choice of law clause contained therein, before the contract, together with that term, has been held to be valid and existing (Article 8), but the existence and validity of consent to the alleged choice of law agreement itself, if in issue, is subjected to the same rule (*hauled up by its bootstraps before it is even known whether it is on firm ground*). (Article 3(4) does not also refer to Article 10(1)(a) applicable law for interpretation of the choice of law term, so that, seemingly, *lex fori* should be resorted to on interpretation – although, presumably, there can be no more objection to bootstrapping interpretation than there is to such treatment of existence and validity.)

Clearly the method is controversial. The choice may be felt to have been between, on the one hand, the rule adopted in Article 3(4) (the US Second Restatement, para. 187, permits bootstrapping – as opposed to objective applicable law – but only so as to *validate* agreements: see Juenger, in North (ed.) (1982), p.298, and below p.272), which, although illogical, is nonetheless a factor in favour of uniformity, and, on the other hand, *lex fori*'s rules on existence, validity, form and capacity, as a matter of procedure and policy-selectivity for the forum, more sound in principle than the preceding, yet potentially disastrous from the unificationist standpoint. (In *Mackender* v. *Feldia AG* [1966] 3 All ER 847, concerning service out of the jurisdiction under RSC Order 11 r.1(1) on the ground of contractual conclusion within England and Wales, LORD DENNING MR (pp.849–50) and DIPLOCK LJ (p.852) seemed to contemplate that English *lex fori* would apply to determine whether a Belgian jurisdiction and law clause was void and non-existent, rather than the chosen Belgian proper law itself (or presumably, any objective foreign proper law in the absence of choice), so as to enable the clause to be discounted as a factor against grant of leave to serve out under Order 11 – compare the decision of the German Federal Supreme Court, III ZR 150/87, that validity of a jurisdiction clause was for the law governing the contract as a whole, whether part of its substantive or procedural law (1989) ELD 252; von Hoffmann, in Lando (ed.) (1975), pp.22–3, mentions further possibilities: objective applicable law, habitual residence of a silent party, discretion of the court, customs between the parties, and usages of international trade; see too Kühne, in Lando (ed.), *European Private International Law of Obligations* (1975) p.124.)

In the present submission, Cheshire and North's support for objective applicable law, otherwise applicable to the contract in the absence of choice, as being appropriate to govern effectiveness of choice of law (p.454 – see too *The Hollandia* [1983] AC 565, p.576, LORD DIPLOCK), could be an acceptable middle route between the two extremes: it is not entirely logical, nor perhaps as jurisprudentially compelling as *lex fori*, in subjecting choice of law's validity to the law objectively governing a contract of which (together with *contracts*-relevant factors objectively taken into account) the very existence may be denied, and which may ultimately be held thereunder to be subject to the different, chosen law (see further below, Chapter 13); nor is the Article 4 process of enquiry as likely to lead to a uniform result on applicable law amongst different Contracting States as would the resort to allegedly chosen law under Article 3 itself. Nevertheless, it does seem to have offered a practical and not wholly objectionable means of avoiding the extremes of the other two methods.

EXPRESS CHOICE OF PRE-EXISTING ENGLISH CONFLICTS SO AS TO DISPLACE THE CONVENTION

F.A.Mann, a critic of the United Kingdom's adoption of the Convention, has suggested that the latter can be sidestepped through parties' agreement on English conflicts as in force on 31 March 1991 ('The Proper Law of the Contract – An Obituary' (1991), 107 *LQR* 353): this is said to be not inconsistent with the Convention's own content and character in favour of party autonomy.

It is seriously doubted whether this argument can run.

In the first place, it is perfectly plain from the Preamble and Article 1(1) that the Convention *is* mandatory, and it is the United Kingdom's international obligation to ensure that it is so applied by its courts.

Secondly, autonomy is certainly central to the Convention, but it is highly questionable whether this may also extend to the very policy law-selection rules which courts – as opposed to arbitrators (see, for example, Article 1496 of the New French Code of Civil Procedure: *L'arbitre tranche le litige conformément aux règles de droit que les parties ont choisies; à défaut d'un tel choix, conformément à celles qu'il estime appropriées...Il tient compte dans tous les cas des usages du commerce*) – must apply to cases before them, at least without courting the charge of attempted ouster. Technically, choice of pre-existing English conflicts law might be given effect to, if permitted in accordance with applicable law under the Convention! Yet difficulties in finding the appropriate solution to the issue thereunder where applicable law is that of a Contracting State – *a fortiori*, the United Kingdom itself – would seem to indicate that such a choice of pre-existing conflicts law should be treated as non-justiciable in the English courts and disregarded in favour of Convention rules.

9 Article 4: Applicable Law in the Absence of Choice

Article 4

Applicable law in the absence of choice

1 To the extent that the law applicable to the contract has not been chosen in accordance with Article 3, the contract shall be governed by the law of the country with which it is most closely connected. Nevertheless, a severable part of the contract which has a closer connection with another country may by way of exception be governed by the law of that other country.

IN THE ABSENCE OF CHOICE

Article 4 concerns those frequent cases where parties have neither expressly nor impliedly selected a law to govern their contract. Private international law has to step in to provide a just and commercially effective solution.

CONTRACT GOVERNED BY LAW OF MOST CONNECTED COUNTRY: ARTICLE 4(1)

This is the fundamental rule of applicable law in the absence of choice laid down by Article 4(1): the contract is governed by

> the law of the country with which it is most closely connected (*méthode du centre de gravité*)

If anything, the rule in Article 4(1) is closest to the pre-existing *English* conflicts approach of applying the *objective proper law*, without reference to any fictitious, hypothetical or presumed intent, in the absence of express or implied choice of law by the parties (see *The Assunzione* [1954] P. 150; *Amin Rasheed Corpn* v. *Kuwait Insurance Co.* [1984] AC 50, 61; *Coast Lines Ltd* v. *Hudig and Veder Chartering NV* [1972] 2 QB 34).

Other European laws, however, varied from one to the other: France and Germany tended to place greater emphasis upon the parties' presumed will, in the absence of an express choice (looking to place of performance and habitual residence of each party where factors were balanced, in the case of Germany: see von Hoffmann, in North (ed.) (1982), p. 226); while, in Italy, courts would resort to fixed rules of parties' common *lex nationalis*, or to *lex loci contractus* in the absence thereof, in such circumstances (Report, pp.19–20).

(a) Country With Which ... Most Closely Connected

There is a degree of uncertainty over whether a contract is to be most closely connected with a particular *law* (*Bonython* v. *Commonwealth of Australia* [1951] AC 201, 219; *Amin Rasheed* [1984] AC 50, 61) or *country* (*Re United Railways of Havana and Regla Warehouses Ltd* [1961] AC 1007, 1068) under pre-existing English conflicts (see *James Miller & Partners Ltd* v. *Whitworth Street Estates (Manchester) Ltd* [1970] AC 583), with recent trends appearing to favour the former (see *Rossano* v. *Manufacturers Life Insurance Company* [1962] 2 All ER 214, 218; 'The Iran Vojdan' [1984] 2 Lloyd's Rep. 380, 383 col. 1; Cheshire and North, p. 463). Article 4 makes it absolutely clear that it is the *country* of closest connection which prevails, should there be a conflict – although, plainly, laws are attached to countries, so that a definite link with a particular law will be a most powerful factor in establishing its host country as being, to that extent, connected with the contract (on the other hand, the German text of Article 1(1) concerning the international scope of the Convention does refer to the requirement of a connection with the *law* of different countries). Country, rather than simply law connections, as the ultimate test, does seem more logical, where parties have chosen applicable law neither expressly nor impliedly.

(b) Contract ... is Most Closely Connected

The reference in Article 4(1) to the law of the country with which 'it', *meaning the contract*, is most closely connected suggests that it is those features and effects of the contract itself which must principally be shown to be connected with a particular country, rather than the more general *situation* as such, including extraneous elements, such as parties' residence and place of business, and previous course of dealing – although, these latter are of course of some relevance, as relating to the parties to the contract themselves, and are consequently attracted, indirectly, into the sphere of the contract itself, and it would certainly seem extraordinary if the pre-existing English practice of seeking to determine objective proper law, as that which is most closely connected with the *transaction* embodied in the contract (Cheshire and North, p.464, as the 'substance of the contractual obligation and what is to be done under the contract') rather than with the technical forms of the latter itself, the province of implied choice of law, were not to be continued with, notwithstanding the textual ambiguity. Those factors usually taken into account by English courts in seeking to ascertain the objective proper law, therefore, include connections such as *locus contractus*, *locus solutionis*, and nature, subject matter and standard terms of the contract (Cheshire and North, p. 465; *Re United Railways of Havana and Regla Warehouses Ltd* [1960] Ch.52) – as well as choice of court or arbitration, as an objective connection with the forum, where this otherwise fails to give rise to an implied choice of the forum's law under Article 3(1). The Report rather confusingly states that, in order to determine country of closest connection, it is also possible 'to take account of factors which supervened after the conclusion of the contract' (p. 20). It is possible that this would be contrary to pre-existing English conflicts practice (see North, in North (ed.) *Contract Conflicts* (1982), p. 13; *James Miller & Partners Ltd. v. Whitworth Street Estates (Manchester) Ltd* [1970] AC 583, 603, 611, 614–15; *Compagnie d'Armement Maritime SA v. Compagnie Tunisienne de Navigation SA* [1971] AC 572, 602–8; *Amin Rasheed Shipping Corpn v. Kuwait Insurance Co.* [1984] AC50, p.69). It may be that a distinction could be drawn in the light of the authorities between, on the one hand, consideration of subsequent conduct in order to infer an implied intention of parties at the time of contracting, which should quite properly be held to be excluded, and, on the other hand, the taking into account of connections established objectively with the transaction subsequent to contract as factors demonstrating the most closely connected law in the absence of express or implied choice of law, the objections to which would in principle be far fewer. Nevertheless, it remains the case that admission of the latter under Article 4(1) or pre-existing English conflicts would create an undesirable risk of manipulation and instability, and, accordingly, it is submitted that in conformity with the general Convention system (see Articles 3(3), 4(2) and 4(4)) and in order to prevent unnecessary uncertainty, subsequent factors should only be taken into account *as evidence of the strength* of connections existing as at the date of contractual conclusion (and even then treated with some reserve), and not as independent factors in their own right. (Certainly, the matter of ascertainment of law of most closely connected country is not one of *contractual interpretation* for decision in accordance with the principles of putative applicable law under Article 10(1)(a). It is rather a question of *application of the Convention*, to be carried out in conformity with unificationist principles under Article 18; and see Chapter 8 preceding, for similar consideration of the question of factors relevant to implied choice of law under Article 3, where the point is made that Article 10(1)(a) is not amongst Convention provisions to be referred to in assessing agreement to choice of law under Article 3(4), so that *lex fori*'s rules would govern the time factor as to relevant facts thereunder, even if the matter were not to be regarded as procedural and evidential in any event.) Nor, in the present writer's view, is it possible to mount an argument to the opposite effect on the basis that the words 'most closely connected' (*liens les plus étroits/die engsten Verbindungen*) in Article 4(1) are wider than 'closest and *most real* connection' which might otherwise have been employed and that the requirement of *relevance* of factors – that is, the *most real* thereof (in respect of time, or otherwise)– need not therefore be found to be satisfied. Convention drafters must surely be taken to have been concerned solely with connections of sufficient substance and materiality to be capable of leading to most appropriate applicable law.

SCOPE OF LAW APPLICABLE IN THE ABSENCE OF CHOICE

Law applicable to the contract under Article 4(1) may apply *severably*, to part only of the contract, in two situations:

(a) To the Extent That ... Has Not Been Chosen in Accordance with Article 3

As previously seen, Article 3(1) permits parties to select the law to apply to the whole or a part only of their contract. In the latter event, the most connected law will govern the remainder of the contract under Article 4(1): must that connection however, still be established with the contract as a whole, including those elements subject to the chosen law, or should it be restricted to the part excluded from the selected law? The latter, surely.

It will be recalled furthermore from the previous discussion in connection with Article 3(1), that such *dépeçage* may only be given effect to where Article 3 and 4 laws are not inconsistent; if they are so, Article 4 alone should apply (Report, p. 17).

(b) Severable Part of Contract More Closely Connected with Another Country

Article 4 itself sanctions operation of more than one law to severable parts of the contract most closely connected with different countries in the absence of choice (presumably, 'closer connection' of the severable part with another country means *most* closely connected therewith, where the severable part has a closer connection with more than one country). Negotiators were anxious not to encourage severability, but decided to make express provision therefor in the text itself, because reference merely in the Report might not have been taken into account in certain Contracting States (Report, p. 23). Nevertheless, in order to discourage severance, the latter possibility is qualified by the expression 'by way of exception' in Article 4(1), which the Report says is to be interpreted 'in the sense that the court must have recourse to severance as seldom as possible' (*ibid.*: and see Pryles, 'An Australian Perspective', in North (ed.) (1982), pp.340–1, on the merits or otherwise of *dépeçage*). The Report also points out that it is a part of the contract, not the dispute, which must be independent and separable for purposes of Article 4(1), examples being contracts for joint ventures and other complex transactions (*ibid.*).

Under previous English conflicts, *scission* of the contract is believed to be possible in principle (see *Hamlyn* v. *Talisker Distillery* [1984] AC 202, 207; *Re United Railways of the Havana and Regla Warehouses Ltd* [1960] Ch.52, 92; *Re Helbert Wagg & Co.Ltd* [1956] Ch.323, 340; *Forsakringsiktieselskapet Vesta* v. *Butcher* [1986] 2 All ER 488, 504–5, affd on other grounds in [1988] 2 All ER 43 and [1989] 1 All ER 402; and *Libyan Arab Foreign Bank* v. *Bankers Trust Co.* [1989] 3 All ER 252, 267 – in the latter case, p.267, Article 4(1) was actually referred to by way of analogy as exceptionally permitting severability), but courts are reluctant to carry it out, save in exceptional, unusual and compelling circumstances, unlikely to include mere different places of performance of the parties (*Kahler* v.*Midland Bank* [1950] AC 24, 42; *Zivnostenska Banka* v. *Frankman* [1950] AC 57, 83).

'Severable' in Article 4(1) is a term without any immediately apparent meaning. *Question*: when is a part of a contract severable for Article 4(1)? *Answer*: when it is sufficiently independent of the remainder of the contract for choice of law policy purposes. *Question*: when is a part of a contract thus sufficiently independent? *Answer*: when it is severable. Clearly, the European Court should be encouraged to flesh out the vacuous concept, for the sake of both uniformity and facilitation of national courts' task of determining applicable law. Presumably, if one part of the contract is socially and economically integrated within a different country from that of the rest of the contract of which it forms part, this, in itself, essentially, *choice of law* form of severability and therefore not necessarily also *substantive* contractual severability, may not be sufficient to amount to severability for purposes of Article 4(1), given the distinction implicit in the very text of Article 4(1) between a 'severable' part of the contract which *has* a closer connection with another country from the rest, and a part – nonetheless 'severable' – which does *not* have such closer connection (nor is mere physical separation of terms within, or from, the contractual document adequate): for example, there may be a joint venture between French and German companies to research and develop a product, and to organize its worldwide marketing, in France and Germany respectively, which is thus choice-of-law, but not substantively, severable. Consequently, it may be the case that an additional element is required – substantive severability, in the sense that each part of the agreement is different from the other and would retain independent commercial viability, even if the other part had never been considered or at least agreed to (a good test might be that the rest of the contract would stand, if the severable part proved void): for example, where X agrees with Y to execute a building lease in France and to introduce Y to sources of finance, for other projects in Germany. (Such a construction is strongly supported by foreign texts of Article 4(1), which require the part to be severable *and* to have a closer connection with another country.) Where a contract is thus held to be severable for purposes of Article 4(1), one supposes furthermore that for 'performance which is characteristic of the contract' under Article 4(2), there should be substituted 'performance which is characteristic *of the severable part* of the contract in question', given that the Article 4(2) presumption may have figured in the Article 4(1)-severability assessment in the first place.

Finally, the word 'may' in the second sentence of Article 4(1) is ambiguous: is it permissive, in the sense that the party to whose advantage it is to claim severability is allowed – though not obliged – to plead separate applicable law thereto; or does it confer a discretion on the court to decline to accede to that party's request to apply such different law to the part established as severable? It can be argued that administration of justice considerations operate in favour of the second interpretation, and that courts should possess an ultimate power to refuse to apply severable law where this would be felt to disrupt the orderly pursuance of contractual relations between the parties. In the present submission, however, this would be wrong and the first interpretation should prevail: the second meaning would add even more uncertainty for parties and lawyers to an already difficult process of determination of applicable law in the absence of choice under Article 4, and any flexibility required by courts to safeguard the internal cohesion of contractual regulation should be present within the test of severability of the contract itself, which, as suggested, may include choice of law consideration, as well as there being a general test of practicability of severance. Furthermore, on a purely textual basis, foreign versions of Article 4(1) (*will be able to/can ... be governed*) lend some support to the view here canvassed.

2   Subject to the provisions of paragraph 5 of this Article, it shall be presumed that the contract is most closely connected with the country where the party who is to effect the performance which is characteristic of the contract has, at the time of conclusion of the contract, his habitual residence, or, in the case of a body corporate or unincorporate, its central administration. However, if the contract is entered into in the course of that party's trade or profession, that country shall be the country in which the principal place of business is situated or, where under the terms of the contract the performance is to be effected through a place of business other than the principal place of business, the country in which that other place of business is situated.

5   Paragraph 2 shall not apply if the characteristic performance cannot be determined, and the presumptions in paragraphs 2, 3 and 4 shall be disregarded if it appears from the circumstances as a whole that the contract is more closely connected with another country.

DISPLACEABLE AND REBUTTABLE PRESUMPTIONS OF APPLICABLE LAW: ARTICLE 4(2)

(a) The Presumptions under Article 4(2)

The following countries are rebuttably presumed to be most closely connected with the contract for purposes of applicability of their laws under Article 4(1):

- *in the case of natural persons*, the country where the party who is to effect the performance which is characteristic of the contract has at the time of contractual conclusion *his habitual residence*;
- *in the case of bodies corporate or unincorporate*, the country where the party who is to effect the performance which is characteristic of the contract has at the time of contractual conclusion *its central administration*;

EXCEPT THAT
- in the case of either natural persons or bodies corporate or unincorporate, *if the contract is entered into in the course of the characteristic performer's trade or profession*, for the country of his

habitual residence or, as the case may be, its central administration, there is substituted:
(i) the country of the principal place of business or,
(ii) where such characteristic contractual performance is to be carried out through a place of business in a country other than that of the principal place of business, the country of the former place of business.

The presumptive method of ascertaining applicable law under Article 4(2) is intended to combine a degree of certainty and uniformity (*rigidité*) with the overall principle of flexibility (*souplesse*) in Article 4(1), in the absence of choice of law (Report, p. 20). National English conflicts law no longer relies on presumptions, with all factors being assessed together, and conclusive weight being accorded to none (see *The Assunzione* [1954] P. 150); and one writer suggests that the presumptive approach in Article 4(2) is in fact more about convenience, in the working of the closest connection test, than justice and operation of most appropriate law (see Jaffey, 'Choice of Law in Relation to *Ius Dispositivum*', in North, (ed.)(1982), pp.38–9). Professor Merkin points out that Article 4(2) leads to the law of the supplier's location, whereas pre-existing English conflicts could frequently result in the law of the place of performance (see (1991) *Journal of Business Law* 205, 216).

It is of course the very basis of the presumptions in Article 4(2) – characteristic performance of the contract – which has proved to be even more controversial than reliance itself upon those presumptions. The meaning of that concept should now therefore be examined.

(b) Party Who is to Effect the Performance Which is Characteristic of the Contract

The 'characteristic performance' is previously unknown to *English* jurisprudence. Latterly, the European Court has utilized the concept in Article 4(2), in its interpretation of place of performance of the *obligation in question* as affording jurisdiction over contracts of employment under Article 5(1) of the Judgments Convention, the employee's obligation to work having been held to be that which characterized the contract (see *Ivenel* v. *Schwab*, Case 133/81 [1982] ECR 1891; *Shenavai v. Kreischer*, Case 266/85 [1987]ECR 239 – note *Union Transport plc* v. *Continental Lines S.A.* [1992] 1 W.L.R. 15, 20–1 (H.L.(E)); *Six Constructions Ltd* v. *Humbert*, Case 32/88 [1989] ECR 341), and this construction has now effectively been incorporated into Article 5(1) of the Judgments Convention, as amended by Article 4 of the San Sebastian Convention on Spanish/Portuguese accession thereto, and into Article 5(1) of the Lugano Convention between the

EC and EFTA states ('where the employee habitually carries out his work'). Yet these decisions have done little to clarify the essential nature of the concept and major difficulties persist (for detailed analysis, see Kaye, *Extension of the Judgments Convention in Europe under the San Sebastian and Lugano Conventions* (1993), Dartmouth).

General considerations

The first problem with 'performance which is characteristic of the contract' in Article 4(2) is that it is devoid of any innate, objectively ascertainable meaning, and must therefore be applied and translated, rather than construed and interpreted – a state of affairs which does little to impede the progress of subjectivity and diversity amongst different Contracting States' courts, ironically the very potential effects of Article 4(1) which Article 4(2) is intended to forestall. In the second place, even when it comes to applying the concept, the crucial term, 'characteristic', is in fact capable of being understood in two different ways, which may not always be reconcilable: that is to say, on the one hand, it may be read as being intended to isolate, internally, within the contract, what may roughly be called *the most important* of all the obligations thereunder, if any one such is ascertainable in the particular case (the presumption being inapplicable under Article 4(5) if it is not), or for that matter, in any case, in practice; whereas, on the other hand, it may be taken as describing the factor which *distinguishes that type of contract*, externally, from other types of contract. Thus, it does not automatically follow that what may loosely be called the *most important* obligation under a contract is also one that *distinguishes* that contract from others (for example, delivery may be regarded as being most important in *all* of contracts of sale, of hire, and of barter of goods, so that it distinguishes none from the others); while, conversely, a *distinguishing* feature may be relatively *minor* in the overall context of the contract (for example, the duty to return any security or deposit paid for goods hired). Wheels and engines may be the most important elements of motor *cars*, but they do not distinguish them from motor *cycles*; a car's boot on the other hand does distinguish it from the latter, but is hardly the most important part of the conveyance. Adoption of the external meaning of 'characteristic', therefore, might not only lead to absurd results (although the latter may be able to be avoided through rebuttal of the presumption of closest connection under Article 4(5) in such cases), but also seems inappropriate in principle, in that applicable law in the absence of choice, one would have thought, ought to derive from the socio-economic impact and internal mechanical working of contracts, rather than from their external, relative position in respect of contracts existing globally and conceptually. It is submitted, consequently, that it is the 'internal' approach towards application of the characteristic performance concept which is the proper method of proceeding: 'characteristic' means most important: or perhaps, because 'important' seems so hopelessly subjective, 'significant' would be preferable. 'Significance' would then be assessed according to dual criteria: (i) the particular performance should be the most significant for the type of contract in question; and (ii) in addition, the performance should be the most significant under the actual contract of that type, which may contain special or unusual or additional terms which have the effect of reducing what might otherwise have been the greatest significance of a particular performance obligation under contracts in general of such type. The first-mentioned criterion is not essential in principle, but only for the sake of certainty and precedent; and classification of 'types' of contract for these purposes should be carried out according to the authorities as they develop, rather than, necessarily, *a priori*, in fulfilment of some scientific scheme: there is little point, for example, in classifying sale of goods and agency contracts as falling within the same broad category, on the basis, say, that both may involve *supply of goods* by manufacturer to, as the case may be, retailer or agent, when clearly, most significant performance obligations in these two types of contract are delivery and agency respectively.

As to which performance obligation under a contract should be held to be *most significant*, it is suggested that the obligation in question should be that whose character is the overwhelming feature of the contract, in the following – admittedly difficult – sense: namely, that it involves activities which are called upon in society or commerce as being essential to the maintenance and development of the fabric of national and international socio-economic coexistence, including the channels of finance. Colloquially, these are the 'fixer' obligations – the socio-economic facilitators – aspects of performance which bring about the greatest change in status under the contract, between a party or parties thereto, in relation to such environmental, tangible, physical, intangible, or mental conditions as previously existed, and to which ancillary obligations of finance and otherwise are made to relate. The Report itself hints at such an underlying meaning (p.20):

> The submission of the contract, in the absence of a choice by the parties, to the law appropriate to the characteristic performance defines the connecting factor of the contract from the inside, and not from the outside by elements unrelated to the essence of the obligation such as the nationality of the contracting parties ....
> In addition it is possible to relate the concept of characteristic performance to an even more general idea, namely the idea that his performance refers to the function which the legal relationship involved fulfils in the economic and social life of any country. The concept of the characteristic performance links the contract to the social and economic environment of which it will form a part.

Reference to 'essence' of the obligation recalls the substance-of-the-cause-of-action-in-tort test of *locus delicti* in the private international law of tort: although, far more certainty than this, however, is required in contract conflicts.

Nevertheless, Vischer too (in Lipstein (ed.) (1978), p.27), harbours similar thoughts as to the nature of the characteristic obligation, in asking 'which is the state in whose socio-legal sphere the contract is embedded ...?'

Concrete applications

Such then, it is believed, is the general policy approach to be adopted in applying the characteristic performance test in Article 4(2). But what of its concrete application? What are the results that are to be reached in practice in respect of different types of contracts?

In the case of the so-called 'unilateral' contracts (Report, p.20), where only one party agrees to confer a benefit, it is clearly the latter which constitutes characteristic performance: for example

- donation (*Schenkung*);
- mandate (*Auftrag*);
- bailee's custody under a bailment;
- gratuitous contract in a deed.

With regard to 'bilateral'/'reciprocal' contracts, the Report stipulates that the obligation to pay money under a contract, as the price of the other party's counter-performance, is *not* the characteristic performance: on the contrary, the latter is the performance for which such payment is due (pp.20 and 21) (see too Vischer, 'The Principle of the Typical Performance in International Contracts and the Draft Convention', in Lipstein (ed.) (1978), *Harmonisation of Private International Law in the EEC*, p.25): for example

- delivery of goods, in sale, hire or hire-purchase (*Vineh Construction Company Limited* v. *Houthandel G. Wijma en Zonen BV* (1989) ELD 252, The Netherlands; *C.M.I. Corporation* v. *ICA (Isis Computer Associates) Europe BV* (1989) ELD 412, The Netherlands; and Case 3 KfH 0 97/98, Landgericht Stuttgart (1990) ELD 112, Germany);
- grant of right to use movable property – subject to extent of user's duties to maintain or employ, beyond mere payment of fee;
- construction;
- provision of a service, such as transport, legal (*S* v. *K*, Recueil Dalloz Sirey, Nos 1–27, 1983, J 146, 147, 'Considérant implicitement que la mission des avocats constituait la prestation caractéristique du contrat'), insurance, and banking operations, and security (one could also mention, for example, employment, agency (*Bata* v. *Beugro* (1984) (Netherlands)) and guarantee: although, the former is the

province of Article 6(2) on applicable law) 'which usually constitutes the centre of gravity and the socio-economic function of the contractual transaction' (p.20);
- to which may be added, the payment of money where this is the service provided, as in a contract for provision of running credit, and in loans and financing operations, whether in the course of banking and other operations mentioned or otherwise (it is disagreed with one writer who insinuates that *repayment* of a loan may be more characteristic than the provision of the money: see Morse (1982) 2 *Yearbook of European Law*, 107, 128; repayment may be a major feature of the debtor's life, especially if many instalments are called for, but it can hardly be described as the essence and most important object of the contract, as a national or global socio-economic facilitator: the *need* for loans precedes the *desire* for interest – and perhaps Biblical, rather than City, perceptions ought therefore to be allowed to prevail on this occasion!).

These formulations seem to correspond with Article 117 of the Swiss Private International Law Statute of 1987, embodying principles developed in previous Swiss case law.

In some types of contract, however, it may not be possible to isolate one particular performance obligation which is more significant and characteristic of the contract than another (see Jaffey, in North (ed.) (1982), p.39): for example,

- joint venture and cooperation agreements between enterprises (such as where one party has to carry out research and development, and the other to finance the experimentation and market the resultant product) (provided, of course, that the contract in question is not held to be severable and subject to different – presumptively ascertained – applicable laws: see earlier, on Article 4(1));
- contracts of exchange;
- contracts between author and publisher of a work, to write and publish respectively.

In these cases, where it is not possible to determine 'the' characteristic performance, Article 4(2) will be inapplicable, under Article 4(5) (in one German case (1989) I.Prax 51, the Landgericht Dortmund held Article 4(5) to be applicable to a contract between a German manufacturer of steel wool and a Dutch manufacturer of scouring sponges, where the former agreed to buy sponges exclusively from the latter for sale in Germany and the latter had exclusive distribution rights over the former's steel wool in Belgium and the Netherlands; the court eventually found the contract, made in Germany and expressed in the German language, to be governed by German law).

Von Hoffmann reveals that there has been some debate in Germany over which is the characteristic obligation under a *contract of licence* (see North (ed.) (1982), p.227): there is support for each of licensor's and licensee's obligations, as well as for regarding neither's performance as characteristic. Von Hoffmann favours the former, and regards the tendency of parties expressly to choose the licensee's law in such contracts as merely representing the typical bargaining power of the parties. There is much to be said for Von Hoffmann's view, although, where the contract is one for a *building* lease or licence in respect of *immovables*, Article 4(2) is then displaced by the special presumption in Article 4(3) (however, possibly only severably, as to the leasing, not the building, obligation: see below, Article 4(3)) (and the position would, it is believed, have been quite different in any event, even without Article 4(3), in that the *lessee's/licensee's* obligation *to build* could then have been looked upon as being characteristic of the contract, or at least as no less so than provision of the lease or licence by the lessor/licensor, or possibly as severable from the latter (although, rather doubtfully so in the case of a mere licence): see below, Article 4(3)).

Exclusive distribution agreements are another difficult case: should it be the grant or the actual distribution which is to be regarded as characteristic thereof, or neither as more than the other? On balance, it is felt that, as in the example of building leases and licences previously mentioned, the activity at the centre of the transaction – here, distribution – is sufficiently significant for it to be said that it is characteristic of the contract (see, however, Jaffey, 'The English Proper Law Doctrine and the EEC Convention' (1984), 22 *ICLQ*, 531, 551).

It is submitted that, since the object of the presumption in Article 4(2) is to add certainty to the rule of flexibility in Article 4(1), courts should be reluctant to find characteristic performance when there is a measure of doubt and certainty has broken down: in such cases, it would seem more appropriate that the party arguing in favour of characteristic performance should instead be put to proof of Article 4(1) closest connection, in accordance with Article 4(5) rendering Article 4(2) inapplicable, than that the other party should be burdened with having to rebut the presumption that characteristic performer's law is most closely connected, again as provided in Article 4(5). The concept of characteristic performance is not so compelling that it need be stretched any further than its obvious limitations permit.

(c) Law of the Characteristic Performer's Habitual Residence, Central Administration, or Relevant Place of Business

It is not the country in which the characteristic performance is to take place whose law is presumed to be most closely connected under Article 4(2): it is that of the country of the characteristic performer which is so presumed. This may seem a most extraordinary state of affairs (see, however, Chapter 44 below): admittedly, it will often be the case that such characteristic performance will be carried out in the habitual residence *et alia* of the performer; but if it is not to be so, the whole scheme and purpose of Article 4(2) would appear to have required that the law of the country of performance (the *internal* contractual factor of greatest significance) should have been presumed to be the most closely connected, subject to rebuttal where, for example, there was more than one such country. Indeed, one may suppose that, in many of the cases of rebuttal of the presumption which will in fact occur under Article 4(5), it will be the law of the country of characteristic performance which displaces that of habitual residence! Such a rule itself, however, would not have been devoid of practical difficulty: where, for example, the parties omitted themselves to make express provision in their contract for country of performance, which country's law would have been referred to in order to determine place of performance, for the purpose of ascertaining applicable law for the decision on the merits? Nevertheless, it remains the case that concentration on characteristic performer's place of business under Article 4(2) is the less likely to promote coincidence of applicable law and jurisdiction of the courts for the place of performance of the obligation in question in non-employment cases under Article 5(1) of the European Judgments Convention, when that person is plaintiff rather than defendant.

It is expressly provided in Article 4(2) that habitual residence and the other connections there mentioned are to be assessed as at the time of conclusion of the contract. This should prevent manipulation of the rules on applicable law and uncertainty at the time of contracting, although, reverting to the previous criticism, one would have thought that, as a matter of principle, law of the habitual residence at the time for performance might be considered to have a greater claim to apply than that of some now-abandoned habitual residence which previously existed at the contract date. (Furthermore, it is suggested that 'time of conclusion' should be taken to mean time at which the characteristic performer executed the offer or, as the case may be, acceptance, rather than technically the moment of final conclusion of the contract, according to applicable law: see below, discussion on Article 9(1).)

'Habitual residence' of natural persons is a fairly factual concept to apply, as the country of their regular abode, which has lasted, or is likely to endure, for some time (*Cruse* v. *Chittum* [1974] 2 All ER 940; Kaye, *Civil Jurisdiction* (1987) pp.547–54).

'Central administration' of legal bodies, corporate or unincorporate, will also involve factual investigation into location of central management and control, rather than place of incorporation as such (*Cesena Sulphur Co. v. Nicholson* (1876) 1 Ex. D 428; *Egyptian Delta Land and Investment Co. v. Todd* [1929] AC 1; Kaye, *Civil Jurisdiction*, pp.412 *et seq*.).

In the case of contracts where the characteristic performer is a trader or a professional, however, and actually enters the contract in the course of that trade or profession, the law of the country of his or its principal place of business, even if different from that of its central administration, will be presumed to be most closely connected: unless, that is, the contractual performance is required to be effected through a place of business in a different country, in which event the latter's law is presumed most closely connected. (It seems logical that the place of business through which the contract is to be *effected* should be so prescribed, rather than that through which it was *negotiated*, if different, given the significance of characteristic 'performance' under Article 4(2).) The situation may not occur too frequently in which a trader executes a contract, involving performance of the characteristic obligation, other than in the course of his business: an example might be where, say, a City solicitor's firm agrees to allow certain members of the public to use its expensive indoor swimming pool, in return for payment of a nominal sum.

'Place of business' (*établissement/Niederlassung/sede/vestiging*) will inevitably give rise to questions of interpretation. In *Cleveland Museum of Art v. Capricorn Art International SA* [1990] 2 Lloyd's Rep. 166, 169, HIRST J reviewed the authorities and concluded that the following characteristics must be present for an oversea company to be held to have an established place of business in Great Britain for purposes of s.695(2) of the Companies Act 1985 (service of process on oversea companies): an identifiable *place* at which the business is carried on, not merely fleetingly or occasionally, but with some degree of *regularity*, and with which the company is *associated*, even if it does not own or lease the premises; carrying on business through an agent or subsidiary is not sufficient.

Finally, it should be reminded that the law of the country of principal or other place of business will only apply, as presumed applicable law, if the trader or professional is the characteristic performer: this follows from the reference to 'that' party's trade or profession in the second sentence of Article 4(2), meaning the party mentioned as characteristic performer in the first sentence (as well as from subsequent reference to 'the' – meaning characteristic – performance to be effected through a place of business other than the principal). Presumably, too, it is the principal place of business at the time of conclusion of the contract which is to be determined, not that at the later date of performance, if different (unless, of course, the latter is otherwise the place through which contractual performance is to be effected).

INAPPLICABILITY AND REBUTTAL OF THE PRESUMPTION IN ARTICLE 4 (2): ARTICLE 4 (5)

(a) Inapplicability

Article 4(5) begins 'Paragraph 2 shall not apply if the characteristic performance cannot be determined ...'. In this event, the court will be required to apply the closest connection test in Article 4(1) without recourse to presumptions, by balancing all relevant connections and assessing their relative significance, individually and cumulatively. Examination of the concept of characteristic performance under Article 4(2), it will be recalled, revealed that its inapplicability may not be too infrequent an occurrence!

(b) Rebuttal

Article 4(5) goes on to specify that the presumption in (*inter alia*) Article 4(2) shall be disregarded 'if it appears from the circumstances as a whole that the contract is more closely connected with another country'. This – what is, essentially, the reintroduction, indirectly, of the pre-existing English contract conflicts approach of weighing all factors – is the get-out clause (the 'margin of discretion' and inevitable counterpart of the general presumption: Report, p.22), where it is found that the country of habitual residence of the party responsible for performance of what is held to be the characteristic obligation under the contract is not in fact the most connected country as a whole: for example, an Englishman goes to Spain for a holiday; the hotel in which he is staying pays the Englishman to change a tyre on one of its coaches which has suffered a puncture; it seems highly likely that the presumption that English law is the most connected, as that of the habitual residence of the characteristic performer under Article 4(2), will be rebutted under Article 4(5) in such circumstances, where on a consideration of all facts and circumstances, Spanish law would seem to qualify as that of the most connected country under Article 4(1); another instance might be where characteristic performance is to take place in a number of different countries, thereby reducing any importance which the performer's country of habitual residence might otherwise have had, as, for example, where an Englishman, intending to drive to Spain for a holiday, is paid by a German businessman to deliver various messages to the latter's contacts in the Netherlands, Belgium and France *en route*. Thus (notwithstanding the preceding example), rebuttal does seem more likely than would have been the case had place of performance of the characteristic obligation instead formed the basis of the presumption in Article 4(2).

It has been argued that rebuttal of the presumption under Article 4(5) should be limited to the most exceptional cases, where *all* contractual connections are with a country other than that of the characteristic performer's habitual residence *et alia*, since otherwise the certainty and predictability advantages of Article 4(2) would be lost (see Schultsz, in North (ed.) (1982), p.187; and Jaffey (1984) 22 *ICLQ*, 531, 554). This view is respectfully disagreed with; if Article 4(2) is indeed about convenience rather than justice, the potential sacrifice of the latter in favour of the former ought not to be accentuated through an excessively restrictive application of Article 4(5) rebuttal. (The further assertion, at pp.555–6, that Article 4(5) rebuttal might be used in order to secure the application of mandatory rules of a foreign country in the United Kingdom, where Article 7(1) is otherwise inapplicable, is quite unacceptable: operation of rebuttal under Article 4(5) turns solely upon the closer connection of another country, not on the mandatory nature of its contract rules; it may be that rebuttal leads to applicability of foreign rules which would have been regarded as mandatory for purposes of Article 7(1), but the latter cannot be the motive for such rebuttal.)

Clearly, then, many Article 4(1) closest connection disputes will in fact be fought out on a presumption-rebuttal claim under Article 4(5). It is curious that the latter merely requires a party wishing to rebut, to prove a *closer* connection with another country, in English and foreign texts; this must therefore be read together with Article 4(1), applying law of the *most closely* connected country.

Finally, it will have been noted that Article 4(5) *requires* the presumptions to be rebutted where the contract appears to be more closely connected with another country; the rule is not merely one of discretion to disregard the presumptions.

CRITICISM OF THE CHARACTERISTIC PERFORMANCE PRESUMPTION

Article 4(2) has been subjected to a great deal of criticism and is probably, therefore, the Convention provision which is the most eligible for revision at some time in the future under Article 26.

It certainly involves pursuance of a rather complicated process in order eventually to arrive at applicable law in the absence of choice. Courts and parties must

- decide which performance obligation is characteristic of the contract; and

- if this is determinable, ascertain where the characteristic performer had his habitual residence, central administration, or relevant place of business at the time of conclusion of the contract, and presume the law thereof to be that of the country most closely connected with the contract (Article 4(2)); and then
- find out if any other country has a closer connection, and, if so, apply that country's law (Article 4(5)).

There are three main species of objection which have been ranged against this system.

(i) First, the characteristic obligation doctrine is said to derive from certain Swiss formulations, designed to avoid the German system, incorporating scission of applicable law in the absence of choice (although, the Swiss more sensibly refer to the law of the country of characteristic performance: see generally Lipstein, in Lipstein (ed.) (1978), p.8, and Vischer, *ibid.*, pp.25–7), and the European Court sanctioned it as the place of contractual performance for jurisdiction over employment contracts, in the Judgments Convention case of *Ivenel* v. *Schwab*, Case 133/81 [1982] ECR 1891, [1983] 1 CMLR 538 (although, note that under Article 5(1) of the Judgments Convention as amended by Article 4 of the San Sebastian Convention on Spanish and Portuguese Accession, place of contractual performance in the case of individual employment contracts is now expressly that in which the employee habitually carries out his work). However, the criticisms have been made that the concept is capable of causing great uncertainty in its application, through its generality and lack of precision, when the whole purpose of its inclusion was to add an element of certainty and predictability to the rule of flexibility in Article 4(1) (see Fletcher, p.163); in England at any rate, it is novel and unfamiliar (see North, in North (ed.) (1982), p.15; Jaffey, *ibid.*, p.39; and Lasok and Stone, pp.352–63); it is arbitrary, fictitious and capricious, encouraging courts to seize on one particular contractual contact point, favouring one party rather than the common interest, and enabling courts to reach the decisions they want (see Juenger, *ibid.*, pp.300–6, and Lipstein, in Lipstein (ed.) (1978), pp.8–9) (hence, the special rules fixing applicable law in the case of *protective* consumer and employment contracts, under Articles 5(3) and 6(2) respectively); specific points of contact, forming the basis of the presumption, in respect of different types of contracts, should have been listed in place of the excessively generalistic characteristic performance test in Article 4(2), as in the case of the US Second Restatement (1971) s.188, which prescribes application of the law having the most significant relationship to the transaction and the parties, in respect of each separate contractual issue (see Overbeck, in North (ed.) (1982), p.276; although, note Juenger, *ibid.*, pp.299–

300, for criticism of this: 'The permutations...would stymie a computer.... Everyone might agree that the search for the proper law should not be a mechanical process of counting contacts. But even a juggler, not to mention a trial judge, can only cope with a finite number of balls in the air').

(ii) Secondly, presumptions take away much of the flexibility gained from the basic rule in Article 4(1), and consequently fell out of fashion, as being wrong in principle, under pre-existing English contract conflicts (see North, in North (ed.) (1982), p.15).

(iii) Thirdly, if there is a presumption as to applicable law, it ought not to have been permitted to be rebutted, which effectively removes whatever certainty – if any – it brings; the rule of closest connection in Article 4(1) might just as well have stood alone, without the need to go through the presumptive process, eventually returning to the original starting point of the closest connection (see Jaffey (1984), 33 *ICLQ* 531, 554; and in North (ed.) (1982), p.39; Schultsz, *ibid.*, p.187; Giardina, *ibid.*, p.241, as to Italian difficulties; Morse (1982) 2 *Yearbook of European Law*, 107, 127–30).

On the other hand, it has to be said, the idea of presumptions – even based upon characteristic performance – usually the subject of criticism for the possibility of rebuttal under Article 4(5), has received a measure of support in various quarters: the Report itself says that it gives specific form and objectivity to the, in itself, too vague concept of 'closest connection' in Article 4(1), and at the same time

> it greatly simplifies the problem of determining the law applicable to the contract in default of choice by the parties ... The place where the act was done becomes unimportant .... There is no longer any need to determine where the contract was concluded, with all the difficulties and the problems of classification that arise in practice.... Seeking the place of performance or the different places of performance and classifying them becomes superfluous (p.21).

Others regard the solution as convenient and efficacious, and as uniform, certain and predictable (see Jaffey, in North (ed.) (1982), p.39; and Schultsz, *ibid.*, p.187); Von Hoffmann (in Lando (ed.) (1975), pp.7–9), drawing attention to both the advantages and the disadvantages, points to the fact that sellers' obligations – probably forming part of the characteristic performance – are usually more complex and subject to greater legal regulation, and that, since the seller enters many contracts, it is expedient that the same law – that of the seller – should govern, thereby reducing costs of legal advice; the seller has also been described as the more active performer, likely to be affected by legal rules, and requiring legal advice, and there is said to be greater certainty from the characteristic performance presumption (more, if it is not rebuttable) than where there is no presumption at all and all facts and circumstances have to be taken into account; and in time, it is claimed, courts themselves will be able to increase the amount of certainty (see Jaffey (1984), 33 *ICLQ*, 531, 548–55; and Vischer, in Lipstein (1978), p.27).

In the present submission, the characteristic performance test should go, and not be replaced by another rule of presumption, for the following reasons.

In the first place, it is patently clear that any certainty said to be provided by this elusive concept is illusory; even if the characteristic performance is ascertained, it is then subject to rebuttal, as it must assuredly be in order to reduce injustice and manipulative, jurisprudentially flawed decisions as to identification of characteristic performance.

Secondly, it has the appearance of a rule of description, but it is in fact a rule of selection, acting as a cover for hidden policy choice of law considerations applied by courts. Such an approach is misleading and promotes instability.

Thirdly, as has been pointed out, to focus on performance, but not to apply the law of the country thereof, may be looked upon as perverse (although, see below Chapter 44, for a defence).

Fourthly, support for presumptions (*a fortiori*, not subject to rebuttal) as being more certain than systems based upon weighing all facts and circumstances betrays the fallacy: where parties do not expressly or impliedly select a law to govern their contract, the situation *is* inherently uncertain, and it is useless to deny that this is so; this is quite different from uncertainty artificially created in the application of rules provided to deal with the former circumstances – which is wholly unacceptable. Contractual uncertainty in the absence of choice of law should therefore be accepted as a fact, and the primary task of courts should then be to apply the most connected law on the basis of whatever arrangements the parties did take the trouble to agree upon under their substantive contract, without risking distortion of this through trying to replace what was never there in the first place: the element of certainty as to applicable law. Furthermore, in the absence of presumptions, at least within the European Community itself, in relation to Community domiciliaries, the Judgments Convention would deflect objections to forum shopping, as courts of each Contracting State developed differing lines of authorities and practices, and the European Court's interpretative jurisdiction under the Brussels Protocols, together with proper reference to comparative Contracting State case law in fulfilment of Article 18 of the Obligations Convention, prescribing uniformity in interpretation and application thereof, would make inter-Contracting State divergence in relation to the closest connection test not a great deal more likely than amongst courts within a single Contracting State itself. (With regard to non-EEC domiciliaries, the problem is their susceptibility to exorbitant national jurisdiction grounds: the solution to this, however, may not necessarily lie in shaping national contracts domestic and conflicts rules specifically so as to cater for this situation!)

Article 4(2) should therefore be removed.

Article 4(1) should be applied without reference to the characteristic performance presumption, although, consistent judicial practice, both within and between states, will always be influential, even if never conclusive.

For the present, certainty should be striven for through inclusion of express contractual provision on choice of law, under Article 3 – or at least implied choice thereunder, from express agreement on jurisdiction or arbitration.

3   Notwithstanding the provision of paragraph 2 of this Article, to the extent that the subject matter of the contract is a right in immovable property or a right to use immovable property it shall be presumed that the contract is most closely connected with the country where the immovable property is situated.

PRESUMPTION THAT *LEX SITUS* GOVERNS CONTRACTS FOR IMMOVABLES

In the case of the sale or lease of ('rights in'), or licence to ('right to use'), immovable property, the presumption in Article 4(2) is inapplicable (nothing seems to turn on the difference in the opening words of Article 4(3) and (4) respectively): Article 4(3) requires the country of the *situs* of the property to be presumed to be most closely connected with the contract. This broadly corresponds with the position under pre-existing national English conflicts, where *lex situs* will be particularly likely to govern the contract as proper law (Dicey and Morris, p.941).

Article 4(3) requires the presumption to operate 'to the extent that' the contract thus relates to immovables. This has two implications worthy of note: (i) where the immovables element of the contract is severable from the rest within the meaning of Article 4(1) – for example, the contract is for the rent of property in Italy by X to Y, and it is further agreed that X is to show Y the places of interest – the presumption in Article 4(3) will govern applicable law in respect of the immovables obligation, whereas arguably that in Article 4(2) will apply to the remainder (see below, p.194); and (ii) it is possible that, if the contract is not held to be severable in accordance with Article 4(1), the effect of Article 4(3) is that *lex situs* will then be presumed to be most closely connected with the contract as a whole, so as to apply even to those parts thereof not solely concerning the use of the property, as, for example, in the case of construction obligations under a building lease, because Article 4(3) does say that 'the contract' is to be presumed to be most closely connected, not merely the part relating to rights in or to use the immovables. However, it is submitted that this would be a regrettable course to follow and that the words 'to the extent that' thereunder are capable of controlling the presumption to the effect that the 'contract' is most closely connected with the *situs*. Accordingly, 'contract' may thus be restricted to that part thereof which is concerned with rights in or to use the immovables, and the rest is a matter for Article 4(2).

Where the contract is purely for the construction or repair of immovable property, without also affecting rights in or to use the latter, Article 4(3) is inapplicable, and Article 4(2) applies: this is because 'the main subject-matter of these contracts is the construction or repair rather than the immovable property itself' (Report, p.21). In such cases, therefore, it may be the law of the country of the constructor's/repairer's habitual residence, central administration, or relevant place of business which is presumed to be most closely connected, as that of the characteristic performer, under Article 4(2) – subject to possible rebuttal under Article 4(5) in favour of, say, common *lex situs* and *lex loci solutionis*. In proceedings involving a building lease, applicability of Article 4(2) or (3) will depend upon whether the claim essentially involves building or possessory and leaseholder obligations respectively (the difference is between builder's law, presumed most connected, and *lex situs*, similarly presumed most closely connected).

Finally, it will be noted that the formula 'right in immovable property or a right to use immovable property' in Article 4(3) is broader than the concepts of *rights in rem in and tenancies of immovable property* which form the subject of exclusive jurisdictional provision for courts of the Contracting State *situs* under Article 16(1)(a) of the Judgments Convention. Nevertheless, it is considered that the same strict interpretation of the special presumption in Article 4(3) of the Obligations Convention will be applied as has been carried out by the European Court in respect of the exclusive *situs* rule in Article 16(1) of the Judgments Convention. Furthermore, it is considered, the decision of the European Court in *Sanders* v. *Van der Putte*, Case 73/77 [1977] ECR 2383 to the effect that Article 16 was inapplicable to a lease essentially of a *business*, as opposed to the premises in which it was carried on, would be followed in the case of Article 4(3) of the Obligations Convention, at least in principle if not on the facts. Certainly too, short-term holiday lettings would be included within the 'right to use' immovable property under Article 4(3) (subject to rebuttal under Article 4(5) – see below), as in the much-criticised Judgments Convention case of *Rösler* v. *Rottwinkel*, Case 241/83 [1985] ECR 99, in respect of exclusive jurisdictional scope of Article 16(1) thereof (subsequently rendered non-exclusive under the amendments in the San Sebastian Convention and in any event successfully circumvented in *Hacker* v. *Euro Relais GmbH*, Case 280/90 (1992) *The Times,* 9 April – see below); and again, as in Rösler, rights of user between the parties, including rent, agreed water, gas and electricity charges and other outgoings, as well as costs of repairs and decorations under the tenancy, would be covered by the presumption in Article 4(3) – subject to where Article 4 was completely replaced by Article 5(3) in a consumer contract in which *travel and accommodation* were provided for an *inclusive* price in accordance with Article 5(5) (see below, p.196).

(However, in *Rösler* the landlord's claim for compensation for lost enjoyment of his own holiday and travel expenses as a result of breach of the user clause in the tenancy agreement was held to fall outside Article 16(1), as only indirectly concerning the immovable property. This finding was inconsistent with Advocate General Slynn's advice in his Opinion to the Court, and is clearly open to criticism: see Kaye, *Civil Jurisdiction,* pp. 925–6. It is by no means certain, therefore, that such a claim resulting from breach of an agreement for use of immovable property would fall outside Article 4(3) on a reconsideration thereof.)

Again, it will be noted that in the Judgments Convention case of *Scherrens* v. *Maenhout*, Case 158/87 [1988] ECR 3791, the European Court held that where there was a dispute as to the existence of a lease relating to immovable property situated in *two* Convention states, other than in special circumstances, exclusive jurisdiction over the immovable property situated in each Contracting State would be held under Article 16(1) by the courts of that state. It seems unclear whether the same principle could operate in respect of Article 4(3) of the Obligations Convention: the latter provision does refer to the *singular* 'country' in which the immovable property is situated (as in fact does Article 16(1), in respect of *Contracting State*), and plainly there is an even more pressing need for determination of single applicable law than resort to a single forum, in relation to such property matters. If Article 4(3) were held to be inapplicable, Article 4(2) would govern instead and law of the characteristic performer would apply. The problem with this outcome, however, is that if the landlord were held to be characteristic performer, the presumed applicable law, as that of his habitual residence, may not correspond with that of either of the *leges situs* of courts seised under Article 16(1), contrary to the very objective of *Scherrens*; whilst, if lessee's obligation under Article 4(2) were found to be characteristic, country of habitual residence would presumably coincide with only one of the *leges situs* of courts hearing the proceedings, and the same result, or worse, would ensue if it were held to be impossible to determine the characteristic obligation under Article 4(5) in such circumstances, so that law of country of closest connection was referred to instead under Article

4(1). In the present writer's submission, given the purpose in *Scherrens*, seen to be to secure coincidence of appropriate law and forum in such cases where immovables situated in two countries are subject to a single leasing contract, the correct application and construction of Article 4 is that which will bring about that result. Accordingly, it is believed, *either* Article 4(3) should be held to be inapplicable in its terms to the circumstances, and Article 4(2) itself then rendered inoperable under Article 4(5) through inability to determine a characteristic obligation, in which event *leges situs* of each of the two states of situation of the immovable property, whose courts are seised, should govern the respective property *severably* as most connected laws under Article 4(1) (alternatively, if Article 4(2) were held to apply, and applicable law thereunder coincided with *lex situs* of only one of the two fora seised, the presumption could be rebutted under Article 4(5) in relation to the property situated in the forum not corresponding with characteristic performer's habitual residence *et alia*, and Article 4(1) could again then apply severably to determine law applicable to the property situated in the country of that forum); *or* a broad construction of Article 4(3) might be adopted in the light of the underlying policy of *Scherrens* and general admission of severability under Article 4(1), so that the presumption in Article 4(3) was permitted to operate separately in respect of law of *each* country in which the immovable property under the lease was situated.

Other cases on the scope of Article 16(1) of the Judgments Convention have held as follows.

In *Hacker* v. *Euro Relais GmbH*, Case 280/90 (1992) *The Times*, 9 April, the European Court avoided the previous application of the then exclusive Article 16(1) to a short-term holiday letting in *Rösler*, by holding that provision to be inapplicable to a *complex* transaction in which a travel agent contracted not only to provide foreign holiday accommodation for a short period, but also to provide other services, such as information and advice, reservation of travel facilities, welcome arrangements at the holiday location and possibly insurance for cancellation, all in return for a *global* price – the principal object of the transaction consequently being unable to be said to be for the renting alone. Under the Obligations Convention, where Article 4 was not simply displaced by Article 5(3) in a consumer contract for combined travel and accommodation within Article 5(5), it would seem, as seen earlier, that Article 4(3) would apply *to the extent that* usage aspects of the contract for immovables were involved, and Article 4(2) to the rest: although, in either case, displacement of the presumptions, under Article 4(5), in favour of a global assessment of closest connection under Article 4(1), would seem a distinct and attractive possibility. It may well be that *Hacker* survives the new Article 16(1)(b) of the Judgments Convention, according alternative jurisdiction to courts of *situs* and defendant's domicile in respect of proceedings principally involving short-term tenancies, when the *non*-tenancy aspects of a complex transaction are held to render the tenancy element subsidiary, as in *Hacker* itself, in which case *situs* jurisdiction will be excluded in such cases (other than in combined proceedings under Article 6(4)), as, correspondingly, would be the presumption of applicability of *lex situs* in Article 4(3) above, on its rebuttal in such circumstances, under Article 4(5) (see below, p. 196).

In *Reichert* v. *Dresdner Bank*, Case 115/88 [1990] ECR 1558, the European Court ruled that an action whereby a creditor seeks to have set aside against him a conveyance of immovable property in defraud of creditors – the French *action paulienne* – does not fall within the scope of Article 16(1), being personal, rather than real, in nature: this meant that the creditor plaintiff bank could only sue the transferors in the courts of their German domicile under Article 2, and not in those of the French *situs* of the immovable property (exclusively or at all) under Article 16(1); the *action paulienne* was said to fall outside the policy of Article 16(1), to safeguard application of local law to govern proprietary matters in respect of immovables (p.113). It is considered that whatever the correctness of this decision by the European Court – and considerable doubts may be felt on that score, depending upon the precise nature and effects of the claim involved – Article 4(3) must obviously still be regarded as applicable to a contract to transfer immovables in defraud of creditors, notwithstanding the transferor's evasionary motive in respect thereof, in the circumstances envisaged: although, of course, any further claim against the third party transferee to restore the property transferred in defraud of creditors, would in essence be one in quasi-contract for unjust enrichment and would therefore fall outside the contractual scope of the Obligations Convention under Article 1(1) (see above, Chapter 6), let alone Article 4(3) itself (nevertheless, according to national English private international law, the proper law of the obligation to restore the benefit of the unjustified enrichment would then govern, as that of the country in which the immovables were situated – see Dicey and Morris, p. 1350, Rule 203(2)(b)).

REBUTTAL

Article 4(5) also requires the presumption in Article 4(3) to be rebutted, where it appears from the circumstances as a whole that the contract is more closely connected with another country. The Report itself provides an example of such rebuttal (p.21): two persons resident in Belgium make a contract for the rent of a holiday home on the island of Elba, Italy; the contract may be held to be most closely connected with Belgium, the country of the contracting parties' residence, not with Italy. One might also imagine the case of two Englishmen in a London pub, one of whom signs his agreement on the back of a beer mat to sell to the other his villa in Benidorm, Spain; here too, England would seem to be the most closely connected country. Furthermore, whereas previously it seemed to be the case that actions, even purely for the recovery of rent, in respect of short holiday lettings of property in EEC countries, were subject to exclusive jurisdiction of courts of the *situs* under Article 16(1) of the Judgments Convention (*Rösler* v. *Rottwinkel* [1985] ECR 99,127), in future, since entry into force of the 1989 San Sebastian Convention on Spanish and Portuguese Accession to the Judgments Convention (O.J. 1989, No. L285), a new paragraph is added by Article 6 of the latter to Article 16(1) of the Judgments Convention, to the effect that in proceedings which have as their object tenancies of immovable property concluded for temporary private use of a maximum period of six consecutive months, the courts of the Contracting State *in which the defendant is domiciled* shall also have jurisdiction, provided that the landlord and the tenant are natural persons and are domiciled in the same Contracting State (Article 16 (1)(b) of the Lugano Convention is similar, but not identical). Accordingly, on rebuttal of the presumption of *lex situs* in Article 4(3) of the Obligations Convention under Article 4(5) thereof in the circumstances envisaged, there would still exist the possibility that non-*situs* jurisdiction and choice of law would correspond (conversely, the new Article 6(4) of the Judgments Convention, added by Article 5 of the San Sebastian Convention, provides for non-exclusive jurisdiction of courts of the Contracting State *situs* of immovable property, where a contract claim is combined with an action against the same defendant concerning rights *in rem* in immovable property). In the case of a complex transaction such as that in *Hacker* v. *Euro Relais GmbH* above, providing for travel *et alia* as well as holiday accommodation, it may be that neither Article 4 of the Obligations Convention nor Article 16(1)(b) of the Judgments Convention would apply in the first place (in the latter case, depending upon what is held to be the *principal* object of the proceedings), and that instead, in accordance with Article 5(5) of the former, law of a consumer plaintiff's habitual residence would govern in place of Article 4, under Article 5(3), in the absence of choice, just as courts of the consumer's own domicile would possess jurisdiction under Article 14 para. 1 of the Judgments Convention (see above, p.194). In non-consumer, or non-Article 5(5) cases, Article 4(3) would only apply, rebuttably, *to the extent that* rights in or to use the holiday property were involved, and Article 4(2), likewise rebuttably, to the rest (see above, pp.191–2).

MANDATORY RULES

Even when the presumption of application of *lex situs* is rebutted in favour of a more closely connected law under Article 4(5), any mandatory rules of the forum, as *situs* (or of the foreign *situs*, in Contracting States where, unlike the United Kingdom, Article 7(1) applies), in relation to contracts for immovables, will nonetheless continue to be referred to under Article 7(2), notwithstanding the absence of closest connection of such *situs*. (Article 9(6) also safeguards mandatory rules on formalities in relation to immovables, under English or foreign *lex situs*, irrespective of *lex loci contractus* and applicable law.)

4 **A contract for the carriage of goods shall not be subject to the presumption in paragraph 2. In such a contract if the country in which, at the time the contract is concluded, the carrier has his principal place of business is also the country in which the place of loading or the place of discharge or the principal place of business of the consignor is situated, it shall be presumed that the contract is most closely connected with that country. In applying this paragraph single voyage charter-parties and other contracts the main purpose of which is the carriage of goods shall be treated as contracts for the carriage of goods.**

REBUTTABLE PRESUMPTION OF APPLICABLE LAW IN CONTRACTS FOR THE CARRIAGE OF GOODS: ARTICLE 4(4)

Applicable law under Article 4(4) is expressly not subject to the characteristic performance presumption in Article 4(2). Instead, most connected applicable law is rebuttably presumed to be that of the country in which at the time of contractual conclusion

- the carrier has his principal place of business; **and**
- the place of loading, *or* the place of discharge, *or* the consignor's principal place of business, is situated.

The Report reveals that after 'long and animated' discussion, it was decided not to exclude transport contracts from the Convention, but to provide a special presumption because of the *peculiarities* of carriage of goods (p.21). (Availability of *arrest* is of course a matter of remedial procedure of the forum, not substantive for the applicable law: see *Barbaros Denizcilik Isletmesi AS* v. *Deval Shipping & Trading Co, Deval Denizcilik V.E. Ticaret SA* (1990) ELD 232, The Netherlands.)

(a) Carriage of Goods

Carriage of passengers remains subject to the general presumption in Article 4(2) (see, however, Article 5 on consumer contracts: contracts of carriage are excluded therefrom, under Article 5(4)(a); except that Article 5 applicable law does apply – to the exclusion of Article 4 therefore – to contracts which, for an inclusive price, provide for a combination of travel and accommodation, under Article 5(5)). Certain negotiators had wanted Article 4(4) to apply to passenger carriage, because sole reference to the law of the country of the carrier's principal place of business (as that of characteristic performer) under Article 4(2) might not be sufficiently significant, as, for example, where a French or English passenger is transported between London and Paris by an American airline (and in mixed carriage of goods and passengers, difficulties of scission arise). However, the majority were against such an approach, for a number of reasons: it might result in the application of several different laws to passengers who were on the same journey; Article 4(4) was not formulated so as to apply to passengers, with the result that Article 4(1) would invariably have to be resorted to; carrier's law under Article 4(2) would normally correspond with choice of the carrier's courts under a jurisdiction clause in the carriage contract; and in any event, the judge would not be able 'to exclude consideration of the country in which the carrier has his principal place of business in seeking the places with which the contract is most closely connected' (Report, p.22).

Schultsz (in 'The Concept of Characteristic Performance and the Effect of the EEC Convention on Carriage of Goods', in North (ed.), *Contract Conflicts* (1982), pp. 188–90) examines whether contracts of carriage by sea which are evidenced by bills of lading are not in fact excluded from the Convention's scope under Article 1(2)(c), as *other negotiable instruments* thereunder, concluding, tentatively, that, as, admittedly, documents of title for purposes of transfer, yet which do not however confer a better title on the transferee than that possessed by the transferor, such contracts do fall within the Convention's scope, except that (a) where the forum state is party to an international convention containing a different choice of law rule on carriage of goods by sea – for example the Hague Rules, under the 1924 Brussels International Convention for the Unification of Certain Rules of Law Relating to Bills of Lading, as amended by the Hague–Visby Rules, Article X, given effect to in the United Kingdom by the Carriage of Goods by Sea Act 1971 (see *The Hollandia* [1983] AC 565) – the rules in that convention take precedence over those in the Obligations Convention in any event under Article 21 thereof; and (b) states not party to such conventions may nevertheless be required to apply the latters' choice of law rules, as mandatory laws of closely connected foreign states, under Article 7(1).

In addition, it is to be noted that in accordance with Article 32 of the Obligations Convention, incorporating the provision made under the Protocol annexed thereto, Denmark retains the rules on applicable law in paragraph 169 of its Statute on Maritime Law (law of the country in which the bill of lading was issued) relating to carriage of goods by sea (see below, Chapters 37 and 39).

Non-maritime international carriage of goods is also generally covered by international conventions within Article 21, which have been ratified by the United Kingdom, and since these conventions either prohibit conflicting choice of law or contain so comprehensive a range of provisions as to leave 'little scope in practice for the application of any other law' (see Dicey and Morris, pp.1270–5), not only the Convention rule in Article 4(4), but also those in Article 4(1) and (2) *et alia*, where carriage of passengers may be involved, are excluded from applying under Article 21 (the Working Group repeatedly stressed in the course of the discussions on transport problems that the international conventions took precedence in the matter: Report, p.22): for example, the Warsaw Convention of 1929, as amended at the Hague in 1955, and supplemented by the Guadalajara Convention of 1961 on the international carriage of persons or goods by aircraft (Carriage by Air Act 1961; Carriage by Air (Supplementary Provision) Act 1962); the 1980 Berne Convention concerning International Carriage by Rail, CIV and CIM Uniform Rules in Appendix A and B (International Transport Conventions Act 1983); 1956 Convention on the Contract for the International Carriage of Goods by Road (CMR) (Carriage of Goods by Road Act 1965); 1973 Convention on the Contract for the International Carriage of Passengers and Luggage by Road (CVR) (Carriage of Passengers by Road Act 1974); (see too 1974 Athens Convention relating to the Carriage of Passengers and their Luggage by Sea – Merchant Shipping Act 1979).

(b) In Applying this Paragraph Single Voyage Charter-parties and Other Contracts 'the Main Purpose of Which is the Carriage of Goods' Shall be Treated as Contracts for the Carriage of Goods.

The Report explains that such wording in the final sentence of Article 4(4) is 'intended to make it clear that charter-parties may be considered to be contracts for the carriage of goods in so far as that is their substance' (p.22). This brings to light the fact that *charters by demise*, operating as a lease of the ship with its master and crew, who act and sign bills of lading on behalf of not the shipowner, but the charterer – himself the 'carrier' – are not within Article 4(4), since the preponderant aspect ('the main purpose') is the hire of the ship rather than the carriage of goods (see Schultsz, pp. 191–2), and are therefore subject to Article 4(2) instead, the characteristic performance being delivery of the ship by the shipowner.

Single voyage charter-parties, realistically, are expressly to be included within Article 4(4) as carriage contracts. Schultsz indicates that time charters and consecutive voyage charters fall outside Article 4(4), as mainly concerning non-carriage of goods (Report, p.192). This argument, however, is open to challenge, and it could be contended, on the contrary, that such non-demise charters fall within the category of 'other contracts' in Article 4(4), *the main purpose* of which is the carriage of goods (similarly, in the case of 'freight contracts' for pure carriage, that is, without charter, of specified quantities of bulk commodities over a given period, using ships of the ship operator's own choice, not necessarily designated in the contract, which Schultsz, p.193, wishes effectively to be treated as consecutive voyage charter-parties, and consequently, according to Schultsz, excluded from Article 4(4)!).

Schultsz's conclusion, therefore, is that Article 4(4) applies to bills of lading and single voyage charters, as contracts for the carriage of goods: demise charters, time charters, consecutive voyage charters and freight contracts are outside Article 4(4) (p.194). With the exception of demise charters, however, doubts are felt, it will be recalled, in respect of the correctness of his finding that the latter contracts are excluded. In the present submission, such charters may be considered to have carriage of goods as their main purpose; and even if there were a *sub-charter* in existence, it would still seem to be the case that, effectively, the predominant purpose of the charter, as between owner and charterer, would remain the carriage of goods – albeit, indirectly – for the contracting party to the charter.

(c) Carrier

The Report states that where a person contracting to carry arranges for a third party to undertake the actual carriage, 'carrier' in Article 4(4) means the former, notwithstanding that he does not perform himself (p.22). Schultsz (p.195) draws attention to the problem of so-called 'demise clauses' or 'identity of carrier clauses' in bills of lading, whereby the bill is deemed to be a contract with the owner or demise charterer through the mere agency of the actual issuer, where the latter is not the owner or demise charterer of the ship: how is the law applicable to the validity and effectiveness of such clauses to be determined, where identification of such law depends upon the very question of which of the owner/demise charterer or issuer is to be regarded as the carrier for purposes of Article 4(4)? Schultsz (*ibid.*) suggests that this is a matter for the forum's national conflicts rules to decide, since such agency is excluded from the Convention's scope under Article 1(2)(f), and it is submitted that his analysis is correct.

(d) Principal Place of Business of Carrier

Is this to be the Panamanian or Liberian place of incorporation, or the country of real management and control (Schultsz p.196)? Surely, it is the latter, if also the principal place in which commercial operations are conducted.

(e) Place of Loading or Discharge

The Report states it to be apparent that places of loading and unloading which enter into consideration are those agreed at the time of conclusion of the contract, and not as subsequently varied (p.22).

(f) Consignor

The Report says that 'consignor' refers in general to any person who consigns goods to the carrier (pp.21–2). Schultsz points out that the language used could cover not only the person entering into the contract of carriage with the carrier, but also a person actually delivering the goods to the ship, as well as a forwarding agent acting in his own name for the account of the contracting party (pp.196–7). It is surely the latter who must be treated as the consignor for purposes of Article 4(4) combined connections forming the basis of the applicable law presumption thereunder.

What if the consignor is not a trader and therefore possesses no 'place of business', let alone a principal one? Is that point of contact abandoned as part of the possible combination? It is thought not. Instead, reasoning backwards by analogy with Article 4(2) containing the general presumption, if the consignor has no place of business, country of his habitual residence should then be referred to for the purpose.

(g) Contract Presumed to be Most Closely Connected with that Country

Carrier's principal place of business as that of characteristic performer under Article 4(2) was thought to be inadequate for applicable law in carriage of goods: so Article 4(4) sets up a combination-based presumption instead. If the required contact elements are lacking, the court falls back on the closest connection under Article 4(1) (Article 4(2) is expressly made inapplicable to carriage of goods, under Article 4(4)). Even if the combination is satisfied, the presumption is rebuttable under Article 4(5) if the contract is more closely connected with another country in all the circumstances: for example, where carrier and consignor have substantial (even though not principal) operations in country X, in which loading or discharge is to take place, notwithstanding their principal places of business in country Y.

5 **Paragraph 2 shall not apply if the characteristic performance cannot be determined, and the presumptions in paragraphs 2, 3 and 4 shall be disregarded if it appears from the circumstances as a whole that the contract is more closely connected with another country.**

Article 4(5), dealing with inapplicability or, as the case may be, rebuttal of presumptions in Article 4(2)–(4), has previously been commented upon in discussion of these latter, in particular, of Article 4(2) (see above, p.186 *et seq*).

Thus, rebuttal under Article 4(5) is described as 'the inevitable counterpart of a general conflict rule intended to apply to almost all types of contract' (Report, p.22).

10 Article 5: Consumer Contracts

Article 5

Certain consumer contracts

1   This Article applies to a contract the object of which is the supply of goods or services to a person ('the consumer') for a purpose which can be regarded as being outside his trade or profession, or a contract for the provision of credit for that object.

4   This Article shall not apply to:

   (a) a contract of carriage;
   (b) a contract for the supply of services where the services are to be supplied to the consumer exclusively in a country other than that in which he has his habitual residence.

5   Notwithstanding the provisions of paragraph 4, this Article shall apply to a contract which, for an inclusive price, provides for a combination of travel and accommodation.

Article 5 is intended to protect the weaker party to a consumer contract – provided that it is international in accordance with Article 1(1) – assumed to be the consumer of goods or services provided (Report, p.23). This is so even if the consumer is a millionaire: any more flexible test of comparative strength and weakness of contracting parties would presumably have been unworkable. The consumer therefore has to be protected under Article 5 against applicability of a potentially unfavourable law which is either pressed upon him or engineered through absence of agreement thereon. Thus, under Article 5

- Article 3-choice of law is limited in its effects (Article 5(2));
- seller's law, otherwise presumed to be most closely connected, as that of the characteristic performer under Article 4(2), is displaced in its entirety by the consumer's law (Article 5(3)).

In adopting this approach, Article 5 has been said to correspond with German, Belgian, French and Dutch laws (Lando, in Lando (ed.) (1975), p.139).

TYPES OF CONSUMER CONTRACT WITHIN ARTICLE 5

(a) Supply of Goods or Services or Provision of Credit for Such

The Report states that a more specific designation of consumer contracts was deliberately avoided in order to prevent possible clashes with national meanings (p.23). This seems wise. Standard consumer transactions of sale of goods (including conditional and credit sales, *ibid.*), hire, and hire-purchase, are included (as to contractual, not proprietary, regulation) (even though, unlike Article 13(1) and (2) of the Judgments Convention, Article 5(1) of the Obligations Convention does not specifically mention instalment credit and loans repayable by instalments: Report, p.24), as well as contracts of exchange. Services, physical or otherwise – for example, advice or, arguably (see above, Article 1(3)), insurance, to the extent that this is not excluded from the Convention's scope under Article 1(3) (see Report, *ibid.*) – are also covered. Unrestricted loans, presumably, are also to be classified as supply of services rather than goods (see Sale of Goods Act 1979 s.61(1)); but the Report states sales of securities to be excluded (p.23 – see too 1979 Act, s.61). Commercial equivalents of services of (credit-) leasing, agency, licensing and reinsurance, however, are unlikely to be supplied to another person who is not acting in the course of a trade or profession (see below, p.205) (similarly, in the case of a contract of pledge, although, the *object* of the latter must surely be taken to be the overall contract of loan of which it forms part, in any event).

Provision of credit for the supply of goods or services is also expressly referred to. Thus, a restricted-use debtor–creditor agreement would fall within this particular category. Arguably, too, an unrestricted-use agreement for such purpose, or unrestricted-use debtor–creditor–supplier agreement, would also be covered – although, these would seem to amount to supply of services in any event under Article 5(1). In the Judgments Convention case of *Bertrand* v.*Ott*, Case 150/77 [1978] ECR 1431, 1446, the European Court adopted an autonomous, rather restrictive, meaning of sale of goods 'on instalment credit terms' under the original Article 13 of the Judgments Convention defining consumer contracts, as a transaction in which the price is discharged by way of several payments or which is linked to a financing contract (see Kaye, *Civil Jurisdiction,* pp.825–41). *Provision of credit* under Article 5(1) of the Obligations Convention seems an altogether broader concept.

(b) One Party a Consumer

Article 5 applies where the person who receives the goods, services or credit under the contract does so for a purpose able to be looked upon as being outside his trade or profession – a 'consumer', so defined. What is the position, however, if the contract is made for the benefit of a third party, by whom it is enforceable according to 'applicable law' (whatever that may be, depending upon operation or not of Article 5!)? Is it the third party who must be a consumer for Article 5 to apply, or the contracting party who seeks to confer the benefit on the former thereunder? It is submitted, somewhat tentatively, that where the action is brought by the third party to enforce the contract, it is he who must be the consumer; where, however, the contracting party sues to enforce the benefit for the third party, applicability of Article 5 should depend upon whether the former is a consumer or not. Furthermore, the wording of Article 5(1) suggests that the recipient of the goods, services or credit may be a consumer, even though he is a trader or professional, provided that the purpose of supply is outside the latter (*'his' trade or profession*). Supply of raw materials to enable the recipient to carry on its manufacturing business is clearly not outside the latter; purchase of a pint of beer at lunchtime in the local public house by the managing director obviously is so. But what of the purchase of a typewriter for the managing director's secretary, or flowers for the reception area outside his office? Presumably, if it can be argued that such supply is genuinely and reasonably required to enable the recipient to conduct – even indirectly – its business, the recipient is not a 'consumer' for such purposes and Article 5 is inapplicable. (The Report appears to agree: p.23. It states that Article 5 does not apply to contracts made by traders, manufacturers or persons in the exercise of a profession (such as doctors), who buy equipment or obtain services for that trade or profession; and if they act partly within and partly outside their trade or profession, Article 5 only applies if they act primarily outside the trade or profession – *ibid.*) Further, it would seem from the text that a contract is a consumer contract under Article 5, *even if the supplier himself is also acting outside his trade or profession*. The Report, however, indicates to the contrary: the opinion of the majority of negotiators was that Article 5 would normally only apply where the person who supplied the goods, services or credit acted in the course of his trade or profession (*ibid.*). In addition, in the Judgments Convention case of *Bertrand v. Ott*, Case 150/77 [1978] ECR 1431, 1447, the European Court appeared to adopt this approach (see Kaye, pp.830–1). Thus, the Report says that the definition of consumer in Article 5(1) should be interpreted in the light of its purpose to protect the weaker party and in accordance with other international instruments with the same purpose, such as the Judgments Convention (p.23). It would, admittedly, seem odd if Article 5 were to apply, when applicable domestic laws themselves were limited to suppliers acting in the course of a business, as, for example, in the case of the Unfair Contract Terms Act 1977 s.12(1)(b) (see, though, s.6(4)) and Sale of Goods Act 1979 s.14(2) and (3) (see too the 1980 Hague Convention on the Law Applicable to Certain Consumer Sales, Article 1); and accordingly, the strict wording of Article 5(1) may have to be ignored in favour of a more commercially realistic approach restricting Article 5's operation to supply by non-consumers.

The next point is that the words 'which can be regarded' in Article 5(1) are rather curious and imprecise (see Kaye, pp.826–8, as to the same expression in Article 13 para. 1 of the Judgments Convention). The purpose of the transaction surely either is or is not outside the recipient's trade or profession. Perhaps the intention is to indicate that, even if there are doubts over whether that party is a consumer, the courts should nonetheless conclude that he is such, unless the contrary is able to be proven: thus, the Report states that Article 5 (corresponding to Article 13 of the Judgments Convention) is to be interpreted in the light of its purpose to protect the weaker party (p.23). On the other hand, the expression may relate to the 'apparent' purpose of the contract in the eyes of the other party (a purpose which *can* be regarded ...): the Report states that Article 5 is inapplicable where 'the receiver of goods or services or credit in fact acted primarily outside his trade or profession but the other party did not know this and, taking all the circumstances into account, should not reasonably have known it' (p.23). In this way, therefore, appearances, it would seem, will count (see Unfair Contract Terms Act 1977, s.12(1)(a): A party to a contract 'deals as a consumer' in relation to another party if – (a) he neither makes the contract in the course of a business nor holds himself out as doing so...). The Report provides an example of where the receiver might be found to have held himself out as a professional, by ordering goods which might well be used in his trade or profession, on his professional notepaper: here, the Report says, 'the good faith of the other party is protected and the case will not be governed by Article 5' (*ibid.*).

Finally, Article 5(1) says that the 'object' of the contract should be for a consumer purpose. Seemingly, then, it is the contract purpose, not actual use, which matters. The problem is, of course, that evidence of subjective intention may frequently be lacking, and the court will have to fall back upon objective criteria. If a driving instructor purchases a motor car, which he thereafter presents as a gift to his wife – who is to know what his real intention may have been at the time of transacting, before his wife threatened to leave him in order to live with his best friend?

EXCLUDED CONSUMER CONTRACTS

(a) Carriage Contracts: Other than for Travel and Accommodation Inclusively

Generally, contracts of carriage – as provision of a service – whether of goods or persons, are outside Article 5: Article 5(4)(a). Protection here is inappropriate (Report, p.24). Such contracts, consequently, are subject to applicable law under Articles 3 and 4, and in particular, to the presumption in Article 4(4) on carriage of goods (to the extent that they are not covered by other international conventions, given precedence under Article 21).

However, as a qualification to this, where the carriage contract is for combined travel *and accommodation* inclusive in the price – the renowned 'package holiday' – Article 5 governs: Article 5(5) (and it would seem that ordinary consumer – rather than *situs* – jurisdiction may exist under the Judgments Convention, see *Hacker* v. *Euro Relais GmbH*, above pp.193–6: application of alternative *situs*/defendant's domicile jurisdiction under Article 16(1)(b) would depend upon whether the letting element was the *principal* object of the proceedings or not). Combination of travel and accommodation is not an entirely problem-free concept: the drafters had difficulty defining the package tour, which they wished to be covered by Article 5, and they therefore confined themselves to underlining the main elements of such type of contract, leaving it to the courts to resolve any doubts (Report, p.25). Thus, for example, at what stage of the trip must accommodation or travel be provided? According to the Report, they must be separate parts of the package, so that, for example, provision of a sleeper on the train would not bring the transport contract within Article 5 (except perhaps where the accommodation is in the course of travel *forming part of the holiday*, rather than simply as transport thereto: as for example, in the case of a cruising holiday, or one where holidaymakers are expected to sleep in a coach, as it conveys them to several different countries over a two-week period!). Further, suppose that, for an inclusive price, the holidaymaker receives accommodation in an hotel in Paris, together with organized excursions by coach to places of interest, but that he had to transport himself to Paris; is this such a combined contract? In the present submission, such a contract, involving possibly substantial transportation within a single country, even though not thereto, should be regarded as falling within Article 5, by virtue of Article 5(5). If it were not – and of course, this will be the case in any event if conditions in Article 5(2) are not satisfied (see below, p.209) – there is a difficulty, in that the right-to-use-accommodation part of the contract might be subject to the presumption of *lex situs* as applicable law in the case of immovables under Article 4(3) (unless the accommodation is a tent on a safari, and depending upon whether a mere licence constitutes a 'right to use' for purposes of Article 4(3)), but the rest to the presumption of characteristic performer's law under Article 4(2); in this eventuality, it would probably be best if each of the presumptions were to be held to be rebutted under Article 4(5) and the general rule of closest connection applied under Article 4(1) (see above, pp.194–6).

Presumably, by inference from express inclusion of combined transport and accommodation within Article 5 under Article 5(5), if transport were combined with a service other than accommodation, such as language teaching, Article 5 *would* then be excluded in relation to the carriage by Article 5(4)(a). Thus, if the language teaching takes place partly in the consumer's habitual residence and partly abroad (say, in the case of university linguistics students), so that Article 5 is not otherwise excluded under Article 5(4)(b), if the supplier throws in the means of transport to the foreign country as part of the cost of the course, Article 5 may be rendered inapplicable. It may be, however, that this is only the case in relation to the carriage part of the contract, and that in accordance with the general Convention principle allowing severability of contracts for applicable law (see Articles 3(1) and 4(1)), the teaching part of the contract is nonetheless subject to Article 5.

(b) Services Supplied Exclusively Outside the Consumer's Habitual Residence

If the consumer is prepared to travel abroad for services (for example hotel accommodation, or a language course: Report, p.24), he ought to expect foreign laws to have a say in regulating his contractual relations (*ibid.*, p.25; see, however, Morse, 'Consumer Contracts, Employment Contracts and the Rome Convention' (1992), 41 *ICLQ* 1, 5, for a contrary view). Article 5 is therefore inapplicable: Article 5(4)(b). But this is only the case where the services are to be supplied to him *exclusively outside his habitual residence*: if any part thereof, however minor in relation to the rest, is to be supplied in the habitual residence of the consumer, Article 5 is brought into play. For example, a foreigner takes an English correspondence course in accountancy; part of the course involves tuition in England; the services are not supplied *exclusively* outside the student's foreign habitual residence, and Article 5 accordingly applies. Again, however, there could be difficulties: thus, an Englishman receives an advertisement for a tax avoidance conference to be held in the Bahamas, transport and accommodation not provided; two weeks prior to the conference date, an outline of the programme content is sent to him in England; is the 'service' exclusively to be carried out in the Bahamas, or is it partly performed in England (assuming the outline to be a service, rather than goods)? It would seem remarkable that so minor an element taking place in England could have the effect of bringing Article 5 into operation (assuming the Englishman to be a consumer and other conditions in Article 5 to be fulfilled), when it would otherwise be excluded. Furthermore, what is the position where by virtue of the contract itself the consumer effectively becomes habitually resident in the foreign country in which the services are to be provided, as, for example, where he is to become an undergraduate for four years? One supposes that in such circumstances, or otherwise, it is habitual residence at the date of conclusion of the contract which matters, irrespective of any subsequent change thereto; yet this is not expressly stated in Article 5(4)(b).

Finally, it will be noted that even where a package holiday starts with transportation from a country other than that of the consumer's habitual residence, so that the services are to be carried out exclusively outside the latter, Article 5 nonetheless governs, by virtue of Article 5(5), expressly overriding provisions of Article 5(4), rather than specifically those in Article 5(4)(a) (see Report, p.25).

2 **Notwithstanding the provisions of Article 3, a choice of law made by the parties shall not have the result of depriving the consumer of the protection afforded to him by the mandatory rules of the law of the country in which he has his habitual residence:**

— **if in that country the conclusion of the contract was preceded by a specific invitation addressed to him or by advertising, and he had taken in that country all the steps necessary on his part for the conclusion of the contract, or**
— **if the other party or his agent received the consumer's order in that country, or**
— **if the contract is for the sale of goods and the consumer trav-**

elled from that country to another country and there gave his order, provided that the consumer's journey was arranged by the seller for the purpose of inducing the consumer to buy.

MANDATORY RULES

Mandatory rules in Article 5(2) are as defined in Article 3(3) *'hereinafter'*, being rules of law 'which cannot be derogated from by contract': but further, according to the consumer protection objective of Article 5, they are also limited to mandatory rules which are *protective of the consumer*, such as those requiring a period for cancellation of agreements to be afforded to the consumer under s.67 of the Consumer Credit Act 1974, or imposing an implied condition of merchantable quality under s.14(2) of the Sale of Goods Act 1979, unable to be excluded by contract, under s.173 of the 1974 Act and s.6(2)(a) of the Unfair Contract Terms Act 1977 (other than in international contracts under 1977 Act s.26 in the latter case), respectively, and are not inclusive of mandatory rules intended to safeguard the economic interests of the state, for example, those imposing credit and price controls or restricting restraint of trade, contravention of which may invalidate a contract (note too for the future, the EC Commission's Draft Directive on Unfair Terms in Consumer Contracts, O.J. 1990, C243/2). However, it is submitted that even those mandatory rules of law which are not solely applicable to consumers are to be regarded as falling within the sphere of Article 5(2), where consumers are involved: for example, contractual terms which purport to exclude s.12(1) of the Sale of Goods Act 1979, implying a condition of title on the part of the seller, are ineffective under s.6(1)(a) of the Unfair Contract Terms Act 1977 (subject to s.26), whether the buyer is a consumer or not (and such 'party'-protection rules may also apply to *non*-consumers by virtue of Article 7). Restrictions on exclusion of party competition and trading may also be seen as partly protective of the individual involved, as well as of society as a whole.

Furthermore, although, as seen in discussion of Article 3(3), certain United Kingdom mandatory rules may be limited to *non-international* cases and the Convention itself is inapplicable in such circumstances under Article 1(1), nevertheless, Article 5(2) is not thereby deprived of any scope in the United Kingdom, since national United Kingdom definitions of international are far more restrictive than the Convention concept in Article 1(1), and accordingly, *non*-international contracts for national United Kingdom mandatory rules (leading to operation of national mandatory restrictions) may well nonetheless amount to *international* contracts for Convention purposes (so that the Convention applies) (nor, it should be added, do the conditions of operation of Article 5 itself, laid down in

Article 5(2) – see below, p.215– in any way restrict the latter's application to cases in which a contract would be international for national United Kingdom mandatory purposes). Thus, basically, under Unfair Contract Terms Act 1977 s.26 and Sale of Goods Act 1979 s.56(3), a contract is international if parties have places of business/habitual residences in different countries *and* the goods are/will be carried between separate states or offer and acceptance are effected in different states or delivery is in a different state from that of offer and acceptance; whereas, as seen, under the Convention, a contract will be international and the Convention – including Article 5 – applicable, if *any* of the factors in ss.26 and 56(3) (for example, different habitual residences) exist, or none does, but some other relevant foreign connection is established (for example, choice of foreign law).

The Convention appears to draw a distinction between, on the one hand, such 'contracts-mandatory' national laws, as have been described, unable to be derogated from directly by contract (see Articles 3(3), 5(2) and 6(1)), and national 'conflicts-mandatory' rules, whereby parties are prohibited from derogating from a particular law either by expressly selecting a foreign legal system to govern the contract ('half-conflicts-mandatory'), or possibly too, even if a foreign legal system applies in the absence of choice ('full-conflicts-mandatory') (see Articles 7 and 9(6)). In the present submission, it is *possible* to construe Article 5(2) (and Articles 3(3) and 6(1)) as also dealing with national half-conflicts-mandatory rules, not merely those which are contracts-mandatory, since the former, as well as the latter, involve attempted derogation *by contract* – albeit, indirectly, through choice of law, in the former case. Furthermore, it is believed that as a matter of construction, if not express statutory provision, it is unlikely that a law found to be contracts-mandatory at national law would not also be held to be unable to be excluded through choice of a foreign legal system, that is to say, half-contracts-mandatory, and vice versa, thereunder (see, for example, Consumer Credit Act 1974 s.173(1), as to protective provisions in that statute; and Carriage of Goods by Sea Act 1971, Schedule, Article III para.8, as applied in *The Hollandia* [1983] A.C. 565).

Thus, for example, the following laws may be classified as contracts-mandatory or, as the case may be, half-conflicts-mandatory, and it is submitted that all are within Article 5(2):

(i) Sale of Goods Act 1979 ss.12–15 (implied conditions in sale of goods contracts) – these are *contracts-mandatory* by virtue of Unfair Contract Terms Act 1977 s.6, which prohibits or restricts their contractual exclusion; and ss.12–15 are also *half-conflicts-mandatory*, by virtue of Sale of Goods Act 1979 s.56 (as substituted by Sched. 1, para.13), which makes a choice of foreign law ineffective in relation thereto,

where the law of a part of the United Kingdom would otherwise apply (in either case, in non-international contracts – see 1977 Act s.26 and 1979 Act s.56(3)).
(ii) Unfair Contract Terms Act 1977 s.6 – this is itself made *half-conflicts-mandatory* by s.27(2), which prevents avoidance of the restriction on contractual exclusion in s.6, through choice of a foreign law in the circumstances there laid down.

MANDATORY CONSUMER PROTECTION LAWS OF COUNTRY OF CONSUMER'S HABITUAL RESIDENCE APPLY NOTWITHSTANDING CHOICE OF ANOTHER LAW

Article 3 continues to apply in principle to choice of law in consumer contracts: but the *result* of application of the chosen law thereunder is not to be to *deprive the consumer of the protection afforded to him* by the mandatory rules of the law of the country of his habitual residence (meaning habitual residence, it is submitted, at the date on which the consumer takes the steps necessary on his part for conclusion of the contract, whether offer or acceptance, rather than that of technical conclusion according to applicable law, or certainly subsequent thereto). 'Habitual residence' (*résidence habituelle/gewöhnlicher Aufenthalt*) is likely to be taken to mean *a regular physical presence which has endured for some time*: see *Cruse* v *Chittum* [1974] 2 All ER 940, 943, under national English conflict of laws, and Kaye, *Civil Jurisdiction*, pp.545–54, for a detailed discussion of the conception, for purposes of Article 5(2) of the Judgments Convention. Were it to be held that a party could have more than one habitual residence, the solution adopted under Article 10(a) and (b) of the United Nations Convention on Contracts for the International Sale of Goods (Vienna, 11 April 1980, Cmnd 8074) is for that which has the closest relationship to the contract and its performance, having regard to the circumstances known to or contemplated by the parties at any time before or at the conclusion of the contract, to be referred to.

(a) Articles 5(2) and 3

Article 5(2) does not provide for ineffectiveness of choice of law, nor even necessarily for its partial replacement by mandatory rules of the consumer's habitual residence. All that is intended is that the result of applying the chosen law should not be to deprive the consumer of protection afforded to him by the mandatory laws of his habitual residence. It is submitted that this provision therefore has two main consequences, as follows:

(i) Article 3 chosen law is only displaced by Article 5(2) mandatory laws when the latter afford *greater protection* to the consumer: it would be wholly contrary to the spirit of Article 5, if the consumer was stopped from being deprived of the 'protection' of mandatory rules of his habitual residence, even when such 'protection' was less than that provided for under the chosen law.

(ii) It may further be argued that Article 3 chosen law and Article 5(2) mandatory rules of the habitual residence should be applied *cumulatively*, on a pick-and-choose basis, selecting the best consumer protection rules from each, in so far as these are compatible and provided that the proper scope and intended effects of *mandatory* provisions of a legal system are not distorted through piecemeal and cumulative application thereof with rules of another law. (In practice, it is thought, even if allowed, the latter limitations would significantly reduce, if not entirely neutralize, any practical scope for cumulation to operate.)

The alternative view of course would state that the mandatory laws of the consumer's habitual residence, with which he is presumably most familiar, should automatically displace the chosen law, whether they are more favourable than the latter or not, and that it is not the function of Article 5 to *confer* substantive consumer protection upon consumers to the maximum degree through the applicable law process, but merely to preserve mandatory rules of the most appropriate law. This argument, however, ignores the fact that even in consumer contracts it is the parties' choice of law which is *prima facie* the most appropriate law to govern, and mandatory law of the habitual residence which brings about the exceptional interruption of the conflicts process, justified solely by consumer protection policies, and that accordingly, a consumer may feel some legitimate concern on discovering that he is to lose the protection afforded to him by the chosen law, in favour of lesser safeguards under his own law. (There might actually have been greater justification, consequently, were Article 5(2) to have provided for application of the law of the consumer's habitual residence *in toto*, as most appropriate applicable law protection, notwithstanding choice of another law, alongside Article 5(3), but subject to mandatory rules of the chosen law where these afforded greater protection!) On the other hand, so far as cumulative application of the most protective rules of chosen law and habitual residence is concerned, it is felt that this would be an incorrect course to follow, and that the one or the other's set of consumer safeguards should govern. The consumer, it is believed, has a choice: either he can confirm the alleged choice of law in relation to the particular issue, and overturn the assumption that he was pressured to assent as the weaker party, in which case the law of his habitual residence has no further part to play; or he can rely on the supposition of pressure, in which event he founds his protection upon mandatory rules of his habitual residence, and not on any of those of the 'renounced' chosen law dealing with the same question. He cannot enjoy both, selectively (see below, for similar arguments in connection with employment protection under Article 6(1)).

(b) Articles 5(2) and 7

It is submitted that similar considerations apply to the relations between Articles 5(2) and 7.

(In the case of Article 3(3), there is little scope for its operation to Article 5 consumer contracts in any event, since *all* connections other than choice – and possibly also agreement on jurisdiction – must be established with the consumer's habitual residence for mandatory rules of the latter's law to apply thereunder, whereas under Article 5(2), mere existence of the habitual residence in a country other than that of which the law is chosen is sufficient: although, in theory, if not in practice, Article 3(3) wholly-connected habitual residence mandatory rules, which are not specifically for the protection of consumers, but, for example, for that of all contracting parties, or of state economies – such as price and credit controls – may nonetheless govern, when these would not otherwise apply under Article 5(2).)

Thus, Article 7 (solely 7(2) in the United Kingdom – 1990 Act s.2(2)), in spite of the wording 'Nothing in this Convention shall restrict ...' in Article 7(2), should only be applied in the alternative to Article 5(2) in relation to mandatory consumer protection laws, rather than automatically displacing habitual residence in Article 5(2), in order to afford consumers maximum protection (although, it is possible that in this case, unlike that of relations between Article 5(2) and Article 3 chosen law, the same objections against *cumulative* application of the best of Article 5(2) and Article 7 consumer-protective laws, where compatible and sufficiently corresponding, do not exist, given the absence of any choice element, and that such cumulation should therefore be permitted in principle, even if unlikely to have much scope for operating in practice). If this were not the case – or at least, if Article 5(2) (and 6(1) – not to mention Articles 5(3) and 6(2): see below, p.219) were not to be permitted to prevail over a different Article 7 law, even if not able to be applied cumulatively therewith – there would have been little point in making the specific provision for protection under Article 5(2), because Article 7(1) would then have been able to be regarded as enabling mandatory provisions of an appropriate law to govern consumer contracts as well as any other.

On the other hand, Article 7 does retain a role. In addition to the fact that a consumer should be permitted to opt for application of mandatory rules of an Article 7 law, in place of those of the Article 5(2) and chosen laws, where the level of protection is higher under the Article 7 law, Article 7, unlike Article 5, does also include within its sphere mandatory rules of a *non*-consumer protective nature, such as restraint of trade and credit controls (as well as 'party'-protection mandatory rules, where not limited to consumers, for example, s.12(1) of the Sale of Goods Act 1979, implying a condition of title on the part of the seller, which is unable to be excluded by contract, under s.6(1)(a) of the Unfair Contract Terms Act 1977, whether the buyer is a 'consumer' within Article 5(1) or not, in non-international cases under s.26), whose contravention may lead to invalidity of offending contracts under the relevant law (within any spatial or other connective limitations laid down thereby), and such rules therefore are preserved specifically by Article 7, alongside mandatory consumer protection rules thereunder which exceed the level of consumer protection afforded by the chosen law under Article 3 or that of the habitual residence under Article 5(2). (Furthermore, in principle, Article 7 would apply to mandatory rules which were unable to be derogated from through choice of foreign law, even if they could otherwise be so by express contractual exclusion, whereas Article 5(2) may *possibly* only be applied to national rules restricting the latter, in accordance with the definition in Article 3(3). In practice, however, it seems most unlikely, at least as a matter of legal construction, if not express statutory provision, that prohibition of choice of law avoidance at national law would not also be accompanied by a corresponding restriction upon contractual exclusion – see below, Article 7.)

Accordingly, Article 5 may be regarded as *lex specialis* in relation to consumer contract-mandatory provision, alongside the general protective provision of Article 7; and, in addition, the latter will have to be resorted to where the particular circumstances for the former's operation, laid down in Article 5(2), now to be considered, are not in existence.

CONDITIONS OF OPERATION OF ARTICLE 5(2) (AND (3))

Article 5(2) contains three alternative conditions ('indents') which must be satisfied for mandatory rules to be brought into operation thereunder (and for the law applicable in the absence of choice to apply under Article 5(3): see below, p. 219). The first two conditions concern types of situation in which the consumer transacts, respectively, in or to, his own country, and where he may therefore justifiably expect any protection afforded to him by his own law to remain available to him in the Convention international context. The third case is where the *wicked* supplier *entices* the *innocent* consumer to travel from the *safety* of his habitual residence to a foreign country and there to place his order: the *Little Red Riding Hood clause*. (Article 13(3) of the Judgments Convention only incorporates the first indent of Article 5(2) of the Obligations Convention.)

(a) First Condition: Conclusion Following Advertising or Specific Invitation in the Consumer's Habitual Residence

This indent is satisfied if the following elements are present:

- prior to conclusion of the contract (it is unclear whether conclusion must also take place in the consumer's habitual residence; both common sense and the second condition below suggest not, but French and Italian texts might indicate otherwise), there was a specific invitation addressed to the consumer in his habitual residence, or advertising there: this is intended to cover *inter alia* mail order (presumably, even if also individually addressed to others!), doorstep selling (whether or not the representative has the power to conclude transactions), direct approaches and canvassing, and advertising in the press and in catalogues, and on radio, television (especially now satellite) and in the cinema (see Report, p.24: Article 5 governs where a German contracts in response to an advertisement published by a French company in a German publication); it is unclear from the text whether the advertising must also be specifically directed to the consumer's habitual residence – the Report suggests that this is the case (*ibid.*), and that if it were not, Article 5 would nonetheless apply, however indirectly an advertisement intended solely for a foreign country was brought to the attention of the consumer in his habitual residence: thus, it might be blown from France to Germany by a strong wind (and even a foreseeability limitation would hardly help the advertiser, since publication in another country could never truly be discounted as unforeseeable); on the other hand, however, it should not be necessary that the supplier directed the advertisement exclusively to the habitual residence, and to no other country; and
- the consumer took all necessary steps to conclude the contract in his habitual residence: this practical test avoids problems over ascertaining the place of technical conclusion and realistically focuses on the consumer's own actions ('steps' include *inter alia* writing, or any action taken in consequence of an offer or advertisement: Report, p.24); as to whether the consumer must have negotiated entirely in his habitual residence ('all the steps'), it is considered that all that

should be required is that the consumer actually made his offer or acceptance in or from his habitual residence, wherever it was that he conducted the prior negotiations ('steps *necessary* on his part for the conclusion'); thus, even though it is admitted that a consumer may therefore satisfy the first indent simply by returning to his habitual residence in order to make his final offer or, as the case may be, acceptance, nevertheless, it is submitted that to require *everything* on his part to have taken place in that country would be excessively restrictive (and the word 'all' is omitted from foreign texts of the first indent) – although, on the other hand, in the converse situation, in which a consumer conducting prior negotiations from his habitual residence actually makes his final offer or acceptance from another country, Article 5 will nonetheless apply if the consumer's order is received in his habitual residence by the other party or the latter's agent, because the *second* indent is then satisfied.

(b) Second Condition: Consumer's Order Received in His Habitual Residence

There is obviously some potential overlap with the first indent: the second indent is meant for the case in which the consumer places his order at the foreign firm's stand at a trade fair or exhibition taking place in the consumer's state, or with the firm's branch or agent in the latter, *even though there was no specific invitation or advertising* (Report, p.24 – 'agent' is intended to cover all persons acting on behalf of the trader); thus, where the consumer's order is made in England, but received abroad, the first indent must be relied on. A further situation in which the second indent may be of use to the consumer is where he operates from his habitual residence but happens to be in another country when he transmits his order to the supplier or to the latter's agent in the consumer's own habitual residence. (Accordingly, therefore, if the supplier (or his agent) goes to the consumer's country to receive the latter's order, the consumer receives Article 5 protection under the second indent; if the consumer sends his order to another country, he is only protected under Article 5 if the supplier had previously advertised or issued a specific invitation to the consumer in the latter's country.) Perhaps the second indent should also have included the case where the supplier is held to have made the offer, and he or his agent goes to the consumer's habitual residence in order to receive there the latter's acceptance: although, it is submitted that the word 'order' in English and foreign texts is in fact not the exact equivalent of *offer* and can therefore be extended so as also to cover *acceptances* by the consumer in the circumstances.

(c) Third Condition: The Seller in a Sale of Goods Contract Arranged for the Consumer to Travel from the Latter's Habitual Residence to Another Country Where He Was Induced to Give His Order

The third indent covers the special situation of 'cross-border excursion-selling' (see *Rewe* v. *Hauptzollamt Kiel*, Case 150/80 [1981] ECR 805, concerning *Butterfahrten* – butter-buying cruises – from Germany to Danish ports), where, for example, a store owner in state X arranges a one-day coach trip for customers in state Y, with the main purpose of inducing them to buy goods in the store: the first indent is inapplicable, because the consumer does not take the steps necessary for conclusion of the contract in his own state, whether or not there was a prior specific invitation or advertising; nor, by its own terms, is the second indent appropriate (although, it should be noted, only sale of goods contracts are covered by the third indent) (Report, p.24). The Report indicates that the requirement for the seller to have *arranged* the consumer's journey does not mean that the seller himself must act as carrier; it is sufficient that he arranged with another to convey the consumer to the foreign country (*ibid.*): the contract of carriage itself, of course, whether undertaken by the seller or by a third party, is excluded from Article 5 by virtue of Article 5(4)(a) (subject to Article 5(5)). As in the case of the second indent, it is submitted that 'gave his order' covers either of offer or acceptance on the part of the consumer, not solely the former.

Finally, it might have been preferable if the third indent had simply stated that the consumer must have given his order in a country other than that of his habitual residence in the circumstances thereunder, rather than specifically in the country to which he travelled. One may imagine, for example, the case, say, of English buyers, arranged to be transported to a motor car showroom in Calais by the French dealers; the latter, in order to prevent application of Article 5, instruct the coach driver to take the scenic route on the return trip to England – through Belgium – during which the English buyers' orders for the cars are taken on the coach by the dealers' representatives! (Since the date of writing, one wonders whether fiction could yet become reality – see *The Times*, 4 May 1991, 'Belgian Bargains for the British Car Buyer', concerning planned day trips to a car theme park at Tournai, on the Belgian–French border!) Presumably, however, the country in which the order is so taken – Belgium, in the example – may also be regarded as a country to which the consumer travelled for the purpose of Article 5, no less than France, in which the goods were viewed, so that Article 5 can be held to apply notwithstanding the lack of clarity in the text.

3 Notwithstanding the provisions of Article 4, a contract to which this Article applies shall, in the absence of choice in accordance with Article 3, be governed by the law of the country in which the consumer has his habitual residence if it is entered into in the circumstances described in paragraph 2 of this Article.

The Report comments that Article 5(3) is sufficiently clear and calls for no additional examination (p.24).

Thus, Article 4 is excluded thereunder ('Notwithstanding the provisions of Article 4'): applicable law, in the absence of choice under Article 3, is that of the

– country of the consumer's habitual residence.

The presumption in favour of the supplier's law, as that of characteristic performer, under Article 4(2), is consequently removed.

This is subject to the proviso that one of the three conditions indented under Article 5(2) is satisfied. (Given the purpose of those indents, being to secure application of the consumer's own law where the consumer is approached on his home ground, or is lured away from the latter, one wonders why Article 5(3) could not also have applied where there *was* a choice of law under Article 3, instead of the provision under Article 5(2), which merely safeguards mandatory rules of the consumer's habitual residence in such cases. Conversely, it could be argued that Article 5(3) ought merely to have provided for the consumer not to be deprived of the protection afforded by mandatory rules of the law of his habitual residence in the absence of choice of law: suppose, for example, that the law applicable under Article 4 confers greater protection upon the consumer than would be the case under the law of his habitual residence.)

Formally speaking, Article 5(3) is no less subject to Article 7 than is Article 5(2): Article 7(2) actually states that '*Nothing* in this Convention' is to prevent application of the forum's mandatory rules. This is so whether the mandatory consumer protection laws under Article 7 are for the protection of the consumer – for example, rights of cancellation, and prohibition on exclusion of liability – or for state-economical reasons – such as invalidity for contravention of price and credit controls, restraint of trade, and compulsory down payments – likely to be subject to express or implied spatial limitations upon their operation. It is submitted, however, that as in the case of Article 5(2), mandatory consumer protection under Article 7 should be optionally available to the consumer – if not even *cumulatively* so (on a pick-and-choose basis) – along with that of applicable law under Article 5(3): it would be wholly inappropriate if looser mandatory consumer protection under Article 7 were automatically to *replace* Article 5(3) consumer protection (or *a fortiori*, if this same principle, governing relations between Articles 5(2) and 7, were not also to apply to Article 5(3), simply because under the latter, the law of the consumer's habitual residence governs in its entirety, not merely specifically in mandatory areas). Thus, the most consumer-protective elements of Article 5(3) and 7(2) (not 7(1) in the United Kingdom) mandatory laws (or at least the most consumer protective *of* the two legal systems, if cumulation were not to be admitted) should govern the consumer contract. In the case of state-protective mandatory rules, such as price and credit controls, and, from one point of view, restraint of trade, it is again considered that these are not the province of Article 5, and that Article 7 should therefore apply within its mandatory laws' own spatial limits of operation in such cases (similarly, in principle too, as seen, Article 7 is applicable to mandatory rules which are solely conflicts-mandatory, even if not also contracts-mandatory, unlike Article 5 – although, construction of laws in such manner is unlikely).

Similar considerations apply in the case of *formal validity* of consumer contracts within Article 5, as to which Article 9(5) provides 'The formal validity of such a contract is governed by the law of the country in which the consumer has his habitual residence' (see below, Chapter 14): that is to say, Article 7(2) mandatory rules of the forum on form should merely be optional – not obligatory – in place of protective rules of form of the law otherwise applicable under Article 9(5).

4   *[Article 5(4) – see above, Article 5(1)]*

5   *[Article 5(5) – see above, Article 5(1)]*

11 Article 6: Individual Employment Contracts

Article 6

INTRODUCTION

Article 6 corresponds broadly with Article 5 on consumer contracts (Report, p.25) – except that applicable law in the absence of choice under Article 6(2) is displaceable by law of a more closely connected country, and, realistically, Article 6 does not require the employee necessarily to have negotiated from, or to have been recruited in, his own country: furthermore, Article 9 contains no special rule governing formal validity of employment contracts by the employee's law, in contrast to Article 9(5) on consumer contracts. The object is to protect the presumed socio-economically weaker party from being deprived indirectly of employment protection under what is considered to be the most appropriate law for that party, either through the choice of law device under Article 3 (Article 6(1)) or through operation of the employee-characteristic-performer's own law, presumptively, under Article 4(2), which may not be the same as that of the place of work in an international context (Article 6(2)); and it is even possible – as a matter of construction – that the effect of Article 6 is to extend and maximize employee protection, so as to enable the employee to rely upon the most protective provisions of *more than one* legal system.

INDIVIDUAL EMPLOYMENT

Operation of Article 6 is confined to individual contracts of employment. 'Collective agreements' between employers and employee associations or unions (under the Trade Union and Labour Relations Act 1974 s.30(1), any agreement or arrangement made by or on behalf of one or more trade unions and one or more employers or employers' associations and relating to one or more of the matters mentioned in section 29(1)) are governed as to binding force and effects by general Convention rules on applicable law (see, for example, Trade Union and Labour Relations Act 1974 s.18, concerning legal enforceability of collective agreements, inapplicable, as a matter of substance not procedure, to collective agreements governed by a *foreign* law, according to *Monterosso Shipping Co. Ltd* v. *ITF* [1982] 3 All ER 841, CA). Nevertheless, by reason of Article 6(1), individual employees cannot be deprived of protection sought to be afforded by these latter by virtue of any mandatory rules of the most appropriate law, through choice of a different, unfavourable law (Report, p.25). Furthermore, it may be implied in certain circumstances that parties to individual employment contracts have chosen the law governing the collective source agreement to apply to their own individual contract under Article 3(1).

EMPLOYMENT CONTRACTS

Whatever the jurisprudential basis of the employment relationship (the latter being the expression used in the original preliminary draft Convention), whether it be founded upon express or implied contract, or derived from creation of a status, or *sui generis*, the Report confirms that such relationship is covered by the term 'contract of employment' (pp.25–6).

Nevertheless, the usual problems of defining employment will exist, and it is imperative that the European Court should give a unificationist lead in shaping the concept, so as to exclude, for example, contracts for services, work and materials, and agency (see *Ready Mixed Concrete (South East) Ltd* v. *Minister of Pensions and National Insurance* [1968] 2 QB 497).

The European Court has held the meaning of workers under Article 48 of the EEC Treaty, concerning freedom of movement for workers, to be a Community, not national, concept (*Hoekstra (née Unger)* v.*BBDA*, Case 75/63 [1964] ECR 177; *Levin* v. *Staatssecretaris van Justitie*, Case 53/81 [1982] ECR 1035). The essential requirement would seem to be the performance of services for and under the direction of another for a certain period of time in return for remuneration (*Lawrie-Blum* v. *Land Baden-Württemberg*, Case 66/85 [1987] 3 CMLR 389). Part-time work is included, provided that the activity constitutes effective and genuine economic activity, rather than marginal or ancillary or merely at the level of rehabilitation and reintegration (*Levin*; *Kempf* v. *Staatssecretaris van Justitie*, Case 139/85 [1987] 1 CMLR 764; *Steymann* v. *Staatssecretaris van Justitie*, Case 196/87 [1989] 1 CMLR 449; *Bettray* v. *Staatssecretaris van Justitie*, Case 344/87 [1991] 1 CMLR 459). Community authorities derived from the EEC Treaty are thus of limited help, which is hardly surprising in view of the fact that even if a person is held not to be a worker for purposes of Article 48, Article 52 of the Treaty nonetheless accords freedom of establishment to, *inter alia*, self-employed persons in any event.

In the Judgments Convention case of *Sanicentral GmbH* v. *René Collin*, Case 25/79 [1979] ECR 3423, 3434, Advocate General Capotorti drew a parallel between operation of the Judgments Convention and Article 6 of the then draft Obligations Convention – of added significance now that the amended Judgments Convention has special provisions on individual contracts of employment in Articles 5(1) and 17 (San Sebastian Convention, Articles 4 and 7). Thus, in the later Judgments Convention decision in *Shenavai* v. *Kreischer*, Case 266/85 [1987] ECR 239, the European Court stated (pp.255–6): '... it should first be observed that contracts of employment, like other contracts for work other than on a self-employed basis, differ from other contracts – even those for the provision of services – by virtue of certain particularities: they create a lasting bond which brings the worker to some extent within the organizational framework of the business of the undertaking or employer, and they are linked to the place where the activities are pursued ...'.

Notwithstanding such help to be derived from existing case law, however, problems will remain: if the contract were classified as employment according to – albeit unified – English *lex fori*, it may nonetheless not be so treated as one of employment under a non-Contracting State law applicable according to Article 6; or conversely, under the law applicable, in accordance with general Convention rules, to a contract not regarded by the forum as being one of employment, the latter may be precisely what the relationship is considered to amount to (see Morse,'The EEC Convention on the Law Applicable to Contractual Obligations' (1982), 2 *Yearbook of European Law*, 107, 146–9). Alternatives to *lex fori* on classification are putative *lex causae* under Article 6(2), with return to the forum and reference to the law applicable to non-employment contracts if the latter is how initial *lex causae* so classifies the relationship; or double classification according to, in the first place, *lex fori* and thereafter in accordance with *lex causae* referred to under the former: the first alternative may be circular, but has the merit of seeming to be consistent with the underlying policy of according at least substantive control to most appropriate employment law under Article 6 (see Morse, *ibid.*). The problem, of course, is what is to happen when initial *lex causae* classifies the contract as non-employment, but the law, say, of a Contracting State thereupon referred to under general Convention rules does regard the contract as one of employment? The court can hardly then refer back and forth to the original Article 6 law on employment *ad infinitum*! All that is possible in such a case is for the forum to apply the general applicable law to what the latter regards as an employment relationship, without reference to any mandatory employment rules of the Article 6(2) law, which may be regarded as non-existent in the particular circumstances in question.

Article 6

Individual employment contracts

1   Notwithstanding the provisions of Article 3, in a contract of employment a choice of law made by the parties shall not have the result of depriving the employee of the protection afforded to him by the mandatory rules of the law which would be applicable under paragraph 2 in the absence of choice.

MANDATORY RULES

(a) Scope

'Mandatory rules' are defined under Article 3(3) *hereinafter* as rules of law 'which cannot be derogated from by contract'. (Thus, they are not simply rules which *give employees a good deal*, for example, by awarding them higher compensation or longer notice of termination than other laws – unless their application were also to be subject to safeguard against exclusion by contractual agreement of parties. Furthermore, it will be recalled that *protective* rules of, for example, minors' incapacity to enter into valid contracts of employment lie outside the Convention's scope, under Article 1(2)(a), without prejudice to Article 11.)

It is submitted, however, that given the underlying purpose of Article 6, being to provide special protective rules in relation to the particular type of contractual relationship classified as one of individual employment, and amounting to *lex specialis* in relation to *general* mandatory provision in Article 7, Article 6(1) should also be held to include those national mandatory employee-protection provisions which prohibit parties from excluding their liability through selection of a foreign law rather than directly by a contractual term: the former, as well as the latter, could be held to amount to (albeit, indirect) derogation by contract, within the definition in Article 3(3) 'hereinafter', and it seems unlikely, in any event, that, as a matter of statutory provision or judicial construction, the two types of restriction would not go hand in hand under the relevant national law.

Accordingly, the view here is that mandatory rules under Article 6(1) will include the following:

(i)   substantive domestic employee-protection laws which are unable to be excluded *directly* by parties' agreement;
(ii)   also those national employee-protection rules – referred to in the present work as 'half-conflicts-mandatory' rules – which (subject to

any national spatial limitations or connections, such as country of the relevant legal system being the employee's place of work, place of contracting, or residence of the employee) parties are prohibited from *indirectly* excluding (instead of or as well as from directly excluding) by agreement on applicable foreign law – the latter, after all, being no less of an attempt to derogate from the domestic rules 'by contract'; further, such half-conflicts-mandatory rules, it is considered, may be treated as such, whether by virtue of a specific statutory provision, or as a result of construction of the substantive rule; and

(iii) even what are referred to in this book as full-conflicts-mandatory laws – namely, those which exclude the law otherwise applicable, whether this is so by virtue of the parties' agreement or in the absence thereof – to the extent that such national extraterritorial provisions therefore also constitute half-conflicts-mandatory rules, prohibited from avoidance through agreement on applicable law, by statute or construction (and subject, again, to any national spatial connections); and doubtless, in any event, in such cases, it would also be possible to argue that as a matter of construction, in the absence of express statutory provision, direct contractual exclusion of the substantive law is also not permitted.

Thus, there are a number of English employment statutes which may be held to fall within these categories. These include, for example:

- the Equal Pay Act 1970 s.1(11) (added by Sex Discrimination Act 1975, Sched. I, Part I, para.1(4)), providing that the terms it implies into employment contracts apply irrespective of whether the proper law of (substituted by the words 'law applicable to' under Contracts (Applicable Law) Act 1990, s.5 and Sched. 4 para.1) the contract is the law of any part of the United Kingdom: and subjecting itself to the spatial limitation under s.1(1) (as amended by Sex Discrimination Act 1975 s.8), to the effect that the equality clause is inserted into contracts of employment of men and women *employed at an establishment in Great Britain*;
- Employment Protection (Consolidation) Act 1978 s.153(5), providing that the Act's provisions (on *inter alia* redundancy, maternity, written particulars of terms of employment, minimum periods of notice and rights against unfair dismissal) apply regardless of whether the law otherwise governing the employment contract is that of a part of the United Kingdom or not: and containing spatial limitations on its written particulars of employment and minimum periods of notice, unfair dismissal, and redundancy payments provisions, in, respectively, s.141 (1), (2) and (3) and (4) (*Cox v.E.L.G. Metals Ltd* [1985] ICR 310 (CA);

Wilson v. *Maynard Shipbuilding Consultants A.B.* [1978] QB 665 (CA)); (note too Trade Union and Labour Relations Act 1974 s.30 (6) – although, as seen, s.18 collective agreements are outside Article 6);
- the Patents Act 1977 ss.39–43, compensating employees for inventions, and subject to spatial limitations under s.43(2), which makes no express provision as to applicable law, but which Dicey and Morris (p.1303) consider to apply irrespective of the proper law of the contract;
- The Wages Act 1986, replacing the Truck Acts, concerning deductions from wages, and subject to spatial limitations under s.30: in *Duncan* v. *Motherwell Bridge and Engineering Co.* 1952 SC 131, a Scottish court held the Truck Act 1831 to apply, without actually determining the proper law of the contract in question (which, admittedly, would probably have been Scottish law), in relation to work to be carried out abroad;
- the general provision of s.27(2) of the Unfair Contract Terms Act 1977, preventing choice of foreign law from evading restrictions on exclusion of general contractual liability under s.3 of the 1977 Act.

(For examples of foreign mandatory rules: see Forde, 'Conflict of Individual Labour Laws and the EEC's Rules' (1979), *Legal Issues* of *European Integration*, 85, 91–3).

All such mandatory rules, it is submitted, may be held to fall within Article 6(1), on the basis that the 'contract-mandatory' definition applicable thereto, laid down in Article 3(3), ought normally to be taken, as a matter of common-sense construction, to be comprised in any specific statutory provision – or, as the case may be, judicial decision – at national law for the full- or half-conflicts-mandatory operation of such substantive employment laws. (Nor, it should be added, is it at all acceptable that the national spatial limitations on the latters' application should themselves be regarded as contract conflicts rules, to be replaced by the Convention's provisions. On the contrary, they are to continue to operate alongside the latter, as they have done in relation to the extraterritorial operation of the substantive rules under pre-existing English conflicts, as self-limiting, negative operational factors.)

Admittedly, it is possible – though, it is felt, not very likely as a matter of construction today, when (partly as a result of discussions on the Convention) there seems to be a greater general awareness of the conflicts dimension in relation to employment statutes *et alia* – that a statutory rule, prohibiting parties from contracting out of liability imposed under a particular law, may be treated as being merely 'contracts-mandatory', and *not* also full- or even half-conflicts-mandatory. Thus, for example, in *Sayers* v. *International Drilling Co. NV* [1971] 1 WLR 1176, a majority of the Court of Appeal held Dutch, rather than English, law to be the proper law of an employment contract, and that accordingly, s.1(3) of the Law Reform (Personal Injuries) Act 1948, making void a contractual exemption clause, was inapplicable, the clause consequently being upheld under Dutch law. (*Quaere* whether the same result would have been reached had English, not Dutch, law been held to be most closely connected, and Dutch law merely agreed to by the parties?) However, in the Scottish case of *Brodin v. A.R.Seljan* 1973 SC 213, a Scottish court held s.1(3) to apply to claims in respect of delicts committed in Scotland regardless of the proper law of the contract (and even indicated *obiter* that s.1(3) might apply to Scottish proceedings, wherever the place of delict), and it is believed that the latter represents the more likely response of courts at the present day towards construction of mandatory rules of national laws: construction of contracts-mandatory and half-conflicts-mandatory together, not the one to the exclusion of the other; and Article 6(1) is to be interpreted and applied in the light of this reality.

(b) Types

The Report indicates that mandatory rules under Article 6(1) are not limited to those relating to the contract of employment itself, but also cover rules on health and safety (see, for example, Factories Act 1961; Offices, Shops and Railway Premises Act 1963; Health and Safety at Work etc. Act 1974) (p.25). It is questioned, however, whether this is correct. Unless such legislation – admittedly, *protective* in nature – actually affects the substantive content of contracts of employment which are subjected thereto, the proper, private civil remedy would seem to lie in tort for breach of statutory duty (unless excluded – see 1974 Act s.47(1), though note s.47(2)), rather than in contract, and so lies beyond the scope of Article 6(1). Furthermore, mandatory rules, the subject of Article 6(1), are limited to those which are for the protection of employees: laws preventing restraint of trade clauses in employment contracts from being given effect to, or avoiding contracts for contravention of, say, statutory restrictions on employment of foreigners, may be felt to fall outside the sphere of Article 6(1), in which case they are subject instead solely to Articles 3(3) and 7 safeguards for application of mandatory rules in general (unless it were considered that controls on restraint of soliciting employers' clients or of competing on termination, were essentially and predominantly – or at least, equally – for ex-employees' protection).

Finally, it could be argued that just as it has previously been put that matters of industrial safety and hygiene are likely to be non-contractual and consequently outside Article 6(1) and the Convention itself, so too should statutory remedies for unfair dismissal and redundancy, not founded on contract, be held to apply outside the Convention and in accordance with their own spatial limitations. This would mean that such issues would be applicable as a legal category *sui generis*, lying halfway between public law and contracts of employment, applicable solely by the courts of the relevant legal system itself. Thus, French, German and Italian courts would not be expected to calculate English redundancy payments, nor to carry out the work of English industrial tribunals in the matter of remedies for unfair dismissal, nor vice versa.

The alternative course would be to regard such rights – for example, the right not to be unfairly dismissed – as in some way constituting implied terms of employees' contracts of employment and consequently subject to the normal processes of contract conflicts, and therefore within the scope of the Convention and Article 6(1) in particular.

The European Court of Justice should be called upon to provide interpretative assistance under the Brussels Protocol in this matter of construction of Article 6(1).

MANDATORY RULES OF EMPLOYMENT LAW APPLY NOTWITHSTANDING CHOICE

(a) Respective Scope of Mandatory Rules and Applicable Law

Chosen law under Article 3 is given effect to according to Article 6(1) (Report, p.25) (see Morse, in North (ed.) (1982), pp.151–2, criticizing implied choice in employment contracts): but only subject to mandatory rules of the law which would be applicable in the absence of choice under Article 6(2).

As in the case of Article 5(2) on consumer protection, the words 'shall not have the result of depriving the [consumer] employee of the protection afforded to him by the mandatory rules of' the relevant law provoke a response.

In the first place, chosen law is not automatically displaced by the mandatory rules, but only if the consumer is afforded inferior protection under the former (*not have the result of depriving*), for example, shorter notice of termination. It would seem quite out of step with the policy of employment protection underlying Article 6(1) and with the principles of party autonomy operating in favour of the employee, for the latter to be regarded as entitled solely to the level of protection afforded by the mandatory rules, whether better or worse than that available under the chosen law. On the other hand, of course, it is conceded that it may be difficult to decide which of chosen and mandatory laws are *superior*: for example, where the chosen law gives a remedy of reinstatement, but not compensation, after wrongful dismissal, whereas the mandatory rules of the law applicable under Article 6(2) only provide compensation (see Morse, in North (ed.) (1982), pp.152–3).

Secondly, it is submitted that the employee should not be permitted to pick and choose from amongst individual rules of an Article 6(2) mandatory law, so as to enjoy maximum protection through the *cumulative* application of chosen law and mandatory rules of the law applicable in the absence of choice. If a statute or decree regulating the particular question at issue is held to be of mandatory nature under the Article 6(2) law, it should be applied to that issue in its entirety, or else not applied at all, in favour of chosen applicable law, and vice versa in favour of Article 6(2) mandatory laws. Thus, the argument has been put that the object – and consequently the effect – of Article 6(1) should not be held to be one of substantive employee protection, but instead, retention of appropriate applicable law, and that cumulative operation should therefore be expressly rejected (if only to prevent its attempted circumvention by courts, through non-mandatory or procedural classification) (Morse, *ibid.*). There is much to be said for the latter view: the employee is to be protected under Article 6(1) by reference to mandatory rules of the Article 6(2) law. If he wishes to rely on his choice, this amounts to negation of the assumption that the choice was forced upon him, and chosen law may thereupon be treated *per se* as most appropriate applicable law, so that he should not then be permitted to rely upon the Article 6(2) law; if the latter is his preference, however, then he effectively denies his assent to the chosen law, and must rely on only so much protection as is available under mandatory rules of the Article 6(2) law. He should not be permitted to rely on elements of both in relation to the particular issue at hand. The European Court should decide accordingly.

Finally, it will be appreciated that applicable laws under Article 6(1) can prove rather complicated and uncertain for employees and their legal advisers: first of all, they have to work out the law which would apply in the absence of choice under Article 6(2), and then they are called upon to determine which of its rules are mandatory; furthermore, under Article 6(2)(b), an employer whose employees do not habitually work in any one country may try to manipulate applicable law thereunder, by engaging the employees through a place of business situated in a country with few mandatory rules (see Fletcher, *Conflict of Laws and European Community Law* (1982), pp.168–9).

(b) Self-limitation of Mandatory Rules

It has previously been seen that national mandatory rules will frequently be subject to their own spatial, self-limitation provision. These are not to be confused with national choice of law rules replaced by the Convention, and the former therefore continue to operate. Thus, for example, mandatory provisions (see above, p.226) on written particulars and minimum notice periods in the Employment Protection (Consolidation) Act 1978 are inapplicable to employees in respect of any period during which they work wholly or mainly outside Great Britain unless they ordinarily work in Great Britain for the same employer (s.141(1)); those concerning *inter alia* written statements of reasons for dismissal, and on unfair dismissal, to employees ordinarily working outside Great Britain (s.141(2)); provisions on redundancy, to employees who are outside Great Britain on the relevant date, unless they ordinarily work in Great Britain, or to employees ordinarily working outside Great Britain, unless they are in Great Britain on the relevant date in accordance with instructions (s.141(3), (4) – see [1991] ELD 372, 4 AZR 238/90, for similar principles in Germany); similarly, the Equal Pay Act 1970 applies to employment at an establishment in Great Britain (s.1(1) as amended by Sex Discrimination Act 1975 s.8), held to be so, unless the employee works wholly or mainly outside Great Britain (Sex Discrimination Act 1975 s.10(1)); and the Patents Act 1977, if the employee was mainly employed in the United Kingdom, or not mainly employed elsewhere, or if his place of employment was unable to be determined but his employer had a place of business in the United Kingdom to which the employee was attached, even if he was also attached elsewhere (s.43(2)).

(c) Articles 6(1) and 3(3)

As in the case of Article 5(2) on consumers, there is little scope for Article 3(3) to operate in respect of mandatory *employment protection* rules with which Article 6(1) is concerned, as opposed to mandatory rules affecting employment which are not intended for protection of employees but are, say, in the interests of the state as a whole: for, clearly, if, in accordance with Article 3(3), all connections are with one country other than that of choice, the former must realistically correspond with that of applicable law under Article 6(2)(a).

(d) Articles 6(1) and 7

Article 7 (not 7(1) in the United Kingdom: 1990 Act s.2(2)) will obviously operate where the mandatory rules are not those for protection of employees, for example, restrictions on employment of foreign nationals and consequent invalidity of contracts of employment thereof; and possibly even invalidity of restraint of competition clauses, if this was considered to be state protective rather than for the benefit of individual employees. In such cases Article 6(1) is inapplicable. However, where it is mandatory employment protection which is in issue:

(i) it is hardly acceptable that courts should exercise their discretion under Article 7(1) – not in the United Kingdom of course – to favour mandatory rules of a foreign country which has merely a close connection thereunder, where the law which would be applicable by virtue of Article 6(2) is considered to be the most appropriate in the absence of choice in relation to employment contracts, and precisely the same arguments apply to Article 7(2), even though in principle the latter – subject to any national spatial limitations – may, and doubtless in practice will, prevail over mandatory Article 6(1) laws ('Nothing in this Convention shall restrict');

(ii) although, notwithstanding the view previously expressed against general cumulation of rules favourable to employees from *chosen* and mandatory laws under Article 6(1), in relation to a particular issue in dispute, it may nevertheless be considered that in principle the same arguments do not apply to cumulation of mandatory protective rules of laws applicable under Articles 6(1) and 7, where not mutually incompatible, in view of the absence of conflict between choice and protection in the latter case. In practice, however, it is considered that there would be very little scope at all, if any, for such cumulation to operate, in view of the narrowness of the concept of mutual compatibility, which must be taken to require that cumulation should not take place in such a way as to distort the proper scope and overall intended effects of the *mandatory* provision of the Article 6(1) or 7 law. Thus, for example, where it is solely the former which holds liability to exist, whereas rules of the Article 7 law alone provide a particular remedy – say, reinstatement, or damages – in respect of such liability not in fact made out *in casu* under the Article 7 law itself, or vice versa, the plaintiff should not be permitted to establish liability under the one law, yet to claim his remedy in accordance with the other, since this would be to interfere with the intended scope of the mandatory rules of whichever legal system is in question. The only situation, consequently, in which cumulation would be feasible is where under a particular legal system, *mandatory* remedies were imposed in respect of *non-mandatory* liability corresponding with established *mandatory* liability under the other legal system, or the converse, an unlikely situation it is felt; and in so far as the amount and quantification of the damages remedy is concerned, this too would in practice be excluded from the cumulation process, since – subject to a contrary reading of Article 10(1)(c) on scope of applicable law, referring *inter alia* to assessment of damages in so far as it is governed by rules of law – measure of damages is in any event a procedural issue for determination according to *lex fori* under national private international law, by virtue of its exclusion from the Convention's scope under Article 1(2)(h).

As in the case of Article 5(2) on consumer protection, therefore, it is submitted that Article 6(1) should be regarded in practice, even if not precisely in accordance with their strict textual interrelationship, as *lex specialis* in relation to Article 7(2), specifically appropriate for employee protection under the employment relationship in case of conflict, but subject to cumulation therewith where possible and desirable.

2   Notwithstanding the provisions of Article 4, a contract of employment shall, in the absence of choice in accordance with Article 3, be governed:

   (a)   by the law of the country in which the employee habitually carries out his work in performance of the contract, even if he is temporarily employed in another country; or
   (b)   if the employee does not habitually carry out his work in any one country, by the law of the country in which the place of business through which he was engaged is situated;

   unless it appears from the circumstances as a whole that the contract is more closely connected with another country, in which case the contract shall be governed by the law of that country.

Article 4, whereunder country of habitual residence of the employee, as characteristic performer, would be presumed to be most closely connected (Article 4(2)), is excluded. Instead, Article 6(2) favours the following rules on applicable law in the absence of choice:

- law of habitual place of work (*locus laboris*) (Article 6(2)(a));
- law of the employer's relevant place of business (that through which the employee was engaged), in the absence of the preceding (Article 6(2)(b));
- SUBJECT TO displacement in either case by the law of a more closely connected country (Article 6(2)).

Law of country of habitual work, or indeed that of engagement through the employer's place of business in the absence of the former, is likely to correspond with *lex fori*, where the appropriate jurisdiction ground (Article 5(1)) is relied on under the Judgments Convention (see *Ivenel* v. *Schwab*, Case 133/81 [1982] ECR 1891; *Shenavai* v. *Kreischer*, Case 266/85 [1987] ECR 239). However, in *Six Constructions Ltd* v. *Humbert*, Case 32/88 [1989] ECR 341, the European Court held that, where an employee did not habitually carry out his work in a single country, it would be contrary to the actual terms of Article 5(1) of the unamended Judgments Convention and to the policy of protecting the employee as the weaker party, for jurisdiction to be given to the courts of the place of business through which the employee was engaged (p.363); and Article 5(1) of the Judgments Convention, as amended by Article 4 of the San Sebastian Convention on Spanish/Portuguese Accession thereto (O.J. 1989 L285/1), specifically limits jurisdiction of courts of the place of business in such cases to actions brought by employees against employers, rather than vice versa, in order to give effect to the principle laid down in *Six Constructions Ltd* v. *Humbert* ('in matters relating to a contract, in the courts for the place of performance of the obligation in question; in matters relating to individual contracts of employment, this place is that where the employee habitually carries out his work, or if the employee does not habitually carry out his work in any one country, the employer may also be sued in the courts for the place where the business which engaged the employee was or is now situated'; see Almeida Cruz/Desantes Real/Jenard Report, O.J. 1990 C189/35 pp.44–5). Article 5(1) of the Lugano Convention between EC Judgments Convention and EFTA countries, on the other hand (O.J. 1988 L319/9), having been drafted prior to the European Court's decision in *Six Constructions Ltd* v. *Humbert*, contains no such restriction upon resort to courts of the country of the place of business through which the employee was engaged (see Jenard/Möller Report, O.J. 1990 C189/57 para. 38).

(a) Habitually Carries Out His Work: Article 6(2)(a)

Concepts of *habitual* place of work, and *temporary* employment elsewhere in Article 6(2)(a) are potentially difficult to operate: how long before work is habitual; how short is temporary? One argument – perhaps controversial – would be that courts, in determining habitual place of work under Article 6(2)(a), should be prepared to undertake an examination of the *prospective* location of employment of the employee in a particular country *as at the date of commencement* thereof, rather than concentrating upon country of employment at the date of proceedings or at any intermediate point in time, even though such subsequent location of actual working activities would nonetheless be taken into account as evidence of the habitual place of work viewed as at the former date; and the related point to be made would be that such assessed habituality would be dependent upon the *terms of the contract* as to required or permissible location of the employee's work, and the likely effectuation thereof, rather than on what had actually occurred with hindsight at the date of proceedings (see *South African Breweries Limited* v. *King* [1900] 1 Ch.273, 274–5; *Moggré* v. *Big Dutchman International AG* (1989) ELD 454, The Netherlands): the level of employment to be carried out in a particular country would then be assessed in relation to competing locations thereof in other countries, and if any country was to be the site of so significant a degree of work in excess of that conducted elsewhere, the former would be regarded as that in which the employee habitually carried out his work in performance of the contract, whilst the other country or countries would merely be those of his temporary employment. If no country enjoyed a sufficient degree of employment activity in excess of the others, the employee would not habitually carry out his work in any one country, and Article 6(2)(b) would apply in place of Article 6(2)(a). Morse, on the other hand (in 'Consumer Contracts, Employment Contracts and the Rome Convention' (1992) 41 *ICLQ* 1, 17), seems to take the contrary view, in favour – tentatively – of applying Article 6(2)(a) to the law of any country in which the employee happens to be habitually working under the contract *at the time of the dispute*.

In favour of the former view, it does seem curious if, instead of focusing on the position as at commencement of the contract, some later date is to be treated as that of assessment of habituality, so that applicable law is then capable of changing every two to three months as the employee is sent to different parts of the world (admittedly, all the less likely to be regarded as habitual for that very reason); and there is even some support for the former construction in the text of Article 6(2)(a), from the words 'his work in performance of the contract', which may be taken to refer not simply to the employee's obligation to carry out for his employer the type of work which he has been engaged to perform, but also to do so in any country to which the employer has the contractual right to send him, *a fortiori*, in that country, if any, where it is most likely, on the evidence as a whole, that the most significant amount of work will be required to take place. This is made even clearer in French, German, Italian and Dutch texts of Article 6(2)(a), which, instead of providing 'in which the employee habitually carries out his work in performance of the contract', state 'in which the employee, in performance of the contract, habitually carries out his work'.

On the whole, however, it is conceded that it is the second possible meaning which may have to be regarded as that which is preferable, and that actual past and current location of work should therefore be primarily assessed for habituality, in the sense described above – yet nonetheless taking full account of likely future country or countries of work *in accordance with the contract*. (Thus, in *Wilson* v. *Maynard Shipbuilding Consultants A.B.* [1978] QB 665 (CA), it was held that in order to determine whether an employee 'ordinarily works' within or outside Great Britain for purposes of what was to become s.141(2) of the Employment Protection (Consolidation) Act 1978 a tribunal should look at the terms of the contract, express or implied, over the whole contemplated period of the contract, not merely at what actually took place prior to termination.) Notional change of applicable law in retrospect under Article 6(2)(a) is likely to be of little concern to parties who omitted to make an express choice of law to govern their contract; whilst, in the case of Article 6(1), it would be highly inappropriate for mandatory rules of law of a country to govern, other than those of that location in which work has *actually* habitually been carried out.

Naturally nevertheless, where investigation into habituality takes place at the beginning of a period of employment, *prospective* contractual location thereof *under the contract* inevitably takes on a correspondingly greater importance. For example, in *Sayers* v. *International Drilling Co.* [1971] 1 WLR 1176 a majority of the Court of Appeal, LORD DENNING MR in the minority, held that Dutch law, not English law, was the most connected where the employee was injured two weeks after beginning work on a Dutch oil drilling rig in Nigerian waters, under a contract which stated that his work was expected to be carried out on the rig in Nigeria, but that he could be sent elsewhere. Under Article 6(2)(a), the court would have to assess the significance of the latter proviso in the contract, and if it were concluded that there was sufficient likelihood as at the date of conclusion of the contract that Sayers would be sent to work in countries other than Nigeria for relatively substantial periods, the court would then be justified in deciding that Sayers was not habitually employed in Nigeria; if, on the other hand, prospects of work elsewhere were minor and insignificant in relation to Nigerian *locus laboris*, the court would have to hold Nigeria to be the place of habitual employment, and its law consequently to be applicable under Article 6(2)(a) (subject to displacement by Dutch law under the proviso to Article 6(2) if it appeared from the circumstances as a whole that the contract was more closely connected with Holland).

Finally, just as Article 6(2)(b) will apply where the employee habitually carries out his work in more than one country, so too, it is thought, this will be the position where he performs his duties substantially in *no* country, that is to say, for example, in the case of an employee who works on a ship or on an oil rig on the high seas, or on an aeroplane flying over the high seas – although, it is clear that in these situations, displacement of Article 6(2)(b) by the rule of closer connection in the proviso, conceivably in favour of laws of countries of ships' flag or ports of registration, may be a distinct possibility. However, reference to laws of flags and ports *as such*, as *deemed* place of habitual employment, under Article 6(2)(a), would hardly seem appropriate (for further discussion, see Kaye, *International Contracts*, Part V, 1993, Barry Rose).

(b) Place of Business Through Which He Was Engaged: Article 6(2)(b)

The usual problems will exist (although, the Report contemplates that the rule is a good one for employees working on rigs or ships on the high seas – p.26: this seems undeniable!) over whether an employer's activities constitute a place of business thereof within a country, even if it is possible to conclude that the 'engagement' of the employee took place there (engagement itself is unclear – place of interview, signing of contract by the employer or employee, or place of technical conclusion of the contract of employment?): presumably, if the employer's sole activity in a country is recruitment (unless of course the employer's business is to run an employment agency!), this will not be sufficient to constitute the venue a place of business (nor, surely, place of closer connection than another under the proviso); however, if the employer conducts its business in a country through an agent or representative – even, it is submitted, lacking authority to conclude contracts without reference to the employer – who operates from a sufficiently fixed and permanent base there (see *Dunlop Pneumatic Tyre Co. Ltd* v.

A.G.Cudell & Co. [1902] 1 KB 342 CA), the latter should be held to amount to a place of business for purposes of Article 6(2)(b) (unless the agent is so independent of the foreign principal that the place of conducting business must be held to be that of the former rather than the latter: see *Cleveland Museum of Art* v. *Capricorn Art International SA* [1990] 2 Lloyd's Rep. 166, 169, HIRST J, and Kaye, 'International Jurisdiction over Companies. When is an Art Gallery not an Art Gallery?' (1992), 1 *International Journal of Cultural Property* 185, 187–189). The matter should ultimately be treated as one of fact (see *South India Shipping Corpn Ltd* v. *Export–Import Bank of Korea* [1985] 1 WLR 585; *Re Oriel Ltd* [1986] 1 WLR 180), although, *some* degree of permanency is clearly a *sine qua non* of 'place' of business, as opposed to mere conduct thereof (*Littauer Glove Corpn* v. *F.W. Millington (1920) Ltd* (1928) 44 TLR 746). In the present writer's opinion, regular attendance of a representative at an hotel for the conduct of transactions should be *capable* of constituting the latter a place of business of the employer in the country concerned, but the point is controversial (see *Cleveland Museum of Art* [1900] 2 Lloyd's Rep. 166, 169) (especially if different hotels are chosen). Occasional use of a customer's (*Littauer*) or subsidiary's (*Sayers*) office is unlikely to be sufficient: indeed, even if this were so held to amount to a place of business under Article 6(2)(b), it would seem likely that applicable law would then be displaced in any event by the law of a more closely connected country under the proviso to Article 6(2) (see below, p.237), possibly that of the employer. Whatever the solutions to these problems, it must surely be the case that place of business in question under Article 6(2)(b) should be that of the employer itself or of its transacting agent, and not that of a third party.

Where it is held that the recruitment of the employee was not carried out through a place of business, then, unless the contract was actually *concluded* through a place of business elsewhere (place where the employee was 'engaged') – and if it was, the latter would clearly be extremely vulnerable to displacement under the proviso in the circumstances – the correct course would seem to be to go immediately to the law of the most closely connected country under the proviso, even though strictly speaking the latter is inapplicable according to its terms (that is, as a *displacement* provision, by virtue of the *more* closely connected law).

(c) Appears from the Circumtances as a Whole that the Contract is More Closely Connected with Another Country: The 'Proviso'

Law applicable under Article 6(2)(a) or (b) is displaceable where it is shown that the contract is more closely connected with another country. This is frequently referred to as the *proviso* to Article 6(2); its object is to provide a degree of flexibility – excessive and too vague in the view of some – in case the law of the place of work, or, more likely, that of the place of business through which the employee was engaged, is not the most satisfactory. In *Sayers* v. *International Drilling Co.*, the employee had only been in Nigeria for a short period at the relevant time, and although he was in England when he was engaged, it may be that the contract would be held most closely connected with the Netherlands seat of the Dutch employer under the Article 6(2) proviso (see earlier, p.235), in which case the majority decision of the Court of Appeal in favour of Dutch law as that governing the contract might be the same today.

Clearly, the burden of proof is upon the party seeking to show a closer connection (qualitatively rather than quantitatively, one suspects) and the proviso permits all circumstances (presumably not just territorial connections) to be taken into account: a previous working relationship governed by a different law would perhaps support displacement; connection with a larger international project run by persons other than the employer might be enough; centre of employer's operations when the employee is very senior (*Re Anglo-Austrian Bank* [1920] 1 Ch.69; Dicey and Morris, p.1298), or when also a place of work (*Coupland* v. *Arabian Gulf Oil Co.* [1983] 1 WLR 1136); common country of habitual residence of employer and employee might even be sufficiently weighty (where the employee remains living in his habitual residence and travels to another country to work there habitually); and obviously, in all events, country of place of business of mere engagement under Article 6(2)(b) is all the more likely to be displaced by the law of a more closely connected country.

One further point concerning the law applicable in accordance with the proviso, as well as that otherwise governing under Article 6(2)(b), is that where the law so determined to be applicable is not in fact that of the country in which the employee ordinarily works, it may well be the case that, as in the United Kingdom, national employment protection legislation of the applicable law may nonetheless still *not* apply, through operation of national spatial limitations upon its scope. Mandatory protective rules of the forum, satisfying spatial conditions of the latter, would then have to be resorted to under Article 7(2) (or alternatively, the employee could try to sue in tort under the English legal system: see *Matthews* v. *Kuwait Bechtel Corpn* [1959] 2 QB 57; *Coupland* v. *Arabian Gulf Petroleum Co.* [1983] 1 WLR 1136, affd [1983] 1 WLR 1151 (CA) – even though the option may not always be available in the alternative under Continental civil laws).

(d) Articles 6(2) and 7

Proceeding from the latter remarks, as indicated, where the law applied under Article 6(2) is not in fact that of the place of work, the latter country's law on employee protection may nevertheless apply as mandatory rules under Article 7(1) (not in the United Kingdom: 1990 Act s.2(2)) and, in the case of the forum's laws, Article 7(2), any spatial qualifications of which are likely to be satisfied in the circumstances.

A Draft Regulation on Provisions of Conflict of Laws in Employment Relationships within the Community was presented by the EEC Commission to the Council in 1972 (O.J. 1972 49/26, 18 May 1972), and amended in 1976 (Com. (1975) 653 Final, 28 April 1976, with Explanatory Memorandum). This was subsequently withdrawn (O.J. 1981, C307/3, 27 November 1981 – see Morse, in North (ed.) (1982), pp.169–72, and 183, note 103; and it would have had precedence over the Obligations Convention under Article 20 of the latter had it been implemented). Article 6, therefore, is evidently regarded as sufficient, at least for the present until its working can be assessed (see though, Hansard, HL Vol.513, col.1265, for criticism). (The Report on the Obligations Convention in fact states that the solution in Article 6(2) was only adopted after a thorough examination of conflicts problems in employment law, 'in the course of which particular consideration was given both to the draft Regulation prepared in this connection by the EEC Commission and to the latest trends in the legal literature and case law of the Member States of the Community': p.26.)

At least in the case of the *locus laboris* rule in Article 6(2)(a), it may be said that, in most cases, law of the country of habitual work will also be likely to be that of the employee's habitual residence, thereby satisfying national spatial limitations, as well as, at the same time, constituting what is perhaps a superior (see too Article 5(3) on consumers' applicable law) choice of law employee-protection rule: law of employee's habitual residence; while, in addition, workers habitually resident in one country, who travel across borders in order to reach their place of habitual employment, daily or weekly, will not always be affluent commuters, and they too, consequently, rightly receive protection under Article 6(2)(a).

12 Article 7: Mandatory Rules of Contract Law

Article 7

Mandatory rules

1 When applying under this Convention the law of a country, effect may be given to the mandatory rules of the law of another country with which the situation has a close connection, if and in so far as, under the law of the latter country, those rules must be applied whatever the law applicable to the contract. In considering whether to give effect to these mandatory rules, regard shall be had to their nature and purpose and to the consequences of their application or non-application. [*Inapplicable in the United Kingdom: 1990 Act, s.2(2); also in Germany, Ireland, and Luxembourg – and possibly in Portugal and Spain when they accede.*]

2 Nothing in this Convention shall restrict the application of the rules of the law of the forum in a situation where they are mandatory irrespective of the law otherwise applicable to the contract. [*Applicable in all Contracting States, including the United Kingdom*]

Article 16

'Ordre public'

The application of a rule of the law of any country specified by this Convention may be refused only if such application is manifestly incompatible with the public policy (*'ordre public'*) of the forum.

OUTLINE OF PRE-EXISTING ENGLISH CONFLICTS

(a) Application of Foreign Mandatory Rules

This is a rare occurrence under pre-existing English conflicts. The one basic circumstance in which it would seem that English courts have a public policy discretion to refuse to uphold a transaction valid according to its applicable law, on the ground of its contravention of foreign mandatory rules of legality, is where it is considered that to do so would be in breach of international comity and likely to compromise the British government's relations with a foreign friendly country whose law has been broken. (In *Lorentzen* v. *Lydden & Co.* [1942] 2 KB 202, however, ATKINSON J appeared to give extraterritorial effect to a Norwegian requisition decree on public policy grounds; but the facts of the case were special owing to wartime exigencies, and in *Bank voor Handel en Scheepvaart NV* v. *Slatford* [1953] 1 QB 248, 263–4, DEVLIN J doubted whether public policy should have been given such positive, rather than the usual negative, operation, in relation to application of foreign laws.) The doctrine of public policy comity is necessarily extremely vague, and it is not wholly clear whether *any* breach of foreign criminal law is sufficient for the doctrine to be invoked, or whether the law in question must be especially imperative, and if so, to what extent; nor is it certain what is meant by a 'friendly' foreign country. Case law is diffuse: in *De Wutz* v. *Hendricks* (1824) 2 Bing 314, the English court refused to enforce an English contract for the loan of money to assist a rebellion by subjects of a foreign friendly state, Crete (the government of the Porte); in *Foster* v. *Driscoll* [1929] 1 KB 470, the Court of Appeal refused to enforce a partnership contract where it was clear that the intention was to export whisky to the United States to be sold in breach of that country's prohibition laws; and in *Regazzoni* v. *K.C. Sethia (1944) Ltd* [1958] AC 301, the House of Lords refused to enforce an English contract between a seller in India and a Swiss buyer to sell jute bags for delivery to Genoa, Italy, because the seller knew that the buyer intended to resell and deliver the bags to South Africa and that it was illegal under Indian law to export jute from India to South Africa. In addition, the well-known case of *Ralli Brothers* v. *Compania Naviera Sota y Aznar* [1920] 2 KB 287 is an example of where an English contract, which had become illegal of performance according to Spanish *lex loci solutionis*, was denied enforcement by the Court of Appeal, although there, comity was admittedly not the – at least, overt – basis of the decision, which has instead been ascribed to the fact that internal English proper law regarded contracts as frustrated by supervening illegality, including, apparently, that occurring under foreign *lex loci solutionis* (see Cheshire and North, p.488, and above, Part II): however, in *Vita Food Products Inc.* v. *Unus Shipping Co* [1939] AC 277, LORD WRIGHT referred to LORD HALSBURY's judgment in *In re Missouri Steamship Co.* (1888) 42 Ch.D 321, as meaning that although, on the one hand, illegality as such under foreign *lex loci contractus* will not render a contract unenforceable, on the other hand, the latter would nonetheless be the case if the foreign law was of such character that it would be against the comity of nations for an English court to give effect to the transaction ([1939] AC 277, 296–8) – reasoning which may equally be used as a more general basis to support the *Ralli* decision.

Nevertheless, clearly not every foreign criminal law will be regarded as sufficiently imperative for the comity public policy doctrine to be invoked, nor even, it would seem, will imperative legality laws of *every* connected law be taken into account. Thus, in *Kleinwort Sons & Co.* v. *Ungarische Baumwolle Industrie A/G* [1939] 2 KB 678, Hungarian exchange control laws were held not to provide a defence for debtors who had promised to pay in London under an English contract, notwithstanding their Hungarian residence, since English law was both proper law and *lex loci solutionis*. In *Lemenda Trading Co.* v. *African Middle East Petroleum Co. Ltd* [1988] 1 All ER 513, PHILLIPS J held that the fact that enforcement of a transaction would be contrary to the public policy of a foreign, friendly country would not be sufficient for the comity doctrine to be invoked against enforcement in the English courts, and that what was required was some violation of a positive rule of law of the foreign state (p.519) – although, the former would nonetheless be a relevant factor in deciding whether the contract offended against public policy of the English forum on general principles of morality.

Finally, a special rule *disapplying* provisions of English law operates under s.27(1) of the Unfair Contract Terms Act 1977: specified restrictions on contractual liability-exclusion under the Act (operating other than in relation to international contracts: s.26) are inapplicable thereunder, where the proper law of the contract is the law of any part of the United Kingdom only by choice of the parties, apart from which the law of a country outside the United Kingdom would apply. (The phrase 'proper law of' in s.27(1) is now substituted by the expression 'law applicable to': 1990 Act s.5 and Sched. 4 para.4.)

(b) Application of the English Forum's Mandatory Rules

There are two main sets of circumstances in which English law will be held to apply in place of pleaded and proven foreign law otherwise applicable under the English conflict of laws.

(i) English laws applied extraterritorially, outside the normal operation of private international law

This may be ordained *either* by express statutory provision *or* judicially held to be so on the basis of social or economic public policy of the forum: and, in either case, the extraterritorial application of such rules will probably be subject to spatial limitations, whereby their operation is dependent upon the existence of certain local connections – place of work, residence, effect on trade – with the forum.

Furthermore, broadly speaking, if one accepts the Convention's own implicit classification, such mandatory rules may be divided into three categories, which can be referred to as follows (see above, Articles 3(3), 5(2) and 6(1)):

(1) Contract-mandatory rules These are domestic rules of law which contracting parties are prohibited from displacing directly by *contractual agreement on exclusion:* for example, s.67 of the Consumer Credit Act 1974 (cancellation period), unable to be excluded by contract, under s.173; ss.12 – 15 of the Sale of Goods Act 1979 (implied conditions of title, description, merchantable quality, fitness for purpose, and correspondence with sample), contractual exclusion of which is controlled by s.6(1)(a) *(s.12)* and (2)(a) and (3) *(ss.13–15)* of the Unfair Contract Terms Act 1977 (other than in international contracts under s.26) (see too Carriage of Goods by Sea Act 1971, Sched., Article III para. 8; and Rent Act 1977 s.126(1)) (outside the purely contractual sphere, one could also point to s.1 (3) of the Law Reform (Personal Injuries) Act 1948, making void a contractual exemption clause: note *Sayers* v. *International Drilling Co. NV* [1971] 1 WLR 1176; and *Brodin* v. *A/R Seljan* 1973 SC 213; and Consumer Protection Act 1987 s.7).

(2) Half-conflicts-mandatory These are domestic English laws which English conflicts rules prohibit – in prescribed circumstances and subject to any spatial limitations – from being excluded through express or implied agreement upon application of a law other than English to govern the contract. The obvious examples are the restrictions on contractual exclusion of liability laid down by the Unfair Contract Terms Act 1977 itself – such as those in s.6 of the 1977 Act, as seen, controlling contractual exclusion of liability under certain provisions of *inter alia* the Sale of Goods Act 1979 (other than in international cases: s.26) – which, by virtue of s.27(2), continue to apply, notwithstanding choice of a foreign law, where either the parties intended to evade the Act, or one of them was a consumer habitually resident in the United Kingdom who took the essential steps to conclude the contract therein; similarly, ss.12–15 of the Sale of Goods Act 1979 themselves are also made half-conflicts-mandatory under s.56 of the 1979 Act (Sched. 1 para. 13) (in

non-international cases thereunder: see s.56(3)), which provides for their continued operation notwithstanding choice of a foreign proper law, where law of a part of the United Kingdom would otherwise have applied apart from the choice; another case, but one of statutory construction rather than express provision, was that of the Hire Purchase and Small Debt (Scotland) Act 1932, as amended by the Hire Purchase Act 1954, which the Scottish Court of Session held in *English* v. *Donnelly* 1958 SC 494 to apply to a hire-purchase contract entered into by a buyer in Scotland, notwithstanding the choice of English law (s.173 of the Consumer Credit Act 1974 would likely be given a similar construction), on the basis that parliament would not have intended such avoidance of protective legislation to be so facilitated; (the Australian case of *Kay's Leasing Corporation* v. *Fletcher* (1964) 116 CLR 124 was not dissimilar, except that there the court adopted a technical construction of place of contracting, as that of acceptance by the supplier in his own state, rather than in that of the forum, from which the non-consumer buyer had contracted); *Golden Acres Ltd* v. *Queensland Estates Pty Ltd* [1969] Qd R. 378, is a further example of a half-conflicts-mandatory (or possibly even full-conflicts-mandatory: see Pryles, in North (ed.) (1982), pp.332–3) rule by construction; however, in *Sayers* v. *International Drilling Co. NV* [1971] 1 WLR 1176, the Court of Appeal held s.1(3) of the Law Reform (Personal Injuries) Act 1948, making void a contractual exemption clause, to be inapplicable where Dutch, not English, law was the proper law of the contract, so that to that extent the English rules of liability, protected by s.1(3), were consequently contracts-mandatory by virtue of the latter, yet not also half-conflicts-mandatory – although, in *Brodin* v. *A/R Seljan* 1973 SC 213, the Scottish court, by contrast, applied s.1(3) regardless of the proper law.

(3) Full-conflicts-mandatory These will comprise both those English rules of statute which, expressly, or impliedly by construction, are required to be applied irrespective of the law governing the contract, whether this be English or foreign, and whether chosen or otherwise applicable in the absence of choice, subject to any prescribed spatial limitations (*'overriding statutes'*), and common law rules so held to apply *extraterritorially*, again restricted to contracts having local effects where necessary. Examples, some of which have previously been noted in connection with Articles 5(2) and 6(1) on consumer and employment contracts, respectively, include various provisions of the Employment Protection (Consolidation) Act 1978, by virtue of s.153(5), safeguarding the Act's application whatever the applicable law, and spatially limited to employees ordinarily working in Great Britain, under s.141; Equal Pay Act 1970, applying under s.1(11) as amended, irrespective of applicable law, limited under s.1(1) to persons employed at an establishment in Great Britain; and, as a matter of statutory

construction, s.1(2) of the Carriage of Goods by Sea Act 1971 ('shall have the force of law in the United Kingdom') (and see Sched., Articles III para. 8 and X), implementing the Hague–Visby Rules in the United Kingdom in relation to *inter alia* carriage from contracting state ports, as interpreted by the House of Lords in *The Hollandia* [1983] AC 565 (although, it is not entirely clear whether, by virtue of Article III para. 8, the same result must be reached where the otherwise applicable foreign proper law is *objective* proper law, rather than that chosen by the parties as in the case of Dutch law in *The Hollandia*; in fact, in relation to that particular example, the 1971 Act would now apply in any event under the Obligations Convention, by virtue of Article 21 thereof, according precedence to rules of other international conventions, such as the Hague–Visby Rules of 1968, regardless of their mandatory nature – see too Carriage by Air Act 1961 s.1(1), Carriage of Goods by Road Act 1965 s.1, Carriage of Passengers by Road Act 1974 s.1(1), Merchant Shipping Act 1979 s.14(1), and *Corocraft Ltd* v. *Pan American Airways Inc* [1969] 1 QB 616, 623); another constructional example is the Emergency Powers (Defence) Act 1939, applicable under s.3(1) to British subjects wherever resident, held by the House of Lords in *Boissevain* v. *Weil* [1950] AC 327 to invalidate contracts in contravention, whatever the governing law; and, as seen, in *English* v. *Donnelly* 1958 SC 494, the Scottish Court of Session construed the Hire Purchase and Small Debt (Scotland) Act 1932, as amended by the Hire Purchase Act 1954 (provision for copies of agreement), as applying to a hire-purchase contract entered into by the buyer in Scotland notwithstanding a choice of English law to govern the contract; the Patents Act 1977 ss.39–43 too (employee compensation for inventions) are to be applied extraterritorially, subject to spatial limitations under s.43(2) (Dicey and Morris, p.1303); and in the common law sphere, of course, there are decisions such as *Grell* v. *Levy* (1864) 9 LT 721, striking down a champertous agreement relating to *English* litigation, notwithstanding its validity under French law; *Rousillon* v. *Rousillon* (1880) 14 Ch.D 351, invalidating a contract in restraint of *English* trade, irrespective of its validity under French proper law; and *Dynamit AG* v. *Rio Tinto Co. Ltd* [1918] AC 292, avoiding a German contract, as involving trade with the enemy.

(Note that where national mandatory rules are restricted in their operation to contracts which are non-international – for example, under Unfair Contract Terms Act 1977 s.26, or Sale of Goods Act 1979 s.56(3) – it by no means follows that the Convention is inapplicable, since its own concept of internationality to be inferred from Article 1(1) is far broader than such national definitions: indeed, most notably, the very factor of choice of a foreign law to govern the contract, where the latter would otherwise be most connected with, or even wholly domestic to, the English forum, is sufficient to constitute the contract an *international* transaction, for regulation by the Convention: see above, p.107.)

(ii) Otherwise applicable foreign law is offensive to fundamental conceptions of English justice

The contract may, for example, be for the promotion of sexual immorality, in which case it will not be upheld, as being contrary to English public policy (*Robinson* v. *Bland* (1760) 2 Burr 1077, p.1084); or the English court may believe that the required degree of consent was lacking, as in *Kaufman* v. *Gerson* [1904] 1 KB 591, where the court refused to enforce a French contract to pay an amount of money misappropriated in return for an agreement not to prosecute in France, on the ground of coercion – although, it would seem from *Addison* v. *Brown* [1954] 2 All ER 213 and *Trendtex Trading Corpn* v. *Crédit Suisse* [1982] AC 679 that, for English courts to strike down such agreements as offending against English notions of justice and public policy, there should be found to be some relevant connection with England itself, such as to justify the offence felt. In addition too, of course, English courts will refuse to enforce directly or indirectly foreign penal, revenue, or other public laws (for example, import and export regulations, price control and anti-trust laws) (*A-G of New Zealand* v. *Ortiz* [1984] AC 1; *Williams and Humbert Ltd* v. *W. and H. Trade Marks (Jersey) Ltd* [1986] 1 AC 368) – although, as seen earlier, English courts will nonetheless *recognize* such foreign public and criminal laws for the purpose of refusing to give effect to a contract in contravention thereof, where these are part of the proper law (*Kahler* v. *Midland Bank Ltd* [1950] AC 24; *Peter Buchanan Ltd and Macharg* v. *McVey* [1954] IR 89, [1955] AC 516n) or otherwise according to the English doctrine of comity and public policy (*Regazzoni* v. *K.C. Sethia (1944) Ltd* [1956] 2 QB 490).

Thus, it may be seen that under pre-existing English conflicts, circumstances in which *mandatory foreign* rules will be applied against applicable law are few and subject to rather imprecise and exceptional principles of discretion, while operation of *mandatory English* provisions outside the normal process of the proper law betrays a somewhat hesitant and diffident approach based on specific express or implied statutory provision and sporadic extraterritorial application of economically significant national rules and fundamental legalo-moral principles, virtually in all such cases, where a local territorial connection is present. The basic – at least, conceptual – difference between on the one hand the, overtly, restrained English (and to some extent, German doctrinal) approach towards extraterritorial operation of its mandatory laws (*lois d'application immédiate/leggi di applicazione necessaria/Vorbehaltsklauseln*), consistent with the view of Savigny, and on the other hand the French, Continental doctrine of *ordre public international*, preferring the views of Mancini, is that the latter – developed within systems giving preference to substantive, rights-based classification and reliance upon *lex nationalis* for status control, in contrast to English concentration on procedure, affording control to *lex fori*, and resort to *lex domicilii*, ensuring application of most connected law to status – proceeds from the standpoint of principled application of the forum's imperative laws as part of the operation of private international law, rather than treating the former as an exceptonal rider to and interruption of the latter (see Wolff, *Private International Law*, 2nd edn (1950), pp.168–71; Forde, 'The Ordre Public Exception and Adjudicative Jurisdiction Conventions' (1980), 29 *ICLQ*, 259, 260; 'Holder, Public Policy and National Preferences: The Exclusion of Foreign Law in English Private International Law' (1968), 17 *ICLQ*, 926, 929; and Kahn-Freund, *Selected Writings* (1978), Chapter 9, pp.241–2).

It will be of some interest to examine the effect of Article 7 upon the pre-existing position in England as described. Before this is done, however, the point should be made that the underlying *constructional* basis of the English approach towards extraterritorial operation of English laws has as its sequel that, potentially, the formally presented categories of contracts-mandatory, half-conflicts-mandatory and full-conflicts-mandatory are not separate at all, but that, in reality, they would invariably be held to cover the same ground, if cases raising the question were ever to come for decision before the courts. Can it be doubted, therefore, that contracts-mandatory rules of English law would simply be permitted by English courts to be avoided through the process of the conflict of laws? Certainly in the case of express or implied choice of a foreign law, the latter agreement could itself be construed, in any event, as *indirectly* falling within the prohibition on contracting out (see *The Hollandia* [1983] A.C. 565, 574, as to Carriage of Goods by Sea Act 1971, Schedule, Article III para. 8); whilst even most connected applicable law in the absence of choice might be said to fall within the mischief at which the contracts-mandatory prohibition is aimed, namely, the avoidance, through *contractual* connections with a foreign country, of provisions considered mandatory in favour of one or other of the parties territorially connected with the forum or third state as prescribed. Similarly, even in the absence of express statutory provision, how could it be thought that a law held to apply extraterritorially, irrespective of subjective or objective applicable law, would not also be found to be unable to be derogated from directly by contractual stipulation of the parties?

These possible truths should be kept in mind in the course of discussion of the scope of Article 7.

Admittedly, *Sayers* v. *International Drilling Co. NV* [1971] 1 WLR 1176 may be cited as an example of where a contract-mandatory rule of English law (imposing liability for personal injuries, unable to be excluded by contract, by virtue of the Law Reform (Personal Injuries) Act 1948) was nonetheless held to be inapplicable where Dutch law was considered to be the law governing the contract (see Morse, in North (ed.) (1982), p.164). However, there seems to have been little attention paid by the majority of the Court of Appeal to possible questions of extraterritoriality in that case, and one wonders whether at the present day a greater awareness of spatial reach of laws might not in fact have been shown.

THE CONVENTION MANDATORY SYSTEM

The Convention contains a network of provisions safeguarding the operation of national mandatory rules from the normal conflicts process:

Article 3(3): *totally connected law apart from choice of law (and, if so, from corresponding or other choice of jurisdiction);*
Article 5(2): *law of consumer's habitual residence;*
Article 6(1): *law of employee's habitual place of work, et alia.*

Features to note about this group of Convention provisions on mandatory rules are:

- they are concerned with rules which are (at least) *contracts-mandatory* at national law;
- their application is *limited* either to specialized types of contract (consumer/individual employment – Article 5(2)/6(1)) or to a specified degree of connection (Article 3(3)), as well as to particular types of mandatory rule (consumer/employee-protective: Article 5(2)/6(1));
- their operation is *obligatory* ('shall');
- their effect is to *convert* national contracts-mandatory laws into half-conflicts-mandatory rules under the Convention, to the extent that this is not also the case at national law, or to *confirm* their half-conflicts-mandatory application under the Convention if this is already the position at national law.

Article 7(1): *law of a closely connected foreign country;*
Article 7(2): *law of the forum.*

Characteristics of interest in this category are:

- they are concerned with *full-conflicts-mandatory* and, it may strongly be argued, also *half-conflicts-mandatory* rules at national law

(which may, of course, in addition, be contracts-mandatory thereunder);
- their application is *general and unlimited* to any particular types of contract or mandatory rule;
- operation of mandatory laws under Article 7(1) is *discretionary*, not obligatory (and even obligatory application of mandatory *leges fori* under Article 7(2) will be subject of course to any *national* law discretion as to their operation);
- their effect is to *confirm* operation of national conflicts-mandatory rules.

Article 9(6): *lex situs*

Aspects for attention are:

- as in the case of Article 7, Article 9(6) is concerned with full- and probably also half-conflicts-mandatory national laws, *but which also apply irrespective of 'lex loci' contractus*, which is probably implicit in Article 7 in any event, even though not express, from the expression therein 'law (otherwise) applicable to the contract', which would seem to cover any governing law, whether applicable to the entire contract or only to a part thereof (notwithstanding which, the description 'conflicts-mandatory-plus' may be appropriate for such Article 9(6)-type national rules!);
- its application is *limited* to contracts for rights in or to use *immovables*, and to laws of *form* of the *situs*;
- its operation is obligatory ('shall');
- the effect of Article 9(6) is to *confirm* national conflicts-mandatory application.

These alternatives and differences should be borne in mind when assessing the scope and effects of Article 7.

Questions needing to be addressed will include:

a which Convention provision on national mandatory rules should be referred to, when more than one seems to be available; and
b is it possible to rely on more than one of them in such a case?

ARTICLE 7(1)

The idea embodied in Article 7(1) of applying mandatory provisions of law of a foreign country having some significant connection with the contract, in derogation from the chosen or otherwise most connected applicable law, was apparently taken from the decision of the Netherlands Supreme Court in the *Alnati* case of 1966 (Hoge Raad 13,5,1966, *Revue Critique de Droit International Privé* (1967), 522 – Diamond, 'Conflict of Laws in the EEC' (1979), 32 *Current Legal Problems*, 155, 173), and from Article 16 of the Hague Convention of 14 March 1978 on the Law Applicable to Agency (Cmnd 7020, Report, pp.26–7; Recognition of Trusts Act 1987, Schedule, Article 15, has a similar, though not identical, provision to that in Article 7(1) of the Obligations Convention).

As seen, it is a principle far removed from the exceptional and forum-based approach of English courts towards extraterritorial application of foreign mandatory rules under pre-existing conflicts (see Holder (1968), 17 *ICLQ*, 926; Forde (1980), 29 *ICLQ*, 259).

Accordingly, Article 7(1) is inapplicable in the United Kingdom, by virtue of the latter's reservation to this effect under Article 22(1)(a) (the latter power having been introduced at the closing stages of negotiations, in order to allay certain negotiators' concerns over the novelty and uncertainty of Article 7(1) – Report, p.28): 1990 Act s.2(2). Germany, Ireland and Luxembourg have also excluded its application (as might Portugal and Spain on accession).

The United Kingdom had a number of objections against Article 7(1) (see North, in North (ed.) (1982), pp.19–20; (1980) *JBL* 382, 387; and Hansard, HL Vol.513, cols 1258, 1270 and 1271 – although, note col. 1263 for the opposite view): (a) it provided a recipe for confusion since courts might have to consider multiple sets of mandatory rules; (b) the discretion would create delays and uncertainty in business, which applicable law was meant to avoid; (c) proof of foreign laws would be expensive; (d) litigants would be deterred from proceeding in the United Kingdom; (e) uniformity would be jeopardized. Further criticisms were of a technical nature, including the complaint that in permitting resort to be made to the mandatory rules of law of a country having a close connection, Article 7(1) effectively provides for the introduction of the United States governmental interests doctrine, whereby examinations are required of courts into the comparative importance to different law districts in having the policies contained in their laws upheld in an inter-state situation (see Mann, 'Contracts: Effect of Mandatory Rules', in Lipstein (ed.), *Harmonisation of Private International Law by the EEC* (1978), p.31). (Mann further states, *ibid.*, that Article 7(1) reflects the German academic theory of the *Sonderstatut* (special law) of the Second World War years, put forward as a defence against United States law's application, in proceedings brought in New York courts against German borrowers on American bonds, who had been prevented from servicing the latter by such 'special' Nazi exchange control laws, in breach of their contracts under United States law: p.32.)

A number of elements of Article 7(1) excite comment.

(A) WHEN APPLYING UNDER THIS CONVENTION THE LAW OF A COUNTRY

Article 7(1) derogates from applicable law 'under this Convention'. Consequently, where the dispute falls outside the Convention's scope, whether as to subject matter or otherwise, Article 7(1) itself is confirmed as inapplicable. It is unclear whether this would be so in relation to natural persons' contractual incapacity subjected to national private international law under Article 11. Technically it might be put that the latter effect is by virtue of the Convention thereunder and should consequently be subject to Article 7(1). The better view, on the other hand, is that Article 11 should be read together with Article 1(2)(a), expressed to be without prejudice to the former, and that it is national private international law, through general exclusion of capacity from the Convention's scope under Article 1(2)(a), which is responsible for applicability of the law governing the contractual incapacity, not Article 11 itself. Whichever of the preceding two views is considered to be correct, however, it seems quite plain that where the law of the country in which both parties are situated at the time of concluding the contract applies to capacity in accordance with Article 11, such application will be able to be regarded as being 'under this Convention' and consequently as subject to mandatory rules under Article 7(1) (and that conversely, where the condition of common situation of parties in the same country at the date of contractual conclusion under Article 11 is failed to be satisfied, national private international law, not the Convention itself, is responsible for applicable law on incapacity).

(B) EFFECT 'MAY' BE GIVEN

Article 7(1) does not oblige courts to give effect to foreign mandatory laws: it is a rule of discretion. This was apparently due to the fact that certain countries might experience constitutional difficulties should their courts actually be required to apply foreign mandatory laws, and the issue proved controversial (Report, p.27 – there would also be problems of necessary selection where two or more such other countries had mandatory rules). Thus the effect of Article 7(1), in the words of the Report, is to 'impose on the court the extremely delicate task of combining the mandatory provisions with the law normally applicable to the contract in the particular situation in question', and some delegations consequently felt the need for the discretionary safeguard (p.28).

(C) EXERCISE OF THE DISCRETION

Article 7(1) itself elaborates on circumstances for exercise of the discretionary application of mandatory rules. It states that, in considering whether to give effect thereto, regard shall be had to

a their nature and purpose; and
b the consequences of their application or non-application.

With regard to the *nature and purpose* of mandatory laws, the drafters rejected the proposal to add a clause stating that such nature and purpose should be established according to internationally recognized criteria, for example similar laws existing in other countries or which serve a generally recognized interest, because it was doubted whether the alleged criteria even existed and the matter involved the sensitive issue of credit to be given to foreign legal systems (Report, p.27). Presumably, therefore, the court should have regard to factors including whether the mandatory rule ought to be construed as being subject to a local spatial limitation, whether it is party or state protective, the former perhaps having greater weight in the Convention context, the number and nature of competing mandatory provisions, in particular, those of applicable law itself, and possibly even the general commercial or moral justifiability of the content of the mandatory rule.

As for the *consequences of application or non-application*, the Report treats this element as defining, clarifying and strengthening, not weakening, the rule in Article 7(1)(p.27). However, the formula appears to add little to the nature and purpose element, except that consequences of *application* would seem to require the court to consider whether a mandatory rule, which is admittedly vital and imperative for the legal system of which it forms part, is nonetheless so inimical in its effects upon the interests of a competing state or of one or both of the parties, as to justify its inapplicability under the Article 7(1) discretion.

(D) MANDATORY RULES OF THE LAW OF ANOTHER COUNTRY ... IF AND IN SO FAR AS, UNDER THE LAW OF THE LATTER COUNTRY, THOSE RULES MUST BE APPLIED WHATEVER THE LAW APPLICABLE TO THE CONTRACT

In the first place, Article 7(1) applies to mandatory rules of *any* country, including in principle that of the forum – although, in practice, Article 7(2) (added at a late stage) can be expected to be relied on for operation of the latter's mandatory rules. Secondly, the mandatory rules to which Article 7(1) applies in its terms are those which are *both*

- contracts-mandatory (as defined under Article 3(3) 'hereinafter'); and
- conflicts-mandatory (it is not expressly clear whether *half*-conflicts-mandatory rules are also included: common sense and the text itself would seem to indicate that they should be so regarded; thus, if Article 3(3) actually *converts* – albeit almost totally connected – contracts-mandatory rules into half-conflicts-mandatory under the Convention, it hardly seems inappropriate for rules – admittedly, not necessarily of an otherwise totally connected law – which are already half-conflicts-mandatory at national law, to be *confirmed* as such under Article 7(1)).

Simply to be the former, therefore, or the latter, is insufficient for Article 7(1) to operate. However, the point has previously been made that in most cases, if only as a matter of construction as opposed to express legislative or previous judicial decree, conflicts-mandatory rules will also be held to be contracts-mandatory, and contracts-mandatory to be at least half-, if not also full-conflicts-mandatory. This is effectively confirmed by the Report, which states that the legal system in question must be examined in order to determine the mandatory nature of its rules, and that the word *loi* (legislation) in the former French text was replaced by *droit* (law generally) 'in order to avoid any doubts as to the scope of the rule, which is to cover both "legislative" provisions of any other country and also common law rules' (p.27).

Von Hoffmann (in Lando (ed.) (1975), pp.17–18) correctly points out that mandatory rules in question will be found to be of two basic types: (1) protective – for example several laws afford protection to commercial agents, through award of compensation where the agency is terminated through no fault of the agent (see von Hoffmann, *ibid.*, p.13, and Graue, *ibid.*, p.100); or (2) economically/politically inspired – for example credit or price controls, exchange control, and prohibition on exports without a licence. In some cases, the mandatory law may satisfy both such policies, for example, restrictions on restraint of trade, or a maximum period of credit. Furthermore, although the Convention is concerned with private law obligations, the effects of contravention of mandatory criminal and other public law regulations of a country, upon contractual existence and remedies, will nonetheless fall within the province of applicable and mandatory laws.

Article 7(1), therefore, presents the courts with some difficult problems, requiring them to construe the law of another country, perhaps before the latter's courts themselves have done so, in order to determine its mandatory nature. One small piece of irony is that the United Kingdom objected to Article 7(1), because it was felt to institutionalize – albeit on a discretionary basis – application of foreign mandatory rules: however, whereas under Article 7(1), for such rules to be given effect to, not only must they belong (as will be seen below) to a closely connected legal system, but also not merely be a matter of legality, but actually contracts- and conflicts-mandatory, by contrast, under pre-existing English conflicts, the doctrine of comity may not in fact require so close a connection as a matter of principle (recall *Regazzoni* v. *Sethia*), and infringement of a foreign friendly state's legality rules as such may justify a refusal to uphold a contract (see *Libyan Arab Foreign Bank* v. *Bankers Trust Co.* [1989] 3 All ER 252, 266). (It is uncertain whether Article 16 on public policy preserves the latter national English practice in Convention cases – see below, Chapter 21.)

(E) LAW OF ANOTHER COUNTRY WITH WHICH THE SITUATION HAS A CLOSE CONNECTION

'A close connection'

Earlier drafts provided for *any* connection, and subsequently a *significant* connection. These were replaced by 'close' in order to prevent courts from having to take large numbers of foreign laws into account: 'close' seemed most suitable to define the case sought to be covered (Report, p.27). Thus, the Report explains 'it is essential that there be a genuine connection with the other country, and that a merely vague connection is not adequate' (p.27). Examples provided (*ibid.*) of such genuine connections are

- *locus solutionis*;
- residence or main place of business of a party.

Accordingly, 'close' is a limiting factor, which, whilst obviously (see Article 4) unable to be equated with 'closest', nevertheless is arguably intended to be restricted to the single most important connection in relation to the area covered by the mandatory rules, notwithstanding that connections with other laws might otherwise be regarded as significant.

It is submitted that Convention connections – that is, those which have been favoured thereunder, such as habitual residence and place of business (Article 4(2)), habitual place of work (Article 6(2)(a)), *lex loci actus* (Article 9) and *lex loci solutionis* (Article 10(2)) – ought to be accorded greater weight than other factors in terms of their deemed closeness of connection under Article 7(1), especially where the law applicable to the contract results from rebuttal of any presumption that the former were most closely connected. Nevertheless, it is conceded that in multinational contracts all connections – even, for example, nationality – are potentially 'close' for purposes of Article 7(1), and that whilst the former should enjoy far more influence, these should not be exclusive. Furthermore, Convention connections may even be important outside their specific Convention sphere: for example, *locus actus* is referred to in matters of formal validity under Article 9; but why should it not also constitute a close connection in matters of material existence and validity of contracts dealt with by reference to applicable law *et alia* under Article 8, for purposes of Article 7(1)?

'The situation'

The close connection has to be that which 'the situation' has with another country. As indicated, therefore, it is considered that it is the country which the contract is connected with in such manner that it is appropriate for operation of its mandatory rules to be safeguarded in the context of Article 7(1), with which 'the situation' has the close connection required thereunder. So, for example, if country X has mandatory rules regarding performance of the contract, 'the situation' may be held to have a 'close connection' with X, if X is *locus solutionis*, but not if it is merely *locus contractus* – and the converse would be the case, if the mandatory rules related to contractual existence; further, if both *locus solutionis* and *locus contractus* have mandatory rules on contractual performance (or, as the case may be, existence), only the former (or latter) is that with which 'the situation' has a 'close connection'. The Report appears to contradict this construction: it states that the connection must exist with 'the contract as a whole', and that although the word 'contract' in an earlier draft had been replaced by 'situation' in Article 7(1), this should not obscure the drafters' rejection of one delegation's proposal that the connection should be between the point in dispute and a specific law, which 'would have given rise to a regrettable dismemberment of the contract and would have led to the application of mandatory laws not foreseeable by the parties' (p.27). With respect to the authors of the Report, it is considered that this is unacceptable: if the subject matter of the dispute is, say, the seller's claim that the buyer failed to pay for goods delivered, the 'situation' is that payment was not forthcoming, and it would be curious if relevant mandatory rules of the country for payment were not referred to, as being those of the country having a close connection under Article 7(1), purely because the close connection of the contract as a whole was with another country, in which the contract had been concluded and where the seller had his main place of business. 'Dismemberment' of contracts does not increase certainty for parties and their legal advisers it is true, but the essential overriding aim must be to apply most appropriate mandatory law, and 'dismemberment' is therefore the inevitable consequence of Article 7(1). Depending upon the number of contractual issues involved in the action, it is submitted that mandatory rules of several different laws may be referred to in respect of particular matters, as those of the countries, with which 'the situation' has, respectively, a close connection under Article 7(1). Mandatory rules of countries X, Y and Z may consequently apply in respect of, respectively, performance, existence and restraint of trade invalidity, under Article 7(1), as those of *locus solutionis, locus contractus* and place of affected trading, with which 'the situation' has a close connection.

In the present writer's opinion, furthermore, it is not necessarily the case that closeness of the situation's connection under Article 7(1) has to be adjudged according to the number of connections which a particular country has with the contract: such would indeed be the probable effect of following the approach advocated in the Report, of looking at the contract as a whole; and, apart from what is here considered to be its incorrectness in principle, it would cause great practical difficulties for courts, in cases where applicable law was not that chosen under Article 3, but most closely connected under Article 4, where they would have to determine which of the *non*-closest-connection countries nevertheless had a close or even the next closest connection on the basis of all facts and circumstances. All that matters, in the present belief, is that a country's mandatory rules are relevant to the issue in question (in accordance with the contract's terms and circumstances at the time of contractual conclusion), in which event it may be concluded that 'the situation' has a 'close connection' with that country, whatever, if any, other contractual connections exist therewith. Indeed, it may be the case that *no* other country's mandatory rules are thus *relevant*, and that consequently, 'the situation' has a 'close connection' with no other country under Article 7(1), however *irrelevantly* connected with the contract a particular country might otherwise be.

It should be re-emphasized, however, as a general rider to the application of mandatory rules of a country of close connection, that, as a matter of discretion, the court should only apply those rules under Article 7(1), in circumstances where, although the law applicable in the absence of choice under Article 4 is that of the country most closely connected with the contract as a whole, the country of which the mandatory rules' application is in question is more significantly connected in respect of the particular matter in issue with which those rules are concerned. Indeed, even in the case of chosen applicable law under Article 3, it is considered that the same principle should be applied under Article 7(1): and certainly, close connection should not then *simply* be taken to be that of the country most closely connected with the contract as a whole and whose law would have been applicable in the absence of choice under Article 4.

'Another country'

It will have been concluded from the preceding that whilst, conceivably, several different countries' mandatory rules could apply to separate issues involved in the claim, under Article 7(1), nevertheless, in respect of each such – or the, if there is only one in the case – issue, 'the situation' should be held to have a 'close connection' with only one country, as the most important in relation to any such issue, as previously explained, both as a matter of principle and practical expedience: it would hardly be practicable to attempt to combine the *most imperative* elements of the mandatory rules of several different laws in respect of an individual issue, concerning, for example, performance.

Finally, 'another' country includes that of the forum. As seen earlier, however, Article 7(2), added at a later stage, is able to be relied on (and must be, of course, in the United Kingdom, in which Article 7(1) is inapplicable) in these circumstances, and will doubtless be so in view of its broader terms and obligatory nature.

Article 7(1) is clearly a difficult provision for both courts and parties to apply: decisions as to closeness of connections, mandatory nature of foreign rules, and exercise of discretion, will not be easy to predict, and practices and attitudes might vary amongst courts of different Contracting States. If, however, the principle of applying foreign mandatory rules extraterritorially is to be accepted, attachment of such difficult conditions to its operation under Article 7(1) is probably justified on the basis that problems and diversity would be considerably increased if the discretion were open-ended. It is the admission of the mandatory rules which is the source of the difficulties, not the devices included as controls thereon.

As to the principle of foreign mandatory rules itself, for what it is worth the present writer is on balance in favour of the general provision for the safeguard of such under Article 7(1). International contracts cannot be isolated within a conceptual vacuum. Convenient and just though it may be to apply a single applicable law to the main part of their regulation, whether on the basis of choice or closest connection, the fact that they have effects in other countries, which may be vitally important for the parties or those countries themselves – and not merely that of *objective* applicable law – cannot simply be ignored in the name of sanctity of the applicable law. The latter doctrine is there to serve justice, not to be shaped and preserved in a pure form so as to satisfy the predilections of theorists – *a fortiori* given the absence of any general Convention safeguard at least in favour of mandatory rules of the country of *objective applicable law*, where governing law has been chosen by the parties (Article 3(3) goes some way towards this, but nevertheless falls short). Applied with appropriate reserve, therefore, Article 7(1) could prove an important additional influence for the cause of justice in the English courts – which the public policy doctrine, embodied in Article 16, may instead be called upon to exercise, involving some uncertainty. It seems churlish of the United Kingdom to have made the reservation.

ARTICLES 7(1) AND 3(3), 5(2), 6(1) AND 9(6)

The following would seem to be the relationship between Article 7(1) and the other Convention provisions on mandatory rules.

1   Where the national rule is purely contracts-mandatory and not even conflicts-mandatory by construction – a somewhat unlikely event, it is thought – Article 7(1) is inapplicable and solely Articles 3(3), 5(2) and 6(1) may be resorted to.

2   Where the rule is both contract-mandatory and conflicts-mandatory, in either case, by express legislative or judicial decree or by construction:

(i) In the case of express or implied choice of applicable law

- obligatory Article 3(3) will be relied on in the case of otherwise total connection with the mandatory country;
- obligatory Article 5(2)/6(1) will be relied on as to mandatory rules
  (a) of a consumer/employee protection nature, and
  (b) in so far as they are rules of the consumer's/employee's habitual residence/place of work (*et alia*);
- discretionary Article 7(1) governs
  (a) where connections other than choice are not all with one country, and
  (b) otherwise, in the case of non-consumer/employee protection mandatory rules, and
  (c) even in respect of mandatory consumer/employee protection rules of a closely connected country other than that of the habitual residence/place of work (hopefully the combination will prove practicable in view of the separate spheres of influence of Articles 5(2)/6(1) and 7(1); if not, courts should then decline

to exercise their discretion under Article 7(1), in favour of the specific protective provisions in Articles 5(2) and 6(1)).

Such, it is submitted, are the respective spheres of influence of Articles 3(3), 5(2) and 6(1) on the one hand, and 7(1) on the other. Clearly, Article 7(1) could also apply in the former cases: it is simply that its application as a general rule, in variance of the special provisions in Articles 3(3), 5(2) and 6(1), would be contrary to the Convention mandatory system. Thus, how may the mandatory employment protection rules of a *closely* connected country (Article 7(1)) (even if spatial conditions are satisfied therein) possibly be held to override those of the *habitual place of work* (Article 6(1))?

(ii) In the case of applicable law in the absence of choice

- Articles 3(3), 5(2) and 6(1) are inapplicable;
- discretionary Article 7(1) applies, although its practical scope of operation in consumer/employment cases will be limited in respect of mandatory consumer/employment protection rules, in view of special Article 5(3)/6(2) objective applicable law connections.

3   Where the national rule is conflicts-mandatory, but, neither by express provision nor by construction, also contracts-mandatory, Articles 3(3), 5(2) 6(1) *and 7(1)* are inapplicable (except possibly in respect of *half*-conflicts-mandatory rules, according to the definition in Article 3(3)).

As seen, it is unlikely that national conflicts-mandatory rules will not also be construed as contracts-mandatory, and vice versa. If the possibility is admitted, however, it is unfortunate that Article 7(1) requires such rules also to be contracts-mandatory, for two reasons:

(i)   in the case of choice of applicable law, it is illogical for Article 7(1) to cover the territory already occupied by Article 3(3), even though the latter only applies to otherwise totally connected laws; and
(ii) the contracts-mandatory criterion in Articles 3(3), 5(2) and 6(1) is hardly sustainable in any event, since Convention treatment of such rules as half-conflicts-mandatory, where they are not already so at national law, seems barely justified, and even less so under Article 7(1), where it is expressly stipulated that the mandatory rules must also be (half-, or full-) conflicts-mandatory at national law.

Article 7(2) does not seem to require rules also to be contracts-mandatory: neither should Article 7(1).

4 In *all* such cases, where any or all of Articles 3(3), 5(2), 6(1) and 7(1) are able to be satisfied: Article 9(6), as the special rule of resort to mandatory rules of form of *lex situs* in the case of immovables, is to be relied upon where

- the mandatory rules in question relate to *formal validity*; and
- whether by construction or otherwise, they are not merely conflicts-mandatory at national law, but also apply thereunder irrespective of the country of contracting (*'conflicts-mandatory-plus'*). It is unclear from the text of Article 9(6) whether mandatory rules thereunder must also be contracts-mandatory: the phrase 'mandatory rules', as defined in Article 3(3), is not used; instead 'mandatory requirements' of form are referred to; foreign texts share the same variation in wording; it is submitted that the difference between 'mandatory rules' and 'mandatory requirements' is minor, and brings about no change in substance; accordingly, the definition in Article 3(3) also applies to Article 9(6), and invariably, it is believed, conflicts-mandatory, whether by construction or otherwise, will also amount to contracts-mandatory.

Again, it would seem curious if the mandatory rules of form of another country were to apply under Article 7(1) instead of or alongside those of *lex situs* under Article 9(6), given the latter's role as a special provision made for the type of contractual issue in question; and it will be recalled that, in the circumstances, the 'situation' in Article 7(1) is hardly likely to be held to be sufficiently close to any country different from *lex situs* in respect of the question of formal validity in any event, so as to bring Article 7(1) into operation.

5 Finally, although Article 7(1) does not use the same formula as appears in Articles 5(2) and 6(1), to the effect that parties are not to be deprived of the benefits of mandatory rules thereunder, it would be remarkable if the same policy were not held to apply to Article 7(1). Accordingly, if parties' or states' interests are better served by application of the rules of applicable law, the latter should then be applied, and the court should exercise its discretion against application of the mandatory rules of a closely connected country under Article 7(1).

Similarly, it is believed, as in the case of Articles 5(2) and 6(1) (and as between the latter themselves and Article 7(1)), *cumulation* of mandatory rules of Article 7(1) laws with those of applicable law, where not incompatible and where the result is not to distort the intended scope and effects of the mandatory rules, might in principle – even if unlikely to have much scope of operation in practice, in view of the latter condition – be permitted so as to afford maximum protection, except where applicable law was chosen by the parties, in which event, in the case of party-protective mandatory rules, parties should be made to opt for those of the chosen law or those of Article 7(1), and should not be allowed to plead both, collectively.

Should the United Kingdom ever decide to withdraw its reservation with respect to Article 7(1) (see Article 22(3), and 1990 Act s.4(1)(b)), all of the preceding considerations should be borne in mind as amounting to the implications of any such decision.

Since Article 7(1) is for the present inapplicable in the United Kingdom, the circumstances in which the United Kingdom's courts must apply *foreign* mandatory rules under the Convention are confined to the following:

- where the contract is totally connected with a foreign country, but for choice of another (possibly even English) law (if not also jurisdiction), the former's contracts-mandatory rules must be applied (Article 3(3));
- where a law, even English, is chosen, English courts must apply contracts-mandatory consumer/employment protection rules of the consumer's/employee's habitual residence/place of work (Article 5(2)/6(1));
- English courts (where jurisdiction exists) must apply conflicts- (as well as possibly also contracts-) mandatory rules of *lex situs* on formal validity in the case of immovables (Article 9(6));
- it may be that validity of a contract according to applicable law will be overturned as being contrary to the English forum's public policy based on comity, by virtue of Article 16, where the contract is illegal according to the law of a foreign country with a legitimate interest in striking it down (a 'close connection' under Article 7(1)); this seems doubtful, however, given Article 16's reference to a 'rule of law' manifestly incompatible with public policy, which may be different from *absence of a rule of law invalidating the contract* or preventing its enforcement (not to mention the existence itself of Article 7(1), generally safeguarding foreign mandatory rules – though, admittedly, not limited to those on legality); if the latter doubts are well-founded, it is interesting that under the Convention, the United Kingdom's courts – in which Article 7(1) is inapplicable – lose their general pre-existing power to refuse to enforce a contract illegal according to the law of a foreign country other than that of applicable law on grounds of comity! (On the other hand, if the *Ralli* decision were construed as meaning that supervening illegality of performance under a foreign

lex loci solutionis will prevent enforcement, as a principle of domestic English law of contract, *Article 7(2)* might be able to be called upon in such circumstances, in effect to safeguard the illegality rule of foreign *lex loci*, provided that such alleged rule of domestic English law were held to be *mandatory* for purposes of Article 7(2): were English law itself to govern the contract of course, the alleged principle would apply in any event.)

In all those cases where the English courts are required to apply foreign mandatory rules under the Convention, it should be recalled that such foreign laws will either be expressed to be mandatory under the foreign legislation, or will be so as a matter of construction in the absence thereof. In the latter case, where courts of the foreign country in question have themselves pronounced on the mandatory nature, or otherwise, of the foreign rule, courts of the forum should follow the foreign courts' construction. If, however, the matter has not yet fallen to be construed by courts of the foreign country itself, it will be for English courts to make an assessment of the mandatory character of the foreign rule in the light of its perceived object and intent.

Finally, there is nothing to prevent parties from reaching an agreement that, in the event of any dispute arising, Article 7(1) shall apply, and clearly the United Kingdom's courts, no less than those of any other Contracting State in which Article 7(1) applies in any event, would have to pay regard to the parties' wishes in this respect. The precise basis on which this would be carried out, however, is less certain: would Article 7(1) mandatory laws then be applied according to the latter provision itself; or as mere terms of the contract, incorporated by reference therein; or as applicable law according to Article 3(1), chosen to apply to part only of the contract? It seems fairly likely that the second possible construction of the parties' agreement would normally be inappropriate and in view of the conflicts, rather than substantive, nature of the rule in Article 7(1), in the present submission, it is the third which is correct – although, such chosen applicable Article 7(1) law will only apply in accordance with the conditions and discretion there set down. It is believed that effects of first and third constructions would not appear to be different (except perhaps that under the latter, but not the former, parties would be able to change their minds and agree that Article 7(1) should be inapplicable, under Article 3(2)). However, the third is considered to be preferable on principle, recalling the view proffered in Chapter 8 to the effect that applicability of *conflicts* rules, as opposed to substantive norms, is a matter of policy for courts, not parties, to decide upon (the position before arbitrators may of course be quite different).

ARTICLE 7(2)

Mandatory rules in general of the forum are safeguarded under Article 7(2): and this is applicable in the United Kingdom, as well as in other Contracting States.

This is the provision which seems to correspond most closely with the French approach towards *règles d'application immédiate*, under the doctrine of *ordre public international*: priority awarded to the forum's laws of extraterritorial application, according to the demands of policy in a private international context. Examples of English statutes and common law rules of extraterritorial application, outside the normal conflicts process of applicable law, and subject to any national spatial limitations, have previously been provided (see above, p.242 *et seq*): recall *The Hollandia, Boissevain v. Weil* and *Rousillon v. Rousillon*, as well as s.6 of the Unfair Contract Terms Act 1977, by virtue of s.27(2) thereof, and the like.

The Report states as the origin of Article 7(2) (which was not in the original draft Convention and was added at a very late stage) the concern of certain delegations to safeguard mandatory rules of the forum, 'notably rules on cartels, competition and restrictive practices, consumer protection and certain rules concerning carriage' (p.28; Recognition of Trusts Act 1987, Schedule, Article 16, has a similar saving for the forum's mandatory laws). It goes on to comment that the paragraph merely deals with the application of mandatory rules in a different way from paragraph 1 (*ibid.*). Thus, doubtless, even without Article 7(2), Contracting States' courts would have applied their own extraterritorial laws in any event by virtue of Article 7(1): however, given the provision for reservation of inapplicability of the latter under Article 22(1)(a), Article 7(2), specifically preserving the forum's mandatory rules, is consequently especially required in the United Kingdom, as a reserving state.

Article 7(2) has three main differences from Article 7(1):

a   in the first place, Article 7(2) is obligatory in nature, rather than affording courts a discretion on whether or not to apply their mandatory laws: however, this is not to say that Article 7(2) is so *dirigiste* as to remove any *national law* discretion which may nonetheless exist as to applicability or otherwise of the mandatory rule;
b   secondly, there is no requirement that the forum should have a close connection with the situation – although, in practice, it may be expected that national mandatory rules will be subject to spatial limitations connecting the case with the forum in the prescribed manner, in any event (see above, p.242 *et seq*); and

c   thirdly, whereas Article 7(1) (as well as 9(6)) appears to require mandatory rules in question to be contracts-mandatory as well as conflicts-mandatory, Article 7(2) seems to be concerned solely with the latter ('mandatory irrespective of the law') – unless the word 'mandatory' can be linked back to the word 'rules' in the preceding line in English and foreign texts, so as to attract the contracts-mandatory definition in Article 3(3) 'hereinafter': in any event, in practice, as seen, the difference should be minimal and the scope of operation of Article 7(2), to that extent, no greater than that of Article 7(1), since either type of mandatory rule is likely to be construed as also constituting the other at national law, if not expressly made so by legislative or judicial decree.

Similarities with Article 7(1) are:

a   first, it is submitted that as a matter of common sense and textual construction of Article 7(2), the latter also applies to national rules of the forum which are merely *half*-conflicts-mandatory – for example, those to which s.27(2) of the Unfair Contract Terms Act 1977 and s.56 of the Sale of Goods Act 1979, preventing avoidance of *lex fori*'s laws through choice of a foreign law (other than in international cases under ss.26 and 56(3) respectively), apply – and not solely to those which are full-conflicts-mandatory;
b   secondly, Article 7(2) covers mandatory rules which may be protective either of parties' or *the state's social, political and economic interests*, not solely the formers'; and
c   thirdly, it is believed that where mandatory rules of the forum are *less* protective of parties or, as the case may be, states, than rules of applicable law itself, the latter should be allowed to prevail over the former.

ARTICLES 7(2) AND 3(3), 5(2), 6(1) AND 9(6)

As seen, Article 7(2) is not restricted to *non*-party-protective mandatory rules, and accordingly, in principle, there is nothing to prevent the forum from applying its own mandatory laws to consumer and employment contracts so as to override otherwise imperative provisions in Articles 5(2) and 6(1) in case of conflict, since Article 7(2) states 'Nothing in this Convention shall restrict': and clearly, where the forum's own spatial limitations are satisfied, it has a legitimate interest in seeing its mandatory rules applied.

In practice, however, the forum should be mindful of the fact that Articles 5(2) (in the circumstances for its operation specified thereunder) and 6(1) are specifically intended for protective consumer and employment cases. It is submitted that courts should therefore apply the mandatory laws most favourable to the party to be protected, whether those of the forum under Article 7(2) or of habitual residence/place of work under Article 5(2)/ 6(1): and if practicable, as well as in accordance with intended scope and effects of mandatory rules – unlikely frequently to be the case it is thought – it is believed that the parties should not necessarily be precluded from picking and choosing favourable mandatory rules from *lex fori* and the others (or indeed from these and applicable law, except where the latter was chosen by the parties, in which case cumulation should be excluded and parties should either stand by or discard the choice *in toto* in respect of areas subject to mandatory provision).

The following is believed to be the relative scope of Article 7(2) and the other Convention mandatory provisions *inter se*.

1   Where a national rule is purely contracts-mandatory, Article 7(2) is inapplicable and the matter is solely for Articles 3(3), 5(2) and 6(1).

2   Where the rule is both contracts-mandatory and conflicts-mandatory, by express provision or construction:

(i) in the case of express or implied choice of applicable law

- Article 3(3) should be relied on in the case of otherwise total connection with a foreign country (Article 7(2) spatial connections with the forum are unlikely to be satisfied in the circumstances, so that forum shopping opportunities otherwise afforded by Article 7(2) are to that extent reduced);
- Article 5(2)/6(1) consumer/employee protection mandatory rules should be relied on where applicable, but Article 7(2) forum's mandatory rules should apply:
  (a)   if they are *more* protective than those under Article 5(2)/6(1) (frequently, the English forum will in fact also be that of a consumer's habitual residence in any event, by virtue of Judgments Convention Article 14 para.1, and Civil Jurisdiction and Judgments Act 1982 s.10(3) – see too Article 5(1) of the Judgments Convention, as amended by Article 4 of the San Sebastian Convention on Spanish and Portuguese accession, in the case of jurisdiction over individual employment contracts); and
  (b)   in the case of *non*-party-protective mandatory rules.

(ii) in the case of applicable law in the absence of choice

- Articles 3(3), 5(2) and 6(1) are inapplicable;

- Article 7(2) applies, although, in the consumer/employee protection sphere, its scope of operation will be limited, since spatial connections with the English forum under conflicts-mandatory laws will frequently correspond with applicable law under Article 5(3) (habitual residence)/ 6(2) (place of habitual work) in any event.

3 Where the national rule is conflicts-mandatory, but not also contracts-mandatory, neither by construction nor otherwise, Articles 3(3), 5(2) and 6(1) are inapplicable (except, possibly, in respect of *half*-conflicts-mandatory rules, according to the definition in Article 3(3)).

ARTICLE 7(2) AND 7(1)

Again, the forum's mandatory rules under Article 7(2) override those of a foreign country under Article 7(1), where a conflict exists ('Nothing in this Convention'), and the latter is of course discretionary.

Nevertheless, it is to be hoped first that in practice, the nature of national spatial limitations will prevent there being such a clash (that is to say, if the forum's spatial connection is satisfied, there is all the less likelihood of there being found to exist a 'close' connection between 'the situation' and another country under Article 7(1)); and further, that English courts would be willing to apply foreign mandatory rules under Article 7(1), where these were more party-protective than the formers' own law, were Article 7(1) ever to be activated in the United Kingdom. In the case of conflicting *non*-party-protective rules, of course, the forum's laws and policies will prevail under Article 7(2).

ARTICLES 7(2) AND 9(6)

In the event that the forum's laws are found to contain conflicts-mandatory rules of form relating to rights in or to use foreign immovables, and that spatial connections laid down therein are satisfied, once again Article 7(2) will prevail – hopefully, subject to where those of the foreign *situs* (and applicable law, if different) afford greater safeguards in the case of party-protective rules.

ARTICLES 7(2) AND 16

It will be recalled that the object of Article 7(2) is to enable specific laws of the forum to override the operation of foreign applicable law under the normal conflicts process, by reason of the extraterritorial reach of the former.

Article 16 differs from this in two main respects:

a in the first place, its functioning is primarily *negative*, in relation to individual rules of an otherwise applicable *foreign law*; and
b secondly, to the extent that its effect is to safeguard the operation of *lex fori*, usually it is only the fundamental underlying principles of the latter which are made to operate through the resort to public policy, rather than any of its specific legal norms; and a mere difference between a rule of foreign applicable law and the corresponding English treatment is insufficient for public policy to be invoked under Article 16 (*Loucks v. Standard Oil Co. of New York* (1918) 224 NY 99, 111). In certain cases, however, where, say, a particular obligation implied into the contract under foreign applicable law is held to be against public policy under Article 16, it may then be that the forum has little alternative other than to substitute the provisions of its own law in respect of matters otherwise dealt with by the inapplicable foreign rule, such as place of delivery, or currency of payment.

ARTICLE 7(2) AND NATIONAL CONFLICTS

In Chapter 16 below, concerning scope of application of national private international law to capacity of natural persons under Articles 1(2)(a) and 11, it is considered whether applicable law thereunder is nonetheless subject to mandatory rules of the forum on incapacity, in accordance with Article 7(2), in the light of the imperative terms of the latter ('Nothing in this Convention ....'). The conclusion is there reached that, whereas the special rule of applicable law of the country of parties' common presence at conclusion in Article 11 should clearly be held to be displaceable by mandatory *lex fori* to the extent laid down in Article 7(2), nevertheless, Article 11 has a purely restrictive role so far as operation of national private international law in relation to capacity of natural persons is concerned, which latter is otherwise excluded from the Convention's scope under Article 1(2)(a) and accordingly no more subject to Article 7(2) than any other excluded area.

The following table serves to demonstrate the interrelationship of Convention provisions safeguarding mandatory rules of national contract laws:

Table 12.1 Order of priority if more than one Convention mandatory provision is satisfied is shown as *horizontal* and *vertical-within-boxes*

		TYPES OF MANDATORY RULE INVOLVED				
		Contracts-mandatory made half-conflicts-mandatory by Convention	Half-conflicts-mandatory	Full-conflicts-mandatory	Full conflicts-mandatory-plus	Requirement of both contracts-mandatory and conflicts-mandatory (plus)
		and/or	and/or	and/or	and/or	
FEATURES OF CONVENTION PROVISIONS ON MANDATORY RULES	Total connection but for choice (and possibly also same or other court)	3 (3)	9 (6) *situs* form 7 (2) forum 7 (1) close connection	9 (6) *situs* form 7 (2) forum 7 (1) close connection	9 (6) *situs* form	9 (6) *situs* form 7 (1) close connection
	Consumer protection	5 (2) habitual residence	9 (6) *situs* form 7 (2) forum 7 (1) close connection	9 (6) *situs* form 7 (2) forum 7 (1) close connection	9 (6) *situs* form	9 (6) *situs* form 7 (1) close connection
	Employment protection	6 (1) habitual place of work et al.	9 (6) *situs* form 7 (2) forum 7 (1) close connection	9 (6) *situs* form 7 (2) forum 7 (1) close connection	9 (6) *situs* form	9 (6) *situs* form 7 (1) close connection
	General non-consumer/employment protection or non-party-protective		7 (2) forum	7 (2) forum	9 (6) *situs* form	9 (6) *situs* form 7 (1) close connection

Table 12.1 continued

FEATURES OF CONVENTION PROVISIONS ON MANDATORY RULES					
Obligatory	3 (3) 5 (2) 6 (1)	9 (6) *situs* form 7 (2) forum	9 (6) *situs* form 7 (2) forum	9 (6) *situs* form	9 (6) *situs* form
Discretionary					7 (1) close connection
Foreign mandatory	3 (3) 5 (2) 6 (1) (16 comity – possibly)	9 (6) *situs* form 7 (1) close connection (16 comity – possibly)	9 (6) *situs* form 7 (1) close connection (16 comity – possibly)	9 (6) *situs* form (16 comity – possibly)	9 (6) *situs* form 7 (1) close connection (16 comity – possibly)
Forum mandatory	3 (3) 5 (2) 6 (1) (16)	9 (6) *situs* form 7 (2) forum 7 (1) close connection (16)	9 (6) *situs* form 7 (2) forum 7 (1) close connection (16)	9 (6) *situs* form 7 (2) forum 7 (1) close connection (16)	9 (6) *situs* form 7 (1) close connection (16)

13 Article 8: Material Validity of Contracts

Article 8

Material validity

1   The existence and validity of a contract, or of any term of a contract, shall be determined by the law which would govern it under this Convention if the contract or term were valid.
2   Nevertheless a party may rely upon the law of the country in which he has his habitual residence to establish that he did not consent if it appears from the circumstances that it would not be reasonable to determine the effect of his conduct in accordance with the law specified in the preceding paragraph.

SCOPE OF ARTICLE 8 : MATERIAL VALIDITY

Article 8(1) deals with all matters of substance of formation and subsisting validity of contracts: this is clear from reference to 'existence and validity' (see Report, p.28 – *existence* was added so as to make it clear that offer and acceptance were included, which might not otherwise have been the case had mention merely been made of *validity*), except that capacity is excluded by Article 1(2)(a) (subject to Article 11) and (e).

The following issues are consequently covered:

- offer and acceptance (*Albeko Schuhmaschinen AG* v. *Kamborian Shoe Machine Co. Ltd* (1961) 111 LJ 519); in *Vineh Construction Company Limited* v. *Houthandel G. Wijma en Zonen BV* (1989) ELD 252, Dutch courts applied Article 8(1) in order to determine whether a

contract had come into being between a Dutch seller and an Iranian buyer of goods, under the law applicable according to Article 4(2);
- consideration (*Re Bonacina* [1912] 2 Ch.394);
- mistake (*Mackender* v. *Feldia* [1967] 2 QB 590);
- duress and undue influence (*Kaufman* v. *Gerson* [1904] 1 KB 591, and see Graveson, p.432);
- legality (*Kahler* v. *Midland Bank Ltd* [1950] AC 24);
- misrepresentation (*British Controlled Oilfields* v. *Stagg* (1921) 127 LT 209);
- validity of exclusion clauses (*P&O Steam Navigation Co.* v. *Shand* (1865) 3 Moo PCNS 272).

Article 8, subjecting material validity primarily to the control of applicable law (see below), thus seems to be in harmony with pre-existing English conflicts with regard to the latter's scope (Briggs (1990), *LMCLQ*, 192, 193, however, doubts the credentials of certain of the usual authorities).

Further, as will be seen, by virtue of Article 3(4), Article 8 governs existence and validity of consent of parties to an agreement on applicable law itself (see von Hoffmann, in Lando (ed.) (1975), p.21, for discussion of alternatives).

The special rule of exception in Article 8(2) applies only to contractual existence *(consent)* not also to validity.

APPLICABLE LAW : THE 'BOOTSTRAPS' RULE

The laws governing contractual existence and essential validity under the Convention are as follows

- the law chosen by the parties in accordance with Article 3 subject to Article 5(2) or 6(1)) : Article 8(1)
- in the absence of choice, the law applicable under Article 4, 5(3) or 6(2) : Article 8(1)
EXCEPT THAT
- in the case of consent as an element of contractual existence, a party can rely instead upon the law of the country of his habitual residence, if different, in order to establish his lack of consent, provided that this appears reasonable in all the circumstances : Article 8(2)

(a) Article 8(1)

This requires reference to applicable law under the Convention for contractual existence and validity (and, also, by way of analogy, for existence and validity of unilateral acts, intended to have legal effect, within Article 9(4) : Report, p.28), notwithstanding that applicable law may depend upon objective assessment *inter alia* of the alleged terms of the alleged contract whose existence and validity is not yet proved, and *even when that law is allegedly chosen by the parties* (whereas, at national law, it is uncertain whether such applicability of the 'putative proper law' – or proper law of the 'putative contract', according to preference – is not instead limited to the objective putative proper law, irrespective of the parties' choice: see Cheshire and North, pp. 471–2 and 473–4, arguing against subjective proper law's application, whereas Dicey and Morris, pp.1200–1, on the other hand, give qualified approval to the latter, citing in support the not very helpful case of *The Parouth* [1982] 1 Lloyd's Rep. 351 (CA), subsequently applied by HIRST J at first instance in *The Atlantic Emperor* [1989] 1 Lloyd's Rep. 548, p.553, col. 1, and thereafter by LLOYD LJ in the appeal proceedings, at p. 554, col. 2, who regarded himself as bound by the Court of Appeal's decision thereon, yet declined to express a view on its correctness). The provision has come to be referred to as the 'bootstraps' rule: it expressly permits the contract's existence and validity to be determined according to a law allegedly agreed to as part of the alleged contract, or objectively ascertained on the basis of *inter alia* alleged terms of the alleged agreement in the absence of an alleged choice of law clause, *before* the existence and validity of the contract and of any choice of law term thereof have been determined – such determination of contractual existence or validity being the very purpose of the efforts undertaken to ascertain and apply applicable law. (The 'bootstraps', therefore, are presumably the choice of law, treated as a term of a valid and existing contract – or, in the absence of alleged choice of law, objective applicable law – in order to decide whether the contract is in fact valid and existing, whereas, strictly, if the contract were thereupon held to be non-existent or invalid according to applicable law, the latter, at least chosen, law ought never to have been applied in the first place. The idea seemingly then, is that the 'body' of the contract is hauled up, somewhat unceremoniously, by its owner's bootstraps, the applicable law, in order to determine whether the body can run!) Article 8(1) expresses the rule to the effect that existence and validity are determined by the law which *would govern it* under the Convention *if* the contract or contractual term *were* valid.

As will also have been noted, Article 8 is expressed to operate in relation to existence and validity of the contract as a whole, or of any particular term thereof.

Furthermore, where the term, of which the existence and validity as an agreement to which consent has been given is in dispute, is the choice of law itself, as opposed to the contract as a whole or any other individual term, it is expressly confirmed by Article 3(4) that the rules *inter alia* on applicable law in Article 8 apply to consent to that choice of law (see Report, p.28). This is therefore almost a 'double-bootstraps' rule: not merely is the choice of law to be applied before existence and validity of the contract of which it forms part – and consequently, *incidentally*, of it itself – has been established, but it is actually *to be applied specifically to its own existence* (in this instance, the bootstraps might not even fit into the holes in the boots provided, and must therefore be strapped underneath the soles, in order to haul up the boots themselves which are attached to the body). Thus, in *The Lankya Abbaya* (1988) I. Prax 26, the German Federal Supreme Court applied Article 31 of the Introductory Law to the German Civil Code, giving effect to Article 8(1) of the Convention in Germany prior to the latter's entry into force at the international level, so as to decide on the effectiveness of a clause in a bill of lading, selecting Sri Lankan law exclusively to govern the contract, in accordance with the chosen Sri Lankan law itself. On the other hand, it may be that subjective choice must necessarily fail where a party itself purporting to conclude the choice of law agreement, is held to be non-existent and a sham device ([1991] ELD 157, 302 0 113/90, Germany).

The 'bootstraps rule' in Article 8(1) will doubtless attract its critics (see, for example, Briggs, 'The Formation of International Contracts' (1990), *LMCLQ*, 192, pp.202–3, who states that cases like *The Parouth* merely followed the path of standard academic opinion in favour of the putative proper law, and usually concerned proceedings under RSC Order 11, in which merely *potentially* applicable law had to be considered, in order to determine whether there was a good arguable case on the merits; *Albeko Schuhmaschinen AG v. Kamborian Shoe Machine Co. Ltd* (1961) 111 LJ 519, was a non-Order 11 decision supporting putative proper law, but even this was merely *obiter*, *ibid*.; and note too Juenger, in North (ed.) (1982) p.298, who points out that the US Second Restatement assumes an express choice of law to have been vitiated by mistake where the contract is void according to chosen law – unjustified, it is here felt, where parties were indifferent as to this outcome at the time of conclusion, through their optimism that no such dispute would ever arise!).

In the present submission:

(a) the most extreme 'bootstrapping' – application of Article 8(1) *to an express choice of law term itself*, by virtue of Article 3(4) – is potentially the most vulnerable to criticism; and it is tempting to support the view that, as part of the forum's choice of law procedure, such alleged agreements on applicable law should have been required to be assessed according to domestic English *lex fori* on contractual existence and validity (and not then reassessed according to applicable law, as if on a *renvoi* thereto – see Briggs, p.203, also citing *Mackender* v. *Feldia AG* [1967] 2 QB 590, as supporting application of *lex fori* to existence and validity of *jurisdiction* clauses ; and a variant of this theme is that *classification* as contractual according to *lex fori* involves ascertainment of consent and contractual intent initially according to English law – see Libling, 'Formation of International Contracts' (1979), 42 *MLR*, 169 – an analysis which critically fails to distinguish between, on the one hand, the forum's contractual classificatory requirement, perfectly admissible, that applicable law should contain *some* rule to establish consent and intention, and, on the other hand, *determination* of whether such consent and intention may be held to exist, a matter of the conflict of laws, referable solely to governing law rather than, automatically, to *lex fori* on classification); (application of *lex fori* could also possibly be justified in jurisprudential principle: thus, simply because *contract* is – allegedly – involved on the merits, it may not be lost sight of that applicable law remains a legal matter, for courts to decide upon in the administration of justice, and ultimately, not for the parties' agreements to oust the courts' jurisdiction in this respect – see *Vita Food Products Inc.* v. *Unus Shipping Co. Ltd* [1939] AC 277; accordingly, whilst courts, in deciding upon applicable law, will usually attach overriding significance to the parties' intentions agreed to, those courts are nonetheless not privy to such agreements, nor bound thereby, as organs of public law, and may therefore apply their own law in order to determine their response to the claim); admittedly, resort to *lex fori* would risk encouraging forum shopping and disunity, but at least Article 8(2) would have helped to reduce those dangers for parties who were falsely and wantonly confronted with the allegation of having entered into an agreement which they denied ever existed; on the other hand, a possible alternative to *lex fori*, in relation to existence and validity of the choice of law term, where validity or existence of the remainder of the contract was not also in issue (or even if it was, if there was no good arguable case thereon according to *lex fori*: see *Effer* v. *Kantner*, Case 38/81 [1982] ECR 825, in the Judgments Convention context), might have been at least to limit the law governing the choice of law clause to that applicable under the Convention *in the absence of choice* (see above, Chapter 8);

(b) the next level of 'bootstrapping' down from the top of the scale which may attract the critics is where there is an *express choice of law clause*, but the existence or validity of the agreement as a whole – of which it forms part – is challenged; unless it is somehow possible to sever the choice of law element from the vice allegedly affecting existence or validity of the remainder of the contract, the same arguments as those preceding will apply, and the choice of law term may be felt to lack authenticity for the purpose; furthermore, in this case it is difficult to justify application even of objective applicable law to existence and validity of the contract, since one of the parties denies existence or validity of agreement upon those very terms of the contract which the court will take into account, *inter alia*, in its determination of objective applicable law; again, therefore, *lex fori* has credentials based on justice and practical expedience;

(c) the lowest level on the scale of 'bootstrapping' is the application of *objective applicable law* to contractual existence or validity, in the absence of express choice of law, on the basis of factors including those contained in, or derived from, the terms of the very contract whose existence or validity is denied; it was previously seen that to permit this is to expose parties to the risk of being confronted with an agreement carefully sculpted to lead to applicability of a law favourable, as to existence or validity, to the party alleging its valid conclusion; a party may receive some protection from Article 8(2), but there is no guarantee that the law of his own habitual residence will afford him any greater safeguards in the matter of contractual consent than the former (he may habitually agree on application of other laws in his genuine contracts for that very reason).

Such, then, is the case which could have been made out in favour of applying *lex fori* to all such instances of bootstrapping under the Convention.

The argument against, of course, is that a plaintiff would invariably choose as the forum a Contracting State whose contract law favoured his claim for existence and validity and which, in addition, possessed jurisdiction over the defendant, and it is impossible to deny the force of this objection – at least in the case of contractual existence and validity as a whole, as opposed to that of choice of law in particular.

The current formulation of Article 8, therefore, seeks to steer a pragmatic, middle route between the opposing camps, even though by no means assured of producing a perfectly just result in all cases: law governing effects of the alleged contract also applies to existence and validity (Article 8(1)), but a party has the chance to block it through the law of his own habitual residence on consent (Article 8(2)). Application of law of each party's habitual residence to his consent as a fixed rule might have been looked on as being far too inflexible. Yet it is nevertheless wondered whether perhaps Article 8(2) ought not to have permitted a party to rely on the law of the other party's habitual residence, as well as his own, in order to establish his lack of consent?

(b) Article 8(2)

This, as seen, enables a party to rely on the absence of his consent under the law of the country of his habitual residence (or presumably, in the case of bodies corporate or unincorporate, of its central administration, or principal or other effective place of business if transacting in the course of a trade or profession, by way of partial generalization of the principle in Article 4(2)), in the circumstances there prescribed.

The Report explains that Article 8(2) is designed *inter alia* to deal with the problem of the implications of silence by a party in receipt of an offer from another: it would seem that under German law, traders may be taken to have accepted an offer which they do not expressly reject, in particular, where new general conditions of agreement are included in subsequent written confirmation of an oral contract (see von Hoffmann, in North (ed.), *Contract Conflicts* (1982), p.228 – and note too *Berghoefer* v. *ASA S.A.*, Case 221/84 [1985] ECR 2699, on jurisdiction agreements under Article 17 of the European Judgments Convention). Thus, Article 8(1) could otherwise operate unfairly where, for example, a person habitually resident in state X goes to stay for a few days in an hotel in state Y, at which he receives a number of offers – selecting German law – to which he gives no reply (see Kühne, in Lando (ed.) (1975), p.122), or where an offer is received by post in X, having been sent by an offeror in Germany (Lagarde, in North (ed.) (1982), p.50): justice seemed to require that the offeree should be protected by absence of consent under the law of X – his own habitual residence – with which he could be presumed to be familiar and able to be advised upon, *a fortiori*, where the offer itself stipulated that silence would be treated as acceptance, ineffective under English law in accordance with *Felthouse* v. *Bindley* (1862) 11 CB (N.S.) 869 (see too *The Leonidas D* [1985] 1 WLR 925; and Owsia, 'Silence: Efficacy in Contract Formation. A Comparative Review of French and English Law' (1991), 40 *ICLQ*, 784, for an analytical survey of different countries' laws on silence) (in addition to which, the new German trend itself is to refer silence to law of the habitual residence of the silent party: see von Hoffmann, p.228, in opposition, on the ground that people engaged in international commerce should bear the risks and not be permitted to fall back on their own law if things go wrong); conversely, an offeror receiving no reply from the offeree could himself be prejudiced on selling the goods to another, if the offeree's law, treating silence as acceptance, were to govern. In such cases, it might be felt, application of the most connected law under Article 4 to consent of a party would be no more equitable thereto than that of the law selected by the other party under Article 3.

CONDITIONS OF OPERATION OF THE ARTICLE 8(2) EXCEPTION

(a) 'A' Party May Rely ...

Article 8(2)'s operation is not limited to the offeree: either party, offeror or offeree, can rely on the law of his own habitual residence thereunder (Report, p.28). But it has to be the allegedly non-consenting party himself who relies on that law of his habitual residence to establish his lack of consent; the other party cannot refer to that law in order to prove that the former did not consent. Nor is the former *obliged* to refer to such law: Article 8(2) merely affords a power to do so ('may' rely).

(b) Law of the Country in which He 'Has' His Habitual Residence ...

The present tense of 'has' (also in the French text – the German avoids the ambiguity) seems inappropriate, and could facilitate manipulation of the rule in Article 8(2), by a party taking up habitual residence in a country whose law regarded him as not having consented, prior to refusing contractual performance and to the consequent litigation. Habitual residence as at the date of concluding the alleged contract is surely the preferable construction.

(c) To Establish That He Did Not Consent ...

Article 8(2) is not concerned with validity of contracts, solely with their existence by reason of mutual consent of the parties (Report, p.28).

Furthermore, law of the habitual residence is only able to be relied on in order to show that a party did *not* consent: it cannot be referred to under Article 8(2) in order to uphold contractual existence when this element is otherwise lacking under the law applicable by virtue of Article 8(1) (*ibid.*).

(d) If it Appears from the Circumstances ...

The Report specifies that the court must have regard to *all* the circumstances of the case, not solely to those in respect of which the party claiming that he has not consented to the contract has acted, and that courts will give particular consideration to the practices followed by the parties *inter se* as well as to their previous business relationships (p.28). The circumstances are thus potentially infinite: relative strength of bargaining power; use of general conditions by a party; omission by a party to obtain legal advice; buyer's or seller's market; otherwise applicable law of an undeveloped country with little commercial expertise. An analogy might be drawn with certain of the factors set out in Schedule 2 to the Unfair Contract Terms Act 1977 as guidelines for determining (in particular, under s.11(2)) whether exclusion of liability is reasonable, as permitted under ss. 6 and 7:

- strength of relative bargaining positions;
- inducements to the customer to agree to the term, and existence of alternative sources of supply;
- whether the customer knew or ought reasonably to have known of the existence and extent of the term (having regard, among other things, to any custom of the trade and any previous course of dealing between the parties);
- whether the goods were manufactured, processed or adapted to the special order of the customer.

(e) It Would Not Be Reasonable ...

Courts of different Contracting States should apply the concept of *reasonableness* in the unificationist spirit required by Article 18, attempting so far as possible not to diverge from one another. Policy decisions are required in respect of the preceding circumstances: it could be argued that considerations of consumer protection should be discounted, because Article 8(1) applicable law already incorporates protective provisions of Articles 5 and 6. However, it is felt that this would be incorrect: first, rules on formation will not necessarily be *mandatory* where a choice of law is made, for purposes of Article 5(2)/6(1); secondly, Article 5(2) conditions of operation may not be satisfied on the facts; and thirdly, under Article 6, law of the employee's place of work, not of his habitual residence, is generally applicable; whereas, in all such cases, Article 8(2) is specifically intended to counteract any unfairness arising from Article 8(1) applicable law, whether the latter is chosen or otherwise, in the particular area of consent.

It is doubtful whether the European Court itself can directly assist, since application – rather than interpretation – of the concept of reasonableness would seem to be in issue; although, indirect help may come from European Court decisions regarding sufficiency of writing and written evidence of jurisdiction agreements under Article 17 of the European Judgments

Convention (see *Salotti* v. *Rüwa*, Case 24/76 [1976] ECR 1831, [1977] 1 CMLR 345; *Segoura* v. *Bonakdarian*, Case 25/76 [1976] ECR 1851, [1977] 1 CMLR 361; *Berghoefer* v. *ASA SA*, Case 221/84 [1985] ECR 2699, [1986] 1 CMLR 13), so that perhaps where one party deals on the other's standard terms and conditions (especially where these are supplied *following* conclusion of the oral contract – and in contrast to Judgments Convention Article 17 on jurisdiction, Article 8(2) will require the *recipient to prove unreasonableness*, rather than the supplier to show reasonableness of their application), or a party is inexperienced in transacting, or – even though capacity exists – a minor, or the contract is oppressive and unfavourable to a party (the German *Knebelvertrag*), choice of the other's law may be held to be unreasonable in relation to consent (nor may the English rule of effectiveness of postal acceptance be considered to be immune from being held to be unreasonable as otherwise applicable law, under Article 8(2) – although, as in the case of silence as acceptance, it is submitted that *reasonableness* of application of applicable law under Article 8(1) should be as dependent upon circumstances of its application as on the content itself of the rule in question). At least it seems clear that unreasonableness of reference to applicable law on consent need not be proved conclusively; all that is required to be shown is that this *appears* to be unreasonable.

In the Court of Appeal proceedings in *George Mitchell (Chesterhall) Ltd* v. *Finney Lock Seeds Ltd* [1983] 1 All ER 108, concerning reasonableness of contractual exclusion under the Sale of Goods Act 1979, KERR LJ indicated that reasonableness required the effect of the parties' bargain to be plain and clear (and not, for example, hidden away in the small print) (see too *The Zinnia* [1984] 2 Lloyd's Rep. 211, 222).

(f) To Determine the Effect of his Conduct ...

Article 8(2) is intended specifically to deal with the problem of silence in response to an offer. 'Conduct' therefore includes such *negative* conduct, as well as positive response (Report, p.28 – under English law, in the absence of estoppel or a course of dealing between the parties, solely conduct, not mere silence, would amount to acceptance: *Brodgen* v. *Metropolitan Ry* (1877) 2 App Cas 666, HL; *Henry Kendall and Sons* v. *William Lillico and Sons* [1969] AC 31; the position is different, however, under German law, whereby according to various statutory provisions, such as Articles 149, 151 and 675 of the Civil Code and 362 of the Commercial Code, as well as under the doctrine of *kaufmännisches Bestätigungsschreiben* – commercial letter of confirmation – silence of the offeree – or even offeror, under Article 145 of the Civil Code – may in particular circumstances amount to acceptance: see Kost's unpublished LL.M thesis, 'Problems Relating to Formation of Contracts under the Rome Convention With Special Regard to English and German Law', 1991, East Anglia/Trier, pp.58–63).

(g) In Accordance with the Law Specified in the Preceding Paragraph

It has to be reference to otherwise applicable law which appears unreasonable, for Article 8(2) to operate. Provided that this is the case, a party may rely on the law of his habitual residence, even if not all other laws would be unreasonable. The question once again arises: if law of the habitual residence is thus assumed to be inherently reasonable, why not a fixed rule requiring it to be applied to consent in all cases, in place of applicable law? The answer of course is that it is not inherently reasonable according to Convention philosophy: it is only *more reasonable than an unreasonable otherwise applicable law*!

14 Article 9: Formal Validity of Contracts

Article 9

Formal validity

1 A contract concluded between persons who are in the same country is formally valid if it satisfies the formal requirements of the law which governs it under this Convention or of the law of the country where it is concluded.

2 A contract concluded between persons who are in different countries is formally valid if it satisfies the formal requirements of the law which governs it under this Convention or of the law of one of those countries.

3 Where a contract is concluded by an agent, the country in which the agent acts is the relevant country for the purposes of paragraphs 1 and 2.

Article 9(1)–(3) offers a liberal regime of alternative laws governing formal validity of contracts, in order to promote validity of contracts in the interests of commerce (*favor negotii/validitatis*) and to prevent contracting parties from being surprised by unexpected formalities of the law applicable to the contract where law of the place of conclusion contained no such requirements (Report, pp.29–30) (although, it was unnecessary to provide the same number of alternatives as in the 1961 Hague Convention on Conflict of Laws Regarding Testamentary Dispositions, because in the latter case, wills could not be re-enacted if successfully challenged after death, *ibid.*). Thus, parties (other than in consumer contracts within Article 5: see below, Article 9(5)) have a choice to comply with formalities of any of

- the law applicable to the contract under the Convention;
- the law of the country of conclusion if concluded between persons in the same country;
- the law of one of the countries where the parties are present at the time of conclusion if they conclude the contract in different countries.

Formal validity under any of the preceding laws is sufficient ('if it satisfies ... or ...'), even if (subject to mandatory provision under Article 6(1) or 7 and public policy under Article 16) the others are not complied with (and regardless, it is submitted, of whether the parties intended to conform with the former or not): Article 9 is thus largely facilitational (Report, p.30). Further alternatives, however, for example, common nationality or (generally) habitual residence, were rejected, because excessive freedom would deprive formal requirements of their effects, and Article 9 must compromise between liberality and due observance; in addition, the connection between Article 9 on formal validity and Article 14(2) on matters of evidence (modes of proof may be referred *inter alia* to Article 9 laws under Article 14(2)) made it desirable to limit laws applicable to formal validity under the former (*ibid.*).

The system of alternatives, moreover, is broadly in accordance with preexisting national systems of private international law of Contracting States: for example, the English (*Guépratte* v. *Young* (1851) 4 De G. & Sm 217 – *lex loci contractus*; *Van Grutten* v. *Digby* (1862) 31 Bear 561 – proper law), German and French (see Lagarde, 'Scope of Applicable Law', in North (ed.) (1982), p.52). Availability of *lex loci actus* offers the particular advantage of enabling parties to obtain local legal advice on form.

The Report itself points out that mandatory rules of form of a law other than those indicated in Article 9 (for example, laws of a country in which a contract of employment is to be carried out, such as those requiring a restraint on competition term to be in writing) will override the latter by virtue of *Article 7* (limited to Article 7(2) *lex fori*, under the 1990 Act s.2(2), in the United Kingdom: *quaere* whether Companies Act 1985 s.36(1)(a) is such a rule) (not to mention Article 6(1)) (p.31).

REFERENCE TO APPLICABLE LAW UNDER THE CONVENTION FOR FORMAL VALIDITY: ARTICLE 9(1) AND (2)

Applicable law will be determined in accordance with Article 3 on choice, or Article 4 in the absence of choice by the parties, or, in the case of individual employment contracts, Article 6 – irrespective of whether the parties are in the same (Article 9(1)) or different (Article 9(2)) countries when the contract is concluded. (Formal validity of consumer contracts is specifically dealt with in Article 9(5) – see below, p.292.)

Four points should be made in this particular respect.

(a) First, Article 3(2) says that parties may subsequently agree to vary the law previously applicable to their contract: and further, that any such variation by the parties made after the conclusion of the contract 'shall not prejudice its formal validity under Article 9 or adversely affect the rights of third parties'. This means that formal validity may be upheld under either of original and subsequent applicable laws: formal invalidity under the former will be cured through compliance with the latter, and, conversely, will not apply under the latter if the contract was formally valid under the former. One writer interestingly combines the formality- and third party-limitations on effectiveness of variation of applicable law in Article 3(2): he points out – taking a broad construction of the concept of 'rights' of third parties, as not necessarily being derived from the contract – that a third party against whom a claim in tort for inducement of breach of contract is made may still argue in defence that the contract in question was formally invalid under the *original* law, even if not also so under the new law, by virtue of Article 3(2) (see Williams, 'The EEC Convention on the Law Applicable to Contractual Obligations' (1986), 35 *ICLQ*, 1, 21)!

(b) Secondly, where more than one applicable law governs the contract – for example, because parties select the law to apply to only part of their contract under Article 3(1), so that another law governs the rest under Article 4(1), or the court exceptionally severs the contract for applicable law under Article 4(1) – will every such applicable law be able to be relied upon for formal validity in the alternative, or must a selection be made for purposes of Article 9? The Report seems to assume that the latter should be the case, and suggests that in these circumstances it would be 'reasonable to apply the law applicable to the part of the contract most closely connected with the disputed condition on which its formal validity depends' (p.30). It is considered that this solution could prove very difficult to apply and is contrary to the liberal spirit of Article 9. Parties should be permitted to comply with either applicable law for formal validity. If the law of one country is selected to govern, say, the payment obligation and the remainder of the contract is subject to a different country's law in the absence of choice, the former but not the latter requiring the contract to be drawn up in writing for it to be valid, which of the two laws can be said to be most closely connected with the proceedings, where, for example, each party alleges breach of contract by the other? (To adopt the characteristic obligation as such from Article 4(2) would be to beg the question in the particular context involved. A possible alternative course would be to apply different applicable laws on formalities separately to each party's claim, holding the contract to be formally invalid under the one and valid in respect of the other – an inelegant solution, it must be confessed.)

(c) Thirdly, the Report asks which of applicable law and *lex loci actus* should be referred to under Article 9(1), as rendering the contract formally invalid, where the latter is the position under *both* these laws (p.30)? It is submitted that for most purposes this is a question not requiring to be answered, since, as seen, Article 9 is concerned with compliance, and only generally with the consequence – invalidity – of non-compliance. The Report considers that the matter is of importance for deciding which of the two laws governs limitation of actions if subject thereto (and, in accordance with Article 9's underlying policy to uphold transactions, suggests that the shorter limitation period for annulment should operate: *ibid.*).

However, in the case of limitation of *actions*, it has to be pointed out that this is not a matter for laws governing formalities under Article 9 at all: for Article 10(1)(d) refers *inter alia* limitation of actions to applicable law under Articles 3 – 6 and 12 of the Convention. Consequently, if the remarks in the Report are limited, for example, to national rules permitting one party to raise an objection with the other, *within a certain time*, requiring a formal defect to be remedied, after which period the formality in question need no longer be complied with for validity, then its view can be accepted.

(d) Fourthly, where the law to be relied on for formal validity under Article 9 is applicable law chosen by the parties under Article 3, Article 3(4) states that existence and validity of consent of parties to the choice of applicable law shall itself be determined in accordance with *inter alia* Article 9. This expressly covers the problem of circularity, whereby an objection might otherwise have been made that chosen applicable law could not be permitted to govern formal validity of the contract, under Article 9, where formal validity of the choice of law provision itself was subject to determination thereunder. The Report further suggests that the expression 'the law which governs it under this Convention' in Article 9(1) and (2), on analogy with the express provision for material validity in Article 8, should similarly be taken to mean the law which *would govern the contract if it were held to be formally valid* ('A contract concluded'), given that the latter, being the very question at issue, is not yet decided (so that there may in fact be no contract for applicable law to 'govern') (p.30).

REFERENCE TO *LEX LOCI ACTUS* FOR FORMAL VALIDITY UNDER THE CONVENTION: ARTICLE 9(1) AND (2)

The problem with referring to *lex loci contractus* – law of the state of conclusion – on formal (or, for that matter, essential) validity of contracts, is that such connecting factor itself raises conflicts questions in the types of case in which it is likely to be required to operate, namely, where the parties have conducted negotiations from different countries: in the circumstances, which law is to apply to determine situation of place of conclusion for such purposes – law governing the contract (thus possibly involving circularity), *lex fori*, or a combination perhaps? Modern technology and telecommunications render the position today far different from when *locus regit actum* first came about, when most 'international' contracts were made *inter praesentes* in the fairs and markets and by travelling sellers (Lando, 'Les Obligations Contractuelles', in Lando (ed.) *European Private International Law of Obligations* (1975), p.150). Since English and Continental laws, respectively, favour countries of dispatch and of receipt of postal acceptances as those of conclusion of contracts (see *Adams* v. *Lindsell* (1818) 1 B. & Ald. 681; Article 130 German Civil Code; Article 932 French Civil Code; Articles 1326 and 1335 Italian Civil Code), resort to law of the place of contracting as the choice of law rule for formal validity is laced with potential difficulty.

Article 9(1) and (2) consequently adopts a liberal solution to the traditional problem: if the parties conclude the contract in the same country, the latter's law may apply (Article 9(1)); if they are in different countries, *each* of those states' laws is allowed to be resorted to for formal validity, thereby dissolving the difficulties. (A number of other possible solutions were rejected, according to the Report, p.31: requiring both laws' formalities to be complied with, cumulatively; artificial selection of one or other of countries of offer and acceptance; application of law of country of offer to formalities of offer, and of law of country of acceptance to formalities of acceptance, unsuitable because formalities could apply to a contract as a whole, for example, signatures and duplicates, and because an offeree might also wish to rely on the offeror's law for formal validity, and vice versa).

Certain points of construction arise.

(a) Persons Who Are in the Same Country/Different Countries

Presumably, fleeting personal presence is sufficient. In the case of companies, the choice of criterion of their presence for such purposes would seem to range between country of incorporation, that of central management and control, and country of the place of business through which the transaction was negotiated, in the absence of agency dealings under Article 9(3). It is submitted that *all* such establishments should be held to amount to a company's presence in a country in the context of Article 9, *but* that, on analogy with Article 9(3) on agents, *only* the country of whichever was actually responsible for having made the offer or acceptance should be taken to be the country of presence in the circumstances. (Clearly, however, in view of the express provision on agents under Article 9(3), mere agent's transacting itself will not amount to presence of the principal for such purposes – and see too Chapter 16 below, concerning similar requirements under Article 11 on contractual capacity of natural persons.)

(b) Time of Presence

It is not wholly clear from Article 9(1) and (2) as to whether the relevant time for presence of the parties is that of, on the one hand, *technical conclusion*, in the sense of effective acceptance of the offer, or, on the other hand, that of the *two-stage* process, comprising both the making of the offer and the dispatch of the acceptance. (Otherwise put, under Article 9(1), is alternative applicable law *lex loci contracus* or *lex loci actus*?)

The text could be taken to support the former construction, but there are problems with this: (1) the old problem of choice of law to determine place of conclusion for such purposes would resurface; (2) peculiar results might ensue – for example, the offeree might send his acceptance by post from state X to the offeror in state Y, and then fly to state Y before his letter arrived, in which case (according to French, German or Italian law) he would be in the same country as the offeror at the date of conclusion, or, conversely, in a different country, were he to have left state Y after posting his acceptance to the offeror in state Y but before its receipt; (3) proceeding from these points, the underlying objective of Article 9 is to enable parties to avail themselves of local forms of the countries in which they actually transact, as opposed to that in which the contract is technically concluded, where these differ; and (4) Article 9(3) refers both to a contract being 'concluded' by an agent and to the country in which the agent 'acts' – it does not seem likely that agent's presence thereunder is only to be adopted in place of the principal's where the agent is that of the offeree, technically *acting* by way of *concluding* the contract through *acceptance*; it seems far more probable that Article 9(3) also operates in relation to an agent's presence when *acting* by way of *making an offer*, not just acceptance.

Accordingly, it is submitted that presence under Article 9(1) and (2) (as well as (3) itself) should preferably be taken to refer to each contracting party's (or agent's, as the case may be) situation at the time of his making the offer or the acceptance. Furthermore, applying the same reasoning, such offer or acceptance should be treated as being 'made' for these purposes at the moment of dispatch rather than that of receipt, since once again the party responsible may change his situation between these two points in time.

Unfortunately, however, in spite of the difficulties with the technical construction, the final words of Article 9(1) 'where it is concluded' suggest that the latter is that which may have to be followed. This is because the two concepts of *parties present and transacting in the same country* and *country where the contract is concluded*, in Article 9(1), do not automatically coincide, and yet Article 9(1) does expressly require the latter's law to be applied, seemingly as *lex loci contractus*. Thus, for example, the offeror might send his offer by post in state X to the offeree who is also in state X; one year later, when the offeror has moved to state Y, the offeree sends his letter of acceptance from state X to state Y: each party has *transacted in the same state X*, but the law of the *country of conclusion* may, according to applicable law, be that of state Y, and since, therefore, the parties are not in the same country at that point in time, Article 9(1) is inapplicable and Article 9(2) governs instead; conversely, if the offeree had received the offer in state Y, from which he dispatched his acceptance to state X, where he also happened to be present on the date of receipt thereof by the offeror, being the point of contractual conclusion according to applicable law, the parties would then be held to be in the same country X when the contract was concluded, and Article 9(1) would apply. Such technical construction of Article 9, here opposed, *might* still be able to be avoided by arguing that even such reference to contractual conclusion in the closing words of Article 9(1) can be taken to denote the country where offeror and offeree effect to make their offer and acceptance, rather than that of technical conclusion if different. Yet the very use of the expression 'where it is concluded' does not help this construction at all, and plainly the final words of Article 9(1) ought to have read 'of the law of that country', rather than 'or of the law of the country where it is concluded', and to have been inserted in the second line immediately after the words 'formal requirements'. Perhaps the European Court should be requested to rule on this rather vital point of interpretation of Article 9. In the meantime, the suggestion here is that, if the technical meaning of contractual conclusion has to be applied, then, for the sake of uniformity, the law (putatively) governing the contract as a whole, rather than *lex fori*, should determine the date of contractual conclusion for purposes of Article 9.

At least under Article 9(2), where parties have transacted from different countries in which they were respectively present at *all* stages, each of their laws will be able to be referred to for formal validity (alternatively to applicable law), rather than that of technical conclusion having to be artificially singled out. (What, however, of those, doubtless, *extremely numerous* cases in which contracts are concluded by radio between persons in England and another, floating in a boat on the high seas? Lasok and Stone, *Conflict of Laws in the European Community* (1987), p.365, suggest a solution based upon the 'policy of validation in case of doubt'. Presumably, therefore, the choice is between, on the one hand, port of registration, as deemed *locus actus* for the sailor – or sailors if both parties are at sea – and, on the other hand, especially if the vessel is not registered, informality of contracting, given the absence of any law to govern in the case of the sailor, let alone rules of form thereof.)

(c) Conclusion by Agents

Article 9(3) substitutes country of an agent's presence for that of the principal contracting party for purposes of Article 9(1) and (2). Thus, if the offeror is in state X and the offeree in state Y, and the latter sends his agent to conclude the contract in state X, the contract is concluded between parties in the same country; conversely, if offeror and offeree are in state X, but their agents conclude the contract on their behalf in states Y and Z respectively, the contract is concluded by parties who are in different countries (Report, pp.30–1). Clearly, it is not sufficient for the agent merely to pass on the other party's offer to the principal for acceptance, or to transmit the principal's offer to the offeree for acceptance: the agent must be capable of acting so as to bind his principal, for Article 9(3) to operate. Furthermore, as has previously been discussed in connection with the meaning of contractual conclusion under Article 9(1), 'conclusion' of contracts by agents and 'acts' in pursuance thereof under Article 9(3) ought to be understood to refer to the two-stage offer and acceptance process, rather than to the technical act of effective acceptance; as seen, however, the latter construction of Article 9(1) may be required to be adopted, in which event agents' presence at the date of technical contractual conclusion would have to be assessed, in applying Article 9(1)–(3), a result even more unappealing than that criticized in respect of contracts concluded by the parties themselves. Finally, what of the agent who concludes a contract in a particular country, under the law of which it is formally valid, nonetheless without possessing authority to do so, or at least to do so in that country, and yet the law governing the principal's liability (outside the Convention, by virtue of Article 1(2)(f)) holds the principal to be bound (even though such contract would be formally invalid under that law)? It seems hard on the principal for the contract to be formally upheld under the law of the country in which the agent acted, when the latter's action in so doing was specifically prohibited under the terms of the agency. The fairer solution would be to construe 'acts' in Article 9(3) (whatever the position on the merits) as meaning *acts with actual authority* according to the law governing the agency contract.

(d) Formally Valid

Article 9 lays down applicable laws in relation to 'formal validity'. Rules to be classified as formalities, rather than substance, are undefined. The Report states that this was deliberately omitted owing to its difficulty (and the law applicable to substance also governs form in any event under Article 9) (p.29). Nevertheless, the Report does go on to indicate a fairly wide meaning of 'form' for the purposes of Article 9, 'as including every external manifestation required on the part of a person expressing the will to be legally bound, and in the absence of which such expression of will would not be regarded as fully effective' (*ibid.*). Clearly, therefore, what is envisaged is form in the nature of writing, written evidence, stamping, registration, and marking in a red box, *et alia*. What are less likely to be included, however, are prescribed actions which do not relate to the physical form in which a contract is concluded, but which require certain steps to be undertaken by parties as a condition of its validity, referable instead to the law governing substance: for example, a requirement to provide copies of a written agreement within a certain time from conclusion, or, as the Report indicates, consent of the family council to a minor's contract under French law, or notice of assignment of a chose in action under English law (see Article 12(2)) (*ibid.*): although, it should be added that these steps may themselves constitute legal 'acts' within the meaning of Article 9(4), so that any form which *they* are required to take – for example, writing, in the case of notice to the debtor of assignment of a legal chose in action under s.136 of the Law of Property Act 1925 – must be complied with according to the law referred to.

Generally speaking, form of contracts is far more important in Continental legal systems – where consideration is not a requirement and notarization of contracts may be called for – than it is in England: this is especially so in Italy (Article 1350 Civil Code) and Germany (Article 125 Civil Code), although, less so in France (Article 1341 Civil Code). Furthermore, the consequence of failure to comply in those systems tends to be invalidity, rather than mere unenforceability. In England few transactions actually have to be *in writing* (for example, regulated agreements, under Consumer Credit

Act 1974 s.61; transfer of a British ship, under Merchant Shipping Act 1894 s.24; contracts for the sale or other disposition of an interest in land, concluded on or after 27 September 1989, under the Law of Property (Miscellaneous Provisions) Act 1989 s.2); certain others must be *evidenced in writing* (for example, contracts of guarantee, Statute of Frauds 1677 s.4; contracts for the sale or other disposition of land or any interest in land, concluded prior to 27 September 1989, under the Law of Property Act 1925 s.40(1), which ceases to have effect in relation to contracts made on or after that date under s.2(8) of the 1989 Act) – but in the case of these latter requirements, whilst they may certainly be held to concern *formalities*, nonetheless they arguably fall outside the sphere of Article 9, because they are not concerned with formal *validity* of the contracts to which they apply, which is the limited function of Article 9: on the contrary, their effect is upon *enforceability* of the contract, without reference to its validity. Article 9 is consequently inapplicable. Instead, such matters *may* be classified as relating to essential validity and as thereby subject to applicable law under the Convention, or more likely, in view of past English authorities (see *Leroux* v. *Brown* (1852) 12 CB 801; *Alves* v. *Hodgson* (1797) 7 Term Rep. 241; *Monterosso Shipping Co. Ltd* v. *ITF* [1982] 3 All ER 841; *G. and H. Montage GmbH* v. *Irvani* [1990] 1 WLR 667), as procedural and, accordingly, as otherwise outside the Convention's scope under Article 1(2)(h) (and for *lex fori* consequently to govern under national conflicts), *but for Article 14(2)*, which expressly refers *modes of proof* either to *lex fori* or to any foreign laws applicable to formal validity under Article 9 (provided that such written evidence requirements are to be classified as 'modes of proof' for the purposes – see below, Article 14(2)). (It seems likely, however, that s.40(1) would always be applicable in any event in respect of English land, even if it were to have been regarded as a matter of formal validity falling within Article 9(1)–(3), by reason of its probable classification as a *mandatory* rule of English *lex situs* under Article 9(6): see further below, p.233 *et seq.*)

4   **An act intended to have legal effect relating to an existing or contemplated contract is formally valid if it satisfies the formal requirements of the law which under the Convention governs or would govern the contract or of the law of the country where the act was done.**

FORMAL VALIDITY OF ACTS INTENDED TO HAVE LEGAL EFFECT: APPLICABLE LAWS

Article 9(4) adapts the principles on formalities of contracts in the preceding provisions of Article 9 to the case of formal validity of unilateral legal acts in reference to existing or contemplated contracts (as opposed, for example, to 'acts' of transfer under involuntary, non-contractual assignment).

Alternative applicable laws are

- the law which governs or would govern the contract under the Convention;
- the law of the country where the act was done.

It should be noted that it is expressed to be the law applicable under the Convention to the contract, rather than to the act itself, which may be referred to for formal validity of the latter. This does not seem to take account of the possibility that a different law may govern, say, notice of termination from that applicable to the rest of the contract, under Articles 3(1) and 4 of the Convention. (Nor is it laws specifically governing *formal* validity of the contract, under Article 9(1)–(3), which are referred to in Article 9(4).)

ACTS

The 'acts' in question are confined to those relating to contracts, existing or contemplated, and falling within the Convention's scope (Report, p.29) (an earlier draft of Article 9 merely referred to 'acts' and not also to contracts, the term *acte juridique*, derived from Roman law, evidently covering both, under Continental legal systems, yet lacking clarity through not being limited to contracts: *ibid.*).

The 'acts' in question are those which are intended to have – and presumably, according to applicable law, are capable of having – legal effect, in the sense of being attended by legal consequences. The concept is extremely wide: it may include any act relating to contract, which might be required to be in a particular form for it to acquire legal effectiveness under the relevant legal system: for example, notice of contractual termination; notice of assignment of an intangible, to be given to the debtor; declaration of rescission or repudiation; even the making of an offer, where the offeror is bound thereby for a fixed or reasonable time according to applicable law, as under Article 145 of the German Civil Code (see too Articles 1328 *et seq.* of the Italian Civil Code) (Report, p.28).

The Report considers that *public* acts – those of public officials, such as the notary of Continental legal systems, authenticating legal transactions – are not included within Article 9(4), because the official may only possess authority to draw up a valid contract in accordance with the forms of the law under which he is appointed. Nevertheless, the contract itself may be formally valid according to any of the laws applicable thereto under Article 9(1)–(3), should the official – as apparently may happen in the Netherlands – think it appropriate to follow the forms laid down by the foreign law governing the substance of the contract (p.29).

5   **The provisions of the preceding paragraphs shall not apply to a contract to which Article 5 applies, concluded in the circumstances described in paragraph 2 of Article 5. The formal validity of such a contract is governed by the law of the country in which the consumer has his habitual residence.**

Where Article 5 applies to the consumer contract, Article 9(1)–(4) is inapplicable. Applicable law for formal validity is

- law of the country of the consumer's habitual residence

This may have been the case in any event, had Article 9(1)–(4) applied, under Article 7, where formalities were regarded as mandatory. According to the Report, however, Article 9(5) (as well as (6)) was included because Article 7(1) is merely discretionary in favour of such mandatory rules (pp.31–2) (form of employment contracts, on the other hand, is left to mandatory Article 7 where necessary – supplementing mandatory rules under Article 6(1), in the case of agreement on applicable law – because whereas Article 5(3) governs consumer contracts in the absence of choice by the law of the consumer's habitual residence, *borrowed* for Article 9(5), Article 6(2) on employment contracts merely has rebuttable presumptions, too uncertain for purposes of compliance with formal requirements : *ibid*). Ironically, however, it might well be necessary to rely upon Article 7(2) for mandatory operation of rules on formalities in ss.60–65 of the Consumer Credit Act 1974 (details of names, price, credit, signatures *et alia*), since non-compliance leads to unenforceability by the creditor, not invalidity (ss. 65 and 127), in view of which Article 9(5), it is submitted, is inapplicable thereto and Article 14(2) refers the mode of proof of contract to *lex fori* or 'any' of Article 9 laws by which the contract is formally valid. In the latter event, therefore, or alternatively, that such 1974 Act formalities were held not to amount to 'modes of proof', but simply to rules of debtor–protection (see Dicey and Morris, pp.1211–12) governed by ordinary Convention applicable law, their application may only be able to be ensured – other than as of English applicable law itself, governing material validity under the Convention (Article 8(1)) in the second eventuality – as being mandatory, by virtue of Article 7(2) (see *English* v. *Donnelly*, 1958 SC 494; *Kay's*

Leasing Corporation Pty Ltd v. *Fletcher* (1964) 116 CLR 124). (Section 173, on the other hand, makes *void* any contractual term which is inconsistent with the Act's protective provisions.)

6   **Notwithstanding paragraphs 1–4 of this Article, a contract the subject matter of which is a right in immovable property or a right to use immovable property shall be subject to the mandatory requirements of form of the law of the country where the property is situated if by that law those requirements are imposed irrespective of the country where the contract is concluded and irrespective of the law governing the contract.**

Article 9(6), apparently requested to be included by the Scottish member of the United Kingdom's negotiating team on the Convention (see Lagarde, in North (ed.) (1982), p.53), means that applicable law on formal validity of the specified contracts relating to immovables is alternatively

- the law applicable to the contract
- *lex loci contractus/actus* : Article 9(1)–(3);
SUBJECT TO
- mandatory rules of form of *lex situs* imposed irrespective of *lex loci contractus* and of applicable law (the latter, in any event, being presumed to be *lex situs* in the absence of choice, under Article 4(3)).

The type of national mandatory rules in issue therefore under Article 9(6) are those which are both conflicts-mandatory and contracts-mandatory at national law. Furthermore, there must be no national limitation on their operation to where they form part of *lex loci contractus*.

There can be few doubts that in England such mandatory rules referred to by Article 9(6) *would* include s.40(1) of the Law of Property Act 1925 (written note or memorandum of sale or other disposition of land or interests in land pre-27 September 1989), in relation to English land (see Dicey and Morris, p.1257: and registration of an estate contract relating to English land as a Class C (iv) land charge under s.2(4) of the Land Charges Act 1972 may have to be treated in the same manner as s.40(1) – although, note that in Canada compliance with notarial form seems to have been treated effectively as a matter of substance for the proper law, rather than as one of form for choice of law purposes: *Lehndorf Property Management* v. *McGrath and Eagle* [1984] 3 WWR 187). It is unclear, however, whether s.40(1) falls within Article 9 at all since in the absence of the requisite written evidence, the contract is unenforceable, not invalid (Article 9 is headed 'formal *validity*', even though Article 9(6) itself simply refers to 'form'); if it is held not to do so, Article 14(2) will arguably apply instead (although, in Chapter 19 below, concerning modes of proof of contract under Article 14(2), it is even questioned whether the latter is intended to cover such written requirements for proof of contract, a matter recommended for submission to the European Court of Justice for interpretation – and if these were then held not to be modes of proof for purposes of Article 14(2), *lex fori* would govern instead under national English private international law, since the matter would be excluded from the Convention's scope, as evidential and procedural under Article 1(2)(h)); if Article 14(2) *does* apply, English *lex fori* will also then be able to re-enter the picture via this indirect route under Article 14(2) (and were an informal contract to be permitted in relation to the English land by one of the Article 9(1)–(3) foreign laws by virtue of Article 14(2), the former, presumably, would nonetheless still be subject to mandatory English *lex situs* under Article 9(6) in any event, so that s.40(1) would remain applicable – unless of course it were to be held, unjustly in the present view, that Article 9(6) was inapplicable in the Article 14(2)–context, through the former's specific reference to mandatory requirements *of form*, meaning formal *validity*, of *lex situs*, in which case reliance would then have to be placed upon Article 7(2) for continued application of s.40(1)). By virtue of s.2(8) of the Law of Property (Miscellaneous Provisions) Act 1989, s.40(1) of the 1925 Act ceases to have effect in relation to contracts made on or after 27 September 1989. Instead, the latter contracts must comply with s.2(1) of the 1989 Act, which requires them to be made *in writing* if they are to exist and to be valid at all (see s.2(4)). There would be no such problem, consequently, over direct inclusion of s.2(1) within the mandatory provision of Article 9(6) on formal *validity* – unless, of course, the distinction between formal validity and modes of proof under Articles 9 and 14(2) respectively, and designation of a requirement as a procedural mode of proof under the latter, were held not merely to turn on the effects of non-compliance as being invalidity or unenforceability, but also upon the policy underlying the particular rule, as being one of party-protection (Article 9) or proof of contractual existence and terms (Article 14(2); see below, Chapter 19). If so, s.2(1) must arguably be considered to fall within Article 14(2) rather than Article 9(6), provided that Article 14(2) itself is broad enough to cover such contracting formalities as 'modes of proof' within the meaning thereof (see below, Chapter 19). In the present submission, however, whereas underlying purpose of formalities should be held to prevent formalities affecting *enforceability* from falling within Article 14(2) as modes of proof where the intention is not to provide evidence of contract but, for example, to protect weaker parties, nevertheless, conversely, the evidential purpose of a rule of formal *validity* of contracts (see Law of Property (Miscellaneous Provisions) Act 1989 s.2(1)) should not be considered to remove the latter from the scope of Article 9. Thus, the overall position should be held to be as follows:

a) if effect of non-compliance consists of formal *invalidity*, Article 9 should apply, not Article 14(2), even if the underlying purpose of the rule of form is to ensure that contractual existence and terms are substantiated;
b) if effect of failure to adopt the prescribed form is *unenforceability* of the contract, Article 9 is clearly inapplicable, and
   (i) where the purpose of the formal requirement is one of proof of contract and terms, Article 14(2) arguably (but if not so held to be included within Article 14(2) as a 'mode of proof', *lex fori* under national English private international law of procedure, since the matter would be excluded from the Convention's scope under Article 1(2)(h), as evidential and procedural), will apply, as to the procedural mode of proof, but
   (ii) where the object of the formal rule is not so evidential, Article 14(2) is also inapplicable and laws generally applicable under the Convention should govern: thus, Article 10 merely lists matters subject to applicable law *in particular* (see below, Chapters 15 and 19).

15 Article 10: Scope of Applicable Law

Article 10

Scope of the applicable law

The law applicable to a contract by virtue of Articles 3 to 6 and 12 of this Convention shall govern in particular:

Article 10 deals with the general scope of applicable law under Articles 3 (choice of law), 4 (applicable law in the absence of choice), 5 (consumer contracts choice of law and applicable law in the absence thereof), 6 (individual employment contracts choice of law and applicable law in its absence) and 12 (law applicable between voluntary assignor and assignee of rights).

Matters listed in Article 10(1) (in conjunction with Article 8) as falling within the scope of applicable law are those generally known as 'substance' or 'essential validity' of contracts.

However, use of the expression 'in particular' thereunder shows that the list is not to be regarded as exhaustive (Report, p.32), but, nevertheless, that aspects included in the list are able to be treated as unquestionably governed by applicable law (Fletcher, p.173).

On the other hand, the list is subject to certain limitations:

a   in accordance with Article 1(2)(h), any aspects of areas referred to, which are held to be procedural in nature, are excluded from the Convention's scope and, consequently, from that of applicable law thereunder, subject to specific provision made in relation to certain matters dealt with under Article 14 (presumptions of law, burden and modes of proof);

b   consent and capacity are the province of special provision for applicable law under Articles 8 and 11 respectively, as are a third person's rights of subrogation under Article 13;
c   formal validity is naturally outside the list and the subject of separate regulation under Article 9.

Thus, Articles 3–6 and 12 show how applicable law is to be determined; Article 10 says what it governs.

(A) INTERPRETATION;

'Interpretation' may be taken to refer to national rules and methods of contractual construction (such as whether terms may be interpreted in the light of earlier or subsequent negotiations: *St Pierre* v. *South American Stores Ltd* [1937] 1 All ER 206, 209), perhaps as influenced by considerations of uniformity, on analogy with Article 18 relating to interpretation of the Convention itself, where contracting parties' intentions are ambiguous or unclear. Such matters of interpretation of contractual terms held to exist, to be carried out in accordance with applicable law under Article 10(1)(a), are to be distinguished from modes of proof of existence of contracts and their terms, which are questions of procedure, for determination by laws referred to in Article 14(2), otherwise excluded from the Convention's substantive scope under Article 1(2)(h) (see *Korner* v. *Witkowitzer* [1950] 2 KB 128, at national English private international law).

Thus, for example, if the parties have used a technical expression which is redolent of a legal system other than that of applicable law, the former's meaning will be applied, and even if the term is known under applicable law itself, the latter's meaning will not automatically be adopted if this is held not to have been intended by the parties, in accordance with applicable law's canons of construction (see *Rowlett Leaky & Co.* v. *Scottish Provident Institution* [1927] 1 Ch.55); and the same principle will be applied in order to determine intended contractual currency, where a multinational currency is agreed upon without further express elaboration: for example, the price is stated to be 'one hundred dollars' (see *Bonython* v. *Commonwealth of Australia* [1951] AC 201); it will be recalled from Chapter 8 that law of the country of the designated currency may itself be found to be the impliedly chosen, severable applicable law under Article 3(1)), and generally, use of technical expressions characteristic of a particular legal system may of course itself also be a factor in deciding upon implied choice of law under Article 3(1) and applicable law in the absence of choice under Articles 4(5) and 6(2).

Presumably, if there is more than one applicable law, because parties have chosen the law to apply to part only of their contract under Article

3(1) (or laws to govern different parts), so that the remainder is subject to applicable law in the absence of choice under Article 4(1), or because the contract is severable under Article 4(1), rules of contractual interpretation of a particular part of the contract are those of applicable law governing that part. This could prove interesting if the seller's delivery obligations were to be subject to the law of state X, and the remainder of the contract, including acceptance and payment, to the law of state Y, and the contract stated that the seller was required to tender delivery of the goods to the buyer and the buyer to accept them within two days. Which law would then govern interpretation if 'tender' meant physical presentation of the goods under Y law, whereas a mere demonstration of the seller's willingness to do so was sufficient under X law?

(B) PERFORMANCE;

(2) IN RELATION TO THE MANNER OF PERFORMANCE AND THE STEPS TO BE TAKEN IN THE EVENT OF DEFECTIVE PERFORMANCE REGARD SHALL BE HAD TO THE LAW OF THE COUNTRY IN WHICH PERFORMANCE TAKES PLACE.

SUBSTANCE OF PERFORMANCE

Matters concerning the substance and initial legality of contracting parties' performance obligations are within the scope of the applicable law, under Article 10(1)(b) (*Jacobs* v. *Crédit Lyonnais* (1884) 12 QBD 589) (see too Article 8(1) on general contractual legality, and Article 10(1)(d) below on supervening illegality leading to discharge).

Excluded therefrom, consequently, are questions relating to the *manner* of performance (Article 10(2)) and issues classified as *procedural* and accordingly as outside the Convention's scope (Article 1(2)(h)): except that, in the latter respect, Article 14 (to which Article 1(2)(h) is expressly subject) specifically brings within the scope of, *inter alia*, applicable law, presumptions of law, burden of proof, and modes of proof.

The Report indicates the following aspects to be included within the *substance* of performance:

- standard of contractual performance and exactness thereof;
- conditions relating to the place and time of performance;
- extent to which the obligations can be performed by a person other than the party liable;
- conditions as to performance of the obligation both in general and in relation to certain categories of obligation (joint and several obliga-

tions, alternative obligations, divisible and indivisible obligations, pecuniary obligations);
- where performance consists of payment of a sum of money, the conditions relating to the discharge of the debtor who has made the payment, appropriation of sums, and receipts.

To the preceding should be added *inter alia*:

- relations between a principal and a third party in a contract effectively concluded by an agent (*Chatenay* v. *Brazilian Submarine Telegraph Co.* [1891] 1 QB 79) (although, see Article 1(2)(f) as to coming into being of such relationship, excluded from the Convention's scope);
- right to, and rate of, interest on a contractual debt (*Mount Albert Borough Council* v. *Australiasian Temperance and General Mutual Life Assurance Society* [1938] AC 224) (right to interest on damages for breach of contract is a matter of 'consequences of breach' under Article 10(1)(c): *Miliangos* v.*George Frank (Textiles) Ltd (No.2)* [1977] QB 489; *Midland International Trade Services Ltd* v. *Sudairy* (1990) *Financial Times*, 2 May; but rate thereof may be procedural for *lex fori*, *ibid.*, and Cheshire and North, pp.96–7);
- money of account, value thereof, and legality of tender (*Re Chesterman's Trusts* [1923] 2 Ch.466); it is submitted that *lex pecuniae* under pre-existing English private international law is translated into severable applicable law, governing those particular matters of currency valuation and designation, under Articles 3 and 4 of the Convention;
- arguably, the requirement of notice of termination or rescission to be given to the party in breach under certain laws (although, *form* thereof is governed by Article 9(4)), unless this is considered to be one of the consequences of breach within Article 10(1)(c), and subject always to *lex loci solutionis* under Article 10(2) in respect of the *manner* of carrying out any such steps to be taken in the event of a defective performance;
- illegality of performance; consequently, illegality – whether of the contract as a whole and affecting existence or validity (see Article 8(1)) or solely of performance and initial (Article 10(1)(b)) or supervening leading to discharge (Article 10(1)(d)) – is not for regulation alternatively according to *lex loci solutionis* as such (see *Ralli Brothers* v. *Compania Naviera Sota y Aznar* [1920] 2 KB 287, and *Libyan Arab Foreign Bank* v. *Bankers Trust Co.* [1989] 3 All ER 252, at national private international law): *except that* Article 7(2) may be

called in aid, in the case of mandatory domestic legality rules of the English forum (which *may* – dependent upon the construction of *Ralli* – themselves include reference to foreign *lex loci solutionis* on supervening illegality of performance) (and possibly – though probably not – subject also to public policy under Article 16 in respect of foreign legality laws).

MANNER OF PERFORMANCE

(a) Meanings

Article 10(2) requires regard to be had to the law of the country in which performance takes place, in relation to the 'manner of performance' and 'steps to be taken in the event of defective performance'. What is the meaning of these expressions?

Manner of performance has no precise and uniform meaning amongst various national laws and is nowhere defined in the Convention. The Report (p.33) states that it is for *lex fori* to determine its meaning, and that normally it might include

- public holidays;
- the manner in which goods are to be examined;
- steps to be taken if goods are refused.

Cheshire and North, in discussing the corresponding rule of national English private international law that *lex loci solutionis* governs mode of performance (*Jacobs* v. *Crédit Lyonnais* (1884) 12 QBD 589, 601), consider that it may be better to abandon any attempt at precision and 'merely to say that the minor details of performance fall to be governed by the law of the place of performance' (pp.495–6). They go on to provide some examples of such minutiae (*ibid.*):

- money of payment;
- date at which a bill of exchange matures for payment;
- date at which lay days begin to run;
- hours during which delivery may be tendered (normal business hours);
- how to effect delivery alongside a steamer.

Another example might be the need to obtain an export licence and customs clearance – no law other than that of the country of export could possibly have so direct an interest (see *A.V.Pound & Co. Ltd* v. *M.W.Hardy & Co.* [1956] 1 All ER 639,642); although, this is a slightly different type of case from the rest, as it relates not to the immediate physical performance of the contractual obligation, but to the steps to be taken in order to gain the necessary authority to effect the latter.

In the present submission, there is in essence no truly independent concept of 'manner of performance', to be subjected in principle to *lex loci solutionis* rather than to applicable law, since the legal obligation, say, to deliver goods under a contract of sale, in a particular place, at a particular time, and in a particular way, is surely a matter for the parties' agreement, to be carried out according to the law governing the contract. All that may be said, therefore, without a great deal of precision, is that if *lex loci solutionis* is to be permitted to have any scope at all in relation to manner of contractual performance, and whether on a mandatory or discretionary basis, under a particular conflicts system, this should be restricted to those legal obligations which have the *closest possible proximity to actual physical performance of the main substance of the contract*, and which thereby touch and concern the established methods of conducting social and economic intercourse in the society in which such performance is to take place, the closest analogy from a different sphere being that of proper classification of marital ceremonial formalities for regulation according to *lex loci celebrationis*. Thus, for example, it is considered, whereas obligations of creditors to deliver goods to the debtor's address, or of debtors to pay at the creditor's address, should be a matter for the law governing the contract, actual hours of delivery – say, whether midnight is reasonable – and the concept of deliverable state, and whether delivery on the path or at the front doorstep is required, are arguably all matters of manner of performing, properly referable to the *lex loci solutionis*, as are public holidays and money of payment. (Less convincing to be so classified, however, are some of the other examples provided by Cheshire and North – see above, p.301.) In essence therefore, the question should not be: is this particular matter an issue of mode of performance, in which case it will be governed according to *lex loci solutionis*; instead, it should be asked whether the particular issue is properly subject to *lex loci solutionis* rather than to any other law, in which case it may then be correctly classified as relating to mode of performance?

Steps to be taken in the event of defective performance should be understood to refer to those formal acts which may have to be undertaken under certain laws as a condition of terminating a contract and proceeding to remedies for breach, such as the giving of notice of termination, or a warning thereof, or protest and time for remedying the defect. 'Defective' performance itself, it is submitted, may also consist of complete failure to perform, as well as partial or incorrect performance. Reference of such matters to *lex loci* may prove controversial, since these are steps which one might normally regard as being appropriate for law governing the contract to regulate, wherever they are a pre-condition to *existence of liability* according to the contract or applicable law (see Article 10(1)(b) and (c)); whilst, when such steps are pre-requisites to the *bringing of proceedings* and do not affect liability itself, their proper classification should strictly be procedural and consequently excluded from the Convention's scope altogether (see Article 1(2)(h); and *General Steam Navigation Co.* v. *Guillou* (1843) IIM. & W. 877). Perhaps, therefore, interpretation of 'steps' as being confined to purely physical acts in relation to contractual performance – for example, procedure for return of defective goods to the transferor – may come to be preferred. Or, at least, if preceding contractual or legal requirements for liability to exist according to applicable law are truly felt to be indicated, such as, for example, notice of termination to the party alleged to be in breach (see Report p.33), scope of *lex loci* in relation to such *steps* to be taken might appropriately be limited to the *mode* of taking the steps in question, according to the spirit of Article 10(2): for instance, to methods by which, and days upon which, such notice of termination may be given (subject always of course to the law applicable to the *form* of any such *acts* in relation to the contract, under Article 9(4): see above, p.300).

(b) Applicable law

Article 10(2) states that in relation to manner of performance and steps to be taken in the event of defective performance regard shall be had to

the law of the country in which performance takes place.

What is the effect of the words 'regard shall be had'?

Three points should be made.

a First, the Report states that Article 10(2) says that a court may have regard to the law of the place of performance and may consider its relevance (p.33); this is not acceptable – English and foreign texts clearly provide that regard 'shall' be had to that law; consequently, the court must at some point at least refer to that law.

b Secondly, however, *must* the court then apply that law? The Report (*ibid.*) says that the court may consider whether such law has any relevance to the manner in which the contract should be performed and has a discretion whether to apply it in whole or in part (*quaere* whether this includes not applying it at all) so as to do justice between the parties, and Article 10(2) does after all merely say regard shall be had to that law, not that it *shall be applied.* Again, this is felt to be unsatisfactory: unless the words 'regard shall be had' are construed as meaning 'are to be applied' (and exclusively of the law applicable to the contract, as well), they are really deprived of all sense; for, what certainty or coherence would there be in respect of law applicable to manner of performance, if courts were to enjoy such discretionary ability to review applicability of *lex loci solutionis* in relation to what is held to be manner of performance, and not even to the exclusion of applicable law? (Suggested exclusive operation of *lex loci solutionis* would seem to conform with pre-existing English conflicts – at least in the absence of evidence that parties intended the proper or any other law to apply: Dicey and Morris, Rule 186(2).)

c   Thirdly, on the other hand, it is believed that the courts will nonetheless possess a 'discretionary', refinement power in the operation of Article 10(2), in a sense that is less likely than the preceding to threaten the stability of contractual relations and the administration of justice in such matters, namely, to decide which elements of contractual performance are to be regarded as sufficiently proximate to the interests of states and parties as to require and justify application of *lex loci solutionis* thereto in the manner described above and on the basis of established and developing precedents (the comments in the Report, above, may even be taken to support such approach, in essence); yet, once it has been so decided that *manner* of performance, within such meaning of Article 10(2), is thus involved, there should then be no discretion as to applicability of *lex loci solutionis* thereunder.

As for the expression in Article 10(2) 'country in which performance takes place', just as it was submitted that *defective* performance, expressly referred to therein, and for which the preceding expression is exactly appropriate, should also be taken to include *non*-performance, so too, it is considered, should the aforementioned expression also be held to refer to countries of the agreed venue in which performance *is to take place* or *ought to have taken place* in such cases of failure to perform the contract (or where the defect is itself performance other than in the agreed country).

(C) WITHIN THE LIMITS OF THE POWERS CONFERRED ON THE COURT BY ITS PROCEDURAL LAW, THE CONSEQUENCES OF BREACH, INCLUDING THE ASSESSMENT OF DAMAGES IN SO FAR AS IT IS GOVERNED BY RULES OF LAW;

THE CONSEQUENCES OF BREACH

'Consequences' is another extremely wide and vague term employed by Article 10(1)(c).

Article 10: Scope of Applicable Law 305

The following two 'consequences' must clearly be taken to be included (see too Report, p.33):

- effects upon the subsistence of the contract itself: for example, automatic discharge and termination; or right of the injured party to rescind, on notice or otherwise;
- effects upon the parties: for example, liability of the guilty party for breach of contract, including matters of causation and remoteness of damage (although, it is debatable whether right of the party in breach to the return of defective property previously delivered should also be covered in the United Kingdom, in view of the latter's reservation under Article 22(1)(b) not to apply Article 10(1)(e), regarding such consequences of *nullity* of contracts, given effect to under 1990 Act, s.2(2) – is it a case of *eiusdem generis*, or *exclusio unius*?).

As to further consequences of breach, however, there is a lack of clarity from the language of the text. Under pre-existing English conflicts (a) types of remedy available in English courts are obviously a matter of procedure for *lex fori* – for example, damages or discretionary specific performance or injunction; (b) similarly as to possibilities of set-off (*Meyer* v. *Dresser* (1864) 16 CB (N.S.) 646); (c) remoteness of damage from breach of contract is substantive, for the proper law (*D'Almeida Araujo Lda* v. *Becker & Co. Ltd* [1953] 2 QB 329); (d) quantification of damages for breach is procedural for *lex fori* (*ibid.*); (e) right to interest on damages for breach is substantive for the proper law (*Miliangos* v. *George Frank (Textiles Ltd (No.2)* [1977] QB 489; *Midland International Trade Services Ltd* v. *Sudairy* (1990) *Financial Times*, 2 May); (f) rate of such interest is probably for *lex fori* (*ibid.*, and see Cheshire and North, pp.96–7).

In principle, all such matters may now have to be regarded as being covered by applicable law under Article 10(1)(c), *a fortiori* by virtue of the express inclusion therein of 'the assessment of damages'.

However, there are restrictions on applicable law's scope of operation in relation thereto, contained in Article 10(1)(c) itself, which may yet serve to undo such consequences.

LIMITATIONS ON APPLICABLE LAW

(a) Within the Limits of the Powers Conferred on the Court by its Procedural Law

Only remedies of applicable law known to *lex fori*, and applicable according to its limitations – for example, on a discretionary basis alone – will be given effect to under Article 10(1)(c) (*Baschet* v. *London Illustrated Standard Co.* [1900] 1 Ch.73; *Phrantzes* v. *Argenti* [1960] 2 QB 19).

(b) ...Assessment of Damages in so far as it is Governed by Rules of Law

As seen, matters of quantification are traditionally for *lex fori*'s procedure: this may comprise features such as fixed or maximum amounts for particular losses (although, if the basis of the limitation is restriction of recoverable loss to certain types of damage, it is submitted that the rule is then one of substance for proper law), reduction through failure to mitigate a loss, and whether damages may be awarded in periodic payments as well as in a lump sum and subsequently increased through further loss. On the other hand, it is considered that effectiveness of agreements on liquidated damages for breach should be held to be a matter of substance for proper law, although, thereafter obviously relevant to assessment of the amount of damages, if any, to be awarded according to *lex fori*. Under pre-existing English conflicts, ability to award damages in a foreign currency is a procedural question for *lex fori* (*Miliangos* v. *George Frank (Textiles) Ltd* [1976] AC 443; *The Despina R* [1979] AC 685), although identification of such currency is a substantive matter for *lex causae* (*Kraut AG* v. *Albany Fabrics Ltd* [1977] QB 182) (the rule of English law as *lex causae* is that the damages should be assessed in the currency of the plaintiff's loss, not, however, automatically the plaintiff's own currency: *The Folias* [1979] AC 685). Seemingly, therefore, as an aspect of assessment of damages within Article 10(1)(c), ability to award damages in a foreign currency may now effectively have to be treated as a substantive matter for applicable law under the Convention (perhaps a more logical classification than at present); except that where the position is that *lex causae* permits damages awards in foreign currency, but *lex fori* does not *and* classifies the question as procedural, it would seem that a foreign damages award would lie outside 'the limits of the powers conferred on the court by its procedural law' within the meaning of Article 10(1)(c).

Apparently, therefore, the above formula in Article 10(1)(c) represents a compromise: the Report explains the division of opinion between, on the one hand, negotiators who believed that assessment of damages was a question of fact, to be carried out according to economic and social conditions in the forum state, possibly by a jury, and, on the other hand, those who pointed to laws or conventions prescribing fixed amounts under definite rules; and accordingly, the Working Group decided to limit Article 10(1)(c) damages-assessment solely to *rules of law* 'given that questions of fact will always be a matter for the court hearing the action' (p.33).

In the present submission, however, this is an inadequate basis for the construction of Article 10(1)(c). Certainly, there are elements in the assessment of damages which should only be dealt with by the court on a factual basis, abstracted from the operation of legal principle: what is the higher market price of goods which the seller failed to deliver; how much did the buyer reasonably have to pay for the repair of faulty goods sold to him? Nevertheless, so obvious and inevitable a restriction upon operation of applicable law surely could not be the sole intention of the *rules of law*-limitation in Article 10(1)(c), which would then leave within the sphere of applicable law as issues of substance all those matters of assessment referred to, normally thought of as procedural and for *lex fori* (though subject of course to the limits of the court's powers under its procedural law) – even though, strictly speaking, such national 'procedural' rules would classify as being governed by 'rules of law' no less than national 'substantive' aspects of damages. The reference to 'rules of law' in Article 10(1)(c), therefore, it is suggested, should be taken to mean *substantive* legal norms concerning assessment of damages, as so classified, rather than *procedural* rules of law relating thereto, although any such classification should be carried out in the light of the fundamental Convention policy of displacing national variations on applicable law of contract, including reduction of the procedural sphere wherever appropriate (perhaps the rules should only be classified as procedural, where a foreign law would be 'intolerably difficult to apply' – see Morse, 'The EEC Convention on the Law Applicable to Contractual Obligations' (1982), 2 *Yearbook of European Law*, 107,155); and accordingly, Article 10(1)(c) should not, it is believed, be construed as effectively bringing about a reclassification of procedural aspects of damages at national law, as substantive under the Convention: indeed, Article 1(2)(h) expressly excludes procedure from the Convention's scope, without prejudice to Article 14, *not 10*. Finally, damages assessment, like other consequences of breach, is also subject to the general limitation under Article 10(1)(c), that operation of foreign applicable laws should be procedurally possible in the forum: if, for example, periodical payments were classified as substantive for Convention purposes, they could still only be awarded if capable of being properly adjudicated upon and administered under *lex fori*.

(D) THE VARIOUS WAYS OF EXTINGUISHING OBLIGATIONS, AND PRESCRIPTION AND LIMITATION OF ACTIONS;

Discharge and extinction of obligations, through frustration or otherwise, is traditionally a matter for the proper law (*Jacobs* v. *Crédit Lyonnais* (1884) 12 QBD 589; *National Bank of Greece and Athens SA* v. *Metliss* [1958] AC 509; *Adams* v. *National Bank of Greece and Athens SA* [1961] AC 255). Limitation of actions was originally classified as procedural for *lex fori* (*British Linen Co.* v. *Drummond* (1830) 10 B. & C. 903).

However, a change was brought about in England and Wales by the Foreign Limitation Periods Act 1984 (and by the Prescription and Limitation (Scotland) Act 1984 in Scotland), s.1(1)(a) of which provides that foreign *lex causae*'s limitation rule shall apply, to the exclusion of English law. It is not entirely clear whether, technically, the Act also brings about a change in the classification of limitation from the original procedural to substantive. If the former remains, it could be argued that Article 10(1)(d) is subject to Article 1(2)(h) generally excluding evidence and procedure from the Convention's scope. The better view, nonetheless, is that s.1(1) of the 1984 Act effectively alters the previous classification to substantive (although, s.4(2) casts certain doubts on this; and furthermore, the Law Commission, in its Report, 'Classification of Limitation in Private International Law' (LAW COM. No.114, 1982), on which the 1984 Act is based, expressly refrained from reclassifying foreign and English limitation periods as substantive rather than procedural, in contrast to the approach taken in the earlier Working Paper (No.75, 1980 para.56(a)), preferring instead the more direct approach of simply stating that limitation provisions of *lex causae* are always to be applied: paras 4.4 and 4.5; however, the Report does indicate that the former course would merely have been declaratory and, consequently, unnecessary, and indeed, one of the factors which led the Law Commission in the direction of altering the previous practice of applying *lex fori* on limitation was the fact that accession by the United Kingdom to the Obligations Convention would bring this step about in relation to contracts – but not to tort, or contracts outside the Convention – in any event (paras 3.9 and 4.41); clearly then, whatever the proper classification of *English* limitation periods might be following the 1984 Act, procedural or otherwise, Article 10(1)(d) has the effect that courts of foreign Contracting States referring to English law as that which is to govern the contract under the Convention are required to treat English limitation provisions as being included amongst those applicable to the contract).

Plainly, where applicable law is severable under Convention Articles 3 and 4, the limitation rule of that law which governs the obligation upon which the plaintiff's action is based must be taken to be that which applies to the proceedings, under Article 10(1)(d): if more than one claim is involved, and these are subject to separate applicable laws, only those which are not out of time according to the relevant applicable law may be proceeded with. (The Report, p.33, simply states that Article 10(1)(d) must be applied 'with due regard to the limited admission of severability (*dépeçage*) in Articles 3 and 4'.)

Finally, operation of applicable law to the 'various ways of extinguishing obligations' under Article 10(1)(d) is consistent with the general English rule that discharge of a debt or contract under a foreign bankruptcy law is only effective if recognized by the proper law of the contract (Dicey and Morris, Rule 169; *Gibbs* v. *Société Industrielle et Commerciale des Métaux* (1890) 25 QBD 399). However, the further rule of pre-existing English conflicts is that English courts will give effect to an English, Scottish or Northern Irish bankruptcy operating under a United Kingdom statute, irrespective of the contract's foreign proper law (Dicey and Morris, Rules 163 and 170; *Sidway* v. *Hay* (1824) 3 B. & C. 12; *Ellis* v. *M'Henry* (1871) LR 6 CP 228). This limitation upon the scope of a non-United Kingdom applicable law under the Convention by virtue of Article 10(1)(d) is thus preserved – *either* on the ground that it concerns a matter of procedure and the administration of justice, excluded from the Convention's scope under Article 1(2)(h), *or* as amounting to mandatory application of the forum's statute law under Article 7(2) (provided that, in the case of Scottish or Northern Irish bankruptcy, the English statute may thus be relied on, and vice versa, given inapplicability of Article 7(1) in the United Kingdom, under 1990 Act s.2(2) and the treatment of separate parts of the United Kingdom as separate countries for purposes of application of the Convention's rules, under Article 19(1) and 1990 Act s.2(3)).

(E) THE CONSEQUENCES OF NULLITY OF THE CONTRACT

Some of the drafters opposed the inclusion of Article 10(1)(e), because, as under English law, rights of restitution on contractual avoidance fell within the realm of quasi-contract, rather than contract, and were consequently outside the strict scope of the Convention (Report, p.33; Hansard, HL Vol. 513, cols 1258–9; and see further, Bennett, 'Choice of Law Rules in Claims of Unjust Enrichment' (1990), 39 *ICLQ*, 136, as to non-contractual nature of quasi-contract, even when arising from, for example, contractual nullity rather than from a different source of unjust enrichment). The majority, however, favoured its retention, and in order to cater for the dissenters, provision is made by Article 22(1)(b) for Contracting States to reserve the right not to apply Article 10(1)(e). The United Kingdom availed itself of the latter facility, and, accordingly, s.2(2) of the 1990 Act prevents *inter alia* Article 10(1)(e) from having the force of law in the United Kingdom. (Section 4(1)(b), however, seems to contemplate that the United Kingdom might withdraw its reservation, under Article 22(3), in which case Article 10(1)(e) may be given the force of law in the United Kingdom by Order in Council.) In the Judgments Convention case of *Kleinwort Benson Ltd and Barclays Bank plc* v. *Glasgow City Council* (1992) *The Times*, 17 March, HIRST J held that claims by two banks for restitution of sums paid to Glasgow City Council under agreements which were *ultra vires* the local authority and consequently void *ab initio* were not to be classified as relating to a *contract*, for the purpose of conferral of jurisdiction upon English courts for the place of performance of the contractual obligation under Article 5(1) of Schedule 4 to the Civil Jurisdiction and Judgments Act 1982 (dealing with internal jurisdiction within the United Kingdom, and based upon Article 5(1) of the Judgments Convention, the latter being applicable to international cases, not confined to the United Kingdom) over the defendant possessing its seat as domicile in Scotland; the opposite construction would have placed a severe strain on the language of Article 5(1), given that the transactions were taken to be void *ab initio*; and HIRST J expressly made the point that, in considering Article 10(1)(e) of the Obligations Convention, as an aid to interpretation of Article 5(1), whilst it was doubtless proper and necessary for the Obligations Convention to have dealt with consequences of nullity of contract thereunder, as a comprehensive conflicts code, nevertheless, it by no means followed that such consequences were matters relating to a contract, since *ex hypothesi* no contract existed – and indeed, the United Kingdom had explicitly excluded Article 10(1)(e) from applying.

Thus, return of money paid, or restoration of property, on nullity of contract, together with the value of any fruits and gains, or interest, less whatever expenses may have been incurred, is a matter for national conflicts rules in the United Kingdom: that is, *lex causae condictionis*, the proper law of the obligation to restore the benefit of unjust enrichment, and in the case of contracts, as under Article 10(1)(e), what would have been the proper law of the contract from which the claim arose, if it had been validly concluded (Dicey and Morris, Rule 203 (2)(a)). North (in North (ed.), *Contract Conflicts* (1982) p.16–17; see too Bennett (1990) 39 *ICLQ*, 136,167–8)) points out that such authorities as exist concern cases in which there has been no choice of law by parties to govern issues of quasi-contractual restitution (*Fibrosa Spolka Akcyjna* v. *Fairbairn Lawson Combe Barbour Ltd* [1943] AC 32; *Arab Bank* v. *Barclays Bank* [1953] 2 QB 527, 572; *BP Exploration Co. (Libya) Ltd* v. *Hunt (No.2)* [1979] 1 WLR 783, affd [1982] 2 WLR 253 (HL); *Etler* v. *Kertesz* (1960) 26 DLR (2d) 209); he doubts whether it would be appropriate to allow parties' express choice in the matter to be given effect to. It seems questionable whether this is correct: in the first place, the objection has been made that the law governing quasi-contractual remedies, if different from the proper law of the contract as a whole, might not itself regard the contract as void (Lasok and Stone, *Conflict of Laws in the European Community* (1987), p.372) (although, admittedly, the point may be an arrow without a head); and secondly, although 'bootstrapping' *might* be said to be inappropriate in the case of consequences of nullity, this is in fact a moot point, given that causes of contractual nullity are unlikely specifically to concern choice of law elements themselves of agreements, which, consequently, may be treated in isolation from the rest of the latter – and at least as superior to any competing applicable law.

16 Article 11: Contractual Incapacity

Article 11

Incapacity

In a contract concluded between persons who are in the same country, a natural person who would have capacity under the law of that country may invoke his incapacity resulting from another law only if the other party to the contract was aware of this incapacity at the time of the conclusion of the contract or was not aware thereof as a result of negligence.

NATIONAL PRIVATE INTERNATIONAL LAW GENERALLY GOVERNS CAPACITY

In principle, capacity of natural (Article 1(2)(a)) and legal (Article 1(2)(e)) persons is excluded from the Convention's scope (civil law countries regarded the matter as one of status, common law as contractual).

National private international law therefore governs.

In the case of natural persons, laws governing capacity to contract, seemingly, may be any of the following:

- *lex domicilii* (*Sottomayor* v. *De Barros (No.1)* (1877) 3 PD 1; *Union Trust Co.* v. *Grosman* 245 US 412 (1918));
- *lex situs* in the case of contracts in respect of immovables (*Bank of Africa* v. *Cohen* [1902] 2 Ch.129 CA);
- *lex loci contractus* (*Male* v. *Roberts*) (1800) 3 Esp. 163;

- (probably objective) proper law (*Charron* v. *Montreal Trust Co.* (1958) 15 DLR (2d) 240; *Bodley Head* v. *Flegon* [1972] 1 WLR 680).

Dicey and Morris, in Rule 182 (p.1202), appear to favour a rule of capacity according to objective proper law and law of a party's domicile and residence, in the alternative.

Capacity of corporations and associations is for their constitutive statutes, as regulated by the law governing their formation – *lex domicilii* (law of incorporation) – and subject to any incapacities imposed according to objective proper law (Dicey and Morris, Rule 174; *Adams* v. *National Bank of Greece SA* [1961] AC 255).

EXCEPTION FOR CAPACITY OF NATURAL PERSONS

In the case of natural persons, Article 11 creates an exception to the operation of national conflicts rules in respect of their contractual incapacity (even where the other party is also a natural person); and this is expressly provided for by Article 1(2)(a), which states that exclusion from the Convention of the status or legal capacity of natural persons is to be 'without prejudice to Article 11'.

The system invoked by Article 11 where a natural person lacks capacity under private international law is that the individual's capacity to contract

> may nonetheless be conferred by the law of the country where contracting parties are situated;

> but the incapacity under the law otherwise applicable according to national conflicts will or can govern instead, where *either* the parties concluded the contract in separate countries *or*, even if not, the other party knew of the individual's incapacity under private international law or should have known but for his negligence.

The method is intended to balance the need to secure protection for incompetent, infirm, feeble-minded, and under-age parties according to applicable *lex nationalis* or *lex domicilii* – as opposed to *lex loci contractus* or the proper law – under national conflicts, with the need to safeguard the other contracting party from discovering that the contract is void for the former's incapacity under the preceding laws, when he dealt in good faith, unaware of the latter, and law of the parties' common country of conclusion conferred capacity thereon (Report, p.34). Apparently, Article 11 is based on the French *Lizardi* case (Cass. (Reg.), 16 January 1861, S.1861.1.305), qualifying the primary French rule of subjecting incapacity to *lex nationalis*.

Commentators are divided as to its merits and in their criticisms: some believe that the needs of international commerce should have been allowed to prevail over protection of the weak (see Lasok and Stone, p.350); others prefer the latter to be favoured at all costs, whatever the good faith of the other party (Hoyer, in Lando (1975), pp.116–17). The present writer himself has called into question the efficacy and justifiability of the underlying mechanism in Article 11 for achieving fairness, whilst endorsing the latter as a meritorious objective (see *International Contracts, 1993*, Barry Rose, and below, pp. 318–19).

The operation of Article 11 in place of national conflicts depends upon a number of conditions being satisfied, as follows.

(a) Contract Concluded Between Persons Who Are in the Same Country

As seen in discussion of Article 9, a *company* may be held to be present in a country for purposes of concluding a contract under the Convention, whenever it is incorporated there, or has its central management and control there, or a place of business there through which the transaction was completed, or even in the absence thereof, if it conducted the business through its representative there. (In view of the express provision under Article 9(3), however, deeming agent's presence to be that of the principal contracting party – corporate or otherwise – for purposes of compliance with contractual formalities, mere transacting through an *agent* in respect of the contract in question, seemingly would not otherwise amount to presence of the principal in the agent's country, neither in the case of Article 9(1) and (2), nor under Article 11 itself. *Quaere*, nevertheless, whether agent's presence, generally, is substituted for that of the principal under Article 11, as in the case of formalities under Article 9(3)? One would have thought not, in the circumstances, specifically requiring reference to be made to the state of mind of a principal contracting party.)

The Report seems to identify the rule of applicable law in Article 11 with that of *lex loci contractus* (p.34) (see too Fletcher, p.158). However, although the latter will frequently be the case, it does not follow automatically under Article 11: for example, parties may contract respectively from states X and Y, and yet, on the day on which the offeree's postal acceptance arrives at the offeror's home in X, having been sent by the offeree from his own home in Y, the offeror happens to be visiting a friend in Y, so that although the parties 'are in the same country' – namely, Y – when the contract is concluded according to applicable law, the latter nevertheless treats the contract as having been concluded on arrival of the letter of acceptance at the offeror's home in X. Capacity is therefore able to be conferred by Y law under Article 11; but X is *lex loci contractus*. (Similarly, if the offeree asks his wife to post his acceptance from their home in Y, but he is in the offeror's state X when she does so, and according to applicable law, acceptance is effective on dispatch of the letter: capacity may be conferred on the offeree by X law under Article 11, but Y is *lex loci contractus*, unless country of *agent's* situation – that of the offeree's wife in Y – is substituted for that of the offeree himself in X under Article 11: see above.) Clearly, it would be better – again, as in the case of Article 9 – if *conclusion* under Article 11 were to be construed as meaning the making of offer and acceptance in the same country by offeror and offeree respectively, rather than in the technical, legal sense of moment of contractual conclusion according to applicable law; if not, then it is suggested that law determining the date of technical conclusion should be that which would apply to contractual existence under the Convention on the assumption that the party in question would be found to possess capacity – *but* that this should be the law which would govern in the absence of choice, rather than in accordance with Article 8(1), given that *capacity* is involved. This is evidently a gap in the Convention's system needing to be filled by the European Court.

If the incapacitated party contracts with several persons undertaking joint liability towards him, and only one of the others is in the same country as the incapacitated party at conclusion, the latter is only restrained as to otherwise applicable law under Article 11 in relation to that party; however, in view of the invalidity of the contract with regard to the other persons by reason of his incapacity under national private international law, the incapacitated party may still be able to claim frustration of the contract with respect to the former party, in accordance with the law otherwise governing the contract.

(b) Law of Common Country Confers Capacity

It has to be the case that capacity exists under the law of the common country, and incapacity under the law otherwise applicable: in the reverse situation, Article 11 is inapplicable, and the party is bound according to private international law and cannot otherwise rely on the incapacity under the law of the common country. If capacity exists under both, Article 11 would seem to be inapplicable, and the law governing under private international law would be the operative law for construction (the Report explains that Article 11 only applies where there is a conflict of laws: p.34).

(c) Only the Party Suffering the Incapacity May Invoke It

This is plain from the wording of the text of Article 11 ('a natural person ... may invoke his incapacity ... if the other party').

WHERE THE EXCEPTION DOES NOT OPERATE

According to Article 11, the party suffering from contractual incapacity under private international law is permitted to invoke that incapacity thereunder, if a number of circumstances exist, as follows.

(a) The Other Party Was Aware of the Incapacity at the Relevant Time

If the other party knew of the incapacity, he has only himself to blame for going ahead with the contract and risking the danger that the incapacitated party would call it off. English and foreign texts of Article 11 refer to the other party's awareness of *this* incapacity: it seems rather futile however not to permit the incapacitated party to rely on an incapacity other than that of which the other party was aware (where perhaps the former is easier to establish), since the effects of his so doing would seem to differ little from the result which would have ensued had the other party known of the precise incapacity relied upon. In all events, as the Report says (p.34), the burden of proving the requisite knowledge or negligence under Article 11 is placed upon the incapacitated party. If there is more than one other party assuming an obligation jointly towards the incapacitated party and only one of them knew of the latter's incapacity, the incapacitated party may only invoke his incapacity against the party with knowledge, but presumably, he might then be able to claim that the entire contract is frustrated in relation to the other contracting parties, by virtue of the law otherwise governing the contract. Finally, it seems clear that knowledge (or negligence) under Article 11 should be as to existence of legal incapacity, rather than merely as to the facts underlying the latter, for example, the relevant party's age – although, conceivably, if that party is *very* young (for example, six years of age!), the other may be fixed with constructive notice of the former's incapacity, or at least be held to fall foul of the negligence condition in Article 11 (see below).

(b) Alternatively, the Other Party was Unaware as a Result of Negligence at the Relevant Time

It seems inconceivable that 'negligence' in the technical sense, embodying all the ingredients of tort, could have been intended. Failure to take reasonable care, in accordance with the usual practices, must surely be the Convention meaning (although, interestingly, the French text uses the word *imprudence*/recklessness rather than *négligence*/carelessness!). The negligence furthermore must be that of the other party (see the French and Italian texts); there would hardly be much point in permitting the incapacitated party to rely thereon where, as a result of the latter's own negligence, the incapacity was not brought to the other party's attention!

As to the circumstances in which lack of reasonable care will be found to have been exercised, this will be a matter of great uncertainty, and depending upon the frequency of their being held to exist, may to that extent take some of the steam out of the Article 11 exception to Article 1(2)(a). The burden, as seen, is on the incapacitated party to show lack of reasonable care as the reason for the other's ignorance: perhaps this would be where the parties had previously transacted and the incapacity had been disclosed, or where the incapacity was fairly notorious in the case of certain nationalities. In the present submission, given the legal and technical nature of the species of knowledge in question, involving issues of private international and domestic law, very few lay persons could reasonably be expected personally to have made themselves aware of another contracting party's capacity. Consequently, the simplest method of proceeding under Article 11 would be for the question of reasonable awareness to be subsumed under the more straightforward test of whether it would have been reasonable to obtain general, professional legal advice on the transaction: if it would have been so, then it should be presumed that the party was negligently ignorant of the incapacity, if he did not seek such advice (it being assumed that the standard English legal practitioner would necessarily have delivered the correct advice on capacity and applicable law); if it would not have been unreasonable not to seek general legal advice (or this was sought, but the relevant information was not then provided), the presumption should be that the party had not been negligent in failing to become aware of the incapacity. Admittedly, the matter of when it is reasonable or not to seek legal advice is still dependent upon policy perceptions of the court applying Article 11, and on which of commercial and weaker parties should receive greater protection. Nevertheless, it is thought that the suggested approach does have the advantage of rendering the difficult provision in Article 11 more *manageable*. Some guidance is to be found in Article 18, requiring Convention rules to be *applied*, not merely interpreted, with regard to its unificationist aims. Presumably, therefore, whereas courts may be willing to conclude that it would have been reasonable to obtain legal advice in the case of many international commercial contracts involving individuals, so that the rule in Article 11 is thus displaced by national private international law in relation thereto, plainly, this would be absurd, for example, in the case of consumer contracts conducted on a large and impersonal scale, or of a holidaymaker purchasing a second-hand car from a native. At least, however, such problems will not have to be faced where the parties actually live in the same country of their common presence and connections with others are lacking, since the Convention, including Article 11 thereof, will itself be inapplicable in accordance with Article 1(1), as the proceedings may then be classified as non-international.

(c) Relevant Time for Knowledge is That of Conclusion of the Contract

The reference to *conclusion*, rather than *concluding*, in English and foreign texts of Article 11 (the French and Italian texts actually refer to the *moment* of the conclusion of the contract) suggests that 'conclusion' therein means technical, legal conclusion, rather than acts of offer and acceptance on the part of offeror and offeree, respectively: and consequently, the moment of conclusion must be determined in accordance with the law which would govern the contract under the Convention if the contract were valid and upheld – although, as will be recalled, the submission was previously made that such investigation into applicable law for these purposes should exclude any choice made by the parties, in view of the fact that its object is to decide upon capacity, a gap in the Convention which needs to be filled. Thus, until that final moment of technical contractual completion, even the offeror will be judged as to the state of his actual or reasonable knowledge in respect of the other party's capacity: if therefore the reasonable means of discovering the other's incapacity only comes to the offeror *after* delivering his final offer, and he does not avail himself thereof, he is then liable to be adjudged negligent as at the subsequent date of acceptance by the offeree, as that of conclusion, for purposes of Article 11.

(d) Foreign Incapacity Not Against Public Policy

Incapacities of a foreign law applicable under private international law (whether the latter applies by virtue of Article 1(2)(a) or in circumstances in Article 11 itself) will of course not be applied if they are regarded as being contrary to public policy: the latter may be resorted to under national English conflicts principles, or arguably, where private international law applies under conditions in Article 11, under Article 16 of the Convention itself, which is expressed to operate in relation to the law of any country 'specified by this Convention' (which may include 'another law' referred to in Article 11). Thus, it *may* be the case from the authorities that contractual incapacity deriving from the general status of prodigality or incompetence under a foreign law will not be recognized (see *Worms v. De Valdor* (1880) 49 LJ Ch.261; *Re Selot's Trusts* [1920] 1 Ch.488; *Re Langley's Settlement Trusts* [1962] Ch.541 – all, however, subjected to much criticism for disregarding essentially protective laws). Again, if law on capacity referred to under national private international law were regarded as *indirectly* applicable by virtue of the Convention in accordance with Articles 1(2)(a) and 11, it may be that its operation could then be held to be subject to resort to mandatory laws on capacity of *lex fori* under Article 7(2) ('Nothing in this Convention shall restrict ...') (although, applicable law of the common state of presence or under private international law in accordance with Article 11, would not also be subject to mandatory rules under Articles 3(3), 5(2) and 6(1), since these deal with safeguards of mandatory rules against applicable *chosen* law, and chosen, seemingly, under Article 3 of the Convention rather than in accordance with any corresponding autonomy provision under national private international law). The contrary – if rather technical – view, of course, would be that the operation of Article 11 in respect of national private international law is purely restrictive and that the latter's operation, subject to the limitation in Article 11, is by virtue of the exclusion of capacity from the Convention's scope under Article 1(2)(a), *not by virtue of Article 11*, and that such excluded matters are not 'in this Convention' and consequently not subject to Article 7(2) (nor to Article 16). In the present writer's opinion, given the main exclusion in Article 1(2)(a), the latter approach should be regarded as correct and ought to prevail (certainly where the condition of common country at conclusion in Article 11 is not satisfied, as well as, it is submitted, where it is so but national conflicts applies by reason of the other party's knowledge or negligence thereunder: see too, earlier pp.250 and 266).

Article 11 has had a fairly bad press amongst the critics because of its adverse effects on certainty and through the need in certain circumstances to discover whether a party's foreign *lex nationalis*, or, as the case may be, *lex domicilii*, under national conflicts, subjects him to an incapacity (see von Hoffmann, in Lando (1975), pp.24–5). The criticism is not entirely justified: reference of capacity to the law applicable to the contract in the absence of choice would be to ignore the protective function of *lex domicilii, et alia*; while abandonment of capacity completely to national conflicts would mean diversity and rejection of unifying, commercially favourable influences. A more sustainable objection to Article 11 would be against the formulation of a contracts choice of law rule based upon proven knowledge or reasonable conduct of a party, the very species of domestic-type legalo-factual complexity which the private international law process is supposed to resolve; nor is it clear why, in principle, a party should be prejudiced through his knowledge of a conflicts rule, since, notwithstanding what must be assumed to be overwhelming support for choice of law rules which promote certainty and familiarity, it is doubtful whether these latter objectives may effectively be converted into the self-fulfilling means themselves. Furthermore, it is not even wholly apparent why an otherwise incapacitated party should be denied that protection simply because the contract is concluded in the same country as that of the other party.

It is submitted, therefore, that the following might be an acceptable alternative to the present Article 11, for possible adoption at some future date:

> The law applicable to the contract in the absence of choice under Article 4 (or 5 or 6) shall govern contractual capacity of a natural person notwithstanding any agreement between the parties as to applicability of that or any other law; except that a natural person may invoke his incapacity resulting from the law of the country of his habitual residence, if that person performed his act towards concluding the contract in that country, and regardless of whether the other party was aware of or ought reasonably to have been aware of the natural person's incapacity under the law of that country.

Article 1(2)(a) would then be amended accordingly so as to exclude reference to contracting capacity of natural persons.

Erratum

Addition to Section (c), p. 315

"A party pleading *the other's* incapacity is thus not the concern of Article 11, although remains subject to the general exclusion of legal capacity of natural persons under Article 1 (2) (a). Accordingly, such party's ability to avoid the contract on the ground of the other's incapacity, and the conditions, if any, for doing so, requiring knowledge or not at the time of contracting, are for the national law applicable under private international law of the forum."

17 Article 12: Voluntary Assignment of Rights

Article 12

Voluntary assignment

1 The mutual obligations of assignor and assignee under a voluntary assignment of a right against another person ('the debtor') shall be governed by the law which under this Convention applies to the contract between the assignor and assignee.

2 The law governing the right to which the assignment relates shall determine its assignability, the relationship between the assignee and the debtor, the conditions under which the assignment can be invoked against the debtor and any question whether the debtor's obligations have been discharged.

Article 12 (and the same may be said of Article 13) is not so much a direct rule of applicable law(s) as one of *internal Convention scope*, dealing with which particular elements and categories of the specified tripartite legal relationship are to be separately treated for purposes of applicable law(s) under the Convention (Article 12(1)), or otherwise (Article 12(2)). Perhaps, therefore, Articles 12 and 13 ought properly to have constituted additional paragraphs in Article 10. The Convention might also have included equivalent provision as to applicable law in respect of novation (and even privity of contract) in order to bring about uniform Contracting State practice (in a novation, under national English conflicts, the discharged and replacement contracts are governed by their respective proper laws: *Re United Railways of the Havana and Regla Warehouses* [1960] Ch.52, 84–5, affd [1961] AC 1007).

VOLUNTARY ASSIGNMENT

Consistent with the overall Convention scope, confined to contractual obligations, Article 12 is concerned with voluntary assignment.

Involuntary assignments, such as garnishment of debts, and their priorities, are consequently matters for national English private international law, which will refer the issue to *lex situs* of the property in question (*Swiss Bank Corporation* v. *Boehmische Industrial Bank* [1923] 1 KB 673; *Re Queensland Mercantile and Agency Co.* [1891] 1 Ch.536).

Assignments by way of subrogation, as an aspect of assignments by operation of law, are governed by Article 13.

LAW APPLICABLE TO ASSIGNOR–ASSIGNEE RELATIONSHIP: ARTICLE 12(1)

Recognizing that in a voluntary assignment of a right against another person ('the debtor'), there are two distinct (though of course related) categories of legal relationship – that existing between assignor and assigneee in the first place, and that between assignee and debtor in the second – which are sought to be created, Article 12 treats of each separately in respect of applicable law.

Article 12(1) concerns the former – the relationship between assignor and assignee – and the second is dealt with under Article 12(2).

Article 12(1) therefore expressly subjects the mutual obligations of assignor and assignee to the law governing *their contract* under the Convention. The Report considers that the provision gives rise to no difficulties of interpretation, and explains that it was not drafted more simply and elegantly – so as to say, for example, *assignment of rights as between assignor and assignee is governed by* – because under German law the word 'assignment' apparently includes effects upon the debtor, the province of Article 12(2).

Accordingly, under the Convention, relations between assignor and assignee may be divided into the following categories for purposes of the laws applicable to their contract.

(a) Capacity to Contract

Subject to the special rule in Article 11 in the case of natural persons, Article 1(2)(a) and (e) excludes legal capacity from the Convention's scope, and consequently national private international law continues to govern this aspect of the assignor–assignee relationship. The old authorities appear to be in a state of some confusion over whether capacity to assign intangible movables is for *lex loci actus* or *lex domicilii* (*Lee* v. *Abdy* (1886) 17 QBD 309; *Republica de Guatemala* v. *Nunez* [1927] 1 KB 669).

Cheshire and North (p.809) suggest that in modern times it ought to be the proper law of the assignment contract which governs capacity.

(b) Formalities

In accordance with Article 9, these (for example, registration) are subject to Article 3- or Article 4- applicable law or *lex loci actus* (*or leges locorum actus*). National English private international law appears to favour *lex loci contractus* alone (*Republica de Guatemala* v. *Nunez* – criticized by Cheshire and North, pp.809–10, as possibly fortuitous, and contrary to modern proper law doctrines in relation to contracts generally).

(c) Essential Validity

Matters of essential validity of the assignment, within Articles 8 and 10(1), are for applicable law under Article 3 or 4, subject to the special rule in respect of consent under Article 8(2). (Cheshire and North suggest that proper law of the assignment should also govern at national private international law, and they cite a dictum in *Trendtex Trading Corpn* v. *Crédit Suisse* [1980] QB 629, 658, affd on other grounds [1982] AC 679, in support. In truth, however, the authorities are at variance with this – see *Re Anziani* [1930] 1 Ch.407: *lex loci actus*, in particular, in the case of intellectual property, such as patents, designs, trademarks and copyright; *Campbell, Connelly & Co.* v. *Noble* [1963] 1 WLR 252: *lex situs*; and Graveson, p.479.)

LAW APPLICABLE TO ASSIGNEE–DEBTOR RELATIONSHIP: ARTICLE 12(2)

This concerns a number of matters affecting the debtor in respect of whose debt the purported assignment is made:

a assignability of the debt in the first place, and the relationship, if any, between assignee and debtor: for example, under English law, life assurance policies, salaries of Crown employees, and certain pensions and rights of action may not be assigned;

b   any conditions which may have to be satisfied before the assignment can be invoked against the debtor: for example, notice of the assignment given to the debtor; joinder of assignor as co-plaintiff in any proceedings brought by the assignee against the debtor;
c   questions of discharge of his obligations by the debtor: including, for example, priorities of assignees of the same debt.

Thus, some laws may actually exclude assignability of intangible movables, or require notice thereof to be given to the debtor for the assignment to be effective, in either case, in order to protect the debtor (see *Linden Gardens Trust Ltd* v. *Lenesta Sludge Disposals Ltd*, and *St Martins Corporation Ltd* v. *Sir Robert McAlpine & Sons Ltd* (1992) *The Times*, 27 February, CA). Article 12(2) subjects such assignability and conditions thereof to *the law governing the right to which the assignment relates*, as opposed to that applicable under the Convention to the assignment as between assignor and assignee under Article 12(1). Thus, law governing the right to which the assignment relates may be, for example, *lex situs* at national private international law, in the case of share transfer, as in *Re Fry* [1946] Ch.312; or that applicable under the Convention itself, if the right is under a contract governed thereby (such as future earnings under a contract of employment subjected to Article 6, *aliter* in the case of excluded EEC insurance) – although, in the latter case, the Report further indicates that, in so far as the right assigned derives from such contract, the latter's terms, if any, govern matters in Article 12(2) as between *assignor* (and presumably also therefore assignee) and debtor, with the exception of their own assignability and subject also to applicable law (p.35).

This regime is in accordance with pre-existing English private international law, subjecting assignability and its conditions to the law governing the original transaction out of which the intangible arose or which created it, for example, the proper law of a transaction creating a debt, as controlling its nature and extent (*Compania Colombiana de Seguros* v. *Pacific Steam Navigation Co.* [1965] 1 QB 101, 128-9; *Kelly* v. *Selwyn* [1905] 2 Ch.117). Thus in *Campbell Connelly & Co. Ltd* v. *Noble* [1963] 1 WLR 252, concerning an agreement subject to English law, assigning US copyright in a musical work, assignability was considered to be a matter for US law, under which the copyright was created, not English proper law of the assignment; again in *Trendtex Trading Corpn* v. *Crédit Suisse* [1982] AC 679, assignability of an English right of action was held to be governed by English law (by which the right was not assignable), notwithstanding the Swiss proper law of the assignment contract – although, the latter would then determine the effects of unassignability upon the continued existence of the contract of assignment as a whole.

However, the principle enshrined in Article 12(2), whereby the assignee–debtor relationship is subjected to the *law governing the right*, should here be elaborated upon in two further respects.

In the first place, the law governing the right assigned is expressed to apply *inter alia* to 'conditions under which the assignment can be invoked against the debtor', under Article 12(2). The question arises, however, of whether that law automatically applies to such matters, or whether Article 12(2) has to be read as being subject to Article 1(2)(h), generally excluding issues of (evidence and) procedure from the Convention's scope. It is submitted that the latter is clearly correct, so that any laws and conditions which are classified as procedural rather than substantive are to be subject to English *lex fori* in accordance with normal practice, and not to the law governing the right (although, the Report – confusingly ('steps' might have been a better word in the circumstances) – indicates that '*procedures*' required to give effect to the assignment in relation to the debtor are also covered by Article 12(2): pp.35–5). On the other hand, however, it would appear to be the case that the domestic English rule whereby an assignee (necessarily equitable) of a chose in action has to join the assignor in an action against the debtor, if notice of the assignment has not been given to the debtor under s.136 of the Law of Property Act 1925 (as well as the latter rule of validity itself of course), may properly have to be classified as substantive, not procedural, and as consequently applicable as part of English law governing the right to which an assignment relates (*Innes* v. *Dunlop* (1800) 8 TR 595; *O'Callaghan* v. *Thomond* (1810) 3 Taunt. 82).

Secondly, the same point may be made with regard to priority of assignees of the same debt, and payment to which amongst whom will discharge the debtor: notwithstanding that the latter issue is expressly included within Article 12(2), law governing the right assigned will not be permitted to regulate priority, *if* the matter is to be classified as procedural – for English *lex fori* – not substantive (foreign laws might give priority to the first in time, unlike English law which favours the first assignee in good faith to give notice to the debtor). Unfortunately, the authorities seem uncertain as to appropriate classification and consequent applicable law under national English conflicts, in the matter of such priorities, and they range between proper law (*Le Feuvre* v. *Sullivan* (1855) 10 Moo. PC 1), *lex situs*, and *lex fori* (*Kelly* v. *Selwyn* [1905] 2 Ch.117). Leading academic opinion appears to favour the proper law (see Cheshire and North, p.813, and Dicey and Morris, pp.964–5; note too Wolff, *Private International Law*, 2nd edn (1950), p.538, as to foreign conflicts systems; Collier, on the other hand, in *Conflict of Laws* (1987), p.223, puts the case for *lex situs*). In view of the artificiality of *situs* in the case of intangibles, it is agreed that the proper law, with concomitant substantive classification of priorities, and resultant applicability of Article 12(2), has much to commend it; and at least, as in the case of the requirement of notice to debtors, the procedural classification, and consequent resort to *lex fori*, would thus be avoided, to the benefit of the Convention's unificationist objectives.

18 Article 13: Subrogation to Contractual Rights

Article 13

Subrogation

1   Where a person ('the creditor') has a contractual claim upon another ('the debtor') and a third person has a duty to satisfy the creditor, or has in fact satisfied the creditor in discharge of that duty, the law which governs the third person's duty to satisfy the creditor shall determine whether the third person is entitled to exercise against the debtor the rights which the creditor had against the debtor under the law governing their relationship and, if so, whether he may do so in full or only to a limited extent.

2   The same rule applies where several persons are subject to the same contractual claim and one of them has satisfied the creditor.

LAW APPLICABLE TO SUBROGATION GENERALLY: ARTICLE 13(1)

(a) Subrogation

Whereas Article 12 deals with voluntary assignment of rights, Article 13 is concerned with the type of assignment by operation of law known as 'subrogation': that is to say, where a third party who has a *duty* towards a creditor to satisfy a debtor's debt to that creditor *must do so or has actually done so*, and thereby becomes entitled (*subrogated*) to the creditor's rights against the debtor according to applicable law. (The Report, p.35, reveals that under the laws of certain legal systems – notably, Articles 1251–3 of the French Civil Code and Articles 1203–3 of the Italian Civil Code – a third party who, though not under a duty to pay the debt, nevertheless has an economic interest in so doing, may be subrogated to the creditor's rights against the debtor, and appears to suggest that Article 13 will consequently also apply thereto. It seems questionable whether this is strictly correct in view of the express reference to 'duty' under Article 13(1), although, on the other hand, the latter is omitted from Article 13(2) – see below. In principle, there is no objection to the approach in the Report; it is simply that there seems no practical scope for its operation: *entitlement* of the third party to be subrogated under national conflicts law (say, of implied contract, quasi-contract, or tort) is not the same as *duty* to satisfy the debt in question and is in fact the very matter for decision according to Article 13(1).)

The standard examples of subrogation are, first, where, according to applicable law, a guarantor (the 'third person') must (that is to say, the obligation has accrued due) fulfil, or has actually fulfilled, his obligation to satisfy the creditor under a contract of guarantee, in the event of the primary debtor's default; and secondly, where an insurer must fulfil, or has fulfilled, his obligation towards the insured, under an insurance policy, to indemnify the insured against loss from breach of a contract with another party. Under English law, in the former case, on payment of what is due under the guarantee, the third-party guarantor is subrogated to the rights of the creditor against the debtor in respect of the debt guaranteed (*Re Lamplugh Iron Ore Co. Ltd* [1927] 1 Ch.308); and in the matter of indemnity insurance, on payment of policy monies to the insured, the third-party insurer is subrogated to the creditor insured's rights against the debtor liable thereto (*Phoenix Assurance Co. v. Spooner* [1905] 2 KB 753). The third-party guarantor or insurer thus becomes vested with the creditor's rights against the debtor according to applicable law.

(b) Limitation to Subrogation to Contractual Claims

Article 13(1) expressly limits its scope to where the creditor's claim against the debtor, to which the third party becomes subrogated, *is in contract*. The reason given is that the Convention is concerned with the law applicable to the exercise of contractual rights of parties against each other (Report, p.35). (Why, therefore, is Article 12 not also so limited to voluntary assignment of *contractual* rights?) Thus, subrogation of an insurer third person to the creditor insured's rights in tort against the debtor tortfeasor is not within Article 13 (to the extent that insurance is otherwise not in any event excluded from the Convention's scope under Article 1(3)). Morse, in *Torts in Private International Law* (1978), p.148, suggests that applicable law in respect of subrogation, in such cases, might be that governing the contract between insurer and insured under national conflicts, rather than that governing the tort. In the present writer's submission, there may be a case for submitting contractual and tortious effectiveness of the subrogation to laws applicable to the contract and tort, respectively.

(c) Applicable Law

Under Article 13(1), the law governing the question whether the third-party payer is subrogated to the rights of the creditor against the debtor existing under the law applicable to the creditor–debtor relationship (the latter being, say, the contract guaranteed) is *that which governs the third-person–creditor relationship* (the latter being the contract of guarantee) and which imposes the duty on the former to satisfy the latter (seemingly, without prejudice to any contract which may exist as between the third person and the debtor, for example an agreement by the former to guarantee the latter's debt, unaffected by Article 13 – see Report, p.35). Whilst at first sight this may appear to differ from Article 12(2) protecting a debtor against voluntary assignment, through continued applicability of the law governing the original assignor–debtor relationship, on closer analysis the subrogation situation is rather different, in that under Article 13 the third person (assignee, under Article 12) has actually *satisfied* the debtor's debt to the creditor, or must do so, in accordance with a *duty* so to act, leading to the assignment *by operation of law* of the creditor's rights to the third person as between the latter: in view of which, application of the third-person–creditor law in relation to the third-person–debtor relationship does not appear objectionable.

Article 13(1) further stipulates – rather unnecessarily, one would have thought – that the law governing the third person's duty to satisfy the creditor not only governs the existence of subrogation as such, but also the extent thereof ('and, if so, whether he may do so in full or only to a limited extent'). Thus, English law would subrogate a guarantor paying *part* of a debt, to the creditor's rights in respect of the latter amount (*Goodwin* v. *Gray* (1874) 22 WR 312).

Naturally, it is only where the third person's duty to satisfy the creditor itself arises from a contract (as opposed to, say, the statutory duty of public authorities to maintain, through social security payments), that *the Convention* – or pre-existing national contract conflicts, in the case of insurance, excluded from the Convention's scope under Article 1(3) in the case of EEC risks – will apply to determine the law governing that relationship, including the question of subrogation. Presumably, in other cases, subrogation will be a matter for whichever law it is which gave rise to the non-contractual duty of the third party to satisfy the creditor.

LAW APPLICABLE TO SUBROGATION ON SATISFACTION OF A COMMON CLAIM: ARTICLE 13(2)

The same rule applies where several persons are subject to the same contractual claim and one of them has satisfied the creditor: that is to say, the law requiring the payer to satisfy the creditor will apply to subrogate the former to the latter's rights against the other debtors, rather than the law(s) governing the other debtors' relationship with the creditor, if different. (Right to contribution from the other debtors would seem to be a matter of substance for that same applicable law governing the payer's right of subrogation: see Graveson, p.614.)

The Report indicates that Article 13(2) operates in relation both to joint and several liability, and to joint alone ('when an indivisible obligation is discharged') (p.35).

Article 13(2) understandably only refers to where the single payer *has satisfied* the claim, since the mere duty to pay *if* called upon, without yet having been so – in contrast to that in Article 13(1) – would be a primary duty, and moreover, could not possibly give rise to subrogation until the debtor had actually been requested to pay and thereafter successfully pursued for payment. (Presumably, where the payer satisfies the entire debt *without* having been under a duty to do so, it would be the law governing his relationship with the creditor in respect of the partial debt which would apply to determine his rights of subrogation.)

Finally, it should be noted that the Convention makes no internal scope provision as to applicability of contract law in relation to questions of (a) contractual exclusion of liability in tort; and (b) direct actions by third-party claimants in tort against insurers. English and Scottish Law Commissions, in their 1990 Report, 'Private International Law. Choice of Law in Tort and Delict' (LAW COM. No. 193 SCOT. LAW COM. No. 129), left open the question of whether such matters were contractual or tortious for applicable law (paras 3.49–3.51; see too Kaye *Private International Law of Tort and Product Liability*, 1991, Dartmouth, pp.184 and 185).

19 Article 14: Presumptions, Burden and Modes of Proof

Article 14

Burden of proof, etc.

1 The law governing the contract under this Convention applies to the extent that it contains, in the law of contract, rules which raise presumptions of law or determine the burden of proof.

2 A contract or an act intended to have legal effect may be proved by any mode of proof recognised by the law of the forum or by any of the laws referred to in Article 9 under which that contract or act is formally valid, provided that such mode of proof can be administered by the forum.

As in the case of Articles 12 and 13 (as well as, of course, Article 10), Article 14 (rather quaintly entitled *'Burden of proof, etc.'* in the English text, as opposed simply to *'Proof'* in the others!) operates as an internal Convention rule of scope of applicable law, in relation to certain matters which may (or may not, according to differing views) be held to amount to questions of procedure according to national conflicts classification: namely, presumptions of law, burden of proof, and modes of proof of contract. (It was, however, decided not to deal with 'evidential value': see Report, p.36.) The result is that applicable law under the Convention may indeed be applied to such issues. However, in view of the possible procedural classification of such matters according to pre-existing national conflicts, Article 14 may also be viewed as having an effect upon the *external* scope of the Convention itself (not merely internally, as to that of applicable law) given the general limitation of the latter's operation to substance rather than procedure; and consequently, in order to make clear the *exceptional* nature of the Convention's application, in this manner, to such possibly procedural questions, Article 1(2)(h) expressly excludes evidence and procedure generally from the Convention's scope, *without prejudice to Article 14* (Report, p.36).

PRESUMPTIONS OF LAW AND BURDEN OF PROOF: ARTICLE 14(1)

Presumptions of law may either be irrebuttable or rebuttable: they are irrebuttable when (usually), on proof of certain facts, the court must presume the existence of other facts *in all events* (for example, the presumption of survivorship of the younger person on proof of commorientes, under s.184 of the Law of Property Act 1925); presumptions of law are rebuttable where, on proof of certain facts, the court must presume the existence of other facts *unless the contrary is proven* (for example, presumption of advancement in the case of gifts to a close relative or dependant). So-called 'presumptions of fact' are those where proof of a certain fact *may* be taken to indicate existence of another, by reason of the frequency with which the latter factor has in the past been found to accompany the former, but does not have to be so as a matter of law: for example, loss of a ship shortly after putting to sea, as evidence of its unseaworthiness on leaving harbour: *Pickup* v. *Thames & Mersey Marine Insurance Co.* (1878) 3 QBD 594. (Thus, the various nomenclatures are really quite misleading, since essentially they *all* concern presumed *facts*. Perhaps, therefore, presumptions of law would be better termed 'legal presumptions of fact', as those required by law to be drawn, and presumptions of fact 'presumptions of fact in practice', or simply 'presumptions of fact', as those which usually are drawn, but need not be so by law.)

Burden of proof places the onus on one of the parties to establish evidence of facts necessary to substantiate a part of his claim or defence: for example, the burden of establishing a defence once breach of contract has been shown (or of proving fault when the defendant pleads frustration: *Joseph Constantine Steamship Line* v. *Imperial Smelting Corporation* [1942] AC 154), or of rebutting a presumption.

Under Article 14(1):

a   applicable law of contract governs presumptions of law and burden of proof;
b   BUT ONLY to the extent that that law contains 'in the law of contract' such rules of presumption and burden.

The proviso is rather confusingly worded. The expression 'in the law of contract' therein is capable of having various possible meanings.

(i) The first would be that applicable law only applies to the extent that presumptions and burdens are classified as substantive rather than procedural rules at national private international law ('that is to say only to the extent to which the rules relating to the burden of proof are in effect rules of substance': Report, p.36). The problem with this interpretation is that whereas, on the one hand, irrebuttable presumptions of law will probably be classified as substantive according to national conflcts (*Re Cohn* [1945] Ch. 5) – and the same is likely to be true in respect of rebuttable presumptions of law, both in the case of those applying in certain contexts alone (for example, advancement and resulting trust: Dicey and Morris, pp.183–4, and Cheshire and North, p.84) and generally to all types of case (for example, validity of marriage, or legitimacy: *Hill* v. *Hibbit* (1871) 25 LT 183, *Mahadervan* v. *Mahadervan* [1964] P.233, 242) – on the other hand, in the case of burden of proof, the effects of Article 14(1) could simply be undone, because, although Morris (p.458) and Cheshire and North (p.85) appear to support a substantive classification of burden of proof at national English law, as being capable of fundamentally affecting the outcome of a case (and even more appropriately, it might be argued, as constituting part of the very fabric of a particular substantive rule of law), nevertheless, the procedural classification, leading to application of *lex fori*, appears to be authoritative (see, for example, *The Roberta* (1937) 58 Ll.L Rep. 159,177; *In the Estate of Fuld (No.3)* [1968] P.675, 696–7); such a result, consequently, would be contrary to the underlying intent of Article 14, since, according to the Report (p.36), as in the case of presumptions (the example provided being that of Article 1731 of the French Civil Code, presuming premises to have been let in good repair in the absence of an inventory or proof to the contrary, thus obliging the lessee to restore them in their rightful condition), burden of proof, logically, in clarifying parties' contractual obligations, is not separable from substantive rules of contract and ought therefore to be subject to the same applicable law as rules of substance (the example given here being Article 1147 of the French Civil Code, whereby a debtor is liable for damages for failure to fulfil his obligations, unless he can prove absence of fault, notwithstanding the creditor's failure to adduce actual evidence of fault).

(ii) The second possible meaning of the Article 14(1) limitation to rules forming part of the 'law of contract' is that only those presumptions of law and rules of burden of proof which specifically form part of the *law of contract* under national legal systems are to be held to be subject to Convention law irrespective of procedural classification at national law, and that any such rules applying not merely to contracts, but generally too, would fall outside Article 14(1) and consequently also, under Article 1(2)(h), the Convention's scope in relation to contracts, if classified as procedural, and not substantive. Such an interpretation, it is submitted, although supported to some extent by foreign authentic texts of Article 14(1), would also, nonetheless, be unacceptable, as restricting the operation of Article 14(1) specifically to those rules on burden of proof which relate solely to the law of contract, for example, the burden of proving frustration in defence of breach, or equity of damages in lieu of rescission for innocent misrepresentation under s.2(2) of the Misrepresentation Act 1967, whilst burdens or presumptions of a more general nature, such as those of undue influence in fiduciary relationships, and absence of intent to create legal relations in social, domestic and family arrangements, which may in principle, if not in practice, also apply beyond the law of contract (for example, in trusts), would consequently be excluded from Article 14(1) (although, in the case of presumptions, classified as substantive, not procedural, in any event, under national English conflicts, not from the Convention's scope as a whole – a difficult and undesirable state of affairs).

(iii) The third possible construction, and that which is here thought to be correct, is that 'law of contract' in Article 14(1) refers to rules of presumption and burden of proof applicable in relation to rules of law under a legal system, whether solely in relation to contract or also concerning other branches of the law, but to the exclusion of presumptions operating in respect of the legal process itself, such as, for example, rules deeming a plaintiff's claim to have been substantiated if the defendant is in default of appearance or fails to take a step in pleadings in response to allegations of fact by the plaintiff which are unsupported by evidence (Report, p.36). This solution would seem to attract within the Convention's unificationist scope, and within that of applicable law itself thereunder, the appropriate type of national rules of presumption and proof, whilst excluding those laws of pleading and procedural process forming part of the administration of justice in a particular country.

MODES OF PROOF: ARTICLE 14(2)

(a) Alternative Applicable Laws : *Lex Fori* and Laws Upholding Formal Validity

Modes of proof of contractual terms under pre-existing English private international law are regarded as procedural for *lex fori* (*Bain* v. *Whitehaven and Furness Ry* (1850) 3 HL Cas. 1). Article 14(2) provides the more liberal solution of offering alternatives to *lex fori*, of laws governing formal validity under Article 9 (previously known in France and the Benelux countries), in order to reconcile the need to confer the protection of *lex fori*, irrespective of more stringent laws governing formal and essential validity, with that of safeguarding the legitimate expectations of parties at the time of concluding the contract, where, for example, the law governing formal validity allows witness evidence of an oral contract, whereas *lex fori* regards such as inadmissible or insufficient (Report, pp.36–7).

Thus, a party may choose to prove the existence of a contract, in accordance with modes permitted by any of

- *lex fori* (Article 14(2));
- applicable law (Articles 14(2) and 9(1) and (2));
- law of the country of conclusion (Articles 14(2) and 9(1));
- law of either of the countries in which the parties are situated at conclusion (Articles 14(2) and 9(2));
- law of the country of a consumer's habitual residence (Articles 14(2) and 9(5));
- (mandatory) *lex situs* in the case of immovable property (Articles 14(2) and 9(6)) (subject to possible *constructional* difficulties – see below, p.340).

However, there are certain limitations upon a party's ability to rely on an Article 9 legal system:

(i) Article 14(2) itself indicates that the contract must be formally *valid* according to the Article 9 law whose mode of proof is to be referred to; thus, a party cannot rely upon, say, applicable law for formal validity under Article 9(1), but use modes of proof of the law of a party's place of conclusion under Article 9(2), when the contract is formally invalid under the latter (Report, p.37); it is not entirely clear from the text whether reliance on modes of *lex fori* is also subject to formal validity thereunder under Article 14(2) – it might seem strange if this were held to be the case, since *lex fori* does not appear in Article 9 as one of the Convention laws governing formal validity, and the German text, at least, militates against such a construction.

(ii) Article 9 foreign modes of proof are only admitted under Article 14(2) if they *can be administered by the forum*. This is a difficult condition to operate. When is the forum incapable of administering a mode of proof? The Report (p.37) says it is where the forum's law of procedure does not generally allow a mode, *such as affidavit evidence, the testimony of a party, or common knowledge*. This comment would seem to have two possible meanings. The first would be that, where the forum *never* allows a particular mode of proof in its courts, whether in contract or otherwise, such mode should be taken to be one which cannot *be administered* by the forum within Article 14(2). Plainly, such an interpretation of the limitation in Article 14 might well be felt to be correct – although, in spite of its apparent liberality, it might well nevertheless be considered to be unduly restrictive in certain respects: for example, presentation of witness evidence say by fax or by telephone, may be difficult to administer, but, with adequate safeguards, not impossible! (English courts themselves now admit evidence given to the court by live video link to a foreign country, under RSC Order 38 rule 3, permitting the court to order that evidence of any particular fact shall be given at the trial in such manner as may be specified by the order – see *Garcin* v. *Amerindo Investment Advisors Ltd* [1991] 4 All ER 655, MORRITT J.) The second possible meaning of the remark in the Report would be that, under Article 14(2), courts must admit particular modes of proof allowed by foreign laws, for example, oral, notwithstanding that *lex fori* itself would require written proof in the case at hand – but only subject to *lex fori*'s rules of evidence of more general application, for example, that a spouse cannot provide such oral testimony against the other's contractual claim, or that uncorroborated oral testimony is never permitted. (According to the Report, a forum whose own law required, say, registration of contracts in a public register as proof thereof, could only recognize such mode of proof provided for by its own law: p.37; and doubtless too, the existing English private international practice against the admission generally of copies of foreign documents – see *Brown* v. *Thornton* (1837) 6 Ad. & El. 185 – would also be upheld, whatever the rule was stated to be under the Article 9 law.) This too may be broadly acceptable, but again it might be thought to render permitted reference to Article 9 laws on mode of proof under Article 14(2) far less liberal than might otherwise be the case. In the present submission, therefore, neither of the two possible meanings in the Report is entirely satisfactory. Instead, the limitation in Article 14(2) should be taken to mean that foreign modes must be permitted – subject, of course, to Article 16 public policy – unless the forum lacks the procedural facilities or the experience required to put such modes into effect (just as, in *Phrantzes* v. *Argenti* [1960] 2 QB 19, the English court felt unable to give effect to an alleged obligation under substantive Greek law to provide an assessed dowry, a concept unknown to English law): thus, extreme – if, with apologies, rather absurd! and, so far as it is known, hypothetical – examples of such cases of impossibility of administration might be those of oral confirmation, under cross-examination, of divine revelation of the existence of a contract, by a priest of the Mundanian Orthodox Church, or proof of a three-day fast undertaken by the party alleging the contract, as evidence of contractual existence under applicable law. Clearly however, in the light of these considerable uncertainties, the matter of interpretation of the concept of *administration of mode of proof* under Article 14(2) is one for the European Court to decide upon at the earliest opportunity.

(iii) The suggestion has been made that where a party seeks to rely upon a mode of proof permitted by an Article 9 law under Article 14(2), he should only be allowed to do so where it can reasonably be established that the particular law played some part in the formation of his original expectations (see Fletcher, p.175). It is felt that, whilst this view (which could even be extended to *lex fori*'s modes of proof, not to mention Article 9 formalities themselves) is basically in accordance with the underlying rationale of Article 14(2), allowing reference to be made to Article 9 laws, in derogation of *lex fori*, it is nonetheless unnecessarily restrictive and out of step with the liberal nature of Article 14(2) (just as, it would seem, in another context, a testator's will may be held formally valid by any of the laws referred to under the Wills Act 1963, s.1, even though not deliberately chosen by the testator: see Cheshire and North, p.839).

(b) Meaning of 'Modes of Proof'

Under pre-existing English private international law, a distinction is drawn between, on the one hand, modes of proof, in order to *determine existence of* contracts or contractual terms, governed according to *lex fori*'s methods and rules (*Korner v. Witkowitzer* [1950] 2 KB 128, 162–3), and, on the other hand, methods of *interpretation* of contractual terms already established as existing, a matter for regulation according to the proper law of the contract (*St Pierre v. South American Stores Ltd* [1937] 1 All ER 206, 209, affd CA [1937] 3 All ER 349). Plainly this division will survive Article 14(2) (see Article 10(1)(a)).

Article 14(2) therefore, subjecting modes of proof to a number of laws, effectively concerns the following types of evidence of contractual existence:

- general rules of *forensic evidence*, applicable to contract or other proceedings: for example, the parol evidence rule, hearsay, competence and compellability of witnesses (provided that these can be administered by the forum) (it might be possible to argue that 'mode' merely goes to the *general type* of evidence or proof sought to be adduced, for example, *oral* testimony, whereas individual rules on competence and compellability within that – according to applicable law – admissible type, are not covered by Article 14(2) and are therefore for procedural *lex fori* at national law: however, it is submitted that this would be incorrect and that the latter – say, oral testimony *by a spouse/party* – as well as the former – oral testimony – are aspects of modes of proof);

- arguably too, contracting *formalities* to be complied with for a contract to be proven and enforceable in court, at least where the purpose of such formalities is held to be one of proof rather than protection; however, it is not wholly clear whether such *formalities* of contract, rendering the latter unenforceable according to the governing law where they are not complied with, are properly to be regarded as *modes of proof* for purposes of Article 14(2), notwithstanding that their underlying purpose may well be that of proof of contractual existence and terms, rather than, say, protection against over-hasty conclusion of contracts, and doubtless this will be another matter for the European Court to rule upon in due course; for the present, it ought at least to be acknowledged that such evidential enforceability-formalities are potentially able to – and, in the present opinion, should – be included as 'modes of proof' within Article 14(2): examples would be written form, written memoranda ('evidence'), stamping, and registration, as evidence of contract (as a result of which, *Leroux* v. *Brown* (1852) 12 CB 801, in which a French contract was unable to be enforced in the English courts by means of oral testimony permitted under French law, due to absence of written evidence required by s.4 of the Statute of Frauds 1677, there classified as procedural and as consequently applicable, may now be able to be circumvented); if such contracting formalities were held to be excluded from the concept of modes of proof under Article 14(2), they would then be subject to procedure of *lex fori* under national English private international law, as being evidential and procedural matters otherwise excluded from the Convention's scope under Article 1(2)(h) (compare *non*-evidential enforceability-formalities, outside Article 14(2) and subject to general Convention rules: see below).

However, what are not included as such 'modes of proof' for purposes of Article 14(2) (notwithstanding that their respective underlying purposes may not be too far removed from the preceding in certain cases) are

a formalities rendering a contract unenforceable if not complied with, but the purpose of which is to provide information and protection for weaker parties to contracts, such as in the case of 'improperly executed' agreements under ss.60–65 and 127 of the Consumer Credit Act 1974, rather than evidence of contractual existence; these are clearly not excluded from the Convention's scope as evidential or procedural according to Article 1(2)(h), and are consequently subject to general Convention rules of applicable law, irrespective of Article 14(2);

b formalities required to be complied with for a contract to be *valid*: 'formal validity' is a substantive matter for laws applicable under Article 9 (see generally, *Monterosso Shipping Co. Ltd* v. *ITF* [1982] 3 All ER 841, 846 and 848, CA, as to the difference between *substantive* validity and *procedural* enforceability requirements); s.2(1) of the Law of Property (Miscellaneous Provisions) Act 1989, requiring a contract for the sale or other disposition of an interest in land to be made in writing, if concluded on or after 27 September 1989 (s.2(8)), for it to be valid and existing (s.2(4)), falls within this category. Contracts made prior to that date continue to be governed by s.40(1) of the Law of Property Act 1925, requiring written evidence for enforceability – clearly, a mode of proof within Article 14(2) (albeit probably mandatory within Articles 7(2) and 9(6), in relation to English land: see below), as seen, if able to be so considered, rather than a rule of formal validity under Article 9.

Thus, but for inclusion of Article 14(2):

a *general* rules of forensic evidence would clearly be excluded from the scope of Article 9 and, by virtue of Article 1(2)(h), from that of the Convention as a whole, as evidential and procedural; and
b *evidential* contracting formalities to be complied with for contracts to be enforceable (as opposed to valid) (i) would also fall outside Article 9 on validity, and (ii) if the procedural classification by English courts of English (*Leroux* v. *Brown* (1852) 12 CB 801) or foreign (*Alves* v. *Hodgson* (1797) 7 TR 214) such requirements were to be followed (compare *Monterosso Shipping Co. Ltd* v. *International Transport Workers' Federation* [1982] 3 All ER 841, CA), these too would also be excluded from the Convention as a whole under Article 1(2)(h).

The effect, then, of Article 14(2) is not merely to bring such matters within the Convention's scope generally, but actually to subject them to Article 9 laws on formal validity, in the matter of modes of proof, as an alternative to what would otherwise have been the exclusive operation of *lex fori* under national procedural law (now *non*-exclusive, under Article 14(2)). Furthermore, it should be clear that Article 14(2) is facilitational: it does not *require* any of *lex fori*'s or of Article 9 laws' formal modes of proof to be complied with, if the contract is otherwise permitted to be proved by means available under any of the other laws' rules.

Accordingly, unless a written evidence requirement of the forum is regarded as mandatory for purposes of Article 7(2), and subject to public policy under Article 16, English courts, by virtue of Article 14(2), would now seem to be required to enforce contracts, capable of being substantiated by modes of proof available under foreign Article 9 laws (provided that they can be administered by the forum), notwithstanding a requirement of written evidence for enforceability under English *lex fori* itself (provided, as seen, that the latter contracting formality is included as a mode of proof under Article 14(2)): for example, guarantee contracts within the meaning of s.4 of the Statute of Frauds 1677 would no longer appear to be unenforceable through failure to comply with written formalities thereunder, if otherwise evidenced by any of the different modes of proof available under Article 9 laws; doubtless, however, s.40(1) of the Law of Property Act 1925 (applicable in relation to contracts for the sale or other disposition of land or an interest in land concluded prior to 27 September 1989, under s.2(8) of the Law of Property (Miscellaneous Provisions) Act 1989), requiring a written note or memorandum of the contract for the latter to be enforceable, would be regarded as a mandatory rule of English *lex situs* in the case of contracts for the disposition of an interest in English land, so as consequently to apply thereto under Article 9(6), whatever the law otherwise to valid mode of proof under Article 14(2) (for example, as a result of parties' choice applicable under Article 9(1) or (2) – these latter themselves presumably also being subject to Article 9(6) in the Article 14(2) context, although, arguably not so, in view of the explicit reference to Mandatory requirements *of form*, meaning formal *validity*, in Article 9(6), in which case reliance would then have to be placed upon Article 7(2) for continued operation of s.40(1)).

In the case of 'improperly executed' agreements under ss. 60–65 and 127 of the Consumer Credit Act 1974, denied enforcement when formalities there prescribed are not complied with, the position is slightly more difficult. Such formalities may not be regarded as matters of formal 'validity' of contracts within Article 9, nor seemingly as modes of proof within Article 14(2), given their protective, rather than evidential, function. It is submitted that such requirements should consequently be regarded, in the first place, as falling within the Convention's scope as substantive, and not as excluded evidential or procedural requirements under Article 1(2)(h), and in the second place, as included within the general scope of (mandatory) applicable law under Article 5 on consumer contracts (where the latter's conditions of operation in Article 5(2) are satisfied : otherwise, under Articles 3 and 4) (note Article 10 merely lists matters subject to Convention applicable law *in particular*).

Finally therefore, the brief summary of the relationship between Articles 9 and 14(2), provided earlier in Chapter 14, is here repeated, as follows.

The main differentiation between matters of formal validity, governed by Article 9, and modes of proof, governed by laws applicable under Article 14(2), must turn upon the effect of non-compliance : *invalidity* means Article 9 applies; *unenforceability* means Article 9 is inapplicable and Article 14(2) governs instead, provided that (a) such contractual formality requirements – for example s.40(1) of the Law of Property Act 1925, applicable to contracts made before 27 September 1989 – are able to be held to be included within the concept of *modes of proof* under Article 14(2), a matter ultimately for the European Court to decide upon (if they are held to fall outside the concept of *modes of proof* in Article 14(2), their evidential and procedural nature will mean that they are excluded from the Convention's scope under Article 1(2)(h), and accordingly are subject to *lex fori* on procedure under national English private international law), and (b) the underlying objective of such enforceability formality is evidential proof of contractual existence and terms, rather than, say, protection of weaker parties to contracts (in the latter case, neither Article 9 nor 14(2) applies, and Convention rules on applicable law in general govern instead). The fact that a rule of formal validity under Article 9 has as its purpose substantiation of contractual existence (for example, Law of Property (Miscellaneous Provisions) Act 1989 s.2(1)) does not affect its status as a law of formal *validity*, and Article 9 continues to apply. If rules of the type laid down in Law of Property Act 1925 s.40(1), not within Article 9, are in fact held to be included within Article 14(2) as modes of proof of contract, then, where a contract in relation to *English* land is subject to a mode of proof varying from the English, under a law according to which the contract is formally (or informally!) valid by virtue of Article 14(2), s.40(1) is thought to be applicable in any event in relation to such contracts concerning English land, as a mandatory rule of the forum's law as *lex situs*, for purposes of Article 9(6), to which the applicable foreign Article 9(1) or (2) law will expressly be subject according to the former, in the case of immovables (provided that this is also so in the Article 14(2)-, as well as in any other, context: see above, pp.294 and 340). In proceedings generally, not involving rights in or to use land (to which, as seen, Article 9(6) may be applicable), mandatory modes of the forum may otherwise of course override less restrictive foreign Article 9 laws, by virtue of Article 7(2)(or 3 (3) and 6(1), where the Article 9(1) or (2) foreign applicable law is on the basis of choice under Article 3).

20 Article 15: Inapplicability of *Renvoi*

Article 15

Exclusion of renvoi

The application of the law of any country specified by this Convention means the application of the rules of law in force in that country other than its rules of private international law.

Renvoi is excluded. Domestic rules of contract of applicable law govern under the Convention, to the exclusion of that law's own rules of private international law.

As a matter of policy, it was considered that domestic rules of contract of a law determined on the basis of localizing factors, in the absence of parties' choice under the Convention, should not be supplanted by a totally different law selected according to conflicts rules of the law indicated by the Convention; and that chosen law under the Convention should be taken to be intended as the domestic, not conflicts, rules of that law (Report, p.37).

It is unclear whether excluded 'private international law' under Article 15 is to be taken to include those rules of national law, probably statutory, which seek to delimit the operation of particular laws to persons or activities having a specific territorial connection with the promulgating state: for example, to consumers resident therein, or employees working there, or to domiciliaries or nationals of that state. The view here held is that such particularized and essentially limiting rules of applicable law are to be regarded as falling outside the exclusion of private international law under Article 15, on the ground that *'renvoi'* and 'private international law' are principally concerned with *selection* of potentially applicable laws, rather than with imposition or spatial delimitation of operation of one particular legal norm or statute. It would seem strange indeed if, by virtue of Article 15, English courts were to find themselves having to apply rules on restraint of trade under English applicable law, in relation to contracts essentially affecting French, not English, markets (see generally, *Rousillon* v. *Rousillon* (1880) 40 Ch. D 351).

Whatever the correctness of the preceding submission, however, at least it is quite plain that Article 7(2), specifically providing for application of *lex fori* according to mandatory provisions of the latter which override normal private international law rules (as well as, presumably, Article 16 on public policy, of similar effect, in a negative sense, in relation to foreign applicable laws otherwise upholding a foreign contract offending local English sensibilities), constitutes an express exception to Article 15 ('Nothing in this Convention shall restrict'), so that spatial delimitations of mandatory rules involved will continue to be applied in all events.

Further, with regard to other Convention provisions preserving application of *mandatory* rules of contract of particular laws (see Articles 3(3), 5(2), 6(1), 7(1) and 9(6)), it would seem to be contrary to the whole process of such Convention safeguards, and to conflict with the very essence of concepts of mandatory nature of domestic rules under national laws, for those norms to be applied other than strictly in accordance with the national spatial or other limitations placed upon their operation by those national legal systems themselves.

Finally, Article 15 on exclusion of *renvoi* is wholly in accord with pre-existing national English private international law of contract (see *Re United Railways of Havana and Regla Warehouses Ltd* [1960] Ch. 52, 96–7 and 115, CA affd [1961] AC 1007; *Amin Rasheed Shipping Corpn* v. *Kuwait Insurance Co.* [1984] AC 50, 61–2, *per* LORD DIPLOCK; and *Dimskal Shipping Co. SA* v. *I.T.W.F.*, *The "Evia Luck" (No.2)* [1990] 1 Lloyd's Rep. 319, 327).

21 Article 16: *Ordre Public* Exception to Applicable Law

Article 16

'Ordre public'

The application of a rule of the law of any country specified by this Convention may be refused only if such application is manifestly incompatible with the public policy ('*ordre public*') of the forum.

This is the ultimate safety-net for any Contracting States which are anxious over the extent of their public international obligations to apply foreign laws under the Convention, previously the subject of their own voluntary relinquishment of the sovereignty of their courts to apply whichever laws they wished in all cases coming before them under national private international laws.

Presumably, the adoption in the English (though not the German) text of the French heading '*ordre public*' is intended to indicate that the provision's scope is limited to public policy of the forum as it operates in a private international context (*ordre public international/externe*), rather than in the sense of including domestic public policy (*ordre public interne*), a distinction which has received much attention in French doctrine. (Graveson, p.165, treats '*ordre*' as meaning 'law and order' rather than policy: that is to say, as necessary to the administration of justice.) French *ordre public international* also has a broader connotation than the English private international public policy approach: the latter is essentially negative in its operation, in relation to the striking down of objectionable foreign rules, whereas the former has both positive scope – assessed extraterritoriality of the forum's laws, conceptually equivalent to the formal processes of private international law – and the negative, interruptive application referred to (see above, Chapter 12; also Kahn-Freund, *Selected Writings* (1978) Chapter 9, 'Reflections on Public Policy in the English Conflict of Laws', 233;and Forde (1980), 29 *ICLQ*, 259). Presumably, it is the negative operation of *ordre public international* which is meant to be indicated, under Article 16.

MAY BE REFUSED ONLY IF

The word 'may' in Article 16 appears to be used in a limiting, permissive sense (emphasis being on the word 'only'), rather than specifically as *conferring* a discretion upon courts nevertheless to apply a foreign rule, notwithstanding that it is against public policy. In fact, there would have been little point in making such provision on discretion, which would always in any event be a matter for courts to decide, in accordance with the forum's principles of public policy. Thus, Article 16 permits refusal of application for public policy; but national principles will determine whether courts must or merely may refuse such application where public policy is found to have been contravened.

APPLICATION OF A RULE OF LAW IS MANIFESTLY INCOMPATIBLE WITH THE FORUM'S PUBLIC POLICY

(a) Rule of Law

It is not the application of a foreign legal system's rules as a whole which has to be against public policy for Article 16 to apply: that of a particular *rule of law* of the legal system must be so. It is difficult, therefore, to state with certainty that Article 16 could be used in order to prevent enforcement of a contract in England, valid according to applicable law, but which is nevertheless illegal under another country's law – *a fortiori* where the latter is the country of performance – whereas comity and public policy might well have led courts to decline to uphold the contract under pre-existing national English conflicts (see *Foster* v. *Driscoll*) (undoubtedly so if England itself was the place of illegal performance); and a similar difficulty in holding application of a foreign *rule of law* to be manifestly contrary to English public policy under Article 16 would arise in a case such as that of *Kaufman* v. *Gerson* [1904] 1 KB 591, in which the Court of Appeal refused to enforce a contract induced by moral pressure and threats of a criminal prosecution in France, alleged to be valid according to the French governing law, on the ground that to do so would contravene an essential universal moral principle of public policy against coercion in contracts (pp.596,597,599,600). The possible grounds for such a finding on the basis of Article 16 are that 'rule of the law' in the latter may be taken to mean the notional, unexpressed rule of the applicable law, according to which the contract is *not* illegal or invalid, and that even though it might otherwise be difficult to establish that a *notional* rule of a legal system was contrary to public policy, nevertheless, under Article 16, it is not the latter which has to be proved, but instead that *application* thereof offends that doctrine. Admittedly, however, the argument is open to challenge, not least in view of specific provision made under Article 7(1) in respect of operation of foreign mandatory rules (though not simply those on legality) of countries with a close connection. (Perhaps if Article 7(1) were to be activated in the United Kingdom and the foreign law on illegality held to be 'mandatory' thereunder, Article 16 would not then be required to be called in aid for non-enforcement – see above, Chapter 12. Alternatively, in the case of illegality under foreign *lex loci solutionis*, it might be possible to construe *Article 7(2)* as, in effect, safeguarding the foreign rule if, in the first place, the *Ralli* case – above, *ibid* – were considered to embody the principle that such supervening foreign illegality of performance would prevent enforcement of the contract as a domestic rule of English law on contracts, and secondly, the latter were held to be mandatory for purposes of Article 7(2): of course, if English law itself were to govern the contract in question, the alleged domestic principle would apply in any event.)

(b) Application Against Public Policy

As noted, it is not the rule itself which must be examined in the abstract, but its concrete application to the particular case (even though, in many instances, the former will almost automatically lead to the latter). Thus, the Report explains (p.38): 'It may therefore happen that a foreign law, which might in the abstract be held to be contrary to the public policy of the forum, could nevertheless be applied, if the actual result of its being applied does not in itself offend the public policy of the forum.' Conceivably then, if a foreign rule of law invalidates the contract for a public-policy-offensive reason, such as the race or religion of a party, English courts should nonetheless apply the foreign law – or at least, not *disapply* it – if (a) in so doing, the court discovers that the party in fact falls within one of the permitted exceptions to the offensive foreign rule, so that the contract is valid thereunder; or (b) the contract would otherwise be held to be invalid, say, for mistake, under another rule of the foreign law, or English law itself, in any event. This distinction between offensiveness of *application* of laws, and that of *substantive norms* themselves, is not unknown to English law (see *Gray* v. *Formosa* [1963] P.259; and *Vervaeke* v. *Smith* [1983] 1 AC 145), and is founded on common sense.

(c) Manifestly Incompatible with Public Policy

The Report explains that this formula, which appeared in all Hague Conventions since 1956, requires the court to find special grounds for upholding the public policy objection (p.38). The usual English test is that application should offend fundamental English conceptions of morality, justice and human liberty (even if no crime would actually be committed according to English law): for example, a contract promoting sexual immorality (*Pearce* v. *Brooks* (1866) LR 1 Exch. 213), or founded on coercion (*Kaufman* v. *Gerson* [1904] 1 KB 591). In addition, it may be the case that public policy will not be applied, where operation of the foreign law upholding the contract has no local effects in England (*Addison* v. *Brown* [1954] 2 All ER 213: agreement to oust jurisdiction of foreign court held not against English public policy; *Saxby* v. *Fulton* [1909] 2 KB 208: recovery of loan of money to be spent on gambling abroad held not to offend English public policy morality) – although, this is not to say that an English court will agree to uphold a contract where the court itself finds it repugnant to lend its aid in enforcement, notwithstanding that its effects may be confined to a foreign country. In all events, Article 16 should be applied very restrictively, for the sake of maintaining uniformity amongst Contracting States (Report, p.38 – and see *Hoffmann* v. *Krieg*, Case 145/86 [1988] ECR 645,668, for a similarly strict approach by the European Court in the case of the public policy exception to recognition of foreign judgments under Article 27(1) of the Judgments Convention): 'manifestly' serves to emphasize this vital consideration.

(d) Of the Forum

Article 16 specifies that it is the forum's public policy which must be contravened – although, hopefully, the latter will correspond with widely, if not universally, accepted principles. Furthermore, the Report points out that Community public policy, which has become an integral part of the forum's public policy, is included (p.38). Frequently, the disapplication of a foreign rule of law on the ground of public policy under Article 16 will simply have the consequence that the contract is upheld or struck down, in contrast to the result which would have ensued from operation of applicable law. In some cases, however, it may be that a substitute rule of law has to be found to replace the inapplicable foreign law: for example, the foreign law implies a condition in the contract that delivery must take place by scaling the Eiffel Tower and leaving the goods at the summit! Presumably, in such a case, if so dangerous and unreasonable a rule were held to be manifestly contrary to English public policy, it would then have to be

English contract rules regarding the delivery obligation which would have to be referred to instead for a solution.

It is submitted that whereas the general scope and meaning of 'public policy' under Article 16 is a matter for reference to the European Court for interpretation under the Brussels Protocol – for example, as to whether public policy therein refers to domestic as well as conflictual, or to political, not merely juridical, policy – the actual decision upon whether a rule of law falls within such public policy exception, as so defined for Article 16, is one solely for the national forum's courts (albeit, in accordance with unificationist principles under Article 18), and not for the European Court to adjudicate upon (as amounting to *application*, not interpretation, of Article 16).

As to the meaning of 'Community public policy', referred to in the Report (p.38) as seen, certain provisions of the EEC Treaty permit departure from the latter's principles on grounds *inter alia* of public policy: thus, Article 36 allows such derogation from prohibition on import–export restrictions, and Article 48(3) enables derogation from freedom of movement of workers (see too Article 56 on freedom of establishment; and Judgments Convention Article 27(1)). European Court case law indicates that (a) whilst public policy will be strictly interpreted and its scope not permitted to be determined unilaterally by member states, nevertheless, in principle, its application is admitted to be a matter for each state's discretion (*Van Duyn* v. *Home Office*, Case 41/74 [1974] ECR 1337, 1350); (b) there must be a genuine and sufficiently serious threat to public policy, operation of which must be necessary (*Rutili* v. *Ministre de l'Intérieur*, Case 36/75 [1975] ECR 1219, 1231–2); (c) further, the threat should affect one of the fundamental interests of society (*R.* v. *Bouchereau*, Case 30/77 [1977] ECR 1999, 2014). (Article 36 also permits derogation on grounds of public *morality*: in *R.* v. *Henn and Darby*, Case 34/79 [1979] ECR 3795, 3813, the European Court considered that it was for each member state to apply its own standards of public morality within its territory; although, in *Conegate Ltd* v. *Customs and Excise Commissioners*, Case 121/85 [1986] ECR 1007, 1022–3, the Court took the view that alleged principles of public morality should apply generally to activities within the territory of a member state, not merely to the actions of foreigners: see too *Adoui and Cornuaille* v. *Belgian State*, Cases 115 and 116/81 [1982] ECR 1665, 1707–8, on Articles 48(3) and 56(1).)

SCOPE OF ARTICLE 16

Article 16 does not apply to matters excluded from the Convention's own scope under Article 1 (see Article 1(2): 'They shall not apply to': 'they' refers to 'rules of this Convention' in Article 1(1), which therefore includes Article 16).

However, what is the position in respect of rules on *incapacity* of natural persons, imposed by laws applicable according to pre-existing private international law under Article 11? Should these be held to be subject to the unificationist constraints of Article 16? At least if they were, this would prevent foreign *protective* incapacities from being held to be penal or against public policy (see the much criticized decisions in *Worms* v. *De Valdor* (1880) 49 LJ Ch. 261; *Re Selot's Trusts* [1901] 1Ch 488; *Re Langley's Settlement* [1963] Ch. 541, under the national English doctrine).

In the present writer's view, the position is the same as that previously described in respect of operation of *Article 7* in relation to Article 11 (see earlier, Chapters 12 and 16): certainly where the common-country-of-parties'-situation-at-contractual-conclusion condition is failed to be satisfied under Article 11, reference to national applicable law on capacity is by virtue of national private international, not Convention Article 11, law, by reason of the exclusion thereof in Article 1(2)(a), and consequently is subject neither to Article 7 nor to Article 16 – and the usual national English principles of public policy then apply, based, for example, upon offensiveness of foreign incapacities founded, say, on race or religion (see *Oppenheimer* v. *Catermole* [1976] AC 249; *Re Metcalfe's Trusts* (1864) 2 De G.J. & S.122); and even where national conflicts on incapacity is referred to under Article 11 through knowledge or negligence of the other party, nevertheless, the belief is retained that this is essentially by virtue of the Article 1(2)(a) exclusion, rather than by that of Article 11 itself which is merely a restriction upon the former, and that consequently Articles 7 and 16 remain inapplicable.

Limitation periods of foreign applicable law are of course applied by the English courts under s.1(1) of the Foreign Limitation Periods Act 1984 and Article 10(1)(d) of the Convention, but this is in any event subject to English public policy 'to the extent that its application would cause undue hardship to a person who is, or might be made, a party to the action or proceedings', under s.2(1) and (2) of the 1984 Act (see *Jones* v. *Trollope Colls Cementation Overseas Ltd* (1990) *The Times*, 26 January, CA).

Finally, a conflict between Article 16 on public policy and Articles 3(3), 5(2), 6(1), 7(1) and 9(6), in so far as these concern mandatory foreign rules, cannot be ruled out, where application of a foreign mandatory rule is considered to be so onerous as to be contrary to the forum's public policy! Presumably, in such an event, the forum's principles must prevail.

22 Article 17: No Retrospective Effect of the Convention

Article 17

No retrospective effect

This Convention shall apply in a Contracting State to contracts made after the date on which this Convention has entered into force with respect to that State.

The Convention came into force for seven states, including the United Kingdom, and in addition Greece, on 1 April 1991 (see The Contracts (Applicable Law) Act 1990 (Commencement No.1) Order 1991, SI 1991 No. 707): but, by virtue of Article 17, its sole effect on that date was to restrict its application to contracts made after midnight on that day, *on 2 April 1991*.

As other states ratify or accede to the Convention, the latter only applies in each such state, to contracts made after the date of its entry into force for the state in question ('with respect to that State': Article 17), in accordance with Article 29(2) (Report, p.38).

An initial problem of applicable law arises, however, in respect of the requirement that the contract be 'made' after the Convention's entry into force, if the latter is to apply thereto under Article 17: will the Convention or pre-existing private international law operate in order to determine when the contract was *made* for such purposes?

Suppose, for example, that at 9 a.m. on 1 April 1991 an offeree posted his acceptance in England to the offeror, also in England, who received the letter of acceptance at 9 a.m. on 2nd April 1991, and that German law was expressly agreed upon to govern the contract, whereas the most connected law, in the absence of such choice, would undoubtedly have been English law; in addition to which, English law is found to regard the acceptance as being effective when it was posted (*Adams* v. *Lindsell* (1818) 1 B. & Ald. 681), whereas German law would hold that it only became complete on its receipt (Article 130 German Civil Code). Which of English and German laws is to apply in the English courts *for the purpose of deciding whether the Convention is applicable to the contract* (as opposed to determining the merits of the contract action, which may or may not concern contractual existence): for, if English law were to govern the matter, the Convention would be inapplicable to choice of law for the merits, because the contract would have been made at the time of posting the letter of acceptance at 9 a.m. on 1 April 1991, the date of the Convention's entry into force with respect to the United Kingdom; whereas, if German law were to be referred to, the Convention would apply, since the contract would then have been made at 9 a.m. on 2 April 1991, the date of receipt of the letter of acceptance?

In the first place, it should be asked: does it in fact even matter whether the Convention, or pre-existing private international law, governs the question or not? Seemingly, it may: if the Convention applies, according to Article 8(1), expressly chosen German law could be referred to in order to determine when the contract came into existence, and the result would then be that since the contract would be found to have been concluded thereunder at 9 a.m. on 2 April 1991, the Convention would thereupon be held to regulate applicable law in order to decide the merits; whereas, if the Convention were inapplicable to the question of date of contractual conclusion under Article 17, it may be the case that, under pre-existing English conflicts, it is the putative proper law *in the objective sense* – that is to say, in the example, English law – which governs contractual existence (Cheshire and North, p.474), so that for the purposes of Article 17, the contract would have been made at 9 a.m. on 1 April 1991 when the letter of acceptance was posted, and consequently the Convention's provisions on applicable law would not operate in relation to the contract action on the merits.

Accordingly, as to which system of conflicts applies, on the one hand, it might be said to be unjust and open to a charge of circularity to apply the Convention to applicable law in relation to conclusion of contracts, even for the limited purpose of Article 17 as opposed to merits adjudication, since this may then directly lead to its application to that and any other questions of contract on the merits; on the other hand, however, it may be responded that parties negotiating contracts in the circumstances described (if they are aware of choice of law at all), and their legal advisers, can hardly be held to have been taken by surprise by imminent entry into force of the Convention, whilst, as for loss of advantages which would have been enjoyed under pre-existing conflicts, the Convention is meant to be a fair and highly desirable improvement upon the pre-existing system of separate national contracts conflicts laws in Europe, so that such a complaint may not be felt to carry a great deal of weight.

On balance, therefore, it is considered that it would be perfectly proper to apply the Convention's own rules of applicable law in order to determine date of conclusion of contracts for purposes of Article 17; although, if courts were to decide otherwise, in favour of pre-existing national private international law, this would be understandable. A possible compromise solution, blessed with simplicity, would be for courts to apply *lex fori*'s domestic rules on contractual conclusion in relation to what may be considered to be an essentially procedural question of effective implementation of new (albeit international, Convention-based) statutory rules. In the present submission, however, this argument is not as appealing as may at first sight seem to be the case: the matter is after all one of applicability of an international, uniform law convention upon the very question at issue, namely, applicable law in contract, even – under Article 3(4) – in respect of the procedural matter of applicable law agreements themselves, as well as to decide the merits; and accordingly, *lex fori* may be unsuitable in the light of the Convention policies which have been in place and effective in relation to contracts since 2 April 1991.

It may well be appropriate that Article 17 should form the basis of the very first reference to the European Court of Justice for an interpretative ruling under the Brussels Interpretation Protocol, when the latter has entered into force. (At least the Protocol itself, under its Article 6, will be in force at the date of proceedings in which any such request is made for exercise of the European Court's Protocol Article 1(a) jurisdiction to interpret the Convention, even though applicability of the Convention at the relevant time – the subject of the reference – is in question. However, as a matter of interest, problems could arise at the end of the Convention's life by reason of Protocol Article 9, whereby the Protocol ceases to have effect in a Contracting State as soon as the Convention itself does so by virtue of Convention Article 30: if the question at that stage concerned whether the Convention remained in force at a particular time, how could it then be known whether the Protocol itself was still operative for purposes of a reference being made on the matter? Moreover, similar problems of Convention applicability to date of conclusion of contracts *could* arise on termination of the Convention, under Article 30, for purposes of deciding upon the Convention's application to the merits or not – see below, Chapter 35.)

Whichever solution is adopted, however, it is clear that pre-existing contract conflicts will continue to be referred to for some time to come in respect of the many contracts which can indubitably be said to have been made prior to 2 April 1991.

23 Article 18: Uniform Interpretation of the Convention

Article 18

Uniform interpretation

In the interpretation and application of the preceding uniform rules, regard shall be had to their international character and to the desirability of achieving uniformity in their interpretation and application.

UNIFORMITY IN INTERPRETATION AND APPLICATION

The unification achieved by the Convention would quickly be lost if national courts were simply to operate without any regard at all to the fact that its provisions are the product of negotiations between several countries and may be the subject of proceedings in different legal systems within the European Community.

REGARD SHALL BE HAD

It might be thought that this requirement is too weak to ensure success for the uniform pan-European development of Convention law (see Fletcher, p.179).

This view, it is considered, would not be wholly correct.

In the first place, it will be noted that the provision requires both *interpretation* and *application* of the Convention to be carried out in a uniform manner (taken from the formula developed by the United Nations Commission on International Trade Law for *inter alia* its international sale of goods convention of 1980, Article 7: Report, p.38). This means that not only must terms and concepts used in the Convention – for example, characteristic performance and habitual residence under Article 4(2), conduct under Article 8(2), and negligence under Article 11 – be given a uniform, Community *meaning*, independent of specific national definitions, *but also* courts are to strive to avoid national divergencies in *applying* those uniform meanings: for instance, English courts should try to reach the same decision upon that which is held to be the characteristic obligation (according to the latter's uniform meaning) under Article 4(2) in a particular type of contract, as would be likely to be the case in French or Italian courts, and vice versa; similarly in respect of circumstances in which it is held not to be reasonable to determine the effect of conduct (as uniformly interpreted) according to applicable law, under Article 8(2); and again in the case of when a party is considered to have been negligent (according to its independent meaning) under Article 11. For this reason, furthermore, it becomes possible for uniformity to be promoted to an even greater extent, through different Contracting States' national courts being sufficiently confident in the homogeneity of the development of Convention law, to refer to each others' case law authorities on the Convention (Report, p.18).

Secondly, even without Article 18, English courts would be expected to adopt broader, internationalist interpretative practices in any event, as they will in the case of (a) statutes giving effect to international conventions, in which context preliminary ambiguity in the statute is no longer required for the latter to be referred to (*James Buchanan & Co. Ltd* v. *Babco Forwarding and Shipping (UK) Ltd* [1978] AC 141; *The Hollandia* [1983] AC 565); (b) legislation intended to give effect to European Community law in general (*Pickstone* v. *Freemans plc* [1989] AC 66; *Lister* v. *Forth Dry Dock and Engineering Co. Ltd* [1989] 2 WLR 634); and (c) European Judgments Convention law (*Newtherapeutics Ltd* v. *Katz* [1991] 2 All ER 151).

Consequently, the fact that the Obligations Convention, unlike the Judgments Convention, includes an express provision requiring *regard to be had* to the needs of uniformity, in interpreting and applying the Convention – far from being noteworthy for its lack of imperative force – actually *adds to* the emphasis placed upon the need for such a Community approach in the case of the Obligations Convention. As the Report says: 'Article 18 operates as a reminder that in interpreting an international convention regard must be had to its international character and that, consequently, a court will not be free to assimilate the provisions of the Convention, in so far as concerns their interpretation, to provisions of law which are purely domestic' (p.38).

Finally, in carrying out the requirement in Article 18, national courts may be expected to follow the guidelines handed down by the European Court of Justice itself in relation to uniform interpretation of the *Judgments Convention*, in the Judgments Convention case of *LTU* v. *Eurocontrol*, Case 29/76 [1976] ECR 1541, [1977] CMLR 88, where the Court ruled that the concept of 'civil and commercial matters' under Article 1 thereof was to be given an independent interpretation, by reference 'first, to the objectives and scheme of the Convention and, secondly, to the general principles which stem from the corpus of the national legal systems', so as to ensure equality and uniformity of rights and obligations thereunder for Contracting States and parties (pp.1551–2) (see too Preamble to Obligations Convention, para.2; and *Ivenel* v. *Schwab*, Case 133/81 [1982] ECR 1891; *Kleinwort Benson Ltd and Barclays Bank plc* v. *Glasgow City Council* (1992) *The Times*, 17 March). This approach is quite consistent with the practice of the European Court in relation to interpretation of Community law generally (see *CILFIT Srl* v. *Ministry of Health*, Case 283/81 [1982] ECR 3415, 3430, [1983] I CMLR 472, 491; *Van Duyn* v. *Home Office*, Case 41/47 [1974] ECR 1337, 1350, [1975] I CMLR 1, 17; *R.* v. *Bouchereau*, Case 30/77 [1977] ECR 1999, 2013, [1977] 2 CMLR 800, 824; *R.* v. *Thompson*, Case 7/78 [1978] ECR 2247, 2273; *Brack* v. *Insurance Officer*, Case 17/16 [1976] ECR 1429, 1451, [1976] 2 CMLR 592, 616).

GENERAL CONVENTION INTERPRETATION SYSTEM

It can now be understood that Article 18 is but one – albeit extremely important – element in the overall Convention system for the uniform application and development of Convention law.

The following, in brief, are the main components of that system:

1   Article 18, prescribing the *principle* of uniform interpretation (and application);
2   Article 33 (see too Luxembourg Convention Articles 2 and 6, Brussels Protocol Article 11), according to which all Community language texts of the Convention are equally authentic, and consequently able to be referred to by national courts of other Contracting States;
3   the power of the European Court to give interpretative rulings on the Convention under the first Brussels Interpretation Protocol, thereby providing the *mechanism* for the principle of uniform interpretation in Article 18 (as well as in the second Joint Declaration of Contracting States annexed to the Convention, calling at that time for an examination of the possibility of conferring an interpretative jurisdiction upon the European Court in Convention cases and for regular meetings, in order to ensure that the Convention would be applied as effectively as possible and impairment of its unifying effect, through differences of interpretation, prevented) to be given full effect and promotion, and without which the latter might simply amount to no more than a pious hope;

4   the general authority of European Court case law on the Convention under s.3(1) and (2) of the 1990 Act (arguably, even including that on the Judgments Convention and EEC law generally, as 'relevant' decisions); reference to 'expression of opinion' by the European Court, under s.3(2), indicates that even *obiter* statements of the Court should be taken into account, to the extent that these can be held to amount to 'principles laid down by' the Court according to s.3(1);

5   statutory authority to consider reports on the Convention and Brussels Protocol in ascertaining the meaning or effect of Convention provisions, under s.3(3) of the 1990 Act (together with any other academic commentaries which the courts may wish to take into account – the latter being the reason for insertion of the words in s.3(3), 'Without prejudice to any practice of the courts as to the matters which may be considered apart from this subsection': see Hansard, HL Vol.515, cols 1488–90; Vol.517, cols 1541–3; naturally, though, other writings, unless internationally referred to, are important merely for the substance of the views expressed therein, rather than as a uniform source for interpretation); s.3(3) omits the words 'and shall be given such weight as is appropriate in the circumstances', to be found in the corresponding provision made in relation to reports on the Judgments Convention under s.3(3) of the Civil Jurisdiction and Judgments Act 1982, but these are surely implicit in any event in the expression 'may be considered', under the former;

6   the ability of national courts to regard Convention case law of foreign Contracting States' courts (proven as fact in the usual way, s.3(2) being inapplicable thereto), as being of persuasive authority, as part of the fundamental Convention system of unified development (on which, see first Joint Declaration annexed to the first Brussels Interpretation Protocol of 1988 – O.J. 1989, No.L48/8 – calling for exchanges of information amongst Contracting States as to national courts' Convention jurisprudence, to be organized through the European Court).

24 Article 19: Application of Convention to and in Composite States

Article 19

States with more than one legal system

1 Where a State comprises several territorial units each of which has its own rules of law in respect of contractual obligations, each territorial unit shall be considered as a country for the purposes of identifying the law applicable under this Convention.

Convention choice of law provisions invariably refer to connections with 'countries': that with which the contract is most closely connected (Article 4), that of a consumer's habitual residence (Article 5), that in which an employee habitually carries out his work (Article 6), that in which contracting parties are present (Article 11). Thus, but for Article 19, in the case of composite countries – for example, the United Kingdom and United States – containing more than one legal system and law of contract within the single political entity, Convention rules would fail to indicate directly the applicable law within such states to govern the contract, and presumably courts seised of proceedings would then be left struggling to apply their pre-existing contract conflicts rules to determine applicable law within the state specified by the Convention, or, alternatively, the Convention's provisions by analogy. Instead, therefore, Article 19(1) requires courts (including those of the composite Contracting State itself, subject to Article 19(2)) to seek prescribed Convention connections with internal law districts, rather than with composite states as a whole: in the absence of a law chosen by the parties, Contracting States' courts will need to determine whether the contract has its closest connections with England and Wales, Scotland or Northern Ireland, not with the United Kingdom as such, and with California, Texas or Michigan, not with the United States, under Article 4(1);

similarly, for example, in the case of consumers' habitual residence (Article 5), employees' habitual place of work (Article 6), and place where parties conclude a contract (Article 11).

A condition of operation of Article 19(1) is that each internal territorial unit of the composite country should have 'its own rules of law in respect of contractual obligations'. Seemingly, therefore, if contracts, or the particular types involved, are universally governed by uniform rules throughout the different law districts of the composite state, connections must then be established with the latter as such, as Article 19(1) is inapplicable. It is believed that this condition is potentially confusing and not wholly desirable; mere existence of separate internal legal systems ought to have been sufficient for Article 19(1) to be brought into application. At least, therefore, for the time being, until the condition can be removed on a revision of the Convention under Article 26, it ought to be clearly understood, as a matter of construction, that solely *constitutional* uniformity, as opposed to mere *substantive* uniformity, of contract rules amongst all territorial units of the state will cause Article 19(1) not to apply: that is to say, that Article 19(1) will nonetheless operate where all states of the union have uniform laws of contract, voluntarily adopted or decided upon by or for them *individually* by their own or federal legal institutions (although, it would admittedly be absurd if such units were also to be regarded as separate countries, and parties to an 'international' convention, for purposes of Article 21 – not to mention Article 24 – according priority to the latter's conflicts rules over those in the Convention, were the units to have concluded an agreement on uniform national contract conflicts amongst themselves: see below, p.362); *a fortiori* too, this will be the case where different units' contract laws simply *happen to* coincide in content, in spite of their separate enunciation thereby or therefor; and Article 19(1) will only then *not* apply when each territorial unit is governed in common by the *same* legal instrument or decisions in contracts promulgated for the entire territory of the composite state. It is *independence* of contract rules, therefore, not their *difference*, if any, which should matter, in the present submission, as a criterion for operation of Article 19(1) as drafted. French and German laws of contract, for example, may be very close in certain respects, not so similar in others. Yet, even in the former case, it is their independent legalo-constitutional provenance which requires the distinct application of *French* or *German* rules of contract law, notwithstanding the absence of any material difference. (This is the answer to those who would object that removal of the offending words from Article 19, or adoption of the construction thereof here advocated, would mean that *Article 11* would fail to apply in a case where a contract was concluded between parties situated in different American states having the same laws of contract, whereas, as things stand, their possible presence in the same 'country' – America – in accordance with Article 19(1), as it is drafted, in fact entails that Article 11 is satisfied and divergent national conflicts avoided, in the circumstances thereunder.) Furthermore, it is submitted – although, it is hardly clear – it is not the *entire* body of contract law of each internal unit which is required to satisfy the constitutional independence test for Article 19(1) to apply: common sense would seem to dictate that, if the laws of contract of separate territorial units were only *partially* independent, for example, in a particular area (say, misrepresentation, left to local regulation and not subject to unification), or even at a certain level (say, state judicial, as opposed to federal), then Article 19(1) must consequently apply to determine the legal rules which are applicable where the claim is founded upon these latter. Thus, in the absence of suggested revision, applicable law may be difficult to predict, where the specific contractual basis on which the case is to be fought, and on which the composite state's internal territorial units' laws may or may not be individually promulgated, is not yet known. A further reason to promote a broader application of Article 19(1), whether by construction as advocated or by revision to remove the own-rules-of-contract condition, is that it might be felt that, in the case of composite states, prescribed connections are more suitable to be ascertained as being established with individual territorial units thereof, rather than with the overall political entity, so that, in practice, even where contract laws are uniform throughout the state, courts will nevertheless find themselves seeking internal connections therein, rather than those established with the state as a whole, notwithstanding that – indeed largely because of the fact that – the former will inevitably involve satisfaction of the latter. Thus, people tend to have connections with Scotland, or with Northern Ireland, or with England and Wales, and rarely solely with the United Kingdom as a whole, without also being, say, habitually resident in one or more of its separate parts; and where Article 19(1) is inapplicable owing to the existence of state-wide uniform contract law, it sits uncomfortably for courts of Contracting States to be required to apply *United Kingdom* law or *American* law of contract as a sort of de-territorialized law of a national legal system lacking total formal existence.

Finally, two points should be made.
(i) Article 19(1) says that *each* of the separate territorial units must satisfy the 'own rules of law in respect of contractual obligations' test. This again seems inappropriate. If some units share a common law of contract, but another or others do not, there exists the need to determine applicable law as between the former and latter. It is believed, therefore, that Article 19(1) should be construed as applying, unless contract law (or the relevant aspect thereof) is *universally* (constitutionally) uniform amongst territorial units within the composite state. Thus, for example, the Misrepresentation

Act 1967 applies in England and Wales and in Scotland, but does not extend to Northern Ireland (s.6(4)). England and Wales, Scotland and Northern Ireland should each be considered a separate country for the purpose of application of laws governing areas of contract covered by the 1967 Act, under Article 19(1) – or at least this should be the case in respect of England and Wales and Scotland together on the one hand, and Northern Ireland on the other.

(ii) Article 19(1) applies 'for the purposes of identifying the law applicable under this Convention'. It does not operate so as to require each territorial unit to be considered a separate country for purposes of applying the final provisions of the Convention, dealing with matters *inter alia* of treaty ratification and duration – which, in any event, as in the case of those in the Brussels Interpretation Protocol, refer to *States* rather than *country* to which latter Article 19(1) itself makes reference – nor for that of deciding whether Convention provisions on applicable law are to operate at all, as under Article 21, according priority to *international* conventions between Contracting *States* (note, not 'countries') and Article 24, regarding consultations.

2 A State within which different territorial units have their own rules of law in respect of contractual obligations shall not be bound to apply this Convention to conflicts solely between the laws of such units.

Where the contract is connected with different territorial units within a single Contracting State, but with no other state, from the point of view of that Contracting State's own courts, the case can be said effectively to be domestic, so that *but for Article 19(1)*, the Convention strictly would be inapplicable in accordance with Article 1(1).

Accordingly, Article 19(2) permits composite Contracting States – notably, the United Kingdom (Report, p.39) – to make appropriate provisions in their implementing legislation for the Convention not to apply to intra-state conflicts, in which event, pre-existing rules will operate.

However, the United Kingdom decided not to avail itself of the power in Article 19(2).

It is expressly provided by s.2(3) of the 1990 Act that, notwithstanding Article 19(2), the Conventions (s.1) shall apply in the case of conflicts between the laws of different parts of the United Kingdom (and where, of course, in accordance with whatever construction is adopted, the condition of 'own rules of law in respect of contractual obligations' in Article 19(1) is satisfied). Convention connections will consequently be sought to be determined by courts in England and Wales in relation to Scotland and

Northern Ireland, and vice versa, as would be done in respect of any other 'country' outside the United Kingdom.

It may be argued that Convention provisions applicable by virtue of Article 19(2) and s.2(3) in relation to pure intra-United Kingdom disputes are technically not those of the Convention as such, as an instrument of international law, but of internal United Kingdom law, albeit derived from the former – one effect of which would be that United Kingdom courts seised of cases involving such rules would be unable to refer to the European Court for preliminary rulings on interpretation under the Brussels Protocol, since Article 1(a) thereof only permits such requests to be made in respect of *the Convention* (see Jayme and Kohler, 'Das Internationale Privat- und Verfahrensrecht der EG auf dem Wege zum Binnenmarkt' (1990), 10 *I Prax*, 353). The Report itself can be taken to lend some credence to this view by describing such a situation as a purely domestic matter for the state concerned which consequently is under no obligation to resolve it by applying the rules of the Convention (p.39).

However, in the present submission, this interpretation is incorrect. The governing provision must be taken to be Article 19(1) itself, which, as has been seen, requires each territorial unit of the United Kingdom to be considered as a country for the purposes of identifying applicable law under the Convention – without any express limitation confining its operation to where proceedings are conducted before courts other than those of the United Kingdom itself. Accordingly, by virtue of Article 19(1), there *is* a conflict of possibly applicable laws of different *countries* within the meaning of Article 1(1) so as to bring *the Convention* into operation, and the effect of Article 19(2) is then simply to allow the Convention – otherwise applicable - to be *disapplied* in relation to intra-United Kingdom disputes before United Kingdom courts themselves, as a pragmatic concession to what might otherwise have been regarded as the domestic nature of the transaction (but which, technically, and in the context of Convention scope, certainly is not so), rather than to permit the Convention's provisions – not otherwise applicable – to be applied in, or at least to be incorporated within the internal legal systems of, the United Kingdom, in accordance with s.2(3).

25 Article 20: Precedence of Community Law over the Convention

Article 20

Precedence of Community law

This Convention shall not affect the application of provisions which, in relation to particular matters, lay down choice of law rules relating to contractual obligations and which are or will be contained in acts of the institutions of the European Communities or in national laws harmonised in implementation of such acts.

This provision, based on Article 57(2) of the Judgments Convention, is intended to avoid the existence of a conflict between the Obligations Convention and any inconsistent acts of Community institutions, by according precedence to the latter (Report, p.39).

The Report explains that *acts* in question, to which priority is thus to be given under Article 20, include

- regulations and directives of the institutions;
- conventions and treaties concluded by them;
- a national law harmonized in implementation of such acts, since that law 'borrows, as it were, from the Directive its Community force, thus justifying the precedence accorded to it' over the Convention (Report, p.39).

The words in Article 20 'are or will be contained in acts of the institutions' demonstrate that precedence is not only to be given to acts already in operation at the date of entry into force of the Convention, but also to those adopted subsequently thereto (*ibid.*).

There are two main characteristics which Community acts are required to possess for them to be accorded precedence over the Convention under Article 20:

1. they, or at least particular provisions thereof, must lay down contracts *choice of law* rules: and presumably, to the extent that particular aspects of contract are not covered by those acts (where, for example, only formation or contractual existence is dealt with), the Convention will continue to operate, rather than resort having to be made to pre-existing national private international law; and
2. the Community choice of law provisions in question must be 'in relation to particular matters' – meaning one or more particular *types* of contract, for example regulations dealing with choice of law in employment contracts or in consumer contracts within the Community – as opposed to those intended to operate more generally, which latter would clearly pose a major threat to the continued operation and purpose of the Convention, if allowed to predominate in relation thereto.

Preference is therefore to be given to Community choice of law rules tailored specifically to the requirements of particular types of contract (*lex specialis*), over the general rules of the Convention (*lex generalis*).

However, in order to prevent a proliferation of different contract choice of law rules in the Community alongside those of the Convention itself, the Contracting States which were signatories to the Convention indicated in the first paragraph of their First Joint Declaration annexed thereto that Article 20 acts should only be made where a real need were to arise and that, even then, inconsistencies with the Convention should be avoided. Thus, it is declared, signatory states

> anxious to avoid, as far as possible, dispersion of choice of law rules, express the wish that the institutions of the European Communities, in the exercise of their powers under the Treaties by which they were established, will, where the need arises, endeavour to adopt choice of law rules which are as far as possible consistent with those of this Convention (O.J. No. L266/14).

26 Article 21: Precedence of Other International Conventions over the Convention

Article 21

Relationship with other conventions

This Convention shall not prejudice the application of international conventions to which a Contracting State is, or becomes, a party

This provision follows the diffident Hague Convention approach of subordinating the Convention's operation to that of any other international convention dealing with contracts conflicts, whether falling wholly or partially within the Convention's own scope, or relating to contracts generally or to particular types thereof, and whether solely concerned with choice of law, or mainly with substantive law, with choice of law rules included perhaps in order to prevent the latter's avoidance.

Other conventions, therefore, prevail over the Obligations Convention.

Thus, for example, the Hague Convention of 15 June 1955 on the Law Applicable to International Sales of Goods (510 U.N.T.S. 147), to which Belgium, Denmark, France and Italy of the Obligations Convention states, are party, applies the law expressly designated by the parties or resulting unambiguously from the provisions of the contract in the absence of such express choice (compare Article 3(1) of the Obligations Convention, permitting choice which is express or even demonstrated with reasonable certainty by the contract *or surrounding circumstances*); where the parties have made no designation, law of the seller's habitual residence at the date of receipt of order governs, except that law of the buyer's habitual residence applies if the order was received there. The 1955 Convention will be replaced by the Hague Convention of 22 December 1986 on the Law Applicable to Contracts for the International Sale of Goods ((1986) 24 I.L.M.1575) for states party to both, when the latter shall have entered into force on its fifth ratification. The latter is intended to amplify the rather piecemeal treatment of the UNCITRAL Vienna Convention on Contracts for the International Sale of Goods of 11 April 1980 (Cmnd 8074; (1980) 19 I.L.M.671), providing a uniform substantive law on international sales of goods (and to which *inter alia* Denmark, France, Germany and Italy are party). Unless it is excluded, the Vienna Convention (in force internationally from 1 January 1988) is expressed to apply where parties' places of business are situated in different Convention states, or in different states and rules of private international law lead to application of the law of a Convention state (Articles 1, 6 and 95). It is in the latter connection, therefore, that rules on applicable law in Articles 7 and 8 of the 1986 Convention were envisaged as fulfilling their supplementary role.

The Hague Convention of 14 March 1978 on the Law Applicable to Agency (Cmnd 7020), ratified by France and Portugal, is not yet in force. Article 1(2)(f) of the Obligations Convention excludes from the latter's scope creation of principal–third party relations, and under the 1978 Convention these are subject to the law of the country in which the agent had his business establishment at the date of his relevant acts. However, the 1978 Convention would also affect principal––agent relations, otherwise within the Obligations Convention's scope, applying the law expressly or impliedly chosen by the parties, and in the absence thereof that of the country in which, at the date of conclusion of the agency agreement, the agent had his business establishment or habitual residence (Articles 5, 6 and 11).

In all such cases, Article 21 of the Obligations Convention – in conjunction with the procedure prescribed under Article 24, in the case of future accession to those other conventions – means that the Obligations Convention must yield where inconsistent.

Presumably, if the other convention to which a Contracting State is or becomes a party makes widescale inroads into the scope of application of the Convention, the proper course for that state to adopt would be to denounce its ratification of the Convention and to cease to be a Contracting State thereto, in accordance with Article 30. Naturally, under the Brussels Interpretation Protocol the European Court of Justice has no power to interpret those other conventions to which a Contracting State may be party (see *Bavaria Fluggesellschaft Schwabe* v. *Eurocontrol*, Cases 9 and 10/77 [1977] ECR 1517, in the context of the European Judgments Convention).

Article 21 applies to both *present and future* ratification of international conventions (existing and future) by a Contracting State as at the date of

Article 21: Precedence of Other International Conventions over the Convention 369

the Convention's entry into force for that State ('international conventions to which a Contracting State is, or becomes, a party').

As the Report points out (p.39), Article 21 has to be read in conjunction with Articles 24 and 25.

Article 21, as seen, lays down the *principle* that other international conventions override the Convention in Contracting States party to the former.

This principle remains unaffected by Articles 24 and 25. However, what Articles 24 and 25 seek to achieve is as follows:

a in the case of Contracting States which wish to become party to another international convention on the private international law of contract *in the future* (that is, subsequent to the Convention's entry into force in any such states), the communication and consultation procedure laid down in Article 23, as reduced from two years to one, is required to be followed, under Article 24(1); and

b notwithstanding that Article 24(1) may be inapplicable – for example, because a Contracting State was *already party* to another international contract conflicts convention on the date of entry into force of the Obligations Convention for that state – consultation may still be requested between Contracting States, if it is considered that the unification achieved by the Obligations Convention is prejudiced by the conclusion of the other international convention, under Article 25 (assuming such *existing* convention to be covered by the words 'conclusion of agreements', in Article 25). Furthermore, under paragraph II of the First Joint Declaration annexed to the Convention, the signatory states declared their intention, as from the date of signature of the Convention until becoming bound by Article 24 thereof (consultation provisions where Contracting States wish to become party to other private international conventions subsequent to the Convention's entry into force), to consult with each other if any one of the signatory states wished to become a party to any convention to which the procedure referred to in Article 24 *would* have applied.

The Report considers that Article 21 will not eliminate all possibilities of difficulties arising from the combined operation of the Convention and other international conventions – especially if the latter themselves include an Article 21-type provision! Nevertheless, states which are parties to several conventions must at least 'seek a solution to these difficulties of application without jeopardizing the observance of their international obligations' (p. 39).

Thus, clearly, an international conflicts convention, such as the Hague Convention of 1955 on the Law Applicable to International Sales of Goods

– containing different applicable law rules from those in the Obligations Convention in the absence of choice, and, as seen, in force in Belgium, Denmark, France and Italy amongst the Contracting States – will doubtless qualify as being entitled to priority under Article 21. However, the question will still nonetheless arise as to whether international conventions which seek to override or to remove the normal process of private international law in respect of application of the substantive legal regulations contained therein should also be held to be covered by Article 21. This will be the case, for example, under the various international transport conventions, such as Article X of the Hague–Visby Rules deriving from the 1924 Brussels Convention on the Unification of Certain Rules relating to Bills of Lading, as amended (carriage between ports in different states *et alia*, construed by the House of Lords in *The Hollandia* [1983] AC 565 as being of extraterritorial application in the United Kingdom, and given the 'force of law' therein under s.1(2) of the Carriage of Goods by Sea Act 1971; and see Dicey and Morris, pp.1270–5, for other such conventions), and under Article 1(1)(a) of the Vienna Convention on Contracts for the International Sale of Goods of 1980 (application to contracts of sale of goods between parties whose places of business are in different Contracting States thereto: see above, p.368). The better view would seem to support the inclusion of these latter within the protection afforded by Article 21, albeit as containing *negative* choice of law rules in conflict with those of the Convention. On the other hand, the Report indicates that an Article 7-type mandatory rule of national law (that is, *mandatory irrespective of the law otherwise applicable to the contract*) would *not* qualify as a 'choice of law rule' for purposes of Article 23 (albeit, seemingly, only on policy, rather than pure textual, grounds, flowing from the strong mandatory nature of such national rules, operation of which should consequently not be subjected to a consultation procedure) (p. 40) – although, of course, the Obligations Convention itself specifically safeguards their operation through a number of its provisions. Whatever the correct classification of mandatory rules may be for Convention purposes, however, the view expressed elsewhere in the present work is nonetheless that any rules of *spatial delimitation* which are attached to such national rules of extraterritoriality should not themselves be treated as national contract conflicts rules, generally overridden by the Convention's operation.

27 Article 22: Reservations to Full Application of the Convention

Article 22

Reservations

1   Any Contracting State may, at the time of signature, ratification, acceptance or approval, reserve the right not to apply:

(a)   the provisions of Article 7(1);
(b)   the provisions of Article 10(1)(e).

Article 7(1) contains a discretionary saving for the application of foreign mandatory laws generally, irrespective of otherwise applicable law; and Article 10(1)(e) extends scope of applicable law under the Convention to *the consequences of nullity of the contract*.

It is not clear from Article 22(1)(a) and (b) whether reservations of inapplicability may cover *either* of Articles 7(1) and 10(1)(e), or whether *both* of these have to be the subject of any reservation made. Articles 7(1) and 10(1)(e) are not especially closely connected, however, and common sense (see too Article 22(2) 'one or more' – below) would seem to suggest that reservations under Article 22 may include either or both of the provisions (and if both, that a withdrawal under Article 22(3) could simply relate to one of them: the words 'either or both' in s.4(1)(b) of the 1990 Act appear to confirm the latter, see below, p.372).

The United Kingdom has made such reservations in respect of both provisions. Section 2(2) of the 1990 Act consequently provides that Articles 7(1) and 10(1)(e) shall not have the force of law in the United Kingdom.

Germany, Ireland and Luxembourg have also made the reservation relating to Article 7(1). Spain and Portugal may do likewise on accession.

2 Any Contracting State may also, when notifying an extension of the Convention in accordance with Article 27(2), make one or more of these reservations, with its effect limited to all or some of the territories mentioned in the extension.

Under Article 27(2), the Convention is inapplicable to the European territories of Contracting States there specified, unless Contracting States make contrary declarations, which, in accordance with Article 27(3), may be carried out at any time. Evidently, from Article 22(2), it would seem that reservations made in respect of the declarant Contracting State itself under Article 22(1) would not also cover Article 27(2) territories to which the Convention was to be extended, and a separate reservation is consequently required for the latter under Article 22(1).

3 Any Contracting State may at any time withdraw a reservation which it has made; the reservation shall cease to have effect on the first day of the third calendar month after notification of the withdrawal.

If the United Kingdom were to withdraw its reservation, say, in the case of Article 7(1), would the latter immediately become applicable to all contracts, or contractual disputes coming before English courts, on the first day of the third month, even in relation to those already concluded or in respect of which proceedings were already pending?

In the present submission, this should not be held to be the position. The need for certainty and settled expectations would seem to make it highly desirable that the withdrawal of the reservation should only affect contracts concluded *subsequently* to the date on which the withdrawal becomes effective, or at least following that of the withdrawal declaration itself, and this would seem to be wholly in line with the policy underlying Article 17, whereby the Convention as a whole is only to apply to contracts made after the date of its entry into force for a state. Unfortunately, however, there is nothing in Article 22 to suggest that this is in fact the case: yet, equally on the other hand, there would also appear to be nothing therein which would prevent the withdrawing state from attaching such a condition to its withdrawal.

In the event of United Kingdom withdrawal, s.2(2) of the 1990 Act would be amended accordingly, by Order in Council: 1990 Act s.4(1)(b).

28 Article 23: Precedence and Procedure for New National Choice of Law Rules

Article 23

FINAL PROVISIONS

1 If, after the date on which this Convention has entered into force for a Contracting State, that State wishes to adopt any new choice of law rule in regard to any particular category of contract within the scope of this Convention, it shall communicate its intention to the other signatory States through the Secretary-General of the Council of the European Communities.

2 Any signatory State may, within six months from the date of the communication made to the Secretary-General, request him to arrange consultations between signatory States in order to reach agreement.

3 If no signatory State has requested consultations within this period or if within two years following the communication made to the Secretary-General no agreement is reached in the course of consultations, the Contracting State concerned may amend its law in the manner indicated. The measures taken by that State shall be brought to the knowledge of the other signatory States through the Secretary-General of the Council of the European Communities.

EFFECTS

Article 23 permits Contracting States unilaterally to adopt any new choice of law rules under their national laws, derogating from those in the Convention, following the Convention's entry into force for those states.

The Report explains that this unusual text, sanctioning the *weakening of the mandatory force* of the Convention, was considered desirable because of the Convention's very wide scope and the very general character of most of its rules.

> The case was envisaged where a State found it necessary for political, economic or social reasons to amend a choice of law rule and it was thought desirable to find a solution sufficiently flexible to enable States to ratify the Convention without having to denounce it as soon as they were forced to disregard its rules on a particular point (p. 40).

Article 23 is therefore a halfway house between requiring total adherence to the Convention's rules by Contracting States, and forced denunciation thereof by the latter in the event of contravention.

CONDITIONS OF OPERATION

Procedures in Article 23 are to be undergone when the following conditions contained therein are satisfied:

(a) the Convention has entered into force for the Contracting State wishing to adopt the new choice of law rule;

(b) the rule which it is desired to adopt at national law must qualify as a 'choice of law rule' for Convention purposes; there seems little doubt that this *would* include a new national mandatory substantive rule whose application was intended to override the normal principles of private international law, in favour of *lex fori* (as opposed to purely spatial or other *limitational* rules, restricting application of the law to contracts performed in a particular place, or to domiciliaries or nationals of the state, which, it is felt, would not qualify), within the meaning of Article 7(2) (as *negative* choice of law rules); however, for policy rather than textual reasons, the Report explains that, in the discussions leading to the Convention, it was decided that Article 23 should *not* apply to Article 7-type extraterritorial choice of law rules and that states should not be bound to submit them-

Article 23: Precedence and Procedure for New National Choice of Law Rules

selves to the Article 23 procedure before adopting such important mandatory rules at national law (although, in order to prevent Article 7 from being used to circumvent Article 23, the national rules in question must truly meet the criteria of Article 7 and 'be explicable by the strong mandatory character of the rule of substantive law which it lays down': thus, it was 'not the intention that the contracting States should be able to avoid the conditions of Article 23 by disguising under the form of a mandatory rule of the Article 7 kind a rule of conflict dealing with matters whose absolute mandatory nature is not established') (p. 40); in addition, the word 'new' in Article 23(1), when taken together with the strict time limits laid down in respect of the consultation process under Article 23(2) and (3), indicates that any such national choice of law rule sought to be introduced under Article 23 in derogation of the Convention's provisions on applicable law may not be permitted to operate retrospectively from the date of amendment of the national law in question;

(c)   the new choice of law rule should relate to a *particular category* (or more than one such category?) of contract *within the scope of the Convention*; the Report emphasizes that derogation permitted by Article 23 is limited to particular categories of contracts – for example contracts made by travel agencies or for correspondence courses – where the specialist nature of the contract may justify such derogation, and that consequently Article 23 is not to be used in order to bring about a general abandonment of the Convention's principles (p. 40); nevertheless, there does not seem to be anything in the text of Article 23 to prevent a Contracting State from derogating thereunder from the *entire* Convention in respect of a particular category of contracts otherwise falling within the Convention's scope (unless the use of the singular 'choice of law rule' in English and foreign texts is taken to have been intended to indicate that the procedure may only be undertaken in respect of a single new choice of law rule to replace the equivalent under the Convention, or at least that separate communications and consultations must take place in the case of each new choice of law rule which it is sought to introduce – unlikely, it is felt); (however, it would seem that a Contracting State still cannot derogate under Article 23 from a particular Convention rule which it finds unpalatable, in relation to contracts *generally*, for example, from the characteristic performance presumption in Article 4(2) – at least, not without undergoing the procedure in respect of each separate category of contracts!); furthermore, contracts categories in question would seem to be able to be defined either broadly – for example, contracts with consumers or with employees, or of re-insurance – or more restrictively – for example, contracts in excess of a certain sum of money, or requiring goods to be delivered in the United States;

(d) the reference in Article 23 to a Contracting State which 'wishes to adopt' any new choice of law rule demonstrates that the state must undergo the procedure laid down thereunder *before* implementing the new rule; it is not sufficient to effect the change and then to invoke consultations thereafter — although, in practice, there would seem to be little difference in the outcome in either event if the state in question is determined to press ahead with adoption of the new rule (or 'newly' to revert to the pre-existing rule thitherto excluded by the Convention).

PROCEDURE

A number of procedural steps must be followed under Article 23 if a new national choice of law rule derogating from the Convention is sought to be adopted:

(a) the state wishing to incorporate the new rule into its law must communicate its intention to the other signatory States *through the Secretary-General of the EC*; any other form of communication, even direct, would seem to contravene prescribed procedure;

(b) the communication is to be made to the 'other' 'signatory' (not merely Contracting) States; presumably, neither the derogating state nor the notified states are confined to the original signatory states to the Convention (which did not include Denmark and the United Kingdom, each of which signed on 10 March 1981 and 7 December 1981 respectively), and will include states which subsequently ratify or accede to the Convention through ratification and signature (*a fortiori*, in view of the fact that Article 31(d) requires the Secretary-General to notify states party to the *EEC Treaty* of such communications);

(c) no more than one signatory state is needed to make the request to the Secretary-General for consultations to take place;

(d) the request for consultations may only be made within six months from the date of the communication made *to* the Secretary-General, not within a period of six months from notification to the signatory States *by* the Secretary-General (Article 31(d) requires the Secretary-General to notify the others of *inter alia* Article 23 communications, but it does not set any maximum time limit for doing so);

(e) if no state requests the consultations within six months, or one or

Article 23: Precedence and Procedure for New National Choice of Law Rules 377

more states do so but no agreement (unanimous, according to the Report, p. 40) is reached in the course of the consultations (in spite of their purpose being 'to reach agreement': Article 23(2)), the derogating state may then simply go ahead and alter its law in the manner indicated, and again it must communicate this step to the others through the Secretary-General; Article 23 therefore is more carrot than stick ('freedom under supervision' – p. 40) and derogating states are ultimately free to amend their law as they choose under Article 23 procedure, provided of course that the eventual amendment is that which was indicated in the communication; in the final analysis, they are able to shut their ears to what the others have to say, although they may nevertheless be expected to act in accordance with the unificationist spirit of the First Joint Declaration annexed to the Convention. (Fletcher, p. 153, concedes that at the end of the day, the individual Contracting State can follow its own predilections, so that the unity achieved initially upon the coming into force of the Convention will not necessarily endure indefinitely; yet the consultative procedure 'should have the virtue of enabling the Member State in question to explain its position to its EEC partners, while they in turn will be enabled to bring to bear whatever moral and persuasive influences lie within their command, with a view to mitigating or even totally avoiding any adverse and disharmonious consequences which may be threatened by the course of action in contemplation': *ibid.*);

(f) Article 23(2) itself does not expressly require the Secretary-General to accede to the request to arrange consultations, although the Report seems to assume that he must do so (p. 40) (yet, curiously, the Report, p. 41, considers that the virtually identical text of Article 25 – albeit lacking any reference to the need to reach agreement – implies that the Secretary-General 'possesses a certain discretionary power'); and since Article 23 omits also to indicate the consequences of his failure to do so within the specified period of two years following communication, it may be concluded that he is obliged to make such arrangements within that time (it would be a different case if the words 'or no consultations are held following the request' had been inserted after 'reached in the course of consultations', in Article 23(3)); nevertheless, the precise nature and form of the 'consultations' to take place remains unclear.

29 Article 24: Procedure for New Multilateral Conflicts Conventions

Article 24

1 If, after the date on which this Convention has entered into force with respect to a Contracting State, that State wishes to become a party to a multilateral convention whose principal aim is or one of whose principal aims is to lay down rules of private international law concerning any of the matters governed by this Convention, the procedure set out in Article 23 shall apply. However, the period of two years, referred to in paragraph 3 of that Article, shall be reduced to one year.

2 The procedure referred to in the preceding paragraph need not be followed if a Contracting State or one of the European Communities is already a party to the multilateral convention, or if its object is to revise a convention to which the State concerned is already a party, or if it is a convention concluded within the framework of the Treaties establishing the European Communities.

CONTRACTING STATE A SUBSEQUENT PARTY TO ANOTHER PRIVATE INTERNATIONAL LAW OF CONTRACTS CONVENTION: ARTICLE 24 (1)

Obviously, where a Contracting State was already party to another contract conflicts convention at the time it became party to the Obligations Convention, the former takes precedence under Article 21 and (subject to paragraph II of the First Joint Declaration annexed to the Convention and to Article 25 of the latter) no further procedure need be undergone.

But where the Contracting State *subsequently* wishes to become party to another such convention, then, in accordance with Article 24(1), the prescribed procedure in Article 23 has to be followed – with the maximum two-year period for consultations in Article 23 para. 3 reduced to one (presumably, so as not to delay unduly progress on the other convention) – in the case of ratification of such other international contracts conflicts conventions, provided that the following conditions are satisfied:

(a) the procedure must be undergone *prior to* ratification of the other convention by the Contracting State, not subsequently thereto ('wishes to become a party');

(b) seemingly, the procedure need not be followed in the case of *bilateral*, as opposed to multilateral, conventions;

(c) the procedure need only be adopted where the other convention's *principal aim* or *one of its principal aims* is to lay down rules of private international law within the scope of the Convention; this could prove difficult to operate: when is private international law the principal aim; how may there be more than one 'principal' aim? (The Report indicates, p. 40, that the procedure would apply where a Contracting State wished to accede to a convention which consolidated the material law of contract with regard to, for example, transport, and which contained, as an ancillary provision, a rule of private international law.) Clearly, where the other convention is solely concerned with private international law in relation to a particular category or categories of contract (or conceivably even to contracts generally, in respect of particular aspects of contract law), the procedure must be followed; conversely, where the convention regulates substantive legal relations, without also providing for conflicts matters either generally or in respect of its own operation, the condition is not satisfied; however, less obvious is the position where the latter convention contains a rule restricting its scope of operation within a particular territorial space or in relation to persons having certain connections with the latter, as an adjunct to the usual processes of private international law – unlikely to be classified as a rule of private international law in the context of Article 24, it is thought, and even less likely to be held to be one of the principal aims of the convention (see too above, p.343); nor is it entirely certain what would be held to be the position in respect of a provision in such a convention requiring the substantive laws laid down therein to operate as overriding regulation of *lex fori*, ousting the normal operation of private international law – a rule, it is submitted, qualifying as a (negative) private international law provision and of sufficient importance to be regarded as one of the convention's principal aims, and yet, in conformity with the view put forward in the Report (see above, Chapter 28) to the effect that Article 7-type mandatory national choice of law rules should not be held to fall within Article 23 procedure as a matter of policy, no more certain to be included amongst those affected by Article 24(1);

(d) the other convention must concern any of the matters governed by the Convention, say, for example, formation or consent, or all aspects of contract but only in relation to certain types thereof, such as those made by travel agencies, or transport undertakings; and

(e) finally, for the procedure to be required to be followed under Article 24(1), it is the *Contracting State* which is required to become a party to the other convention subsequent to becoming a Contracting State to the Obligations Convention; the other convention itself need not also have come into force *subsequently* thereto (see Report, pp. 40–1, notwithstanding the heading 'New Conventions' in the Report).

If the procedure in Article 24(1) is incorrectly carried out, or not followed at all, there appears to be no sanction, other than for the Contracting State concerned to be held to be in breach of its treaty obligations at public international law. (Article 169 of the EEC Treaty concerns non-fulfilment of obligations *under the latter.*) Most important, the other multinational convention to which it has improperly become a party will nonetheless be accorded precedence over the Convention under Article 21, since the latter's effects are not expressed to be subject to the procedure laid down in Article 24(1) having been kept to.

EXCEPTIONS WHERE ARTICLE 24 (1) PROCEDURE IS INAPPLICABLE: ARTICLE 24(2)

In three cases under Article 24(2), the Article 24(1) procedure *need not* (so that it *can*, if all parties so desire: the German text is consistent, but the French less so) be followed in relation to Contracting States subsequently wishing to become party to another contract conflicts convention:

a where another Contracting State (by virtue of Article 24(1) or otherwise) or one of the European Communities themselves (as opposed to a member state thereof, not also a Contracting State to the Convention, which would be an incorrect construction of the wording – see French and German texts : the feminine *l'une/eine* ...... des Communautés européennes/der Europäischen Gemeinschaften, referring to these latter, rather than to the preceding masculine *un État contractant/ein Vertragsstaat*) is already party to the other convention (so that the breach already exists in the Convention wall, and only the first Contracting State to become party to the other convention need undergo the procedure – unless prior to the Convention's entry into force, although, see below in this event – and further, repeated consultations are unnecessary): for example, Belgium, Denmark, France and Italy are among states already party to the Hague Convention on the Law Applicable to International Sales of Goods of 15 June 1955 (510 U.N.T.S. 147), should the United Kingdom decide to accede thereto; or

b if the object of the new convention is to *revise* a convention to which the state concerned is already a party – otherwise modernization of conventions would be obstructed (Report, p. 41); it has to be the Contracting State wishing to become party to the revised convention ('the State concerned'), not any other Contracting State, which is already a party to the unrevised other convention (unless, presumably, any other Contracting State or one of the European Communities is already party to the revised convention, see above); or

c if the other convention itself is concluded within the framework of the Treaties establishing the European Communities (even – as in the case of the Obligations Convention itself – where the convention forms part of the overall Community legal structure and corpus of Community legal rules, although not required to be concluded under any specific provision of a Community treaty), 'particularly in the case of a multilateral convention to which one of the Communities is already party' (Report, p. 41: 'These rules are in harmony with the precedence of Community law provided for under Article 20').

However, there are two cases where a convention to which the procedure in Article 24(1) itself is inapplicable may nonetheless become subject to consultation procedure: first, where Article 24 is inapplicable because the Contracting State concerned wished to become a party to the other convention *before* becoming a Contracting State to the Obligations Convention, paragraph II of the First Joint Declaration annexed to the Convention declares that, as from the date of signature of the Convention and until Article 24 were to become binding on entry into force of the Convention for a Contracting State, signatory states were intended to consult with each other if any one of them wished to become a party to any convention to which Article 24 procedure would have applied, had it already been a

State; and secondly, Article 25 provides that, even in relation to conventions not covered by Article 24(1), if a Contracting State considers that the unification achieved by the Convention is prejudiced thereby, that state may request the Secretary-General of the Council of the European Communities to arrange consultations between the signatory states to the Convention.

30 Article 25: Procedure in Respect of Certain International Agreements

Article 25

If a Contracting State considers that the unification achieved by this Convention is prejudiced by the conclusion of agreements not covered by Article 24(1), that State may request the Secretary-General of the Council of the European Communities to arrange consultations between the signatory States of this Convention.

Whereas paragraph II of the First Joint Declaration annexed to the Convention seeks to encourage states to apply Article 24(1) procedure where they wish to become parties to other conventions *prior to* the date at which they become Contracting States to the Obligations Convention, Article 25 tries to achieve a similar objective at the opposite end of the time scale: that is, where a state is already party to the Obligations Convention and yet the other convention is not covered by Article 24(1).

SCOPE

Article 25 applies to the 'conclusion of agreements not covered by Article 24(1)'.

This presumably includes conventions falling within Article 24(2), as well as those in any event not covered by the terms of Article 24(1), such as those where private international law is not one of the principal aims of the other convention, or conceivably even where a strict rule of private international law is not involved at all, for example a rule limiting the other convention's application solely to convention state domiciliaries.

It is not clear why the word 'agreements' is used by Article 25, instead of 'convention' appearing in Article 24 (French and Italian texts are equivalent to the English; German and Dutch, however, use the same term as is contained in Article 24). One supposes that 'agreement' is to be taken to be wider than 'convention', so as to cover multilateral and bilateral agreements between states of a less formal nature than that of international treaties and conventions (possibly even including mere concerted harmonization of national laws, so that Denmark may not be entirely safeguarded against consultation procedure in respect of its harmonized national rules referred to in the Protocol annexed to the Convention: see below, Chapter 39).

Whether inclusion of the term 'conclusion' is also indicative of the fact that Article 25 is limited to *new* conventions, to the exclusion of those already in existence when a state became party to the Obligations Convention, is again doubtful. The better view, it is thought, is that 'conclusion' refers to the point at which an Obligations Convention Contracting State becomes party to another convention, whether the latter is completely new or already in force between other states prior thereto.

CONDITION

The condition for requesting consultations is that any Contracting State 'considers that the unification achieved by this Convention is prejudiced by' the other agreement. (Presumably, even the Contracting State itself which has become party to the other convention not covered by Article 24 may make the request! – although, in the case of Article 24(2) excluded conventions, the latter itself seems to allow for *Article 24(1)* procedure to be voluntarily undertaken: see above, p.381.)

This is of course a very subjective and vague test (although 'unification achieved' has objective form: Convention rules themselves!) and, provided that the Contracting State is able to put forward a reasonable *prima facie* case in favour of its contention, the request need not be turned down out of hand. Conceivably, what has to be shown is that the other convention differs from the Obligations Convention in some fundamental respect – for example, by prohibiting express or implied choice of law in contracts generally.

Article 25 appears to indicate that the other agreement must actually have been concluded ('is' prejudiced by the 'conclusion'), but it would seem unduly restrictive to exclude from its scope cases where a Contracting State intends to conclude (or become party to) such an agreement.

EFFECTS

The Report draws from the text of Article 25 the implication that the Secretary-General has a certain discretion over whether to accede to the request for consultations (p. 41).

This may simply mean that the Secretary-General must be satisfied in his own mind that the requesting state has reasonable grounds for considering the prejudice condition to be satisfied. As to whether he has a further discretion to do nothing even where that condition is met, on the one hand it will be noted that Article 25 merely refers to consultations, in contrast to Article 23, which requires consultations 'in order to reach agreement', perhaps suggesting that the former is less of an imperative rule, and merely directory upon the Secretary-General; on the other hand, however, this may be reading too much into what is, after all, in either case, a not particularly compulsive procedure, which, certainly in the case of Article 25, has to be accepted for what it is: a *therapeutic* opportunity for government delegates to bash heads together and make rude faces at one another. Article 25, therefore, it is considered, should be held to be no less obligatory upon the Secretary-General than Article 23(2).

31 Article 26: Revision of the Convention

Article 26

Any Contracting State may request the revision of this Convention. In this event a revision conference shall be convened by the President of the Council of the European Communities.

In the event of a request for revision, a conference *must* be convened. Clearly, therefore, the issue of revision should be one which is sufficiently important and which has a reasonable prospect of being adopted following serious discussions, before any request is made. Given the fact that Contracting States which were *seriously* dissatisfied with particular aspects of the Convention need not have ratified it in the first place, presumably, the reasons for a request for revision in practice will include *inter alia* the fact that a particular provision is eventually shown to be incapable of fulfilling Convention policies of uniform interpretation and application in relation to applicable law (as, say, in the case of the presumption of closest connection of law of the country of habitual residence of the characteristic performer under Article 4(2)) so as to prejudice the unification achieved by the Convention, or that a gap is shown to exist in the system of regulation, or that the European Court renders an interpretation of the Convention to which objection is taken and more immediate action to reverse the effects of its decision is preferred to that of hoping that it will change its position in a subsequent ruling.

Where the Convention is agreed to be revised at the international level under Article 26, consequent amendment of the 1990 Act is brought about by Order in Council under s.4(1)(a) thereof.

32 Article 27: Extensions of the Convention to European Territories of Contracting States

Article 27

1 This Convention shall apply to the European territories of the Contracting States, including Greenland, and to the entire territory of the French Republic.

2 Notwithstanding paragraph 1:

   (a) this Convention shall not apply to the Faroe Islands, unless the Kingdom of Denmark makes a declaration to the contrary;

   (b) this Convention shall not apply to any European territory situated outside the United Kingdom for the international relations of which the United Kingdom is responsible, unless the United Kingdom makes a declaration to the contrary in respect of any such territory;

   (c) this Convention shall apply to the Netherlands Antilles, if the Kingdom of the Netherlands makes a declaration to that effect.

3 Such declarations may be made at any time by notifying the Secretary-General of the Council of the European Communities.

4 Proceedings brought in the United Kingdom on appeal from courts in one of the territories referred to in paragraph 2(b) shall be deemed to be proceedings taking place in those courts.

Under paragraph 1, courts of European territories (see EEC Treaty Article 227(4)) of Contracting States are to apply the Convention. As seen, by virtue of Article 2, from the point of view of other Contracting States, it is immaterial whether the country whose law is applicable under the Convention is itself a Contracting State or not.

In the case of the United Kingdom, under paragraph 2(b), the Convention is *inapplicable in* (surely more accurate than 'to' in Article 27 – the German text uses the word 'for', although, others, for example, French and Dutch, also say 'to') its 'European territories', unless it makes a declaration to the contrary in respect of any such territory. (Obviously, the Convention is also inapplicable in those *non*-European territories for whose international relations the United Kingdom is responsible, a useful list of which may be found in the Jenard/Möller Report on the Lugano Convention on Jurisdiction and the Enforcement of Judgments in Civil and Commercial Matters of 1988 between EC and EFTA states: see O.J. 1990, No.C189/120 note 8.)

Accordingly, provision is made under s.8(2) of the 1990 Act for the Act's rules to be extended in whole or in part by Order in Council to any of the Isle of Man, Channel Islands, Gibraltar, and the Sovereign Base Areas of Akrotiri and Dhekelia (that is, areas mentioned in s.2(1) of the Cyprus Act 1960). Section 8(3) further provides that such Order in Council may modify (including additions, omissions and alterations – s.4(3)) the Act in its application to any such territories and contain such supplementary provisions as are considered appropriate.

Appeal proceedings from such European territories of the United Kingdom taking place before the Judicial Committee of the Privy Council are deemed to be conducted under Article 27(4) in courts in the territories against whose decision the appeal was lodged.

In respect of the Convention's operation for France, it will be noted that Article 27(1) specifically states that it shall apply to 'the entire territory of the French Republic', not merely to the *European* territories thereof.

Denmark extended the Convention to the Faroe Islands in accordance with Article 27(2)(a) under an order of 1986.

On ratifying the Convention, the Netherlands made a declaration under Article 27(2)(c) in respect of its application to the Netherlands Antilles.

(As to the geographical areas covered in the references to foreign countries under Article 27, see O.J. 1990 No. C189/85 paras 91–96, and O.J. 1990 No. C189/49 para 33.)

The Brussels Interpretation Protocols make no corresponding provision as to their independent geographical scope, seemingly owing to Spanish sensibilities concerning their possible extension by the United Kingdom to Gibraltar's courts. According to the Tizzano Report (p.15), the omission accords with recent practice under the San Sebastian Convention on accession of Spain and Portugal to the Judgments Convention (Article 21 of which deleted Article 60 of the Judgments Convention regarding its geographical scope) and the Lugano Convention with the EFTA countries, and the report's author indicates that the Brussels Protocols are related but separate from the Obligations Convention itself, so that the latter's territorial extensions are not applicable to the former. Presumably, for this to happen, a revision conference would have to be convened under Article 10 of the first Brussels Protocol – unless it were otherwise to be considered by national courts of Contracting States and by the European Court itself that such result should follow in any event in accordance with the fundamental underlying unificationist objectives of the Convention system and overall Community legal order.

33 Article 28: Ratification of the Convention

Article 28

1 This Convention shall be open from 19 June 1980 for signature by the States party to the Treaty establishing the European Economic Community.

2 This Convention shall be subject to ratification, acceptance or approval by the signatory States. The instruments of ratification, acceptance or approval shall be deposited with the Secretary-General of the Council of the European Communities.

By international custom, methods of incorporation of the Convention into national law are left to the states concerned (Report, p. 41).

The United Kingdom gives the force of law to the Convention under s.2 of the 1990 Act, itself brought into effect by Order in Council (SI 1991 No. 707) under s.7 thereof.

Germany, on the other hand, adopted the Convention as its national private international law as from 1 September 1986 (see [1985] 2 CMLR 49, 281, for EC Commission's criticisms of the method of *internalization* adopted) before it actually came into effect on the international level, and the Convention was also implemented in France (1983), Denmark (1984), Italy (1984), Luxembourg (1986), Belgium (1987) and Greece (1988).

Finally, the Convention is stated in Article 28(1) to be open for signature by States party to the EEC Treaty. Under paragraph III of the First Joint Declaration annexed to the Convention, the signatory states express the view that, having regard to the contribution of the Convention to the unification of choice of law rules within the European Communities, any state becoming a member of these latter should (according to the Report, p.

42, 'be under an obligation also to') accede to the Convention. This may be contrasted with the Judgments Convention's regulation in Article 63, whereby any new member state of the EEC is *required* by that provision of the Convention itself to accept that Convention, subject to necessary adjustments. (The Obligations Convention Report, p. 42, takes the line that such matter is not for the Obligations Convention itself, as falling within the scope of any Accession Convention with new members.) Apparently, there was also some discussion of whether accession to the Obligations Convention by non-EEC states should be provided for, but agreement could not be reached. The issue would therefore fall for further consultation amongst Contracting States were it ever to arise.

34 Article 29: Entry into Force of the Convention

Article 29

1 This Convention shall enter into force on the first day of the third month following the deposit of the seventh instrument of ratification, acceptance or approval.

2 This Convention shall enter into force for each signatory State ratifying, accepting or approving at a later date on the first day of the third month following the deposit of its instrument of ratification, acceptance or approval.

The Report explains that to have required ratification by all signatory states might have risked delaying the Convention's entry into force for too long a period (p. 41).

The United Kingdom's ratification on 29 January 1991 was the seventh, and thus brought the Convention into force on 1 April 1991 for the United Kingdom, Belgium, Denmark, France, Germany, Italy, and Luxembourg: Article 29(1).

In the case of the remaining signatory states (Ireland and the Netherlands), the Convention would enter into force for each, on the first day of the third month following its ratification thereby: Article 29(2). Thus, for the Netherlands, the Convention came into operation on 1 September 1991; for Ireland on 1 January 1992.

Greece acceded to the Obligations Convention under the Luxembourg Convention (see 1990 Act Schedule 2), not under Article 29 of the former. Article 3 of the Luxembourg Convention required its signatory states to ratify it, and Article 4 para. 1 provided for its entry into force for ratifying states on the first day of the third month following the last ratification by Greece and seven states which had ratified the Obligations Convention; it would then enter into force for any other Contracting State which subsequently ratified it, under Article 4 para. 2, on the first day of the third month following such ratification. Thus, the Luxembourg Convention also entered into force for the original seven Rome Convention ratifying States and Greece on 1 April 1991; for the Netherlands, the date was 1 September 1991; for Ireland, 1 January 1992.

The Luxembourg Convention is given the force of law in the United Kingdom under 1990 Act s.2(1), as from 1 April 1991 (SI 1991 No. 707).

In accordance with paragraph III of the First Joint Declaration annexed to the Convention, Spain and Portugal will also be expected to accede to the Convention.

Signatures, ratifications and date (date*s*, for the Luxembourg Convention) of entry into force of the Convention are notified to *EEC states* by the Secretary-General of the Council of the European Communities under Article 31(a), (b) and (c) (see too Luxembourg Convention, Article 5, and first Brussels Interpretation Protocol, Article 7 – each in relation to notification of *Signatory* States).

35 Article 30: Duration of the Convention

Article 30

1 This Convention shall remain in force for 10 years from the date of its entry into force in accordance with Article 29(1), even for States for which it enters into force at a later date.

2 If there has been no denunciation it shall be renewed tacitly every five years.

3 A Contracting State which wishes to denounce shall, not less than six months before the expiration of the period of 10 or five years, as the case may be, give notice to the Secretary-General of the Council of the European Communities. Denunciation may be limited to any territory to which the Convention has been extended by a declaration under Article 27(2).

4 The denunciation shall have effect only in relation to the State which has notified it. The Convention will remain in force as between all other Contracting States.

INITIAL DURATION OF CONVENTION

The Convention will remain in force initially for a period of ten years: that is, until midnight on 31 March 2001. (Whereas *contractual* time stipulations may, as a matter of contractual interpretation, be held to be a question for applicable law, under Article 10(1)(a) – see the Australian case of *White Cliffs Opal Mines* v. *Miller* (1904) 4 SR (NSW) 150 – time of expiration of the Convention as private international law is surely for *lex fori*'s time zone to govern. The matter would be all the more important if, on the expiration of the ten-year period, the Convention – otherwise no longer in force – were nonetheless required to apply to contracts concluded prior to its expiration: see below.)

By reason of the words 'for 10 years from the date of its entry into force *in accordance with Article 29(1)*', the ten-year period runs from 1 April 1991 not only for the seven Contracting States and Greece for which it entered into force on that date by reason of their ratification under Article 29(1) of the Obligations Convention and Article 4 para. 1 of the Luxembourg Convention, but also for any other Contracting States for which it entered into force at a later date under Article 29(2) and Article 4 para. 2, for example, the Netherlands or Ireland: Article 30(1).

The Report explains the limited duration of the Convention on the basis that, unlike the EC Judgments Convention, which contains no equivalent to Article 30, the Obligations Convention is not founded directly upon Article 220 of the EEC Treaty, concerning equalization of certain legal rights and processes within the EEC, and was freely concluded between Contracting States, not imposed by the Treaty (p. 41).

ON THE EXPIRATION OF TEN YEARS

1 Where There Has Been *No* Effective Denunciation of the Convention by Any Contracting State

The Convention is tacitly renewed for a period of five years, and thereafter every five years under the same conditions: Article 30(2).

2 Effective Denunciation by *One or More*, but Not All, Contracting States

(a) In the denunciating state(s)

— the denunciation takes effect in that (those) state(s) and the Convention is inapplicable therein: Article 30(4);

— the denunciation only has effect on the expiration of the ten-year period specified in Article 30(1) (or, as the case may be, five-year period in Article 30(2)), even if it is made a considerable time before that date (see

Report, p. 41) (although, this is not made particularly clear in the text of Article 30); and

— whereas, under Article 17, on its entry into force, the Convention only applies to contracts made after that date, there is no corresponding provision in Article 30, continuing the Convention's application in relation to contracts made prior to the expiration of the ten- or five-year period, following denunciation, and consequently pre-existing national conflicts will govern all contracts after that date, irrespective of the date of their conclusion (curiously, therefore, at one minute past midnight on 31 March 2001, a contracting party may find that a different law now governs, say, his capacity, or that he must now seek out and collect payment from the debtor, rather than waiting for the latter to tender payment according to previously applicable law; if the Convention were to be made applicable to pre-expiration contracts, presumably, date of their conclusion for this purpose should be determined in accordance with the Convention's rules – see Article 8(1) – as the *incumbents*, rather than with those of the superseding national law!).

(b) In the non-denunciating states

The Convention remains in force for them: Article 30(4) EXCEPT THAT

— it is not entirely clear whether the five-year tacitly renewable extension period under Article 30(2) operates in such circumstances, because the latter does stipulate that there has been *no* denunciation; however, it is submitted that the five-year period is indeed applicable in the case at hand, first, because it would be rather peculiar if the Convention were to be renewed indefinitely where some states had denounced it, but only for five years where none had done so, and secondly, the word 'no' in Article 30(2) may be taken to relate specifically to the *non*-denunciating states (significantly too, 'no' is absent from French, German, Italian and Dutch texts); and

— the reference, in the singular, to 'the' state which has denounced, under Article 30(4), might be taken to suggest that only one Contracting State is permitted to denounce, if the Convention is to be tacitly renewed for the others, and that more than one denunciation will lead to the Convention's termination for all Contracting States; this would plainly be incorrect, and the Convention should be understood, as seen, to continue in operation for all states other than those which have denounced, if more than one, even if the number is below the minimum set for entry into force of the Convention under Article 29(1) (presumably, however – from the words in Article 30(4) *'as between all other* Contracting States' – the

Convention must lapse, if one Contracting State alone has failed to denounce – of practical importance only in relation to jurisdiction of the European Court to accept interpretative references from courts of the remaining state, since Article 9 of the first Brussels Interpretation Protocol provides that it shall have effect for as long as the Obligations Convention remains in force under conditions laid down in Article 30 thereof).

3 Denunciation by *All* Contracting States

In this momentous event, the Convention may be *formally* consigned to the annals of legal history (and there may be those in the United Kingdom who will not mourn its passing).

ON THE EXPIRATION OF FURTHER FIVE-YEAR PERIODS

Denunciation and extension procedures and periods are those for the initial ten-year duration: Article 30(2).

PROCEDURE FOR EFFECTIVE DENUNCIATIONS: ARTICLE 30(3)

Contracting States cannot denounce when there is less than *six months* to go before the expiration of the relevant ten- or five-year period: if they do so, they will continue to be bound by the Convention for the succeeding five-year period (although, presumably, the ineffective denunciation will then take effect at the expiration of the latter period).

Denunciation is by notice to the Secretary-General of the Council of the European Communities; and the latter must notify other EEC states under Article 31(d).

The denunciation may be limited to any territory of a Contracting State to which the Convention has been extended by a declaration under Article 27(2).

As seen, it would appear that denunciations are to take effect upon the expiration of the relevant ten-year or five-year period, not at the earlier date of notice of denunciation.

36 Article 31: Notifications in Respect of the Convention

Article 31

The Secretary-General of the Council of the European Communities shall notify the States party to the Treaty establishing the European Economic Community of:

(a) the signatures;
(b) the deposit of each instrument of ratification, acceptance or approval;
(c) the date of entry into force of this Convention;
(d) communications made in pursuance of Articles 23, 24, 25, 26, 27 and 30;
(e) the reservations and withdrawals of reservations referred to in Article 22.

Communications referred to in Articles 23–7 and 30 are those concerning the desire of a Contracting State to deviate from Convention provisions, or to become party to a multilateral contracts conflicts convention, objection to conclusion of international conflicts agreements by other Contracting States, requests for revision, extension of the Convention to European territories of certain Contracting States, and denunciation of the Convention within the permitted period.

Article 22, referred to in Article 31(e), deals with reservations that either or both of Articles 7(1) and 10(1)(e) are not to apply in a particular Contracting State, and with the withdrawal of such reservations.

Thus, Article 31 (together with Article 33) entrusts the management of the Convention (Report, p. 41) to the Secretary-General of the EC Council. The Secretary-General is merely required to 'notify' the states of matters listed thereunder, without any stipulation as to the time for doing so being expressly laid down. However, given the fact that in certain cases – for example Article 23(2) – specific time limits are prescribed for action to be taken following the date of communication made *to* the Secretary-General, rather than that of notification *by* the latter, it may be argued that in accordance with the spirit and objectives and general scheme of the Convention, the Secretary-General should notify communications referred to under Article 31(d) *without delay* following his receipt thereof.

(Interestingly, Article 31 requires notification to states party to the *EEC Treaty*; Article 23 requires communication to other *signatory* states to the Obligations Convention, via the Secretary-General.)

37 Article 32: Integration of Annexed Protocol

Article 32

The Protocol annexed to this Convention shall form an integral part thereof.

The Protocol annexed to the Convention (O.J. 1980, No. L 266/11), regarding retention of certain elements of pre-existing Danish conflicts law relating to law applicable to the carriage of goods by sea (see below, Chapter 39), is to be treated as part of the Convention for all purposes, such as duration, revision and interpretation. Accordingly, for 'Convention', read 'Convention and annexed Protocol'.

38 Article 33: Authentic Texts of the Convention

Article 33

This Convention, drawn up in a single original in the Danish, Dutch, English, French, German, Irish and Italian languages, these texts being equally authentic, shall be deposited in the archives of the Secretariat of the Council of the European Communities. The Secretary-General shall transmit a certified copy thereof to the Government of each signatory State.

Article 2 para. 2 of the Luxembourg Convention on Greek Accession provides that the Greek text of the Obligations Convention is equally authentic with the others.

Under Article 33, Irish and Dutch texts were equally authentic from entry into force of the Convention, notwithstanding their ratification subsequent thereto.

In the natural course of things, United Kingdom courts may be expected to work *primarily* from the English text of the Convention. But should it be discovered that English and foreign texts are not identical, it cannot then be assumed that the English text must prevail, since all are equally authentic: Article 33 (see too Luxembourg Convention, Article 6; first Brussels Interpretation Protocol, Article 11; the English texts are only set out in Schedules 1–3 to the 1990 Act for *ease of reference* (s.2(4)), and it is the Convention as an international instrument which is given the force of law in the United Kingdom under s.2(1), see above, Chapter 4). Instead, any such discrepancies between authentic texts must be dealt with through the process of interpretation, so as to arrive at a single, uniform meaning of the relevant Convention rule, based on a reading of all language texts.

In this way, Article 33, on its own a technical rule concerning authoritative source of Convention law, to be applied, like any other Convention provision, according to proper, uniform Convention interpretative process, laid down in Article 18, is itself an essential instrument in the general operation of the latter uniform Convention interpretative system prescribed by Article 18.

It is desirable, consequently, that national courts, and the European Court itself in exercise of its interpretative jurisdiction under the Brussels Protocol, should make positive efforts *not* to base decisions too closely upon a particular language text without also making some reference to the others.

This interpretative practice will therefore take its place alongside other mechanisms – authority of European Court judgments (1990 Act s.3(1) and (2)), reference to the Giuliano/Lagarde and Tizzano Reports (s.3(3)), and consideration of other Contracting States' laws and case law on the Convention (Article 18) – which together will increase the prospects of unified development of Convention law amongst the different Contracting States.

39 Annexed Protocol

PROTOCOL

The High Contracting Parties have agreed upon the following provision which shall be annexed to the Convention:

Notwithstanding the provisions of the Convention, Denmark may retain the rules contained in Søloven (Statute on Maritime Law) paragraph 169 concerning the applicable law in matters relating to carriage of goods by sea and may revise these rules without following the procedure prescribed in Article 23 of the Convention.

The annexed Protocol has two intended effects:

1. preservation of the relevant choice of law provisions of the Danish maritime law statute, notwithstanding the Convention's entry into force; and
2. ability of Denmark to revise those provisions without having to follow the communication and consultation procedure in respect of subsequent changes to national private international law in general, laid down by Article 23 (although, presumably, *Article 25* will apply where the revision is a result of Scandinavian agreement).

The Report gives the reasons for the Protocol: certain of the choice of law rules contained in paragraph 169 of the Danish maritime law statute – a uniform law, common to the Scandinavian countries, relating to carriage of goods by sea – are not founded upon an international *convention*, but are the result of simultaneous introduction of identical bills into the Scandinavian parliaments (the usual method of Scandinavian harmonization) (others, based on the International Convention for the Unification of Certain Rules of Law relating to Bills of Lading, signed at Brussels on 25 August 1924, as amended by the 1968 Protocol, are preserved under Article 21 of the Obligations Convention); consequently, Article 21 does not apply to accord them precedence over the Convention, and Article 24(2) of the Convention, concerning preservation of application of multinational conflicts 'conventions' *without* the consultation procedure in Article 23 having to be followed, is itself inapplicable to the Danish law – not a 'convention' – in the event of revision thereof, so that the effects of Article 24(2) are required to be expressly repeated in the annexed Protocol (p. 42: '... the fact that another method of cooperation has been followed should not prevent Denmark from retaining this result of Scandinavian cooperation in the field of uniform legislation').

The main effect of paragraph 169 of the Danish law is that law applicable to carriage of goods by sea is that of the country in which the bill of lading was issued, and the provision may therefore be applied in Danish courts in place of the combination-based rule of presumption in the absence of express or implied choice, otherwise operating under Article 4(4) of the Obligations Convention.

40 Schedule 2 1990 Act: The Luxembourg Convention on Greek Accession

SCHEDULE 2

THE LUXEMBOURG CONVENTION

Article 1

The Hellenic Republic hereby accedes to the Convention on the law applicable to contractual obligations, opened for signature in Rome on 19 June 1980.

In paragraph III of their First Joint Declaration annexed to the Obligations Convention, signatory states, having regard to the Obligations Convention's contribution to the unification of choice of law rules within the European Communities, expressed the view that any state becoming a member of the EC should accede to the Obligations Convention (see too Preamble to the Luxembourg Convention: below, Appendix). Hence, Greece acceded thereto by virtue of the Luxembourg Convention (O.J. 1984, No.L146/1).

Article 2

[*Transmission of authentic texts of the Obligations Convention to the government of Greece. Equal authenticity of Greek text of the Obligations Convention: see too Obligations Convention, Article 33.*]

Article 3

[Luxembourg Convention to be ratified by its signatory states. Deposit of ratification.]

Article 4

This Convention shall enter into force, as between the States which have ratified it, on the first day of the third month following the deposit of the last instrument of ratification by the Hellenic Republic and seven States which have ratified the Convention on the law applicable to contractual obligations.

This Convention shall enter into force for each Contracting State which subsequently ratifies it on the first day of the third month following the deposit of its instrument of ratification.

Greek accession to the Obligations Convention was to take place by virtue of entry into force of the Luxembourg Convention between Greece and seven Contracting States to the Obligations Convention (para. 1), on the first day of the third month following the last of Greece and the others to ratify (para. 1).

After that, the Luxembourg Convention would enter into force as between Greece and any other Obligations Convention Contracting State on the first day of the third month following its ratification by the latter (para. 2). Since, under the Obligations Convention, in contrast to the Judgments Convention, the former's rules govern irrespective of whether a party or a law is that of a Contracting or non-Contracting State (see Obligations Convention, Article 2), Article 4 para. 2 of the Luxembourg Convention would only seem to have any significance on the public international level, as binding Obligations Convention Contracting States as between themselves and Greece, and vice versa, to the effect that they and Greece, parties to the Luxembourg Convention, will observe the provisions of the latter and of the Obligations Convention.

The Luxembourg Convention entered into force for Greece and the seven other original Rome Convention ratifying states – Belgium, Denmark, France, Germany, Italy, Luxembourg and the United Kingdom – on 1 April 1991; for the Netherlands on 1 September 1991; and for Ireland on 1 January 1992.

Article 5

[*Notifications of ratifications by, and of dates of entry into force for, Luxembourg Convention states.*]

Article 6

[*Danish, Dutch, English, French, German, Greek, Irish and Italian texts of Luxembourg Convention equally authentic.*]

41 Schedule 3 1990 Act: The First Brussels Interpretation Protocol

SCHEDULE 3

THE BRUSSELS PROTOCOL

Having regard to the Joint Declaration annexed to the Convention on the law applicable to contractual obligations, opened for signature in Rome on 19 June 1980

The (*second*) Joint Declaration referred to [O.J. 1980, No. L266/17] provides that signatory states:

> Desiring to ensure that the Convention is applied as effectively as possible;
> Anxious to prevent differences of interpretation of the Convention from impairing its unifying effect;
> Declare themselves ready:
> 1. to examine the possibility of conferring jurisdiction in certain matters on the Court of Justice of the European Communities and, if necessary, to negotiate an agreement to this effect;
> 2. to arrange meetings at regular intervals between their representatives.

Thus, the first Brussels Interpretation Protocol (referred to in the 1990 Act as 'the Brussels Protocol': 1990 Act s.1(c)) is the outcome of the desire expressed to confer interpretative jurisdiction upon the European Court in respect of the Obligations Convention.

The system has attracted its critics because of *inter alia* the delays which may be caused in commercial cases (see, for example, Mann (1991) 107 *LQR*, 353, 354).

One commentator, on the other hand, actually laments the exclusion of first instance national courts (see below, p.420, Article 2) from those having power to request the European Court to deliver interpretative rulings on the Convention under the Brussels Protocol: 'since otherwise the elucidation of its by no means exiguous number of points of obscurity or ambiguity may become dependent upon the appearance upon the litigious scene of parties wealthy enough – or perverse enough – to pursue points of interpretation on appeal' (Fletcher, *Conflict of Laws and European Community Law* (1982), p.178).

However, whatever its shortcomings may be considered to be, what has to be appreciated is that there were a number of special problems encountered in the formulation of the Brussels Interpretation Protocol, and that the system ultimately adopted for signature in December 1988, some eight years after the signing of the Obligations Convention itself in June 1980, was a compromise, to enable the requisite jurisdiction to be conferred upon the European Court and the Convention to come into force.

The background to the Brussels Protocol is explained in full in the Tizzano Report thereon (O.J. 1990, C219/1: see 1990 Act s. 3(3)(b)).

The basic technical problem regarding European Court jurisdiction over the Obligations Convention was that since the latter (in contrast to the Judgments Convention) was not founded upon Article 220 of the EEC Treaty, the European Court strictly lacked the institutional power under the Treaty to carry out any such function.

Nevertheless, those in favour of such activity, including the European Court itself, based their support for conferral of the jurisdiction on two main grounds (Tizzano Report, pp. 3 and 5–6):

(i) the need to ensure uniform interpretation of the Convention; and
(ii) the desirability for non-Article 220 conventions nonetheless to be linked to the Community legal order in this manner, as being inseparable from attainment of EC objectives, in particular, in the case of the Obligations Convention which was viewed as the logical complement to the Judgments Convention.

Some delegations opposed the scheme: the Convention's application was universal under Article 2 and use of delaying tactics might deter non-EC parties from litigating in EC courts; the Irish government also had the constitutional difficulty of being unable to confer jurisdiction belonging to its national courts upon a supranational entity, where authority to do so was not founded on the EEC Treaty Article 220.

However, many of the objections were able to be discounted: experience with the Judgments Convention had shown fears of abuse to be groundless and risks of delays should not lead to a failure of European Court jurisdiction, where the real need for the latter was due not to compliance with Article 220 of the EEC Treaty, but to the basic requirement of uniformity (Tizzano Report, pp. 7–9; Hansard, HL Vol. 518, col.440).

The problem of lack of Treaty authority of the European Court to interpret a non-EEC Treaty convention was a difficult one. The Report is sceptical over the argument which was put, to the effect that revision of the Treaty to enable such was unnecessary because interpretation of the Obligations Convention was merely an extension, not an amendment, of the Court's Treaty powers (pp. 7–8). Accordingly, any such conferral of jurisdiction upon the European Court would require the *unanimous* consent of the EC member states. The problem with this, of course, would be that the process of giving effect to such powers would inevitably then be delayed because of *inter alia* the Irish constitutional difficulty referred to.

The solution, therefore, adopted at a late stage, was reasonably sophisticated and, as said, embodied certain compromises.

It was decided to draw up *two* Protocols:

1 the *first* Brussels Protocol (O.J. 1989, No. L48/1), which is set out in Schedule 3 to the 1990 Act, for ease of reference, defines the conditions of referral to the European Court for interpretative rulings, and accepts the latter's jurisdiction on the part of the ratifying Contracting State; to enter into force, the Protocol must be ratified by seven Obligations Convention Contracting States, provided that the second Brussels Protocol (see below) shall also have entered into force at such date (first Protocol, Article 6(1));
2 the *second* Brussels Protocol (O.J. 1989, No. L48/17), which does not appear in the 1990 Act, actually confers the institutional power upon the European Court to interpret the Convention, and this requires the unanimous ratification of EC member states (see Tizzano Report, p. 16; and second Protocol, Articles 2 and 3). It provides as follows:

Article 1

1. The Court of Justice of the European Communities shall, with respect to the Rome Convention, have the jurisdiction conferred upon it by the first Protocol on the interpretation by the Court of Justice of the European Communities of the Convention on the law applicable to contractual obli-

gations, opened for signature in Rome on 19 June 1980, concluded in Brussels on 19 December 1988. The Protocol on the Statute of the Court of Justice of the European Communities and the Rules of Procedure of the Court of Justice shall apply.

2. The Rules of Procedure of the Court of Justice shall be adapted and supplemented as necessary in accordance with Article 188 of the Treaty establishing the European Economic Community.

Article 2

This Protocol shall be subject to ratification by the Signatory States. The instruments of ratification shall be deposited with the Secretary-General of the Council of the European Communities.

Article 3

This Protocol shall enter into force on the first day of the third month following the deposit of the instrument of ratification of the last Signatory State to complete that formality.

Article 4

This Protocol, drawn up in a single original in the Danish, Dutch, English, French, German, Greek, Irish, Italian, Portuguese and Spanish languages, all 10 texts being equally authentic, shall be deposited in the archives of the General Secretariat of the Council of the European Communities. The Secretary-General shall transmit a certified copy to the Government of each signatory.

In this way, therefore, the Irish government, for example, may ratify the *second Protocol* (which it actually did, on 29 October 1991), granting power to the European Court to interpret, but need not itself *accept* that jurisdiction through ratification of the *first Protocol*, until it has overcome its constitutional difficulties. In the meantime, European Court jurisdiction could be brought into effect for the other Contracting States through the ratification of the first Protocol by seven of the latter (provided, of course, that the second Protocol has been unanimously ratified).

In addition finally, the obligation of last instance courts to refer to the European Court, to be found in the 1971 Interpretation Protocol on the Judgments Convention, is replaced in the first Brussels Protocol by a discretion (see below), in order further to reduce potential difficulties at national law.

The result thus produced did not meet with universal approval: objections were that changes from the Judgments Convention approach meant a further proliferation of different European-Court-interpretation methods in Europe; allowing courts of last instance a discretion amounted to 'authorised evasion'; and the two-Protocols solution could lead to forum shopping (Tizzano Report, p.11). However, each of the criticisms was able to be answered: (a) the course adopted was the only one which was practicable; (b) the European Court's judgment in *CILFIT Srl* v. *Ministry of Health*, Case 283/81 [1982] ECR 3415, in the general EEC law context, itself showed that the trends were in favour of permitting highest national courts a certain discretion in making references to the Court, albeit subject to restraints set down by the latter in that case; (c) the two-Protocol system was not meant to be permanent and would merely get the process started; and (d) even in Contracting States which had not yet ratified the first Protocol, courts would undoubtedly still be influenced by European Court rulings, especially since Article 18 of the Obligations Convention required a uniform interpretation and application thereof (*ibid.*).

Article 1

[This accepts the jurisdiction of the European Court of Justice to give rulings on interpretation of (a) the Obligations Convention, (b) the Luxembourg Convention on Greek accession and any future accession Convention by EC states (the reference to 'Convention' in the singular in the English text of Article 1(b) is curious – foreign texts refer to 'Conventions' in the plural), and (c) the first Brussels Protocol itself. The second Protocol, actually conferring power on the European Court to accept references, is not mentioned, which seems quite logical. Nor are joint declarations annexed to the Convention and first Brussels Protocol referred to, which – given their nature, as propositional, rather than dispositive – again appears to be appropriate.]

It was previously argued in Chapter 24 preceding that, by virtue of Article 19, and s.2(3) of the 1990 Act, the Convention continues to apply even in relation to conflicts of laws solely between different parts of the United Kingdom, and that consequently the latter's courts may make requests for an interpretative ruling by the European Court under Article 1(a) of the Brussels Protocol in such cases. Provisions to be interpreted remain those of the Convention, and are not to be regarded as somehow having been converted into mere internal rules of United Kingdom laws (compare those of Schedule 4 to the Civil Jurisdiction and Judgments Act 1982).

Article 2

Any of the courts referred to below may request the Court of Justice to give a preliminary ruling on a question raised in a case pending before it and concerning interpretation of the provisions contained in the instruments referred to in Article 1 if that court considers that a decision on the question is necessary to enable it to give judgment:

[*Other Contracting States' courts listed: note Italian Council of State is included in contrast to Judgments Convention 1971 Protocol, because Obligations Convention cases could come before the highest administrative court.*]

(a) **in the United Kingdom:**

the House of Lords and other courts from which no further appeal is possible;

(b) [*in all Contracting States*] **the courts of the Contracting States when acting as appeal courts.**

COURTS WHICH CAN MAKE REQUESTS

Difficulties arose from the formula in Article 177 of the EEC Treaty 'court ... against whose decisions there is no judicial remedy under national law': did this mean only those courts against whose decisions there could *never* be an appeal (abstract theory), or were courts whose decisions were not appealable *in a particular case* (concrete theory) also included? In England there was the particular complication that (a) in a case where the Court of Appeal may refuse leave to appeal to the House of Lords, it is not yet known whether the latter itself will also refuse, thereby making the Court of Appeal the final court *in the case*; and (b) a court deciding as the final court on interlocutory relief may nonetheless be held not to be the final court in the case, if *prospective merits* adjudication, where the provisional issues may be re-examined, were included. In respect of these problems, European Court case law seemed to support the concrete approach (*Costa v. ENEL*, Case 6/64 [1964] ECR 585), and the Court had declined to treat final interlocutory courts as courts of last resort against whose decisions there was no further remedy (*Hoffmann-La Roche AG v. Centrafarm*, Case 107/76 [1977] ECR 957). In England, however, there were indications that the abstract theory might find favour, notwithstanding need for leave to appeal from the Court of Appeal to the House of Lords (*Bulmer v. Bollinger*

[1974] Ch.401, 421; *R. v. Pharmaceutical Society of Great Britain, ex parte Association of Pharmaceutical Importers* [1987] 3 CMLR 951, 969); although, as in the European Court, interlocutory decisions were not to be treated as final – in spite of their not being appealable – where they were subject to reconsideration in the main proceedings (*Garden Cottage Foods Ltd v. Milk Marketing Board* [1984] AC 130).

The Brussels Protocol sought to avoid these difficulties of definition. Article 2 specifies for the United Kingdom or, as the case may be, generally:

- the House of Lords, and
- other courts from which no further appeal is possible (*in the United Kingdom*) (Article 2(a))
- courts acting as appeal courts (*in Contracting States generally*) (Article 2(b))

as being able to make references. (Thus, the Inner House of the Court of Session in Scotland, civilly appellate from the Outer House and, in certain cases, from the sheriff courts, but from whose decisions civil appeals may yet be taken to the House of Lords, falls within Article 2(b), rather than 2(a).)

Effectively, therefore, as in the case of the Judgments Convention, and in contrast to the system adopted by Article 177 of the EEC Treaty, references to the European Court under the first Brussels Protocol are restricted to the appellate level, to the exclusion of first instance adjudication – *elles statuent en appel/sie als Rechtsmittelinstanz entscheiden* – and the 'concrete' approach is adopted under Article 2(b) (*acting as*). (Furthermore, by virtue of Convention Article 27(4), proceedings in the United Kingdom, before the Privy Council, on appeal from courts in Article 27(2)(b) territories, are of course not those from which a reference may be made to the European Court, being treated as proceedings taking place in the courts of the overseas territory itself, to which the Convention is inapplicable in the absence of the necessary declaration. Presumably, however, if the latter were ever to be made, the Privy Council should then have the power to refer to the European Court, albeit as an appeal court of the particular overseas territory to which the Convention had been declared applicable – see too, the Tizzano Report, p.14 – although, strictly, extension of the *Obligations Convention* under Article 27(2) does not automatically import the same in relation to the Brussels Protocol: see above, Chapter 32, pp. 392–3.)

Such 'courts' able to refer must be part of the official state machinery, and private arbitral tribunals are therefore not included (*Nordsee v. Reederei Mond*, Case 102/81 [1982] ECR 1095 – notwithstanding use of the broad term 'juridictions' in the French text of Article 2).

Furthermore, it is submitted, the concept of 'appellate' within the reference context should be taken to denote the judicial consideration of law or facts on appeal from a jurisdiction which would itself qualify as a 'court' on the preceding basis for such purposes, as, for example, in the case of the Employment Appeal Tribunal, sitting as an appeal *court* (see Employment Protection Act 1975, Sch. 6) on questions of law from industrial tribunals – and such an appeal need only relate to mere procedural objections if such be the case, as with the German *Beschwerde* (see Kaye, *Civil Jurisdiction*, p.1715). Thus, it is felt, appeals to the High Court on questions of law arising out of an arbitration award under s.1 of the Arbitration Act 1979 or applications to the High Court to determine preliminary points of law in the course of arbitration under s.2 of the 1979 Act ought not to be held to fall within the provision for *appellate* judicial references under Article 2(b) of the Brussels Protocol (compare the position for purposes of Article 177 of the EEC Treaty, where references are not so restricted to *appeal* courts: see *Bulk Oil (Zug) AG v. Sun International Ltd* [1984] 1 All ER 386); and likewise, judicial review of decisions of professional disciplinary bodies, lacking the statutory function to give judgment in proceedings intended to lead to decisions of a judicial nature, and which consequently are themselves not to be regarded as *courts* for reference purposes (see *Borker*, Case 138/80 [1980] ECR 1975), can hardly be looked upon as being *appellate* in nature. On the other hand, sufficient state involvement in the membership or procedure of a body, or absence of any recourse to the ordinary courts after full adversarial argument, could lead to the opposite conclusion, to the effect that such body does in fact possess juridical status (see *Broekmeulen v. Huisarts Registratie Commissie*, Case 246/80 [1981] ECR 2311) – although, even in these circumstances, there remain doubts over whether judicial review thereof should nonetheless still be considered to be *appellate* in character for such purposes (see Kaye, *Civil Jurisdiction*, pp. 1715–16).

Finally, there appears to be an overlap between Article 2(a) and (b) in respect of appellate courts (including, strictly, the House of Lords itself of course!) permitted to make references in the United Kingdom: courts from which no *further* (ne sont *plus* susceptibles de/kein Rechtsmittel *mehr*) appeal is possible in the United Kingdom, under Article 2(a), and generally, courts acting as *appeal* courts, under Article 2(b), are accorded a power to request interpretative rulings under the Protocol. The former seems to be the result of an earlier contemplation, later dropped, that as in the case of the Judgments Convention, references by final courts should be obligatory, and it is consequently expected that United Kingdom courts other than the expressly-referred-to House of Lords will simply rely upon the easier and more general provision in Article 2(b) for their power to refer – which could actually have an effect upon the arrangements to be made for exchange of information on certain national courts' Convention judgments as between Contracting States (see below, pp.427-8). (It is considered that an attempt to distinguish between the two, by reference to the French text, stipulating that other courts' judgments under Article 2(a) should no longer be *susceptibles de recours* and that courts under Article 2(b) are those which *statuent en appel*, on the ground that *recours* (unless specifically meaning a *recours en révision* under Article 593 of the New French Code of Civil Procedure) is a broader procedural concept than *appel* under French law, would be excessively subtle, since it is perfectly possible to construe *recours* as having been used in a general, non-technical sense and, consequently, as linked to and limited by the subsequent term *appel* when the text is taken as a whole. The position might have been different had the French system of *cassation* applied in the United Kingdom, whereby a subsequent *first instance* court – itself not appellate for 2(b) – will eventually be bound to follow the highest court's decision to quash a former's judgment, so as arguably to come within 2(a). As it is, therefore, in the United Kingdom, reference in Article 2(a) to courts from which no further appeal is possible should be taken to indicate that such courts are appellate, rather than unappealable-first-instance.)

'MAY' REQUEST

A difference from *both* the Judgments Convention and Article 177 is that under the Brussels Protocol, in no case is a reference to the European Court *obligatory*, even where the House of Lords is involved: there is simply a discretion to make the request.

In the context of Article 177, the European Court has tried to encourage national courts only to refer at the appropriate point in time, when all facts and issues are clear (*Irish Creamery Milk Suppliers Association* v. *Ireland* [1981] ECR 735), and in England, in *Bulmer* v. *Bollinger* [1974] Ch.401, 423-5, LORD DENNING MR set forth a number of 'guidelines' to be taken into account in the exercise of the discretion: the delay and expense of obtaining rulings (the European Court may take anything from a year or eighteen months to three years to deliver a ruling); the need to formulate questions clearly; difficulty and importance of the point; wishes of the parties (see Tizzano Report, p.14); the importance of not overloading the European Court. Nevertheless, the national courts' discretion is ultimately a matter for those courts themselves to decide upon (*Adoui and Cornuaille* v. *Belgium*, Cases 115 and 116/81 [1982] ECR 1665; *Lord Bethell* v. *Sabena* [1983] 3 CMLR 1), even against the wishes of parties to the litigation (see *Maxim's Ltd* v. *Dye* [1978] 2 All ER 55; *The Atlantic Emperor* [1989] 1 Lloyd's Rep. 548).

QUESTION RAISED IN A CASE PENDING BEFORE IT AND CONCERNING INTERPRETATION

(a) Question Raised

National courts may not ask hypothetical questions. The matter referred must actually be in issue in the proceedings. As to whether the issue raising the question has to be genuinely the subject of a dispute between the parties, the European Court in *Foglia* v. *Novello (Nos 1 and 2)*, Cases 104/79 and 244/80 [1980] ECR 745 and [1981] ECR 3045, held that it must refuse to rule where there is no genuine dispute and the proceedings are merely a device to secure an advisory opinion from the Court (see too *Meilicke* v. *ADV/OGA F.A. Meyer AG*, Case C-83/91 (1992) *The Times*, 20 October). However, in subsequent cases the Court has shown a more cautious approach, reinforcing the principle that the decision to refer is one for the national courts alone to take, not the European Court itself (*Chemial Farmaceutici SpA* v. *DAF SpA*, Case 140/79 [1981] ECR 1; *Vinal SpA* v. *Orbat SpA*, Case 46/80 [1981] ECR 77). Further, the case must be 'pending' (*pendante/schwebend*) before the referring national court, according to Article 2. Difficult questions have arisen from time to time in connection with Articles 21 and 22 of the Judgments Convention, concerning the moment at which the courts of a Contracting State thereto became *seised* of proceedings, for the purpose of fulfilling the obligation, or, as the case may be, exercising their discretion, to decline or to stay their jurisdiction otherwise possessed thereunder, in favour of courts of the Contracting State which were first *seised* of the same cause of action (see *The Freccia del Nord* [1989] 1 Lloyd's Rep. 388; *Kloeckner & Co. AG* v. *Gatoil Overseas Inc* [1990] 1 Lloyd's Rep. 177; *Dresser UK Limited* v. *Falcongate Freight Management Limited* [1992] 2 WLR 319). In *Zelger* v. *Salinitri* [1984] ECR 2397, the European Court ruled that *seised* meant *definitively seised* for Article 21, and English courts have variously favoured date of *service* of process (*The Freccia del Nord*; *Dresser* v. *Falcongate*) or of *issue* of the writ (*Kloeckner*) as date of definitive seisin – with academic opinion having hitherto been largely in favour of the latter. Thus, in *Kloeckner* (p.204, col.1), HIRST J stated '... the critical moment when an action has been brought in this country, and therefore becomes pending, is the moment of the issue of the writ.' Naturally, the meaning, on the one hand, of 'pending' for purposes of references to the European Court under Article 2 of the Brussels Protocol, and, on the other hand, of 'definitively seised' for decline or stay of jurisdiction under the Judgments Convention will not necessarily be subject to identical considerations. It is believed that at least in the former case, date of issue should be taken to be that at which the case becomes pending – although, given the limitation of requests for interpretation thereunder to appellate jurisdictions (not to mention doubts previously expressed over whether judicial review should be held to be *appellate* in nature for such purposes), in practice the issue should not arise with great frequency and the greater attention may be focused upon the question of whether proceedings have as yet not been *terminated* in the appellate court which has heard the case, at the relevant date of the reference, rather than upon whether they have been commenced in the first place.

(b) Concerning Interpretation

In principle, the European Court is only permitted to rule on a reference if it involves *interpretation* of the Convention (Article 1), and not also its *application* to the facts of the case (*De Geus* v. *Bosch*, Case 13/61 [1962] ECR 45). The English court could not therefore ask the Court to rule on which party's performance obligation was characteristic of the contract in the proceedings before it, under Convention Article 4(2), or on whether it was unreasonable for applicable law to govern a party's consent, under Article 8(2): these questions would involve asking the Court to *apply* the Convention. However, the Court could be asked to *interpret* the Convention by specifying the particular factors to be taken into account by national courts in defining whether an obligation was 'characteristic', or applicable law on consent 'not reasonable', and in practice the Court will be quite willing to reshape an incorrectly referred question so as to confine its ruling to the interpretative sphere (*Van Gend en Loos* v. *Nederlandse Administratie der Belastingen*, Case 26/62 [1963] ECR 1).

(c) Of the Provisions Contained in the Instruments Referred to in Article 1

Article 2 refers to *provisions contained in* the instruments in Article 1, rather than to the latter themselves. This is because certain countries – notably, Germany (see Articles 27–37 of the Introductory Law to the Civil Code) – prefer to transform the substance of the Convention into national legislation, rather than simply incorporating it with direct effect; and accordingly, through the wording in Article 2, it is made possible to request the European Court to rule on interpretation of such national provisions derived from the Convention (Tizzano Report, p.13).

(d) If the National Court Considers that a Decision on the Question is Necessary to Enable it to Give Judgment

In the first place, it is for the national court to decide upon necessity, and not for the European Court itself to assess this question (*Rijksdienst voor Werknemerspensionen v. Vlaeminck*, Case 132/81 [1982] ECR 2953). Secondly, it is the *decision* itself on the question of interpretation, and *not the reference* to the European Court for a ruling, which must be necessary for judgment. Nevertheless, in respect of cases concerning the duty of certain courts to make a reference under Article 177(3) of the EEC Treaty for interpretation of the latter, the European Court has indicated that a reference need not be made where (a) there has been a prevous ruling by the Court on the same or a similar question (*Da Costa*, Cases 28–30/62 [1963] ECR 31); or (b) the meaning is so obvious and free from doubt on the basis of different language texts of the provision in question that no scope for interpretation remains – that is to say, there is a finding of *acte clair* (*CILFIT Srl v. Ministry of Health*, Case 283/81 [1982] ECR 3415); and presumably, therefore, in such circumstances as these, in which it is the reference to the European Court which appears to be unnecessary, the national court will (and arguably is obliged to, in the absence of 'interpretation') exercise its discretion against making a reference under the first Brussels Protocol, unless it considers that the Court should be asked to alter its previous ruling (*Molkerei-Zentrale*, Case 28/67 [1968] ECR 143). Thirdly, as to when a decision on the issue *is* necessary for judgment, LORD DENNING MR in *Bulmer v. Bollinger* [1974] Ch. 401, 422, actually suggested that the point should be capable of being *conclusive* as to the court's eventual decision in the case, but this very strict test is not without its critics.

Once delivered, the European Court's ruling is binding upon the referring national court (*Milchkontor v. Hauptzollamt Saarbrücken*, Case 29/68 [1969] ECR 165, 180). If the latter is dissatisfied, it can make a fresh reference. With regard to other courts, in the United Kingdom, s. 3(1) of the 1990 Act provides that any question as to the meaning or effect of a Convention provision shall, if not referred to the European Court under the Brussels Protocol, 'be determined in accordance with the principles laid down by, and any relevant decision of, the European Court'; and s. 3(2) requires judicial notice to be taken of any decision of, or expression of opinion by, the European Court on any such question.

Article 3

[*Competent authorities of Contracting States have the power to request interpretative rulings if res judicata judgments of courts in the requesting state conflict with the interpretation of the European Court or with a res judicata judgment of a Protocol-Article 2 court of another Contracting State.*

Conflicting judgments themselves remain unaffected. United Kingdom courts are bound by Article 3 rulings, under 1990 Act s. 3(1) and (2).]

This provision is very similar to Article 4 of the 1971 Protocol on Interpretation of the Judgments Convention. It makes up in part for the inability of first instance courts to refer and may be more likely to be used under the Brussels Protocol in view of highest courts' discretion (Tizzano Report, pp.14 and 15).The requirement in Article 3(1) is that *judgments* – that is, more than one – of the requesting state's courts conflict with a European Court or specified foreign Contracting State's court's *judgment* in the singular. *Competent authorities* in the United Kingdom would seem to be the Attorney General in England and Wales and Lord Advocate in Scotland.

The First Joint Declaration annexed to the first Brussels Protocol (O.J. 1989 No. L48/8), which does not appear in Schedule 3 to the 1990 Act, may be read in conjunction with Article 3.

It states that signatory states:

Desiring to ensure that the Convention is applied as effectively and as uniformly as possible,

Declare themselves ready to organize, in cooperation with the Court of Justice of the European Communities, an exchange of information on judgments which have become *res judicata* and have been handed down pursuant to the Convention on the law applicable to contractual obligations by the courts referred to in Article 2 of the said Protocol. The exchange of information will comprise:

— the forwarding to the Court of Justice by the competent national authorities of judgments handed down by the courts referred to in Article 2(a) and significant judgments handed down by the courts referred to in Article 2 (b),

— the classification and the documentary exploitation of these judgments by the Court of Justice including, as far as necessary, the drawing up of abstracts and translations, and the publication of judgments of particular importance,

— the communication by the Court of Justice of the documentary material to the competent national authorities of the States parties to the Protocol and to the Commission and the Council of the European Communities.

Note that whereas *all* Article 2(a) final court judgments are to be forwarded, only the 'significant' judgments of Article 2(b) appellate courts need to be so; and under the final paragraph, documentation is only communicated to *inter alia* states party to the Protocol, not to Contracting States to the Convention as such.

Article 4

[EEC Treaty and Court of Justice Statute Protocol provisions on preliminary rulings apply, subject to any necessary adjustments to the Court's Rules of Procedure.]

Article 20 of the European Court Statute's Protocol deals with matters which include notification of parties, member states and EC institutions, and submission of written observations thereby (even in the case of member states which have not yet ratified the first Brussels Protocol: Tizzano Report, p. 15). Article 35 empowers the Court to adjudicate on costs.

It is the national court seised, not the parties, which submits the reference to the Court.

RSC Order 114 governs references to the European Court by High Court and Court of Appeal, in the case of the EEC Treaty and European Judgments Convention, and doubtless the Brussels Protocol will be included as appropriate.

Article 5

[Deposit of instruments of ratification of the Brussels Protocol by signatory states.]

Article 6

[The first Brussels Protocol enters into force on the first day of the third month following the seventh ratification by the Contracting States to the Convention (see Tizzano Report, p. 15).

EXCEPT THAT if the second Brussels Protocol on Interpretation of 19 December 1988 (O.J. 1989, No. L48/17) is to enter into force at a later date, the first Protocol enters into force on the same date as that on which the second Protocol so enters into force.

Ratifications subsequent to entry into force of the first Protocol take effect on the first day of the third month thereafter, provided that the Convention has also entered into force in the state in question.]

The first and second Brussels Protocols have yet to enter into force in accordance – in the former case – with 1990 Act ss. 2(1) and 7. As at September 1992, only Greece, the Netherlands and the United Kingdom were said to have ratified the two interpretation Protocols. Ireland ratified the Second Protocol on 29 October 1991.

Article 7

[*Notification to states by the Secretary-General of the Council of the European Communities of ratifications, date of entry into force of the Protocol, designations of competent authority of a state under Article 3, communications by states under Protocol Article 8, necessitating amendments to courts listed in Article 2(a).*]

Article 8

[*States must inform the Secretary-General of the text of any of their laws necessitating an amendment to courts listed in Article 2(a)*: see Kaye, *International Contracts* (1993), Part V, for further discussion.]

Article 9

This Protocol shall have effect for as long as the Rome Convention remains in force under the conditions laid down in Article 30 of that Convention.

The ten- and five-year periods of Article 30 apply (see Tizzano Report, p. 15). That is to say, when the Brussels Protocol enters into force, its duration will be whatever period of time is outstanding on the ten- or five-year period applicable to the Obligations Convention. Presumably, if Convention proceedings were commenced prior to expiration and consequent termination of the Convention in a Contracting State in the course thereof, reference could nonetheless subsequently be made to the European Court under the Protocol in those proceedings?

Article 10

[*Requests for revision conference.* A request by a single Contracting State is sufficient. It is not entirely clear whether 'Contracting State' means simply Contracting State to the Obligations Convention, or whether the state concerned must also have ratified the Brussels Protocol. In view of the fact that the latter cannot enter into force under Article 6, unless the second Protocol, requiring unanimous ratification by member states, has first come into operation, it seems likely that the reference is to Contracting States to the Obligations Convention, and that, consequently, a Contracting State which has not itself ratified the first Brussels Protocol (nor even the second, if the Protocols were not yet in force), could nevertheless request revision thereof.]

Article 11

[*Danish, Dutch, English, French, German, Greek, Irish, Italian, Portuguese and Spanish texts of Protocol all equally authentic. Note that 'all' EEC member state language texts are authoritative in the case of the first, not merely the second, Brussels Protocol.*]

FIRST JOINT DECLARATION

[*See above, p.427. Not set out in 1990 Act Schedule 3.*]

SECOND JOINT DECLARATION

The second Joint Declaration annexed to the first Brussels Protocol (O.J. 1989, No. L48/13) does not appear in Schedule 3 to the 1990 Act.
  It states that signatory states:

> Having regard to the Joint Declaration annexed to the Convention on the law applicable to contractual obligations,
>   Desiring to ensure that the Convention is applied as effectively and as uniformly as possible,
>   Anxious to prevent differences of interpretation of the Convention from impairing its unifying effect,
>   Express the view that any State which becomes a member of the European Communities should accede to this Protocol.

Since the Convention is not based upon the EEC Treaty, neither the Convention nor the Protocol has a provision *requiring* new EEC states to accede (Tizzano Report, p. 16).

42 Schedule 4 1990 Act: Revisions to Other Enactments

S.5 The enactments specified in Schedule 4 to this Act shall have effect subject to the amendments specified in that Schedule.

SCHEDULE 4
CONSEQUENTIAL AMENDMENTS

THE EQUAL PAY ACT 1970 (C.41)

THE EQUAL PAY ACT (NORTHERN IRELAND) 1970 (C.32 (N.I.))

1. In Section 1(11) of the Equal Pay Act 1970 and section 1(12) of the Equal Pay Act (Northern Ireland) 1970, for the words 'proper law of' there shall be substituted the words 'law applicable to'.

THE CONSUMER CREDIT ACT 1974 (C.39)

2. In sections 43(2)(c) and 145(3)(c) and (4)(b) of the Consumer Credit Act 1974, for the words 'proper law of', in each place where they occur, there shall be substituted the words 'law applicable to'.

THE PATENTS ACT 1977 (C.37)

3. In Section 82(5) and (6) of the Patents Act 1977, for the words 'proper law of' there shall be substituted the words 'law applicable to'.

THE UNFAIR CONTRACT TERMS ACT 1977 (C.50)

4. In section 27(1) of the Unfair Contract Terms Act 1977, for the words 'proper law of' there shall be substituted the words 'law applicable to' and for the words 'the proper law' there shall be substituted the words 'of the law applicable to the contract'.

THE AVIATION SECURITY ACT 1982 (C.36)

5. In section 19(5) of the Aviation Security Act 1982, for the words 'of which the proper law' there shall be substituted the words 'the law applicable to which'.

THE INCOME AND CORPORATION TAXES ACT 1988 (C.1)

6. In section 347B(1)(a) of the Income and Corporation Taxes Act 1988, for the words 'proper law of' there shall be substituted the words 'law applicable to'.

The Convention (see Preamble para. 3) and 1990 Act (see short and long titles) refer to the *law applicable* to contracts. The term 'proper law', belonging to pre-existing English conflicts, is no longer used in relation to post-1 April 1991 choice of law in contract.

Accordingly, s.5 and Schedule 4 to the 1990 Act substitute for the old phrase 'proper law' the new term 'applicable law' in the statutory provisions listed which make reference to the law applicable to contract.

Therefore, those statutes now read as follows:

EQUAL PAY ACT 1970

S.1(11). For the purposes of this Act it is immaterial whether the law which (apart from this subsection) is the *law applicable to* a contract is the law of any part of the United Kingdom or not.

EQUAL PAY ACT (NORTHERN IRELAND) 1970

S.1(12). For the purposes of this Act it is immaterial whether the law which (apart from this subsection) is the *law applicable to* a contract is the law of any part of the United Kingdom or not.

CONSUMER CREDIT ACT 1974

S.43(2). An advertisement does not fall within subsection (1) if the advertiser does not carry on–
   (a)
   (b)

   (c) a business which comprises or relates to unregulated agreements where–
       (i) the *law applicable to* the agreement is the law of a country outside the United Kingdom, and
       (ii) if the *law applicable to* the agreement were the law of a part of the United Kingdom it would be a regulated agreement.

S.145(3). Subsection (2)(a)(i) applies to–
   (a)
   (b)

   (c) a business which comprises or relates to unregulated agreements where–
       (i) the *law applicable to* the agreement is the law of a country outside the United Kingdom, and
       (ii) if the *law applicable to* the agreement were the law of a part of the United Kingdom it would be a regulated consumer credit agreement.

(4) Subsection (2)(b) applies to–
   (a)
   (b) a business which comprises or relates to unregulated agreements where–
       (i) the *law applicable to* the agreement is the law of a country outside the United Kingdom, and
       (ii) if the *law applicable to* the agreement were the law of a part of the United Kingdom it would be a regulated consumer hire agreement.

PATENTS ACT 1977

S.82(5). The court and the comptroller shall have jurisdiction to determine an employer–employee question if either of the following conditions is satisfied, that is to say–

(a) the employee is mainly employed in the United Kingdom; or
(b) the employee is not mainly employed anywhere or his place of main employment cannot be determined, but the employer has a place of business in the United Kingdom to which the employee is attached (whether or not he is also attached elsewhere);

and also if in either of those cases there is no written evidence that the parties have agreed to submit to the jurisdiction of the competent authority of a relevant contracting state other than the United Kingdom or, where there is such evidence of such an agreement, if the *law applicable to* the contract of employment does not recognise the validity of the agreement.

(6) Without prejudice to subsections (2) to (5) above, the court and the comptroller shall have jurisdiction to determine any question to which this section applies if there is written evidence that the parties have agreed to submit to the jurisdiction of the court or the comptroller, as the case may be, and, in the case of an employer–employee question, the *law applicable to* the contract of employment recognises the validity of the agreement.

UNFAIR CONTRACT TERMS ACT 1977

S.27(1). Where the *law applicable to* a contract is the law of any part of the United Kingdom only by choice of the parties (and apart from that choice would be the law of some country outside the United Kingdom) sections 2 to 7 and 16 to 21 of this Act do not operate as part *of the law applicable to the contract.*

AVIATION SECURITY ACT 1982

S.19(5). In this section 'United Kingdom court' means a court exercising jurisdiction in any part of the United Kingdom under the law of the United Kingdom or of part of the United Kingdom, and 'United Kingdom contract' means a contract which is either expressed to have effect in accordance with the law of the United Kingdom or of part of the United Kingdom or (not being so expressed) is a contract *the law applicable to which* is the law of the United Kingdom or of part of the United Kingdom.

INCOME AND CORPORATION TAXES ACT 1988

S.347B(1) In this section 'qualifying maintenance payment' means a periodical payment which–
    (a) is made under an order made by a court in the United Kingdom, or under a written agreement the *law applicable to* which is the law of a part of the United Kingdom.

There are two comments which may be made in respect of the preceding drafting amendments.

In the first place, whilst the term 'proper law' is a legal term of art of which the meaning is perfectly well known, as that law which – by choice or closest connection – governed the whole or major part of contracts under pre-existing English contract conflicts, the new term 'law applicable to' is only assured of such interpretation within the context of the 1990 legislation itself, and outside the latter may have a certain ambiguity: different laws may 'apply' to various parts of a contract under the new law as under the old, for example, *lex loci solutionis* in relation to mode of contractual performance (Article 10(2)) and *lex fori* to procedure, but under the former phraseology these would be clearly distinguished from the 'proper law'. (At least, however, it is clear that discretionary English *jurisdiction* under RSC Order 11 rule 1(1)(d)(iii) is based on express or implied *choice* of English law – 'by its terms, or by implication' – to govern the contract under Article 3 of the Convention, and not on applicability of English law merely to certain aspects of the contract, under different Convention provisions, or, for example, to mandatory safeguards by virtue of Article 5(2) or 6(1) – although, this is not to say that these *partially* applicable laws would not be taken into account as factors in the exercise of the court's Order 11 and *forum conveniens* discretion: see *Spiliada* [1987] AC 460, 478).

Secondly, the problem is exacerbated where the contract in question falls outside the Convention's temporal scope because it was not concluded *after* the date on which the Convention entered into force (Article 17), so that pre-existing conflicts, with its reference to proper law of contracts, continues to govern. For, s.5 and the amendments in Schedule 4, which entered into force on 1 April 1991 (S.I. 1991 No. 707), do not appear to be limited in their operation to contracts falling within the temporal or other scope of the Convention, and consequently will operate in relation to contracts retrospectively.

Accordingly, it might have been more appropriate for the amendments in Schedule 4 to have been limited by the words 'in relation to contracts governed by the Contracts (Applicable Law) Act 1990'.

PART IV

43 Comparison of Convention and Pre-existing English Private International Rules of Contract

Contract choice of law rules relating to certain aspects or types of agreement remain subject to pre-existing national private international law, by virtue of their exclusion from the Convention's scope under Article 1, namely: legal capacity of individuals (subject to Article 11); internal corporate affairs and capacity; certain maintenance and matrimonial obligations; negotiable instruments; jurisdiction and arbitration agreements; binding of principals by agents' contracts; trust obligations; procedure and evidential matters, subject to exceptions; and EC insurance (but not reinsurance) risks.

Where the Convention does apply, the pre-existing rules permitting express or implied choice of law, and requiring most connected law to apply in the absence thereof, generally continue to operate (Articles 3 and 4), as does (basically) the rule that *lex loci contractus* or applicable law governs formal validity (Article 9) and that *lex loci solutionis* regulates mode of performance (Article 10(2)).

However, there are differences:

a) presumptions exist as to most connected applicable law (Article 4(2)–(5)), and it is possible – although, in the present writer's belief, not the position (see Chapter 9 above) – that *post*-conclusion factors may establish the most closely connected country, as well as those existing as at the date of contract;

b) general protective provisions operate so as to affect choice of law and applicable law in the absence thereof, in the case of consumer and employment contracts (Articles 5 and 6);

c) law governing existence (and validity) of contracts and terms (and of

439

choice of law itself) is subjective, not merely objective, applicable law, and law of the habitual residence can also apply (Article 8);
d) *lex loci contractus* is defined broadly for purposes of formal validity (Article 9(1) and (2));
e) quantification of damages *may* be required to be referred to applicable law (although, it is thought not) (Article 10(1)(c));
f) there is a special choice of law rule (in effect) of common place of contracting for individuals' contractual capacity, operating in prescribed circumstances (Article 11);
g) (at least in the UK, where Article 7(1) is inoperative) illegality of performance is not subject to *lex loci solutionis* as such;
h) burden of proof in contract is for applicable law (Article 14(1)), and modes of proof are for the law of the forum or laws conferring formal validity (Article 14(2));
i) there are specific safeguards for the operation of mandatory rules:

(i) **under pre-existing conflicts**, application of mandatory *English* laws is safeguarded from choice, or, as the case may be, otherwise the application of a foreign law by (1) the choice having to be a *bona fide* and legal choice in any event (*Vita*), which will possibly not be the case, if the contract is totally connected with England; (2) s.27(2) Unfair Contract Terms Act 1977 (*et alia*) expressly preserving prescribed rules of English law (see, for example, s.6) irrespective of chosen law (other than in international cases under s.26); (3) statutes or other laws of extraterritorial operation, applying outside normal conflicts (*The Hollandia*; *Boissevain* v. *Weil*; *Rousillon* v. *Rousillon*), and (4) public policy where a rule of foreign applicable law is repugnant or against comity.**These remain under the Convention**: (1) Article 7(2) (as well as, arguably, Articles 3(3), 5(2) and 6(1)) safeguards English contract rules protected by the likes of s.27 (2) Unfair Contract Terms Act 1977 and other extraterritorial English laws ('private international/conflicts-mandatory'), and Article 9(6) applies mandatory English (or otherwise, foreign) rules of form to contracts for immovables, where English (or foreign) law is *lex situs*, and (2) Article 16 preserves public policy as a ground to refuse to apply a foreign rule. There is no express general provision rendering ineffective the choice of a totally unconnected law; but, in such a case, Article 3(3) provides that *mandatory* rules – in the sense of those national laws (for example, by virtue of s.6 UCTA 1977, in cases other than international under s.26, ss.12–15 of the Sale of Goods Act 1979) which are not permitted thereunder to be derogated from by contractual exclusion ('contracts-mandatory') – of another country (England or otherwise) with which all relevant connections (but for corresponding or other choice of jurisdiction, if such be the case) are established, will nonetheless apply, and Articles 5(2) and 6(1) also preserve application of mandatory rules ('contracts-mandatory') of consumers' laws and laws of employees' places of work (English or foreign) in spite of an inconsistent choice; (ii) **under pre-existing English conflicts**, application of mandatory *foreign* laws is safeguarded from breach, by (1) the doctrine of comity and public policy, calling for contracts in contravention of the laws of a foreign and friendly country not to be enforced (*Foster v. Driscoll*); and (2) the special case of s.27(1) UCTA 1977, preventing English restrictions on contractual exclusion in the Act from being chosen in evasion of the most connected foreign law. **Under the Convention** (1) Article 7(1), enabling application of foreign rules of a closely connected country, which are both contracts-mandatory and private international-mandatory under that country's law, whatever the applicable law (chosen or otherwise), is in fact inapplicable in the United Kingdom under s.2(2) of the 1990 Act (see Article 22(1)(a)); (2) however, Article 3(3), previously seen to safeguard operation of mandatory rules of a wholly connected law from *choice* of another law (but possibly not *English*, from the terms of Article 3(3), although, in the present writer's view, including such), applies to foreign – not just English – mandatory rules (contracts-mandatory), as do Articles 5(2), 6(1) and 9(6) preservation of mandatory rules of *particular* laws, also referred to; and (3) arguably, Article 16 public policy *might* provide the grounds for refusal to enforce a contract valid under the rules of foreign applicable law, where the contract is in breach of the mandatory rules of *another* foreign and friendly country – although, this seems doubtful in view of the specific provision to like effect made by Article 7(1), and Article 16's primary purpose is to strike down individual foreign rules manifestly unsuitable or repugnant to the sensitivities of the forum; (however, if the *Ralli* case can be construed as safeguarding application of laws on supervening illegality of performance under foreign *lex loci solutionis*, as a *domestic* principle of the English forum, it is possible that such procedure may be preserved under *Article 7(2)*, should the alleged English rule in question be held to be mandatory for purposes thereof: if English law itself governs the contract of course, the alleged principle will apply in any event).

The following table gives expression to some of the differences and similarities between pre-existing English and Convention rules on contracts conflicts, as described above:

Table 43.1

Pre-existing English Conflicts	Obligations Convention
Two or more proper laws can apply to different aspects of contract (*Hamlyn & Co. v. Talisker Distillery*)	Likewise (*Article 3(1)*)
Renvoi is excluded (*Re United Railways*)	Likewise (*Article 15*)
Uncertain whether parties can subsequently alter proper law	Parties can alter applicable law (*Article 3(2)*)
Express or implied choice of law is given effect to, if *bona fide*, legal and not against public policy (*Vita Food Products Inc.*), and subject to *inter alia* Unfair Contract Terms Act 1977 s.27 and the Carriage of Goods by Sea Act 1971 (*The Hollandia*), and to general operation of public policy and comity and other mandatory rules of the forum	Likewise: applicable law can be expressly or impliedly chosen (*Article 3(1)*), subject to mandatory rules of law of another state with which all other relevant elements are connected (*Article 3(3)*) and to mandatory rules of the forum (*Article 7(2)*), consumers' (*Article 5(2)*) and employees' (*Article 6(1)*) laws, *lex situs* on form (*Article 9(6)*) and general rules of public policy (*Article 16*)
Objective proper law governs in the absence of express or implied choice of law, as most closely connected on all facts and circumstances (*The Assunzione*)	Likewise: most closely connected country's law governs in the absence of express or implied choice of law (*Article 4(1)*) BUT rebuttable *presumptions* apply as to most connected country (*Article 4(2)–(5)*); AND special applicable law rules govern consumer (*Article 5(3)*) and employment (*Article 6(2)*) contracts
Creation of the contract is for the putative – possibly solely the objective – proper law (*The Parouth*), including the question of validity of the choice of law agreement itself (*Compagnie Tunisienne*)	Likewise: applicable law – however, *chosen* or otherwise – governs validity and existence of the contract (*Article 8(1)*) and of the choice of law agreement itself (*Article 3(4)*) EXCEPT THAT a party may rely on

Table 43.1 continued

Pre-existing English Conflicts	Obligations Convention
	the law of his habitual residence, if reasonable, to show that he did not consent (*Article 8(2)*)
Essential validity, substance of performance, interpretation, limitation and discharge are for the proper law (*Mount Albert, Bonython, National Bank of Greece and Athens SA*)	Likewise (*Articles 8 and 10(1)*)
Formal validity is for *lex loci contractus* (*Guépratte*) or proper law (*Van Grutten*)	Likewise (*Article 9(1)*): subject to variants where the parties were in different countries, and in consumer contracts, and in contracts for immovables (*Article 9(2)–(6)*)
Capacity of individuals to contract is subject to *lex loci contractus* (*Male*), *lex domicilii* (*Sottomayor*), *lex situs* (*Bank of Africa*), or proper law (probably objective) (*Charron*)	Likewise: since such capacity is excluded from the Convention (*Article 1(2)(a)*) EXCEPT THAT *lex loci contractus* may confer capacity regardless of proper law (*Article 11*)
Capacity of companies is for law of place of incorporation, as domicile, and corporate statute and proper law (*Baroness Wenlock*)	Likewise: since corporate capacity is excluded from the Convention (*Article 1(2)(e)*)
Illegality is governed by the proper law (*Kahler*), or by *any* law on comity and public policy grounds (*Foster*), and possibly by *lex loci solutionis* (*Ralli, Libyan Arab Foreign Bank*)	The Convention contains no express ground specifically covering illegality, which is therefore subject to applicable law (*Articles 8 and 10(1)(b) and (d)*). The forum's rules – and possibly also, indirectly, those of foreign *lex loci solutionis* (see below) – may be safeguarded however (*Article 7(2)*), and general foreign rules *may* also be protected on comity and public policy grounds (*Article*

Table 43.1 continued

Pre-existing English Conflicts	Obligations Convention
	16) (as well as in particular contracts under *Articles 5(2)* and *6(1)*).
Mode of performance and money of payment are for *lex loci solutionis* (*Jacobs*; *Miliangos*)	Likewise: (*Article 10(2)*)
Value and validity of money of account is for *lex pecuniae* (*Re Chesterman's Trusts*)	Likewise: as severable choice of law applicable to that aspect (*Article 3(1)*)
Procedural aspects are for *lex fori* (*D'Almeida*)	Likewise: since procedure is excluded (*Article 1(2)(h)*) EXCEPT THAT *Article 14(1)* treats contracts burden of proof as substantive, for applicable law, and under *Article 14(2)* modes of proof are subject to laws on formal validity, in the alternative to *lex fori*; it is further possible – though, in the present writer's opinion, not so – that quantification of damages is made subject to applicable law on substance, under *Article 10(1)(c)*
Application of English law might be safeguarded expressly against operation of otherwise applicable foreign law (see e.g. s.27(2) Unfair Contract Terms Act 1977), or construed as having extraterritorial effect (*Boissevain*; *The Hollandia*), or on the ground of public policy in not enforcing a contract in breach of imperative English law (*Rousillon*; *Robinson*)	*Article 7(2)* generally safeguards application of mandatory English rules, as does *Article 9(6)* in the case of form where England is the *situs*, in respect of contracts for immovables; and *Article 16* prevents operation of foreign rules where this would be manifestly incompatible with public policy; *Article 3(3)* provides for *mandatory* rules of English (or any other) law to apply notwithstanding choice of a different law, if all relevant connections are with England

Table 43.1 continued

Pre-existing English Conflicts	Obligations Convention
	(or other country, as the case may be), and *Articles 5 and 6* preserve application of mandatory provisions of consumers' and employees' laws (English or foreign) respectively, against inconsistent chosen applicable law
Application of a foreign mandatory law may be safeguarded on the ground of comity (*Foster* v. *Driscoll, Libyan Arab Foreign Bank*), or as a consequence of s.27(1) Unfair Contract Terms Act 1977 (as amended by 1990 Act, Sch. 4, para. 4)	*Article 7(1)*, enabling application of mandatory rules of a closely connected foreign country, regardless of applicable law (chosen or otherwise), does not operate in the United Kingdom. But *Article 3(3)* safeguarding mandatory rules of a wholly connected law from choice of another law (even English, in the present submission, in spite of textual uncertainty), and *Articles 5, 6* and *9* also preserving mandatory rules, whatever the (chosen, in the case of *Articles 5* and *6*) applicable law, apply to foreign – not just English – mandatory rules; and arguably, *Article 16* might preserve the national comity basis of refusing to enforce contracts in breach of mandatory rules of a foreign friendly country other than that of applicable law, but this seems doubtful (alternatively, *Article 7(2) might* apply to supervening *illegality* of performance under foreign *lex loci solutionis*, if the *Ralli* case is construed as prohibiting enforcement in such cases as a principle *of domestic English law*, and the latter is held to be mandatory for purposes of *Article 7(2)*: if English

Table 43.1 continued

Pre-existing English Conflicts	Obligations Convention
	law itself governs the contract, of course, the alleged principle will apply in any event, whether mandatory or otherwise).

PART V

44 Conclusions

In the Introduction to this book, there were stated to be four central pillars of the Convention system of regulation of international contracts conflicts: (1) autonomy; (2) law of closest connection in the absence of choice; (3) safeguards for mandatory rules; (4) uniformity of interpretation.

It is felt to be permissible at this stage, following a long and detailed consideration of the Convention's provisions, to take a few brief moments to muse upon whether it was justifiable for the negotiators to base the Convention upon these cardinal rules.

AUTONOMY

Why should contracting parties be entitled to select a law to govern their contract – even to the extent that courts will seek to determine whether they have impliedly opted for a particular country's legal system to regulate their relations, in the absence of express agreement, under Article 3(1) of the Convention? If the law of the country with which the contract is most closely connected is to be referred to in the absence of express or implied choice, as the most appropriate on policy to govern under Article 4(1), how may it then be that intervention of the parties in the matter can so drastically alter the position, in accordance with Article 3?

Because one is dealing with *contracts*, comes the answer. Contracts are all about giving effect to parties' communal wills and agreements, which therefore extends to applicable law itself: just as parties may agree on substantive rights and duties under their contracts, so too should they be enabled effectively to decide upon these latter indirectly through selection of applicable law conferring the same.

But should they? Is this type of party-autonomy necessarily acceptable in contract (or for that matter in any other field, such as formal validity of marriage, or wills)? Cheshire and North seem to think not, on technical and social policy grounds, in the case of *creation* of contracts and parties' contractual *capacity* (pp. 472–3). The real objection, however, is neither of these: technical and logical objections against giving effect to parties' 'agreement' upon applicable law before it has been ascertained whether agreement has actually been reached on that or any other matter may simply be met with the riposte that the chosen law ultimately is applied *by the court*, as a choice of law rule, rather than strictly *by virtue of* parties' agreement, and that accordingly, to that extent, although as open to comment and criticism as any alternative rule of applicable law, such rule of applicability is nonetheless technically *no less* valid than any of the latter; and as regards social policy of protecting, say, minors, against choice of a law conferring capacity and consequently denying their protection, again it can be argued that protection is the preserve of substantive applicable law, should it be disposed to confer it, and not part of the conflicts process itself. Thus, the true and legitimate basis of any criticism which may be levelled at party autonomy is that of *legal policy*: courts should apply what *they* consider to be the most appropriate law to govern contractual or other legal relations, not that which the parties believe to be so or otherwise wish the court to apply – just as it is not for contracting parties to a purely domestic transaction to reconstruct a notional English law of contract for English courts to apply *as law* in the event of disputes arising. According to this argument, the most that may be contemplated as falling within the scope of parties' autonomy over their contract is that the allegedly chosen 'law' should be allowed to govern – but only subject to initial operation of the most connected law as applicable law, and then only as *terms* of the contract, not strictly as law (commonly referred to as mere incorporation of terms by reference, as opposed to choice of law, the two different processes being distinguished by the Germans as *materiellrechtlich* and *kollisionsrechtlich*, respectively). Thus, for example, in order to decide upon creation of the contractual bond, it would initially have to be determined according to most connected applicable law that the contract had come into being, after which, parties' own choice of 'law' could then be referred to in order to determine the very same question as a matter of parties' agreement upon terms; the same procedure would be involved in matters of capacity and illegality. Where, however, the approach – at least in principle – goes beyond that of Cheshire and North, is that even questions of standard, content and discharge of contractual performance would first be subjected to most connected applicable law, and chosen law only permitted to override the former's rules where the former's law so decreed. In practice, it should be said, this would be unlikely to differ a great deal from Cheshire and North, given the generally optional nature of such rules (especially in an international context). Nevertheless, certain differences would exist: were chosen law to be regarded as mere terms rather than law as such, it is possible that it would have to be applied as it stood at the date of contracting, in the event of subsequent changes thereto (unless it were to be argued that parties had selected it to apply as terms in whatever condition it might be at the date of any dispute – difficult, one would have thought, in view of uncertainties involved as to impliedly agreed date for its content to be established, and, in any event, on normal principles of contractual certainty of terms: see *Scammell v. Ousten* [1941] AC 251); in the matter of interpretation of the incorporated provisions of a foreign legal system, technically, if these were to be treated as terms, their interpretation would be a matter for most connected applicable law's principles or meanings (for example, as under Article 10(1)(a) of the Obligations Convention), whereas, if instead they were to be regarded as law, they would have to be pleaded and proved in the usual manner by resort to foreign experts therein, or be considered to be the same as English *lex fori* in the absence of such evidence (although, even in the former case, foreign experts might have to be called upon in order to interpret the contractual terms); and finally, if chosen law were deemed to be terms, rather than law, in the case of performance obligations, any mandatory rules of the most connected applicable law thereon would automatically apply so as to prevent operation of the inconsistent 'terms' of selected law, whereas, under the narrower Cheshire and North approach, confining most connected law to the *logical* areas of creation, capacity and legality, mandatory rules of law on performance under that latter law would require to be applied extraterritorially, irrespective of otherwise applicable (chosen) law, a far more uncertain prospect, in particular where mandatory laws of most connected *foreign* countries are in issue rather than those of the forum, both under pre-existing national English conflicts and even under the Convention in the case of proceedings in the United Kingdom's courts (see 1990 Act s.2(2); and Convention, Article 22(1)(a)).

Accordingly, as said, the question of scope, if any, to be given to party autonomy in contract choice of law is one of *legal policy* in the administration of justice: which of most connected law and law chosen by the parties, where these differ, ought to be applied *by courts as their choice of law rule* on most appropriate governing law?

Against autonomy, arguments based upon logic and circularity, protection of the weak, and preservation of courts' control over applicability of legal norms, were previously cited; and in addition, it might be said that if most connected law were to apply irrespective of parties' choice of law, most appropriate law to safeguard consumers' and employees' rights would then govern automatically, and there would be no need for inclusion of special choice of law exceptions for mandatory rules, such as those in Articles 5(2) and 6(1) of the Obligations Convention.

In the present submission, however, in the case of performance (and capacity too), such considerations ought not to be permitted to prevail over the clear commercial benefits of allowing party autonomy to be given effect to in applicable law, and, as seen, the writ of logic still runs in any event where law chosen is viewed as being applicable by virtue of *courts'* policy finding in favour of giving overriding significance to such established agreement between the parties as to applicable law – no less of a *connection* than any others constituting a link between a contract and a territory; and if parties wish to have their relations regulated according to norms of a society other than that in which the socioeconomic effects of their transaction are principally felt, then, except in the case of mandatory provisions of the latter's laws, neither the forum's nor any of the other two legal systems' interests would seem to require their wishes in this respect to be ignored.

Articles 3(1) and 10(1) of the Convention give effect to this principle.

Yet not so easily dismissed are those objections relating to applicability of 'chosen' law to creation of the contractual bond – not purely on technical and logical grounds, since, as seen, it is courts' prerogative to apply laws based upon any point of contact considered suitable, whether founded upon parties' intervention or otherwise, but because, until a main agreement and choice of law are established as having been concluded, it can hardly be possible for courts to treat such a policy *connection* as established, so as to give effect to a choice of law rule according overriding significance thereto: and so, doubts may occur over the justification for rules in Articles 3(4) and 8 of the Convention, subjecting such matters to the 'chosen' law connection (see Part III, Chapters 8 and 13). The proper course, it would seem, would have been to subject existence of choice of law to an appropriate legal system in the first place, and thereafter there could have been few objections against applying such chosen law, established as existing according to the former, to the question of main contractual existence (or even to that of choice of law itself, as secondary applicable law thereon).

LAW OF MOST CLOSELY CONNECTED COUNTRY

Article 4 enshrines the principle that most appropriate law to govern contracts in the absence of agreement thereon between the parties is, as under pre-existing English contract conflicts, that of the country with which the contract is most closely connected, and it provides rebuttable presumptions as to determination of such law, based on the characteristic performance obligation under the contract, *et alia*.

Various technical difficulties surrounding the Convention's rule were considered in Chapter 9. The question now posed is whether such an approach is justified in any event, as a matter of principle.

The system of *rebuttable presumptions* as to most connected applicable law under Article 4, and in particular resort to the characteristic performance concept thereunder, have proved easy targets for critics. In truth, *initially* at any rate, the level of uncertainty created through inclusion of the latter and its difficulty of construction are fairly disastrous from the point of view of commercial convenience.

On the other hand, however, would the credentials of a pure rule of closest connection in the absence of parties' choice, as exists under pre-existing national English conflicts, have been any more justified than the method adopted? Where two parties to an international contract establish connections with a number of countries thereunder, is it really an appropriate and 'objective' aproach to conclude that the law of the country having, on balance, the most – even most 'significant' – connections with the contract should be referred to, as that which reasonable parties or businessmen ought to have decided upon had they thought about it? In *The Assunzione* [1954] P. 150, did the edge in favour of overall Italian connections truly justify the drastic consequences that the contract would be governed by Italian, rather than French, law? In cases other than those in which an overwhelming balance of factors is established with one particular country in an international transaction, why should the socio-economic interests of a society having the lesser connections – as well as those of the party or parties to whose benefit it would be for such state's laws to apply – be disregarded, in favour of those of the country having the *closest* connection? The latter type of international contract does not really 'belong' or have its 'seat' anywhere, and it is purely for forensic convenience – rather than logic, principle, socio-economic policy, or even commercial convenience in view of uncertainties involved – that courts may seek to apply the *winner* amongst those laws having competing connections therewith. It is both extremely presumptuous to suggest that reasonable parties would have chosen such law as most appropriate to govern their relations had they thought about it (if choice were even to be admitted as a valid influencing factor: see above, p.449 *et seq.*), and also questionable whether such law is justified in principle in any event more than, for example, *lex loci contractus* or *lex loci solutionis* as such in multinational cases.

Accordingly, viewed in the preceding light, law of the most closely connected country would not appear to enjoy the sort of superiority over Article 4(2) which the latter's detractors would have us believe. On the contrary, it is perfectly possible to mount an argument to the effect that as a matter both of presumed intent and of socio-economic and legal policy, it is the law of the country of each contracting party's base of operations – habitual residence in the case of individuals or central administration of legal entities, or principal place of business of traders, or, if different, that through which the transaction is effected in the latter case – which should be turned to, at least presumptively, as that most suitable to govern a party's legal relations in contract; and further, that since it is essential for commercial convenience that one of the parties' laws alone should be selected to govern, it is not wholly unreasonable that it should be that of the party who can in some way be said to be responsible for the most *significant* of the obligations imposed by the contract if ascertainable – perhaps that which may be said to be *characteristic* of the overall contractual undertaking – in other words, precisely that which is prescribed by Article 4(2)!

The problem, of course, with all of this is very simple: as was demonstrated at some length in Chapter 9, it is not possible to identify, nor even for that matter to prove the conceptual existence of, the *characteristic obligation* of a contract, and consequently, whereas the idea of the latter as the basis of presumptively applicable law may – as its most vociferous critics should perhaps note – be considered to be correct on the purist level of socio-economic and legal policy, nevertheless, from a practical point of view it is quite unworkable without being altered beyond recognition in its actual application.

Accordingly, it has to be concluded that a pure closest connection test would at least have enabled courts to give effect to what they considered to be the most important and significant connection, or overall balance of connections, in each individual case, albeit without much certainty in advance in many cases. The characteristic obligation system, it is true, may – and probably should (see above, Chapter 9) – be operated in precisely the same way, merely as a different *code word* to apply as describing the most appropriate law to govern on the facts of the case, in the light of numbers of connections with particular countries and the individual and collective significance of each such element. However, the difference between the latter and the former *code* is that the former carries out its task openly, rather than in the guise of operating according to some more exact scientific formula for securing the application of the most suitable law. Certainty, as seen, is a casualty in either case – at least, frequently on the facts, if not also in respect of legal principles to be applied thereto in the absence of sufficient precedents. However, if parties to non-consumer contracts (Article 4 is inapplicable to consumer contracts: Article 5(3)) do not make provision as to applicable law expressly or impliedly in their contracts, the situation is inherently uncertain, and the appropriate choice of law rule is simply likely to reflect this (see above, Chapter 9).

MANDATORY SAFEGUARDS

Much has been written about the Convention's mandatory safeguards. Those in Article 3(3) on mandatory rules of the law of the otherwise wholly connected country apart from choice, and in Articles 5(2) and 6(1) on consumer and employee protection respectively, are the result of Article 3 itself, permitting full party autonomy in choice of law. Only the mandatory rules of what is considered to be the most appropriate law are safeguarded, however, not the latter in its entirety. Safeguards in Article 7 in favour of mandatory rules of closely connected countries in general and those of the forum, as well as those in respect of mandatory laws of form of the *situs* of immovable property under Article 9(6), are not specifically the product of Article 3, but instead give effect to what are seen as essential interests of parties or states that particular laws should be applied – although, again, only in the case of their mandatory rules as opposed to such laws as a whole.

It is regrettable that the Convention mandatory system has had to be constructed in so complex and overlapping a manner. A single provision to the effect that mandatory rules of the law otherwise applicable in the absence of choice should continue to apply notwithstanding the latter would surely have sufficed in place of Articles 3(3), 5(2) and 6(1) (a mere formal change in the latter two cases, and it hardly seems conceivable that the wholly connected Article 3(3) law would not be applicable under Article 4), together with the existing safeguard for the forum's mandatory laws in Article 7(2), and presumably also that in respect of *lex situs*'s mandatory laws of form under Article 9(6) in the case of immovables (although, in this instance, *lex situs* is invariably likely to be applicable law under Article 4(3) in any event, and frequently too, *lex fori*, covered by Article 7(2), in EEC Contracting States to the Judgments Convention, under Article 16(1) thereof, conferring exclusive jurisdiction upon courts of the *situs*, and according to national jurisdiction grounds in the case of non-EEC immovables – except that, in accordance with Article 6 of the San Sebastian Convention on Spanish and Portuguese Accession to the Judgments Convention, courts of the Contracting State of the defendant's domicile will also have jurisdiction over disputes involving short tenancies of immovables in circumstances prescribed under Article 16(1)(b) of the amended Judgments Convention, so that the situation could then arise in which *lex situs* was not also *lex fori*: again, however, in this situation, the presumption of applicability of *lex situs* under Article 4(3) would in fact be likely to be rebutted in favour of law of the country of the defendant's domicile as most closely connected law under Article 4(1) by virtue of Article 4(5), that is, once more, *lex fori*). As for Article 7(1), providing safeguards for mandatory rules of the law of *any* country having a close connection, one argument would be that whilst, doubtless (though, evidently, not in the view of the United Kingdom, Germany, Ireland and Luxembourg, which have all made reservations of inapplicability under Article 22(1)(a)) politic, this provision would have no real place in a system giving effect to mandatory rules of the law having the closest connection with the contract, and except in the most serious cases of manifest contravention of a state's public policy under Article 16, *Regazzoni v. K.C. Sethia (1944) Ltd* might thus usefully have been allowed to fall into desuetude. In the author's opinion, however, this would be a mistake. It is not simply the *most* connected country which may have an interest in seeing its mandatory laws applied irrespective of applicable law, and an ultimate discretion in the forum to apply such rules of other states, which have a close and compelling connection with the contract, a useful and important element in the effective regulation of international contractual relations (see above, p.256).

One further noteworthy feature in the Convention's mandatory regime is that under Article 3(3) it is only the mandatory rules of the otherwise wholly connected law which are made to apply notwithstanding an inconsistent choice by the parties. This may perhaps be viewed as rather surprising when compared with the pre-existing English rule whereby, in principle at least, choice of a wholly unconnected law *may* be regarded as a sham, not seriously intended, and accordingly wholly inapplicable (*Vita Foods*). Furthermore, under Article 3(3), a party can openly admit to his agreement upon a particular law, and yet subsequently seek to rely upon the mandatory rules of the most connected law in the course of contentious proceedings (to respond that this is justified because application of such rules is mandatory merely begs the question; it further stretches the imagination to argue that operation of mandatory law under Article 3(3) is an exception implied into parties' agreements on choice of law). What of the case moreover where neither party wishes the mandatory rules to apply? Such an exclusionary *choice of law agreement* at the time of contracting or subsequently under Article 3(2) will doubtless be subject to Article 3(3) (or 5(2) or 6(1)), no less than any purely positive agreement upon application of a particular country's law. But supposing neither party wishes mandatory rules to apply under Article 3(3) at the date of the proceedings? Presumably, this will simply be achieved through their failure to plead the applicability of the mandatory rules of the foreign legal system – although, this writer has considerable doubts over whether the stratagem will prove effective, first because Article 3(3) specifies no time limit restricting its operation and objective to the period prior to proceedings, nor, secondly, is it clear that the court would not be obliged – following upon the Contracting State's public international obligations – to apply the Convention's rules on applicable law *of its own motion*, that is, to call for necessary pleadings by the parties. (At least where the chosen law was English, parties might achieve inapplicability of mandatory rules of the connected foreign law by pleading the latter, yet providing no evidence as to its content, upon which it would be deemed to be the same as English law of the forum – chosen applicable law *in casu!*)

UNIFORM INTERPRETATION AND APPLICATION

The Convention is the present. Uniform mechanisms for its interpretation are the future. The latter, however, are what distinguish the Convention from lesser international efforts at contract conflicts unification. When the Brussels Interpretation Protocol has entered into force, the means for greatly increasing the prospects of enduring uniformity will then exist. There will be a natural reluctance by parties to commercial contracts to see this discretionary interpretative jurisdiction of the European Court exercised: their immediate interests will be in avoidance of extra costs and delays, rather than in the homogeneous development of Community law. Yet it hardly needs repeating that the latter is precisely the prerequisite of greater equalization and harmonization of legal protections under the legal processes of different states of the EC. It is significant, therefore, that under Article 2 of the Brussels Protocol it is for national courts there indicated, not contracting parties, to decide whether to refer to the European Court (albeit that the parties' wishes may be treated as relevant to a court's decision in this respect: see *Bulmer* v. *Bollinger* [1974] Ch. 401, 425, in the context of references under Article 177 of the EEC Treaty), and it is to be hoped that, as in the case of such references for interpretation of the Judgments Convention (see *Marc Rich & Co. AG* v. *Società Italiana Impianti P.A.* [1989] 1 Lloyd's Rep. 548, p. 555), our courts will not flinch from requesting the European Court's assistance, when considered necessary and desirable, in spite of the parties' objections. In terms of posterity, consequently, it may be that the three most important elements in the whole of Rome Convention law will be found to be the following: Article 18, requiring uniform interpretation and application of the Convention's provisions, in the light of their international character and the desirability of achieving uniformity; the Brussels Interpretation Protocol, hopefully soon to be brought into force without any further delays in securing the required number of ratifications by Convention states, and providing the essential unifying influence and impetus at the centre; and such arrangements as are made, in accordance with the First Joint Declaration annexed to the Brussels Protocol (O.J. 1989, No. L48/8), for the exchange of information amongst Contracting States as to judgments of certain of their courts concerning the Obligations Convention. Upon these three preceding components may largely depend the substantial long-term success of the Convention, as a unifying force in international contract conflicts, and the hoped-for absence of denunciations of the Convention by Contracting States on the expiration of its initial ten-year period of duration under Article 30.

Some elements within the English legal profession have publicly lamented the transition, under the Convention, from that magnificent judge-made edifice that is the English conflict of laws in the matter of contracts, built up over the last 150 years by our courts and sought after by those engaged in commerce throughout the world as a common lingua franca.

It is true to say, however – without wishing in any way to detract from the considerable force of such arguments – that gaps and uncertainties there were, and one suspects that on more than one occasion counsel and businessmen have perhaps mutually combined with their contracting counterparts to resist the cost and delays involved in seeking judicial clarification of the rules – splendid, ostensibly, from the point of view of consensus-motivated transacting, but more dubious from that of availability, where needed, of developed legal doctrine for the governance of international contracts.

Viewed against this background, therefore, what the Convention's introduction would actually seem to achieve, through its systematic presentation of a comprehensive corps of legal principle to regulate the applicable law of contracts in a relatively candid and explicit manner, is to invite renewed consideration of some old and familiar questions, which had undergone a deal of scrutiny in the past, and yet still depended upon their random treatment by the courts and the commercial willingness of parties to litigate over uncertainties. Accordingly, the mystery has not disappeared; it is merely repackaged as *Euro-mystery*.

The reassuring thought for those Convention sceptics, however, must be that the pre-existing law remains, that is to say, outside the Convention's subject matter and temporal scope, and it will admittedly be of some interest to observe how the two systems are able to compete, when operating side by side in the same English courts. Convention critics' dream must be that its rules will eventually be found to be so unattractive, when compared with those of our pre-existing system, that the United Kingdom will be eager to denounce, once the ten-year sentence under Article 30 has been served.

Sheer terror of being viewed as an enemy by one of the opposing camps prevents this writer from revealing his unworthy sentiments respecting the above. Let the following simply be declared, therefore: *The king is not dead. Long live the king* – from which, readers may divine whatever they wish.

Appendix A
The Contracts (Applicable Law)* Act 1990

*Reproduced by kind permission of Her Majesty's Stationery Office.

ELIZABETH II   c. 36

Contracts (Applicable Law) Act 1990

1990 CHAPTER 36

An Act to make provision as to the law applicable to contractual obligations in the case of conflict of laws.   [26th July 1990]

B<small>E IT ENACTED</small> by the Queen's most Excellent Majesty, by and with the advice and consent of the Lords Spiritual and Temporal, and Commons, in this present Parliament assembled, and by the authority of the same, as follows:—

    1. In this Act—   Meaning of "the
       (a) "the Rome Convention" means the Convention on the law   Conventions".
applicable to contractual obligations opened for signature in Rome on 19th June 1980 and signed by the United Kingdom on 7th December 1981;

       (b) "the Luxembourg Convention" means the Convention on the accession of the Hellenic Republic to the Rome Convention signed by the United Kingdom in Luxembourg on 10th April 1984; and

       (c) "the Brussels Protocol" means the first Protocol on the interpretation of the Rome Convention by the European Court signed by the United Kingdom in Brussels on 19th December 1988;

and the Rome Convention, the Luxembourg Convention and the Brussels Protocol are together referred to as "the Conventions".

    2.—(1) Subject to subsections (2) and (3) below, the Conventions shall   Conventions to
have the force of law in the United Kingdom.   have force of law.

    (2) Articles 7(1) and 10(1)(e) of the Rome Convention shall not have the force of law in the United Kingdom.

    (3) Notwithstanding Article 19(2) of the Rome Convention, the Conventions shall apply in the case of conflicts between the laws of different parts of the United Kingdom.

(4) For ease of reference there are set out in Schedules 1, 2 and 3 to this Act respectively the English texts of—

(a) the Rome Convention;

(b) the Luxembourg Convention; and

(c) the Brussels Protocol.

Interpretation of Conventions.

3.—(1) Any question as to the meaning or effect of any provision of the Conventions shall, if not referred to the European Court in accordance with the Brussels Protocol, be determined in accordance with the principles laid down by, and any relevant decision of, the European Court.

(2) Judicial notice shall be taken of any decision of, or expression of opinion by, the European Court on any such question.

(3) Without prejudice to any practice of the courts as to the matters which may be considered apart from this subsection—

O.J.1980
No.C282/1.

(a) the report on the Rome Convention by Professor Mario Giuliano and Professor Paul Lagarde which is reproduced in the Official Journal of the Communities of 31st October 1980 may be considered in ascertaining the meaning or effect of any provision of that Convention; and

(b) any report on the Brussels Protocol which is reproduced in the Official Journal of the Communities may be considered in ascertaining the meaning or effect of any provision of that Protocol.

Revision of Conventions etc.

4.—(1) If at any time it appears to Her Majesty in Council that Her Majesty's Government in the United Kingdom—

(a) have agreed to a revision of any of the Conventions (including, in particular, any revision connected with the accession to the Rome Convention of any state); or

(b) have given notification in accordance with Article 22(3) of the Rome Convention that either or both of the provisions mentioned in section 2(2) above shall have the force of law in the United Kingdom,

Her Majesty may by Order in Council make such consequential modifications of this Act or any other statutory provision, whenever passed or made, as Her Majesty considers appropriate.

(2) An Order in Council under subsection (1) above shall not be made unless a draft of the Order has been laid before Parliament and approved by a resolution of each House.

(3) In subsection (1) above—

"modifications" includes additions, omissions and alterations;

"revision" means an omission from, addition to or alteration of any of the Conventions and includes replacement of any of the Conventions to any extent by another convention, protocol or other description of international agreement; and

"statutory provision" means any provision contained in an Act, or in any Northern Ireland legislation, or in—

(a) subordinate legislation (as defined in section 21(1) of the Interpretation Act 1978); or

1978 c. 30.

(b) any instrument of a legislative character made under any Northern Ireland legislation.

5. The enactments specified in Schedule 4 to this Act shall have effect subject to the amendments specified in that Schedule.

Consequential amendments.

6. This Act binds the Crown.

Application to Crown.

7. This Act shall come into force on such day as the Lord Chancellor and the Lord Advocate may by order made by statutory instrument appoint; and different days may be appointed for different provisions or different purposes.

Commencement.

8.—(1) This Act extends to Northern Ireland.

Extent.

(2) Her Majesty may by Order in Council direct that all or any of the provisions of this Act shall extend to any of the following territories, namely—

(a) the Isle of Man;

(b) any of the Channel Islands;

(c) Gibraltar;

(d) the Sovereign Base Areas of Akrotiri and Dhekelia (that is to say, the areas mentioned in section 2(1) of the Cyprus Act 1960).

1960 c. 52.

(3) An Order in Council under subsection (2) above may modify this Act in its application to any of the territories mentioned in that subsection and may contain such supplementary provisions as Her Majesty considers appropriate; and in this subsection "modify" shall be construed in accordance with section 4 above.

9. This Act may be cited as the Contracts (Applicable Law) Act 1990.

Short title.

SCHEDULES

Section 2.

SCHEDULE 1

THE ROME CONVENTION

The High Contracting Parties to the Treaty establishing the European Economic Community,

Anxious to continue in the field of private international law the work of unification of law which has already been done within the Community, in particular in the field of jurisdiction and enforcement of judgments,

Wishing to establish uniform rules concerning the law applicable to contractual obligations,

Have agreed as follows:

TITLE I

SCOPE OF THE CONVENTION

Article 1

Scope of the Convention

1. The rules of this Convention shall apply to contractual obligations in any situation involving a choice between the laws of different countries.

2. They shall not apply to:

(a) questions involving the status or legal capacity of natural persons, without prejudice to Article 11;

(b) contractual obligations relating to:

-wills and succession,

-rights in property arising out of a matrimonial relationship,

-rights and duties arising out of a family relationship, parentage, marriage or affinity, including maintenance obligations in respect of children who are not legitimate;

(c) obligations arising under bills of exchange, cheques and promissory notes and other negotiable instruments to the extent that the obligations under such other negotiable instruments arise out of their negotiable character;

(d) arbitration agreements and agreements on the choice of court;

(e) questions governed by the law of companies and other bodies corporate or unincorporate such as the creation, by registration or otherwise, legal capacity, internal organisation or winding up of companies and other bodies corporate or unincorporate and the personal liability of officers and members as such for the obligations of the company or body;

(f) the question whether an agent is able to bind a principal, or an organ to bind a company or body corporate or unincorporate, to a third party;

(g) the constitution of trusts and the relationship between settlors, trustees and beneficiaries;

(h) evidence and procedure, without prejudice to Article 14.

3. The rules of this Convention do not apply to contracts of insurance which cover risks situated in the territories of the Member States of the European Economic Community. In order to determine whether a risk is situated in these territories the court shall apply its internal law.

4. The preceding paragraph does not apply to contracts of re-insurance.

Article 2
Application of law of non-contracting States

Any law specified by this Convention shall be applied whether or not it is the law of a Contracting State.

TITLE II
UNIFORM RULES
Article 3
Freedom of choice

1. A contract shall be governed by the law chosen by the parties. The choice must be express or demonstrated with reasonable certainty by the terms of the contract or the circumstances of the case. By their choice the parties can select the law applicable to the whole or a part only of the contract.

2. The parties may at any time agree to subject the contract to a law other than that which previously governed it, whether as a result of an earlier choice under this Article or of other provisions of this Convention. Any variation by the parties of the law to be applied made after the conclusion of the contract shall not prejudice its formal validity under Article 9 or adversely affect the rights of third parties.

3. The fact that the parties have chosen a foreign law, whether or not accompanied by the choice of a foreign tribunal, shall not, where all the other elements relevant to the situation at the time of the choice are connected with one country only, prejudice the application of rules of the law of that country which cannot be derogated from by contract, hereinafter called "mandatory rules".

4. The existence and validity of the consent of the parties as to the choice of the applicable law shall be determined in accordance with the provisions of Articles 8, 9 and 11.

Article 4
Applicable law in the absence of choice

1. To the extent that the law applicable to the contract has not been chosen in accordance with Article 3, the contract shall be governed by the law of the country with which it is most closely connected. Nevertheless, a severable part of the contract which has a closer connection with another country may by way of exception be governed by the law of that other country.

2. Subject to the provisions of paragraph 5 of this Article, it shall be presumed that the contract is most closely connected with the country where the party who is to effect the performance which is characteristic of the contract has, at the time of conclusion of the contract, his habitual residence, or, in the case of a body corporate or unincorporate, its central administration. However, if the contract is entered into in the course of that party's trade or profession, that country shall be the country in which the principal place of business is situated or, where under the terms of the contract the performance is to be effected through a place of business other than the principal place of business, the country in which that other place of business is situated.

3. Notwithstanding the provisions of paragraph 2 of this Article, to the extent that the subject matter of the contract is a right in immovable property or a right to use immovable property it shall be presumed that the contract is most closely connected with the country where the immovable property is situated.

4. A contract for the carriage of goods shall not be subject to the presumption in paragraph 2. In such a contract if the country in which, at the time the contract is concluded, the carrier has his principal place of business is also the country in which the place of loading or the place of discharge or the principal place of business of the consignor is situated, it shall be presumed that the contract is most

closely connected with that country. In applying this paragraph single voyage charter-parties and other contracts the main purpose of which is the carriage of goods shall be treated as contracts for the carriage of goods.

5. Paragraph 2 shall not apply if the characteristic performance cannot be determined, and the presumptions in paragraphs 2, 3 and 4 shall be disregarded if it appears from the circumstances as a whole that the contract is more closely connected with another country.

Article 5

Certain consumer contracts

1. This Article applies to a contract the object of which is the supply of goods or services to a person ("the consumer") for a purpose which can be regarded as being outside his trade or profession, or a contract for the provision of credit for that object.

2. Notwithstanding the provisions of Article 3, a choice of law made by the parties shall not have the result of depriving the consumer of the protection afforded to him by the mandatory rules of the law of the country in which he has his habitual residence:

- -if in that country the conclusion of the contract was preceded by a specific invitation addressed to him or by advertising, and he had taken in that country all the steps necessary on his part for the conclusion of the contract, or
- -if the other party or his agent received the consumer's order in that country, or
- -if the contract is for the sale of goods and the consumer travelled from that country to another country and there gave his order, provided that the consumer's journey was arranged by the seller for the purpose of inducing the consumer to buy.

3. Notwithstanding the provisions of Article 4, a contract to which this Article applies shall, in the absence of choice in accordance with Article 3, be governed by the law of the country in which the consumer has his habitual residence if it is entered into in the circumstances described in paragraph 2 of this Article.

4. This Article shall not apply to:

(a) a contract of carriage;

(b) a contract for the supply of services where the services are to be supplied to the consumer exclusively in a country other than that in which he has his habitual residence.

5. Notwithstanding the provisions of paragraph 4, this Article shall apply to a contract which, for an inclusive price, provides for a combination of travel and accommodation.

Article 6

Individual employment contracts

1. Notwithstanding the provisions of Article 3, in a contract of employment a choice of law made by the parties shall not have the result of depriving the employee of the protection afforded to him by the mandatory rules of the law which would be applicable under paragraph 2 in the absence of choice.

2. Notwithstanding the provisions of Article 4, a contract of employment shall, in the absence of choice in accordance with Article 3, be governed:

(a) by the law of the country in which the employee habitually carries out his work in performance of the contract, even if he is temporarily employed in another country; or

(b) if the employee does not habitually carry out his work in any one country, by the law of the country in which the place of business through which he was engaged is situated;

unless it appears from the circumstances as a whole that the contract is more closely connected with another country, in which case the contract shall be governed by the law of that country.

SCH. 1

Article 7

Mandatory rules

1. When applying under this Convention the law of a country, effect may be given to the mandatory rules of the law of another country with which the situation has a close connection, if and in so far as, under the law of the latter country, those rules must be applied whatever the law applicable to the contract. In considering whether to give effect to these mandatory rules, regard shall be had to their nature and purpose and to the consequences of their application or non-application.

2. Nothing in this Convention shall restrict the application of the rules of the law of the forum in a situation where they are mandatory irrespective of the law otherwise applicable to the contract.

Article 8

Material validity

1. The existence and validity of a contract, or of any term of a contract, shall be determined by the law which would govern it under this Convention if the contract or term were valid.

2. Nevertheless a party may rely upon the law of the country in which he has his habitual residence to establish that he did not consent if it appears from the circumstances that it would not be reasonable to determine the effect of his conduct in accordance with the law specified in the preceding paragraph.

Article 9

Formal validity

1. A contract concluded between persons who are in the same country is formally valid if it satisfies the formal requirements of the law which governs it under this Convention or of the law of the country where it is concluded.

2. A contract concluded between persons who are in different countries is formally valid if it satisfies the formal requirements of the law which governs it under this Convention or of the law of one of those countries.

3. Where a contract is concluded by an agent, the country in which the agent acts is the relevant country for the purposes of paragraphs 1 and 2.

4. An act intended to have legal effect relating to an existing or contemplated contract is formally valid if it satisfies the formal requirements of the law which under this Convention governs or would govern the contract or of the law of the country where the act was done.

5. The provisions of the preceding paragraphs shall not apply to a contract to which Article 5 applies, concluded in the circumstances described in paragraph 2 of Article 5. The formal validity of such a contract is governed by the law of the country in which the consumer has his habitual residence.

6. Notwithstanding paragraphs 1 to 4 of this Article, a contract the subject matter of which is a right in immovable property or a right to use immovable property shall be subject to the mandatory requirements of form of the law of the country where the property is situated if by that law those requirements are imposed irrespective of the country where the contract is concluded and irrespective of the law governing the contract.

SCH. 1

Article 10

Scope of the applicable law

1. The law applicable to a contract by virtue of Articles 3 to 6 and 12 of this Convention shall govern in particular:

   (a) interpretation;

   (b) performance;

   (c) within the limits of the powers conferred on the court by its procedural law, the consequences of breach, including the assessment of damages in so far as it is governed by rules of law;

   (d) the various ways of extinguishing obligations, and prescription and limitation of actions;

   (e) the consequences of nullity of the contract.

2. In relation to the manner of performance and the steps to be taken in the event of defective performance regard shall be had to the law of the country in which performance takes place.

Article 11

Incapacity

In a contract concluded between persons who are in the same country, a natural person who would have capacity under the law of that country may invoke his incapacity resulting from another law only if the other party to the contract was aware of this incapacity at the time of the conclusion of the contract or was not aware thereof as a result of negligence.

Article 12

Voluntary assignment

1. The mutual obligations of assignor and assignee under a voluntary assignment of a right against another person ("the debtor") shall be governed by the law which under this Convention applies to the contract between the assignor and assignee.

2. The law governing the right to which the assignment relates shall determine its assignability, the relationship between the assignee and the debtor, the conditions under which the assignment can be invoked against the debtor and any question whether the debtor's obligations have been discharged.

Article 13

Subrogation

1. Where a person ("the creditor") has a contractual claim upon another ("the debtor"), and a third person has a duty to satisfy the creditor, or has in fact satisfied the creditor in discharge of that duty, the law which governs the third person's duty to satisfy the creditor shall determine whether the third person is entitled to exercise against the debtor the rights which the creditor had against the debtor under the law governing their relationship and, if so, whether he may do so in full or only to a limited extent.

2. The same rule applies where several persons are subject to the same contractual claim and one of them has satisfied the creditor.

Article 14

Burden of proof, etc.

1. The law governing the contract under this Convention applies to the extent that it contains, in the law of contract, rules which raise presumptions of law or determine the burden of proof.

2. A contract or an act intended to have legal effect may be proved by any mode of proof recognised by the law of the forum or by any of the laws referred to in Article 9 under which that contract or act is formally valid, provided that such mode of proof can be administered by the forum.

Article 15

Exclusion of renvoi

The application of the law of any country specified by this Convention means the application of the rules of law in force in that country other than its rules of private international law.

Article 16

"Ordre public"

The application of a rule of the law of any country specified by this Convention may be refused only if such application is manifestly incompatible with the public policy ("ordre public") of the forum.

Article 17

No retrospective effect

This Convention shall apply in a Contracting State to contracts made after the date on which this Convention has entered into force with respect to that State.

Article 18

Uniform interpretation

In the interpretation and application of the preceding uniform rules, regard shall be had to their international character and to the desirability of achieving uniformity in their interpretation and application.

Article 19

States with more than one legal system

1. Where a State comprises several territorial units each of which has its own rules of law in respect of contractual obligations, each territorial unit shall be considered as a country for the purposes of identifying the law applicable under this Convention.

2. A State within which different territorial units have their own rules of law in respect of contractual obligations shall not be bound to apply this Convention to conflicts solely between the laws of such units.

Article 20

Precedence of Community law

This Convention shall not affect the application of provisions which, in relation to particular matters, lay down choice of law rules relating to contractual obligations and which are or will be contained in acts of the institutions of the European Communities or in national laws harmonised in implementation of such acts.

SCH. 1

Article 21

Relationship with other conventions

This Convention shall not prejudice the application of international conventions to which a Contracting State is, or becomes, a party.

Article 22

Reservations

1. Any Contracting State may, at the time of signature, ratification, acceptance or approval, reserve the right not to apply:

   (a) the provisions of Article 7(1);

   (b) the provisions of Article 10(1)(e).

2. Any Contracting State may also, when notifying an extension of the Convention in accordance with Article 27(2), make one or more of these reservations, with its effect limited to all or some of the territories mentioned in the extension.

3. Any Contracting State may at any time withdraw a reservation which it has made; the reservation shall cease to have effect on the first day of the third calendar month after notification of the withdrawal.

TITLE III

FINAL PROVISIONS

Article 23

1. If, after the date on which this Convention has entered into force for a Contracting State, that State wishes to adopt any new choice of law rule in regard to any particular category of contract within the scope of this Convention, it shall communicate its intention to the other signatory States through the Secretary-General of the Council of the European Communities.

2. Any signatory State may, within six months from the date of the communication made to the Secretary-General, request him to arrange consultations between signatory States in order to reach agreement.

3. If no signatory State has requested consultations within this period or if within two years following the communication made to the Secretary-General no agreement is reached in the course of consultations, the Contracting State concerned may amend its law in the manner indicated. The measures taken by that State shall be brought to the knowledge of the other signatory States through the Secretary-General of the Council of the European Communities.

Article 24

1. If, after the date on which this Convention has entered into force with respect to a Contracting State, that State wishes to become a party to a multilateral convention whose principal aim or one of whose principal aims is to lay down rules of private international law concerning any of the matters governed by this Convention, the procedure set out in Article 23 shall apply. However, the period of two years, referred to in paragraph 3 of that Article, shall be reduced to one year.

2. The procedure referred to in the preceding paragraph need not be followed if a Contracting State or one of the European Communities is already a party to the multilateral convention, or if its object is to revise a convention to which the State concerned is already a party, or if it is a convention concluded within the framework of the Treaties establishing the European Communities.

Article 25

If a Contracting State considers that the unification achieved by this Convention is prejudiced by the conclusion of agreements not covered by Article 24(1), that State may request the Secretary-General of the Council of the European Communities to arrange consultations between the signatory States of this Convention.

Article 26

Any Contracting State may request the revision of this Convention. In this event a revision conference shall be convened by the President of the Council of the European Communities.

Article 27

1. This Convention shall apply to the European territories of the Contracting States, including Greenland, and to the entire territory of the French Republic.

2. Notwithstanding paragraph 1:

   (a) this Convention shall not apply to the Faroe Islands, unless the Kingdom of Denmark makes a declaration to the contrary;

   (b) this Convention shall not apply to any European territory situated outside the United Kingdom for the international relations of which the United Kingdom is responsible, unless the United Kingdom makes a declaration to the contrary in respect of any such territory;

   (c) this Convention shall apply to the Netherlands Antilles, if the Kingdom of the Netherlands makes a declaration to that effect.

3. Such declarations may be made at any time by notifying the Secretary-General of the Council of the European Communities.

4. Proceedings brought in the United Kingdom on appeal from courts in one of the territories referred to in paragraph 2(b) shall be deemed to be proceedings taking place in those courts.

Article 28

1. This Convention shall be open from 19 June 1980 for signature by the States party to the Treaty establishing the European Economic Community.

2. This Convention shall be subject to ratification, acceptance or approval by the signatory States. The instruments of ratification, acceptance or approval shall be deposited with the Secretary-General of the Council of the European Communities.

Article 29

1. This Convention shall enter into force on the first day of the third month following the deposit of the seventh instrument of ratification, acceptance or approval.

2. This Convention shall enter into force for each signatory State ratifying, accepting or approving at a later date on the first day of the third month following the deposit of its instrument of ratification, acceptance or approval.

SCH. 1

Article 30

1. This Convention shall remain in force for 10 years from the date of its entry into force in accordance with Article 29(1), even for States for which it enters into force at a later date.

2. If there has been no denunciation it shall be renewed tacitly every five years.

3. A Contracting State which wishes to denounce shall, not less than six months before the expiration of the period of 10 or five years, as the case may be, give notice to the Secretary-General of the Council of the European Communities. Denunciation may be limited to any territory to which the Convention has been extended by a declaration under Article 27(2).

4. The denunciation shall have effect only in relation to the State which has notified it. The Convention will remain in force as between all other Contracting States.

Article 31

The Secretary-General of the Council of the European Communities shall notify the States party to the Treaty establishing the European Economic Community of:

 (a) the signatures;

 (b) the deposit of each instrument of ratification, acceptance or approval;

 (c) the date of entry into force of this Convention;

 (d) communications made in pursuance of Articles 23, 24, 25, 26, 27 and 30;

 (e) the reservations and withdrawals of reservations referred to in Article 22.

Article 32

The Protocol annexed to this Convention shall form an integral part thereof.

Article 33

This Convention, drawn up in a single original in the Danish, Dutch, English, French, German, Irish and Italian languages, these texts being equally authentic, shall be deposited in the archives of the Secretariat of the Council of the European Communities. The Secretary-General shall transmit a certified copy thereof to the Government of each signatory State.

PROTOCOL

The High Contracting Parties have agreed upon the following provision which shall be annexed to the Convention:

Notwithstanding the provisions of the Convention, Denmark may retain the rules contained in Søloven (Statute on Maritime Law) paragraph 169 concerning the applicable law in matters relating to carriage of goods by sea and may revise these rules without following the procedure prescribed in Article 23 of the Convention.

Section 2.

SCHEDULE 2

THE LUXEMBOURG CONVENTION

The High Contracting Parties to the Treaty establishing the European Economic Community,

Considering that the Hellenic Republic, in becoming a Member of the Community, undertook to accede to the Convention on the law applicable to contractual obligations, opened for signature in Rome on 19 June 1980,

Have decided to conclude this Convention, and to this end have designated as their plenipotentiaries:

(Designation of plenipotentiaries)

Who, meeting within the Council, having exchanged their full powers, found in good and due form,

Have agreed as follows:

Article 1

The Hellenic Republic hereby accedes to the Convention on the law applicable to contractual obligations, opened for signature in Rome on 19 June 1980.

Article 2

The Secretary-General of the Council of the European Communities shall transmit a certified copy of the Convention on the law applicable to contractual obligations in the Danish, Dutch, English, French, German, Irish and Italian languages to the Government of the Hellenic Republic.

The text of the Convention on the law applicable to contractual obligations in the Greek language is annexed hereto. The text in the Greek language shall be authentic under the same conditions as the other texts of the Convention on the law applicable to contractual obligations.

Article 3

This Convention shall be ratified by the Signatory States. The instruments of ratification shall be deposited with the Secretary-General of the Council of the European Communities.

Article 4

This Convention shall enter into force, as between the States which have ratified it, on the first day of the third month following the deposit of the last instrument of ratification by the Hellenic Republic and seven States which have ratified the Convention on the law applicable to contractual obligations.

This Convention shall enter into force for each Contracting State which subsequently ratifies it on the first day of the third month following the deposit of its instrument of ratification.

Article 5

The Secretary-General of the Council of the European Communities shall notify the Signatory States of:

(a) the deposit of each instrument of ratification;

(b) the dates of entry into force of this Convention for the Contracting States.

Article 6

This Convention, drawn up in a single original in the Danish, Dutch, English, French, German, Greek, Irish and Italian languages, all eight texts being equally authentic, shall be deposited in the archives of the General Secretariat of the Council of the European Communities. The Secretary-General shall transmit a certified copy to the Government of each Signatory State.

SCHEDULE 3
THE BRUSSELS PROTOCOL

The High Contracting Parties to the Treaty establishing the European Economic Community,

Having regard to the Joint Declaration annexed to the Convention on the law applicable to contractual obligations, opened for signature in Rome on 19 June 1980,

Have decided to conclude a Protocol conferring jurisdiction on the Court of Justice of the European Communities to interpret that Convention, and to this end have designated as their Plenipotentiaries:

(Designation of plenipotentiaries)

Who, meeting within the Council of the European Communities, having exchanged their full powers, found in good and due form,

Have agreed as follows:

Article 1

The Court of Justice of the European Communities shall have jurisdiction to give rulings on the interpretation of—

(a) the Convention on the law applicable to contractual obligations, opened for signature in Rome on 19 June 1980, hereinafter referred to as "the Rome Convention";

(b) the Convention on accession to the Rome Convention by the States which have become Members of the European Communities since the date on which it was opened for signature;

(c) this Protocol.

Article 2

Any of the courts referred to below may request the Court of Justice to give a preliminary ruling on a question raised in a case pending before it and concerning interpretation of the provisions contained in the instruments referred to in Article 1 if that court considers that a decision on the question is necessary to enable it to give judgment:

(a) - in Belgium:

la Cour de cassation (het Hof van Cassatie) and le Conseil d'Etat (de Raad van State),

- in Denmark:

Højesteret,

- in the Federal Republic of Germany:

die obersten Gerichtshöfe des Bundes,

- in Greece:

τα ανώτατα Δικαστήρια,

- in Spain:

el Tribunal Supremo,

- in France:

la Cour de cassation and le Conseil d'Etat,

- in Ireland:

the Supreme Court,

- in Italy:

la Corte suprema di cassazione and il Consiglio di Stato,

- in Luxembourg:

    la Cour Supérieure de Justice, when sitting as Cour de cassation,

- in the Netherlands:

    de Hoge Raad,

- in Portugal:

    o Supremo Tribunal de Justiça and o Supremo Tribunal Administrativo,

- in the United Kingdom:

    the House of Lords and other courts from which no further appeal is possible;

(b) the courts of the Contracting States when acting as appeal courts.

Article 3

1. The competent authority of a Contracting State may request the Court of Justice to give a ruling on a question of interpretation of the provisions contained in the instruments referred to in Article 1 if judgments given by courts of that State conflict with the interpretation given either by the Court of Justice or in a judgment of one of the courts of another Contracting State referred to in Article 2. The provisions of this paragraph shall apply only to judgments which have become *res judicata*.

2. The interpretation given by the Court of Justice in response to such a request shall not affect the judgments which gave rise to the request for interpretation.

3. The Procurators-General of the Supreme Courts of Appeal of the Contracting States, or any other authority designated by a Contracting State, shall be entitled to request the Court of Justice for a ruling on interpretation in accordance with paragraph 1.

4. The Registrar of the Court of Justice shall give notice of the request to the Contracting States, to the Commission and to the Council of the European Communities; they shall then be entitled within two months of the notification to submit statements of case or written observations to the Court.

5. No fees shall be levied or any costs or expenses awarded in respect of the proceedings provided for in this Article.

Article 4

1. Except where this Protocol otherwise provides, the provisions of the Treaty establishing the European Economic Community and those of the Protocol on the Statute of the Court of Justice annexed thereto, which are applicable when the Court is requested to give a preliminary ruling, shall also apply to any proceedings for the interpretation of the instruments referred to in Article 1.

2. The Rules of Procedure of the Court of Justice shall, if necessary, be adjusted and supplemented in accordance with Article 188 of the Treaty establishing the European Economic Community.

Article 5

This Protocol shall be subject to ratification by the Signatory States. The instruments of ratification shall be deposited with the Secretary-General of the Council of the European Communities.

SCH. 3

O.J.1989
No.L48/17.

Article 6

1. To enter into force, this Protocol must be ratified by seven States in respect of which the Rome Convention is in force. This Protocol shall enter into force on the first day of the third month following the deposit of the instrument of ratification by the last such State to take this step. If, however, the Second Protocol conferring on the Court of Justice of the European Communities certain powers to interpret the Convention on the law applicable to contractual obligations, opened for signature in Rome on 19 June 1980, concluded in Brussels on 19 December 1988, enters into force on a later date, this Protocol shall enter into force on the date of entry into force of the Second Protocol.

2. Any ratification subsequent to the entry into force of this Protocol shall take effect on the first day of the third month following the deposit of the instrument of ratification provided that the ratification, acceptance or approval of the Rome Convention by the State in question has become effective.

Article 7

The Secretary-General of the Council of the European Communities shall notify the Signatory States of:

(a) the deposit of each instrument of ratification;

(b) the date of entry into force of this Protocol;

(c) any designation communicated pursuant to Article 3(3);

(d) any communication made pursuant to Article 8.

Article 8

The Contracting States shall communicate to the Secretary-General of the Council of the European Communities the texts of any provisions of their laws which necessitate an amendment to the list of courts in Article 2(a).

Article 9

This Protocol shall have effect for as long as the Rome Convention remains in force under the conditions laid down in Article 30 of that Convention.

Article 10

Any Contracting State may request the revision of this Protocol. In this event, a revision conference shall be convened by the President of the Council of the European Communities.

Article 11

This Protocol, drawn up in a single original in the Danish, Dutch, English, French, German, Greek, Irish, Italian, Portuguese and Spanish languages, all 10 texts being equally authentic, shall be deposited in the archives of the General Secretariat of the Council of the European Communities. The Secretary-General shall transmit a certified copy to the Government of each Signatory State.

Section 5.

SCHEDULE 4

CONSEQUENTIAL AMENDMENTS

The Equal Pay Act 1970 (c.41)

The Equal Pay Act (Northern Ireland) 1970 (c.32 (N.I.))

1. In section 1(11) of the Equal Pay Act 1970 and section 1(12) of the Equal Pay Act (Northern Ireland) 1970, for the words "proper law of" there shall be substituted the words "law applicable to".

The Consumer Credit Act 1974 (c.39)

2. In sections 43(2)(c) and 145(3)(c) and (4)(b) of the Consumer Credit Act 1974, for the words "proper law of", in each place where they occur, there shall be substituted the words "law applicable to".

The Patents Act 1977 (c.37)

3. In section 82(5) and (6) of the Patents Act 1977, for the words "proper law of" there shall be substituted the words "law applicable to".

The Unfair Contract Terms Act 1977 (c.50)

4. In section 27(1) of the Unfair Contract Terms Act 1977, for the words "proper law of" there shall be substituted the words "law applicable to" and for the words "of the proper law" there shall be substituted the words "of the law applicable to the contract".

The Aviation Security Act 1982 (c.36)

5. In section 19(5) of the Aviation Security Act 1982, for the words "of which the proper law" there shall be substituted the words "the law applicable to which".

The Income and Corporation Taxes Act 1988 (c.1)

6. In section 347B(1)(a) of the Income and Corporation Taxes Act 1988, for the words "proper law of" there shall be substituted the words "law applicable to".

© Crown copyright 1990

PRINTED IN THE UNITED KINGDOM BY PAUL FREEMAN
Controller and Chief Executive of Her Majesty's Stationery Office
and Queen's Printer of Acts of Parliament

Appendix B
Some Authentic Foreign Texts of the Rome Contracts Convention*

*Reproduced from O.J. L 266, 9.10.1980 by kind permission of the European Community.

FRENCH TEXT OF ROME CONVENTION

CONVENTION
SUR LA LOI APPLICABLE AUX OBLIGATIONS CONTRACTUELLES

ouverte à la signature à Rome le 19 juin 1980

(80/934/CEE)

PRÉAMBULE

LES HAUTES PARTIES CONTRACTANTES au traité instituant la Communauté économique européenne,

SOUCIEUSES de poursuivre, dans le domaine du droit international privé, l'œuvre d'unification juridique déjà entreprise dans la Communauté, notamment en matière de compétence judiciaire et d'exécution des jugements,

DÉSIRANT établir des règles uniformes concernant la loi applicable aux obligations contractuelles,

SONT CONVENUES DES DISPOSITIONS QUI SUIVENT :

TITRE PREMIER
CHAMP D'APPLICATION

Article premier

Champ d'application

1. Les dispositions de la présente convention sont applicables, dans les situations comportant un conflit de lois, aux obligations contractuelles.

2. Elles ne s'appliquent pas :

a) à l'état et à la capacité des personnes physiques, sous réserve de l'article 11 ;

b) aux obligations contractuelles concernant :

— les testaments et successions,

— les régimes matrimoniaux,

— les droits et devoirs découlant des relations de famille, de parenté, de mariage ou d'alliance, y compris les obligations alimentaires envers les enfants non légitimes ;

c) aux obligations nées de lettres de change, chèques, billets à ordre ainsi que d'autres instruments négociables, dans la mesure où les obligations nées de ces autres instruments dérivent de leur caractère négociable ;

d) aux conventions d'arbitrage et d'élection de for ;

e) aux questions relevant du droit des sociétés, associations et personnes morales, telles que la constitution, la capacité juridique, le fonctionnement interne et la dissolution des sociétés, associations et personnes morales, ainsi que la responsabilité personnelle légale des associés et des organes pour les dettes de la société, association ou personne morale ;

f) à la question de savoir si un intermédiaire peut engager envers les tiers la personne pour le compte de laquelle il prétend agir ou si un organe d'une société, d'une association ou d'une personne morale peut engager envers les tiers cette société, association ou personne morale ;

g) à la constitution des *trusts,* aux relations qu'ils créent entre les constituants, les *trustees* et les bénéficiaires ;

h) à la preuve et à la procédure, sous réserve de l'article 14.

3. Les dispositions de la présente convention ne s'appliquent pas aux contrats d'assurance qui couvrent des risques situés dans les territoires des États membres de la Communauté économique européenne. Pour déterminer si un risque est situé dans ces territoires, le juge applique sa loi interne.

4. Le paragraphe précédent ne concerne pas les contrats de réassurance.

Article 2

Caractère universel

La loi désignée par la présente convention s'applique même si cette loi est celle d'un État non contractant.

TITRE II

RÈGLES UNIFORMES

Article 3

Liberté de choix

1. Le contrat est régi par la loi choisie par les parties. Ce choix doit être exprès ou résulter de façon certaine des dispositions du contrat ou des circonstances de la cause. Par ce choix, les parties peuvent désigner la loi applicable à la totalité ou à une partie seulement de leur contrat.

2. Les parties peuvent convenir, à tout moment, de faire régir le contrat par une loi autre que celle qui le régissait auparavant soit en vertu d'un choix antérieur selon le présent article, soit en vertu d'autres dispositions de la présente convention. Toute modification quant à la détermination de la loi applicable, intervenue postérieurement à la conclusion du contrat, n'affecte pas la validité formelle du contrat au sens de l'article 9 et ne porte pas atteinte aux droits des tiers.

3. Le choix par les parties d'une loi étrangère, assorti ou non de celui d'un tribunal étranger, ne peut, lorsque tous les autres éléments de la situation sont localisés au moment de ce choix dans un seul pays, porter atteinte aux dispositions auxquelles la loi de ce pays ne permet pas de déroger par contrat, ci-après dénommées « dispositions impératives ».

4. L'existence et la validité du consentement des parties quant au choix de la loi applicable sont régies par les dispositions établies aux articles 8, 9 et 11.

Article 4

Loi applicable à défaut de choix

1. Dans la mesure où la loi applicable au contrat n'a pas été choisie conformément aux dispositions de l'article 3, le contrat est régi par la loi du pays avec lequel il présente les liens les plus étroits. Toutefois, si une partie du contrat est séparable du reste du contrat et présente un lien plus étroit avec un autre pays, il pourra être fait application, à titre exceptionnel, à cette partie du contrat de la loi de cet autre pays.

2. Sous réserve du paragraphe 5, il est présumé que le contrat présente les liens les plus étroits avec le pays où la partie qui doit fournir la prestation caractéristique a, au moment de la conclusion du contrat, sa résidence habituelle ou, s'il s'agit d'une société, association ou personne morale, son administration centrale. Toutefois, si le contrat est conclu dans l'exercice de l'activité professionnelle de cette partie, ce pays est celui où est situé son principal établissement ou, si, selon le contrat, la prestation doit être fournie par un établissement autre que l'établissement principal, celui où est situé cet autre établissement.

3. Nonobstant les dispositions du paragraphe 2, dans la mesure où le contrat a pour objet un droit réel immobilier ou un droit d'utilisation d'un immeuble, il est présumé que le contrat présente les liens les plus étroits avec le pays où est situé l'immeuble.

4. Le contrat de transport de marchandises n'est pas soumis à la présomption du paragraphe 2. Dans ce

contrat, si le pays dans lequel le transporteur a son établissement principal au moment de la conclusion du contrat est aussi celui dans lequel est situé le lieu de chargement ou de déchargement ou l'établissement principal de l'expéditeur, il est présumé que le contrat a les liens les plus étroits avec ce pays. Pour l'application du présent paragraphe, sont considérés comme contrats de transport de marchandises les contrats d'affrètement pour un seul voyage ou d'autres contrats lorsqu'ils ont principalement pour objet de réaliser un transport de marchandises.

5. L'application du paragraphe 2 est écartée lorsque la prestation caractéristique ne peut être déterminée. Les présomptions des paragraphes 2, 3 et 4 sont écartées lorsqu'il résulte de l'ensemble des circonstances que le contrat présente des liens plus étroits avec un autre pays.

Article 5

Contrats conclus par les consommateurs

1. Le présent article s'applique aux contrats ayant pour objet la fourniture d'objets mobiliers corporels ou de services à une personne, le consommateur, pour un usage pouvant être considéré comme étranger à son activité professionnelle, ainsi qu'aux contrats destinés au financement d'une telle fourniture.

2. Nonobstant les dispositions de l'article 3, le choix par les parties de la loi applicable ne peut avoir pour résultat de priver le consommateur de la protection que lui assurent les dispositions impératives de la loi du pays dans lequel il a sa résidence habituelle :

— si la conclusion du contrat a été précédée dans ce pays d'une proposition spécialement faite ou d'une publicité, et si le consommateur a accompli dans ce pays les actes nécessaires à la conclusion du contrat, ou

— si le cocontractant du consommateur ou son représentant a reçu la commande du consommateur dans ce pays, ou

— si le contrat est une vente de marchandises et que le consommateur se soit rendu de ce pays dans un pays étranger et y ait passé la commande, à la condition que le voyage ait été organisé par le vendeur dans le but d'inciter le consommateur à conclure une vente.

3. Nonobstant les dispositions de l'article 4 et à défaut de choix exercé conformément à l'article 3, ces contrats sont régis par la loi du pays dans lequel le consommateur a sa résidence habituelle, s'ils sont intervenus dans les circonstances décrites au paragraphe 2 du présent article.

4. Le présent article ne s'applique pas :

a) au contrat de transport ;

b) au contrat de fourniture de services lorsque les services dus au consommateur doivent être fournis exclusivement dans un pays autre que celui dans lequel il a sa résidence habituelle.

5. Nonobstant les dispositions du paragraphe 4, le présent article s'applique au contrat offrant pour un prix global des prestations combinées de transport et de logement.

Article 6

Contrat individuel de travail

1. Nonobstant les dispositions de l'article 3, dans le contrat de travail, le choix par les parties de la loi applicable ne peut avoir pour résultat de priver le travailleur de la protection qui lui assurent les dispositions impératives de la loi qui serait applicable, à défaut de choix, en vertu du paragraphe 2 du présent article.

2. Nonobstant les dispositions de l'article 4 et à défaut de choix exercé conformément à l'article 3, le contrat de travail est régi :

a) par la loi du pays où le travailleur, en exécution du contrat, accomplit habituellement son travail, même s'il est détaché à titre temporaire dans un autre pays, ou

b) si le travailleur n'accomplit pas habituellement son travail dans un même pays, par la loi du pays où se trouve l'établissement qui a embauché le travailleur,

à moins qu'il ne résulte de l'ensemble des circonstances que le contrat de travail présente des liens plus étroits avec un autre pays, auquel cas la loi de cet autre pays est applicable.

Article 7

Lois de police

1. Lors de l'application, en vertu de la présente convention, de la loi d'un pays déterminé, il pourra être donné effet aux dispositions impératives de la loi d'un autre pays avec lequel la situation présente un lien étroit, si et dans la mesure où, selon le droit de ce dernier pays, ces dispositions sont applicables quelle que soit la loi régissant le contrat. Pour décider si effet doit être donné à ces dispositions impératives, il sera tenu compte de leur nature et de leur objet ainsi que des conséquences qui découleraient de leur application ou de leur non-application.

2. Les dispositions de la présente convention ne pourront porter atteinte à l'application des règles de la

loi du pays du juge qui régissent impérativement la situation quelle que soit la loi applicable au contrat.

Article 8

Consentement et validité au fond

1. L'existence et la validité du contrat ou d'une disposition de celui-ci sont soumises à la loi qui serait applicable en vertu de la présente convention si le contrat ou la disposition étaient valables.

2. Toutefois, pour établir qu'elle n'a pas consenti, une partie peut se référer à la loi du pays dans lequel elle a sa résidence habituelle s'il résulte des circonstances qu'il ne serait pas raisonnable de déterminer l'effet du comportement de cette partie d'après la loi prévue au paragraphe précédent.

Article 9

Forme

1. Un contrat conclu entre des personnes qui se trouvent dans un même pays est valable quant à la forme s'il satisfait aux conditions de forme de la loi qui le régit au fond en vertu de la présente convention ou de la loi du pays dans lequel il a été conclu.

2. Un contrat conclu entre des personnes qui se trouvent dans des pays différents est valable quant à la forme s'il satisfait aux conditions de forme de la loi qui le régit au fond en vertu de la présente convention ou de la loi de l'un de ces pays.

3. Lorsque le contrat est conclu par un représentant, le pays où le représentant se trouve au moment où il agit est celui qui doit être pris en considération pour l'application des paragraphes 1 et 2.

4. Un acte juridique unilatéral relatif à un contrat conclu ou à conclure est valable quant à la forme s'il satisfait aux conditions de forme de la loi qui régit ou régirait au fond le contrat en vertu de la présente convention ou de la loi du pays dans lequel cet acte est intervenu.

5. Les dispositions des paragraphes précédents ne s'appliquent pas aux contrats qui entrent dans le champ d'application de l'article 5 conclus dans les circonstances qui y sont décrites au paragraphe 2. La forme de ces contrats est régie par la loi du pays dans lequel le consommateur a sa résidence habituelle.

6. Nonobstant les dispositions des quatre premiers paragraphes du présent article, tout contrat ayant pour objet un droit réel immobilier ou un droit d'utilisation d'un immeuble est soumis aux règles de forme impératives de la loi du pays où l'immeuble est situé, pour autant que selon cette loi elles s'appliquent indépendamment du lieu de conclusion du contrat et de la loi le régissant au fond.

Article 10

Domaine de la loi du contrat

1. La loi applicable au contrat en vertu des articles 3 à 6 et de l'article 12 de la présente convention régit notamment :

a) son interprétation ;

b) l'exécution des obligations qu'il engendre ;

c) dans les limites des pouvoirs attribués au tribunal par sa loi de procédure, les conséquences de l'inexécution totale ou partielle de ces obligations, y compris l'évaluation du dommage dans la mesure où des règles de droit la gouvernent ;

d) les divers modes d'extinction des obligations, ainsi que les prescriptions et déchéances fondées sur l'expiration d'un délai ;

e) les conséquences de la nullité du contrat.

2. En ce qui concerne les modalités d'exécution et les mesures à prendre par le créancier en cas de défaut dans l'exécution on aura égard à la loi du pays où l'exécution a lieu.

Article 11

Incapacité

Dans un contrat conclu entre personnes se trouvant dans un même pays, une personne physique qui serait capable selon la loi de ce pays ne peut invoquer son incapacité résultant d'une autre loi que si, au moment de la conclusion du contrat, le cocontractant a connu cette incapacité ou ne l'a ignorée qu'en raison d'une imprudence de sa part.

Article 12

Cession de créance

1. Les obligations entre le cédant et le cessionnaire d'une créance sont régies par la loi qui, en vertu

de la présente convention, s'applique au contrat qui les lie.

2. La loi qui régit la créance cédée détermine le caractère cessible de celle-ci, les rapports entre cessionnaire et débiteur, les conditions d'opposabilité de la cession au débiteur et le caractère libératoire de la prestation faite par le débiteur.

Article 13

Subrogation

1. Lorsqu'en vertu d'un contrat, une personne, le créancier, a des droits à l'égard d'une autre personne, le débiteur, et qu'un tiers a l'obligation de désintéresser le créancier ou encore que le tiers a désintéressé le créancier en exécution de cette obligation, la loi applicable à cette obligation du tiers détermine si celui-ci peut exercer en tout ou en partie les droits détenus par le créancier contre le débiteur selon la loi régissant leurs relations.

2. La même règle s'applique lorsque plusieurs personnes sont tenues de la même obligation contractuelle et que le créancier a été désintéressé par l'une d'elles.

Article 14

Preuve

1. La loi régissant le contrat en vertu de la présente convention s'applique dans la mesure où, en matière d'obligations contractuelles, elle établit des présomptions légales ou répartit la charge de la preuve.

2. Les actes juridiques peuvent être prouvés par tout mode de preuve admis soit par la loi du for, soit par l'une des lois visées à l'article 9, selon laquelle l'acte est valable quant à la forme, pour autant que la preuve puisse être administrée selon ce mode devant le tribunal saisi.

Article 15

Exclusion du renvoi

Lorsque la présente convention prescrit l'application de la loi d'un pays, elle entend les règles de droit en vigueur dans ce pays à l'exclusion des règles de droit international privé.

Article 16

Ordre public

L'application d'une disposition de la loi désignée par la présente convention ne peut être écartée que si cette application est manifestement incompatible avec l'ordre public du for.

Article 17

Application dans le temps

La convention s'applique dans un État contractant aux contrats conclus après son entrée en vigueur pour cet État.

Article 18

Interprétation uniforme

Aux fins de l'interprétation et de l'application des règles uniformes qui précèdent, il sera tenu compte de leur caractère international et de l'opportunité de parvenir à l'uniformité dans la façon dont elles sont interprétées et appliquées.

Article 19

Systèmes non unifiés

1. Lorsqu'un État comprend plusieurs unités territoriales dont chacune a ses propres règles en matière d'obligations contractuelles, chaque unité territoriale est considérée comme un pays aux fins de la détermination de la loi applicable selon la présente convention.

2. Un État dans lequel différentes unités territoriales ont leurs propres règles de droit en matière d'obligations contractuelles ne sera pas tenu d'appliquer la présente convention aux conflits de lois intéressant uniquement ces unités territoriales.

Article 20

Priorité du droit communautaire

La présente convention ne préjuge pas l'application des dispositions qui, dans des matières particulières, règlent les conflits de lois en matière d'obligations contractuelles et qui sont ou seront contenues dans les actes émanant des institutions des Communautés européennes ou dans les législations nationales harmonisées en exécution de ces actes.

Article 21

Relations avec d'autres conventions

La présente convention ne porte pas atteinte à l'application des conventions internationales auxquelles un État contractant est ou sera partie.

Article 22

Réserves

1. Tout État contractant, au moment de la signature, de la ratification, de l'acceptation ou de l'approbation, pourra se réserver le droit de ne pas appliquer :

a) l'article 7 paragraphe 1 ;

b) l'article 10 paragraphe 1 sous e).

2. Tout État contractant pourra également, en notifiant une extension de la convention conformément à l'article 27 paragraphe 2, faire une ou plusieurs de ces réserves avec effet limité aux territoires ou à certains des territoires visés par l'extension.

3. Tout État contractant pourra à tout moment retirer une réserve qu'il aura faite ; l'effet de la réserve cessera le premier jour du troisième mois du calendrier après la notification du retrait.

TITRE III
CLAUSES FINALES

Article 23

1. Si, après la date d'entrée en vigueur de la présente convention à son égard, un État contractant désire adopter une nouvelle règle de conflit de lois pour une catégorie particulière de contrats entrant dans le champ d'application de la convention, il communique son intention aux autres États signataires par l'intermédiaire du secrétaire général du Conseil des Communautés européennes.

2. Dans un délai de six mois à partir de la communication faite au secrétaire général, tout État signataire peut demander à celui-ci d'organiser des consultations entre États signataires en vue d'arriver à un accord.

3. Si, dans ce délai, aucun État signataire n'a demandé la consultation ou si, dans les deux ans qui suivront la communication faite au secrétaire général, aucun accord n'est intervenu à la suite des consultations, l'État contractant peut modifier son droit. La mesure prise par cet État est portée à la connaissance des autres États signataires par l'intermédiaire du secrétaire général du Conseil des Communautés européennes.

Article 24

1. Si, après la date d'entrée en vigueur de la présente convention à son égard, un État contractant désire devenir partie à une convention multilatérale dont l'objet principal ou l'un des objets principaux est un règlement de droit international privé dans l'une des matières régies par la présente convention, il est fait application de la procédure prévue à l'article 23. Toutefois, le délai de deux ans, prévu au paragraphe 3 de l'article 23, est ramené à un an.

2. La procédure prévue au paragraphe précédent n'est pas suivie si un État contractant ou l'une des Communautés européennes sont déjà parties à la convention multilatérale ou si l'objet de celle-ci est de réviser une convention à laquelle l'État intéressé est partie ou s'il s'agit d'une convention conclue dans le cadre des traités instituant les Communautés européennes.

Article 25

Lorsqu'un État contractant considère que l'unification réalisée par la présente convention est compromise par la conclusion d'accords non prévus à l'article 24 paragraphe 1, cet État peut demander au secrétaire général du Conseil des Communautés européennes d'organiser une consultation entre les États signataires de la présente convention.

Article 26

Chaque État contractant peut demander la révision de la présente convention. Dans ce cas, une conférence de révision est convoquée par le président du Conseil des Communautés européennes.

Article 27

1. La présente convention s'applique au territoire européen des États contractants, y compris le

Groenland, et à l'ensemble du territoire de la République française.

2. Par dérogation au paragraphe 1 :

a) la présente convention ne s'applique pas aux îles Féroé, sauf déclaration contraire du royaume de Danemark ;

b) la présente convention ne s'applique pas aux territoires européens situés hors du Royaume-Uni et dont celui-ci assume les relations internationales, sauf déclaration contraire du Royaume-Uni pour un tel territoire ;

c) la présente convention s'applique aux Antilles néerlandaises, si le royaume des Pays-Bas fait une déclaration à cet effet.

3. Ces déclarations peuvent être faites à tout moment, par voie de notification au secrétaire général du Conseil des Communautés européennes.

4. Les procédures d'appel introduites au Royaume-Uni contre des décisions rendues par les tribunaux situés dans un des territoires visés au paragraphe 2 sous b) sont considérées comme des procédures se déroulant devant ces tribunaux.

Article 28

1. La présente convention est ouverte à compter du 19 juin 1980 à la signature des États parties au traité instituant la Communauté économique européenne.

2. La présente convention sera ratifiée, acceptée ou approuvée par les États signataires. Les instruments de ratification, d'acceptation ou d'approbation seront déposés auprès du secrétariat général du Conseil des Communautés européennes.

Article 29

1. La présente convention entrera en vigueur le premier jour du troisième mois suivant le dépôt du septième instrument de ratification, d'acceptation ou d'approbation.

2. La convention entrera en vigueur pour chaque État signataire ratifiant, acceptant ou approuvant postérieurement, le premier jour du troisième mois suivant le dépôt de son instrument de ratification, d'acceptation ou d'approbation.

Article 30

1. La convention aura une durée de dix ans à partir de la date de son entrée en vigueur conformément à l'article 29 paragaphe 1, même pour les États pour qui elle entrerait en vigueur postérieurement.

2. La convention sera renouvelée tacitement de cinq ans en cinq ans sauf dénonciation.

3. La dénonciation sera notifiée, au moins six mois avant l'expiration du délai de dix ans ou de cinq ans selon le cas, au secrétaire général du Conseil des Communautés européennes. Elle pourra se limiter à l'un des territoires auxquels la convention aurait été étendue par application de l'article 27 paragraphe 2.

4. La dénonciation n'aura d'effet qu'à l'égard de l'État qui l'aura notifiée. La convention restera en vigueur pour les autres États contractants.

Article 31

Le secrétaire général du Conseil des Communautés européennes notifiera aux États parties au traité instituant la Communauté économique européenne :

a) les signatures ;

b) le dépôt de tout instrument de ratification, d'acceptation ou d'approbation ;

c) la date d'entrée en vigueur de la présente convention ;

d) les communications faites en application des articles 23, 24, 25, 26, 27 et 30 ;

e) les réserves et le retrait des réserves mentionnées à l'article 22.

Article 32

Le protocole annexé à la présente convention en fait partie intégrante.

Article 33

La présente convention, rédigée en un exemplaire unique en langues allemande, anglaise, danoise, française, irlandaise, italienne et néerlandaise, ces textes faisant également foi, sera déposée dans les archives du secrétariat général du Conseil des Communautés européennes. Le secrétaire général en remettra une copie certifiée conforme à chacun des gouvernements des États signataires.

GERMAN TEXT OF ROME CONVENTION

ÜBEREINKOMMEN
ÜBER DAS AUF VERTRAGLICHE SCHULDVERHÄLTNISSE ANZUWENDENDE RECHT

aufgelegt zur Unterzeichnung am 19. Juni 1980 in Rom

(80/934/EWG)

PRÄAMBEL

DIE HOHEN VERTRAGSPARTEIEN des Vertrages zur Gründung der Europäischen Wirtschaftsgemeinschaft —

IN DEM BESTREBEN, die innerhalb der Gemeinschaft insbesondere im Bereich der gerichtlichen Zuständigkeit und der Vollstreckung gerichtlicher Entscheidungen bereits begonnene Rechtsvereinheitlichung auf dem Gebiet des internationalen Privatrechts fortzusetzen,

IN DEM WUNSCH, einheitliche Normen für die Bestimmung des auf vertragliche Schuldverhältnisse anzuwendenden Rechts zu schaffen —

SIND WIE FOLGT ÜBEREINGEKOMMEN:

TITEL I
ANWENDUNGSBEREICH

Artikel 1

Anwendungsbereich

(1) Die Vorschriften dieses Übereinkommens sind auf vertragliche Schuldverhältnisse bei Sachverhalten, die eine Verbindung zum Recht verschiedener Staaten aufweisen, anzuwenden.

(2) Sie sind nicht anzuwenden auf

a) den Personenstand sowie die Rechts-, Geschäfts- und Handlungsfähigkeit von natürlichen Personen, vorbehaltlich des Artikels 11;

b) vertragliche Schuldverhältnisse betreffend

— Testamente und das Gebiet des Erbrechts,

— die ehelichen Güterstände,

— die Rechte und Pflichten, die auf einem Familien-, Verwandschafts- oder eherechtlichen Verhältnis oder auf einer Schwägerschaft beruhen, einschließlich der Unterhaltsverpflichtungen gegenüber einem nichtehelichen Kind;

c) Verpflichtungen aus Wechseln, Schecks, Eigenwechseln und anderen handelbaren Wertpapieren, sofern die Verpflichtungen aus diesen anderen Wertpapieren aus deren Handelbarkeit entstehen;

d) Schieds- und Gerichtsstandsvereinbarungen;

e) Fragen betreffend das Gesellschaftsrecht, das Vereinsrecht und das Recht der juristischen Personen, wie z. B. die Errichtung, die Rechts- und Handlungsfähigkeit, die innere Verfassung und die Auflösung von Gesellschaften, Vereinen und juristischen Personen sowie die persönliche gesetzliche Haftung der Gesellschafter und der Organe für die Schulden der Gesellschaft, des Vereins oder der juristischen Person;

f) die Frage, ob ein Vertreter die Person, für deren Rechnung er zu handeln vorgibt, Dritten gegenüber verpflichten kann, oder ob das Organ einer Gesellschaft, eines Vereins oder einer juristischen Person diese Gesellschaft, diesen Verein oder dieser juristische Person gegenüber Dritten verpflichten kann;

g) die Gründung von „Trusts" sowie die dadurch geschaffenen Rechtsbeziehungen zwischen den Verfügenden, den Treuhändern und den Begünstigten;

h) den Beweis und das Verfahren, vorbehaltlich des Artikels 14.

(3) Die Vorschriften dieses Übereinkommens sind nicht anzuwenden auf Versicherungsverträge, die in den Hoheitsgebieten der Mitgliedstaaten der Europäischen Wirtschaftsgemeinschaft belegene Risiken decken. Ist zu entscheiden, ob ein Risiko in diesen Hoheitsgebieten belegen ist, so wendet das Gericht sein innerstaatliches Recht an.

(4) Absatz 3 gilt nicht für Rückversicherungsverträge.

Artikel 2

Anwendung des Rechts von Nichtvertragsstaaten

Das nach diesem Übereinkommen bezeichnete Recht ist auch dann anzuwenden, wenn es das Recht eines Nichtvertragsstaats ist.

TITEL II

EINHEITLICHE BESTIMMUNGEN

Artikel 3

Freie Rechtswahl

(1) Der Vertrag unterliegt dem von den Parteien gewählten Recht. Die Rechtswahl muß ausdrücklich sein oder sich mit hinreichender Sicherheit aus den Bestimmungen des Vertrages oder aus den Umständen des Falles ergeben. Die Parteien können die Rechtswahl für ihren ganzen Vertrag oder nur für einen Teil desselben treffen.

(2) Die Parteien können jederzeit vereinbaren, daß der Vertrag nach einem anderen Recht zu beurteilen ist als dem, das zuvor entweder aufgrund einer früheren Rechtswahl nach diesem Artikel oder aufgrund anderer Vorschriften dieses Übereinkommens für ihn maßgebend war. Die Formgültigkeit des Vertrages im Sinne des Artikels 9 und Rechte Dritter werden durch eine nach Vertragsabschluß erfolgende Änderung der Bestimmung des anzuwendenden Rechts nicht berührt.

(3) Sind alle anderen Teile des Sachverhalts im Zeitpunkt der Rechtswahl in ein und demselben Staat belegen, so kann die Wahl eines ausländischen Rechts durch die Parteien — sei sie durch die Vereinbarung der Zuständigkeit eines ausländischen Gerichtes ergänzt oder nicht — die Bestimmungen nicht berühren, von denen nach dem Recht jenes Staates durch Vertrag nicht abgewichen werden kann und die nachstehend „zwingende Bestimmungen" genannt werden.

(4) Auf das Zustandekommen und die Wirksamkeit der Einigung der Parteien über das anzuwendende Recht sind die Artikel 8, 9 und 11 anzuwenden.

Artikel 4

Mangels Rechtswahl anzuwendendes Recht

(1) Soweit das auf den Vertrag anzuwendende Recht nicht nach Artikel 3 vereinbart worden ist, unterliegt der Vertrag dem Recht des Staates, mit dem er die engsten Verbindungen aufweist. Läßt sich jedoch ein Teil des Vertrages von dem Rest des Vertrages trennen und weist dieser Teil eine engere Verbindung mit einem anderen Staat auf, so kann auf ihn ausnahmsweise das Recht dieses anderen Staates angewendet werden.

(2) Vorbehaltlich des Absatzes 5 wird vermutet, daß der Vertrag die engsten Verbindungen mit dem Staat aufweist, in dem die Partei, welche die charakteristische Leistung zu erbringen hat, im Zeitpunkt des Vertragsabschlusses ihren gewöhnlichen Aufenthalt oder, wenn es sich um eine Gesellschaft, einen Verein oder eine juristische Person handelt, ihre Hauptverwaltung hat. Ist der Vertrag jedoch in Ausübung einer beruflichen oder gewerblichen Tätigkeit dieser Partei geschlossen worden, so wird vermutet, daß er die engsten Verbindungen zu dem Staat aufweist, in dem sich deren Hauptniederlassung befindet oder in dem, wenn die Leistung nach dem Vertrag von einer anderen als der Hauptniederlassung zu erbringen ist, sich die andere Niederlassung befindet.

(3) Ungeachtet des Absatzes 2 wird, soweit der Vertrag ein dingliches Recht an einem Grundstück oder ein Recht zur Nutzung eines Grundstücks zum Gegenstand hat, vermutet, daß der Vertrag die engsten Verbindungen zu dem Staat aufweist, in dem das Grundstück belegen ist.

(4) Die Vermutung nach Absatz 2 gilt nicht für Güterbeförderungsverträge. Bei diesen Verträgen wird vermu-

tet, daß sie mit dem Staat die engsten Verbindungen aufweisen, in dem der Beförderer im Zeitpunkt des Vertragsabschlusses seine Hauptniederlassung hat, sofern sich in diesem Staat auch der Verladeort oder der Entladeort oder die Hauptniederlassung des Absenders befindet. Als Güterbeförderungsverträge gelten für die Anwendung dieses Absatzes auch Charterverträge für eine einzige Reise und andere Verträge, die in der Hauptsache der Güterbeförderung dienen.

(5) Absatz 2 ist nicht anzuwenden, wenn sich die charakteristische Leistung nicht bestimmen läßt. Die Vermutungen nach den Absätzen 2, 3 und 4 gelten nicht, wenn sich aus der Gesamtheit der Umstände ergibt, daß der Vertrag engere Verbindungen mit einem anderen Staat aufweist.

Artikel 5

Verbraucherverträge

(1) Dieser Artikel gilt für Verträge über die Lieferung beweglicher Sachen oder die Erbringung von Dienstleistungen an eine Person, den Verbraucher, zu einem Zweck, der nicht der beruflichen oder gewerblichen Tätigkeit des Verbrauchers zugerechnet werden kann, sowie für Verträge zur Finanzierung eines solchen Geschäfts.

(2) Ungeachtet des Artikels 3 darf die Rechtswahl der Parteien nicht dazu führen, daß dem Verbraucher der durch die zwingenden Bestimmungen des Rechts des Staates, in dem er seinen gewöhnlichen Aufenthalt hat, gewährte Schutz entzogen wird: -

— wenn dem Vertragsabschluß ein ausdrückliches Angebot oder eine Werbung in diesem Staat vorausgegangen ist und wenn der Verbraucher in diesem Staat die zum Abschluß des Vertrages erforderlichen Rechtshandlungen vorgenommen hat oder

— wenn der Vertragspartner des Verbrauchers oder sein Vertreter die Bestellung des Verbrauchers in diesem Staat entgegengenommen hat oder

— wenn der Vertrag den Verkauf von Waren betrifft und der Verbraucher von diesem Staat ins Ausland gereist ist und dort seine Bestellung aufgegeben hat, sofern die Reise vom Verkäufer mit dem Ziel herbeigeführt worden ist, den Verbraucher zum Vertragsabschluß zu veranlassen.

(3) Abweichend von Artikel 4 ist mangels einer Rechtswahl nach Artikel 3 für Verträge, die unter den in Absatz 2 bezeichneten Umständen zustande gekommen sind, das Recht des Staates maßgebend, in dem der Verbraucher seinen gewöhnlichen Aufenthalt hat.

(4) Dieser Artikel gilt nicht für

a) Beförderungsverträge,

b) Verträge über die Erbringung von Dienstleistungen, wenn die dem Verbraucher geschuldeten Dienstleistungen ausschließlich in einem anderen als dem Staat erbracht werden müssen, in dem der Verbraucher seinen gewöhnlichen Aufenthalt hat.

(5) Ungeachtet des Absatzes 4 gilt dieser Artikel für Reiseverträge, die für einen Pauschalpreis kombinierte Beförderungs- und Unterbringungsleistungen vorsehen.

Artikel 6

Arbeitsverträge und Arbeitsverhältnisse von Einzelpersonen

(1) Ungeachtet des Artikels 3 darf in Arbeitsverträgen und Arbeitsverhältnissen die Rechtswahl der Parteien nicht dazu führen, daß dem Arbeitnehmer der Schutz entzogen wird, der ihm durch die zwingenden Bestimmungen des Rechts gewährt wird, das nach Absatz 2 mangels einer Rechtswahl anzuwenden wäre.

(2) Abweichend von Artikel 4 sind mangels einer Rechtswahl nach Artikel 3 auf Arbeitsverträge und Arbeitsverhältnisse anzuwenden:

a) das Recht des Staates, in dem der Arbeitnehmer in Erfüllung des Vertrages gewöhnlich seine Arbeit verrichtet, selbst wenn er vorübergehend in einen anderen Staat entsandt ist, oder

b) das Recht des Staates, in dem sich die Niederlassung befindet, die den Arbeitnehmer eingestellt hat, sofern dieser seine Arbeit gewöhnlich nicht in ein und demselben Staat verrichtet,

es sei denn, daß sich aus der Gesamtheit der Umstände ergibt, daß der Arbeitsvertrag oder das Arbeitsverhältnis engere Verbindungen zu einem anderen Staat aufweist; in diesem Fall ist das Recht dieses anderen Staates anzuwenden.

Artikel 7

Zwingende Vorschriften

(1) Bei Anwendung des Rechts eines bestimmten Staates aufgrund dieses Übereinkommens kann den zwingenden Bestimmungen des Rechts eines anderen Staates, mit dem der Sachverhalt eine enge Verbindung aufweist, Wirkung verliehen werden, soweit diese Bestimmungen nach dem Recht des letztgenannten Staates ohne Rücksicht darauf anzuwenden sind, welchem Recht der Vertrag unterliegt. Bei der Entscheidung, ob diesen zwingenden Bestimmungen Wirkung zu verleihen ist, sind ihre Natur und ihr Gegenstand sowie die Folgen zu berücksichtigen, die sich aus ihrer Anwendung oder ihrer Nichtanwendung ergeben würden.

(2) Dieses Übereinkommen berührt nicht die Anwendung der nach dem Recht des Staates des angerufenen

Gerichtes geltenden Bestimmungen, die ohne Rücksicht auf das auf den Vertrag anzuwendende Recht den Sachverhalt zwingend regeln.

Artikel 8

Einigung und materielle Wirksamkeit

(1) Das Zustandekommen und die Wirksamkeit des Vertrages oder einer seiner Bestimmungen beurteilen sich nach dem Recht, das nach diesem Übereinkommen anzuwenden wäre, wenn der Vertrag oder die Bestimmung wirksam wäre.

(2) Ergibt sich jedoch aus den Umständen, daß es nicht gerechtfertigt wäre, die Wirkung des Verhaltens einer Partei nach dem in Absatz 1 bezeichneten Recht zu bestimmen, so kann sich diese Partei für die Behauptung, sie habe dem Vertrag nicht zugestimmt, auf das Recht des Staates ihres gewöhnlichen Aufenthaltsorts berufen.

Artikel 9

Form

(1) Ein zwischen Personen, die sich in demselben Staat befinden, geschlossener Vertrag ist formgültig, wenn er die Formerfordernisse des auf ihn nach diesem Übereinkommen materiell-rechtlich anzuwendenden Rechts oder des Rechts des Staates, in dem er geschlossen wurde, erfüllt.

(2) Ein zwischen Personen, die sich in verschiedenen Staaten befinden, geschlossener Vertrag ist formgültig, wenn er die Formerfordernisse des auf ihn nach diesem Übereinkommen materiell-rechtlich anzuwendenden Rechts oder des Rechts eines dieser Staaten erfüllt.

(3) Wird der Vertrag durch einen Vertreter geschlossen, so muß bei Anwendung der Absätze 1 und 2 der Staat berücksichtigt werden, in dem sich der Vertreter befindet.

(4) Ein einseitiges Rechtsgeschäft, das sich auf einen geschlossenen oder zu schließenden Vertrag bezieht, ist formgültig, wenn es die Formerfordernisse des Rechts, das nach diesem Übereinkommen für den Vertrag maßgebend ist oder maßgebend wäre, oder die Formerfordernisse des Rechts des Staates erfüllt, in dem dieses Rechtsgeschäft vorgenommen worden ist.

(5) Die Absätze 1 bis 4 sind nicht anzuwenden auf Verträge, für die Artikel 5 gilt und die unter den in Artikel 5 Absatz 2 bezeichneten Umständen geschlossen worden sind. Für die Form dieser Verträge ist das Recht des Staates maßgebend, in dem der Verbraucher seinen gewöhnlichen Aufenthalt hat.

(6) Abweichend von den Absätzen 1 bis 4 beurteilen sich Verträge, die ein dingliches Recht an einem Grundstück oder ein Recht zur Nutzung eines Grundstücks zum Gegenstand haben, nach den zwingenden Formvorschriften des Staates, in dem das Grundstück belegen ist, sofern diese nach dem Recht dieses Staates ohne Rücksicht auf den Ort des Abschlusses des Vertrages und auf das auf ihn anzuwendende Recht gelten.

Artikel 10

Geltungsbereich des auf den Vertrag anzuwendenden Rechts

(1) Das nach den Artikeln 3 bis 6 und nach Artikel 12 dieses Übereinkommens auf einen Vertrag anzuwendende Recht ist insbesondere maßgebend für

a) seine Auslegung,

b) die Erfüllung der durch ihn begründeten Verpflichtungen,

c) die Folgen der vollständigen oder teilweisen Nichterfüllung dieser Verpflichtungen, einschließlich der Schadensbemessung, soweit sie nach Rechtsnormen erfolgt, in den Grenzen der dem Gericht durch sein Prozeßrecht eingeräumten Befugnisse,

d) die verschiedenen Arten des Erlöschens der Verpflichtungen sowie die Verjährung und die Rechtsverluste, die sich aus dem Ablauf einer Frist ergeben,

e) die Folgen der Nichtigkeit des Vertrages.

(2) In bezug auf die Art und Weise der Erfüllung und die vom Gläubiger im Falle mangelhafter Erfüllung zu treffenden Maßnahmen ist das Recht des Staates, in dem die Erfüllung erfolgt, zu berücksichtigen.

Artikel 11

Rechts-, Geschäfts- und Handlungsunfähigkeit

Bei einem zwischen Personen, die sich in demselben Staat befinden, geschlossenen Vertrag kann sich eine natürliche Person, die nach dem Recht dieses Staates rechts-, geschäfts- und handlungsfähig wäre, nur dann auf ihre aus dem Recht eines anderen Staates abgeleitete Rechts-, Geschäfts- und Handlungsunfähigkeit berufen, wenn der andere Vertragsteil bei Vertragsabschluß diese Rechts-, Geschäfts- und Handlungsunfähigkeit kannte oder infolge Fahrlässigkeit nicht kannte.

Artikel 12

Übertragung der Forderung

(1) Für die Verpflichtungen zwischen Zedent und Zessionar einer Forderung ist das Recht maßgebend, das

nach diesem Übereinkommen auf den Vertrag zwischen ihnen anzuwenden ist.

(2) Das Recht, dem die übertragene Forderung unterliegt, bestimmt ihre Übertragbarkeit, das Verhältnis zwischen Zessionar und Schuldner, die Voraussetzungen, unter denen die Übertragung dem Schuldner entgegengehalten werden kann, und die befreiende Wirkung einer Leistung durch den Schuldner.

Artikel 13

Gesetzlicher Forderungsübergang

(1) Hat eine Person, der Gläubiger, eine vertragliche Forderung gegen eine andere Person, den Schuldner, und hat ein Dritter die Verpflichtung, den Gläubiger zu befriedigen, oder befriedigt er den Gläubiger aufgrund dieser Verpflichtung, so bestimmt das für die Verpflichtung des Dritten maßgebende Recht, ob der Dritte die Forderung des Gläubigers gegen den Schuldner gemäß dem für deren Beziehungen maßgebenden Recht ganz oder zu einem Teil geltend zu machen berechtigt ist.

(2) Dies gilt auch, wenn mehrere Personen dieselbe vertragliche Forderung zu erfüllen haben und der Gläubiger von einer dieser Personen befriedigt worden ist.

Artikel 14

Beweis

(1) Das nach diesem Übereinkommen für den Vertrag maßgebende Recht ist insoweit anzuwenden, als es für vertragliche Schuldverhältnisse gesetzliche Vermutungen aufstellt oder die Beweislast verteilt.

(2) Zum Beweis eines Rechtsgeschäfts sind alle Beweisarten der lex fori oder eines jener in Artikel 9 bezeichneten Rechte, nach denen das Rechtsgeschäft formgültig ist, zulässig, sofern der Beweis in dieser Art vor dem angerufenen Gericht erbracht werden kann.

Artikel 15

Ausschluß der Rück- und Weiterverweisung

Unter dem nach diesem Übereinkommen anzuwendenden Recht eines Staates sind die in diesem Staat geltenden Rechtsnormen unter Ausschluß derjenigen des internationalen Privatrechts zu verstehen.

Artikel 16

Öffentliche Ordnung

Die Anwendung einer Norm des nach diesem Übereinkommen bezeichneten Rechts kann nur versagt werden, wenn dies offensichtlich mit der öffentlichen Ordnung des Staates des angerufenen Gerichtes unvereinbar ist.

Artikel 17

Ausschluß der Rückwirkung

Dieses Übereinkommen ist in einem Vertragsstaat auf Verträge anzuwenden, die geschlossen worden sind, nachdem das Übereinkommen für diesen Staat in Kraft getreten ist.

Artikel 18

Einheitliche Auslegung

Bei der Auslegung und Anwendung der vorstehenden einheitlichen Vorschriften ist ihrem internationalen Charakter und dem Wunsch Rechnung zu tragen, eine einheitliche Auslegung und Anwendung dieser Vorschriften zu erreichen.

Artikel 19

Staaten ohne einheitliche Rechtsordnung

(1) Umfaßt ein Staat mehrere Gebietseinheiten, von denen jede für vertragliche Schuldverhältnisse ihre eigenen Rechtsnormen hat, so gilt für die Bestimmung des nach diesem Übereinkommen anzuwendenden Rechts jede Gebietseinheit als Staat.

(2) Ein Staat, in dem verschiedene Gebietseinheiten ihre eigenen Rechtsnormen für vertragliche Schuldverhältnisse haben, ist nicht verpflichtet, dieses Übereinkommen auf Kollisionen zwischen den Rechtsordnungen dieser Gebietseinheiten anzuwenden.

Artikel 20

Vorrang des Gemeinschaftsrechts

Dieses Übereinkommen berührt nicht die Anwendung der Kollisionsnormen für vertragliche Schuldverhältnisse auf besonderen Gebieten, die in Rechtsakten der Organe der Europäischen Gemeinschaften oder in dem in Ausführung dieser Akte harmonisierten innerstaatlichen Recht enthalten sind oder enthalten sein werden.

Artikel 21

Verhältnis zu anderen Übereinkommen

Dieses Übereinkommen berührt nicht die Anwendung internationaler Übereinkommen, denen ein Vertragsstaat angehört oder angehören wird.

Artikel 22

Vorbehalte

(1) Jeder Vertragsstaat kann sich bei der Unterzeichnung, der Ratifizierung, der Annahme oder der Zustimmung das Recht vorbehalten, folgende Bestimmungen nicht anzuwenden:

a) Artikel 7 Absatz 1,

b) Artikel 10 Absatz 1 Buchstabe e).

(2) Jeder Vertragsstaat kann außerdem bei der Notifizierung einer Ausdehnung des Übereinkommens gemäß Artikel 27 Absatz 2 einen oder mehrere dieser Vorbehalte einlegen, deren Wirkung auf die oder einige der Gebiete begrenzt ist, die von der Ausdehnung erfaßt werden.

(3) Jeder Vertragsstaat kann jederzeit einen von ihm eingelegten Vorbehalt zurückziehen; der Vorbehalt wird am ersten Tag des dritten Kalendermonats nach Notifizierung der Rücknahme unwirksam.

TITEL III

SCHLUSSVORSCHRIFTEN

Artikel 23

(1) Wünscht ein Vertragsstaat, nachdem dieses Übereinkommen für ihn in Kraft getreten ist, eine neue Kollisionsnorm für eine bestimmte Gruppe von Verträgen einzuführen, die in den Anwendungsbereich des Übereinkommens fallen, so teilt er seine Absicht den anderen Unterzeichnerstaaten über den Generalsekretär des Rates der Europäischen Gemeinschaften mit.

(2) Innerhalb von sechs Monaten nach der Mitteilung an den Generalsekretär des Rates kann jeder Unterzeichnerstaat bei diesem beantragen, Konsultationen mit den Unterzeichnerstaaten einzuleiten, um zu einem Einvernehmen zu gelangen.

(3) Hat innerhalb dieser Frist kein Unterzeichnerstaat Konsultationen beantragt oder haben die Konsultationen innerhalb von zwei Jahren nach Mitteilung an den Generalsekretär des Rates nicht zu einem Einvernehmen geführt, so kann der betreffende Vertragsstaat sein Recht ändern. Die von diesem Staat getroffene Maßnahme wird den anderen Unterzeichnerstaaten über den Generalsekretär des Rates der Europäischen Gemeinschaften zur Kenntnis gebracht.

Artikel 24

(1) Wünscht ein Vertragsstaat, nachdem dieses Übereinkommen für ihn in Kraft getreten ist, einem mehrseitigen Übereinkommen beizutreten, dessen Hauptziel oder eines seiner Hauptziele eine international-privatrechtliche Regelung auf einem der Gebiete dieses Übereinkommens ist, so findet das Verfahren des Artikels 23 Anwendung. Jedoch wird die in Artikel 23 Absatz 3 vorgesehene Frist von zwei Jahren auf ein Jahr verkürzt.

(2) Das in Absatz 1 bezeichnete Verfahren braucht nicht befolgt zu werden, wenn ein Vertragsstaat oder eine der Europäischen Gemeinschaften dem mehrseitigen Übereinkommen bereits angehört oder wenn sein Zweck darin besteht, ein Übereinkommen zu revidieren, dem der betreffende Staat angehört, oder wenn es sich um ein im Rahmen der Verträge zur Gründung der Europäischen Gemeinschaften geschlossenes Übereinkommen handelt.

Artikel 25

Ist ein Vertragsstaat der Auffassung, daß die durch dieses Übereinkommen erzielte Rechtsvereinheitlichung durch den Abschluß anderer als in Artikel 24 Absatz 1 bezeichneter Übereinkommen gefährdet ist, so kann dieser Staat beim Generalsekretär des Rates der Europäischen Gemeinschaften beantragen, Konsultationen zwischen den Unterzeichnerstaaten dieses Übereinkommens einzuleiten.

Artikel 26

Jeder Vertragsstaat kann die Revision dieses Übereinkommens beantragen. In diesem Fall beruft der Präsident des Rates der Europäischen Gemeinschaften eine Revisionskonferenz ein.

Artikel 27

(1) Dieses Übereinkommen gilt für das europäische Hoheitsgebiet der Vertragsstaaten einschließlich Grön-

lands und für das gesamte Hoheitsgebiet der Französischen Republik.

(2) Abweichend von Absatz 1

a) gilt dieses Übereinkommen nicht für die Färöer, sofern nicht das Königreich Dänemark eine gegenteilige Erklärung abgibt;

b) gilt dieses Übereinkommen nicht für die europäischen Gebiete außerhalb des Vereinigten Königreichs, deren internationale Beziehungen dieses wahrnimmt, sofern nicht das Vereinigte Königreich eine gegenteilige Erklärung in bezug auf ein solches Gebiet abgibt;

c) gilt dieses Übereinkommen für die Niederländischen Antillen, sofern das Königreich der Niederlande eine Erklärung in diesem Sinn abgibt.

(3) Diese Erklärungen können jederzeit durch Notifikation an den Generalsekretär des Rates der Europäischen Gemeinschaften abgegeben werden.

(4) Rechtsmittelverfahren, die im Vereinigten Königreich gegen Entscheidungen von Gerichten in einem der in Absatz 2 Buchstabe b) genannten Gebiete angestrengt werden, gelten als Verfahren vor diesen Gerichten.

Artikel 28

(1) Dieses Übereinkommen liegt vom 19. Juni 1980 an für die Vertragsstaaten des Vertrages zur Gründung der Europäischen Wirtschaftsgemeinschaft zur Unterzeichnung auf.

(2) Dieses Übereinkommen bedarf der Ratifizierung, Annahme oder Zustimmung durch die Unterzeichnerstaaten. Die Urkunden über die Ratifizierung, Annahme oder Zustimmung werden beim Generalsekretär des Rates der Europäischen Gemeinschaften hinterlegt.

Artikel 29

(1) Dieses Übereinkommen tritt am ersten Tag des dritten Monats in Kraft, der auf die Hinterlegung der siebten Urkunde über die Ratifizierung, Annahme oder Zustimmung folgt.

(2) Das Übereinkommen tritt für jeden Unterzeichnerstaat, der später ratifiziert, annimmt oder zustimmt, am ersten Tag des dritten Monats in Kraft, der auf die Hinterlegung seiner Urkunde über die Ratifizierung, Annahme oder Zustimmung folgt.

Artikel 30

(1) Dieses Übereinkommen wird für zehn Jahre vom Zeitpunkt seines Inkrafttretens nach Artikel 29 Absatz 1 an geschlossen; dies gilt auch für die Staaten, für die es nach diesem Zeitpunkt in Kraft tritt.

(2) Vorbehaltlich einer Kündigung verlängert sich die Dauer dieses Übereinkommens stillschweigend jeweils um fünf Jahre.

(3) Die Kündigung ist dem Generalsekretär des Rates der Europäischen Gemeinschaften mindestens sechs Monate vor Ablauf der zehnjährigen oder fünfjährigen Frist zu notifizieren. Sie kann auf eines der Gebiete beschränkt werden, auf das dieses Übereinkommen nach Artikel 27 Absatz 2 erstreckt worden ist.

(4) Die Kündigung hat nur Wirkung gegenüber dem Staat, der sie notifiziert hat. Für die anderen Vertragsstaaten bleibt das Übereinkommen in Kraft.

Artikel 31

Der Generalsekretär des Rates der Europäischen Gemeinschaften notifiziert den Vertragsstaaten des Vertrages zur Gründung der Europäischen Wirtschaftsgemeinschaft

a) die Unterzeichnungen,

b) die Hinterlegung jeder Urkunde über die Ratifizierung, Annahme oder Zustimmung,

c) den Tag, an dem dieses Übereinkommen in Kraft tritt,

d) die Mitteilungen gemäß den Artikeln 23, 24, 25, 26, 27 und 30,

e) die Vorbehalte und deren Rücknahme gemäß Artikel 22.

Artikel 32

Das im Anhang enthaltene Protokoll ist Bestandteil des Übereinkommens.

Artikel 33

Dieses Übereinkommen ist in einer Urschrift in dänischer, deutscher, englischer, fanzösischer, irischer, italienischer und niederländischer Sprache abgefaßt, wobei jeder Wortlaut gleichermaßen verbindlich ist; es wird im Archiv des Generalsekretariats des Rates der Europäischen Gemeinschaften hinterlegt. Der Generalsekretär übermittelt der Regierung jedes Unterzeichnerstaats eine beglaubigte Abschrift.

ITALIAN TEXT OF ROME CONVENTION

CONVENZIONE
SULLA LEGGE APPLICABILE ALLE OBBLIGAZIONI CONTRATTUALI

aperta alla firma a Roma il 19 giugno 1980

(80/934/CEE)

PREAMBOLO

LE ALTE PARTI CONTRAENTI del trattato che istituisce la Comunità economica europea,

SOLLECITE di continuare, nel campo del diritto internazionale privato, l'opera di unificazione giuridica già intrapresa nella Comunità, in particolare in materia di competenza giurisdizionale e di esecuzione delle sentenze,

DESIDEROSE d'adottare delle regole uniformi concernenti la legge applicabile alle obbligazioni contrattuali,

HANNO CONVENUTO LE DISPOSIZIONI SEGUENTI :

TITOLO I

CAMPO D'APPLICAZIONE

Articolo 1

Campo d'applicazione

1. Le disposizioni della presente convenzione si applicano alle obbligazioni contrattuali nelle situazioni che implicano un conflitto di leggi.

2. Esse non si applicano :

a) alle questioni di stato e di capacità delle persone fisiche, fatto salvo l'articolo 11 ;

b) alle obbligazioni contrattuali relative a :

— testamenti e successioni,

— regimi matrimoniali,

— diritti e doveri derivanti dai rapporti di famiglia, di parentela, di matrimonio o di affinità, compresi gli obblighi alimentari a favore dei figli naturali ;

c) alle obbligazioni che derivano da cambiali, assegni, vaglia cambiari nonché da altri strumenti negoziabili, qualora le obbligazioni derivanti da tali strumenti risultino dal loro carattere negoziabile ;

d) ai compromessi, alle clausole compromissorie e alle convenzioni sul foro competente ;

e) alle questioni inerenti al diritto delle società, associazioni e persone giuridiche, quali la costituzione, la capacità giuridica, l'organizzazione interna e lo scioglimento delle società, associazioni e persone giuridiche, nonché la responsabilità legale personale dei soci e degli organi per le obbligazioni della società, associazione o persona giuridica ;

f) alla questione di stabilire se l'atto compiuto da un intermediario valga a obbligare di fronte ai terzi la persona per conto della quale egli ha affermato di agire, o se l'atto compiuto da un organo di una società, associazione o persona giuridica valga ad obbligare di fronte ai terzi la società, l'associazione o la persona giuridica ;

g) alla costituzione di « trusts » né ai rapporti che ne derivano tra i costituenti, i « trustees » e i beneficiari ;

h) alla prova e alla procedura, fatto salvo l'articolo 14.

3. Le disposizioni della presente convenzione non si applicano ai contratti di assicurazione per la copertura di rischi localizzati nei territori degli Stati membri della Comunità economica europea. Al fine di determinare se un rischio è localizzato in questi territori, il giudice applica la propria legge interna.

4. Il paragrafo 3 non concerne i contratti di riassicurazione.

Articolo 2

Carattere universale

La legge designata dalla presente convenzione si applica anche se è la legge di uno Stato non contraente.

TITOLO II

NORME UNIFORMI

Articolo 3

Libertà di scelta

1. Il contratto è regolato dalla legge scelta dalle parti. La scelta dev'essere espressa, o risultare in modo ragionevolmente certo dalle disposizioni del contratto o dalle circostanze. Le parti possono designare la legge applicabile a tutto il contratto, ovvero a una parte soltanto di esso.

2. Le parti possono convenire, in qualsiasi momento, di sottoporre il contratto ad una legge diversa da quella che lo regolava in precedenza, vuoi in funzione di una scelta anteriore secondo il presente articolo, vuoi in funzione di altre disposizioni della presente convenzione. Qualsiasi modifica relativa alla determinazione della legge applicabile, intervenuta posteriormente alla conclusione del contratto, non inficia la validità formale del contratto ai sensi dell'articolo 9 e non pregiudica i diritti dei terzi.

3. La scelta di una legge straniera ad opera delle parti, accompagnata o non dalla scelta di un tribunale straniero, qualora nel momento della scelta tutti gli altri dati di fatto si riferiscano a un unico paese, non può recare pregiudizio alle norme alle quali la legge di tale paese non consente di derogare per contratto, qui di seguito denominate « disposizioni imperative ».

4. L'esistenza e la validità del consenso delle parti sulla legge applicabile al contratto sono regolate dagli articoli 8, 9 e 11.

Articolo 4

Legge applicabile in mancanza di scelta

1. Nella misura in cui la legge che regola il contratto non sia stata scelta a norma dell'articolo 3, il contratto è regolato dalla legge del paese col quale presenta il collegamento più stretto. Tuttavia, qualora una parte del contratto sia separabile dal resto e presenti un collegamento più stretto con un altro paese, a tale parte del contratto potrà applicarsi, in via eccezionale, la legge di quest'altro paese.

2. Salvo quanto disposto dal paragrafo 5, si presume che il contratto presenti il collegamento più stretto col paese in cui la parte che deve fornire la prestazione caratteristica ha, al momento della conclusione del contratto, la propria residenza abituale o, se si tratta di una società, associazione o persona giuridica, la propria amministrazione centrale. Tuttavia, se il contratto è concluso nell'esercizio dell'attività economica o professionale della suddetta parte, il paese da considerare è quello dove è situata la sede principale di detta attività oppure, se a norma del contratto la prestazione dev'essere fornita da una sede diversa dalla sede principale, quello dove è situata questa diversa sede.

3. Quando il contratto ha per oggetto il diritto reale su un bene immobile o il diritto di utilizzazione di un bene immobile, si presume, in deroga al paragrafo 2, che il contratto presenti il collegamento più stretto con il paese in cui l'immobile è situato.

4. La presunzione del paragrafo 2 non vale per il contratto di trasporto di merci. Si presume che questo con-

tratto presenti il collegamento più stretto col paese in cui il vettore ha la sua sede principale al momento della conclusione del contratto, se il detto paese coincide con quello in cui si trova il luogo di carico o di scarico o la sede principale del mittente. Ai fini dell'applicazione del presente paragrafo sono considerati come contratti di trasporto di merci i contratti di noleggio a viaggio o altri contratti il cui oggetto essenziale sia il trasporto di merci.

5. È esclusa l'applicazione del paragrafo 2 quando la prestazione caratteristica non può essere determinata. Le presunzioni dei paragrafi 2, 3 e 4 vengono meno quando dal complesso delle circostanze risulta che il contratto presenta un collegamento più stretto con un altro paese.

Articolo 5

Contratto concluso dai consumatori

1. Il presente articolo si applica ai contratti aventi per oggetto la fornitura di beni mobili materiali o di servizi a una persona, il consumatore, per un uso che può considerarsi estraneo alla sua attività professionale, e ai contratti destinati al finanziamento di tale fornitura.

2. In deroga all'articolo 3, la scelta ad opera delle parti della legge applicabile non può aver per risultato di privare il consumatore della protezione garantitagli dalle disposizioni imperative della legge del paese nel quale risiede abitualmente :

— se la conclusione del contratto è stata preceduta in tale paese da una proposta specifica o da una pubblicità e se il consumatore ha compiuto nello stesso paese gli atti necessari per la conclusione del contratto o

— se l'altra parte o il suo rappresentante ha ricevuto l'ordine del consumatore nel paese di residenza o

— se il contratto rappresenta una vendita di merci e se il consumatore si è recato dal paese di residenza in un paese straniero e vi ha stipulato l'ordine, a condizione che il viaggio sia stato organizzato dal venditore per incitare il consumatore a concludere una vendita.

3. In deroga all'articolo 4 ed in mancanza di scelta effettuata a norma dell'articolo 3, tali contratti sono sottoposti alla legge del paese nel quale il consumatore ha la sua residenza abituale sempreché ricorrano le condizioni enunciate al paragrafo 2 del presente articolo.

4. Il presente articolo non si applica :

a) al contratto di trasporto,

b) al contratto di fornitura di servizi quando i servizi dovuti al consumatore devono essere forniti esclusivamente in un paese diverso da quello in cui egli risiede abitualmente.

5. In deroga al paragrafo 4, il presente articolo si applica al contratto che prevede per un prezzo globale prestazioni combinate di trasporto e di alloggio.

Articolo 6

Contratto individuale di lavoro

1. In deroga all'articolo 3, nei contratti di lavoro, la scelta della legge applicabile ad opera delle parti non vale a privare il lavoratore della protezione assicuratagli dalle norme imperative della legge che regolerebbe il contratto, in mancanza di scelta, a norma del paragrafo 2.

2. In deroga all'articolo 4 ed in mancanza di scelta a norma dell'articolo 3, il contratto di lavoro è regolato :

a) dalla legge del paese in cui il lavoratore, in esecuzione del contratto compie abitualmente il suo lavoro, anche se è inviato temporaneamente in un altro paese, oppure

b) dalla legge del paese dove si trova la sede che ha proceduto ad assumere il lavoratore, qualora questi non compia abitualmente il suo lavoro in uno stesso paese,

a meno che non risulti dall'insieme delle circostanze che il contratto di lavoro presenta un collegamento più stretto con un altro paese. In questo caso si applica la legge di quest'altro paese.

Articolo 7

Disposizioni imperative e legge del contratto

1. Nell'applicazione, in forza della presente convenzione, della legge di un paese determinato potrà essere data efficacia alle norme imperative di un altro paese con il quale la situazione presenti uno stretto legame, se e nella misura in cui, secondo il diritto di quest'ultimo paese, le norme stesse siano applicabili quale che sia la legge regolatrice del contratto. Ai fini di decidere se debba essere data efficacia a queste norme imperative, si terrà conto della loro natura e del loro oggetto nonché delle conseguenze che deriverebbero dalla loro applicazione o non applicazione.

2. La presente convenzione non può impedire l'applicazione delle norme in vigore nel paese del giudice, le

quali disciplinano imperativamente il caso concreto indipendentemente dalla legge che regola il contratto.

Articolo 8

Esistenza e validità sostanziale

1. L'esistenza e la validità del contratto o di una sua disposizione si stabiliscono in base alla legge che sarebbe applicabile in virtù della presente convenzione se il contratto o la disposizione fossero validi.

2. Tuttavia un contraente, al fine di dimostrare che non ha dato il suo consenso, può riferirsi alla legge del paese in cui ha la sua residenza abituale, se dalle circostanze risulti che non sarebbe ragionevole stabilire l'effetto del comportamento di questo contraente secondo la legge prevista nel paragrafo 1.

Articolo 9

Requisiti di forma

1. Un contratto concluso tra persone che si trovano nello stesso paese è valido quanto alla forma se soddisfa i requisiti di forma della legge del luogo che ne regola la sostanza in forza della presente convenzione o della legge del luogo in cui viene concluso.

2. Un contratto concluso tra persone che si trovano in paesi differenti è valido quanto alla forma se soddisfa i requisiti di forma della legge che ne regola la sostanza in forza della presente convenzione o della legge di uno di questi paesi.

3. Quando il contratto è concluso da un rappresentante, il paese in cui il rappresentante agisce è quello che deve essere preso in considerazione per l'applicazione dei paragrafi 1 e 2.

4. Un atto giuridico unilaterale relativo ad un contratto concluso o da concludere è valido quanto alla forma se soddisfa i requisiti di forma della legge del luogo che regola o regolerebbe la sostanza del contratto in forza della presente convenzione o della legge del luogo in cui detto atto è compiuto.

5. I paragrafi da 1 a 4 non si applicano ai contratti cui si applica l'articolo 5, conclusi nelle circostanze enunciate nell'articolo 5, paragrafo 2. La forma di questi contratti è regolata dalla legge del paese in cui il consumatore ha la sua residenza abituale.

6. In deroga ai paragrafi da 1 a 4, qualsiasi contratto che ha per oggetto un diritto reale su un immobile o un diritto di utilizzazione di un immobile è sottoposto alle regole imperative di forma della legge del paese in cui l'immobile è situato sempreché, secondo questa legge, esse si applichino indipendentemente dal luogo di conclusione del contratto e dalla legge che ne regola la sostanza.

Articolo 10

Portata della legge del contratto

1. La legge che regola il contratto in forza degli articoli da 3 a 6 e dell'articolo 12 regola in particolare :

a) la sua interpretazione ;

b) l'esecuzione delle obbligazioni che ne discendono ;

c) nei limiti dei poteri attribuiti al giudice dalla sua legge processuale, le conseguenze dell'inadempimento totale o parziale di quelle obbligazioni, compresa la liquidazione del danno in quanto sia governata da norme giuridiche ;

d) i diversi modi di estinzione delle obbligazioni nonché le prescrizioni e decadenze fondate sul decorso di un termine ;

e) le conseguenze della nullità del contratto.

2. Per quanto concerne le modalità di esecuzione e le misure che il creditore dovrà prendere in caso di esecuzione difettosa, si avrà riguardo alla legge del paese dove l'esecuzione ha luogo.

Articolo 11

Incapacità

In un contratto concluso tra persone che si trovano in uno stesso paese, una persona fisica, capace secondo la legge di questo paese, può invocare la sua incapacità risultante da un'altra legge soltanto se, al momento della conclusione del contratto, l'altra parte contraente era a conoscenza di tale incapacità o l'ha ignorata soltanto per imprudenza da parte sua.

Articolo 12

Cessione del credito

1. Le obbligazioni tra cedente e cessionario di un credito sono regolate dalla legge che, in forza della pre-

sente convenzione, si applica al contratto tra essi intercorso.

2. La legge che regola il credito ceduto determina la cedibilità di questo, i rapporti tra cessionario e debitore, le condizioni di opponibilità della cessione al debitore e il carattere liberatorio della prestazione fatta dal debitore.

Articolo 13

Surrogazione

1. Quando una persona, il creditore, ha diritti derivanti da contratto nei confronti di un'altra persona, il debitore, ed una terza persona ha l'obbligo di soddisfare il creditore oppure lo ha soddisfatto in esecuzione di detto obbligo, la legge applicabile a questo obbligo del terzo stabilisce se costui possa totalmente o solo in parte far valere i diritti che il creditore ha contro il debitore in forza della legge che regola i loro rapporti.

2. La stessa regola si applica quando più persone sono sottoposte alla stessa obbligazione contrattuale ed una di esse abbia soddisfatto il creditore.

Articolo 14

Prova

1. La legge regolatrice del contratto in forza della presente convenzione è applicabile in quanto, in materia di obbligazioni contrattuali, essa stabilisca presunzioni legali o ripartisca l'onere della prova.

2. Gli atti giuridici possono essere provati con ogni mezzo di prova ammesso tanto dalla legge del foro quanto da quella tra le leggi contemplate all'articolo 9 secondo la quale l'atto è valido quanto alla forma, sempreché il mezzo di prova di cui si tratta possa essere impiegato davanti al giudice adito.

Articolo 15

Esclusione del rinvio

Quando la presente convenzione prescrive l'applicazione della legge di un paese, essa si riferisce alle norme giuridiche in vigore in questo paese, ad esclusione delle norme di diritto internazionale privato.

Articolo 16

Ordine pubblico

L'applicazione di una norma della legge designata dalla presente convenzione può essere esclusa solo se tale applicazione sia manifestamente incompatibile con l'ordine pubblico del foro.

Articolo 17

Applicazione nel tempo

La presente convenzione si applica in ogni Stato contraente ai contratti conclusi dopo la sua entrata in vigore in questo Stato.

Articolo 18

Interpretazione uniforme

Nell'interpretazione e applicazione delle norme uniformi che precedono, si terrà conto del loro carattere internazionale e dell'opportunità che siano interpretate e applicate in modo uniforme.

Articolo 19

Sistemi giuridici non unificati

1. Se uno Stato si compone di più unità territoriali di cui ciascuna ha le proprie norme in materia d'obbligazioni contrattuali, ogni unità territoriale è considerata come un paese ai fini della determinazione della legge applicabile secondo la presente convenzione.

2. Uno Stato, in cui differenti unità territoriali abbiano le proprie norme di diritto in materia d'obbligazioni contrattuali, non sarà tenuto ad applicare la presente convenzione ai conflitti di leggi che riguardano unicamente queste unità territoriali.

Articolo 20

Primato del diritto comunitario

La presente convenzione non pregiudica l'applicazione delle disposizioni che, in materie particolari, regolano i conflitti di leggi nel campo delle obbligazioni contrattuali e che sono contenute in atti emanati o da emanarsi dalle istituzioni delle Comunità europee o nelle legislazioni nazionali armonizzate in esecuzione di tali atti.

Articolo 21

Rapporti con altre convenzioni

La presente convenzione non pregiudica l'applicazione delle convenzioni internazionali di cui uno Stato contraente è o sarà parte.

Articolo 22

Riserve

1. Ogni Stato contraente potrà, al momento della firma, della ratifica, dell'accettazione o dell'approvazione, riservarsi il diritto di non applicare :

a) l'articolo 7, paragrafo 1,

b) l'articolo 10, paragrafo 1, lettera e).

2. Nel notificare l'estensione dell'applicazione della convenzione conformemente all'articolo 27, paragrafo 2, ogni Stato contraente potrà anche esprimere una o più riserve con effetto limitato ai territori o a taluni dei territori previsti dall'estensione.

3. Ogni Stato contraente potrà in ogni momento ritirare una riserva che avrà fatto ; l'effetto della riserva cesserà il primo giorno del terzo mese di calendario dopo la notifica del ritiro.

TITOLO III

CLAUSOLE FINALI

Articolo 23

1. Se uno Stato contraente, dopo l'entrata in vigore della presente convenzione nei suoi confronti, desidera adottare una nuova norma di conflitto di leggi per una categoria particolare di contratti che rientrano nel campo di applicazione della convenzione, esso comunica la sua intenzione agli altri Stati firmatari per il tramite del segretario generale del Consiglio delle Comunità europee.

2. Nel termine di sei mesi dalla comunicazione fatta al segretario generale, ogni Stato firmatario potrà domandargli di organizzare consultazioni tra gli Stati firmatari allo scopo di raggiungere un accordo.

3. Se, entro questo termine, nessuno Stato firmatario ha domandato la consultazione o se, nei due anni successivi alla comunicazione fatta al segretario generale, non è intervenuto nessun accordo in seguito alle consultazioni, lo Stato contraente può modificare la sua legislazione. La modificazione è comunicata agli altri Stati firmatari per il tramite del segretario generale del Consiglio delle Comunità europee.

Articolo 24

1. Se uno Stato contraente, dopo l'entrata in vigore della presente convenzione nei suoi confronti, desidera divenire parte di una convenzione multilaterale che ha quale suo oggetto principale, o comprende tra i suoi oggetti principali, una disciplina di diritto internazionale privato concernente una delle materie disciplinate dalla presente convenzione, si applica la procedura prevista all'articolo 23. Tuttavia il termine di due anni, previsto all'articolo 23, paragrafo 3, è ridotto a un anno.

2. Non si segue la procedura prevista al paragrafo 1 se uno Stato contraente o una delle Comunità europee sono già parti alla convenzione multilaterale o se l'oggetto di questa è la revisione di una convenzione cui lo Stato interessato è parte, ovvero se si tratta di una convenzione conclusa nel quadro dei trattati istitutivi delle Comunità europee.

Articolo 25

Se uno Stato contraente ritiene che l'unificazione realizzata dalla presente convenzione è compromessa dalla conclusione di accordi non previsti all'articolo 24, paragrafo 1, esso può domandare al segretario generale del Consiglio delle Comunità europee di organizzare consultazioni tra gli Stati firmatari della presente convenzione.

Articolo 26

Ogni Stato contraente può chiedere la revisione della presente convenzione. In tal caso, il presidente del Consiglio delle Comunità europee convoca una conferenza di revisione.

Articolo 27

1. La presente convenzione si applica al territorio europeo degli Stati contraenti, ivi compresa la Groen-

landia, e all'insieme del territorio della Repubblica francese.

2. In deroga al paragrafo 1 :

a) la presente convenzione non si applica alle Isole Færøer, salvo dichiarazione contraria del Regno di Danimarca,

b) la presente convenzione non si applica ai territori europei situati fuori del Regno Unito, di cui il Regno Unito assume la rappresentanza nei rapporti con l'estero, salvo dichiarazione contraria del Regno Unito relativamente ad uno o più territori,

c) la presente convenzione si applica alle Antille olandesi, se il Regno dei Paesi Bassi fa una dichiarazione a tale effetto.

3. Queste dichiarazioni possono essere fatte in ogni momento mediante notifica al segretario generale del Consiglio delle Comunità europee.

4. I procedimenti d'appello proposti nel Regno Unito avverso decisioni pronunciate dai tribunali situati in uno dei territori di cui al paragrafo 2, lettera b), sono considerati come procedimenti pendenti davanti a tali tribunali.

Articolo 28

1. La presente convenzione è aperta dal 19 giugno 1980 alla firma degli Stati parti del trattato che istituisce la Comunità economica europea.

3. La presente convenzione sarà ratificata, accettata o approvata dagli Stati firmatari. Gli strumenti di ratifica, di accettazione o di approvazione saranno depositati presso il segretario generale del Consiglio delle Comunità europee.

Articolo 29

1. La presente convenzione entrerà in vigore il primo giorno del terzo mese successivo al deposito del settimo strumento di ratifica, di accettazione o di approvazione.

2. Per ogni Stato firmatario che la ratifichi, accetti o approvi posteriormente, la convenzione entrerà in vigore il primo giorno del terzo mese successivo al deposito del suo strumento di ratifica, di accettazione o di approvazione.

Articolo 30

1. La convenzione avrà una durata di dieci anni a partire dalla sua entrata in vigore conformemente all'articolo 29, paragrafo 1, anche per gli Stati per i quali essa entri in vigore posteriormente.

2. La convenzione si rinnoverà tacitamente di cinque anni in cinque anni, salvo denuncia.

3. La denuncia sarà notificata, almeno sei mesi prima della scadenza del termine fissato in dieci o cinque anni secondo il caso, al segretario generale del Consiglio delle Comunità europee. Essa potrà essere limitata ad uno dei territori ai quali la convenzione sia stata estesa in applicazione dell'articolo 27, paragrafo 2.

4. La denuncia avrà effetto unicamente nei confronti dello Stato che l'ha notificata. La convenzione resterà in vigore per gli altri Stati contraenti.

Articolo 31

Il segretario generale del Consiglio delle Comunità europee notificherà agli Stati parti del trattato che istituisce la Comunità economica europea :

a) le firme,

b) il deposito di ogni strumento di ratifica, di accettazione o di approvazione,

c) la data di entrata in vigore della presente convenzione,

d) le comunicazioni fatte in applicazione degli articoli 23, 24, 25, 26, 27 e 30,

e) le riserve ed il ritiro delle riserve di cui all'articolo 22.

Articolo 32

Il protocollo allegato alla presente convenzione ne costituisce parte integrante.

Articolo 33

La presente convenzione, redatta in un unico esemplare in lingua danese, francese, inglese, irlandese, italiana, olandese e tedesca, ciascun testo facente ugualmente fede, sarà depositata negli archivi del segretariato generale del Consiglio delle Comunità europee. Il segretario generale provvederà a trasmetterne copia certificata conforme al governo di ciascuno degli Stati firmatari.

DUTCH TEXT OF ROME CONVENTION

VERDRAG

INZAKE HET RECHT DAT VAN TOEPASSING IS OP VERBINTENISSEN UIT OVEREENKOMST

ter ondertekening opengesteld te Rome op 19 juni 1980

(80/934/EEG)

PREAMBULE

DE HOGE VERDRAGSLUITENDE PARTIJEN bij het Verdrag tot oprichting van de Europese Economische Gemeenschap,

GELEID door de wens om op het gebied van het internationaal privaatrecht verder te gaan met de in de Gemeenschap reeds begonnen eenmaking van het recht, met name ter zake van de rechterlijke bevoegdheid en de tenuitvoerlegging van beslissingen,

VERLANGENDE eenvormige regels op te stellen voor het recht dat van toepassing is op verbintenissen uit overeenkomst,

HEBBEN OVEREENSTEMMING BEREIKT OMTRENT DE VOLGENDE BEPALINGEN:

TITEL I

TOEPASSINGSGEBIED

Artikel 1

Toepassingsgebied

1. De bepalingen van dit Verdrag zijn van toepassing op verbintenissen uit overeenkomst in gevallen waarin uit het recht van verschillende landen moet worden gekozen.

2. Zij zijn niet van toepassing op:

a) de staat en bevoegdheid van natuurlijke personen, behoudens artikel 11;

b) verbintenissen uit overeenkomst betreffende:

— testamenten en erfenissen

— huwelijksgoederenrecht

— rechten en verplichtingen uit familierechtelijke betrekkingen tussen ouders en kinderen, uit bloedverwantschap, huwelijk en aanverwantschap, met inbegrip van onderhoudsverplichtingen jegens onwettige kinderen;

c) verbintenissen uit wissels, cheques, orderbriefjes, alsmede andere verhandelbare waardepapieren, voor zover de verbintenissen uit deze andere papieren het gevolg zijn van hun verhandelbaarheid;

d) overeenkomsten tot arbitrage en tot aanwijzing van een bevoegde rechter;

e) kwesties behorende tot het recht inzake vennootschappen, verenigingen en rechtspersonen, zoals de oprichting, de rechts- en handelingsbevoegdheid, het inwendig bestel en de ontbinding van vennootschappen, verenigingen en rechtspersonen, alsmede de persoonlijke aansprakelijkheid van de vennoten en de organen voor de schulden van de vennootschap, vereniging of rechtspersoon;

f) de vraag of een vertegenwoordiger zijn principaal, dan wel of een orgaan van een vennootschap, vereniging of rechtspersoon deze vennootschap, vereniging of rechtspersoon jegens een derde kan binden;

g) de oprichting van „trusts", alsmede de daardoor ontstane rechtsbetrekkingen tussen oprichters, „trustees" en begunstigden;

h) het bewijs en de rechtspleging, behoudens artikel 14.

3. De bepalingen van dit Verdrag zijn niet van toepassing op verzekeringsovereenkomsten waarin risico's worden gedekt die op het grondgebied van de Lid-Staten van de Europese Economische Gemeenschap zijn gelegen. Bij de beoordeling van de vraag of een risico op deze grondgebieden is gelegen past de rechter zijn eigen recht toe.

4. Het voorgaande lid is niet van toepassing op herverzekeringsovereenkomsten.

Artikel 2

Toepassing van het recht van niet-verdragsluitende Staten

Het door dit Verdrag aangewezen recht is toepasselijk, ongeacht de vraag of het recht is van een verdragsluitende Staat.

TITEL II

EENVORMIGE REGELS

Artikel 3

Rechtskeuze door partijen

1. Een overeenkomst wordt beheerst door het recht dat partijen hebben gekozen. De rechtskeuze moet uitdrukkelijk zijn gedaan of voldoende duidelijk blijken uit de bepalingen van de overeenkomst of de omstandigheden van het geval. Bij hun keuze kunnen partijen het toepasselijke recht aanwijzen voor de overeenkomst in haar geheel of voor slechts een onderdeel daarvan.

2. Partijen kunnen te allen tijde overeenkomen de overeenkomst aan een ander recht te onderwerpen dan het recht dat deze voorheen, hetzij op grond van een vroegere rechtskeuze overeenkomstig dit artikel, hetzij op grond van een andere bepaling van dit Verdrag, beheerste. Een wijziging in de rechtskeuze door partijen na de totstandkoming van de overeenkomst is niet van invloed op de formele geldigheid van de overeenkomst in de zin van artikel 9 en doet geen afbreuk aan rechten van derden.

3. De keuze door partijen van een buitenlands recht, al dan niet gepaard gaande met de aanwijzing van een buitenlandse rechter, laat, wanneer alle overige elementen van het geval op het tijdstip van deze keuze met een enkel land zijn verbonden, onverlet de bepalingen waarvan volgens het recht van dit land niet bij overeenkomst mag worden afgeweken, hierna „dwingende bepalingen" te noemen.

4. De vraag of er overeenstemming tussen partijen tot stand is gekomen over de keuze van het toepasselijke recht en of deze overeenstemming geldig is, wordt beheerst door de artikelen 8, 9 en 11.

Artikel 4

Het recht, dat bij gebreke van een rechtskeuze door partijen toepasselijk is

1. Voor zover geen keuze overeenkomstig artikel 3 van het op de overeenkomst toepasselijke recht is gedaan, wordt de overeenkomst beheerst door het recht van het land waarmee zij het nauwst is verbonden. Indien evenwel een deel van de overeenkomst kan worden afgescheiden en dit deel nauwer verbonden is met een ander land, kan hierop bij wijze van uitzondering het recht van dat andere land worden toegepast.

2. Behoudens het vijfde lid wordt vermoed dat de overeenkomst het nauwst is verbonden met het land waar de partij die de kenmerkende prestatie moet verrichten, op het tijdstip van het sluiten van de overeenkomst haar gewone verblijfplaats, of, wanneer het een vennootschap, vereniging of rechtspersoon betreft, haar hoofdbestuur heeft. Indien de overeenkomst evenwel in de uitoefening van het beroep of het bedrijf van deze partij werd gesloten, is dit het land waar zich haar hoofdvestiging bevindt of, indien de prestatie volgens de overeenkomst door een andere vestiging dan de hoofdvestiging moet worden verricht, het land waar zich deze andere vestiging bevindt.

3. Voor zover de overeenkomst een zakelijk recht op of een recht tot gebruik van een onroerend goed tot onderwerp heeft wordt, ongeacht het tweede lid, vermoed dat de overeenkomst het nauwst is verbonden met het land waar het onroerend goed is gelegen.

4. Het vermoeden van het tweede lid geldt niet voor de overeenkomst tot vervoer van goederen. Wanneer bij

een dergelijke overeenkomst het land waar de vervoerder zijn hoofdvestiging heeft ten tijde van de sluiting, tevens het land is waar de plaats van de inlading of lossing, dan wel de hoofdvestiging van de verzender is gelegen, wordt vermoed dat de overeenkomst het nauwst is verbonden met dat land. Voor de toepassing van dit lid wordt als overeenkomst tot vervoer van goederen beschouwd de bevrachting voor een enkele reis en iedere andere overeenkomst die hoofdzakelijk het vervoer van goederen betreft.

5. Het tweede lid vindt geen toepassing indien niet kan worden vastgesteld welke de kenmerkende prestatie is. De vermoedens van het tweede, derde en vierde lid gelden niet wanneer uit het geheel der omstandigheden blijkt dat de overeenkomst nauwer is verbonden met een ander land.

Artikel 5

Door consumenten gesloten overeenkomsten

1. Dit artikel is van toepassing op overeenkomsten die betrekking hebben op de levering van roerende lichamelijke zaken of de verstrekking van diensten aan een persoon, de consument, voor een gebruik dat als niet bedrijfs- of beroepsmatig kan worden beschouwd, alsmede op overeenkomsten ter financiering van een dergelijke levering of verstrekking.

2. Ongeacht artikel 3 kan de rechtskeuze van partijen er niet toe leiden dat de consument de bescherming verliest welke hij geniet op grond van de dwingende bepalingen van het recht van het land waar hij zijn gewone verblijfplaats heeft, indien:

— de sluiting van de overeenkomst in dat land is voorafgegaan door een bijzonder voorstel of publiciteit en indien de consument in dat land de voor de sluiting van die overeenkomst noodzakelijke handelingen heeft verricht,

— de wederpartij van de consument of zijn vertegenwoordiger de bestelling van de consument in dat land heeft ontvangen, of

— het een koopovereenkomst betreft en de consument vanuit dat land naar een ander land is gereisd en daar de bestelling heeft gedaan, mits de reis door de verkoper is georganiseerd met het doel de consument tot koop te bewegen.

3. Ongeacht artikel 4 worden deze overeenkomsten, bij gebreke van een rechtskeuze overeenkomstig artikel 3, beheerst door het recht van het land waar de consument zijn gewone verblijfplaats heeft, indien zij zijn gesloten in de in het tweede lid beschreven omstandigheden.

4. Dit artikel is niet van toepassing op

a) de vervoerovereenkomst;

b) de overeenkomst tot verstrekking van diensten, wanneer de diensten aan de consument uitsluitend moeten worden verstrekt in een ander land dan dat waar hij zijn gewone verblijfplaats heeft.

5. Ongeacht het vierde lid is dit artikel van toepassing op de overeenkomst waarbij voor één enkele prijs zowel vervoer als verblijf wordt aangeboden.

Artikel 6

Individuele arbeidsovereenkomsten

1. Ongeacht artikel 3 kan de rechtskeuze van partijen in een arbeidsovereenkomst er niet toe leiden dat de werknemer de bescherming verliest welke hij geniet op grond van de dwingende bepalingen van het recht dat ingevolge het tweede lid van het onderhavige artikel bij gebreke van een rechtskeuze op hem van toepassing zou zijn.

2. Ongeacht artikel 4 wordt de arbeidsovereenkomst, bij gebreke van een rechtskeuze overeenkomstig artikel 3, beheerst door :

a) het recht van het land waar de werknemer ter uitvoering van de overeenkomst gewoonlijk zijn arbeid verricht, zelfs wanneer hij tijdelijk in een ander land te werk is gesteld, of

b) het recht van het land waar zich de vestiging bevindt die de werknemer in dienst heeft genomen, wanneer deze niet in een zelfde land gewoonlijk zijn arbeid verricht,

tenzij uit het geheel der omstandigheden blijkt dat de arbeidsovereenkomst nauwer is verbonden met een ander land, in welk geval het recht van dat andere land toepasselijk is.

Artikel 7

Bepalingen van bijzonder dwingend recht

1. Bij de toepassing ingevolge dit Verdrag van het recht van een bepaald land kan gevolg worden toegekend aan de dwingende bepalingen van het recht van een ander land waarmede het geval nauw is verbonden, indien en voor zover deze bepalingen volgens het recht van het laatstgenoemde land toepasselijk zijn, ongeacht het recht dat de overeenkomst beheerst. Bij de beslissing of aan deze dwingende bepalingen gevolg moet worden toegekend, wordt rekening gehouden met hun aard en strekking, alsmede met de gevolgen die uit de toepassing of niet-toepassing van deze bepalingen zouden voortvloeien.

2. Dit Verdrag laat de toepassing onverlet van de bepalingen van het recht van het land van de rechter die

ongeacht het op de overeenkomst toepasselijke recht, het geval dwingend beheersen.

Artikel 8

Bestaan en materiële geldigheid

1. Het bestaan en de geldigheid van de overeenkomst of van een bepaling daarvan worden beheerst door het recht dat ingevolge dit Verdrag toepasselijk zou zijn, indien de overeenkomst of de bepaling geldig zou zijn.

2. Niettemin kan een partij zich, voor het bewijs dat zij haar toestemming niet heeft verleend, beroepen op het recht van het land waar zij haar gewone verblijfplaats heeft, indien uit de omstandigheden blijkt dat het niet redelijk zou zijn de gevolgen van haar gedrag te bepalen overeenkomstig het recht, bedoeld in het voorgaande lid.

Artikel 9

Vorm

1. Een overeenkomst die is gesloten tussen personen die zich in een zelfde land bevinden, is wat de vorm betreft geldig indien zij voldoet aan de vormvereisten van het recht dat ingevolge dit Verdrag op de overeenkomst zelve van toepassing is, of van het recht van het land waar de overeenkomst is gesloten.

2. Een overeenkomst die is gesloten tussen personen die zich in verschillende landen bevinden, is wat de vorm betreft geldig indien zij voldoet aan de vormvereisten van het recht dat ingevolge dit Verdrag op de overeenkomst zelve van toepassing is, of van het recht van een van die landen.

3. Wanneer de overeenkomst is gesloten door een vertegenwoordiger, wordt onder het land, bedoeld in het eerste en tweede lid, verstaan het land waar de vertegenwoordiger zich bevindt op het tijdstip dat hij optreedt.

4. Een eenzijdige rechtshandeling die betrekking heeft op een reeds gesloten of nog te sluiten overeenkomst, is wat de vorm betreft geldig indien zij voldoet aan de vormvereisten van het recht dat de overeenkomst zelve ingevolge dit Verdrag beheerst of zou beheersen, of van het recht van het land waar die rechtshandeling is verricht.

5. De voorgaande leden zijn niet van toepassing op overeenkomsten waarop artikel 5 van toepassing is en die onder de in het tweede lid van dat artikel beschreven omstandigheden zijn gesloten. Deze overeenkomsten worden wat de vorm betreft beheerst door het recht van het land waar de consument zijn gewone verblijfplaats heeft.

6. Ongeacht het eerste tot en met het vierde lid van dit artikel wordt de overeenkomst die een zakelijk recht op of een recht tot gebruik van een onroerend goed tot onderwerp heeft, beheerst door de dwingende vormvoorschriften van het recht van het land waar het onroerend goed is gelegen, voor zover die voorschriften volgens dat recht toepasselijk zijn ongeacht de plaats waar de overeenkomst werd gesloten en ongeacht het daarop toepasselijke recht.

Artikel 10

De onderwerpen die het toepasselijke recht beheerst

1. Het recht dat ingevolge de artikelen 3 tot en met 6 en 12 van dit Verdrag op de overeenkomst toepasselijk is, beheerst met name:

a) de uitlegging ervan;

b) de nakoming ervan;

c) de gevolgen van gehele of gedeeltelijke tekortkoming, daaronder begrepen de vaststelling van de schade voor zover hiervoor rechtsregels gelden, een en ander binnen de grenzen welke het procesrecht van de rechter aan diens bevoegdheden stelt;

d) de verschillende wijzen waarop verbintenissen tenietgaan, alsmede de verjaring en het verval van rechten als gevolg van het verstrijken van een termijn;

e) de gevolgen van de nietigheid van de overeenkomst.

2. Ten aanzien van de wijze van nakoming en de door de schuldeiser in geval van tekortkoming te nemen maatregelen, wordt rekening gehouden met het recht van het land waar de overeenkomst wordt nagekomen.

Artikel 11

Handelingsonbekwaamheid

Bij een overeenkomst die is gesloten tussen personen die zich in een zelfde land bevinden, kan een natuurlijke persoon die volgens het recht van dat land handelingsbekwaam is, zich slechts beroepen op het feit dat hij volgens een ander recht handelingsonbekwaam is, indien de wederpartij ten tijde van de sluiting van de overeenkomst deze onbekwaamheid kende of door nalatigheid niet kende.

Artikel 12

Cessie

1. De verbintenissen tussen cedent en cessionaris van een vordering worden beheerst door het recht dat inge-

volge dit Verdrag op de tussen hen bestaande overeenkomst van toepassing is.

2. Het recht dat de gecedeerde vordering beheerst, bepaalt of zij voor cessie vatbaar is, alsmede de betrekkingen tussen cessionaris en schuldenaar, de voorwaarden waaronder de cessie aan de schuldenaar kan worden tegengeworpen en of de schuldenaar door betaling is bevrijd.

Artikel 13

Subrogatie

1. Indien een persoon, de schuldeiser, een vordering uit overeenkomst heeft jegens een andere persoon, de schuldenaar, en een derde verplicht is de schuldeiser te voldoen, dan wel deze reeds door de derde op grond van deze verplichting is voldaan, bepaalt het recht dat op de verplichting van de derde toepasselijk is, of deze de rechten die de schuldeiser jegens de schuldenaar heeft overeenkomstig het recht dat hun betrekkingen beheerst, kan uitoefenen en zo ja, in welke mate.

2. Hetzelfde geldt wanneer verschillende personen door dezelfde overeenkomst zijn gebonden en een van hen de schuldeiser heeft voldaan.

Artikel 14

Bewijs

1. Het recht dat ingevolge dit Verdrag de overeenkomst beheerst, is van toepassing voor zover het ten aanzien van verbintenissen uit overeenkomst wettelijke vermoedens vestigt of regels over de verdeling van de bewijslast bevat.

2. Rechtshandelingen kunnen worden bewezen door ieder middel dat is toegelaten door het recht van de rechter of door een der in artikel 9 bedoelde rechtsstelsels volgens hetwelk de rechtshandeling wat haar vorm betreft geldig is, voor zover dit middel van bewijsvoering kan worden opgedragen door de rechter bij wie de zaak aanhangig is.

Artikel 15

Uitsluiting van herverwijzing

Wanneer dit Verdrag de toepassing van het recht van een land voorschrijft, worden daaronder verstaan de rechtsregels die in dat land gelden met uitsluiting van het internationaal privaatrecht.

Artikel 16

Openbare orde

De toepassing van een bepaling van het door dit Verdrag aangewezen recht kan slechts terzijde worden gesteld indien deze toepassing kennelijk onverenigbaar is met de openbare orde van het land van de rechter.

Artikel 17

Overgangsbepaling

Dit Verdrag is in een verdragsluitende Staat van toepassing op overeenkomsten die zijn gesloten nadat het voor deze Staat in werking is getreden.

Artikel 18

Eenvormige uitlegging

Bij de uitlegging en de toepassing van de voorgaande eenvormige regels moet rekening worden gehouden met het internationale karakter ervan en de wenselijkheid om eenheid te bereiken in de wijze waarop zij worden uitgelegd en toegepast.

Artikel 19

Staten met meer dan een rechtssysteem

1. Indien een Staat uit meer dan een territoriale eenheid bestaat en elke eenheid daarvan eigen rechtsregels voor verbintenissen uit overeenkomst bezit, wordt voor de bepaling van het overeenkomstig dit Verdrag toe te passen recht iedere territoriale eenheid als een land beschouwd.

2. Een Staat waarbinnen verschillende territoriale eenheden eigen rechtsregels voor verbintenissen uit overeenkomst bezitten, is niet verplicht dit Verdrag toe te passen in gevallen waarin uitsluitend rechtsregels van deze territoriale eenheden voor toepassing in aanmerking komen.

Artikel 20

Voorrang van het gemeenschapsrecht

Dit Verdrag laat onverlet de toepassing van bepalingen die voor bijzondere gebieden regels van internationaal privaatrecht met betrekking tot verbintenissen uit overeenkomst bevatten en die zijn of zullen worden neergelegd in besluiten van de Instellingen van de Europese Gemeenschappen of in ter uitvoering van deze besluiten geharmoniseerde nationale wetgevingen.

Artikel 21

Verhouding tot andere verdragen

Dit Verdrag laat onverlet de toepassing van internationale verdragen waarbij een verdragsluitende Staat partij is of zal worden.

Artikel 22

Voorbehouden

1. Iedere verdragsluitende Staat kan zich op het tijdstip van ondertekening, bekrachtiging, aanvaarding of goedkeuring, het recht voorbehouden niet toe te passen:

a) artikel 7, eerste lid;

b) artikel 10, eerste lid, onder e).

2. Iedere verdragsluitende Staat kan tevens, bij de verklaring met betrekking tot een uitbreiding van de toepasselijkheid van het Verdrag overeenkomstig artikel 27, tweede lid, een of meer van deze voorbehouden maken waarvan de werking is beperkt tot de of sommige van de gebieden bedoeld in de uitbreiding.

3. Iedere verdragsluitende Staat kan een door hem gemaakt voorbehoud op elk moment intrekken; het voorbehoud verliest zijn gevolg op de eerste dag van de derde kalendermaand na de kennisgeving van de intrekking.

TITEL III

SLOTBEPALINGEN

Artikel 23

1. Indien een verdragsluitende Staat, nadat het Verdrag voor hem in werking is getreden, een nieuwe verwijzingsregel wenst vast te stellen voor een speciale categorie van overeenkomsten die onder het Verdrag vallen, geeft hij de andere Staten die het Verdrag hebben ondertekend, van zijn voornemen kennis door tussenkomst van de Secretaris-generaal van de Raad van de Europese Gemeenschappen.

2. Binnen zes maanden na de kennisgeving aan de Secretaris-generaal kan elke Staat die het Verdrag heeft ondertekend, hem verzoeken te bevorderen dat de Staten die het Verdrag hebben ondertekend, met elkaar in overleg treden ten einde tot een akkoord te komen.

3. Indien geen enkele Staat die het Verdrag heeft ondertekend binnen deze termijn om overleg heeft verzocht of indien binnen twee jaar na de kennisgeving aan de Secretaris-generaal het overleg niet tot overeenstemming heeft geleid, kan de verdragsluitende Staat zijn recht wijzigen. De door deze Staat getroffen regeling wordt door tussenkomst van de Secretaris-generaal van de Raad van de Europese Gemeenschappen ter kennis gebracht van de overige Staten die het Verdrag hebben ondertekend.

Artikel 24

1. Indien een verdragsluitende Staat, nadat het onderhavige Verdrag voor hem in werking is getreden, partij wenst te worden bij een meerzijdig verdrag waarvan het voornaamste onderwerp of een der voornaamste onderwerpen een regeling van internationaal privaatrecht is betreffende een van de onderwerpen die door het onderhavige Verdrag worden beheerst, is de procedure van artikel 23 van toepassing. De termijn van twee jaar, bedoeld in artikel 23, derde lid, wordt evenwel teruggebracht tot een jaar.

2. De in het voorgaande lid bedoelde procedure wordt niet gevolgd wanneer een verdragsluitende Staat of een van de Europese Gemeenschappen reeds partij is bij het meerzijdige verdrag, of wanneer daarmee wordt beoogd een verdrag te wijzigen waarbij de betrokken Staat partij is, of wanneer het een verdrag betreft dat werd gesloten in het kader van de Verdragen tot oprichting van de Europese Gemeenschappen.

Artikel 25

Wanneer een verdragsluitende Staat van oordeel is dat de door dit Verdrag tot stand gekomen eenmaking van het recht in gevaar wordt gebracht door het sluiten van andere dan de in artikel 24, eerste lid, bedoelde verdragen, kan deze Staat aan de Secretaris-generaal van de Raad van de Europese Gemeenschappen verzoeken te bevorderen dat de Staten die dit Verdrag hebben ondertekend, met elkaar in overleg treden.

Artikel 26

Iedere verdragsluitende Staat kan verzoeken om herziening van dit Verdrag. In dat geval roept de Voorzitter van de Raad van de Europese Gemeenschappen een herzieningsconferentie bijeen.

Artikel 27

1. Dit Verdrag is van toepassing op het Europese gebied van de verdragsluitende Staten, met inbegrip van

Groenland en het volledige grondgebied van de Franse Republiek.

2. In afwijking van het eerste lid:

a) is dit Verdrag niet van toepassing op de Faeröer, tenzij het Koninkrijk Denemarken anders verklaart;

b) is dit Verdrag niet van toepassing op de Europese gebieden buiten het Verenigd Koninkrijk, waarvan het Verenigd Koninkrijk de buitenlandse betrekkingen verzorgt, tenzij het Verenigd Koninkrijk anders verklaart ten aanzien van een zodanig gebied;

c) is dit Verdrag van toepassing op de Nederlandse Antillen, indien het Koninkrijk der Nederlanden een verklaring in deze zin aflegt.

3. Deze verklaringen kunnen op elk tijdstip worden afgelegd door middel van een kennisgeving aan de Secretaris-generaal van de Raad van de Europese Gemeenschappen.

4. Beroepsprocedures die in het Verenigd Koninkrijk worden ingesteld tegen beslissingen van gerechten die zijn gelegen in een van de in het tweede lid, onder b), bedoelde gebieden, worden beschouwd als procedures die voor die gerechten worden gevoerd.

Artikel 28

1. Dit Verdrag staat met ingang van 19 juni 1980 open voor ondertekening door de Staten die Partij zijn bij het Verdrag tot oprichting van de Europese Economische Gemeenschap.

2. Dit Verdrag wordt door de ondertekenende Staten bekrachtigd, aanvaard of goedgekeurd. De akten van bekrachtiging, aanvaarding of goedkeuring worden nedergelegd bij de Secretaris-generaal van de Raad van de Europese Gemeenschappen.

Artikel 29

1. Dit Verdrag treedt in werking op de eerste dag van de derde maand volgende op het nederleggen van de zevende akte van bekrachtiging, aanvaarding of goedkeuring.

2. Voor elke ondertekenende Staat die het Verdrag nadien bekrachtigt, aanvaardt of goedkeurt, treedt het in werking op de eerste dag van de derde maand die volgt op het nederleggen van zijn akte van bekrachtiging, aanvaarding of goedkeuring.

Artikel 30

1. Dit Verdrag heeft een looptijd van tien jaar, te rekenen vanaf het tijdstip waarop het overeenkomstig artikel 29, eerste lid, in werking treedt; het voorgaande geldt ook voor Staten waarvoor dit Verdrag op een later tijdstip in werking treedt.

2. Behoudens opzegging wordt het Verdrag stilzwijgend verlengd, telkens voor een tijdvak van 5 jaar.

3. De opzegging wordt ten minste zes maanden voor het verstrijken van de termijn van tien jaar of, al naar het geval, van vijf jaar, ter kennis gebracht van de Secretaris-generaal van de Raad van de Europese Gemeenschappen. Zij kan worden beperkt tot een van de gebieden waarop het Verdrag krachtens artikel 27, tweede lid, van toepassing wordt verklaard.

4. De opzegging geldt slechts ten aanzien van de Staat die haar heeft gedaan. Voor de andere verdragsluitende Staten blijft het Verdrag van kracht.

Artikel 31

De Secretaris-generaal van de Raad van de Europese Gemeenschappen stelt de Staten die partij zijn bij het Verdrag tot oprichting van de Europese Economische Gemeenschap in kennis van :

a) de ondertekeningen;

b) het nederleggen van iedere akte van bekrachtiging, aanvaarding of goedkeuring;

c) het tijdstip van inwerkingtreding van dit Verdrag;

d) de kennisgevingen, gedaan ingevolge de artikelen 23, 24, 25, 26, 27 en 30;

e) de voorbehouden en de intrekking van de voorbehouden bedoeld in artikel 22.

Artikel 32

Het aan dit Verdrag toegevoegde protocol maakt een wezenlijk onderdeel van het Verdrag uit.

Artikel 33

Dit Verdrag, opgesteld in één exemplaar in de Deense, de Duitse, de Engelse, de Franse, de Ierse, de Italiaanse en de Nederlandse taal, welke teksten gelijkelijk authentiek zijn, zal worden nedergelegd in het archief van het Secretariaat-generaal van de Raad van de Europese Gemeenschappen. De Secretaris-generaal zendt een voor eensluidend gewaarmerkt afschrift daarvan toe aan de Regeringen van de ondertekenende Staten.

Select Bibliography

Baxter, 'International Business and Choice of Law' (1987) 36 *I.C.L.Q.* 92.
Bennett, 'The Draft Convention on the Law Applicable to Contractual Obligations' (1980) 17 *C.M.L. Rev.* 269.
Blaikie, 'Choice of Law in Contract: "Characteristic Performance" and the EEC Contracts Convention' (1983) 43 *S.L.T.* 241.
Briggs, 'The Formation of International Contracts' (1990) *LMCLQ* 192.
Cheshire and North, *Private International Law*, 11th ed (1987), Chapter 18.
Collier, 'The Draft Convention and Restitution or Quasi-Contract', in Lipstein (ed.) (1978) 41.
Collins, 'Contractual Obligations – The EEC Preliminary Draft Convention on Private International Law' (1976) 25 *I.C.L.Q.* 35.
Collins, 'Practical Implications in England of the EEC Convention on the Law Applicable to Contractual Obligations', in *Contract Conflicts*, North (ed.) (1982) 205.
Delaume, 'The European Convention on the Law Applicable to Contractual Obligations: Why a Convention?' (1981) 22 *Virginia J.Int.L.* 105.
Diamond, 'Conflict of Laws in the EEC' (1979) 32 *Curr. Leg Problems* 155.
Diamond, 'Harmonisation of Private International Law relating to Contractual Obligations', 199 *Hague Recueil* (1986–IV) 233.
Dicey and Morris, *The Conflict of Laws*, 11th ed (1987), Chapters 32 and 33.
Fletcher, *Conflict of Laws and European Community Law* (1982), Chapter 5.
Forde, 'The "Ordre Public" Exception and Adjudicative Jurisdiction Conventions' (1980) 29 *I.C.L.Q.* 259
Giardina, 'The Impact of the EEC Convention on the Italian System of Conflict of Laws', in *Contract Conflicts*, North (ed.) (1982) 237.
Gill, 'The EEC Convention on the Law Applicable to Contractual Obligations' (1982–3) 6 *Jo.Ir.Soc.Eur.L.* 1.
Graveson, *Conflict of Laws. Private International Law*, 7th ed (1974), Chapter 12.

Haak, 'International Contract Law and the Draft EEC Convention' (1975) 22 *Neths.Int.L.Rev.* 183.

Hartley, 'Beyond the Proper Law. Mandatory Rules under Draft Convention on the Law Applicable to Contractual Obligations' (1979) 4 *E.L.Rev* 236.

Hartley, 'Consumer Protection Provisions in the EEC Convention' in *Contract Conflicts* North (ed.) (1982) 111.

von Hoffmann, 'Assessment of the EEC Convention from a German Point of View', in *Contract Conflicts*, North (ed.)(1982) 221.

von Hoffmann, 'General Report on Contractual Obligations', Lando (ed.) (1975) 1.

Holder, 'Public Policy and National Preferences: The Exclusion of Foreign Law in English Private International Law' (1968) 17 *I.C.L.Q.* 926.

Jackson, 'Mandatory Rules and Rules of *Ordre Public*', in *Contracts Conflicts*, North (ed.) (1982) 59.

Jaffey, 'Choice of Law in relation to *ius dispositivum* with Particular Reference to the EEC Convention on the Law Applicable to Contractual Obligations', in *Contracts Conflicts*, North (ed.) (1982) 33.

Jaffey, 'The English Proper Law Doctrine and the EEC Convention' (1984) 33 *I.C.L.Q.* 531.

Jayme and Kohler, *Das Internationale Privat- und Verfahrensrecht der EG Aug dem Wege zum Binnenmarkt* (1990) 10 I Prax 353.

Jessurun d'Oliveira, 'International Contract Law: Observations concerning the Preliminary Draft EEC Convention on the Law Applicable to Contractual and Extra-Contractual Obligations' (1975) 22 *Neths.Int.L.Rev.* 194.

Jessurun d'Oliveira, 'Characteristic Obligation' in the Draft EEC Obligation Convention' (1977) 25 *Am.J.Comp.L.* 303.

Juenger, 'The European Convention on the Law Applicable to Contractual Obligations: Some Critical Observations' (1981) 22 *Virginia J.Int.L.* 123.

Juenger, 'The EEC Convention on the Law Applicable to Contractual Obligations: An American Assessment', in *Contract Conflicts*, North (ed.) (1982) 295.

Kaye, *Civil Jurisdiction and Enforcement of Foreign Judgments* (1987) (Butterworths, London).

Kaye, *Extension of the Judgments Convention in Europe under the San Sebastian and Lugano Conventions* (1993) (Dartmouth, Aldershot).

Kaye, *International Contracts* (1993) (Barry Rose, Chichester).

Kaye, *Private International Law of Tort and Product Liability* (1991) (Dartmouth, Aldershot).

Lagarde, 'The European Convention on the Law Applicable to Contractual Obligations. An Apologia' (1981) 22 *Virginia J.Int.L.* 91.
Lagarde, 'The Scope of the Applicable Law in the EEC Convention', in *Contract Conflicts*, North (ed.) (1982) 49.
Lando, von Hoffmann and Siehr (eds) *European Private International Law of Obligations* (1975).
Lando, 'The EC Draft Convention on the Law Applicable to Contractual Obligations: Introduction and Contractual Obligations' (1974) 38 *Rabels Zeitschrift* 6.
Lando, 'International Situations and "Situations Involving a Choice between the Laws of Different Legal Systems"', in Lipstein (ed.) (1978) 15.
Lando, 'New American Choice-of-Law Principles and the European Conflict of Laws of Contracts' (1982) 30 *Am.J.Comp.L.* 19.
Lando, 'The EEC Convention on the Law Applicable to Contractual Obligations' (1987) 24 *C.M.L.Rev.* 159.
Lasok and Stone, *Conflict of Laws in the European Community* (1987), Chapter 9.
Leslie, 'Contract in Scottish Private International Law: EEC Contracts Convention' (1983) 28 *Jo.L.Soc.Scot.* 311.
Lipstein, *Harmonisation of Private International Law by the EEC* (1978).
Lipstein, 'The Preliminary Draft Convention on the Law Applicable to Contractual and Non-Contractual Obligations', in Lipstein (ed.) (1978) 1.
Lipstein, 'Characteristic Performance: A New Concept in the Conflict of Laws in Matters of Contract for the EEC' (1981) 3 *Northwestern J.Int.L. and Bus.* 102.
F.A. Mann, 'Contracts: Effect of Mandatory Rules', in Lipstein (ed.) (1978) 31.
Merkin, 'Contracts (Applicable Law) Act 1990' (1991) *Journal of Business Law* 205.
Morse, 'Contracts of Employment and the EEC Contractual Obligations Convention', in *Contract Conflicts*, North (ed.) (1982) 143.
Morse, 'The EEC Convention on the Law Applicable to Contractual Obligations' (1982) 2 *Yearbook of European Law* 107.
Nadelmann, 'The EEC Draft of a Convention on the Law Applicable to Contractual and Non-Contractual Obligations' (1973) 21 *Am.J.Comp.L.* 584.
Nadelmann, 'Impressionism and Unification of Law: The EEC Draft Convention on the Law Applicable to Contractual and Non-Contractual Obligations' (1976) 24 *Am.J.Comp.L.* 1.

North, 'The EEC Convention on the Law Applicable to Contractual Obligations' (1980) *Journal of Business Law* 382.
North, *Contract Conflicts* (1982).
North, 'The EEC Convention on the Law Applicable to Contractual Obligations 1980: Its History and Main Features', in *Contract Conflicts*, North (ed.) (1982) 3.
von Overbeck, 'Contracts: The Swiss Draft Statute compared with the EEC Convention', in *Contract Conflicts*, North (ed.) (1982) 269.
Philip, 'Mandatory Rules, Public Law (Political Rules) and Choice of Law in the EEC Convention on the Law Applicable to Contractual Obligations', in *Contract Conflicts*, North (ed.) (1982) 81.
Plender, *The European Contracts Convention* (1991)
Pryles, 'Reflections on the EEC Contractual Obligations Convention – An Australian Perspective', in *Contract Conflicts*, North (ed.) (1982) 323.
Ross Williams, 'The EEC Convention on the Law Applicable to Contractual Obligations' (1986) 35 *I.C.L.Q.* 1.
Samuel, 'The New Swiss Private International Law Act' (1988) 37 *I.C.L.Q.* 681.
Schultsz, 'The Concept of Characteristic Performance and the Effect of the EEC Convention on Carriage of Goods', in *Contract Conflicts*, North (ed.) (1982) 185.
Schultsz, 'Dutch Antecedents and Parallels to Article 7 of the EEC Contracts Convention of 1980' (1983) 47 *Rabels Zeitschrift* 267.
Triebel, 'The Choice of Law in Commercial Relations: A German Perspective' (1988) 37 *I.C.L.Q.* 935.
Vischer, 'The Principle of the Typical Performance in International Contracts and the Draft Convention', in Lipstein (ed.) (1978) 25.

Index

Absence of choice of law 55–60, 171–201
  characteristic performance 57–58, 85, 178–185, 187–191
  consumers 219–220
  most closely connected country 3, 56–59, 171–174,
  presumptions 11, 56–59
Acceptance 269
Affreightment 12
Agency 42–43
Agent's contracts 12, 127–131, 300
Agreement on applicable law 50, 147–170
Amiable compositeur 150–152
Annexed Protocol 37, 405, 409–410
Arbitration agreements 11, 40–41, 118, 119–121
Assignment of rights 47, 321–326
  assignee-debtor relationship 323–326
  assignor-assignee relationship 322–323
  voluntary 322
Authentic texts 357, 407–408
Autonomy 449–452

Bills of exchange 40, 116–118
Bills of lading 14, 117
'Bootstraps rule' ('bootstrapping') 103, 168–170, 270–274
Breach of contract 304
  consequences of breach 304–305
  quantification of damages 305–307

Brussels Convention 2, 38, 40, 41, 98–99, 115, 120, 165, 178, 192–195, 206, 223, 233, 273, 309, 356, 424, 457
Brussels Interpretation Protocols 392–393, 415–430
  entry into force 428–429
  first Protocol 415–417
    competent authorities 427–428
    conditions of reference 424–426
    discretion 423
    duration 429
    entry into force 428–429
    jurisdiction of European Court 419–420
    national courts which can refer 420–423
    revision 430
  second Protocol 417–419
Burden of proof 44, 48–49, 136, 331–334
  applicable law 332–334
  meaning 332

Capacity 9, 19, 42, 64–65, 112–113, 168, 311–319, 322–323
  applicable law 312–319
  individuals 311–319
  national law 311–312
Carriage 14, 54, 58–59, 196–201, 207–208, 370
  carrier 200
  consignor 200–201
Central administration 184

Characteristic performance 57–58, 85, 178–185, 187–191, 452–454
Charter parties 12, 58, 199–200
Cheques 40, 116, 118
Choice of de-localised law 152–153
Closest connection 3, 56–59, 171–174, 452–454
Communications 403–404
Companies 41–42, 121–127
  Ultra vires 123–124
Composite states 359–363
Consent to contract 60, 275
Consequences of breach of contract 46, 304–307
Consequential amendments to other enactments 431–435
Consideration 270
Consumer contracts 14, 24, 45, 53–55, 59, 62, 203–220
  applicable law 210–215, 219–220, 292–293
  consumer 205–207
  definition 204–205
  excluded categories 207–209
  mandatory rules 201–215
  types 215–218
Currency 12
Customs clearance 301

Danish national maritime law 405, 409–410
Date of operation 34
  not retrospective 34–35
  termination 35
Delivery 13
Discharge of contracts 18, 46, 307–309
Duration of Convention 4, 399–402
  Brussels Protocols 429
  denunciation 400–402
  initial 399–400
  subsequent 400–402
Duress 15, 270

EC laws and acts 37, 365–366
  meaning 366

Employment contracts 55, 59–60, 221–238
  applicable law 224–232, 232–238
  employment 221–224
  habitual place of work 233–235
  mandatory rules 224–232
  most connected country 237–238
  place of engagement 235–236
Entry into force 1, 31, 395–396, 397–398
  Brussels Protocols 428–429
  Luxembourg Convention 413
  no retrospective operation 351–353
Essential validity 18, 168, 270–279, 323
European Court interpretative jurisdiction 81–83, 357–358
Evidence 43–44, 133–138, 337–341
Excluded subject-matter 39
Exclusion clauses 11, 13, 270
Existence of consent to choice of law 168–170
Existence of contracts 10, 15, 16, 46, 270–279
Export licence 301
Express choice of law 11

Family relations 39, 115–116
Floating choice of law 148–149, 151
Form of contracts 9, 11, 60–63
Formal validity 18, 133–135, 157–159, 168, 281–295, 323, 337–341
  acts 290–293
  applicable law 282–285
  conclusion by agents 288–289
  consumers 292–293
  immovables 293–295
  meaning of formal validity 289–290
Frustration of contracts 307–309

Geographical scope 372, 391–393
  European territories 392
Gifts 38
Greek accession 397, 407–408, 411–413

Index 513

Habitual residence 14, 45, 183–184, 212
Hague Rules 14

Illegality 19, 21, 22, 23, 46, 47, 68–69, 270, 299, 440–441, 444–445
Immovables 58, 62, 191–196, 293–295
Implied choice of law 11, 13, 149–154
  reasonable certainty 150–154
Insurance
  General 2, 12, 45, 138–142
  Life 140
  Non-life 139
  Situation of risk 141–142
Interest on damages 24, 300
Interpretation 2, 3, 18, 44, 46, 77–83, 190, 298–299, 355–358
  general Convention system 357–358
  principles 355–357, 457–458
  procedure to obtain European Court rulings 81–83, 357, 415–430
  sources 78–81, 92, 357–358

Jurisdiction agreements 11, 40–41, 119

Legal capacity 39
Lex loci solutionis 20–22, 69, 302–305, 435
Limitation of actions 44, 46, 436, 307–309
Luxembourg Convention
  authentic texts 407–408, 411, 413
  entry into force 397, 412
  Greek accession 411

Maintenance agreements 115–116
Mandatory rules 3, 22, 24–25, 52, 29–76, 85, 148, 158, 159–168, 196, 210–215, 224–232, 239–267, 371–372, 440–441, 444–445, 454–457
  close connection 253–256
  Convention system 247–249, 256–259
  discretion 250–251
  foreign rules 249–261

forum's rules 261–266
pre-existing law 240–247
Material validity of contracts 269
  applicable law 270–279
  effect of conduct 278–279
  meaning 269–270
Matrimonial property 39, 113, 114–115
Misrepresentation 18, 270
Mistake 15, 270
Mode of performance 9, 23, 47, 48, 63–64, 435
Modes of proof 44, 65–68, 137, 293–295, 331
  applicable laws 334–337
  meaning 337–341
Money of account 9, 23, 46, 300
Money of payment 301

National laws 36–37, 373–377
  procedures 376–377
Negotiable instruments 40, 116–118
Notifications and communications 403–404, 413, 429
Nullity of contract 309–310, 371–372

Offer and acceptance 269
Other conventions and agreements 37, 367–370
  exceptions 381–383
  principles 367–369, 370
  procedures 369, 373–377, 379–381

Payment 12
Performance 13
  mode 301–304
  substance 299–301
Place of business 185
Place of performance 20
Preamble to Convention 95–96
Pre-existing private international law 2, 9–25, 439–445
Presumptions as to applicable law
  carriage of goods 196–201
  general 11, 56–59, 85, 176–185, 452–454

immovables 191–195
  rebuttal 186–187, 195 –196, 201
Presumptions of law 44, 48–49,136, 331–334
  applicable law 332–334
  meaning 332
Principal 12
Procedure 24, 43–44, 46, 49, 133–138, 293–295, 337–341
Promissory notes 40, 116–118
Proper law 2, 9–25, 31, 93, 431–435
  Objective 12, 13, 14, 15
Public policy (*ordre public*) 13, 19, 20, 24–25, 68, 76, 239, 245–246, 265–266, 317–319, 345–350, 444–445
  effects on applicable law 346–350
  meaning 345–346, 349
  scope of operation 350
Putative applicable law 15, 16, 17

Quantification of damages 24, 44, 46, 135
Quasi-contract (restitution) 39, 47,100, 101, 309–310, 371–372

Ratification 395–396, 413, 428–429
Re-insurance 12, 45, 142
Remedies 136
Remoteness of damage 24,135
Renvoi 10, 50, 343–344
Reports 358
Reservations 92, 371–372
  consequences of nullity 371–372
  foreign mandatory rules 371–372
  withdrawal 372
Retrospective operation 351–353
Revision of Convention 36, 389
  Brussels Protocols 430

Sale of goods 14, 53–55, 369
Scission of applicable law (dépeçage) 9, 51,174–176
Scope
  Contractual obligations 38, 98–105

General 2, 97–98, 102–103
International contracts 32–33, 106–110, 161–162
Obligations 105–106
Other conventions 2
Subject-matter 2
  agents' contracts 12, 127–131, 300
  arbitration agreements 11, 40–41, 118, 119–121
  bills of exchange 40, 116–118
  capacity 9, 19, 42, 64–65, 112–113, 168, 311–319, 322–323
  companies 41–42, 121–127
  evidence 43–44, 133–138, 337–341
  family relations 39, 115–116
  insurance 2, 12, 45, 138–142
  jurisdiction agreements 11, 40–41, 119
  maintenance 115–116
  matrimonial property 39, 113, 114–115
  negotiable instruments 40, 116–118
  procedure 24, 43–44, 46, 49, 133–138, 293–295, 337–341
  promissory notes 40, 116–118
  re-insurance 12, 45, 142
  status 39, 111–112
  succession 39, 114
  trusts 43, 131–133
  wills 39, 113, 114
Temporal 2, 435
Universal application 34, 143–146
Scope of applicable law 297–310
  consequences of breach 304–307
  consequences of nullity of contract 309–310, 371–372
  discharge and limitation and pre-scription 307–309
  interpretation 298–299
  performance 299–304
    mode 301–304
    substance 299–301

Severable applicable law 154–155
Status 39, 111–112
Subrogation 47–48, 327–330
    applicable law 329–330
    types 328–329
Succession 39, 114

Third party rights 157–159
Trusts
    General 43, 131–132
    Meaning 132–133

Undue influence 270

United Kingdom (intra) choice of law 53, 111, 359–363, 392, 395, 397–398
    reservations 371–372

Validity of consent to choice of law 168–170, 272–275
Validity of contracts 10, 16, 17, 270–279
Variation of applicable law 51–52, 155–159

Wills 39, 113, 114